Directory of

MILITARY BASES

in the U.S.

edited by
William R. Evinger

ORYX PRESS
1991

The rare Arabian Oryx is believed to have inspired the myth of the unicorn. This desert antelope became virtually extinct in the early 1960s. At that time several groups of international conservationists arranged to have 9 animals sent to the Phoenix Zoo to be the nucleus of a captive breeding herd. Today the Oryx population is nearly 800, and over 400 have been returned to reserves in the Middle East.

Copyright © 1991
The Oryx Press
4041 N. Central at Indian School Road
Phoenix, Arizona 85012

Published simultaneously in Canada

Printed and Bound in the United States of America

∞ The paper used in this publication meets the minimum requirements of American National Standard for Information Science—Permanence of Paper for Printed Library Materials, ANSI Z39.48, 1984.

Library of Congress Cataloging-in-Publication Data

Directory of military bases in the U.S. / edited by William R. Evinger.
    p.   cm.
  Includes index.
  ISBN 0-89774-531-0
  1. Military bases—United States—Directories. 2. United States—
-Armed Forces—Facilities—Directories. I. Evinger. William R.,
1943- .
UA26.A26 1991
355.7′025′73—dc20   90-7680
                                                     CIP

CONTENTS

ACKNOWLEDGEMENTS

This *Directory* would not have been possible without the help of the hundreds of Public Affairs Officers throughout the country who took the time to fill out my surveys, send me information on their base/installation, and/or answer my telephone inquiries. I am especially indebted to the Public Affairs Officers of the NAS Oceana, SMR Camp Pendleton, and Ft Story for taking time out of their busy schedules to see me on short notice and to answer my questions. The author is grateful for the support for this project provided by Alice Thomson and the other members of The Oryx Press staff.

—*William R. Evinger*

INTRODUCTION

The *Directory of Military Bases* lists over 700 bases and installations in the continental United States, Alaska, and Hawaii. It is the only single source to comprehensively list the Army, Navy, Air Force, Marines, Coast Guard, National Guard, Reserve, and Joint Service Installations, as well as Department of Defense agencies, military camps and stations, recruiting offices, and command headquarters offices.

The *Department of Defense Dictionary of Military and Associated Terms* defines military bases as "areas or localities containing installations that provide logistics or other support." It defines installations as "groupings of facilities located in the same vicinity, which support particular functions."

The research for this volume began in late 1988 when survey forms were sent to the public affairs offices for the bases/installations that were identified from lists obtained from the armed services, ZIP code listings, and other references. Several follow-up mailings were done and many telephone calls were made to ensure as complete a coverage as possible. In many cases, the bases/installations returned the survey forms. In other cases, they supplied pamphlets or publications from which the information was extracted. Some listings are the result of researching other published sources.

The main section of this *Directory* lists the bases/installations alphabetically, first by state, then by city, and by name. Information in each entry profiles the base's location and size; key contact persons and telephone and Autovon numbers; branch(es) of service; major units; visitor attractions; brief history; personnel and contract expenditures; and services including housing, temporary housing, commissary and exchange, child care facilities, schools, libraries, medical facilities, and recreational opportunities on base or nearby.

The appendix lists the domestic bases/installations that were identified in the report of the Defense Secretary's Commission on Base Realignments and Closure (Public Law 100-526), issued on December 29, 1988, and in a news release from the Department of Defense entitled "Defense Secretary Proposed Base Closings on January 29, 1990." Except where noted, all those bases are found in the directory.

There are three indexes in the *Directory:* An alphabetical listing of all bases by the official base name; a branch of service index, listing the bases by state; and an index of states with the bases located in them by branch of service.

The editor of this *Directory* has made every effort to identify and list as many bases/installations as possible and he plans to update and expand the database continuously in the future. Users of the *Directory* are urged to notify the editor of additional information which will update the files and help complete the inventory of this *Directory.* Succeeding editions will feature these additional listings, as well as expanded entries with more detailed information.

While every effort has been made to ensure that all information is both accurate and current within the confines of format and scope, the publisher does not assume and hereby disclaims any liability to any party for loss or damage caused by errors or omissions in the *Directory of Military Bases* whether such errors or omissions resulted from negligence, accident, or any other cause. In the event of a publication error, the sole responsibility of the publisher will be the entry of corrected information in succeeding editions. Please direct such information to: Editor, *Directory of Military Bases*, The Oryx Press, 4041 N. Central at Indian School Road, Phoenix, Arizona 85012.

HOW TO USE THIS DIRECTORY

The main section of this *Directory* is organized alphabetically by state. Within each state section, the information is alphabeticized first by city and then by the official name of the base or installation, regardless of branch of service. Each entry contains the following descriptive information:

BASIC INFORMATION

Official name of the base/installation: This is not always the name by which a particular base/installation is referred to in ordinary usage. For example, the Marine Corps Combat Development Command is commonly known in the Washington, DC area as Quantico or Quantico Marine Base.

Address and telephone number: This is the mailing address of the base/installation and commercial and Autovon (or FTS) telephone numbers. Autovon is the military telephone network and FTS is the Federal Telecommunications System.

Officer-of-the-day: This telephone number is often usable 24 hours a day. Sometimes it is referred to by other names: (Navy) Duty Officer, Command Duty Officer, Officer of the Deck, Quarterdeck; (Coast Guard) Group Duty Officer, Operations Center; (Air National Guard) Command Post; and (Army) Staff Duty Officer.

BASE PROFILE

Branch (of service): The *Directory* covers the Army, Navy, Air Force, Marine Corps, Army National Guard, Army Reserve, Naval Reserve, Air National Guard, Air Force Reserve, Air Force Civil Air Patrol, Joint Service Installations, Department of Defense agencies such as the Defense Logistics Agency, and the U.S. Coast Guard.

Size and location: The approximate land area of the base/installation is given in acres. Some facilities are located in buildings listed as "Offices only." Directions to the base are included, giving main highways and/or distances from airports or nearby towns.

Major units (located on the base/installation): Major commands, host commands, and tenant activities are listed. Some of the most important units may also have separate entries in the *Directory*, particularly if they have a separate geographic location, although they may be assigned to a particular base.

Base history: A brief history of the base/installation is given.

Visitor attractions: Visitor attractions and museums, on or off base but on land owned/leased by the base, are identified.

KEY CONTACTS

This section lists key personnel and their addresses and telephone numbers if different from the main base. Included are **Base Commander, Public Affairs Officer, Procurement Officer, Transportation Officer,** and **Director of Personnel and Community Activities.**

PERSONNEL AND EXPENDITURES

This section lists the numbers of **Active Duty Personnel, Dependents** living on the base/installation, and **Civilian Personnel.** Total **Military Payroll Expenditures** and total **Contract Expenditures** for fiscal year 1987 in approximate and rounded dollar amounts are provided where available. When bases supplied this information for other fiscal years, that is indicated.

SERVICES

This part of the entry contains information on the services available on the base/installation including: **Housing and Temporary Housing** for officers, enlisted personnel, families, and visitors; **Base commissary,** equivalent to a supermarket, with sizes varying depending on the base; **Base exchange,** equivalent to a shopping center offering a variety of products and services, and which is generally run on nonappropriated funds. **Child care facilities and capacities, Schools, Libraries, Medical care facilities,** and **Recreational facilities** are all listed when known.

SAMPLE ENTRY

FORT MONMOUTH

OFFICIAL BASE NAME ⎯

ADDRESS AND TELEPHONE NUMBER

FORT MONMOUTH
Fort Monmouth, NJ 07703-5000
(201) 532-9000; Autovon 922-9000
OFFICER-OF-THE-DAY: (201) 532-2110,
Autovon 992-2110 ⎯ OFFICER OF THE DAY

Profile

BRANCH(ES) OF SERVICE FOUND ON THE BASE ⎯ BRANCH: Army.

SIZE AND LOCATION: 1560 acres. NJ Tpke to I-95; E to Garden State Pkwy; N to Exit 105 for Eatontown & Fort Monmouth; nearest city, New Brunswick, 23 mi NW; 10 min from Atlantic Ocean beaches; nearby Monmouth Park Race Track; 1.5 hrs S of New York City. ⎯ LAND AREA AND GROUND TRANSPORTATION DIRECTIONS TO THE BASE

MAJOR COMMANDS, HOST COMMANDS, AND TENANT ACTIVITIES ⎯ MAJOR UNITS: Communications-Electronics Command; 513th Military Intelligence Brigade; US Military Academy Preparatory School; US Army Chaplain Center and School; Information Systems Engineering Command; 235th Signal Detachment; 535th Engineering Detachment; 54th Explosive Ordnance Detachment; Army Recruiting Battalion; 389th Army Band; Joint Tactical C3 Agency; Army Aviation R&D Activity; Army Electronics Technology and Devices Laboratory.

BASE HISTORY: July 20, 1917, Army established reserve officers training battalion at Signal Corps Camp, Little Silver. Sept 1917, renamed Camp Alfred Vail. Aug 1925, made permanent military post, Fort Monmouth, in honor of soldiers of American Revolution who fought in nearby fields. Leading military technological and logistics center. ⎯ BRIEF HISTORY OF BASE

VISITOR ATTRACTIONS ON OR NEAR THE BASE ⎯ VISITOR ATTRACTIONS: Communications-Electronics Museum has equipment and documents that trace the development of Army communications from 1860 to the present; US Army Chaplains Museum; Post Chapel.

Key Contacts

NAMES AND TELEPHONE NUMBERS OF FIVE KEY CONTACTS OF THE BASE ⎯

COMMANDER: Maj Gen Billy M Thomas; Commander Communications-Electronics Command and Fort Monmouth, (201) 532-1515, Autovon 922-1515.
PUBLIC AFFAIRS: Alvin M Schwartz; Public Affairs Office (AMSEL-IO), (201) 532-1258, Autovon 992-1258.
PROCUREMENT: J Levanson; (201) 532-5601, Autovon 992-5601.
TRANSPORTATION: L Wilson; (201) 532-3545, Autovon 992-3545.
PERSONNEL/COMMUNITY ACTIVITIES: Lt Col Lynn Fleury; (201) 532-7810, Autovon 992-7810.

Personnel and Expenditures
ACTIVE DUTY PERSONNEL: 2535
DEPENDENTS: 5200
CIVILIAN PERSONNEL: 8143
MILITARY PAYROLL EXPENDITURE: $47.2 mil
CONTRACT EXPENDITURE: $4.5 bil ⎯ NUMBERS OF PERSONNEL INCLUDING ACTIVE DUTY, DEPENDENT, AND CIVILIANS; AND PAYROLL AND CONTRACT EXPENDITURES

SUMMARY OF TYPES AND NUMBER OF HOUSING UNITS, SHOPPING SERVICES, CHILDCARE AND EDUCATIONAL FACILITIES, LIBRARIES, SCHOOLS, MEDICAL AND RECREATIONAL FACILITIES ⎯

Services *Housing:* Family units 881; Duplex units 186; Senior NCO units 100; Trailer spaces 24. *Temporary Housing:* VIP cottages 6; VOQ cottages 60; Guesthouse units 70; off-base hotel/motel rooms w/year round rates 135. *Commissary:* Base commissary; Retail store; Barber shop; Dry cleaners; Food shop; Banking; Service station; Furniture store; Military clothing sales; Jewelry/watch sales and repair; Cafeteria; Optical shop; Tailor; Laundry; Credit union. *Child Care/Capacities:* Day care center 250; Home day care program; Certified child care homes 57. *Base Library:* Yes. *Medical Facilities:* Hospital 49; Medical clinic; Dental clinic. *Recreational Facilities:* Bowling; Movie theater; Pool; Gym; Recreation center; Golf; Tennis; Racquetball; Fitness center; Softball field; Football field; Auto shop; Crafts; Officers club; NCO club; Fishing/Hunting; Marina.

ABBREVIATIONS USED IN THIS DIRECTORY

A1c	Airman First Class	COM	Consolidated Open Mess
ABFC	Advanced Base Functional Component	DARCOM	Army Materiel Development and Readiness Command
ABG	Air Base Group	DESCOM	Army Depot System Command
adj	adjacent	Det	Detachment
Adj	Adjutant	Div	Division
Adj Gen	Adjutant General	DLA	Defense Logistics Agency
Adm	Admiral	DOD	Department of Defense
AF	Air Force	DVQ	Distinguished Visitors Quarters
AFB	Air Force Base	E	East
AFRES	Air Force Reserve	EMC	Electrician's Mate, Chief
AFS	Air Force Station	Ens	Ensign
AKC	Aviation Storekeeper	ext	extension
AMC	Air Materiel Command	FIG	Fighter Interceptor Group
ANG	Air National Guard	FIS	Fighter Interceptor Squadron
approx	approximately	FIW	Fighter Interceptor Wing
AT	Annual Training	ft	feet
AV	Autovon	Ft	Fort
Ave	Avenue	FY	Fiscal year
BAQ	Basic Allowance for Quarters	Gen	General
BEQ	Bachelor Enlisted Quarters	GOCO	Government Owned, Contractor Operated
bil	billion	GOGO	Government Owned, Government Operated
Blvd	Boulevard	HMC	Hospital Corpsman, Chief
BMW	Bombardment Wing	HQ	Headquarters
Bn	Battalion	hr(s)	hour(s)
BOQ	Bachelor Officers Quarters	Hwy	Highway
Brig Gen	Brigadier General	IAP	International Airport
BUC	Chief Builder	IDT	Inactive Duty Training
Capt	Captain	Intl	International
CDR	Commander	ITT	Information, Tickets, Tours (Service)
CEVG	Combat Evaluation Group	JO#	Journalist, # Class
CMS	Central Materiel Service Team	LCDR	Lieutenant Commander
CMSgt	Chief Master Sergeant	Lt	Lieutenant
Col	Colonel	LTC	Lieutenant Colonel
Cpl	Corporal	Lt Gen	Lieutenant General
CSM	Command Sergeant Major	LTjg	Lieutenant Junior Grade
Ctr	Center	MAC	Military Airlift Command
CWO	Chief Warrant Officer	MACM	Master Chief Machine Accountant
CW#	Chief Warrant Officer		

MACS	Marine Air Control Squadron	*St*	Street
Maj	Major	*TAC*	Tactical Air Command
Maj Gen	Major General	*TAG*	Tactical Airlift Group
MAP	Municipal Airport	*TAS*	Tactical Airlift Squadron
MATS	Military Air Transport Service	*TAW*	Tactical Airlift Wing
MAW	Military Airlift Wing	*TFG*	Tactical Fighter Group
MCAS	Marine Corps Air Station	*TFW*	Tactical Fighter Wing
MEWS	Early Warning Station Missile	*TRG*	Tactical Reconnaissance Group
mi	mile(s)	*TMDE*	test, measurement, and diagnostic equipment
mil	million	*Tpke*	Turnpike
MMCM	Machinist's Mate, Master Chief	*TSgt*	Technical Sergeant
MSgt	Master Sergeant	*Twp*	Township
N	North	*USA*	United States Army
NAS	Naval Air Station	*USAF*	United States Air Force
NCO	Noncommissioned Officer	*USAR*	United States Army Reserve
PAO	Public Affairs Officer	*USCG*	United States Coast Guard
PCS	Permanent Change of Station	*USCGC*	United States Coast Guard Cutter
Pfc	Private First Class	*USCGR*	United States Coast Guard Reserve
PHCS	Senior Chief Photographer's Mate	*USMC*	United States Marine Corps
Pkwy	Parkway	*USN*	United States Navy
PO	Petty Officer	*USNR*	United States Navy Reserve
Pvt	Private	*USPFO*	United States Property and Fiscal Office
Rear Adm	Rear Admiral	*VA*	Attack Squadron
Rte	Route	*VAQ*	Visiting Airmen's Quarters
RV	Recreational vehicle	*VEQ*	Visiting Enlisted Quarters
S	South	*VF*	Fighter Squadron
SAC	Strategic Air Command	*VFA*	Fighter Attack Squadron
SAR	Search and Rescue	*VIP*	Very Important Person
SFC	Specialist First Class	*VMA*	Marine All Weather Attack Squadron
Sgt	Sergeant	*VMFA*	Marine Fighter Attack Squadron
SK#	Storekeeper, # class	*VOQ*	Visiting Officers Quarters
SKCM	Master Chief Storekeeper	*VP*	Patrol Squadron
SMSgt	Senior Master Sergeant	*VQ*	Fleet Air Reconnaissance Squadron
sq	square	*W*	West
Sq	Squadron	*WO*	Warrant Officer
SRW	Strategic Reconnaissance Wing	*WWI*	World War I
SSG	Staff Sergeant	*WWII*	World War II
SSgt	Staff Sergeant	*YNC*	Yeoman, Chief

ALABAMA

ANNISTON

ANNISTON ARMY DEPOT
Anniston, AL 36201-5000
(205) 235-7501; Autovon 571-7501
Profile
BRANCH: Army.
SIZE AND LOCATION: 18,233 acres. Approx 50 mi E of Birmingham, AL and 90 mi W of Atlanta just off I-20.
MAJOR UNITS: An industrial base with 99% civilian workforce.
BASE HISTORY: Installation currently closed.
Key Contacts
PUBLIC AFFAIRS: Joan C Gustafson; ATTN: SDSAN-PA, Anniston, AL 36201-5006, (205) 235-6281, Autovon 571-6281.
PROCUREMENT: H Y Cullefer; ATTN: SDSAN-DOC, Anniston, AL 36201-5003, (205) 235-7638, Autovon 571-7638.
TRANSPORTATION: M H Rhodes; ATTN: SDSAN-DSP-TD, Anniston, AL 36201-5021, (205) 235-6031, Autovon 571-6031.
PERSONNEL/COMMUNITY ACTIVITIES: H R Turpin; ATTN: SDSAN-DPCA, Anniston, AL 36201-5007, (205) 235-6159, Autovon 571-6159.
Personnel and Expenditures
ACTIVE DUTY PERSONNEL: 65
CIVILIAN PERSONNEL: 4646
MILITARY PAYROLL EXPENDITURE: $136 mil
CONTRACT EXPENDITURE: $133.1 mil
Services *Medical Facilities:* Medical clinic. *Recreational Facilities:* Pool; Tennis; Racquetball; Fitness center; Softball field; Crafts; Fishing/Hunting.

FORT MCCLELLAN
Fort McClellan, Anniston, AL 36205-5000
(205) 848-4611; Autovon 865-4611
OFFICER-OF-THE-DAY: (205) 848-3821, Autovon 865-3821
Profile
BRANCH: Army.
SIZE AND LOCATION: 46,000 acres. On Hwy 21, at the N edge of Anniston, AL; 7 mi N of US 20, use the Anniston-Oxford-Ft McClellan Exit, I-85.
MAJOR UNITS: US Army Chemical School; US Army Military Police School; DOD Polygraph Institute; US Army Training Brigade; US Army Reception Station; 701st Military Police Battalion; Fort McClellan Military Police Company; Headquarters Battalion; 14th Army Band; Company D, 46th Engineer (Combat) (Heavy); 365th Transportation Company (Light Truck); 142nd Ordnance Detachment; US Army Medical Department Activity; Noble Army Community Hospital.
BASE HISTORY: 1912, National Guardsmen trained in area. 1917, federal government purchased land and began construction and mobilization. 1929, Camp McClellan became fort. WWII, trained soldiers and served as POW camp for Germans and Italians. Following WWII, inactivated and facilities deteriorated. 1951, reactivated as Chemical Corps School and Women's Army Corps Center and School. Later, Military Police Corps.
VISITOR ATTRACTIONS: Women's Army Corps Museum; Military Police Corps Regimental Museum; Chemical Corps Museum.
Key Contacts
PUBLIC AFFAIRS: Lt Col Andrew Coffey; (205) 848-5377, Autovon 865-5377.
PROCUREMENT: (205) 848-3622, Autovon 865-3622.
TRANSPORTATION: (205) 848-3020, Autovon 865-3020.
PERSONNEL/COMMUNITY ACTIVITIES: (205) 848-3827, Autovon 865-3827.
Personnel and Expenditures
ACTIVE DUTY PERSONNEL: 10,000
DEPENDENTS: 1976
CIVILIAN PERSONNEL: 4500
MILITARY PAYROLL EXPENDITURE: $166 mil
CONTRACT EXPENDITURE: $303 mil
Services *Housing:* Family units 570; BOQ cottages (double occupancy) 6; BEQ units 80; BAQ units 1. *Temporary Housing:* VIP cottages 3; VOQ cottages 342; VEQ units 80; Guesthouse units 138; Guest cottages 4; Apartment units 50; Lodge units 1. *Commissary:* Base commissary; Retail store; Barber shop; Dry cleaners; Food shop; Florist; Banking; Service station. *Child Care/Capacities:* Day care center. *Schools:* Elementary. *Base Library:* Yes. *Medical Facilities:* Hospital 100; Dental clinic. *Recreational Facilities:* Bowling; Movie theater; Pool; Gym; Recreation center; Golf; Tennis; Racquetball; Fitness center; Softball field; Football field; Auto shop; Crafts; Officers club; NCO club; Camping; Fishing/Hunting; Roller skating rink.

BIRMINGHAM

SMITH AIR NATIONAL GUARD BASE
Birmingham Municipal Airport, Birmingham, AL 35217
(205) 591-8160; Autovon 694-2260
Profile
BRANCH: Air National Guard.
SIZE AND LOCATION: 86 acres. Within corporate limits of Birmingham off I-59, use Airport Hwy, exit 129.
MAJOR UNITS: 117th Tactical Reconnaissance Wing (ANG).
BASE HISTORY: Named for Col Sumpter Smith who played important part in promoting development of Birmingham's airport.
Personnel and Expenditures
ACTIVE DUTY PERSONNEL: 1152
CIVILIAN PERSONNEL: 252
MILITARY PAYROLL EXPENDITURE: $12.7 mil

FORT RUCKER

FORT RUCKER
US Army Aviation Center, Fort Rucker, AL 36362-5000
(205) 255-3100; Autovon 558-3400; 558-3100
Profile
BRANCH: Army.
SIZE AND LOCATION: 64,349 acres. In SE AL, approx 90 mi S of Montgomery and 30 mi NW of Dothan, AL, between US 231 and 84.
MAJOR UNITS: US Army Aviation Center; 1st Aviation Brigade; Aviation Training Brigade; Directorate of Aviation Proponency; Directorate of Combat Developments; Directorate of Evaluation and Standardization; Directorate of Logistics; Directorate of Plans, Training, Mobilization and Security; Directorate of Training and Doctrine; Department of Combined Arms Tactics; Department of Enlisted Training; Department of Gunnery and Flight Systems; Army Air Traffic Control Activity; Army Aviation Center Noncommissioned Officer Academy; TRADOC Systems Managers; TRADOC Project Office; Army Aeromedical Center; Army Aeromedical Research Laboratory; Army Aviation Development Test Activity; Army Dental Activity; Army Information Systems Command-Ft Rucker; Army National Guard Aviation Division Multi-Media Branch; Army Research Institute Aviation R&D Activity; Army Safety Center; Army School of Aviation Medicine; Defense Reutilization and Marketing Office; Medical Evacuation Proponency Division; TEXCOM Aviation Board; 3588th Flying Training Squadron.
BASE HISTORY: 1935, land bought by federal government as Pea River Cooperative Land Use Area. 1942, opened as Ozark Triangular Division Camp, infantry training site. 1943, renamed Camp Rucker, to honor Gen Edmund Winchester Rucker, Confederate Army officer from TN and businessman, Montgomery, AL. 1946-50, Camp Rucker on inactive status until reactivated for Korean War. 1954, closed May-July, until US Army Aviation School moved from Ft Sill, OK. 1955, designated fort. Vietnam Conflict, provided primary training for Army Aviation.
VISITOR ATTRACTIONS: Army Aviation Museum.
Personnel and Expenditures
ACTIVE DUTY PERSONNEL: 7958
DEPENDENTS: 4012
CIVILIAN PERSONNEL: 3189
MILITARY PAYROLL EXPENDITURE: FY 89, $109.3 mil
CONTRACT EXPENDITURE: FY 89, $67.6 mil

FORT RUCKER (continued)
Services *Housing:* Family units 1515; Trailer spaces 43. *Temporary Housing:* VIP cottages 8; VOQ cottages 256; Guesthouse units; TDY reservations only, 15 days in advance. *Commissary:* Base commissary; Retail store; Barber shop; Dry cleaners; Food shop; Florist; Banking; Service station; Military clothing sales; Convenience store/Shopette; Video rental; Photo finishing; Laundry; Beauty shop; Jewelry/watch sales and repair; Optical shop; Car rental; Shoe repair; Tailor; Package beverages; Rent all; Toys; Garden center; Ice cream; Snacks. *Child Care/Capacities:* Day care center; Home day care program; Latch key. *Schools:* Kindergarten/Preschool; Elementary; College courses. *Base Library:* Yes. *Medical Facilities:* Hospital 72; Dental clinic; Lyster USA Community Hospital; Air Ambulance Division; Veterinary services. *Recreational Facilities:* Bowling; Movie theater; Pool; Gym; Recreation center; Golf; Stables; Tennis; Racquetball; Skating rink; Fitness center; Softball field; Football field; Auto shop; Crafts; Officers club; NCO club; Camping (day); Fishing/Hunting; Post Wildlife Association; Lake Tholocco on post; Beach; Water sports; Squash; Equestrian center; Basketball; Florida Recreation Area; Skeet Club; ITT.

GUNTER AFB

GUNTER AIR FORCE BASE
Gunter AFB, AL 36114
(205) 293-1110; Autovon 446-1110
Profile
BRANCH: Air Force.
SIZE AND LOCATION: 348 acres. Central AL, approx 5 mi NE of downtown Montgomery; between US-80 and US-231, off Dalraide.
MAJOR UNITS: AF Air University; Extension Course Institute; AF Senior Noncommissioned Officer Academy; 3800th Air Base Squadron; AF Communications Command, Standard Systems Center; Military Entrance Processing Station; US Army Recruiting Center; 3308th Technical Training Squadron; 3531st AF Recruiting Squadron.
BASE HISTORY: 1940, Army Air Corps Basic Flying Training School activated at Montgomery Municipal Airport and next year named Gunter Field for a mayor of Montgomery, William A Gunter. Flyer training began with American, British, Canadian, French, and Chinese pilots. Following WWII, transferred to Army Air Force's School, later Air University; used originally to house Maxwell AFB's personnel and tenant organizations. 1950, received first major educational mission with Extension Course Institute. 1960s, nearly became base of tenant units. 1970s, revival of Gunter as major AF installation.
Key Contacts
COMMANDER: 3800th Air Base Squadron.
PUBLIC AFFAIRS: Maxwell AFB, AL 36112, (205) 293-2016.
Personnel and Expenditures
ACTIVE DUTY PERSONNEL: 1505
DEPENDENTS: 1400
CIVILIAN PERSONNEL: 895
MILITARY PAYROLL EXPENDITURE: $322.3 mil (including Maxwell AFB)
CONTRACT EXPENDITURE: $184.6 mil (including Maxwell AFB)
Services *Housing:* Family units 324; BEQ units 152. *Temporary Housing:* Apartment units 3; PCS priority. *Commissary:* Base commissary; Service station. *Child Care/Capacities:* Day care center 180. *Schools:* Kindergarten/Preschool. *Medical Facilities:*

Dental clinic; Dispensary. *Recreational Facilities:* Bowling; Movie theater; Pool; Gym; Crafts; Picnic area.

HUNTSVILLE

US ARMY CORPS OF ENGINEERS, HUNTSVILLE DIVISION
PO Box 1600, Huntsville, AL 35807
(205) 895-5460
Profile
BRANCH: Army.
SIZE: Offices only.
Key Contacts
COMMANDER: Col Charles T Myers; Division Engineer.

MAXWELL AFB

MAXWELL AIR FORCE BASE
3800th ABW, Maxwell AFB, AL 36112-5000
(205) 293-1110; Autovon 875-1110
Profile
BRANCH: Air Force.
SIZE AND LOCATION: 2487 acres. In central AL, between I-65, US Hwy 82 and the Alabama River, approx 3 mi N-NW of downtown Montgomery.
MAJOR UNITS: 3800th Air Base Wing; Headquarters AF Reserve Officer Training Corps; Community College of the AF; USAF Historical Research Center; 1973rd Communications Group; Detachment 3, 1402nd Military Airlift Squadron; Detachment 9, 24th Weather Squadron; 908th Tactical Airlift Group (AF Reserve); 280th Combat Information Systems Squadron (Air National Guard); District 8, AF Office of Special Investigations; AF Management Engineering Team; Detachment 3, 1361st Audiovisual Squadron; Detachment 8, AF Commissary Service; USAF Trial Judiciary, 2d Circuit; Federal Prison Camp.
BASE HISTORY: 1910, Orville Wright came to Montgomery to start first school for instruction in aviation; Army purchased Wright Field. 1918, established aircraft engine and repair depot. 1922, named Maxwell Field for 2nd Lt William C Maxwell, Atmore, AL, native and aircraft accident victim. 1928, first permanent buildings completed. 1946, Air University established. 1978-83 subordinate unit of Air Training Command.
Key Contacts
COMMANDER: 3800th ABW/CC.
PUBLIC AFFAIRS: 3800th ABW/PA.
Personnel and Expenditures
ACTIVE DUTY PERSONNEL: 2000
DEPENDENTS: 7400
CIVILIAN PERSONNEL: 4000
MILITARY PAYROLL EXPENDITURE: $322.3 (military and civilian)
CONTRACT EXPENDITURE: $184.6 mil
Services *Housing:* Family units 515; BOQ cottages 25; BAQ units 731; Trailer spaces 24. *Temporary Housing:* VIP cottages 20; VOQ cottages 1300; VAQ units 28; Transient living quarters 30. *Commissary:* Base commissary; Barber shop; Dry cleaners; Convenience store/Shopette; Tailor; Beauty shop; Laundry; Optical shop; Jewelry/watch sales and repair. *Child Care/Capacities:* Day care center 180. *Schools:* Elementary. *Medical Facilities:* Hospital 240. *Recreational Facilities:* Bowling; Pool; Golf; Skating rink; Crafts; Youth center; Aero club; Lake Pippin, 165 mi away.

MOBILE

MOBILE COAST GUARD AVIATION TRAINING CENTER
Bates Field, Mobile, AL 36608-9258
(205) 694-6610; Autovon 436-3635
OFFICER-OF-THE-DAY: (205) 694-6110
Profile
BRANCH: Coast Guard.
SIZE AND LOCATION: 231 acres. 2 mi W of the Mobile city limits on the Bates Field airport facility across the field from the Municipal Airport; 7 mi W of I-65 on Tanner-Williams Rd.
MAJOR UNITS: ATC Mobile; CG Atlantic Area Strike Team.
BASE HISTORY: 1966, commissioned with establishment of fixed-wing and rotary-wing pilot training unit. 1969, Helicopter Icebreaker Support Unit (IBSU) created and Aviation Training Center assumed current name and came under direct control of USCG HQ. Operational divisions: Search & Rescue (supporting Eighth District), Training (providing training to all USCG pilots), and Polar Operations (deployed on Icebreakers in AK, Arctic, and Antarctic). Largest air unit in Coast Guard.
VISITOR ATTRACTIONS: Pterodactyl Hall of Fame (Memorial to Coast Guard aviators).
Key Contacts
COMMANDER: Capt R D Herr; (205) 694-6101.
PUBLIC AFFAIRS: LTjg R M Kenin; (205) 694-6428.
PROCUREMENT: CDR G Calhoun; Comptroller Officer, (205) 694-6300.
TRANSPORTATION: CWO2 C Brown; (205) 694-6126.
PERSONNEL/COMMUNITY ACTIVITIES: CDR D Benefield; Director of Personnel, (205) 694-6101.
Personnel and Expenditures
ACTIVE DUTY PERSONNEL: 420
CIVILIAN PERSONNEL: 20
MILITARY PAYROLL EXPENDITURE: $6.5 mil
Services *Housing:* BEQ (PCS rooms) 20. *Temporary Housing:* VIP cottages (rooms) 2; VEQ units (flight crew space as req'd); BOQ units (transient rooms) 2. *Commissary:* Base commissary; Retail store; Barber shop; Dry cleaners; Banking; Service station. *Base Library:* Yes. *Medical Facilities:* Medical clinic; Dental clinic. *Recreational Facilities:* Pool; Gym; Tennis; Fitness center; Softball field; Auto shop; Officers club; NCO club; Camping; Fishing/Hunting; Rental cottages and RV sites at Dauphin Island recreation area 25 mi S on the Gulf of Mexico.

MOBILE COAST GUARD BASE
S Broad St, Mobile, AL 36615-1390
(205) 690-2217; 690-2218
OFFICER-OF-THE-DAY: (205) 690-2214
Profile
BRANCH: Coast Guard.
SIZE AND LOCATION: 25 acres. S of I-10 in Mobile in the Brookley Industrial Complex on Mobile Bay.
MAJOR UNITS: USCG Group Mobile, AL; USCG Station Mobile, AL; USCGC *Whitepine*; USCGC *Axe*; USCGC *Salvia*; USCGC *Saginaw*; USCGC *Cushing*; USCGC *Chincoteague*; USCG Fire and Safety Test Detachment.
VISITOR ATTRACTIONS: Cutters located at base.
Key Contacts
COMMANDER: Capt Larry R Hyde; (205) 690-2217.
PUBLIC AFFAIRS: LTjg Seven D Poulin; (205) 690-2210.
PROCUREMENT: CWO4 Ron Badeaux; (205) 690-3008.

MOBILE COAST GUARD BASE *(continued)*
TRANSPORTATION: CWO3 Keith Koch; Administrative Officer, (205) 690-2234.
Personnel and Expenditures
ACTIVE DUTY PERSONNEL: 150
CIVILIAN PERSONNEL: 23
MILITARY PAYROLL EXPENDITURE: $3 mil
CONTRACT EXPENDITURE: $1.54 mil
Services *Temporary Housing:* Guest cottages (at Dauphin Island, AL); Transient living quarters (for single military members not to exceed 3 days). *Commissary and Exchange:* Retail store; Barber shop; Banking; Service station. *Medical Facilities:* Medical clinic. *Recreational Facilities:* Tennis; Softball field; All servicemen's club; Weight room; Outdoor basketball court.

US ARMY CORPS OF ENGINEERS, MOBILE DISTRICT
PO Box 2288, 109 St Joseph St, Mobile, AL 36628-0001
(205) 690-2500
Profile
BRANCH: Army.
LOCATION: In Mobile, AL.
MAJOR UNITS: Army Corps of Engineers.
BASE HISTORY: 1815, first Corps of Engineers officers reported to Mobile Gulf coastal area. 1888, present structure established. Mobile District 1 of 7 district level areas of South Atlantic Division, Atlanta. Performs both civil works (water resources) and military construction/installation support. District includes parts of AL, MS, TN, FL, GA, and Central America.
Key Contacts
COMMANDER: Col Larry S Bonine; District Commander, (205) 690-2511.
PUBLIC AFFAIRS: Samuel R Green; (205) 690-3320.
PROCUREMENT: James A Campbell; (205) 690-2501.
TRANSPORTATION: Gloria Liggett; (205) 690-2405.
PERSONNEL/COMMUNITY ACTIVITIES: Evelyn I Cave; Director of Personnel, (205) 690-2521.
Personnel and Expenditures
ACTIVE DUTY PERSONNEL: 13
DEPENDENTS: 32
CIVILIAN PERSONNEL: 1850
MILITARY PAYROLL EXPENDITURE: $62 mil
CONTRACT EXPENDITURE: $400 mil
Services *Base Library:* Yes.

MONTGOMERY

ALABAMA STATE MILITARY DEPARTMENT
PO Box 3711, Office of the Adjutant General, Montgomery, AL 36193-4701
Profile
BRANCH: Army National Guard.
SIZE: Offices only.
Key Contacts
PUBLIC AFFAIRS: Col George A Dawson; (205) 271-7244.

187TH TACTICAL RECONNAISSANCE GROUP (ANG)
Dannelly Field, Montgomery, AL 36105
(205) 281-7770; Autovon 485-9210
Profile
BRANCH: Air National Guard.
SIZE AND LOCATION: 42 acres. 7 mi SW of Montgomery, off US-80.
MAJOR UNITS: 187th Tactical Reconnaissance Group (ANG); 232nd Combat Communications Group.
BASE HISTORY: Named for Ens Clarence Dannelly, Navy pilot killed at Pensacola NAS during WWII.

Personnel and Expenditures
ACTIVE DUTY PERSONNEL: 1129
CIVILIAN PERSONNEL: 271
MILITARY PAYROLL EXPENDITURE: $12.9 mil
Services *Medical Facilities:* Dispensary.

REDSTONE ARSENAL

REDSTONE ARSENAL
Redstone Arsenal, AL 35898
(205) 876-4161; Autovon 746-4161
Profile
BRANCH: Army.
SIZE AND LOCATION: 38,000 acres. Adj to Huntsville, off Rte 231 on AL-20.
MAJOR UNITS: Army Missile Command; Army Missile and Munitions Center and School.
BASE HISTORY: 1941, established to make conventional ammunition and toxic chemicals. 1949-50, began work on missiles, with arrival of missile experts from Ft Bliss.
Personnel and Expenditures
ACTIVE DUTY PERSONNEL: 2500
CIVILIAN PERSONNEL: 25,000
Services *Housing:* Family units 1273. *Temporary Housing:* VIP cottages 6; VOQ cottages 76; VEQ units 16; Guesthouse units 21; No pets. *Commissary:* Base commissary; Retail store; Service station; Convenience store/Shopette; Package beverages; Credit union. *Child Care/Capacities:* Day care center 191; Home day care program. *Medical Facilities:* Hospital 42; Medical clinic; Dental clinic; Veterinary services. *Recreational Facilities:* Bowling; Movie theater; Pool; Gym; Golf; Tennis; Racquetball; Fitness center; Auto shop; Crafts; Camping; Fishing/Hunting; Youth center (activities); Boating; Aero Club.

ALASKA

ADAK

ADAK NAVAL AIR STATION

Box 2, NAVSTA, Adak, FPO Seattle, WA, Adak, AK 98791
(907) 592-4102; Autovon 317-692-4102
OFFICER-OF-THE-DAY: (907) 592-4201, Autovon 317-692-4201

Profile
BRANCH: Navy.
SIZE AND LOCATION: 52,180 acres. On Adak Island in Andreanof Islands of Aleutian Chain. Approx 1200 mi from Anchorage; 2000 mi from Tokyo and Seattle.
MAJOR UNITS: Naval Security Group Activity, Adak; Naval Facility, Adak.
BASE HISTORY: Provides base for ships and aircraft operating in North Pacific; deployment of P-3 Orion aircraft flies antisubmarine patrols, ice patrols, search missions and routine surveillance flights; harbor at Sweeper Cove provides full services for US ships; Naval Security Group Activity's mission is fleet communications and Naval Facility's mission is oceanographic research.
VISITOR ATTRACTIONS: Closed installation and travel to Adak requires security clearance from security police, 907-592-8051. No off-base, only off-island; no civilian community.

Key Contacts
COMMANDER: Capt James E Dulin; (907) 592-8031, Autovon 317-692-4208.
PUBLIC AFFAIRS: Jane Surmi.

Personnel and Expenditures
ACTIVE DUTY PERSONNEL: 2500
DEPENDENTS: 1500-2000
CIVILIAN PERSONNEL: 500
CONTRACT EXPENDITURE: $24.8 mil
Services *Housing:* Family units 1028; BOQ cottages 47; BEQ units 40. *Temporary Housing:* BOQ units; BAQ units; Lodge units 8. *Commissary:* Base commissary; Retail store; Barber shop; Dry cleaners; Food shop; Florist; Service station; Bakery; Book store; Credit union. *Child Care/Capacities:* Day care center 200; Home day care program. *Schools:* Kindergarten/Preschool; Elementary; Intermediate/Junior high; High school. *Base Library:* Yes. *Medical Facilities:* Hospital 15; Medical clinic; Dental clinic. *Recreational Facilities:* Bowling; Movie theater; Pool; Gym; Recreation center; Tennis; Racquetball; Skating rink; Fitness center; Softball field; Auto shop; Crafts; Officers club; NCO club; Camping; Fishing/Hunting; Caribou hunting; Shooting range.

ADAK NAVAL SECURITY GROUP ACTIVITY

FPO Seattle, WA, Adak, AK 98777-1801
(907) 592-6248; 592-6222; Autovon 317-692-6248; 692-6222
OFFICER-OF-THE-DAY: (907) 592-6211, 592-4293, Autovon 317-692-6211, 692-4293

Profile
BRANCH: Navy.
SIZE AND LOCATION: 8800 acres. On Adak Island in Andreanof Islands in Aleutian Islands, approx 1200 air mi SW of Anchorage. Island shared with NAS, Adak, which occupies central portion of island; southern half of island controlled by US Fish and Wildlife Service as National Wildlife Refuge. Closed installation and travel to Adak requires security clearance from security police, 907-592-8051. No off-base, only off-island; no civilian community.
MAJOR UNITS: Naval Electronics Center Detachment, Adak; Company "I" Marine Support Battalion; "True Blue" Detachment, 704th MI Brigade.
BASE HISTORY: 1942, established as Naval Operating Base on Adak; evolved into communications supplementary activity at Clam Lagoon. During and after WWII provided communications support. 1948, Communications Station established as separate command on island. 1977, Communications Station decommissioned and Naval Security Group, Adak, commissioned under COMNAVSECGRU.
VISITOR ATTRACTIONS: Fish and Wildlife Center/Museum; Adak Museum.

Key Contacts
COMMANDER: Capt Thomas P Traughber; (907) 592-4109, Autovon 317-692-4109.
PUBLIC AFFAIRS: ENS Swede Larson.
PROCUREMENT: Lt B B Bates; (907) 592-6471, 592-6472, Autovon 317-692-6471, 692-6472.
TRANSPORTATION: Lt S A Bessette; (907) 592-6397, 592-6377, Autovon 317-692-6397, 692-6377.
PERSONNEL/COMMUNITY ACTIVITIES: Robert Winckler; (907) 592-6314, 592-6235, Autovon 317-692-6314, 692-6235.

Personnel and Expenditures
ACTIVE DUTY PERSONNEL: 600
DEPENDENTS: 550
CIVILIAN PERSONNEL: 25
Services *Housing:* BEQ units 4; Dormitory spaces 300; All BOQ and family housing are located on the NAS, Adak approx 10 mi S. *Temporary Housing:* Transient dormitory spaces for bachelor enlisted are available on a limited basis on the NAS, Adak approx 10 mi S. *Commissary:* Base commissary; Retail store; Barber shop; Dry cleaners; Food shop; Florist; Banking; Service station; Bakery; Book store; Most services available at the NAS Adak. *Child Care/Capacities:* Day care center At NAS Adak, 200; Home day care program. *Schools:* Kindergarten/Preschool Located at NAS, Adak; Elementary Located at NAS, Adak; Intermediate/Junior high Located at NAS, Adak; High school Located at NAS, Adak. *Base Library:* Yes. *Medical Facilities:* Medical clinic; Dental clinic; Hospital at NAS, Adak, 15 beds. *Recreational Facilities:* Bowling; Movie theater; Pool; Gym; Recreation center; Tennis; Racquetball; Fitness center; Softball field; Football field; Auto shop; Crafts; Camping; Fishing/Hunting (Charter fishing program); Boating; All hands club; Some facilities located at NAS, Adak.

ANCHORAGE

ELMENDORF AIR FORCE BASE

Anchorage, AK 99506-5000
(907) 552-1110; Autovon 317-552-1110
OFFICER-OF-THE-DAY: (907) 552-5748, Autovon 317-552-5748

Profile
BRANCH: Air Force.
SIZE AND LOCATION: 13,130 acres. N edge of Anchorage; turn N off the Glenn Hwy on to Boniface Pkwy.
MAJOR UNITS: Headquarters, Alaskan Air Command; 21st Tactical Fighter Wing; 11th Tactical Control Wing; 1931st Communications Wing; 21st Combat Support Group; 616th Military Airlift Group; 962nd Airborne Warning Control Squadron; 6981st Electronic Security Squadron.
BASE HISTORY: 1940, activated and named for Capt Hugh M Elmendorf, test pilot killed flying new pursuit plane at Wright Field, OH, 1933. Base originally Ft Richardson but in 1951, Ft Richardson moved to present location and base redesignated Elmendorf.
VISITOR ATTRACTIONS: Elmendorf Natural Wildlife Museum; Seward Recreation Camp, 120 mi S of base, open mid-May to mid-Sept, features: cabins, trailers, motels, dining facilities, campgrounds, scenic views, and fishing charters, for info call (907) 552-4015, reservations 552-5526, space limited on weekends.

Key Contacts
COMMANDER: Col Richard D Brown; 21 CSG/CC, (907) 552-4660, Autovon 317-552-4660.
PUBLIC AFFAIRS: Maj Douglas D McCoy Jr; 21 TFW/PA, (907) 552-8151, Autovon 317-552-8151.
PROCUREMENT: LTC Joseph C Hannigan; 5000 CONS/CC, (907) 552-2610, Autovon 317-552-2810.
TRANSPORTATION: Maj Ronald Daniels; 21 TFW/LGT, (907) 552-2312, Autovon 317-552-2312.
PERSONNEL/COMMUNITY ACTIVITIES: LTC Donald S Buriff; 21 CSG/SS, (907) 552-2468, Autovon 317-552-2468.

Personnel and Expenditures
ACTIVE DUTY PERSONNEL: 6400
DEPENDENTS: 5500
CIVILIAN PERSONNEL: 2400
MILITARY PAYROLL EXPENDITURE: $148 mil

ELMENDORF AIR FORCE BASE (continued)
CONTRACT EXPENDITURE: $83 mil
Services *Housing:* Family units 1532; Barracks spaces; Dormitory spaces 2608; Senior NCO units 230; Junior NCO units 1070; RV/Camper sites 200; The total number of houses include duplexes, 4-plexes, townhouses, and other units. *Temporary Housing:* VIP cottages 5; VOQ cottages 80; VEQ units 300; VAQ units; BOQ units; BAQ units; Transient living quarters 48. *Commissary:* Base commissary; Retail store; Barber shop; Dry cleaners; Food shop; Florist; Banking; Service station; Furniture store; Bakery; Computer store; Optical shop; Video rental. *Child Care/Capacities:* Day care center 250; Home day care program. *Schools:* Kindergarten/Preschool; Elementary; Special education. *Base Library:* Yes. *Medical Facilities:* Hospital 90; Dental clinic; Satellite pharmacy. *Recreational Facilities:* Bowling; Movie theater; Pool; Gym; Recreation center; Golf; Stables; Tennis; Racquetball; Skating rink; Fitness center; Softball field; Football field; Auto shop; Crafts; Officers club; NCO club; Camping; Fishing/Hunting; Parks; Frame shop; Snow sports; Seward Recreation Camp.

KULIS AIR NATIONAL GUARD BASE
6000 Air Guard Rd, Anchorage, AK 99502-1998
(907) 249-1176; Autovon 317-626-1176
Profile
BRANCH: Air National Guard.
SIZE AND LOCATION: 125 acres. In Anchorage off Raspberry Rd, approx 5 mi from downtown.
MAJOR UNITS: 176th Composite Group (COMPGP); 144th Tactical Airlift Squadron (TAS); 168th Air Refueling Squadron (AREFS).
BASE HISTORY: 1952, organized as 8144th Air Base Squadron. 1953, redesignated 144th Fighter-Bomber Squadron with unit training at Elmendorf AFB. 1955, ANG moved to its own base by Anchorage Airport. Kulis ANGB named after 1st Lt Albert Kulis, ANG pilot killed during training mission. 1957, mission changed to airlift. 1969, Squadron raised to group level; renamed 176th TAG with 144th TAS as mission unit. 1986, new flying squadron established and redesignated 176th Composite Group; missions of refueling and airlift under one group commander.
Key Contacts
COMMANDER: Col Kenneth M Taylor Jr.
PUBLIC AFFAIRS: Lt Michael Haller; State Public Affairs Officer, 3601 C St, Ste 620, Anchorage, AK 99503, (907) 249-1253, Autovon 317-626-1253.
PROCUREMENT: TSgt Tony Miller; (907) 249-1288, Autovon 317-626-1288.
TRANSPORTATION: Capt Sharon Antisdell; (907) 249-1158, Autovon 317-626-1158.
PERSONNEL/COMMUNITY ACTIVITIES: Maj Marshall Calvert; Director of Personnel, (907) 249-1137, Autovon 317-626-1137.
Personnel and Expenditures
ACTIVE DUTY PERSONNEL: 287
CIVILIAN PERSONNEL: 268
MILITARY PAYROLL EXPENDITURE: $19.4 mil
CONTRACT EXPENDITURE: $1.8 mil
Services *Medical Facilities:* Medical clinic; Dental clinic. *Recreational Facilities:* Softball field; Officers club; NCO club.

CAMPION AIR FORCE STATION

CAMPION AIR FORCE STATION
APO Seattle, WA, Campion Air Force Station, AK 98703
Autovon 317-743-1200
Profile
BRANCH: Air Force.
MAJOR UNITS: Campion AFS (AAC).

CAPE LISBURNE AIR FORCE STATION

CAPE LISBURNE AIR FORCE STATION
APO Seattle, WA, Cape Lisburne Air Force Station, AK 98716
Autovon 317-725-1200
Profile
BRANCH: Air Force.
MAJOR UNITS: Cape Lisburne AFS (AAC).

CAPE NEWENHAM AIR FORCE STATION

CAPE NEWENHAM AIR FORCE STATION
APO Seattle, WA, Cape Newenham Air Force Station, AK 98745
Autovon 317-794-1200
Profile
BRANCH: Air Force.
MAJOR UNITS: Cape Newenham AFS (AAC).

CAPE ROMANZOF AIR FORCE STATION

CAPE ROMANZOF AIR FORCE STATION
APO Seattle, WA, Cape Romanzof Air Force Station, AK 98706
Autovon 317-795-1200
Profile
BRANCH: Air Force.
MAJOR UNITS: Cape Romanzof AFS (AAC).

COLD BAY

COLD BAY AIR FORCE STATION
APO Seattle, WA, Cold Bay, AK 98711
Autovon 317-469-7200
Profile
BRANCH: Air Force.
MAJOR UNITS: Cold Bay AFS (AAC).

EIELSON AFB

EIELSON AIR FORCE BASE
343rd TFW, Eielson AFB, AK 99702-5000
(907) 377-2116; Autovon 317-377-2116
Profile
BRANCH: Air Force.
SIZE AND LOCATION: 63,110 acres. 26 mi SE of Fairbanks on the Richardson Hwy.
MAJOR UNITS: 343rd Tactical Fighter Wing.
BASE HISTORY: 1943, known as Mile 26 when it opened. 1948, named after Carl Ben Eielson, famed arctic pioneer and aviator. Until 1961, satellite of Ladd Field, taken over by Army and renamed Ft Wainwright. Today, mission: training and equipping tactical air support and close air support for Army forces in AK.
Key Contacts
COMMANDER: Col David Dingee; 343 TFW/CC, (907) 377-6101, Autovon 317-377-6101.

PUBLIC AFFAIRS: Capt Peter D Kirk; 343 TFW/PA, (907) 377-2116, Autovon 317-377-2116.
PROCUREMENT: Maj George O'Neal; Det 1, 5000th Contracting Squadron, (907) 377-2441, Autovon 317-377-2441.
TRANSPORTATION: LTC John Kiland; 343 TRANS Squ/CC, (907) 377-3376, Autovon 317-377-3376.
PERSONNEL/COMMUNITY ACTIVITIES: Capt Gary Olds; 343 MSSq/CC, (907) 377-1132, Autovon 317-377-1132.
Personnel and Expenditures
ACTIVE DUTY PERSONNEL: 3261
DEPENDENTS: 3171
CIVILIAN PERSONNEL: 794
MILITARY PAYROLL EXPENDITURE: FY 88, $83.6 mil
CONTRACT EXPENDITURE: FY 88, $51.5 mil
Services *Housing:* Family units 1463; BOQ cottages 8; Dormitory spaces 1266; Senior NCO units 8; Trailer spaces 84. *Temporary Housing:* VIP cottages 8; VOQ cottages 45; VAQ units 40; BOQ units 8; Transient living quarters 40. *Commissary:* Base commissary; Retail store; Barber shop; Dry cleaners; Food shop; Florist; Service station. *Child Care/Capacities:* Day care center 94; Home day care program. *Schools:* Elementary; Intermediate/Junior high; High school. *Base Library:* Yes. *Medical Facilities:* Medical clinic; Dental clinic. *Recreational Facilities:* Bowling; Movie theater; Pool; Gym; Recreation center; Tennis; Racquetball; Skating rink; Fitness center; Softball field; Football field; Auto shop; Crafts; Officers club; NCO club; Camping; Fishing/Hunting (hunting on federal lands away from base proper).

FORT GREELY

FORT GREELY
APO Seattle, WA, Fort Greely, AK 98733
(907) 872-1121; Autovon 317-872-1121
Profile
BRANCH: Army.
SIZE AND LOCATION: 661 acres. 105 mi S of Fairbanks on Richardson Hwy; near end of ALCAN (Alaska/Canadian Hwy) at Delta Junction.
MAJOR UNITS: Headquarters and Headquarters, US Army Garrison; Headquarters Northern Warfare Training Center; 526th Military Police Detachment; Cold Regions Test Center; US Army Information Systems Command, Ft Greely.
BASE HISTORY: 1942, Army AFB established at Station 17, Alaskan Wing, Air Transport Command. Throughout WWII, transfer point for American and Russian pilots under Lend-Lease. 1945, put on inactive status. 1947, designated site for first postwar cold weather maneuver, Exercise Yukon. 1948, transferred to Army and redesignated Army post, named US Troops, Big Delta, AK. 1948, named site for Arctic Training Center. Originally, Center consisted of: Army Arctic Indoctrination School, Army Training Company, and Test and Development Section. 1952, renamed Army Arctic Center and US Army Chemical Corps-Arctic Test Team established. 1955, designated Ft Greely for Maj Gen Adolphus Washington Greely, arctic explorer and founder of AK Communications System. 1956, Chemical Corps-Arctic Test Team redesignated Class II activity and renamed US Army Chemical Corps-Arctic Test Activity; Arctic Test Group renamed Arctic Test Board and Arctic Indoctrination School became Army Cold Weather and Mountain School which in 1963, became Northern Warfare Training Center. 1964, Arctic Test Board renamed Arctic Test Center. 1974, Ft Greely became part of

FORT GREELY *(continued)*
172nd Infantry Brigade. 1986, with activation of 6th Infantry Division (Light) and US Army Garrison, AK, Ft Greely became one of three posts in single installation concept.
Key Contacts
COMMANDER: Col Donald F Borden; (907) 872-2106, Autovon 317-872-2106.
PUBLIC AFFAIRS: SFC Ron Pruitt; (907) 872-4206, 873-4161, Autovon 317-872-4206, 873-4161.
TRANSPORTATION: SFC Burns; (907) 873-1124, Autovon 317-873-1124.
PERSONNEL/COMMUNITY ACTIVITIES: Capt Lambert; (907) 872-4140, Autovon 317-872-4140.
Personnel and Expenditures
ACTIVE DUTY PERSONNEL: 630
DEPENDENTS: 960
CIVILIAN PERSONNEL: 350
MILITARY PAYROLL EXPENDITURE: $12.8 mil
CONTRACT EXPENDITURE: $3 mil
Services *Housing:* Family units 361; BOQ cottages 20; BEQ units 28. *Temporary Housing:* VOQ cottages 3; VEQ units 32. *Commissary:* Base commissary; Retail store; Barber shop; Dry cleaners; Food shop; Service station; Credit union. *Child Care/Capacities:* Day care center; Home day care program. *Schools:* Kindergarten/Preschool; Elementary. *Base Library:* Yes. *Medical Facilities:* Medical clinic; Dental clinic. *Recreational Facilities:* Bowling; Movie theater; Pool; Gym; Recreation center; Tennis; Racquetball; Skating rink; Fitness center; Softball field; Football field; Auto shop; Crafts; Officers club; NCO club; Fishing/Hunting.

FORT RICHARDSON

FORT RICHARDSON
Fort Richardson, AK 99505
(907) 864-0121; Autovon 317-864-0121
OFFICER-OF-THE-DAY: (907) 864-0133, Autovon (317) 864-0133
Profile
BRANCH: Army.
SIZE AND LOCATION: 64,470 acres. Approx 8 mi N of Anchorage on the Glenn Hwy.
MAJOR UNITS: Headquarters, 6th Infantry Division (Light); 1st Brigade; Division Artillery; Division Support Command; 6th Signal Battalion; 106th Military Intelligence Battalion; US Army Information Systems Command-Alaska.
BASE HISTORY: 1940-41, built on site of what is now post's sister installation, Elmendorf AFB; named for military pioneer explorer, Brig Gen Wilds P Richardson, who served 3 tours of duty in AK Territory, 1897-1917. 1947, established as HQs of US Army AK (USARAL). 1950, moved to present location. 1959, 3 off-post Nike Hercules missiles built. 1961-73, home to US Modern Biathlon Training Center. 1990, 6th Infantry Division (Light) scheduled to move to Ft Wainwright.
VISITOR ATTRACTIONS: Fish and Wildlife Center (museum); Ft Richardson National Cemetery; State-operated fish hatchery.
Key Contacts
COMMANDER: Col Kenneth W Northamer Jr; ATTN: APVR-GC, (907) 862-5197, Autovon (317) 862-5197; Maj Gen Harold T Fields Jr; 6th Infantry Division (Light).
PUBLIC AFFAIRS: Maj George D Lennon; Public Affairs Office, 6th Infantry Division (Light), ATTN: APVR-PO-MR, Ft Richardson, AK 99505-5320, (907) 862-9298, Autovon (317) 862-9298.
PROCUREMENT: Hazen Kramer; ATTN: APVR-DOC, (907) 863-6287, Autovon (317) 863-6287.

TRANSPORTATION: Maj Grady Manning; ATTN: APVR-DL-T, (907) 862-2117, Autovon (317) 862-2117.
PERSONNEL/COMMUNITY ACTIVITIES: LTC William B Lindsey; ATTN: APVR-PA, (907) 862-4100, Autovon (317) 862-4100.
Personnel and Expenditures
ACTIVE DUTY PERSONNEL: 3300
DEPENDENTS: 3900
CIVILIAN PERSONNEL: 1550
MILITARY PAYROLL EXPENDITURE: $117.3 mil
CONTRACT EXPENDITURE: $33 mil
Services *Housing:* Family units 1757; BOQ cottages 24; Barracks spaces 2463; Senior NCO units 39. *Temporary Housing:* VIP cottages 13; VOQ cottages 82; VEQ units 20; Guest cottages 2. *Commissary:* Base commissary; Retail store; Barber shop; Dry cleaners; Florist; Service station; Furniture store. *Child Care/Capacities:* Day care center 117; Home day care program; Before/After school care; Preschool hourly care. *Schools:* Kindergarten/Preschool; Elementary. *Base Library:* Yes. *Medical Facilities:* Medical clinic; Dental clinic. *Recreational Facilities:* Bowling; Movie theater; Pool; Gym; Recreation center; Golf; Tennis; Racquetball; Skating rink; Fitness center; Softball field; Football field; Auto shop; Crafts; Officers club; NCO club; Camping; Fishing/Hunting.

FORT WAINWRIGHT

FORT WAINWRIGHT
Fort Wainwright, AK 98731
(907) 353-7500, ext 907; Autovon 312-353-7500
Profile
BRANCH: Army.
SIZE AND LOCATION: 656,250 acres. Approx 0.25 mi from downtown Fairbanks off Rte 2 (Steese Hwy).
MAJOR UNITS: 4th Battalion, 9th Infantry Regiment; 5th Battalion, 9th Infantry Regiment; 5th Battalion, 11th Field Artillery Regiment; Cold Regions Research and Engineering Laboratory; 6th Infantry Division (Light), 2d Brigade; 6th Infantry Division (Light), 4-9 Infantry; 6th Infantry Division (Light), 5-9 Infantry; 6th Infantry Division (Light), 6th S&T Battalion; 6th Infantry Division (Light), 6th Medical Battalion; 6th Infantry Division (Light), Aviation Brigade; 6th Infantry Division (Light), 4th Squadron, 9th Cavalry; 6th Infantry Division (Light), 4th Battalion, 123rd AVN; DENTAC; US Army Garrison, HQ; US Army Garrison, 42nd Military Police Company; US Army Garrison, 16th Military Police.
BASE HISTORY: Late 1941, originally begun as Ladd Army Airfield, link in AK Siberia Lend Lease route. 1947, became part of Eielson AFB and used as resupply base for Distant Early Warning radar sites and experimental ice stations in Arctic Ocean. 1961, Army reassumed command of Ladd Field; renamed Fort Wainwright for Gen Jonathan M Wainwright, defender of Bataan Peninsula in WWII. Home of 171st Infantry Brigade (Mechanized); Nike-Hercules Battalion; and, 172nd Infantry Brigade.
Personnel and Expenditures
ACTIVE DUTY PERSONNEL: 3500
DEPENDENTS: 4100
CIVILIAN PERSONNEL: 722
CONTRACT EXPENDITURE: $81.2 mil
Services *Housing:* Family units 1725; BOQ cottages 40; BEQ units 32. *Temporary Housing:* VIP cottages 4; VOQ cottages 43; VEQ units 27. *Commissary:* Base commissary; Retail store; Barber shop; Food shop; Florist; Service station; Furniture store; Bakery; Convenience store/Shopette; Four seasons store; Optical shop; Beauty shop; Specialty

concessions; Video rental; Credit union; Laundry; Clothing sales; Construction materiels. *Child Care/Capacities:* Day care center 291; Home day care program; Latch key program. *Schools:* Kindergarten/Preschool. *Medical Facilities:* Hospital (Bassett Army Community Hospital, 58); Dental clinic; Veterinary clinic. *Recreational Facilities:* Bowling; Movie theater; Pool; Gym; Recreation center; Golf; Tennis; Racquetball; Skating rink; Fitness center (weight room); Softball field; Auto shop; Crafts; Officers club; NCO club; Camping; Fishing/Hunting; Youth center; Track facilities; Snow sports; SATO; Skeet shooting; Information, tour and registration office; Outdoor adventure center; Harding Lake, 40 mi SE.

FORT YUKON

FORT YUKON AIR FORCE STATION
APO Seattle, WA, Fort Yukon, AK 98710
Autovon 317-732-1200
Profile
BRANCH: Air Force.
MAJOR UNITS: Fort Yukon AFS (AAC).

GALENA

GALENA AIRPORT
Galena, AK 99741
(907) 446-3309; Autovon 317-446-3309
Profile
BRANCH: Air Force.
SIZE AND LOCATION: 173 acres. 350 mi NW of Anchorage; 270 mi W of Fairbanks.
MAJOR UNITS: 5072nd Combat Support Squadron; Detachment 2, 1931st Information Systems Squadron; 11th Weather Squadron.
VISITOR ATTRACTIONS: Remote location, unaccompanied tours of duty only.
Personnel and Expenditures
ACTIVE DUTY PERSONNEL: 325
Services *Housing:* BOQ cottages 1; Senior NCO units 1; Junior NCO units 1. *Temporary Housing:* VIP cottages 4; VOQ cottages 6; VAQ units 66. *Commissary and Exchange:* Small exchange. *Medical Facilities:* Aid station. *Recreational Facilities:* Bowling; Movie theater; Pool; Gym; Golf; Stables; Tennis; Fitness center; Crafts; Camping; Fishing/Hunting; Aero Club; Skeet shooting; Snow sports.

INDIAN MOUNTAIN AIR FORCE STATION

INDIAN MOUNTAIN AIR FORCE STATION
APO Seattle, WA, Indian Mountain Air Force Station, AK 98748
Autovon 317-722-1200
Profile
BRANCH: Air Force.
MAJOR UNITS: Indian Mountain AFS (AAC).

KODIAK

KODIAK COAST GUARD SUPPORT CENTER
Box 22, Kodiak, AK 99619
(907) 487-5760; Autovon 487-5760
OFFICER-OF-THE-DAY: (907) 487-5267, Autovon 487-5267
Profile
BRANCH: Coast Guard.
SIZE AND LOCATION: 23,000 acres. On NE corner of Kodiak Island, 7 mi S of Kodiak, 1 mi S of Airport; 1 hr flight from Anchorage.

KODIAK COAST GUARD SUPPORT CENTER
(continued)
MAJOR UNITS: Support Center Kodiak; Air
Station Kodiak; Communication Station
Kodiak; Marine Safety Detachment
Kodiak; Loran Station Narrow Cape;
Loran Monitor Station Kodiak; USCGC
Yocona (WMEC 168); USCGC *Ironwood*
(WLB 297); USCGC *Storis* (WMEC 38);
USCGC *Firebush* (WLB 393).
BASE HISTORY: 1939, built by Navy as part of
Aleutian campaign with small USCG de-
tachment assigned as tenant command.
1972, Coast Guard acquired base from
Navy; changed to Support Center Kodiak.
VISITOR ATTRACTIONS: Historic site; strategic
Navy base during WWII, bunkers and ar-
tillery sites still on base; Excellent hunt-
ing, fishing, crabbing, hiking and photo-
graphic opportunities nearby.
Key Contacts
COMMANDER: Capt Joseph S Blackett; Box
14.
PUBLIC AFFAIRS: LTjg Tom Saint; Box 22,
(907) 487-5542, Autovon 487-5542.
PROCUREMENT: Carole Johnson; Box 18,
(907) 487-5818, Autovon 487-5818.
TRANSPORTATION: CWO3 Larry DeMarchi;
Box 1, (907) 487-5761, Autovon 487-
5761.
PERSONNEL/COMMUNITY ACTIVITIES: ENS Su-
san Workman; Box 22, (907) 487-5542,
Autovon 487-5542.
Personnel and Expenditures
ACTIVE DUTY PERSONNEL: 1000
DEPENDENTS: 1500
CIVILIAN PERSONNEL: 320
CONTRACT EXPENDITURE: $4 mil
Services *Housing:* Family units 413; BOQ
cottages 8; BEQ units 213. *Temporary Housing:* BOQ units 8; Guesthouse units 44;
Apartment units 27. *Commissary:* Base com-
missary; Retail store; Barber shop; Dry
cleaners; Food shop; Banking; Service station; Furniture store; Book store; Sporting
goods. *Child Care/Capacities:* Day care center 100. *Schools:* Kindergarten/Preschool;
Elementary. *Base Library:* Yes. *Medical Facilities:* Medical clinic; Dental clinic. *Recreational Facilities:* Bowling; Movie theater;
Gym; Recreation center; Golf; Tennis; Racquetball; Fitness center; Softball field; Football field; Auto shop; Crafts; Officers club;
NCO club; Fishing/Hunting; Sporting equipment & morale boats; Indoor gazebo and
Buskin River beach house for rent; Outdoor
gazebo; Skeet shooting.

KOTZEBUE

KOTZEBUE AIR FORCE STATION
APO Seattle, WA, Kotzebue, AK 98709
Autovon 317-748-1200
Profile
BRANCH: Air Force.
MAJOR UNITS: Kotzebue AFS (AAC).

MCGRATH

TATALINA AIR FORCE STATION
GE Government Services, Tatalina,
McGrath, AK 99627-9999
(907) 728-9001; Autovon 728-1203
Profile
BRANCH: Air Force.
SIZE AND LOCATION: 4970 acres. Approx 230
air mi NW of Anchorage; 150 mi W of
Mt McKinley.
MAJOR UNITS: GE Government Services-elec-
tronics site.
BASE HISTORY: Long-Range Radar (LRRS)
Site.

Key Contacts
COMMANDER: William L Morgan; Site Su-
pervisor.
PUBLIC AFFAIRS: R Johnson; Site Chief, (907)
728-9001, Autovon 728-1248.
Personnel and Expenditures
CIVILIAN PERSONNEL: 10
Services *Temporary Housing:* BAQ units 6.
Recreational Facilities: Softball field.

MURPHY DOME AIR FORCE STATION

MURPHY DOME AIR FORCE STATION
APO Seattle, WA, Murphy Dome Air Force
Station, AK 98750
Autovon 317-744-1200
Profile
BRANCH: Air Force.
MAJOR UNITS: Murphy Dome AFS (AAC).

SHEMYA AFB

SHEMYA AIR FORCE BASE
APO Seattle, WA, Shemya AFB, AK 98736
(907) 392-3000; Autovon 317-392-3000
Profile
BRANCH: Air Force.
SIZE AND LOCATION: 5120 acres. Remote
AFB, 1500 mi W of Anchorage, AK, at
the westernmost top of the Aleutian Is-
lands.
MAJOR UNITS: 5073rd Air Base Group; 16th
Surveillance Squadron; 2064th Commu-
nications Squadron; Detachment 1, 6th
Strategic Wing (SAC).
Key Contacts
COMMANDER: Personnel rotates every 12
months.
Services *Commissary and Exchange:* Retail
store. *Base Library:* Yes. *Medical Facilities:*
Medical clinic. *Recreational Facilities:* Bowl-
ing; Movie theater; Gym; Recreation center;
Racquetball; Fitness center; Softball field.

SPARREVOHN AIR FORCE STATION

SPARREVOHN AIR FORCE STATION
APO Seattle, WA, Sparrevohn Air Force
Station, AK 98746
Autovon 317-731-1200
Profile
BRANCH: Air Force.
MAJOR UNITS: Sparrevohn AFS (AAC).

TIN CITY AIR FORCE STATION

TIN CITY AIR FORCE STATION
APO Seattle, WA, Tin City Air Force
Station, AK 98715
Autovon 317-724-1200
Profile
BRANCH: Air Force.
MAJOR UNITS: Tin City AFS (AAC).

ARIZONA

BELLEMONT

NAVAJO DEPOT ACTIVITY
Bellemont, AZ 86015-5000
(602) 774-7161; Autovon 790-8161
Profile
BRANCH: Army National Guard.
SIZE AND LOCATION: 28,000 acres. 10 mi W of Flagstaff off US 40.
BASE HISTORY: 1942, construction of Navajo Ordnance Depot began; Navajo Indian Reservation furnished much of unskilled labor; first Navajo "town" on record built to house workers, later replaced by Indian Village, including trading post, sheep, weaving looms, and Navajo interpreters. 1942, first ammunition received. 1953, strategic and critical materiels mission assigned. 1955, general supply mission became back-up to Erie Ordnance Depot and then to Benicia Arsenal. 1961, general supplies mission phased out. 1967, assigned physical distribution mission of Defense Logistics Administration. 1971, reserve status assigned and placed under Pueblo Army Depot. 1975, reassigned to Tooele Army Depot Complex. 1982, AZ Army NG took over direct command of depot for training guard units in ammunition operations.
Key Contacts
COMMANDER: LTC Larry Triphan; (602) 774-7161, ext 205, Autovon 790-8205.
PUBLIC AFFAIRS: Maj Timothy J Cowan; ATTN: AZXA-AS, (602) 774-7161, ext 229, Autovon 790-8229.
PROCUREMENT: CW2 William Meyer; (602) 774-7161, ext 294, Autovon 790-8294.
TRANSPORTATION: Sgt Cheryl Mott; (602) 774-7161, ext 209, Autovon 790-8209.
PERSONNEL/COMMUNITY ACTIVITIES: See Public Affairs Officer.
Personnel and Expenditures
ACTIVE DUTY PERSONNEL: 1
CIVILIAN PERSONNEL: 113
Services *Commissary and Exchange:* Retail store; Food shop.

FORT HUACHUCA

FORT HUACHUCA
Commander, ATTN: AS-PI, Fort Huachuca, AZ 85613-5000
(602) 538-8604; Autovon 879-8604
OFFICER-OF-THE-DAY: (602) 538-6100, Autovon 879-6100
Profile
BRANCH: Army.
SIZE AND LOCATION: 73,315 acres. 70 mi SE of Tucson. Take I-10, Exit 302 (Hwy 90); approx 30 mi to Sierra Vista/Fort Huachuca after you pass through Huachuca City.

MAJOR UNITS: US Army Information Systems Command; US Army Electronic Proving Ground; US Army Intelligence Center & School; Joint Test Element (JTC3A).
BASE HISTORY: Arizona's only active Army post, established 1877, when Capt Samuel Marmaduke Whitside and 2 companies of Sixth Cavalry built post in foothills of Huachuca Mountains. 1886, Gen Nelson A Miles' headquarters and forward supply base for campaign against Geronimo and Apaches, captured Geronimo after a 5-month, 3000 mile pursuit throughout SE AZ.
VISITOR ATTRACTIONS: Museum; WWII buildings; Military cemetery dating to 1877; Old post area designated a National Historical Landmark.
Key Contacts
COMMANDER: Lt Gen Thurman D Rodgers; ATTN: AS-CG, (602) 538-6161, Autovon 879-6161.
PUBLIC AFFAIRS: Maj Dennis M Seely; ATTN: ASH-PAO, Ft Huachuca, AZ 85613-6000, (602) 533-2714, Autovon 821-2714.
PROCUREMENT: Ron L Kilby; ATTN: ASH-DOC, Ft Huachuca, AZ 85613-6000, (602) 533-1061, Autovon 821-1061.
TRANSPORTATION: Tom Sochan; ATTN: ASH-DOL, Ft Huachuca, AZ 85613-6000, (602) 533-2041, Autovon 879-2041.
PERSONNEL/COMMUNITY ACTIVITIES: Dan Valle; ATTN: ASH-PCA, Ft Huachuca, AZ 85613-6000, (602) 533-3107, Autovon 821-3107.
Personnel and Expenditures
ACTIVE DUTY PERSONNEL: 6880
DEPENDENTS: 4826
CIVILIAN PERSONNEL: 5234
MILITARY PAYROLL EXPENDITURE: $139.5 mil
CONTRACT EXPENDITURE: $229.4 mil
Services *Housing:* Family units 3524; Duplex units; Townhouse units; Barracks spaces; Senior NCO units 265; Junior NCO units 1304. *Temporary Housing:* VOQ cottages 111; VEQ units 58; BOQ units 147; Guesthouse units 33. *Commissary:* Base commissary; Retail store; Barber shop; Dry cleaners; Food shop; Florist; Banking; Service station; Furniture store. *Child Care/Capacities:* Day care center 200; Home day care program; Latch key programs before and after school. *Schools:* Kindergarten/Preschool; Elementary; Intermediate/Junior high. *Base Library:* Yes. *Medical Facilities:* Hospital 104; Medical clinic; Dental clinic. *Recreational Facilities:* Bowling; Movie theater; Pool; Gym; Recreation center; Golf; Stables; Tennis; Racquetball; Skating rink; Fitness center; Softball field; Football field; Auto shop; Crafts; Officers club; NCO club; Camping; Fishing/Hunting; Hiking.

GILA BEND AF AUXILIARY FIELD

GILA BEND AIR FORCE AUXILIARY FIELD
832nd Combat Support Squadron (TAC), Gila Bend AF Auxiliary Field, AZ 85337-5000
(602) 683-6200
OFFICER-OF-THE-DAY: (602) 683-6220
Profile
BRANCH: Air Force.
SIZE AND LOCATION: 2.7 mil acres. In Sonoran Desert of AZ, 65 mi SW of Luke AFB; 80 mi SW of Phoenix Skyharbor IAP.
MAJOR UNITS: 832nd Combat Support Squadron (TAC).
BASE HISTORY: 1941, site selected for gunnery range to serve advanced flying training for Luke Field and Williams Field. 1940s, control and use of range varied as requirements changed. 1942, small support established S of Gila Bend. 1946-51, military site deactivated; upon reactivation, range remained Williams Bombing and Gunnery Range. 1963, range redesignated Luke Air Force Range. 1986, range redesignated Barry M Goldwater Air Force Range. Today, Gila Bend Air Force Auxiliary Field supports world's largest gunnery range.
VISITOR ATTRACTIONS: Gillespie Dam; Painted Rocks; Butterfield stage route; Sonoran Desert; Oatman graves.
Key Contacts
COMMANDER: Rotates on 2 year tours.
PERSONNEL/COMMUNITY ACTIVITIES: (602) 683-6108, Autovon 853-5108.
Personnel and Expenditures
ACTIVE DUTY PERSONNEL: 250 (military & civilian)
Services *Housing:* Family units 1; Duplex units 10; Dormitory spaces; Trailer spaces 20; Two/Three bedroom units 65. *Temporary Housing:* Guesthouse units 3; Transient living quarters. *Commissary:* Base commissary; Barber shop; Convenience store/Shopette; Credit union; Laundry; Thrift shop; Video rental. *Child Care/Capacities:* Day care center. *Schools:* Kindergarten/Preschool; College courses. *Base Library:* Yes. *Medical Facilities:* Medical clinic; Dental clinic. *Recreational Facilities:* Bowling; Movie theater; Pool; Gym; Racquetball; Fitness center; Auto shop; Crafts; Youth center; Equipment rental.

LUKE AFB

LUKE AIR FORCE BASE
Luke AFB, AZ 85309-5000
(602) 856-6011; Autovon 853-6011
Profile
BRANCH: Air Force.
SIZE AND LOCATION: 4200 acres. 20 mi W of Phoenix, off I-10 on Glendale Ave and Litchfield Rd.
MAJOR UNITS: 832nd Air Division; 58th Tactical Training Wing; 405th Tactical Training Wing; 832nd Combat Support Group; 607th Tactical Control Training Squadron; 2037th Communications Squadron; 944th Tactical Fighter Group (Reserve); Detachment 1, 4444th Operations Squadron; Detachment 832, 4400th Management Engineering Squadron; Detachment 15, 25th Weather Squadron; 527th Field Training Detachment; Detachment 1815 Air Force Office of Special Investigations; Area Defense Counsel; Detachment 51 Central Audit Region.
BASE HISTORY: 1941, Army Air Corps advanced training facility for pilots of fighter aircraft, Luke Field, named for Lt Frank Luke Jr, Phoenix native and WWI pilot, first aviator to receive Medal of Honor. During WWII, nicknamed, "Home of the Fighter Pilot." 1946, closed. 1951, reactivated as Luke AFB under Air Training Command, home to 127th Pilot Training Wing. 1958, transferred to TAC, parent unit 4510th Combat Crew Training Wing, later, 58th Tactical Fighter Training Wing, 1969. 1977, HQs Tactical Training Luke (TTL) activated. 1980, HQs TTL became 832nd Air Division.
Key Contacts
COMMANDER: Brig Gen Daniel J Sherlock; Air Division Commander, 832AD/CC, (602) 856-5832, Autovon 853-5832.
PUBLIC AFFAIRS: Capt Joseph Davis; 832AD/PA, (602) 856-6011, Autovon 853-6011.
TRANSPORTATION: LTC F L Bennett; 832TRANS/CC, (602) 856-7743, Autovon 853-7743.
PERSONNEL/COMMUNITY ACTIVITIES: LTC G Williams; Director of Personnel, 832MSP/CC, (602) 856-7001, Autovon 853-7001.
Personnel and Expenditures
ACTIVE DUTY PERSONNEL: 6500
DEPENDENTS: 15,000
CIVILIAN PERSONNEL: 2000
Services Housing: Dormitory spaces 1472. Temporary Housing: VIP cottages 2; BOQ units 162; BAQ units 85; Transient living quarters 40; TLQ for families 40. Commissary: Base commissary; Retail store; Barber shop; Dry cleaners; Food shop; Florist; Banking; Service station. Child Care/Capacities: Day care center. Schools: Elementary. Base Library: Yes. Medical Facilities: Hospital; Medical clinic; Dental clinic. Recreational Facilities: Bowling; Movie theater; Pool; Gym; Recreation center; Stables; Tennis; Racquetball; Fitness center; Softball field; Auto shop; Crafts; Officers club; NCO club.

PHOENIX

PAPAGO MILITARY INSTALLATION
5636 E McDowell Rd, Phoenix, AZ 85008-3495
(602) 267-2897; Autovon 853-2897
OFFICER-OF-THE-DAY: (602) 267-2739, Autovon 853-2739

Profile
BRANCH: Air National Guard; Army National Guard.
SIZE AND LOCATION: 75 acres. In Phoenix at 52nd St and McDowell Rd.
MAJOR UNITS: Headquarters Military Affairs for Air and Army National Guard; Headquarters 385th Aviation Group; Arizona Military Academy.
Key Contacts
COMMANDER: Brig Gen Peter D Tosi; (602) 267-2713, Autovon 853-2713.
PUBLIC AFFAIRS: Army National Guard of Arizona, 123rd Public Affairs Detachment, 1335 N 52nd St, Phoenix, AZ 85008-3433.
PROCUREMENT: LTC Burns; (602) 267-2819, Autovon 853-2819.
PERSONNEL/COMMUNITY ACTIVITIES: Col Austin Graton; (602) 267-2790, Autovon 853-2790.
Personnel and Expenditures
ACTIVE DUTY PERSONNEL: 40
CIVILIAN PERSONNEL: 100

161ST AIR REFUELING GROUP (ANG)
Sky Harbor IAP, Phoenix, AZ 85034
(602) 244-9841; Autovon 853-9211
Profile
BRANCH: Air National Guard.
SIZE AND LOCATION: 51 acres. At Sky Harbor IAP, off Maricopa Fwy, I-17.
MAJOR UNITS: 161st Air Refueling Group (ANG).
Personnel and Expenditures
ACTIVE DUTY PERSONNEL: 927
CIVILIAN PERSONNEL: 243
MILITARY PAYROLL EXPENDITURE: $10.5 mil

TUCSON

DAVIS-MONTHAN AIR FORCE BASE
Tucson, AZ 85707
(602) 750-4717; Autovon 361-4717
Profile
BRANCH: Air Force.
SIZE AND LOCATION: 10,763 acres. In Tucson, approx 20 min from Tucson IAP.
MAJOR UNITS: 836th Air Division; 355th Tactical Training Wing; 602nd Tactical Air Control Wing; 868th Tactical Training Missile Group.
BASE HISTORY: 1927, Army Air Corps established airfield; named for 2 Air Corps officers, Lt Samuel H Davis, who died in air crash at Carlstrom Field, FL, 1921, and Lt Oscar Monthan, who died in crash near Honolulu, HI, 1924.
VISITOR ATTRACTIONS: Tours of Aerospace Maintenance and Regeneration Center, storage yard for US military aircraft; reservations required approx 4 weeks in advance. Tours given on Mon/Wed (one a day); 2nd Sat of each month, 4-hr photographers tour, reservations required.
Key Contacts
COMMANDER: Col Joseph Sugg; Combat Support Group Commander, (602) 750-3444, Autovon 361-3444.
PUBLIC AFFAIRS: Capt Mark Besich; (602) 750-3204, Autovon 361-3204.
PROCUREMENT: Maj Virgil DeArmand; (602) 750-3131, Autovon 361-3131.
TRANSPORTATION: Maj J D Hamilton Jr; (602) 750-3542, Autovon 361-3542.
Personnel and Expenditures
ACTIVE DUTY PERSONNEL: 5348
DEPENDENTS: 3055
CIVILIAN PERSONNEL: 2421
MILITARY PAYROLL EXPENDITURE: FY 88, $116.5 mil
CONTRACT EXPENDITURE: FY 88, $8.6 mil

Services Housing: Family units 1239; Dormitory spaces 1397; Mobile home units 102. Temporary Housing: VIP cottages 8; VOQ cottages 178; VEQ units 408; Transient living quarters 16. Commissary: Base commissary; Retail store; Barber shop; Dry cleaners; Food shop; Florist; Banking; Service station; Furniture store; Bakery; Book store; Optical shop. Child Care/Capacities: Day care center. Schools: Kindergarten/Preschool; Elementary. Base Library: Yes. Medical Facilities: Hospital; Dental clinic. Recreational Facilities: Bowling; Movie theater; Pool; Gym; Recreation center; Golf; Stables; Tennis; Racquetball; Skating rink; Fitness center; Softball field; Auto shop; Crafts; Officers club; NCO club.

162ND TACTICAL FIGHTER GROUP
Tucson IAP, Tucson, AZ 85706
(602) 573-2192; Autovon 853-4192
OFFICER-OF-THE-DAY: Capt George Rutter; (602) 573-2193, Autovon 853-4193
Profile
BRANCH: Air National Guard.
SIZE AND LOCATION: 84 acres. NW of Tucson IAP.
MAJOR UNITS: 162nd Tactical Fighter Group; 152nd Tactical Fighter Squadron; 195th Tactical Fighter Training Squadron; 148th Tactical Fighter Training Squadron.
BASE HISTORY: 152nd Observation Squadron, predecessor to 162nd, originated with RIANG, 1939. 1956, 152nd FIS of AZANG organized, Tucson. Began with old adobe farmhouse and hangar for one airplane. End of 1950s, grew to Group status, first ANG unit designated Tactical Fighter Training Group; ANG Fighter Weapons School formed for advanced tactics and weapons employed for systems used by reserve air forces. Only A-7 and F-16 Combat Air-Crew Training Base in US.
Key Contacts
COMMANDER: Col Glen W Van Dyke; (602) 573-2100, Autovon 853-4100.
PUBLIC AFFAIRS: Capt Neil L Talboff; 162 TAC FTR GP (TAC), PO Box 11037, Tucson, AZ 85734-1037.
PROCUREMENT: See Officer-of-the-Day.
TRANSPORTATION: See Officer-of-the-Day.
PERSONNEL/COMMUNITY ACTIVITIES: See Officer-of-the-Day.
Personnel and Expenditures
ACTIVE DUTY PERSONNEL: 2198
CIVILIAN PERSONNEL: 88
MILITARY PAYROLL EXPENDITURE: $31.3 mil
CONTRACT EXPENDITURE: $15.9 mil
Services Medical Facilities: Medical clinic. Recreational Facilities: Officers club; NCO club.

WILLIAMS AFB

WILLIAMS AIR FORCE BASE
Williams AFB, AZ 85240-5000
(602) 988-2611; Autovon 474-1011
OFFICER-OF-THE-DAY: (602) 988-6811, Autovon 474-6811
Profile
BRANCH: Air Force.
SIZE AND LOCATION: 4758 acres. 10 mi E of Chandler, AZ; 12 mi SE of Mesa; 30 mi SE of Phoenix; 25 mi from Sky Harbor IAP; 16 mi E of Exit 160 on I-10.
MAJOR UNITS: 82nd Flying Training Wing; 425th Tactical Fighter Training Squadron; Air Force Human Relations Laboratory/Operations Training Division; 1922nd Communications Squadron; Field Training Detachment 528; 96th Flying Training Squadron; 97th Flying Training Squadron "Devil Cats"; Detachment 17, 24th Weather Squadron (MAC); Detachment 13, 3314th Management Engineer-

WILLIAMS AIR FORCE BASE (continued)
ing Squadron; Detachment 1817, Office of Special Investigations.
BASE HISTORY: 1941, construction of Higley Field began; variously known as Higley Field, Mesa Air Base, and Mesa Military Airport before named Williams Field, 1942, for 1st Lt Charles Linton Williams, AZ native killed in air crash, 1927. WWII, basic flying training, bombardment training in B-17s, instrument bombing specialist training in B-24s, and fighter gunnery school, in addition to training British and Chinese pilots. 1946, first jet pilot training base. 1958-60, TAC in charge. 1960s, Air Training Command resumed control. 1976, first women officers entered AF Undergraduate Pilot Training.

Key Contacts
COMMANDER: Col Ronald E Smith; 82nd Air Base Group/CC, (602) 988-5311, Autovon 474-5311.
PUBLIC AFFAIRS: Capt Linda L Britt; 82nd Flying Training Wing/PA, Williams AFB, AZ 85240-5154, (602) 988-5808, Autovon 474-5808.
PROCUREMENT: Maj Joseph Goldblatt; 82nd Flying Training Wing/LGC, (602) 988-5856, Autovon 474-5856.
TRANSPORTATION: Maj Donald Carrico; 82nd Flying Training Wing/LGC, (602) 988-5517, Autovon 474-5517.
PERSONNEL/COMMUNITY ACTIVITIES: LTC John Cleveland; 82nd Air Base Group/ DP, (602) 988-6918, Autovon 474-6918.

Personnel and Expenditures
ACTIVE DUTY PERSONNEL: 3047
DEPENDENTS: 6554
CIVILIAN PERSONNEL: 1577
MILITARY PAYROLL EXPENDITURE: $89.5 mil
CONTRACT EXPENDITURE: $46.8 mil
Services *Housing:* Family units 700; BOQ cottages 160; Dormitory spaces 671. *Temporary Housing:* VIP cottages 10; VOQ cottages 28; VEQ units 39; Guesthouse units 40. *Commissary:* Base commissary; Retail store; Barber shop; Dry cleaners; Food shop; Florist; Banking; Service station; Beauty shop; Computer store. *Child Care/Capacities:* Day care center 122; Home day care program. *Schools:* Kindergarten/Preschool; Elementary; Intermediate/Junior high. *Base Library:* Yes. *Medical Facilities:* Hospital 20; Dental clinic. *Recreational Facilities:* Bowling; Movie theater; Pool; Gym; Recreation center; Golf; Tennis; Racquetball; Fitness center; Softball field; Football field; Auto shop; Crafts; Officers club; NCO club; Camping; Fishing/Hunting.

YUMA

YUMA MARINE CORPS AIR STATION
Yuma, AZ 85369-5000
(602) 726-2224; Autovon 951-2224
OFFICER-OF-THE-DAY: (602) 726-2252, Autovon 951-2252
Profile
BRANCH: Marines.
SIZE AND LOCATION: 3060 acres. In SW corner of AZ, 20 mi N of Mexican border, within Yuma city limits; 2 mi E of Yuma IAP.
MAJOR UNITS: Marine Aircraft Group-13; Headquarters and Maintenance Squadron-13; Marine Attack Squadron-211; Marine Attack Squadron-214; Marine Attack Squadron-311; Marine Attack Squadron-513; Marine Wing Support Squadron-371; Marine Fighter Training Squadron-401; 2nd Light Antiaircraft Missile Battalion; Marine Air Control Squadron-7.
BASE HISTORY: 1928, federal government leased 640 acres of desert land for flying field, Fly Field. WWII, taken over by

Army Air Corps, renamed Yuma Army Airfield and site of flying school. Following WWII, all flight activities ceased. 1951, reactivated as weapons proficiency center for fighter-interceptor units; named Yuma Air Base. 1956, renamed Vincent Air Force Base for Brig Gen Clinton D Vincent. 1959, facility signed over to Navy, and designated Marine Corps Auxiliary Air Station. 1962, designation changed to current Marine Corps Air Station.

Key Contacts
COMMANDER: Col F Mack Luckie.
PUBLIC AFFAIRS: 1st Lt M H Baldwin; Joint Public Affairs Office, (602) 726-2275, Autovon 951-2275.
PROCUREMENT: LCDR G R Schafer; Supply Officer, Supply Dept, (602) 726-2722, Autovon 951-2722.
TRANSPORTATION: 1st Lt M K Hayden; Traffic Management Officer, Traffic Management Office, (602) 726-2019, Autovon 951-2019.
PERSONNEL/COMMUNITY ACTIVITIES: LTC H C Geren II; MWR Officer, (602) 726-2278, Autovon 951-2278.

Personnel and Expenditures
ACTIVE DUTY PERSONNEL: 5316
DEPENDENTS: 2040
CIVILIAN PERSONNEL: 1266
MILITARY PAYROLL EXPENDITURE: $70.2 mil
CONTRACT EXPENDITURE: $33.8 mil
Services *Housing:* Family units 908; BOQ cottages (barracks 34 rms); BEQ units (barracks 887 rms); BAQ units; Senior NCO units (barracks 90 rms). *Temporary Housing:* VIP cottages 1; VOQ cottages 282; VEQ units 594; VAQ units; BOQ units; BAQ units; Guesthouse units 13. *Commissary:* Base commissary; Retail store; Barber shop; Dry cleaners; Banking; Service station. *Child Care/Capacities:* Day care center 306; Home day care program. *Base Library:* Yes. *Medical Facilities:* Medical clinic; Dental clinic. *Recreational Facilities:* Bowling; Movie theater; Pool; Gym; Stables; Tennis; Racquetball; Fitness center; Softball field; Football field; Auto shop; Officers club; NCO club; Camping; Fishing/Hunting.

YUMA PROVING GROUND
Yuma, AZ 85365
(602) 328-1110
OFFICER-OF-THE-DAY: (602) 328-2020, Autovon 899-2020
Profile
BRANCH: Army.
SIZE AND LOCATION: 1 mil acres. Approx 26 mi NE of Yuma and accessible from US-95, clearly marked.
MAJOR UNITS: Medical Department Activity (MEDDAC); Dental Activity (DENTAC); US Army Information Systems Command (USAISC).
BASE HISTORY: 1943, activated as Yuma Test Branch under Corps of Engineers to test bridges, boats, vehicles, and well drilling equipment. 1944, Imperial Dam Engineer Station established. 1945, abolished but continued as Engineer Board, Engineer Research and Development Laboratories, Yuma Test Branch, until deactivation, 1950. 1951, reactivated as Yuma Test Station, Class I installation under Sixth US Army. 1956, designated permanent Class I installation. 1962, redesignated and reassigned Yuma Test Station as Class II installation, under AMC, and TECOM. 1963, redesignated Yuma Proving Ground.
VISITOR ATTRACTIONS: US Army Parachute Team, Golden Knights, conduct winter training during Jan-Feb; Asian-Pacific Islander Week (May); Hispanic Week (Sept); American Indian Pow-Wow; Black

History Week (Jan); Military Appreciation Days (MADays).
Key Contacts
COMMANDER: Col William J Miller; Commander, USAYPG, (602) 328-2163, Autovon 899-2163.
PUBLIC AFFAIRS: Bernard J Duffy; Commander, USAYPG, ATTN: STEYP-PA, (602) 328-2533; 328-2167, Autovon 899-2533, 899-2167.
PROCUREMENT: Loren D Cady; Commander, USAYPG, ATTN: STEYP-CR, (602) 328-3285, Autovon 899-3285.
TRANSPORTATION: Commander, USAYPG, (602) 328-2654, Autovon 899-2654.
PERSONNEL/COMMUNITY ACTIVITIES: Maj Wayne Y Katayama; Commander, USAYPG, ATTN: STEYP-CA, (602) 328-2183, Autovon 899-2183.

Personnel and Expenditures
ACTIVE DUTY PERSONNEL: 375
DEPENDENTS: 570
CIVILIAN PERSONNEL: 1000
MILITARY PAYROLL EXPENDITURE: $89.5 mil
CONTRACT EXPENDITURE: $31.1 mil
Services *Housing:* Family units 290; Barracks spaces 435; Mobile home units 8. *Temporary Housing:* BOQ units 9; BAQ units 8; Guesthouse units 8. *Commissary:* Base commissary; Retail store; Barber shop; Dry cleaners; Food shop; Banking; Service station; Bakery. *Child Care/Capacities:* Day care center 100. *Schools:* Kindergarten/Preschool; Elementary, grades 1-5. *Base Library:* Yes. *Medical Facilities:* Medical clinic; Dental clinic. *Recreational Facilities:* Bowling; Movie theater; Pool; Gym; Recreation center; Tennis; Racquetball; Fitness center; Softball field; Auto shop; Crafts; Fishing/Hunting; Combined Community Club.

ARKANSAS

BLYTHEVILLE

EAKER AIR FORCE BASE
97 BMW, Blytheville, AR 72317-5000
(501) 762-7000; Autovon 721-7000
Profile
BRANCH: Air Force.
SIZE AND LOCATION: 3931 acres. In NE AR; From I-55 exit to US 61 N through Blytheville to Gosnell to the main gate; 70 mi N of Memphis off I-55.
MAJOR UNITS: 97th Bombardment Wing.
BASE HISTORY: 1942, activated as Army airfield; used as advanced flying school in Southeastern Training Command's pilot training program. After WWII, used as discharge processing center. 1945, inactivated, land placed under administrative control of AMC. 1955, TAC assumed control and 461st BMW moved from Hill AFB, UT. 1959, 97th Combat Support Group took charge as 97th BMW. 1988, renamed for Gen Ira C Eaker, air pioneer and first commander of 8th Air Force during WWII.
Key Contacts
COMMANDER: Col Peter J Giroux; 97 CSG/CC, (501) 762-7211, Autovon 721-7211.
PUBLIC AFFAIRS: Capt Thomas L Pander III; 97 BMW/PA, (501) 762-7232, Autovon 721-7232.
PROCUREMENT: Capt Van Matthews; 97 CPTS/LGC, (501) 762-6213, Autovon 721-6213.
TRANSPORTATION: Maj Douglas P Baird; 97 TRNS/CC, (501) 762-7387, Autovon 721-7387.
PERSONNEL/COMMUNITY ACTIVITIES: Maj James K Evernham; 97 CSG/DP, (501) 762-7753, Autovon 721-7753; Community Activities see Public Affairs Officer.
Personnel and Expenditures
ACTIVE DUTY PERSONNEL: 2996
DEPENDENTS: 4400
CIVILIAN PERSONNEL: 336
MILITARY PAYROLL EXPENDITURE: $67 mil (military and civilian)
CONTRACT EXPENDITURE: $20.9 mil
Services *Housing:* Family units 195; Senior NCO units 82; Junior NCO units 650. *Temporary Housing:* VOQ cottages 22; VEQ units 24; Transient living quarters 4. *Commissary:* Base commissary; Retail store; Barber shop; Dry cleaners; Food shop; Florist; Banking; Service station. *Child Care/Capacities:* Day care center; Home day care program. *Schools:* Kindergarten/Preschool. *Base Library:* Yes. *Medical Facilities:* Hospital; Dental clinic. *Recreational Facilities:* Bowling; Movie theater; Pool; Gym; Recreation center; Golf; Tennis; Racquetball; Fitness center; Softball field; Football field; Auto shop; Crafts; Officers club; NCO club; Fishing/Hunting.

FORT CHAFFEE

FORT CHAFFEE
US Army Garrison, Fort Chaffee, AR 72905-5000
(501) 484-2141; Autovon 962-2141
OFFICER-OF-THE-DAY: (501) 484-2666, Autovon 962-2666
Profile
BRANCH: Army.
SIZE AND LOCATION: 72,000 acres. 5 mi SE of Ft Smith, AR, on AR State Hwy-22; From IH-40, take exit for IH-540 W, then take Exit No 8 for AR State Hwy 22 E.
MAJOR UNITS: Joint Readiness Training Center (JRTC); 5th Army Consolidated Training Activity.
BASE HISTORY: 1941, construction began; most of present buildings date from that time; named for Maj Gen Adna R Chaffee, first Chief of Armored Forces; first mission to train armored divisions. 1942-1945, German POWs imprisoned. 1946-48, placed on inactive status until designated home of 5th Armored Division (deactivated 1950, resumed operations with Korean Conflict). 1956, redesignated as Fort Chaffee. 1957, 5th again deactivated and fort became US Army Training Center, Field Artillery; additional mission of training Reserve forces. 1959, placed in caretaker status with HQ XIX US Army Corps remaining. 1961, reopened as training center. 1965, inactivated; used for NG and Reserve summer training. 1975, Refugee Processing Center for Vietnamese Refugees. 1980-82, Resettlement Center for Cuban Refugees. 1986, Joint Readiness Training Center established. Currently, training begins in May and continues through Aug. Regional Medical Training Center and Regional Maintenance Training Site approved for implementation in FY 1990 and 1991 respectively.
Key Contacts
COMMANDER: Col Henry S Larsen Jr; (501) 484-2282, Autovon 962-2282.
PUBLIC AFFAIRS: (501) 484-2905, Autovon 962-2905.
PROCUREMENT: (501) 484-2818, Autovon 962-2818.
TRANSPORTATION: (501) 484-2068, Autovon 962-2068.
PERSONNEL/COMMUNITY ACTIVITIES: Personnel and Administration Division, (501) 484-3130, Autovon 962-3130.
Personnel and Expenditures
ACTIVE DUTY PERSONNEL: 185
CIVILIAN PERSONNEL: 400
MILITARY PAYROLL EXPENDITURE: $17 mil
Services *Housing:* Barracks spaces 200; RV/Camper sites 20. *Temporary Housing:* VIP cottages 4; VOQ cottages 5; VEQ units 6; BOQ units 6. *Commissary and Exchange:* Retail store; Barber shop; Service station; Clothing sales. *Base Library:* Yes. *Medical Facilities:* Troop medical clinic staffed by medic. *Recreational Facilities:* Bowling; Movie theater; Pool; Gym; Recreation center; Golf; Tennis; Racquetball; Softball field; Football field; Officers club; NCO club; Camping; Fishing/Hunting; (hunting on days specified by the State, with license); All ranks club.

FORT SMITH

188TH TACTICAL FIGHTER GROUP
AR ANG Municipal Airport, Fort Smith, AR 72903-6096
(501) 648-5100
Profile
BRANCH: Air National Guard.
LOCATION: In S Fort Smith, AR, off I-540.
MAJOR UNITS: 184th Tactical Fighter Squadron; 188th Consolidated Aircraft Maintenance Squadron; 188th Mission Support Squadron; 188th Tactical Clinic; 188th Civil Engineering Squadron; 188th Resource Management Squadron.
BASE HISTORY: 1953, 184th Tactical Reconnaissance Squadron federally recognized at Fort Smith, AR. 188th TFG activated during Berlin Crisis of 1961, supported Vietnamese airlift in 1975, and Cuban boatlift in 1980.
Key Contacts
COMMANDER: LTC Robert R Hardy.
PUBLIC AFFAIRS: 188th TAC FTR GP/PA.
Personnel and Expenditures
ACTIVE DUTY PERSONNEL: 1000
CIVILIAN PERSONNEL: 332
MILITARY PAYROLL EXPENDITURE: $4.4 mil
CONTRACT EXPENDITURE: $1.3 mil
Services *Medical Facilities:* Medical clinic; Dental clinic.

LITTLE ROCK

US ARMY CORPS OF ENGINEERS, LITTLE ROCK DISTRICT
PO Box 867, 700 W Capitol St, Little Rock, AR 72203-0867
(501) 378-5551
Profile
BRANCH: Army.
LOCATION: Near the center of Little Rock.
MAJOR UNITS: Corps of Engineers.
BASE HISTORY: 1881, established for work on limited navigation projects and investigations on Arkansas, St Francis, L'Anguille, Saline, White, Black, Current, and Fourche LaFave Rivers; dredging and channeling main projects. 1923, combined with Memphis District. 1937, reorganized as Little Rock District. 1939, Denison District formed, and Tulsa District activated from Little Rock territory. 1980, territory added to District. Today, manages Ar-

US ARMY CORPS OF ENGINEERS, LITTLE ROCK DISTRICT *(continued)*

kansas River watershed between Fort Smith and Pine Bluff, White River watershed above Peach Orchard Bluff, near Georgetown, AR, and Little River Basin in SW AR; both civil works and military construction missions. Additionally, responsible for developing and operating water resource projects in most of AR and southern MO, for flood control, recreation, hydroelectric power generation, and improvement of fish and wildlife. Current projects: Beaver, Blue Mountain, Bull Shoals, Clearwater, DeQueen, Dierks, Gillham, Greers Ferry, Millwood, Nimrod, Norfolk, and Table Rock plus entire McClellan-Kerr Arkansas River Navigation System.

Key Contacts

COMMANDER: Col Anthony V Nida; (501) 378-5531.

PUBLIC AFFAIRS: David G McNully; ATTN: Public Affairs Office CESWL-PA.

PROCUREMENT: Ian Snyder; (501) 378-5720.

TRANSPORTATION: Judy Greenwood; (501) 378-5651.

PERSONNEL/COMMUNITY ACTIVITIES: Larry Fincher; Director of Personnel, (501) 378-6350.

Personnel and Expenditures

ACTIVE DUTY PERSONNEL: 6
CIVILIAN PERSONNEL: 875
MILITARY PAYROLL EXPENDITURE: $30 mil
CONTRACT EXPENDITURE: $94 mil
Services *Base Library:* Yes.

LITTLE ROCK AFB

LITTLE ROCK AIR FORCE BASE

Little Rock AFB, AR 72099-5000
(501) 988-3601; Autovon 731-3601
OFFICER-OF-THE-DAY: (501) 988-3200, Autovon 731-3300

Profile

BRANCH: Air Force.

SIZE AND LOCATION: 6898 acres. 17 mi NE of Little Rock, adj to Jacksonville, AR.

MAJOR UNITS: 314th Tactical Airlift Wing; 314th Combat Support Group; 189th Tactical Airlift Group (AR ANG); Joint Readiness Training Center (Army); 2151st Communications Squadron (AFCC); Air Force Office of Special Investigations, Detachment 0813; Detachment 9, 1365th Audiovisual Squadron, Aerospace Audiovisual Service; Detachment 20, 17th Weather Squadron; Field Training Detachment 310; 96th Mobile Aerial Port Squadron; Detachment 243, Air Force Audit Agency; 22nd Air Force NCO Leadership School.

BASE HISTORY: 1953, construction began, part of SAC. 1960s, support base for Titan II ICBMs around N central AR, as 308th Strategic Missile Wing. 1970, came under TAC, with 64th TAW host until replaced by 314th TAW, 1971. 1970, transferred from SAC to TAC again, and 64th TAW, Stewart AFBS, TN, became host. 1971, unit redesignated 314th TAW, MAC. 1974, MAC assumed control. 1986, Army's Joint Readiness Training Center (JRTC) established; trains non-mechanized infantry battalion task forces. 1986, AR ANG became 189th TAG.

Key Contacts

COMMANDER: Col Donald E Loranger Jr; Commander, 314 TAW, (501) 988-6401, Autovon 731-6401.

PUBLIC AFFAIRS: Capt Richard J Reibeling.

PROCUREMENT: Capt Anthony McCoy; (501) 988-3303, Autovon 731-3303.

TRANSPORTATION: Maj Clarence J Evans; (501) 988-6755, Autovon 731-6755.

PERSONNEL/COMMUNITY ACTIVITIES: LTC Gary Rowland; (501) 988-6349, Autovon 731-6349.

Personnel and Expenditures

ACTIVE DUTY PERSONNEL: 6700
DEPENDENTS: 3575
CIVILIAN PERSONNEL: 817
MILITARY PAYROLL EXPENDITURE: $280 mil
CONTRACT EXPENDITURE: $28.2 mil
Services *Temporary Housing:* VIP cottages; VOQ cottages; VEQ units; VAQ units; BOQ units; BAQ units; Guesthouse units; Guest cottages; Apartment units; Lodge units; Dormitory units; Mobile home units; Transient living quarters. *Commissary:* Base commissary; Barber shop; Dry cleaners; Food shop; Florist; Banking; Service station; Bakery. *Child Care/Capacities:* Day care center. *Schools:* Kindergarten/Preschool; Elementary. *Base Library:* Yes. *Medical Facilities:* Hospital. *Recreational Facilities:* Bowling; Movie theater; Pool; Gym; Recreation center; Golf; Stables; Tennis; Racquetball; Fitness center; Softball field; Football field; Auto shop; Crafts; Officers club; NCO club; Camping; Fishing/Hunting.

NORTH LITTLE ROCK

CAMP JOSEPH T ROBINSON

Arkansas National Guard Headquarters, North Little Rock, AR 72118-2200
(501) 771-5100; Autovon 731-5100
OFFICER-OF-THE-DAY: Fire & Security Office, (501) 771-5280, Autovon 731-5280

Profile

BRANCH: Army National Guard.

SIZE AND LOCATION: 48,188 acres. In N Little Rock with connecting roads from I-40, follow the signs, or from Hwy 176; 12 mi to Little Rock Regional Airport; 8 mi to Little Rock AFB.

MAJOR UNITS: HQ, Arkansas National Guard; HQ, 39th Infantry Brigade; State Area Command; Detachment 1, State Area Command (Troop Command); Professional Education Center.

BASE HISTORY: 1917, War Department constructed huge post named Camp Pike in honor of explorer, Zebulon Pike. After WWI, closed. 1922, used as NG training area. 1937, renamed Camp Joseph T Robinson for US Senator Robinson of AR; basic training base and POW camp. In past decade, many of prewar structures replaced; open for year round training. All branches train here; brigade-sized infantry, artillery, engineer, or combat service support units in non-live fire exercises can be accommodated one at a time.

VISITOR ATTRACTIONS: Aircraft, flag, artillery, and equipment display on 7th St.

Key Contacts

COMMANDER: Maj Gen James A Ryan; Adjutant General, TAG, (501) 771-5200, Autovon 731-5200; Training Site Manager: Maj Larry W Haltom; Camp Robinson Training Site, ATTN: TSM-D, (501) 771-5260, Autovon 731-5260.

PUBLIC AFFAIRS: Maj Alicia C Lashbrook; State Public Affairs Officer, TAG-AZ-PA, (501) 771-5207, Autovon 731-5207.

PROCUREMENT: Bill Stenson; State Purchasing Agent, State Personnel/Purchasing, (501) 771-5241, Autovon 731-5241.

TRANSPORTATION: Maj Nathaniel McGee; State Maintenance Office, (501) 771-5171, Autovon 731-5171.

PERSONNEL/COMMUNITY ACTIVITIES: Col Alf Langston; Director of Personnel, DPA, (501) 771-5101; Autovon 731-5101; Community Activities see Public Affairs Officer.

Personnel and Expenditures

ACTIVE DUTY PERSONNEL: 561 Guard (AGR); 523 Army Technicians
CIVILIAN PERSONNEL: 148
MILITARY PAYROLL EXPENDITURE: $128.3 mil
CONTRACT EXPENDITURE: $3.1 mil
Services *Housing:* Family units 1136. *Temporary Housing:* VIP cottages 2; VOQ cottages 26; VEQ units 100; Dormitory units 360; Mobile home units 7. *Commissary and Exchange:* Canteen. *Medical Facilities:* Medical clinic. *Recreational Facilities:* Pool; Gym; Recreation center; Golf; Tennis; Fitness center; Softball field; Fishing/Hunting; All ranks club; Fitness trail.

CALIFORNIA

ALAMEDA

ALAMEDA COAST GUARD ISLAND
Alameda, CA 94501-5100
(415) 437-3324
OFFICER-OF-THE-DAY: (415) 437-3156 ,
Profile
BRANCH: Coast Guard.
SIZE AND LOCATION: 43 acres. In middle of Oakland Estuary between cities of Alameda and Oakland, CA. I-880 runs N-S only 2 blocks E of Island. Oakland IAP approx 5 mi S of Island.
MAJOR UNITS: Coast Guard Pacific Area Headquarters; Maintenance & Logistics Command Pacific; Coast Guard Support Center Alameda; Marine Safety Office San Francisco Bay.
Key Contacts
COMMANDER: Capt Paul Resnick; Support Center Alameda, Bldg 21, Coast Guard Island, (415) 437-3171.
PUBLIC AFFAIRS: LCDR Jack L Hardin; Commander (Ppa), Coast Guard Pacific Area, Coast Guard Island, (415) 437-3324.
PROCUREMENT: Capt Ralph E Anderson; (415) 437-3011.
TRANSPORTATION: (415) 437-3051.
PERSONNEL/COMMUNITY ACTIVITIES: Capt Alan Rosebrook; Maintenance & Logistics Command Pacific, (415) 437-3925.
Personnel and Expenditures
ACTIVE DUTY PERSONNEL: 600
CIVILIAN PERSONNEL: 300
Services *Temporary Housing:* BOQ units 10; Barracks 2. *Commissary and Exchange:* Retail store; Barber shop; Dry cleaners; Food shop; Service station. *Medical Facilities:* Medical clinic; Dental clinic. *Recreational Facilities:* Pool; Gym; Tennis; Racquetball; Fitness center; Softball field; Football field; Auto shop; NCO club.

ALAMEDA NAVAL AIR STATION
Alameda, CA 94501-5000
(415) 869-0111; Autovon 686-0111
OFFICER-OF-THE-DAY: (415) 869-4197, Autovon 686-4197
Profile
BRANCH: Navy.
SIZE AND LOCATION: 2842 acres. On E side of San Francisco Bay off US-880, just S of Oakland.
MAJOR UNITS: Naval Air Station Alameda; Naval Aviation Depot; Navy Regional Automation Center, San Francisco; Naval Air Reserve, HM 15; USS *Carl Vinson* (CVN-70); USS *Enterprise* (CVN-65); USS *California* (CGN-36); USS *Arkansas* (CGN-41); USS *Texas* (CGN-39); USS *Samuel Gompers* (AD-37).
BASE HISTORY: 1936, city of Alameda gave federal government land on which station was built.

Key Contacts
COMMANDER: Capt Roger P Boennighausen; (415) 869-4046, Autovon 686-4046.
PUBLIC AFFAIRS: Virginia Felker-Thorpe; (415) 869-4101, Autovon 686-4101.
PROCUREMENT: LCDR Keith Nostrant; (415) 869-3956, Autovon 686-3956.
TRANSPORTATION: LCDR Robert Steimer; (415) 869-4731, Autovon 686-4731.
PERSONNEL/COMMUNITY ACTIVITIES: LCDR Shin Nakazawa; Family Service Center, (415) 869-4111, Autovon 686-4111.
Personnel and Expenditures
ACTIVE DUTY PERSONNEL: 2100
DEPENDENTS: 1213
CIVILIAN PERSONNEL: 5100
MILITARY PAYROLL EXPENDITURE: $17.7 mil
CONTRACT EXPENDITURE: $0.3 mil
Services *Housing:* Family units 1213; BOQ cottages 62; BEQ units 1286. *Temporary Housing:* VOQ cottages 1; VEQ units 352; BOQ units 163; Lodge units 70. *Commissary:* Base commissary; Retail store; Barber shop; Dry cleaners; Food shop; Florist; Banking; Service station; Bakery; Convenience store/Shopette; Auto hobby shop. *Child Care/Capacities:* Day care center 134. *Schools:* Elementary. *Base Library:* Yes. *Medical Facilities:* Medical clinic; Dental clinic. *Recreational Facilities:* Bowling; Movie theater; Pool; Gym; Recreation center; Tennis; Racquetball; Fitness center; Softball field; Football field; Auto shop; Crafts; Officers club; NCO club; Airline ticket office; Bass tickets, baseball, football, etc; Pitch & Putt golf.

BARSTOW

BARSTOW MARINE CORPS LOGISTICS BASE
Barstow, CA 92311-5011
(619) 577-6611; Autovon 282-6611
OFFICER-OF-THE-DAY: (619) 577-6611, Autovon 282-6611
Profile
BRANCH: Marines.
SIZE AND LOCATION: 5687 acres. Near Barstow, CA, served by Hwys I-15 and I-40 and State Hwys 58 and 247; nearest commercial airport is Ontario IAP, 90 mi SW.
MAJOR UNITS: Headquarters Battalion; Resources Management Division; Facilities and Services Division; Personnel and Administrative Division; Materiel Division; Repair Division; Defense Reutilization and Marketing Office; Naval Investigative Service; Marine Reserve Organic Property Control Training Unit, 4th MAW.
BASE HISTORY: 1942, established as naval supply depot but transferred to Marine Corps as storage site for supplies and equipment for Fleet Marine Forces in Pacific; known as Marine Corps Depot of

Supplies and under Commanding General, Marine Corps Depot of Supplies, San Francisco. 1946, outgrew original facilities and holding and reconsignment point belonging to Army annexed, Yermo Annex. 1954, Commanding General, San Francisco moved to Barstow. 1978, redesignated to present title. Divided into Nebo and Yermo Annex. HQs, administrative, storage, shopping, recreational and housing facilities at Nebo. Repair Division, stables, Obregon Park, and bulk of Materiel Division's outdoor storage at Yermo Annex.
Key Contacts
PUBLIC AFFAIRS: SSgt Sylvia M Bowron; (619) 577-6449, Autovon 282-6449.
Personnel and Expenditures
ACTIVE DUTY PERSONNEL: 600
CIVILIAN PERSONNEL: 2090
MILITARY PAYROLL EXPENDITURE: $8.4 mil
CONTRACT EXPENDITURE: $28.6 mil
Services *Housing:* Family units 439; BOQ cottages 7; BEQ units; Senior NCO units 20. *Temporary Housing:* BOQ units 17; Oasis temporary lodging 4. *Commissary:* Base commissary; Retail store; Credit union; Snacks. *Child Care/Capacities:* Child development center. *Schools:* Chapman College. *Base Library:* Yes. *Medical Facilities:* Medical clinic; Dental clinic. *Recreational Facilities:* Bowling; Movie theater; Pool; Gym; Golf (driving range); Stables; Tennis; Racquetball; Softball field; Football field; Auto shop; Crafts; Officers club; NCO club; Youth center; Enlisted club; Skeet shooting; Picnicking; Handball; Motocross/ATV track; Equipment issue; Cabin at Big Bear.

BEALE AFB

BEALE AIR FORCE BASE
9th SRW, Beale AFB, CA 95903-5000
(916) 634-2137; Autovon 368-2137
Profile
BRANCH: Air Force.
SIZE AND LOCATION: 23,000 acres. Approx 40 mi N of Sacramento; 8 mi E of Marysville, CA. Hwy 65 runs S of Beale; Hwy 20 runs N (E-W); Hwy 70 runs W of Beale (N-S); and, Hwy 99 runs W of Beale (N-S).
MAJOR UNITS: 14th Air Division; 9th Strategic Reconnaissance Wing (SRW); 9th Combat Support Group; 7th Missile Warning Squadron.
BASE HISTORY: 1942, construction of Camp Beale began; named for founder of US Camel Corps, Edward Fitzgerald Beale, Naval Academy graduate, Commissioner of Indian Affairs, Army Brig Gen, Surveyor Gen of CA and NV, and Minister to Austria. WWII, 13th Armored, 81st and 96th Infantry Divisions trained here; at various times, also served as personnel

BEALE AIR FORCE BASE (*continued*)
replacement depot, German POW camp, and at war's end, West Coast separation center. After WWII, declared surplus. 1948, USAF used base for bombardier-navigator training. 1951, designated AFB; underwent several jurisdictional changes before becoming part of SAC. 1957, construction of first runway. 1958, 14th Air Division transferred in; became support base for 851st Strategic Missile Squadron and three Titan I missile sites (discontinued, 1965). 1965, 4200th SRW (later 9th SRW) activated, flying SR-71. 1975, 17th BMW host unit. 1976, 100th SRW reassigned as 100th Air Refueling Wing and 99th Strategic Reconnaissance Squadron brought U-2s and later TR-1 aircraft. 1979, became SAC unit. 1980, site for PAVE PAWS (Phased Array Radar) with 7th Missile Warning Squadron. 1983, 100th ARW inactivated; all personnel consolidated with 9th SRW; and transferred to newly-formed Space Command.
VISITOR ATTRACTIONS: Edward F Beale Museum; WWII POW Cell Block (Historic Monument); Aircraft exhibits.
Key Contacts
COMMANDER: Col Roger L Jacks; 9th CSG/CC, (916) 634-2311, Autovon 368-2311.
PUBLIC AFFAIRS: Capt Antonio Ronquillo; 9th SRW/PA.
PROCUREMENT: Maj Robert C Socik; Bldg 2529, (916) 634-2952, Autovon 368-2952.
TRANSPORTATION: Maj David A Barnes; Bldg 2491, (916) 634-4126, Autovon 368-4126.
PERSONNEL/COMMUNITY ACTIVITIES: Maj D Jean Mason; Bldg 2145, (916) 634-2106, Autovon 368-2106.
Personnel and Expenditures
ACTIVE DUTY PERSONNEL: 4458
DEPENDENTS: 5531
CIVILIAN PERSONNEL: 446
MILITARY PAYROLL EXPENDITURE: $82.2 mil
CONTRACT EXPENDITURE: $33.2 mil
Services *Housing:* Family units 1712; BOQ cottages; Duplex units; Dormitory spaces; Senior NCO units; Junior NCO units; Trailer spaces 176; RV/Camper sites. *Temporary Housing:* Transient living quarters. *Commissary:* Base commissary; Retail store; Barber shop; Dry cleaners; Food shop; Florist; Banking; Beauty shop; Jewelry/watch sales and repair; Video rental; Fast food. *Child Care/Capacities:* Day care center; Home day care program. *Schools:* Kindergarten/Preschool; Elementary. *Base Library:* Yes. *Medical Facilities:* Hospital; Dental clinic. *Recreational Facilities:* Bowling; Movie theater; Pool; Gym; Recreation center; Golf; Stables; Tennis; Racquetball; Fitness center; Softball field; Auto shop; Crafts; Officers club; NCO club; Fishing/Hunting; Rod and Gun Club; Dry Creek Saddle Club.

BOLINAS

COAST GUARD COMMUNICATION AREA MASTER STATION PACIFIC TRANSMITTER SITE
525 Mesa Rd, Bolinas, CA 94924
(415) 868-2514; (707) 765-7162
Profile
BRANCH: Coast Guard.
SIZE AND LOCATION: 75 acres. 25 mi SE of Point Reyes housing site near town of Bolinas.
BASE HISTORY: See USCG Communication Area Master Station Pacific, San Francisco
Services *Housing:* See USCG CAMSPAC.

BRIDGEPORT

US MARINE CORPS MOUNTAIN WARFARE TRAINING CENTER
Bridgeport, CA 93517
(619) 932-7761; Autovon 855-7204
OFFICER-OF-THE-DAY: (619) 932-7761, ext 231, Autovon 855-7231
Profile
BRANCH: Marines.
SIZE AND LOCATION: 475,000 acres. In the Sweetwater Mts of E central CA, 21 mi N of Bridgeport, CA; 4 mi W of the intersection of Hwy 395 and Sonora Junction 108.
Key Contacts
COMMANDER: Phillip E Tucker; (619) 932-7061.
PUBLIC AFFAIRS: Raymond Johnson; 203 Vittori Ct, Coleville, CA 96107, (916) 495-2129, Autovon 855-7204.
PROCUREMENT: Robert L Woodruff Jr; 1428 Leonard Rd, Gardnerville, NV 89410, Autovon 855-7245.
TRANSPORTATION: Alfred E Napier; 731 Hornet St, Gardnerville, NV 89410, (702) 265-4468, Autovon 855-7238.
PERSONNEL/COMMUNITY ACTIVITIES: See Public Affairs Officer.
Personnel and Expenditures
ACTIVE DUTY PERSONNEL: 246
DEPENDENTS: 211
CIVILIAN PERSONNEL: 20
CONTRACT EXPENDITURE: $1.2 mil
Services *Housing:* Family units 80; BEQ units 98; Senior NCO units 34; Junior NCO units 32. *Temporary Housing:* Lodge units 1. *Commissary and Exchange:* Retail store; Barber shop; Dry cleaners. *Medical Facilities:* Medical clinic. *Recreational Facilities:* Movie theater; Gym; Recreation center; Stables; Fitness center; Softball field; Auto shop; Camping; Fishing/Hunting; All ranks club.

CAMP PENDLETON

CAMP PENDLETON MARINE CORPS BASE
Camp Pendleton, CA 92055-5001
(619) 725-5566; Autovon 365-5566
OFFICER-OF-THE-DAY: (619) 725-5617, Autovon 365-5617
Profile
BRANCH: Marines.
SIZE AND LOCATION: 125,000 acres. 35 mi N of San Diego; just off I-5 in the city of Oceanside.
MAJOR UNITS: Marine Corps Base; Headquarters Battalion; Support Battalion; Schools Battalion; Military Police Battalion; Corrections Battalion; School of Infantry; Field Medical Service School; Reserve Support Unit; Marine Corps Mountain Warfare Training Center; I Marine Amphibious Force (I MAF); 1st Marine Division; 1st Force Service Support Group (1st FSSG); Marine Aircraft Group-39 (MAG-39); Marine Air Control Group 38; Marine Corps Air Station, Camp Pendleton; Marine Corps Tactical Systems Activity (MCTSSA); Assault Craft Unit Five (Navy); US Army Reserve Center; Naval Hospital.
BASE HISTORY: 1941, Navy bought SE corner of Rancho Santa Margarita to establish a Naval Ammunition Depot. Mid-1942, government purchased remainder of Rancho and 9th Marines and 1st Battalion, 12th Marines arrived. Named after Gen Joseph H Pendleton, Corps veteran. General's full name used including initial to distinguish between Army East Coast facility, Camp Pendleton. For years, correspondence from Base maintained Santa

Margarita Rancho designation part of address. WWII, training site for elements of 3rd Marine Division, entire 4th and 5th Marine Divisions and replacements for all divisions. Korean War, 1st Provisional Brigade replaced by reservists. Mid-1950s to mid-1960s, site of variety of training exercises. 1965, 1st Marine Division departed for Vietnam. 1969, 4th Marine Division moved to New Orleans; and 5th Marine Division deactivated.
VISITOR ATTRACTIONS: Rancho Santa Margarita y Las Flores (built circa 1830); El Camino Real ruins; Amphibian Vehicle Museum; Las Flores Adobe; Las Flores Asistencia (auxiliary mission).
Key Contacts
COMMANDER: Brig Gen Richard H Huckaby; (619) 725-5012, Autovon 365-5012.
PUBLIC AFFAIRS: LTC John Shotwell; Joint Public Affairs Office, Bldg #1160, (619) 725-5566, Autovon 365-5566.
PROCUREMENT: Maj Kevin Sankuhler; Contracting Office.
PERSONNEL/COMMUNITY ACTIVITIES: See Public Affairs Officer.
Personnel and Expenditures
ACTIVE DUTY PERSONNEL: 35,000
DEPENDENTS: 12,700
CIVILIAN PERSONNEL: 3700
MILITARY PAYROLL EXPENDITURE: $714.9 mil
CONTRACT EXPENDITURE: $141.5 mil
Services *Housing:* Family units 4565; Mobile home units (spaces only); Trailer spaces 249; RV/Camper sites 237. *Temporary Housing:* VIP cottages 5; VOQ cottages 99; VEQ units 42; BOQ units 117; Lodge units 66; Transient living quarters. *Commissary:* Base commissary; Retail store; Barber shop; Dry cleaners; Food shop; Florist; Banking; Service station; Bakery. *Child Care/Capacities:* Day care center 900. *Schools:* Kindergarten/Preschool; Elementary. *Base Library:* Yes. *Medical Facilities:* Hospital; Medical clinic; Dental clinic. *Recreational Facilities:* Bowling; Movie theater; Pool; Gym; Recreation center; Golf; Stables; Tennis; Racquetball; Fitness center; Softball field; Football field; Auto shop; Crafts; Officers club; NCO club; Camping; Fishing/Hunting.

CASTLE AFB

CASTLE AIR FORCE BASE
93rd Bombardment Wing, Castle AFB, CA 95342
(209) 726-4735; Autovon 347-4735
Profile
BRANCH: Air Force.
SIZE AND LOCATION: 3257 acres. 7 mi NW of Merced, CA, in central CA in town of Atwater, off Hwy 99, take Buhach Exit directly to main gate approx 2 mi from freeway. Approx 2 hrs from San Francisco; 6 hrs from Los Angeles.
MAJOR UNITS: 93rd Bombardment Wing; 93rd Air Refueling Squadron; 328th Bombardment Squadron; 329th Combat Crew Training Squadron; 924th Air Refueling Squadron; Central Flight Instructor Course; Linebacker II Training Center; SAC Instrument Flight Course; Deputy Commander for Logistics; 93rd Avionics Maintenance Squadron; 93rd Field Maintenance Squadron; 93rd Munitions Maintenance Squadron; 93rd Organizational Maintenance Squadron; 693rd Organizational Maintenance Squadron; Deputy Commander for Resource Management; 93rd Comptroller Squadron; 93rd Supply Squadron; 93rd Transportation Squadron; 93rd Combat Support Group; 93rd Civil Engineering Squadron; 93rd Combat Support Group Headquarters Squadron; 93rd Mission Support Squadron; 93rd Security Police Squadron; 93rd Services Squadron;

CASTLE AIR FORCE BASE (continued)

2035th Communications Squadron; Detachment 1, 31st Test and Evaluation Squadron; Detachment 1, 323rd Flying Training Wing; 318th Fighter Interceptor Squadron, Detachment 1; Detachment 2, 9th Weather Squadron; Detachment 412, Air Force Audit Agency; Field Training Detachment 514; Detachment 1902, Air Force Office of Special Investigations; SAC Management Engineering Team; 93rd Strategic Hospital.

BASE HISTORY: 1941, activated by 89th Bombardment Group; first HQs of Merced Army Flying School set up in Hotel Tioga. 1943, name changed to Merced Army Air Field, part of Western Flying Training Command; also operated auxiliary fields at Potter, Howard, Ballico, Athione, and Mariposa. 1945, flying personnel and aircraft transferred to Minter Field, CA. 1946, name changed to Castle Army Air Field, for Brig Gen Frederick W Castle, killed in action, 1944. 1947, 93rd BMW reduced to one officer and airman. 1948, SAC redesignated installation Castle AFB. 1954, SAC converted 93rd Bomb Group to B-52 training wing with training of tanker crews added. 1982, 924th AFRES performed first all-female mission (weather, air traffic control, ground fuel service, and supply).

VISITOR ATTRACTIONS: Castle Air Museum; Castle Memorial Parade Ground.

Key Contacts

COMMANDER: Col John F Fowler; 93 CSG/CCQ, (209) 726-2361, Autovon 347-2361.

PUBLIC AFFAIRS: Maj Linda L Leong; 93 BMW/PA, (209) 726-4735, Autovon 347-4735.

PROCUREMENT: Maj Mark D Rogers; 93 CSG/LGC, (209) 726-2555, Autovon 347-2555.

TRANSPORTATION: LTC Robert F Martin; 93rd TRANS/CC, (209) 726-2134, Autovon 347-2134.

PERSONNEL/COMMUNITY ACTIVITIES: LTC Joseph E Link; Director of Personnel, 93rd MSSg/CC, (209) 726-2701, Autovon 347-2701.

Personnel and Expenditures

ACTIVE DUTY PERSONNEL: 4982
DEPENDENTS: 2412
CIVILIAN PERSONNEL: 367
MILITARY PAYROLL EXPENDITURE: $112 mil
CONTRACT EXPENDITURE: $11.7 mil

Services *Housing:* Family units 934; BAQ units 28; Duplex units 302; Dormitory spaces 1346; Senior NCO units 4. *Temporary Housing:* VIP cottages 12; VOQ cottages 40; VAQ units 28; Mobile home units 42; Transient living quarters 12; Student Officer quarters 240. *Commissary:* Base commissary; Retail store; Barber shop; Dry cleaners; Food shop; Florist; Banking; Service station. *Child Care/Capacities:* Day care center. *Base Library:* Yes. *Medical Facilities:* Hospital 25. *Recreational Facilities:* Bowling; Movie theater; Pool; Gym; Recreation center; Tennis; Racquetball; Fitness center; Softball field; Football field; Auto shop; Crafts; Officers club; NCO club; Camping.

CHINA LAKE

CHINA LAKE NAVAL WEAPONS CENTER

China Lake, CA 93555
(619) 939-9011; Autovon 437-9011
OFFICER-OF-THE-DAY: (619) 939-2303, Autovon 437-2303

Profile

BRANCH: Navy.

SIZE AND LOCATION: 1,126,000 acres. In Mojave Desert, S-central CA, next to Ridgecrest, CA; 8 mi from US 395; 11 mi from Hwy 14; 150 mi N of Los Angeles.

MAJOR UNITS: Air Test and Evaluation Squadron Five (VX-5).

BASE HISTORY: 1943, established. Includes vast complex of laboratories and test-range facilities. Center situated under restricted military airspace of nearly 17,000 sq mi, making NWC Navy's largest research development, test, and evaluation (RDT&E) activity. Complex covers 2 areas: China Lake Complex, in north; and, Randsburg Wash/Mojave "B" Complex, in south. Principal Navy RDT&E center for air warfare systems (except anti-submarine warfare systems), missile weapon systems, and national range/facility for parachute test and evaluation; permanent activity of Space and Naval Warfare Systems Command.

Key Contacts

COMMANDER: Capt John Burt; Code 00, (619) 939-2201, Autovon 437-2201.

PUBLIC AFFAIRS: Denny Kline; Code 00, (619) 939-3511, Autovon 437-3511.

PROCUREMENT: CDR S C Nyland; Code 25, (619) 939-2053, Autovon 437-2053.

TRANSPORTATION: D B Hams; Code 26B2, (619) 939-3411, Autovon 437-3411.

PERSONNEL/COMMUNITY ACTIVITIES: E W Bien; Director of Personnel, Code 22, (619) 939-2434, Autovon 437-2434.

Personnel and Expenditures

ACTIVE DUTY PERSONNEL: 1000
DEPENDENTS: 2587
CIVILIAN PERSONNEL: 5200
MILITARY PAYROLL EXPENDITURE: $16 mil
CONTRACT EXPENDITURE: $197 mil

Services *Housing:* Family units 500; BOQ cottages; BEQ units; BAQ units; Duplex units; Barracks spaces. *Temporary Housing:* VIP cottages 4; VOQ cottages 7; VEQ units; BOQ units 24. *Commissary:* Base commissary; Retail store; Barber shop; Food shop; Credit union. *Child Care/Capacities:* Day care center; Home day care program. *Schools:* Kindergarten/Preschool; Elementary; Intermediate/Junior high. *Base Library:* Yes. *Medical Facilities:* Medical clinic; Dental clinic. *Recreational Facilities:* Bowling; Movie theater; Pool; Gym; Recreation center; Golf; Stables; Tennis; Racquetball; Skating rink; Fitness center; Softball field; Football field; Auto shop; Crafts; Officers club; NCO club; Camping; Fishing/Hunting.

CONCORD

CONCORD NAVAL WEAPONS STATION

Concord, CA 94520-5000
(415) 671-0111; Autovon 253-0111
OFFICER-OF-THE-DAY: (415) 671-5531, Autovon 253-5531

Profile

BRANCH: Navy.

SIZE AND LOCATION: 12,000 acres. 35 mi NE of San Francisco; main gate on Port Chicago Hwy.

MAJOR UNITS: Ordnance Department; Weapons Quality Engineering Center; Data Systems Department; Explosive Ordnance Disposal Detachment; US Coast Guard Port Safety Station, Concord; Public Works Department; Naval Reserve Units; Marine Corps Security Company; USS *Pyro* (AE-24); USS *Mount Hood* (AE-29); USS *Flint* (AE-32); USS *Shasta* (AE-33); USS *Kiska* (AE-35); USS *Mauna Kea* (AE-22).

BASE HISTORY: 1942, established as annex to Naval Ammunition Depot, Mare Island. Today, largest military facility on West Coast for transshipment of ammunition and other hazardous cargo; also provides materiel and technical support for ammunition, weapons and weapons systems; and, homeport and logistic support agency for Pacific Fleet auxiliary ammunition ships used for replenishment of Navy ships at sea. Divided into Tidal Area and Inland Area. Tidal Area has facility for sorting returned ordnance, railroad and truck classification yards, and three ocean terminal piers capable of berthing six large cargo ships simultaneously. Inland Area consists of administration buildings, military barracks, storage magazines, and extensive and guided missile facilities.

VISITOR ATTRACTIONS: Tule Elk and other wild life conservation area.

Key Contacts

COMMANDER: Capt L F Cagle.

PUBLIC AFFAIRS: J Dan Tikalsky; (415) 671-5066, Autovon 253-5066.

PROCUREMENT: (415) 671-5056, Autovon 253-5056.

PERSONNEL/COMMUNITY ACTIVITIES: (415) 671-5722, Autovon 253-5722.

Personnel and Expenditures

ACTIVE DUTY PERSONNEL: 360
CIVILIAN PERSONNEL: 1100

Services *Housing:* Family units; Barracks spaces. *Commissary and Exchange:* Barber shop; Service station. *Base Library:* Yes. *Medical Facilities:* Medical clinic; Dental clinic. *Recreational Facilities:* Movie theater; Pool; Gym; Recreation center; Tennis; Racquetball; Fitness center; Softball field; Football field; Auto shop; Officers club; Morale, Welfare, & Recreation Dept; Recreation gear issue; Picnic area; Lending closet; Golf course nearby.

CORONA

CORONA NAVAL WEAPONS STATION

Corona, CA 91720
(714) 736-5000

Profile

BRANCH: Navy.

LOCATION: 40 mi E of Seal Beach.

MAJOR UNITS: Fleet Analysis Center.

BASE HISTORY: Division of Naval Weapons Center Seal Beach. Serves as HQs for Fleet Analysis Center. Responsible for evaluating performance, reliability, and readiness of missiles and combat systems. Performance history of every weapon in fleet maintained. Administers metrology and calibration program, serving more than 700 calibration laboratories worldwide. Operates and maintains telemetry facilities in Okinawa, Crete, Puerto Rico, and Philippines; track missile firings. Home of Government-Industry Data Exchange Program (GIDEP); acts as clearinghouse for existing technical knowledge.

Key Contacts

COMMANDER: See Naval Weapons Center Seal Beach.

PUBLIC AFFAIRS: Tracey Schwarze; ATTN: Code 01P, Naval Weapons Center Seal Beach, Seal Beach, CA 90740-5000, (213) 594-7215, Autovon 873-7215.

CROWS LANDING

CROWS LANDING NAVAL AUXILIARY LANDING FIELD

Crows Landing, CA 95313-5000
(209) 837-4781; Autovon 462-5175

**CROWS LANDING NAVAL AUXILIARY
LANDING FIELD** (continued)
Profile
BRANCH: Navy.
SIZE AND LOCATION: 1500 acres. 23 mi SW
  of Modesto, CA; 5 mi E off of I-5 on the
  Crows Landing Exit.
MAJOR UNITS: Under control of NAS Moffett
  Field.
BASE HISTORY: 1942, constructed. 1943, commissioned under control of NAS Alameda. 1944, renamed Naval Auxiliary Air
  Station, Crows Landing. 1946, disestablished. 1950, reactivated as Naval Auxiliary Landing Field, Crows Landing for
  field carrier landing practice. 1954, transferred to control of NAS, Moffett Field
  and permanent control tower built. 1965,
  first West Coast installation of Mirror
  Landing System completed to provide pilot training for shipboard landings. 1960,
  helicopter assigned and TACAN (Tactical
  Air Navigation) Site erected. 1965, transferred to control of NAS, Lemoore, CA.
  1970, reverted back to NAS Alameda;
  since reactivation, an average of 100,000
  landings and takeoffs a year. 1978, once
  again placed under NAS, Moffett Field.
Key Contacts
COMMANDER: LCDR Danny B Kelley; (209)
  837-4782, Autovon 462-5175.
PUBLIC AFFAIRS: BM3 Mary J Delawder;
  (209) 837-4782, Autovon 462-5175.
PROCUREMENT: AKC Tamberlane Kennedy;
  (209) 837-4782, Autovon 462-5227.
TRANSPORTATION: ABFC Nestor Olaes; (209)
  837-4782, Autovon 462-5227.
PERSONNEL/COMMUNITY ACTIVITIES: See Base
  Commander.
Personnel and Expenditures
ACTIVE DUTY PERSONNEL: 35
CIVILIAN PERSONNEL: 6
Services *Housing:* Trailer spaces 6; RV/
Camper sites 10. *Temporary Housing:* Camp-
er trailers, 6. *Commissary and Exchange:*
Barber shop. *Medical Facilities:* Medical
trailer. *Recreational Facilities:* Pool; Tennis;
Softball field; All hands club.

DUBLIN

**PARKS RESERVE FORCES
TRAINING AREA**
Bldg 790, 5th St, Dublin, CA 94568-5201
(415) 828-1822; Autovon 586-6262
Profile
BRANCH: Army.
SIZE AND LOCATION: 2650 acres. In the Liver-
  more Valley, central to the greater San
  Francisco Bay Area; 18 mi E of Oakland
  and 44 mi E of San Francisco. Nearest
  major population centers are Dublin,
  Pleasanton, San Ramon and Livermore.
  Served by both I-580 and I-680. Nearest
  airports in Livermore and Oakland.
MAJOR UNITS: Headquarters US Army Garrison (Detachment of Presidio of San
  Francisco); 91st USA MTC; 91st Division
  Training Group; 6237th USARF School;
  124th ARCOMs AMSA/ECS 30.
BASE HISTORY: 1942, comprised of two major
  areas, Camp Parks and Camp Shoemaker;
  served as Navy basic training center
  through WWII when deactivated and
  leased to Alameda County. Korean Conflict, became known as Parks AFB, until
  1958; declared excess to USAF requirements, then passed to Army control and
  became Camp Parks. 1975, redesignated
  sub-installation of Presidio of San Francisco and assigned mission of supporting
  Reserve Components training and readiness. 1983, status changed from inactive
  to semi-active; reserve forces local train-

ing area. Currently, studies underway to
renovate installation.
Key Contacts
COMMANDER: LTC Richard Speidel; (415)
  828-1823, Autovon 586-4238.
PUBLIC AFFAIRS: Capt Kym H E Fleet; Public
  Affairs Officer/Executive & Operations
  Officer, (415) 828-1823, Autovon 586-
  4238.
Personnel and Expenditures
ACTIVE DUTY PERSONNEL: 65
DEPENDENTS: 25
CIVILIAN PERSONNEL: 476
MILITARY PAYROLL EXPENDITURE: Combined
  with Presidio of San Francisco
CONTRACT EXPENDITURE: Combined with
  Presidio of San Francisco
Services *Housing:* Family units 15; Barracks
spaces 1150; Senior NCO units 23; Junior
NCO units 23; Family units are controlled
by Presidio of SF. *Temporary Housing:* VEQ
units 476. *Commissary and Exchange:* Retail
store; Barber shop. *Base Library:* Yes. *Medical Facilities:* Small seasonal troop clinic. *Recreational Facilities:* Gym; Recreation center;
Tennis; Softball field; Football field; Officers
club; NCO club; Model airplane club; Square
dance club.

EDWARDS AFB

EDWARDS AIR FORCE BASE
Edwards AFB, CA 93523
(805) 277-1110; Autovon 350-1110
Profile
BRANCH: Air Force.
SIZE AND LOCATION: 301,000 acres. In SW
  CA on western edge of Mojave Desert
  approx 100 mi NE of Los Angeles, 90 mi
  NW of San Bernardino, 80 mi SE of Ba-
  kersfield.
MAJOR UNITS: Air Force Flight Test Center
  (AFFTC); 6510th Test Wing; USAF Test
  Pilot School; 6545th Test Group; Utah
  Test and Training Range; Deputy Com-
  mander for Operations; 6510th Test
  Group; Programs and Resources Division;
  Deputy Commander for Technical Sup-
  port; Deputy Commander for Maintenance DCM Complex; Logistic Plans and
  Programs Division; Maintenance Division; Quality Assurance Division; Maintenance Control Division; 6515th Avionics Maintenance Squadron; 6515th Logis-
  tics Test Squadron; 6515th Field Main-
  tenance Squadron; 6515th Munition
  Maintenance Squadron; 6515th Organiza-
  tional Maintenance Squadron; 6505th
  Supply Squadron; 6500th Air Base Wing;
  6500th Mission Support Squadron;
  6500th Security Police Squadron; 6500th
  Civil Engineering Squadron; Astronautics
  Laboratory; NASA Ames-Dryden Flight
  Research Facility; Army Aviation Engineering Flight Activity; 31st Test and
  Evaluation Squadron; Directorate of
  Communications and Computer Systems;
  Detachment 21, 2d Weather Squadron;
  Detachment 5, Air Force Operational
  Test and Evaluation Center; Air Force
  Acquisitions Logistics Center; 3306th Test
  and Evaluation Squadron.
BASE HISTORY: 1933, bombing and gunnery
  training began at Muroc, CA, with de-
  tachment, March Field, CA. WWII, S end
  of dry lake used to train fighter pilots and
  bomber crews. 1942, portion of Muroc
  Dry Lake assigned to Materiel Command
  Flight Test Base; America's first jet test-
  ed. 1944, redesignated Muroc Flight Test
  Base. 1946, facilities merged into single
  flight test activity at Muroc Army Air
  Field under AMC. 1948, redesignated
  Muroc AFB. 1949, redesignated Edwards
  AFB for Capt Glen W Edwards, resident
  of Lincoln, CA, killed during performance

test of YB-49, Flying Wing. 1950, Air
Research and Development Command
(ARDC) replaced AMC. 1951, AF Flight
Test Center activated. 1961, ARDC be-
came AF Systems Command, responsible
for research and development of aero-
space weapons systems, from drawing
board to operational readiness. Flight
Test Center also provides support func-
tions to NASA space shuttle program, in-
cluding prime landing site for all space
shuttle flights.
VISITOR ATTRACTIONS: Flight Test Center
  Museum; Jimmy Doolittle Airpark.
Key Contacts
PUBLIC AFFAIRS: (805) 277-2345.
Personnel and Expenditures
ACTIVE DUTY PERSONNEL: 4460
DEPENDENTS: 6100
CIVILIAN PERSONNEL: 7200
MILITARY PAYROLL EXPENDITURE: $141.2 mil
CONTRACT EXPENDITURE: $293 mil
Services *Housing:* Family units 1989; Dor-
mitory spaces 208; Senior NCO units; Trail-
er spaces 164; Apartments 50. *Temporary
Housing:* VOQ cottages 85; VAQ units 82;
Transient living quarters. *Commissary:* Base
commissary; Retail store; Barber shop; Dry
cleaners; Florist; Banking; Service station;
Military clothing sales; Beauty shop; Laun-
dry; Credit union; Snacks. *Child Care/Ca-
pacities:* Child development center. *Schools:*
Kindergarten/Preschool; Elementary;
Intermediate/Junior high; High school. *Base
Library:* Yes. *Medical Facilities:* Hospital;
Medical clinic; Dental clinic; Veterinary clin-
ic. *Recreational Facilities:* Bowling; Movie
theater; Pool; Gym; Recreation center; Golf;
Stables; Tennis; Racquetball; Skating rink;
Fitness center; Softball field; Football field;
Auto shop; Crafts; Officers club; NCO club;
Camping; Youth center; Aero club; Rod and
Gun Club; Tours and Tickets; Recreation
equipment rental; Lake Isabella, 2 hr drive
N; SATO.

EL CENTRO

EL CENTRO NAVAL AIR FACILITY
El Centro, CA 92243-5001
(619) 339-2524; Autovon 958-8524
OFFICER-OF-THE-DAY: (619) 339-2524,
  Autovon 958-8524
Profile
BRANCH: Navy.
SIZE AND LOCATION: 2289 acres (plus control
  of additional 54,000 acres). 120 mi E of
  San Diego off I-8, take Drew Rd Exit at
  Seeley, CA; 62 mi W of Yuma, AZ off I-
  8.
MAJOR UNITS: Personnel Support Detach-
  ment (PSD); Chief of Naval Air Training
  Detachment (CNATRA STRIKE DET);
  Medium Attack Weapons Detachment;
  NAVSTAR.
BASE HISTORY: Since 1942, NAF El Centro
  has had several names: Marine Corps Air
  Station, Naval Air Facility, Naval Auxil-
  iary Landing Field, Naval Air Station,
  and National Parachute Test Range. Facility involved in aeronautical escape system testing, evaluation and design. 1947,
  Parachute Experimental Division moved
  from Lakehurst, NJ. 1949, Fleet Gunnery
  Unit assigned. 1951, Joint Parachute Facility established. 1959, ejection seat from
  high-speed jet at altitudes under 1000 ft
  successfully tested; parachute system for
  Mercury Space Program. 1964, US Naval
  Aerospace Recovery Facility designated
  (later combined with Naval Air Facility to
  form National Parachute Test Range).
  1979, parachute test function transferred
  to Naval Weapons Center, China Lake;
  and El Centro again NAF. 1986, much of
  film "Top Gun" shot here.

EL CENTRO NAVAL AIR FACILITY
(continued)
VISITOR ATTRACTIONS: Winter Home of the Blue Angels Air Demonstration Team.
Key Contacts
COMMANDER: (619) 339-2401, Autovon 958-8401.
PUBLIC AFFAIRS: (619) 339-2519, Autovon 958-8519.
PROCUREMENT: (619) 339-2283, Autovon 958-8283.
TRANSPORTATION: (619) 339-2218, Autovon 958-8218.
PERSONNEL/COMMUNITY ACTIVITIES: (619) 339-2618, Autovon 958-8618.
Personnel and Expenditures
ACTIVE DUTY PERSONNEL: 200
CIVILIAN PERSONNEL: 120
MILITARY PAYROLL EXPENDITURE: $5 mil
Services *Housing:* Family units 230; BOQ cottages 10; BEQ units 105; BAQ units 67; Dormitory spaces 56; Senior NCO units 15; Mobile home units 4; RV/Camper sites 40. *Temporary Housing:* VIP cottages 10; VOQ cottages 67; BOQ units 105; Lodge units 4; Dormitory spaces 56; Mobile home units; Transient living quarters 270. *Commissary:* Base commissary; Retail store; Barber shop; Dry cleaners; Service station; Furniture store. *Child Care/Capacities:* Day care center 80. *Base Library:* Yes. *Medical Facilities:* Medical clinic; Dental clinic. *Recreational Facilities:* Bowling; Movie theater; Pool; Recreation center; Tennis; Racquetball; Fitness center; Softball field; Football field; Auto shop; Crafts; Officers club; NCO club; Go-Kart track; Golf driving range.

EL GRANADA

PILLAR POINT AIR FORCE STATION
PO Box 609, El Granada, CA 94018-0609
Profile
BRANCH: Air Force.
MAJOR UNITS: Pillar Point AFS.

EL SEGUNDO

LOS ANGELES AIR FORCE BASE
El Segundo, CA 90009
(213) 643-1000; Autovon 833-1110
Profile
BRANCH: Air Force.
SIZE AND LOCATION: 100 acres. 2 mi S of Los Angeles IAP in El Segundo.
MAJOR UNITS: Headquarters Space Division; 6592nd Air Base Group.
BASE HISTORY: July 1964, established. Mission to develop satellite communication, navigation, and launch systems.
Personnel and Expenditures
ACTIVE DUTY PERSONNEL: 1954
DEPENDENTS: 7120
CIVILIAN PERSONNEL: 2000
Services *Housing:* Family units 33; Townhouse units 370; Dormitory spaces 27; Housing at Ft MacArthur Annex 19 mi S. *Temporary Housing:* VOQ cottages 60; Transient living quarters 25. *Commissary:* Base commissary; Dry cleaners; Florist; Service station; Shoppette at Ft MacArthur Annex. *Child Care/Capacities:* Day care center 92. *Medical Facilities:* Medical clinic; Veterinary services. *Recreational Facilities:* Bowling; Movie theater; Pool; Gym; Golf; Tennis; Auto shop; Crafts; Officers club; NCO club; Camping; Fishing/Hunting; Youth center (activities); Boating; Skeet shooting; Skiing.

FALLBROOK

FALLBROOK NAVAL WEAPONS STATION
Fallbrook, CA 92028
(619) 728-3306
Profile
BRANCH: Navy.
LOCATION: 80 mi S of Seal Beach; adj to Camp Pendleton Marine Corps Base.
BASE HISTORY: Division of Naval Weapons Center Seal Beach. Stores, issues, and performs intermediate repair of air-launched weapons, including Phoenix, Sidewinder, Walleye, HARM, Hellfire, Maverick, Skipper, and Shrikes missiles. Statistical performance analysis of various air, surface, and sub-surface launched weapons conducted. Primary provisioner of conventional ordnance to Marine Corps.
Key Contacts
COMMANDER: See Naval Weapons Center Seal Beach.
PUBLIC AFFAIRS: Tracey Schwarze; ATTN: Code 01P, Naval Weapons Center Seal Beach, Seal Beach, CA 90740-5000, (213) 594-7215, Autovon 873-7215.

FERNDALE

CENTERVILLE BEACH NAVAL FACILITY
General Delivery, Ferndale, CA 95536-9766
(707) 786-9531; Autovon 896-3381
OFFICER-OF-THE-DAY: (707) 786-9531, Autovon 896-3381
Profile
BRANCH: Navy.
SIZE AND LOCATION: 37 acres. On 320 ft cliff overlooking Eel River Valley to N and bordered by Pacific Ocean to W; approx 260 mi N of San Francisco and 100 mi S of OR border; Ferndale 6 mi E.
BASE HISTORY: Mar 5, 1958, commissioned as shore activity and assigned to operating forces of US Pacific Fleet.
Key Contacts
COMMANDER: CDR R T Bridges.
PUBLIC AFFAIRS: Lt R N Gates; (707) 786-9531, ext 490.
PROCUREMENT: Lt K Cuyler.
TRANSPORTATION: Lt M Myrum.
PERSONNEL/COMMUNITY ACTIVITIES: Ray Anderson; MWR Director.
Personnel and Expenditures
ACTIVE DUTY PERSONNEL: 250
DEPENDENTS: 600
CIVILIAN PERSONNEL: 20
Services *Housing:* Family units 52. *Temporary Housing:* BOQ units. *Commissary and Exchange:* Retail store. *Base Library:* Yes. *Medical Facilities:* Medical clinic (for active duty only). *Recreational Facilities:* Gym; Recreation center; Racquetball; Fitness center; Softball field; Football field; Auto shop.

FORT HUNTER LIGGETT

FORT HUNTER LIGGETT
Fort Hunter Liggett, CA 93928
(408) 385-2533; 385-2502; Autovon 8-949-2533; 949-2502
Profile
BRANCH: Army.
SIZE AND LOCATION: 164,636 acres. 23 mi SW of King City at the intersection of Hwy G14 and G18 near Jolon, CA.
MAJOR UNITS: Army Garrison, Ft Hunter Liggett; Combat Development Experimentation Center.
VISITOR ATTRACTIONS: Ranch house of William Randolph Hearst (used as guesthouse).

Personnel and Expenditures
ACTIVE DUTY PERSONNEL: 500
DEPENDENTS: 250
Services *Housing:* Family units 8; BEQ units 1; Trailer spaces 50; Prefabricated housing units 180. *Temporary Housing:* Guesthouse units. *Commissary:* Base commissary; Small, combined with commissary. *Child Care/Capacities:* Day care center; Home day care program. *Medical Facilities:* Medical clinic; Uses Ft Ord Hospital, 86 mi away. *Recreational Facilities:* Bowling; Movie theater; Pool; Gym; Recreation center; Golf; Auto shop; Crafts; Fishing/Hunting.

FORT IRWIN

FORT IRWIN, NATIONAL TRAINING CENTER
Fort Irwin, CA 92310
(619) 386-3916; Autovon 470-3916
OFFICER-OF-THE-DAY: (619) 386-3750, Autovon 470-3750
Profile
BRANCH: Army.
SIZE AND LOCATION: 640,000 acres. In Mojave Desert along I-15, halfway between Los Angeles and Las Vegas, 37 mi NE of Barstow, CA; only access via Ft Irwin Rd which joins I-15 just N of Barstow.
MAJOR UNITS: National Training Center; 177th Armored Brigade; Detachment 2, 602nd Tactical Air Control Wing (USAF).
BASE HISTORY: 1940, originally subpost of Camp Haan, adjacent to what is now March AFB, named for Maj Gen George Leroy Irwin, commander of 57th Field Artillery Brigade in WWI. Deactivated and reactivated over the years, thousands of soldiers have completed rotational training since NTC established in 1981.
VISITOR ATTRACTIONS: Foreign Materiel Intelligence Group (FMTG).
Key Contacts
COMMANDER: Brig Gen Wesley K Clark; (619) 386-3260, Autovon 470-3260.
PUBLIC AFFAIRS: Maj John Wagstaffe; (619) 386-4511, Autovon 470-4511.
PROCUREMENT: LTC Al Tio; (619) 386-3660, Autovon 470-3660.
TRANSPORTATION: Maj Roger Kays; (619) 386-3817, Autovon 470-3817.
PERSONNEL/COMMUNITY ACTIVITIES: LTC Randall Lancaster; (619) 386-5111, Autovon 470-5111.
Personnel and Expenditures
ACTIVE DUTY PERSONNEL: 4387
DEPENDENTS: 5326
CIVILIAN PERSONNEL: 2414
MILITARY PAYROLL EXPENDITURE: $120.9 mil
CONTRACT EXPENDITURE: $331.6 mil
Services *Housing:* Family units 1103; BOQ cottages 128; BAQ units 30; Barracks spaces 1834; Senior NCO units 70; Mobile home units 40; Trailer spaces 78. *Temporary Housing:* BOQ units 70; BAQ units 30; Guesthouse units 30; Mobile home units 78; Transient living quarters 30. *Commissary:* Base commissary; Retail store; Barber shop; Dry cleaners; Food shop; Florist; Banking; Service station; Furniture store; Bakery; Fast food; Mini-mall; Pizza; Delicatessen. *Child Care/Capacities:* Day care center; Home day care program. *Schools:* Kindergarten/Preschool; Elementary. *Base Library:* Yes. *Medical Facilities:* Hospital 20; Dental clinic; Preventive medicine. *Recreational Facilities:* Bowling; Movie theater; Pool; Gym; Recreation center; Stables; Tennis; Racquetball; Fitness center; Softball field; Football field; Auto shop; Crafts; Officers club; NCO club; Camping.

FORT ORD

FORT ORD
7th Infantry Division (Light), Fort Ord, CA 93941-5000
(408) 242-2211; Autovon 929-2211-Operator
OFFICER-OF-THE-DAY: (408) 242-3432; 242-4209, Autovon 929-3432; 929-4209
Profile
BRANCH: Army.
SIZE AND LOCATION: 28,057 acres. On coast in central CA, 105 mi S of San Francisco; 320 mi N of Los Angeles; a few miles W of Salinas and N of Monterey. Main gate fronts on US Hwy 1, coastal and sometimes mountainous route.
MAJOR UNITS: 7th Infantry Division; 1st Brigade; 2d Brigade; 3rd Brigade; DIVARTY; Combat Aviation Brigade; Bayonet Combat Support Brigade; DISCOM; Law Enforcement Command; 127th Signal Battalion; 107th MI Battalion; 2/62nd Air Defense Artillery Battalion; 13th Engineer Battalion.
BASE HISTORY: Originally established as maneuver area and field artillery range. Named for Maj Gen Edward Ord, served at Presidio of Monterey and later commanded Union troops in Civil War. 1972, designated home of 7th Infantry Division. 1974, Division reactivated to increase Army strength to 16 combat units.
VISITOR ATTRACTIONS: Ft Ord Museum.
Key Contacts
COMMANDER: Maj Gen Carmen J Cavezza; Commanding General, (408) 242-3500, Autovon 929-3500.
PUBLIC AFFAIRS: Capt Guy T Shields; Public Affairs Officer, ATTN: AFZW-PO, 7th Infantry Division (Light) and Ft Ord, Ft Ord, CA 93941-5660, (408) 242-3804; 242-3133, Autovon 929-3133; 929-3804.
PROCUREMENT: LTC Shackelford; Director of Contracting, (408) 242-2611, 242-2717, Autovon 929-2611, 929-2717.
TRANSPORTATION: Col Johnson; Director of Logistics, (408) 242-2007, 242-2009, Autovon 929-2007, 929-2009.
PERSONNEL/COMMUNITY ACTIVITIES: Col Weirich; (408) 242-3911, 242-5683, Autovon 929-3911, 929-5683.
Personnel and Expenditures
ACTIVE DUTY PERSONNEL: 20,264
DEPENDENTS: 26,434
CIVILIAN PERSONNEL: 3000
MILITARY PAYROLL EXPENDITURE: $297.2 mil
CONTRACT EXPENDITURE: $34.9 mil
Services
Housing: Family units 5399; BEQ units 181; Duplex units 1048; Townhouse units 380; Barracks spaces 7997; Senior NCO units 676; Junior NCO units 3960; Mobile home units 220; RV/Camper sites 62 (27 w/o hookups). *Temporary Housing:* VIP cottages 6; VOQ cottages 279; VEQ units 63; BOQ units 177; Guesthouse units 137; Guest cottages 25; Apartment units 33; Lodge units 30. *Commissary:* Base commissary; Retail store; Barber shop; Dry cleaners; Food shop; Florist; Banking; Service station. *Child Care/Capacities:* Day care center 289; Home day care program. *Schools:* Elementary; Intermediate/Junior high. *Base Library:* Yes. *Medical Facilities:* Hospital 227; Medical clinic; Dental clinic. *Recreational Facilities:* Bowling; Movie theater; Pool; Gym; Recreation center; Golf; Stables; Tennis; Racquetball; Fitness center; Softball field; Football field; Auto shop; Crafts; Officers club; NCO club; Camping; Fishing/Hunting; Enlisted club.

FRESNO AIR TERMINAL

FRESNO AIR NATIONAL GUARD BASE
5425 E McKinley Ave, Fresno Air Terminal, CA 93727-2199
(209) 445-5350
Profile
BRANCH: Air National Guard.
SIZE AND LOCATION: 85 acres. Within city limits of Fresno, bounded by city on three sides and just S of Clovis, CA; main portion of base lies in E-W orientation adj to McKinley Ave and runway shared with Fresno Air Terminal on N.
MAJOR UNITS: 144th Fighter Interceptor Wing; 194th Fighter Interceptor Squadron; 144th Consolidated Aircraft Maintenance Squadron; 144th Civil Engineering Squadron; 144th Mission Support Squadron; 144th Resource Management Squadron; 144th Security Police Flight; 144th USAF Clinic; Detachment 1, 144th Fighter Interceptor, George AFB, CA.
BASE HISTORY: 1955, first three buildings built on site. 1975, current facility development program started when refueling function unified into single facility. Weapons storage area inherited from Marines and lies across runway on N portion of base.
VISITOR ATTRACTIONS: Static display of former aircraft.
Key Contacts
COMMANDER: Brig Gen Paul L Carrol Jr.
PUBLIC AFFAIRS: Maj Sally P Riley; 144th FIW/HO.
PROCUREMENT: LTC Joe Oliphant; Chief of Supply.
Personnel and Expenditures
ACTIVE DUTY PERSONNEL: 1050
CIVILIAN PERSONNEL: 290
Services *Medical Facilities:* Medical clinic.

GEORGE AFB

GEORGE AIR FORCE BASE
George AFB, CA 92394-5000
(619) 269-1110; Autovon 353-1110
Profile
BRANCH: Air Force.
SIZE AND LOCATION: 6000 acres; plus 7583 acres in Cuddeback Range. 4.5 mi NE of Victorville, CA, between State Rte 395 and I-15.
MAJOR UNITS: 831st Air Division; 37th Tactical Fighter Wing; 35th Tactical Training Wing; 27th Tactical Air Support Squadron; 2067th Communications Squadron.
BASE HISTORY: 1941, began as Victorville Army Flying School; named after Brig Gen Harold S George, WWI fighter ace, killed in aircraft crash at Darwin, Australia, Apr 1942.
Key Contacts
COMMANDER: Col Ralph Duncan; 831st CSG/CC, (619) 269-2120, Autovon 353-2120.
PUBLIC AFFAIRS: 1st Lt Ed Glaize; 831st AD/PA, (619) 269-2800, Autovon 353-2800.
PROCUREMENT: Capt Paul Botts; 831st RM/CC, (619) 269-2445, Autovon 353-2445.
TRANSPORTATION: Maj Douglas Coltharp; 831st TRNS/LGT, (619) 269-2046, Autovon 353-2046.
PERSONNEL/COMMUNITY ACTIVITIES: Capt John Gawrysiak; 831st CSG/SS, (619) 269-2865, Autovon 353-2865.
Personnel and Expenditures
ACTIVE DUTY PERSONNEL: 5200
DEPENDENTS: 6300
CIVILIAN PERSONNEL: 520
MILITARY PAYROLL EXPENDITURE: $109 mil

Services *Housing:* Family units 1641; Dormitory spaces 1639. *Temporary Housing:* VOQ cottages 20; VAQ units 2; Transient living quarters 40. *Commissary:* Base commissary; Retail store; Barber shop; Dry cleaners; Food shop; Banking; Service station. *Child Care/Capacities:* Day care center. *Schools:* Kindergarten/Preschool; Elementary. *Base Library:* Yes. *Medical Facilities:* Hospital 25; Medical clinic; Dental clinic. *Recreational Facilities:* Bowling; Movie theater; Pool; Gym; Recreation center; Golf; Tennis; Racquetball; Fitness center; Softball field; Auto shop; Crafts; Officers club; NCO club; Facilities at Lake Isabella.

HERLONG

SIERRA ARMY DEPOT
Herlong, CA 96113
(916) 827-2111; Autovon 830-9910
Profile
BRANCH: Army.
SIZE AND LOCATION: 36,000 acres. In Honey Lake Valley among foothills of Sierra Nevadas; approx 55 mi NW of Reno, NV; 40 mi SE of Susanville, CA, off Hwy 395.
BASE HISTORY: 1942, designated Sierra Reserve Arsenal; primary mission receipt, storage and issue of ammunition; also general supplies. 1947-1951, mission expanded to include renovation and demilitarization of ammunition and demolition of outdated and dangerous ammunition. 1962, renamed Sierra Army Depot; supply mission: ammunition; strategic and critical elements such as chromium, manganese, and tungsten; and, packed and crated household goods stored for military service personnel (only Army installation storing household goods for DOD personnel on nontemporary basis). Today, under DESCOM; also provides training and facilities for Army Reserve and NG units; Amadee Army Airfield in northern part of depot.
Key Contacts
PUBLIC AFFAIRS: Larry Rogers; (916) 827-4343, Autovon 830-9343.
Personnel and Expenditures
ACTIVE DUTY PERSONNEL: 450
CIVILIAN PERSONNEL: 600
Services *Housing:* Family units. *Temporary Housing:* Lodge units. *Commissary:* Base commissary; Barber shop; Dry cleaners; Food shop; Service station; Credit union. *Child Care/Capacities:* Day care center; Home day care program. *Schools:* Kindergarten/Preschool; Elementary; Intermediate/Junior high; High school. *Base Library:* Yes. *Medical Facilities:* Medical clinic. *Recreational Facilities:* Bowling; Movie theater; Pool; Gym; Recreation center; Stables; Tennis; Racquetball; Fitness center; Softball field; Football field; Auto shop; Crafts; Community Club.

KLAMATH

CRESCENT CITY AIR FORCE STATION
Klamath, CA 95548
Autovon 670-2352
Profile
BRANCH: Air Force.
MAJOR UNITS: Crescent City AFS (TAC).

LATHROP

SHARPE ARMY DEPOT
Lathrop, CA 95331
(209) 982-2000; Autovon 462-2000
OFFICER-OF-THE-DAY: (209) 982-2008; 982-2213; Autovon 462-2008; 462-2213
Profile
BRANCH: Army.
SIZE AND LOCATION: 724 acres. 75 mi E of San Francisco; 60 mi S of Sacramento; 7 mi S of Stockton, CA. 1 mi E off Hwy 5 and 2 mi W off Hwy 99; Stockton Airport 5 mi N; Modesto Airport 35 mi S from Depot.
MAJOR UNITS: Armed Forces Reserve Center; 5th Battalion, 361st Regiment; California Army Aviation National Guard.
BASE HISTORY: 1942, Lathrop Holding and Reconsignment Point commissioned. 1943, became major wartime installation. 1948, renamed Sharpe General Depot for Maj Gen Henry Granville Sharpe, Commissionary and Quartermaster General of Army, 1905-1918. 1959, airstrip, hangar, and shop facilities built to support air maintenance support mission for Army aircraft. 1962, final name change, Sharpe Army Depot; depot assigned to Army Supply and Maintenance Command; petroleum lab dedicated. 1965, mission expanded to include maintenance of air delivery items and personnel parachutes for depot stocks. During past 10 years, depot has lost and gained missions, built new facilities, remodeled others and been part of several reorganizations.
Key Contacts
COMMANDER: Col John Michael Chessnoe; ATTN: SDSSH-C, Lathrop, CA 95331-5000, (209) 982-2001, 982-2002, Autovon 462-2001, 462-2002.
PUBLIC AFFAIRS: Ronald F Fournier; ATTN: SDSSH-CPA, Public Affairs Officer, Lathrop, CA 95331-5122, (209) 982-2030, 982-2031, Autovon 462-2030, 462-2031.
PROCUREMENT: Bertie Hopkins; ATTN: SDSSH-DC, Lathrop, CA 95331-5000, (209) 982-2401, 982-2402, Autovon 462-2401, 462-2402.
TRANSPORTATION: Capt Sandra Belden; ATTN: SDSSH-STD, Lathrop, CA 95331-5000, (209) 982-3110, Autovon 462-3110.
PERSONNEL/COMMUNITY ACTIVITIES: Edward Enfield; Director of Family and Community Activities, ATTN: SDSSH-M, Lathrop, CA 95331-5000, (209) 982-2201, Autovon 462-2201.
Personnel and Expenditures
ACTIVE DUTY PERSONNEL: 38
DEPENDENTS: 66
CIVILIAN PERSONNEL: 1100
MILITARY PAYROLL EXPENDITURE: $0.7 mil
CONTRACT EXPENDITURE: $18.5 mil
Services *Housing:* Family units 30; BEQ units 6; Barracks spaces 100; RV/Camper sites 12. *Temporary Housing:* Barracks spaces 100. *Commissary and Exchange:* Retail store. *Child Care/Capacities:* Home day care program. *Schools:* Civilian Personnel Learning Ctr. *Base Library:* Yes. *Medical Facilities:* Medical clinic. *Recreational Facilities:* Pool; Gym; Recreation center; Tennis; Racquetball; Fitness center; Softball field; Crafts; NCO club.

LEMOORE

LEMOORE NAVAL AIR STATION
Lemoore, CA 93246
(209) 998-2211; Autovon 949-4110
Profile
BRANCH: Navy.
SIZE AND LOCATION: 18,000 acres; 12,000 leased back to farmers. 40 mi S of Fresno at Lemoore off Hwy 198, 19 mi E of I-5; 30 mi W of Hwy 99 in the San Joaquin Valley in central CA.
MAJOR UNITS: Headquarters Commander, Light Attack Wing, US Pacific Fleet (COMLAT-WINGPAC); Carrier Air Wing-9 (CVW-9); Attack Squadron-22 (VA-22); Strike Fighter Squadron-25 (VFA-25); Attack Squadron-27 (VA-27); Attack Squadron-94 (VA-94); Attack Squadron-97 (VA-97); Strike Fighter Squadron-113 (VFA-113); Attack Squadron-122 (VA-122); Strike Fighter Squadron-125 (VFA-125); Strike Fighter Squadron-127 (VFA-127); Attack Squadron-146 (VA-146); Attack Squadron-147 (VA-147); Strike Fighter Squadron-151 (VFA-151); Strike Fighter Squadron-161 (VFA-161); Strike Fighter Squadron-192 (VFA-192); Strike Fighter Squadron-195 (VFA-195); Strike Fighter Squadron-303 (VFA-303); Aircraft Intermediate Maintenance Department (AIMD); Air Traffic Control Facility; Construction Battalion Unit 406 (CBU-406); Fleet Aviation Specialized Operational Training Group, Pacific, Detachment Lemoore; Light Attack Weapons School, Pacific (LAWSP); Naval Aviation Engineering Service Unit Detachment Lemoore (NAESU); Naval Air Maintenance Training Detachments (NAMTRA); Naval Oceanography Command Detachment Lemoore (NOCD); Naval Air Reserve Center (NAS Lemoore 3490, LATWINGPAC 0190, NAVHOSP Lemoore 0190, VTU-9076); Search & Rescue.
BASE HISTORY: 1958, construction began about 1 mi W of Lemoore Army Air Field (LAAF), active during WWII. 1961, commissioned and originally named Reeves Field for Rear Adm Joseph M Reeves, laid groundwork for modern aircraft carrier strike force. Primary mission to support fleet carrier squadrons and serve as master training center for carrier based light attack squadrons of US Pacific Fleet.
Key Contacts
PUBLIC AFFAIRS: Andrea V Harper; Community Relations Officer, (209) 998-3140, Autovon 949-3140.
Personnel and Expenditures
ACTIVE DUTY PERSONNEL: 5717
DEPENDENTS: 9100
CIVILIAN PERSONNEL: 1200
Services *Housing:* Family units 1590. *Temporary Housing:* Lodge units 46. *Commissary:* Base commissary; Retail store; Barber shop; Dry cleaners; Food shop; Service station; Hobby store; Fast food; Laundry; Ice cream; Package beverages; Optical shop; Credit union. *Child Care/Capacities:* Day care center 135; Home day care program. *Schools:* Elementary. *Base Library:* Yes. *Medical Facilities:* Hospital 20; Dental clinic. *Recreational Facilities:* Bowling; Movie theater; Pool; Gym; Recreation center; Stables; Tennis; Racquetball; Fitness center; Softball field; Auto shop; Crafts; Officers club; NCO club; Camping; Fishing/Hunting; Youth center; Archery; Pistol range; Picnicking; Gear locker rental equipment; Cross country track; Flying club; Skeet shooting; Tours and travel.

LONG BEACH

LONG BEACH COMBINED SUPPORT MAINTENANCE SHOP
3500 Stearns St, Long Beach, CA 90822-1093
(213) 597-4064; Autovon 972-2855
Profile
BRANCH: Army National Guard.
SIZE AND LOCATION: 9.5 acres. In Long Beach.
Key Contacts
COMMANDER: LTC Manuel F Silva.
Personnel and Expenditures
CIVILIAN PERSONNEL: 87

LONG BEACH NAVAL STATION
Long Beach, CA 90822-5000
(213) 547-7840; Autovon 360-7840
OFFICER-OF-THE-DAY: (213) 547-6817; 547-6818; Autovon 360-6817; 360-6818
Profile
BRANCH: Navy.
SIZE AND LOCATION: 614 acres. 17 mi from Los Angeles IAP; 22 mi from downtown LA; 3 mi from downtown Long Beach; Fwys 710, 47 or 110 nearby station; Fwys 405, 101, 605 and 5, all within 8 to 20 mi of station.
MAJOR UNITS: Commander, Naval Surface Group Long Beach (COMNAVSURFGRU); Naval Supply Center Detachment, Long Beach; Supervisor of Shipbuilding, Conservation & Repair (SUPSHIP); Naval Regional Contracting Center Long Beach (NRCC); Destroyer Squadron Nine (DESRON 9); Military Sealift Command; Naval Telecommunications Center Long Beach (NTCC); Personnel Support Activity; Naval Reserve Readiness Center; Long Beach Naval Shipyard; SIMA (NRMF) Command Mission; Surface Squadron One (SURFRON 1); Naval Hospital; Naval Brig; CBU-409; USS *Missouri* (BB-63); USS *New Jersey* (BB-62); USS *Peleliu* (LHA-5); USS *Prairie* (AD-15).
BASE HISTORY: 1938, first naval activity on Terminal Island, Naval Air Facility Reeves Field, commissioned to provide support for seaplanes, battleships, and cruisers in Pacific. 1940, land purchased from city of Long Beach for present site of Naval Station. 1942, designated "Roosevelt Base." 1974, Naval Station Long Beach disestablished and redesignated Naval Support Activity. 1979, Naval Support Activity disestablished and again redesignated Naval Station; reopening of Long Beach as home port for units of Pacific Fleet and gradual return of ships, personnel, and support activities.
VISITOR ATTRACTIONS: USS *Missouri*; USS *New Jersey*; USS *Prairie* (Oldest commissioned ship in Navy); ships information provided on a 24-hr basis 547-6801.
Key Contacts
COMMANDER: Capt Gerald W Dunne; (Code 00), (213) 547-7825, Autovon 360-7825.
PUBLIC AFFAIRS: Chief Smith; (Code 005), (213) 547-7219, Autovon 360-7219.
PROCUREMENT: Lt R Newkirk (SC); (Code N7), (213) 547-6855, Autovon 360-6855.
TRANSPORTATION: LCDR L Serafini (CEC); (Code N4), (213) 547-7513, Autovon 360-7513.
PERSONNEL/COMMUNITY ACTIVITIES: Lt P Terry; (Code N1), (213) 547-7967, Autovon 360-7967.
Personnel and Expenditures
ACTIVE DUTY PERSONNEL: 17,000
DEPENDENTS: 14,200
CIVILIAN PERSONNEL: 2000
MILITARY PAYROLL EXPENDITURE: $515.4 mil
CONTRACT EXPENDITURE: $1.2 bil

LONG BEACH NAVAL STATION (continued)
Services *Housing:* Family units 2139; BOQ cottages 49; Barracks spaces 1133. *Temporary Housing:* Lodge units 50; Transient living quarters 142. *Commissary:* Base commissary; Retail store; Barber shop; Dry cleaners; Food shop; Florist; Service station; Furniture store; Teller machine. *Child Care/Capacities:* Day care center 240; Home day care program. *Base Library:* Yes. *Medical Facilities:* Medical clinic; Dental clinic; Long Beach Naval Hospital, 12 mi away. *Recreational Facilities:* Bowling; Movie theater; Pool; Gym; Recreation center; Golf; Tennis; Racquetball; Fitness center; Softball field; Football field; Auto shop; Crafts; Officers club; NCO club; Fishing/Hunting; Marina.

LONG BEACH NAVY REGIONAL MEDICAL CENTER
7500 E Carson St, Long Beach, CA 90822
(213) 420-5503
Profile
BRANCH: Navy.
LOCATION: In Long Beach approx 12 mi from Long Beach Naval Station; near intersection of I-605 and Carson St.
MAJOR UNITS: Naval Hospital.
BASE HISTORY: Offers wide range of services to active duty personnel and their dependents, retired personnel and dependents. No Emergency Medical Department/Emergency Room; no trauma services available.
Key Contacts
COMMANDER: See Naval Station Long Beach.
Personnel and Expenditures
ACTIVE DUTY PERSONNEL: 750
DEPENDENTS: 1000
Services *Housing:* Family units 28; BEQ units 89. *Commissary and Exchange:* Convenience store/Shopette; Small main exchange. *Medical Facilities:* Hospital 210. *Recreational Facilities:* Gym; Tennis; Basketball; Large sports field.

LONG BEACH SUPERVISOR OF SHIPBUILDING, CONVERSION AND REPAIR
Long Beach, CA 90822-5093
(213) 547-8117; Autovon 360-8117
OFFICER-OF-THE-DAY: (213) 547-6226, Autovon 360-6226
Profile
BRANCH: Navy.
SIZE AND LOCATION: 204 acres. At Long Beach Naval Shipyard on Terminal Island, 1 mi W of Long Beach, CA.
MAJOR UNITS: Supervisor of Shipbuilding, Conversion and Repair.
BASE HISTORY: 1943, Naval Dry Docks, Terminal Island, first ship dry docked. WWII, provided routine and battle damage repairs. 1945, name changed to Terminal Island Naval Shipyard. 1948, current name. One of eight shipyards in US.
Key Contacts
COMMANDER: Capt William M Donnelly; (213) 547-8118, Autovon 360-8118.
PUBLIC AFFAIRS: Gil Bond; Long Beach Naval Shipyard, Long Beach, CA 90822-5099, (213) 547-6146, Autovon 360-6146.
PERSONNEL/COMMUNITY ACTIVITIES: See Public Affairs Officer.
Personnel and Expenditures
ACTIVE DUTY PERSONNEL: 22
CIVILIAN PERSONNEL: 160
CONTRACT EXPENDITURE: $122.4 mil
Services *Commissary:* Base commissary; Retail store; Barber shop; Dry cleaners; Food shop; Banking; Service station; Post office. *Child Care/Capacities:* Day care center 100. *Schools:* Kindergarten/Preschool. *Medical Facilities:* Medical clinic; Dental clinic. *Recreational Facilities:* Bowling; Movie theater;

Pool; Gym; Recreation center; Tennis; Fitness center; Softball field; Auto shop; Crafts; Officers club; NCO club.

MARCH AFB

MARCH AIR FORCE BASE
March AFB, CA 92518
(714) 655-1110; Autovon 947-1110
OFFICER-OF-THE-DAY: (714) 655-2944, Autovon 947-2944
Profile
BRANCH: Air Force.
SIZE AND LOCATION: 6950 acres. In the cities of Riverside and Moreno Valley; approx 8 mi from downtown Riverside; 22 mi from Ontario IAP. Base 2 mi S of intersection of CA Hwy 60 and I-215.
MAJOR UNITS: 22nd Air Refueling Wing; 452nd Air Refueling Wing; 943rd Tactical Airlift Group; 163rd Tactical Fighter Group; Southwest Air Defense Sector Operations Control Center; Headquarters 15th Air Force; US Customs Service C3I West; 22nd Combat Support Group.
BASE HISTORY: Over 70 years ago, Alessandro Aviation Field established; part of national build-up of aviation training facilities. Field renamed March Field for Lt Peyton C March, killed in aircraft accident, 1918. First base established in W; continues with motto of 22nd Bombardment Group, 1940, DUCEMUS, "WE LEAD."
VISITOR ATTRACTIONS: March Field Museum, displays of military aircraft.
Key Contacts
COMMANDER: Col Harry A Stafford; Base Commander, 22nd Combat Support Group, (714) 655-4735, Autovon 947-4735.
PUBLIC AFFAIRS: Capt Aubrey V "Joe" Stephenson; (714) 655-4137, Autovon 947-4137.
PROCUREMENT: Maj John Murphy; (714) 655-2046, Autovon 947-2046.
TRANSPORTATION: Maj David Cook; (714) 655-4120, Autovon 947-4120.
PERSONNEL/COMMUNITY ACTIVITIES: LTC Gary Baugh; Director of Personnel, (714) 655-4076, Autovon 947-4076.
Personnel and Expenditures
ACTIVE DUTY PERSONNEL: 3982
DEPENDENTS: 2226
CIVILIAN PERSONNEL: 1616
MILITARY PAYROLL EXPENDITURE: $89.3 mil
CONTRACT EXPENDITURE: $35.5 mil
Services *Housing:* Family units 711; Dormitory spaces 710; Townhouse units off base in Perris, CA 200. *Temporary Housing:* VIP cottages 17; VOQ cottages 215. *Commissary:* Base commissary; Retail store; Barber shop; Dry cleaners; Food shop; Florist; Banking; Service station; Beauty shop; Optical shop; Alterations shop; Video rental. *Child Care/Capacities:* Day care center 120. *Schools:* Kindergarten/Preschool; Elementary. *Base Library:* Yes. *Medical Facilities:* Hospital 50; Dental clinic. *Recreational Facilities:* Movie theater; Pool; Gym; Recreation center; Golf; Stables; Tennis; Racquetball; Fitness center; Softball field; Football field; Auto shop; Crafts; Officers club; NCO club; Camping; Fishing/Hunting; Lake Perris, 6 mi E.

MATHER AFB

MATHER AIR FORCE BASE
Mather AFB, CA 95655-5000
(916) 364-1110; Autovon 674-1110
Profile
BRANCH: Air Force.
SIZE AND LOCATION: 5845 acres. Off US Hwy 50 near Rancho Cordova, CA, take Mather AFB Exit.

MAJOR UNITS: 323rd Flying Training Wing (Air Training Command); 320th Bombardment Wing (Strategic Air Command); 940th Air Refueling Group (Air Force Reserve); Naval Air Training Unit; 3506th USAF Recruiting Group; Army Aviation Support Facility.
BASE HISTORY: 1918, aviation training base, originally called Mills Field, constructed; name changed to Mather Field for Lt Carl Mather of Paw Paw, MI, killed in aircraft accident, Ellington Field, TX. 1923-41, closed with exception of series of maneuvers, 1930. WWII, home of pilot and navigator/observer trainees. Navigator training mission continues. 323rd Flying Training Wing single supplier of DOD basic navigation training and AF advanced navigator training.
VISITOR ATTRACTIONS: Silver Wings Aviation Museum.
Key Contacts
COMMANDER: Col Grady H Hawkins.
PUBLIC AFFAIRS: Capt Ronald A Lovas; 323 FTW/PA, (916) 364-2908, Autovon 674-2908.
Personnel and Expenditures
ACTIVE DUTY PERSONNEL: 6183
DEPENDENTS: 3578
CIVILIAN PERSONNEL: 2094
MILITARY PAYROLL EXPENDITURE: $163.8 mil
CONTRACT EXPENDITURE: $56.7 mil
Services *Housing:* Family units; BEQ units; BAQ units; Duplex units; Barracks spaces; Dormitory spaces; Junior NCO units. *Temporary Housing:* VOQ cottages; VEQ units; VAQ units; BOQ units; BAQ units; Transient living quarters. *Commissary:* Base commissary; Retail store; Barber shop; Dry cleaners; Food shop; Florist; Banking; Service station; Bakery. *Child Care/Capacities:* Day care center; Home day care program. *Schools:* Kindergarten/Preschool; Elementary. *Base Library:* Yes. *Medical Facilities:* Hospital 70; Dental clinic. *Recreational Facilities:* Bowling; Movie theater; Pool; Gym; Recreation center; Golf; Stables; Tennis; Racquetball; Fitness center; Softball field; Football field; Auto shop; Crafts; Officers club; NCO club; Fishing/Hunting.

MCCLELLAN AFB

MCCLELLAN AIR FORCE BASE
McClellan AFB, CA 95652-5990
(916) 643-1110; Autovon 633-1110
Profile
BRANCH: Air Force.
SIZE AND LOCATION: 3755 acres. In NE section of Sacramento, main gate on Watt Ave, just N of I-880.
MAJOR UNITS: Sacramento Air Logistics Center; Coast Guard Air Station Sacramento; 2951st Combat Logistics Support Squadron; 2852nd Air Base Group; 41st Rescue and Weather Reconnaissance Wing; 55th Weather Reconnaissance Squadron; Detachment 1, 1400th Military Airlift Squadron; Detachment 8, 17th Weather Squadron; 431st Test and Evaluation Squadron; Detachment 2, 2d Aircraft Delivery Group; Technical Operations Division; Defense Reutilization and Marketing Office; Headquarters 4th Air Force; 2049th Communications Group (AFCC); Air Rescue Service; 1849th Electronics Installation Squadron; Air Force Audit Agency, Detachment 415; Field Training Detachment 510.
BASE HISTORY: 1937, Sacramento Air Depot commissioned. 1939, renamed McClellan Field for Maj Hezekiah McClellan, pioneer in charting Alaskan air routes; depot kept name and became primary unit at McClellan. During WWII, bore brunt of air logistics to Pacific. Following WWII,

McCLELLAN AIR FORCE BASE (continued)
stored surplus aircraft and supplies. 1947,
renamed McClellan AFB. One of five centers of AF Logistics Command; assumed
world-wide responsibility for management
of USAF electrical components,
communications-electronics systems, flight
control instruments, fluid drive accessories, and tactical shelters. 1985, complet-
ed land exchange, selling Splinter City, S
of base and across railroad and Roseville
Rd, in exchange for land W of base.
Growth of space logistics continued; sup-
ports Space Shuttle. 1988, assigned F-15
Eagle workload.
VISITOR ATTRACTIONS: McClellan Aviation
Museum (open Mon-Sat 9-3).
Key Contacts
COMMANDER: Col James Wilson; 2852 ABG/
CC.
PUBLIC AFFAIRS: LTC Duane C Roberts; SM-
ALC/PA, (916) 643-6127, Autovon 633-
6127.
Personnel and Expenditures
ACTIVE DUTY PERSONNEL: 3500
CIVILIAN PERSONNEL: 15,000
MILITARY PAYROLL EXPENDITURE: $545 mil
CONTRACT EXPENDITURE: $1 bil
Services *Housing:* Family units 645; BAQ
units 14; Senior NCO units 24. *Temporary
Housing:* VIP cottages 8; VOQ cottages 63;
VAQ units 48; Transient living quarters 21.
Commissary: Base commissary; Retail store;
Barber shop; Dry cleaners; Food shop; Flo-
rist; Banking; Service station; Bakery; Video
rental. *Child Care/Capacities:* Day care cen-
ter 99. *Base Library:* Yes. *Medical Facilities:*
Medical clinic; Dental clinic. *Recreational
Facilities:* Bowling; Movie theater; Pool;
Gym; Recreation center; Golf; Tennis; Rac-
quetball; Softball field; Auto shop; Crafts;
Officers club; NCO club.

MOFFETT FIELD

**MOFFETT FIELD NAVAL AIR
STATION**
Naval Air Station, Moffett Field, CA 94035
(415) 966-4887; Autovon 462-4887
OFFICER-OF-THE-DAY: (415) 966-5326,
Autovon 462-5326
Profile
BRANCH: Navy.
SIZE AND LOCATION: 3000 acres. 34 mi S of
San Francisco off Hwy 101, near the in-
tersection with State Rte 85.
MAJOR UNITS: Commander Patrol Wings Pa-
cific Fleet; Commander Patrol Wing Ten;
Naval Air Station; Commander Reserve
Patrol Wing; California Air National
Guard.
BASE HISTORY: 1933, commissioned as
Sunnyvale NAS. 1942, renamed for Rear
Adm William A Moffett, killed in crash
of dirigible *Akron*. Visitors today from
airship era would still recognize many
buildings. Hangar One, built to hold diri-
gible USS *Macon*, and Hangars Two and
Three, built in WWII era for blimps, to-
day hold fleet of Orions. Today, hub of
anti-submarine warfare patrol operations
in Pacific and largest P-3 Orion base.
VISITOR ATTRACTIONS: George Carroll History Room (by appointment only); Base
Tours for schools/organized groups (by
appointment only).
Key Contacts
COMMANDER: (415) 966-5746 Autovon 462-
5746.
PUBLIC AFFAIRS: Public Affairs Office, Bldg
23, (415) 966-5976, Autovon 462-5976.
PROCUREMENT: Supply Officer, (415) 966-
5926, Autovon 462-5926.
TRANSPORTATION: Transportation Officer,
(415) 966-5856, Autovon 462-5856.

PERSONNEL/COMMUNITY ACTIVITIES: Military
Personnel, Bldg 23, (415) 966-5561, Auto-
von 462-5561; Civilian Personnel, Bldg
23, (415) 966-5027, Autovon 462-5027.
Personnel and Expenditures
ACTIVE DUTY PERSONNEL: 5500
DEPENDENTS: 8500
CIVILIAN PERSONNEL: 1500
MILITARY PAYROLL EXPENDITURE: $90 mil
Services *Housing:* Family units 650; BOQ
cottages 100; BEQ units 1600. *Commissary:*
Base commissary; Retail store; Barber shop;
Dry cleaners; Food shop; Banking; Service
station; Furniture store. *Child Care/Capac-
ities:* Day care center. *Base Library:* Yes.
Medical Facilities: Medical clinic; Dental
clinic. *Recreational Facilities:* Bowling; Mov-
ie theater; Pool; Gym; Recreation center;
Golf; Stables; Tennis; Fitness center; Softball
field; Football field; Auto shop; Crafts; Officers club; NCO club.

MONTEREY

NAVAL POSTGRADUATE SCHOOL
Monterey, CA 93940-5000
(408) 646-2411; Autovon 878-2411
OFFICER-OF-THE-DAY: (408) 646-2441,
Autovon 878-2441
Profile
BRANCH: Navy.
SIZE AND LOCATION: 620 acres. In Monterey,
CA, on Hwy 1; 60 mi S of San Jose; 120
mi S of San Francisco; 5 mi N of Carmel;
300 mi N of Los Angeles. Monterey has a
small commercial airport.
MAJOR UNITS: Naval Postgraduate School;
Fleet Numerical Oceanography Center;
Naval Environmental Prediction Research
Facility; Personnel Support Activity De-
tachment; Defense Resources Management Education Center; Aviation Safety
Programs; Naval Security Group Detachment; Defense Manpower Data Center;
Naval Telecommunication Center.
BASE HISTORY: 1909, started as separate department of Naval Academy, Annapolis,
MD. 1951, NPS officially moved to Monterey; old hotel renamed Herrmann Hall
and used for administrative offices, bachelor officer's quarters, Commissioned Officers' and Faculty Club, and some classrooms. Presently, more than 1700 students enrolled in over 30 academic programs, representing all services, NOAA,
DOD civilians, and 20 allied countries.
VISITOR ATTRACTIONS: Part of school in old
Del Monte Hotel, historic site; small mu-
seum in old hotel.
Key Contacts
COMMANDER: Rear Adm Robert Austin;
(408) 646-2511, Autovon 878-2511.
PUBLIC AFFAIRS: CDR Allen Sherwood; (408)
646-2023, Autovon 878-2023.
PROCUREMENT: LCDR Barry Boyd; (408)
646-2183, Autovon 878-2183.
TRANSPORTATION: (408) 646-2151, Autovon
878-2151.
PERSONNEL/COMMUNITY ACTIVITIES: E V
Morin; Director of Personnel, (408) 646-
3236, Autovon 878-3236.
Personnel and Expenditures
ACTIVE DUTY PERSONNEL: 800
DEPENDENTS: 2141
CONTRACT EXPENDITURE: $28 mil
Services *Housing:* Family units 1021; BEQ
units 60; Duplex units; Townhouse units.
Temporary Housing: VOQ cottages 8; BOQ
units 50; BAQ units; Temporary housing for
families at Ft Ord nearby. *Commissary and
Exchange:* Retail store; Barber shop; Dry
cleaners; Florist; Banking; Service station;
Book store. *Child Care/Capacities:* Day care
center. *Schools:* Kindergarten/Preschool.
Base Library: Yes. *Medical Facilities:* Dental
clinic; Hospital at Ft Ord & Monterey; Clin-

ic at Presidio of Monterey. *Recreational Facilities:* Pool; Gym; Recreation center; Golf;
Tennis; Racquetball; Fitness center; Softball
field; Auto shop; Officers club; NCO club;
Sailing; Flying club; Other activities available at Ft Ord & Presidio of Monterey.

PRESIDIO OF MONTEREY
Monterey, CA 93944-5006
(408) 647-5312; Autovon 878-5312
OFFICER-OF-THE-DAY: (408) 647-5119,
Autovon 878-5119
Profile
BRANCH: Air Force; Army; Marines; Navy;
Coast Guard.
SIZE AND LOCATION: 128 acres. On Light-
house Ave, in the city limits of Monterey.
MAJOR UNITS: Defense Language Institute;
Foreign Language Center; Army Research
Institute.
BASE HISTORY: 1941, Army instituted formal
Japanese language instruction for
Japanese-American recruits in abandoned
airplane hangar at San Francisco's Crissy
Field; school named 4th Army Intelli-
gence School; Navy began teaching Japa-
nese to officers at Berkeley. 1942, Navy
moved to Univ of Colorado, Boulder;
Army moved to Camp Savage, MN, and
later to Ft Snelling; renamed Military Intelligence Service Language School. After
WWII, Navy school combined with Naval
Intelligence School, Anacostia, Washington, DC. 1947, Army school moved to
Presidio of Monterey; renamed Army
Language School. 1963, consolidation of
all service language programs resulted in
establishment of Defense Language Institute; East Coast Branch established in
Washington, DC; Army Language School
in Monterey became West Coast Branch.
1974, branches merged into Defense Lan-
guage Institute Foreign Language Center,
Presidio of Monterey. DLI now offers 41
foreign languages and dialects and enrolls
approximately 5000 students annually.
VISITOR ATTRACTIONS: Museum.
Key Contacts
COMMANDER: Col Todd Robert Poch; Commandant.
PUBLIC AFFAIRS: (408) 647-5104, Autovon
878-5104.
PROCUREMENT: See Ft Ord.
TRANSPORTATION: See Ft Ord.
PERSONNEL/COMMUNITY ACTIVITIES: See Ft
Ord.
Personnel and Expenditures
ACTIVE DUTY PERSONNEL: 3000
DEPENDENTS: 250
CIVILIAN PERSONNEL: 1000
Services *Housing:* Family units 20; Addi-
tional facilities available through Ft Ord
nearby. *Temporary Housing:* Facilities avail-
able through Ft Ord. *Commissary and Ex-
change:* Retail store; Barber shop; Dry clean-
ers; Service station. *Child Care/Capacities:*
Day care center 100. *Base Library:* Yes.
Medical Facilities: Primus clinic. *Recreational Facilities:* Movie theater; Gym; Recreation
center; Fitness center; Softball field; Football
field; Officers club; NCO club.

NORTON AFB

NORTON AIR FORCE BASE
Norton AFB, CA 92409-5154
(714) 382-1110; Autovon 867-1110
Profile
BRANCH: Air Force.
SIZE AND LOCATION: 2410 acres. In the city
of San Bernardino; 60 mi E of Los
Angeles; 109 mi NE of San Diego; 470 mi
SE of San Francisco.
MAJOR UNITS: 63rd Military Airlift Wing
(MAW); 63rd Air Base Group (ABG);
Headquarters Air Force Inspection and

COAST GUARD COMMUNICATION AREA MASTER STATION PACIFIC, SAN FRANCISCO (continued)
Services *Housing:* BEQ units; Townhouse units 36; Additional housing at Hamilton AFB in Novato. *Temporary Housing:* Guest house at TRACEN, Petaluma 8. *Commissary and Exchange:* This is a satellite exchange of TRACEN, Petaluma. *Medical Facilities:* Dispensary at Petaluma; Letterman Hospital is 1 hr away. *Recreational Facilities:* Recreation center (pool table); Fitness center (weight room; hot tub); Tennis; Auto shop; Morale locker equipment checkout; Participates with TRACEN, Petaluma; Bear Valley Visitor Center, 5 mi away.

POMONA

POMONA NAVAL WEAPONS STATION
Pomona, CA 91769
(714) 868-1000
Profile
BRANCH: Navy.
LOCATION: 40 mi NE of Seal Beach.
MAJOR UNITS: Gage and Standards Center.
BASE HISTORY: Division of Naval Weapons Center Seal Beach. Navy's Gage and Standards Center for developing and maintaining more than 18,000 unique ordnance gages that ensure weapons can be assembled into ready-to-fire rounds. Quality assurance agent for Navy's metrology and calibration program; design and apply measurement science disciplines to national standards.
Key Contacts
COMMANDER: See Naval Weapons Center Seal Beach.
PUBLIC AFFAIRS: Tracey Schwarze; ATTN: Code 01P, Naval Weapons Center Seal Beach, Seal Beach, CA 90740-5000, (213) 594-7215, Autovon 873-7215.

PORT HUENEME

NAVAL CIVIL ENGINEERING LABORATORY
Port Hueneme, CA 93043
(805) 982-5336
Profile
BRANCH: Navy.
LOCATION: Across the harbor from Port Hueneme, Naval Construction Battalion Center.
MAJOR UNITS: Naval Civil Engineering Laboratory (R&D center for Naval Facilities Engineering Command).
BASE HISTORY: 1948, established at Solomons, MD. 1950, moved to present site. Today, full spectrum laboratory.
Key Contacts
COMMANDER: (805) 982-4528.
PUBLIC AFFAIRS: (805) 982-5787.
Personnel and Expenditures
ACTIVE DUTY PERSONNEL: 400 (military & civilian)
Services *Housing:* See Port Hueneme, Naval Construction Battalion Center. *Temporary Housing:* See Port Hueneme, Naval Construction Battalion Center.

NAVAL SHIP WEAPONS SYSTEMS ENGINEERING STATION
Port Hueneme, CA 93043
(805) 982-4493
Profile
BRANCH: Navy.
LOCATION: On Port Hueneme, Naval Construction Battalion Center.
MAJOR UNITS: Systems Engineering Directorate; Logistics Directorate.

BASE HISTORY: 1963, established for inservice engineering and logistics support of Terrier, Tartar, and Talos missile systems. Today, supports Naval Sea Systems Command in development testing of combat system for *Arleigh Burke* class Aegis destroyer.
Personnel and Expenditures
ACTIVE DUTY PERSONNEL: 2000 (military & civilian)
MILITARY PAYROLL EXPENDITURE: $74 mil
CONTRACT EXPENDITURE: $625 mil
Services *Housing:* See Port Hueneme, Naval Construction Battalion Center. *Temporary Housing:* See Port Hueneme, Naval Construction Battalion Center. *Base Library:* Yes.

PORT HUENEME, NAVAL CONSTRUCTION BATTALION CENTER
Port Hueneme, CA 93043-5000
(805) 982-4493; Autovon 360-5309
OFFICER-OF-THE-DAY: (805) 982-4571, Autovon 360-4571
Profile
BRANCH: Navy.
SIZE AND LOCATION: 1600 acres. In Oxnard and Port Hueneme communities; 60 mi NW of Los Angeles; on coast on Pacific Coast Hwy and 101 Fwy.
MAJOR UNITS: Naval Construction Battalion; Thirty-First Construction Regiment; Naval Mobile Construction Battalion Three; Naval Mobile Construction Battalion Four; Naval Mobile Construction Battalion Five; Naval Mobile Construction Battalion Forty; Underwater Construction Team Two; Reserve Naval Mobile Construction Battalion Seventeen; Naval Support Force Antarctica; Naval Construction Training Center; Naval Energy and Environmental Support Activity; USNS *Curtiss*; Naval Reserve Information Office; Naval School, Civil Engineer Corps Officers; NAVFAC Contracts Training Center; Defense Reutilization and Marketing Office; Marine Corps Reserve Training Center; Naval Ship Weapons Systems Engineering Station; Naval Civil Engineering Laboratory.
BASE HISTORY: 1942, began operations to train, stage, and supply newly created Seabees. During WWII, shipped more construction supplies than any other port in US. Also in Korean War and Vietnam Conflict. Mission remains same today, support for Seabees.
VISITOR ATTRACTIONS: CEC/Seabee Museum.
Key Contacts
COMMANDER: Capt Brian J O'Connell; (805) 982-4741, Autovon 360-4741.
PUBLIC AFFAIRS: Connie Taylor; (805) 982-4493, Autovon 360-5309.
PERSONNEL/COMMUNITY ACTIVITIES: Civilian Personnel Office; (805) 982-4511.
Personnel and Expenditures
ACTIVE DUTY PERSONNEL: 4500
DEPENDENTS: 1500
CIVILIAN PERSONNEL: 4500
MILITARY PAYROLL EXPENDITURE: $194 mil (military & civilian)
CONTRACT EXPENDITURE: $73.5 mil
Services *Housing:* Family units 500; BOQ cottages 48; BEQ units 1549; Trailer spaces 20; Units under construction 398. *Temporary Housing:* VIP cottages 1; Lodge units 22. *Commissary:* Base commissary; Retail store; Barber shop; Dry cleaners; Florist; Service station; Furniture store. *Child Care/Capacities:* Day care center 153; Home day care program. *Schools:* Kindergarten/Preschool. *Base Library:* Yes. *Medical Facilities:* Medical clinic. *Recreational Facilities:* Bowling; Movie theater; Pool; Gym; Recreation center; Golf; Tennis; Skating rink; Fitness

center; Softball field; Auto shop; Crafts; Officers club; NCO club; Youth center; Gear issue-rental.

SACRAMENTO

SACRAMENTO ARMY DEPOT
8350 Fruitridge Rd, Sacramento, CA 95813-5000
(916) 388-2211; Autovon 839-1110
Profile
BRANCH: Army.
SIZE AND LOCATION: 485 acres. In SE corner of Sacramento; approx 3 mi E of US 99, and 1 mi S of US 50, intersection of Power Inn Rd and Fruitridge Rd.
MAJOR UNITS: 1118th CASA Battalion; Army Television-Audio Support Activity (TASA); High-Tech Regional Training Site.
BASE HISTORY: 1942, established as Sacramento Advanced Communications Zone Depot on site of old CA State Fairgrounds. Quartermaster Corps established depot in Sacramento to relieve congestion at Port of San Francisco; dismantled and moved to Tracy, CA; communications (signal) equipment moved from fairgrounds to old warehouse on N 7th St downtown. 1943, Sacramento Signal Depot established. 1944, additional warehouse space leased. 1945, present site chosen and construction began. Korean and Vietnam Wars brought depot to full strength.
Key Contacts
COMMANDER: Col John F Donahoe; (916) 388-3125, Autovon 839-3125.
PUBLIC AFFAIRS: Dick Dyer; (916) 388-2324, Autovon 839-2324.
PROCUREMENT: Otis Osborne; (916) 388-3161, Autovon 839-3161.
PERSONNEL/COMMUNITY ACTIVITIES: Pat Hansen; (916) 388-3222, Autovon 839-3222.
Personnel and Expenditures
ACTIVE DUTY PERSONNEL: 300
CIVILIAN PERSONNEL: 3000
MILITARY PAYROLL EXPENDITURE: FY 88, $100 mil
CONTRACT EXPENDITURE: FY 88, $64.6 mil
Services *Housing:* Family units 2. *Commissary and Exchange:* Retail store; Barber shop; Service station; Credit union. *Base Library:* Yes. *Medical Facilities:* Health clinic. *Recreational Facilities:* Pool; Recreation center; Racquetball; Fitness center; Softball field; Auto shop; Community club.

US ARMY CORPS OF ENGINEERS, SACRAMENTO DISTRICT
650 Capitol Mall, Sacramento, CA 95814
(916) 551-2526
Profile
BRANCH: Army.
SIZE AND LOCATION: Offices only. In the city of Sacramento.
BASE HISTORY: 1929, became a separate District of Corps of Engineers. Before 1929, known as Sacramento Sub-office of San Francisco District. 1929-41, performed civil works projects only. Currently, military works call for design and construction of projects at 34 military installations. 1968, became second largest in contiguous US when territory transferred from Los Angeles District. Covers all or part of 9 western states, CA, NV, UT, OR, ID, WY, CO, NM, and AZ; also operates 13 recreation areas in CA.
Personnel and Expenditures
ACTIVE DUTY PERSONNEL: 1300
CONTRACT EXPENDITURE: $200 mil

SAN DIEGO

CORONADO NAVAL AMPHIBIOUS BASE

San Diego, CA 92155-5000
(619) 437-2011; Autovon 577-2011
OFFICER-OF-THE-DAY: (619) 437-3432,
Autovon 577-3432

Profile

BRANCH: Navy.

SIZE AND LOCATION: 1006 acres. On Silver Strand between San Diego Bay and Pacific Ocean. Take Hwy 5 S over Coronado-San Diego Bay Bridge, left on Orange (becomes Hwy 75), turn left at sign to front gate. Approx 7 mi from downtown San Diego; 10 mi from San Diego Airport; 1 mi from Coronado.

MAJOR UNITS: Naval Surface Force; Landing Force Training Command; Surface Warfare Officer School; Naval Special Warfare Command; Amphibious Construction Battalion One; Assault Craft Unit One; Special Boat Unit 12; Special Boat Unit 13; Beachmaster Unit One; Tactical Air Squadron 11; Tactical Air Squadron 12; Naval Amphibious School; SEAL Team 1; SEAL Team 3; SEAL Team 5; Fleet Tactical Deception Group.

BASE HISTORY: 1943, establishment of Amphibious Training Base to train landing craft crews. 1946, renamed Naval Amphibious Base (NAB), Coronado; mission changed to providing administrative and logistical support to amphibious units on base and to conduct research and test amphibious equipment; property formed by land fill, dredged from bottom of San Diego Bay; remained in active operational status since initial establishment. Today, major shore command supporting some 30 tenant commands and units.

Key Contacts

COMMANDER: Capt Glenn Welch Jr; Commanding Officer, Bldg 16, (619) 437-2078, Autovon 577-2078.

PUBLIC AFFAIRS: William C Bartkus; Bldg 16, (619) 437-3024, Autovon 577-3024.

PROCUREMENT: LCDR James Cote; Bldg 16, (619) 437-2096, Autovon 577-2096.

TRANSPORTATION: LCDR Paul Newport; Bldg 16, (619) 437-3025, Autovon 577-3025.

PERSONNEL/COMMUNITY ACTIVITIES: Lt Patrick Tezak; Director of Personnel, Bldg 16, (619) 437-3230, Autovon 577-3230.

Personnel and Expenditures

ACTIVE DUTY PERSONNEL: 4500
DEPENDENTS: 3500

Services Housing: Family units 29; BEQ units 10; Barracks spaces 2927; Senior NCO units 62. Temporary Housing: VOQ cottages (in BOQ) 10; BOQ units 3; BAQ units; Transient living quarters 40. Commissary and Exchange: Retail store; Barber shop; Dry cleaners; Food shop; Florist; Service station; Credit union. Child Care/Capacities: Day care center 20. Base Library: Yes. Medical Facilities: Medical clinic; Dental clinic. Recreational Facilities: Bowling; Movie theater; Pool; Gym; Tennis; Racquetball; Fitness center; Softball field; Football field; Auto shop; Officers club; NCO club; Marina; Beach; Recreation gear locker, rentals.

FLEET ANTISUBMARINE WARFARE TRAINING CENTER, PACIFIC

San Diego, CA 92147-5000
(619) 524-1689; Autovon 957-4011
OFFICER-OF-THE-DAY: (619) 225-4405,
Autovon 957-4405

Profile

BRANCH: Navy.

SIZE: Offices only.

BASE HISTORY: 1939, Fleet Sound School established at Destroyer Base (now Naval Station) San Diego. 1942, Fleet Sound School, San Diego constructed and occupied. 1960, name changed to Fleet Anti Submarine Warfare School. 1973, changed to present name. Currently, primary center for training sonar technicians.

Key Contacts

PUBLIC AFFAIRS: (619) 524-0664.

Services Housing: BEQ units; Barracks spaces; 10 Housing areas with 5852 units in San Diego. Temporary Housing: Lodge units in area 3. Commissary and Exchange: Retail store; Barber shop; Dry cleaners; Food shop; Military clothing sales. Medical Facilities: Medical clinic; Dental clinic. Recreational Facilities: Bowling; Movie theater; Pool; Recreation center; Tennis; Racquetball; Softball field; Officers club; Weight room; Equipment rental.

FLEET COMBAT TRAINING CENTER, PACIFIC

200 Catalina Blvd, San Diego, CA 92147-5080
(619) 553-8330; Autovon 553-8330
OFFICER-OF-THE-DAY: (619) 553-8330,
Autovon 553-8330

Profile

BRANCH: Navy.

SIZE AND LOCATION: 95 acres. Ocean-front property on Point Loma in San Diego approx 4 mi from intersection of I-5 & I-8 and approx 6 mi from downtown San Diego.

MAJOR UNITS: Fleet Combat Training Center; Fleet Combat Direction Systems Support Activity (FCDSSA); Tactical Training Group, Pacific (TTGP); Navy Interoperability Support Activity (NTISA).

BASE HISTORY: Origin of FCTC dates back to 1943 with a series of informal lectures on radar and Combat Information Center (CIC) concept. 1943-45, CIC instruction expanded to meet fleet's need to understand capabilities and tactical use of radar. 1945, CIC section established as separate command and designated CIC Indoctrination School. 1946, School moved to present location; designated CIC Group Training Center (later redesignated US Fleet Air Defense Training Center in 1954, Fleet Anti-Air Warfare Training Center in 1960, and FCTC in 1976). Newest developments: include integration of electronic warfare and long range, over-the-horizon weapons applications to counter changing threats, and Battlex, a multi-warfare area scenario simulation exercising battle group command and control.

VISITOR ATTRACTIONS: Beautiful view overlooking the Pacific.

Key Contacts

COMMANDER: Capt L P Amborn; (619) 553-8324, Autovon 553-8324.

PUBLIC AFFAIRS: Lt G T Pennell; (619) 553-8112, Autovon 553-8112.

PROCUREMENT: LCDR E F Panado; (619) 553-8160, Autovon 553-8160.

TRANSPORTATION: MACS J J Howell; (619) 553-8226, Autovon 553-8226.

PERSONNEL/COMMUNITY ACTIVITIES: CDR R W McClung; (619) 553-8324, Autovon 553-8324.

Personnel and Expenditures

ACTIVE DUTY PERSONNEL: 510
CIVILIAN PERSONNEL: 70
MILITARY PAYROLL EXPENDITURE: $12.75 mil
CONTRACT EXPENDITURE: $2.8 mil

Services Commissary and Exchange: Retail store; Barber shop; Dry cleaners; Food shop; Banking; Cafeteria. Recreational Facilities: Tennis; Fitness center; Softball field; PAR course; Basketball, volleyball facilities.

MIRAMAR NAVAL AIR STATION

San Diego, CA 92145
(619) 271-3011; Autovon 959-0111
OFFICER-OF-THE-DAY: (619) 537-1227,
Autovon 577-1227

Profile

BRANCH: Navy.

SIZE AND LOCATION: 24,000 acres. 10 mi N of San Diego near I-15 and I-805.

MAJOR UNITS: Commander Fighter Airborne Early Warning Wing, US Pacific Fleet (COMFITAEW-WINGPAC); Carrier Air Wing 2 (CVW-2); Carrier Air Wing 5 (CVW-5); Carrier Air Wing 11 (CVW-11); Carrier Air Wing 14 (CVW-14); Carrier Air Wing 15 (CVW-15); VF-124 Gunfighters; Navy Fighter Weapons School (TOPGUN); VF-126 Bandits; VAW-110 Firebirds; VF-1 Wolfpack; VF-2 Bounty Hunters; VF-21 Freelancers; VF-24 Fighting Renegades; VF-51 Screaming Eagles; VF-111 Sundowners; VF-114 Fighting Aardvarks; VF-154 Black Knights; VF-211 Fighting Checkmates; VF-213 Blacklions; VAW-112 Golden Hawks; VAW-113 Black Eagles; VAW-114 Hormel Hawgs; VAW-115 Liberty Bells; VAW-116 Sun Kings; VAW-117 Nighthawks; Naval Air Reserve Center Miramar; VF-301 Devil's Disciples; VF-302 Stallions; VC-13 Saints; VAW-88 Cottonpickers; Fleet Aviation Specialized Operational Training Group Pacific, Detachment Miramar; Fourth Tank Battalion (Marine Corps Reserves); Naval Aviation Engineering Service Unit; Naval Air Maintenance Training Group Detachments, Miramar; Naval Oceanography Command Detachment; Naval Drug Rehabilitation Center; Naval Telecommunications Center Miramar; Operations, Mitscher Field; Pacific Fleet Audiovisual Center; Tactical Aircrew Combat Training System.

BASE HISTORY: Present site owned by US Government since WWI, when purchased for Camp Kearny, Army Infantry Training Center. Also used for variety of military functions, including lighter-than-air aircraft base and target bombing range. WWII, southern half of station commissioned auxiliary air station, North Island and northern half designated Marine Corps Air Depot Miramar. 1946, activities combined; designated Marine Corps Air Station Miramar. 1947, Marine air units moved to MCAS El Toro. 1952, designated NAS Miramar. 1961, became support base for fighter squadrons only. Today, home base for all Pacific Fleet fighter and airborne early warning squadrons.

Key Contacts

COMMANDER: Rear Adm J B Best; Commander (COMFITAEW-WINGPAC); (619) 537-1227, Autovon 577-1227.

PUBLIC AFFAIRS: (619) 537-4084, Autovon 577-4084.

Personnel and Expenditures

ACTIVE DUTY PERSONNEL: 10,000
CIVILIAN PERSONNEL: 2000

Services Housing: Family units 88; BOQ cottages 200; BEQ units 26; Trailer spaces 108. Temporary Housing: BOQ units 1; Lodge units 90. Commissary: Base commissary; Retail store; Barber shop; Dry cleaners; Food shop; Florist; Banking; Service station; Furniture store; Bakery; Military clothing sales; Convenience store/Shopette; Beauty shop; Laundry; Toys; Snacks; Car rental; Jewelry/watch sales and repair; Optical shop;

MIRAMAR NAVAL AIR STATION (*continued*)
Package beverages; Tailor; Video rental. *Child Care/Capacities:* Day care center 90. *Base Library:* Yes. *Medical Facilities:* Medical clinic; Dental clinic; San Diego Naval Hospital, 15 mi away. *Recreational Facilities:* Bowling; Movie theater; Pool; Gym; Recreation center; Golf; Stables; Tennis; Racquetball; Fitness center; Softball field; Auto shop; Crafts; Officers club; NCO club; Camping; Fishing/Hunting; Picnic area; Jogging course; Camp gear; RV storage lot; RV park spaces, 24; Youth center.

NORTH ISLAND NAVAL AIR STATION
San Diego, CA 92135
(619) 545-8123; Autovon 735-8123
OFFICER-OF-THE-DAY: (619) 545-8123, Autovon 735-8123
Profile
BRANCH: Navy.
SIZE AND LOCATION: 2802 acres. Off Hwy I-5; take Coronado Bay Bridge Exit, go through toll booths, continue down Third St to main gate. Coronado approx 5 min from base; San Diego Airport approx 15 min N.
MAJOR UNITS: Commander Naval Air Force US Pacific Fleet; Commander Antisubmarine Warfare Wing Pacific; Commander Carrier Group One; Commander Carrier Group Seven; USS *Ranger* (CV-61); USS *Independence* (CV-65); USS *Constellation* (CV-64); Naval Air Station, North Island; Naval Auxiliary Landing Field San Clemente Island; Antisubmarine Warfare Operations Center (ASWOC); Commander Helicopter Wing Reserve; Fleet Area Control and Surveillance Facility (FACSFAC); Fleet Aviation Specialized Operational Training Group, Pacific Fleet (FASOTRAGRUPAC); Fleet Electronic Warfare Support Group; Marine Corps Security Company; Naval Air Maintenance Training Group Detachments North Island (NAMTRAGRUDETS North Island); Naval Aviation Depot (NAVAVNDEPOT); Naval Aviation Engineering Service Unit (NAESU); Naval Oceanography Command Facility; Navy Regional Data Automation Center San Diego; Naval Telecommunications Center; Nuclear Weapons Training Group, Pacific (NUWPNTRAGRUPAC); Operational Test and Evaluation Force, Pacific (OPTEVFOR); Pacific Fleet Imaging Command (FLTIMAGCOMPAC); Personnel Support Activity Detachment; Submarine Rescue Unit; US Customs Service.
BASE HISTORY: 1910, Curtiss Pusher made emergency landing on North Island. 1917, North Island commissioned and, until 1937, Navy shared facilities with Army Signal Corps. 1927, Charles Lindbergh took off from North Island for St Louis on way to Paris. Before WWII, area called Spanish Bight separated base from city of Coronado; filled in with sand from San Diego harbor, 1940s. Important training, staging, and deployment center, especially during WWII, and Korean Conflict.
Key Contacts
COMMANDER: Capt J R DeNigro; (619) 545-8163, Autovon 735-8163.
PUBLIC AFFAIRS: Ken Mitchell; Code OB, (619) 545-8167, Autovon 735-8167.
PROCUREMENT: CDR Archer; Code 19, (619) 545-3247, Autovon 735-3247.
PERSONNEL/COMMUNITY ACTIVITIES: Joe Mauro; Code 22, (619) 545-8033, Autovon 735-8033.

Personnel and Expenditures
ACTIVE DUTY PERSONNEL: 16,200
DEPENDENTS: 7044
CIVILIAN PERSONNEL: 7300
Services *Housing:* BOQ cottages; BEQ units; No base housing at NAS North Island. *Temporary Housing:* VIP cottages; BOQ units; Lodge units. *Commissary:* Base commissary; Retail store; Barber shop; Dry cleaners; Food shop; Florist; Banking; Service station. *Child Care/Capacities:* Day care center 90. *Base Library:* Yes. *Medical Facilities:* Medical clinic; Dental clinic. *Recreational Facilities:* Bowling; Movie theater; Pool; Gym; Recreation center; Golf; Tennis; Racquetball; Fitness center; Softball field; Football field; Auto shop; Crafts; Officers club.

SAN DIEGO COAST GUARD GROUP
2710 N Harbor Dr, San Diego, CA 92101-1079
(619) 557-5870
OFFICER-OF-THE-DAY: (619) 557-6644
Profile
BRANCH: Coast Guard.
SIZE AND LOCATION: 11.3 acres. Directly across N Harbor Dr from San Diego Lindbergh Field.
MAJOR UNITS: Coast Guard Group San Diego; Coast Guard Air Station San Diego; Coast Guard Marine Safety Office San Diego.
BASE HISTORY: 1935, tideland adjacent to Lindbergh Field acquired for construction of Coast Guard base. 1936, constructed with funds from Federal Public Works Administration. Today, Air Station maintains 3 HH65A helicopters and 3 falcon jets. 1985, extensive renovation and remodeling campaign began. 1986, small boat station redesignated, Station San Diego.
Key Contacts
COMMANDER: Capt Richard S Jarombek.
PUBLIC AFFAIRS: LTjg C William Mello Jr; (619) 557-6556.
PROCUREMENT: Lt Richard Gromlich; (619) 557-6613.
TRANSPORTATION: See Procurement Officer.
PERSONNEL/COMMUNITY ACTIVITIES: LCDR Patrick Gregory; Director of Personnel, (619) 557-6510.
Personnel and Expenditures
ACTIVE DUTY PERSONNEL: 225
Services *Housing:* Dormitory spaces. *Commissary and Exchange:* Retail store. *Medical Facilities:* Medical clinic. *Recreational Facilities:* Tennis; Racquetball.

SAN DIEGO MARINE CORPS RECRUIT DEPOT
San Diego, CA 92140-5000
(619) 524-1276; Autovon 524-1276
OFFICER-OF-THE-DAY: (619) 524-1276
Profile
BRANCH: Marines.
SIZE AND LOCATION: 433 acres. Off I-5 just S of I-8; joined by Washington St, Pacific Hwy, Witherby St (also joined by Old Town Ave), and Barnett St; 2 mi from downtown San Diego, between I-5 and Lindbergh Field Airport.
MAJOR UNITS: Recruit Training Regiment; Headquarters and Service Battalion; Recruiters School; Drill Instructor School.
BASE HISTORY: Marine Corps' oldest operating installation on West Coast. 1921, designated as Advance Marine Corps Expeditionary Base. 1923, Recruit Depot for western half of US moved to San Diego. Served as home for both Marine Expeditionary Forces in China and Fleet Marine Forces between two world wars; During WWII, trained about 223,000 recruits. 1948, designated MCRD.

VISITOR ATTRACTIONS: Command Museum; Graduation ceremonies.
Key Contacts
COMMANDER: Brig Gen F J Breth.
PUBLIC AFFAIRS: Maj J Broeckert.
Personnel and Expenditures
ACTIVE DUTY PERSONNEL: 6000
DEPENDENTS: 2100
CIVILIAN PERSONNEL: 600
MILITARY PAYROLL EXPENDITURE: $71.2 mil
Services *Housing:* Family units 5; BEQ units 636; Navy housing available off base. *Temporary Housing:* VIP cottages 2; VOQ cottages 18. *Commissary and Exchange:* Convenience store/Shopette; Household store; Garden center. *Child Care/Capacities:* Day care center 100. *Medical Facilities:* Dispensary; San Diego Naval Hospital, 8 mi away. *Recreational Facilities:* Bowling; Movie theater; Fitness center; Auto shop; Boat house.

SAN DIEGO NAVAL STATION
San Diego, CA 92136
(619) 556-2400; Autovon 526-2400
OFFICER-OF-THE-DAY: (619) 556-1246, Autovon 526-1246
Profile
BRANCH: Navy.
SIZE AND LOCATION: 1000 acres. In city of San Diego at intersection of Harbor Dr and 32nd St, portions of southern end of base in National City.
MAJOR UNITS: Fleet Training Center; Navy Public Works Center; Shore Intermediate Maintenance Activity; Personnel Support Activity Detachment; Transient Personnel Unit; Navy Brig.
BASE HISTORY: 1923, commissioned as destroyer base, then repair base. 1945, named Naval Station, San Diego. Currently homeport to 74 surface warships.
Key Contacts
COMMANDER: Capt D F Berkebile; (619) 556-2400, Autovon 526-2400.
PUBLIC AFFAIRS: Julie Swan; (619) 556-7356, Autovon 526-7356.
Personnel and Expenditures
ACTIVE DUTY PERSONNEL: 7000 shore; 34,000 fleet
CIVILIAN PERSONNEL: 5000
Services *Housing:* Family units 1; BEQ units 4363; Barracks spaces; Dormitory spaces. *Temporary Housing:* VOQ cottages; VEQ units; VAQ units; BOQ units 132; BAQ units; Lodge units 45. *Commissary:* Base commissary; Retail store; Barber shop; Dry cleaners; Food shop; Florist; Service station; Furniture store. *Child Care/Capacities:* Day care center 300; Home day care program. *Base Library:* Yes. *Medical Facilities:* Active duty clinic only. *Recreational Facilities:* Bowling; Movie theater; Pool; Gym; Recreation center; Golf; Tennis; Racquetball; Fitness center; Softball field; Auto shop; Crafts; Officers club; NCO club.

SAN DIEGO NAVAL SUBMARINE BASE
140 Sylvester Rd, San Diego, CA 92106-3521
(619) 553-7208; Autovon 553-7208
Profile
BRANCH: Navy.
SIZE AND LOCATION: 330 acres. At tip of Ballast Point (harbor entrance) on Point Loma peninsula; approx 8 mi from downtown San Diego, Lindbergh Field and I-5 & I-8.
MAJOR UNITS: Submarine Group 5; Submarine Squadron 3; Submarine Squadron 11; Submarine Development Group 1; Submarine Training Facility.
BASE HISTORY: 1852, President Fillmore set aside southern portion of Point Loma for military use. Subsequently, land assigned

SAN DIEGO NAVAL SUBMARINE BASE
(continued)

to Army and named for Civil War Gen William Rosecrans. 1959, Ft Rosecrans, designated historic landmark, turned over to Navy. 1963, Submarine Support Facility established. 1974, Submarine Support Facility became shore command. 1981, redesignated Naval Submarine Base.

VISITOR ATTRACTIONS: Ft Rosecrans/Cabrillo National Monument nearby.

Personnel and Expenditures

ACTIVE DUTY PERSONNEL: 2000
DEPENDENTS: 25
CIVILIAN PERSONNEL: 5000
MILITARY PAYROLL EXPENDITURE: $7.9 mil
CONTRACT EXPENDITURE: $9.3 mil

Services *Housing:* Duplex units 4; Barracks spaces 1745. *Commissary and Exchange:* Retail store; Barber shop; Dry cleaners; Food shop; Florist; Banking; Service station; Convenience store/Shopette; Video rental; Laundry. *Base Library:* Yes. *Medical Facilities:* Dental clinic; First aid office with one corpsman, supported by Naval Training Center, San Diego. *Recreational Facilities:* Bowling; Pool; Gym; Recreation center (game room); Tennis; Racquetball; Fitness center; Softball field; Auto shop; Crafts; Officers club; NCO club; Fishing/Hunting; Enlisted Club; Gear issue; Tour/ticket office; SATO.

SAN DIEGO NAVAL SUPPLY CENTER

937 N Harbor Dr, San Diego, CA 92132-5044
(619) 532-2203; Autovon 522-2203
OFFICER-OF-THE-DAY: (619) 556-8318, Autovon 526-8318

Profile

BRANCH: Navy.

SIZE AND LOCATION: 16 acres. HQ at Broadway Complex, downtown San Diego; Offices at: Naval Station, San Diego; NAS, North Island; Point Loma; Long Beach.

MAJOR UNITS: Navy Regional Contracting Center; Naval Base San Diego; Fleet Accounting & Disbursing Pacific; Naval Communications Station.

BASE HISTORY: 1904, coaling station at Point Loma, first permanent Navy logistics shore establishment in San Diego. Today, site occupied by NSC Fuel Department. 1922, Naval Supply Depot opened; Supply Depot building also HQ, Commander, Naval Base, San Diego. 1952, redesignated Naval Supply Center. 1973, sister Supply Center in Long Beach closed. 1980, consolidation gave NSC responsibility for functions previously accomplished by supply department, NAS North Island. Today, provides direct logistic support to ships homeported in San Diego and Long Beach and over 250 shore activities.

Key Contacts

COMMANDER: Capt Charles W Stone Jr; (619) 532-2203, Autovon 522-2203.
PUBLIC AFFAIRS: Mary Markovinovic; (619) 532-1931, Autovon 522-1931.
PROCUREMENT: (619) 556-8953, Autovon 526-8953.
TRANSPORTATION: (619) 556-8457, Autovon 526-8457.
PERSONNEL/COMMUNITY ACTIVITIES: (619) 532-2743, Autovon 522-2743.

Personnel and Expenditures

ACTIVE DUTY PERSONNEL: 35
CIVILIAN PERSONNEL: 1400

Services *Commissary and Exchange:* Barber shop; Dry cleaners; Banking; Mini-exchange; Credit union. *Medical Facilities:* Medical clinic. *Recreational Facilities:* Gym.

SAN DIEGO NAVAL TRAINING CENTER

San Diego, CA 92133-5000
(619) 524-4210; Autovon 524-4210
OFFICER-OF-THE-DAY: (619) 524-5796, Autovon 524-5796

Profile

BRANCH: Navy.

SIZE AND LOCATION: 666 acres. Point Loma near downtown San Diego; 2 min to San Diego Airport, Hwy 8/Harbor Dr.

MAJOR UNITS: Naval Training Center (NTC); Service School Command; Recruit Training Command.

BASE HISTORY: 1921, NTC construction began. 1923, commissioned; shore line considerably further inland then and Preble Field, N athletic area and Camp Farragut was under water. 1936, Camp Lawrence completed. 1939, land added by filling in eastern boundaries of Station. 1944, Training Station redesignated Naval Training Center, San Diego. 1953, land SE of estuary developed into recruit training area, Camp Nimitz. NTC San Diego is historic landmark.

VISITOR ATTRACTIONS: Recruit graduation held every Fri at 1:00 pm, open to the public; Recruit Training Command has POW/MIA Memorial.

Key Contacts

COMMANDER: Capt P M Reber; (619) 524-5428, Autovon 524-5428.
PUBLIC AFFAIRS: Lt Kenneth E Luchka; Public Affairs Officer (Code 07).

Services *Housing:* BEQ units; Barracks spaces. *Temporary Housing:* BOQ units. *Commissary:* Base commissary; Retail store; Barber shop; Dry cleaners; Food shop; Florist; Banking; Service station. *Child Care/Capacities:* Day care center. *Base Library:* Yes. *Medical Facilities:* Medical clinic; Dental clinic. *Recreational Facilities:* Bowling; Movie theater; Pool; Gym; Recreation center; Golf; Fitness center; Softball field; Football field; Auto shop; Crafts; Officers club; NCO club.

SAN DIEGO RECRUIT TRAINING COMMAND, NAVAL TRAINING CENTER

San Diego, CA 92133-2000
(619) 524-1157; Autovon 514-1157
OFFICER-OF-THE-DAY: (619) 524-1150, Autovon 524-1150

Profile

BRANCH: Navy.

SIZE AND LOCATION: 666 acres. Point Loma near downtown San Diego; 2 min to San Diego Airport, Hwy 8/Harbor Dr.

MAJOR UNITS: Recruit Training Command; Personnel Support Detachment/Attachment; Service School Command.

BASE HISTORY: See San Diego Naval Training Center

VISITOR ATTRACTIONS: POW/MIA Memorial.

Key Contacts

COMMANDER: Capt P M Reber; (619) 524-5428, Autovon 524-5428.
PUBLIC AFFAIRS: Lt Kenneth E Luchka; Public Affairs Officer (Code 07).

Personnel and Expenditures

ACTIVE DUTY PERSONNEL: 500
CIVILIAN PERSONNEL: 10

Services *Housing:* Family units 4; BEQ units 2100; Senior NCO units 168; Junior NCO units 100. *Temporary Housing:* BOQ units 345. *Commissary:* Base commissary; Retail store; Barber shop; Dry cleaners; Food shop; Florist; Banking; Service station; Furniture store. *Child Care/Capacities:* Day care center 76. *Base Library:* Yes. *Medical Facilities:* Medical clinic; Dental clinic. *Recreational Facilities:* Bowling; Movie theater; Pool; Gym; Recreation center; Golf; Tennis; Racquetball; Fitness center; Softball field;

Football field; Auto shop; Crafts; Officers club; NCO club; Basketball courts; Race track; Barbecue/picnic areas; Game room.

SAN FRANCISCO

FORT MASON

San Francisco, CA 94123
(415) 441-5705
OFFICER-OF-THE-DAY: See Presidio of San Francisco

Profile

BRANCH: Army.

SIZE AND LOCATION: 30 acres. At intersection of Bay and Franklin Sts, 3 blocks N of Hwy 101, San Francisco.

MAJOR UNITS: Golden Gate National Recreation Area; Fort Mason Center.

BASE HISTORY: 1851, site reserved by President Fillmore; used as coastal artillery batteries during Civil War through WWII. Transportation Corps port of embarkation through Korean War. 1972, deactivated and transferred to National Park Service. Presidio of San Francisco maintains housing and officer's club at Fort Mason. Presidio of San Francisco scheduled to be closed. Until then, Army maintains housing at Forts Baker, Mason, and Barry, all subposts of Presidio of San Francisco until transferred to National Park Service.

VISITOR ATTRACTIONS: Civil War and later coast artillery batteries; Headquarters Golden Gate National Recreation Area; Fort Mason Center.

Key Contacts

COMMANDER: Col Joseph V Rafferty; Headquarters, Presidio of San Francisco, CA 94123, (415) 561-2044.
PUBLIC AFFAIRS: Robert Mahoney; Headquarters, Presidio of San Francisco, CA 94123, (415) 561-3995.
PROCUREMENT: See Presidio of San Francisco.
TRANSPORTATION: See Presidio of San Francisco.
PERSONNEL/COMMUNITY ACTIVITIES: See Presidio of San Francisco.

Personnel and Expenditures

ACTIVE DUTY PERSONNEL: Included in Presidio of San Francisco
DEPENDENTS: Included in Presidio of San Francisco
CIVILIAN PERSONNEL: Included in Presidio of San Francisco

Services *Housing:* Family units 20. *Recreational Facilities:* Officers club.

LETTERMAN ARMY MEDICAL CENTER

Presidio of San Francisco, San Francisco, CA 94129-6700
(415) 561-2231; Autovon 586-2231
OFFICER-OF-THE-DAY: (415) 561-2231, Autovon 586-2231

Profile

BRANCH: Army.

LOCATION: In NW corner of San Francisco, adj to S end of Golden Gate Bridge; Within city and Golden Gate National Recreation Area, Department of Interior; Approx 15 mi from San Francisco and Oakland Airports.

MAJOR UNITS: Letterman Army Medical Center; US Army Dental Activity (DENTAC); Regional Veterinary Lab.

BASE HISTORY: 1898, construction began on hospital to provide primary health care to soldiers en route to combat duty in the Philippines. 1906, earthquake, provided care for victims. 1911, US Army General Hospital renamed for Maj Jonathan Letterman, Surgeon General of Army of the Potomac during Civil War. WWI, world's largest military hospital with 2200 beds

LETTERMAN ARMY MEDICAL CENTER
(continued)

(expanded to 3,500); known for Orthopedics and Psychiatry specialties. Mid-1960s, new hospital constructed; dedicated in 1969. 1973, redesignated Letterman Army Medical Center. 1988, LAMC, "Lam see," part of new joint San Francisco Medical Command, uniting Army and Navy medical resources in Bay Area. A major teaching hospital with 16 major graduate medical education programs and serves total beneficiary population of over 400,000 mainly military retirees and families in CA and NV.

VISITOR ATTRACTIONS: See Presidio of San Francisco.

Key Contacts

COMMANDER: Col Paul L Shetler; Commander, Letterman AMC (ATTN: HSHH CDR), (415) 561-2153, Autovon 586-2153.

PUBLIC AFFAIRS: Michael G Meines; ATTN: HSHH-PAO, (415) 561-4427, Autovon 586-4427.

Personnel and Expenditures

ACTIVE DUTY PERSONNEL: 1100

CIVILIAN PERSONNEL: 750

Services *Housing:* See Presidio of San Francisco. *Temporary Housing:* See Presidio of San Francisco. *Commissary and Exchange:* Retail store (through Presidio of San Francisco); Barber shop (through Presidio of San Francisco); Banking (through Presidio of San Francisco). *Child Care/Capacities:* Through the Presidio of San Francisco. *Schools:* Preschool part of Presidio Child Development Ctr. *Base Library:* Yes. *Medical Facilities:* Hospital 354; Medical clinic; Dental clinic; Veterinary activities. *Recreational Facilities:* Bowling (through Presidio of San Francisco); Movie theater (through Presidio of San Francisco); Pool (through Presidio of San Francisco); Gym (through Presidio of San Francisco); Recreation center (through Presidio of San Francisco); Golf (through Presidio of San Francisco); Tennis (through Presidio of San Francisco); Racquetball (through Presidio of San Francisco); Fitness center (through Presidio of San Francisco); Softball field (through Presidio of San Francisco); Football field (through Presidio of San Francisco); Auto shop (through Presidio of San Francisco); Crafts (through Presidio of San Francisco); Officers club (through Presidio of San Francisco); NCO club (through Presidio of San Francisco).

PRESIDIO OF SAN FRANCISCO

Bldg 37, San Francisco, CA 94129-6520
(415) 561-3770, Autovon 586-3770
OFFICER-OF-THE-DAY: (415) 561-2780, Autovon 586-2045

Profile

BRANCH: Army.

SIZE AND LOCATION: 1700 acres. In NW corner of San Francisco, adj to S end of Golden Gate Bridge; Within city and Golden Gate National Recreation Area, Department of Interior; Approx 15 mi from San Francisco and Oakland Airports.

MAJOR UNITS: Headquarters, Sixth US Army; Letterman Army Medical Center; Letterman Army Institute of Research; US Army Sixth Recruiting Brigade.

BASE HISTORY: 1776, Spanish established northernmost of their CA posts at point that is now center of main post. "Presidio" is derived from Roman word, "praesidium," meaning garrison or fortified camp. 1846, US took forceable possession. During Civil War, Union Army trained regiments and maintained defense for Western frontiers during Indian campaigns of 1870-80s. Spanish American

War, volunteers trained on Infantry Terrace. 1906 earthquake, Presidio troops helped to keep order, assist refugees, and fight fire; refugee camps set up on Presidio grounds. WWI, officers' training camp; HQ for Fourth Army and Western Defense Command. 1946, Sixth Army stationed at Presidio. 1963, named Registered National Historic Landmark. Also see Letterman Army Medical Center.

VISITOR ATTRACTIONS: Presidio Army Museum; Historic Trail, includes Pershing Square, Inspiration Point; Ft Point (Ft Winfield Scott); coastal artillery gun emplacements; San Francisco National Cemetery; Spanish-American War Campground; 400 historic structures on post.

Key Contacts

COMMANDER: Lt Gen William Harrison; CG, 6th Army, Bldg 38, PSF, (415) 561-2044, Autovon 586-2044; Col William Swift; Garrison Commander, Bldg 220, PSF.

PUBLIC AFFAIRS: Col Charles O'Brien; 6th Army, (415) 561-3995, Autovon 586-3995; Robert Mahoney; Garrison PAO.

PROCUREMENT: Richard Gore; Director, Logistics, Bldg 220, (415) 561-2740, Autovon 586-2740.

TRANSPORTATION: Elaine Bielecki; Bldg 35, (415) 561-3116, Autovon 586-3116.

PERSONNEL/COMMUNITY ACTIVITIES: Col Le Ester Alexander; Bldg 220, (415) 561-2451, Autovon 586-2451.

Personnel and Expenditures

ACTIVE DUTY PERSONNEL: 2500

DEPENDENTS: 6200

CIVILIAN PERSONNEL: 3500

Services *Housing:* Family units 1368; Senior NCO units 60. *Temporary Housing:* VIP cottages 3; VOQ cottages 18; VEQ units 39; BOQ units 28; Guesthouse units 42; Guest cottages 6. *Commissary:* Base commissary; Retail store; Barber shop; Food shop; Florist; Banking; Service station; Fast food. *Child Care/Capacities:* Day care center 354. *Base Library:* Yes. *Medical Facilities:* Hospital 500; Dental clinic. *Recreational Facilities:* Bowling; Movie theater; Pool; Gym; Recreation center; Golf; Stables; Tennis; Racquetball; Fitness center; Softball field; Auto shop; Crafts; Officers club; NCO club; Camping; Fishing/Hunting; Activities throughout northern CA and the Sierras, Lake Tahoe, etc..

SAN FRANCISCO COAST GUARD AIR STATION

San Francisco International Airport, San Francisco, CA 94128-5000
(415) 876-2925; Autovon 859-6925
OFFICER-OF-THE-DAY: (415) 876-2929, Autovon 859-6929

Profile

BRANCH: Coast Guard.

SIZE AND LOCATION: 24 acres. 1 mi N of San Francisco IAP Exit, off North Access Rd between United Airlines and Flying Tigers Airlines.

BASE HISTORY: 1941, established at Mills Field, CA. Through WWII, placed under operational command of Navy and conducted search and rescue (SAR) missions and coastal patrols. Mission: maritime search and rescue along 300 miles of coastline, from Point Conception to Ft Bragg, CA; drug and fisheries law enforcement missions; aids to navigation, such as offshore lighthouses; and, aerial surveillance for marine environmental protection.

Key Contacts

COMMANDER: CMDR Terry M Cross; (415) 876-2910, Autovon 859-6910.

PUBLIC AFFAIRS: LTjg Tim N Scoggins; (415) 876-2925, Autovon 859-6925.

PROCUREMENT: Lt Mike Quinn; (415) 876-2970, Autovon 859-6970.

TRANSPORTATION: See Procurement Officer.

PERSONNEL/COMMUNITY ACTIVITIES: Ens Felix Danz; (415) 876-2936, Autovon 859-6936.

Personnel and Expenditures

ACTIVE DUTY PERSONNEL: 99

CIVILIAN PERSONNEL: 2

CONTRACT EXPENDITURE: $0.7 mil

Services *Housing:* All government quarters located at Hamilton AFB. *Temporary Housing:* All government quarters located at Hamilton AFB. *Medical Facilities:* Clinic limited to assigned personnel. *Recreational Facilities:* Gym; Recreation center; Tennis; Racquetball; Fitness center; Auto shop.

SAN FRANCISCO COAST GUARD BASE

Yerba Buena Island, San Francisco, CA 94130-5000
(415) 399-3500
OFFICER-OF-THE-DAY: (415) 399-3529

Profile

BRANCH: Coast Guard.

LOCATION: Yerba Buena Island in center of entrance to San Francisco Bay connected to Treasure Island and access to I-80 San Francisco Oakland Bay Bridge, with San Francisco and Oakland 5 min away; bus service available.

MAJOR UNITS: ANT San Francisco; USCGC *Blackhaw*.

BASE HISTORY: Yerba Buena is a natural island. Treasure Island was built for 1939-40 Golden Gate International Exposition and was to become San Francisco's airport after the fair. Spaniards named island Yerba Buena for "good herb" growing there, mint used to flavor tea. Americans called it "Goat Island," for goat herds kept there by ship captains. Island's history includes tales of pirates, buried treasure, and ghosts. 1866, government set aside Yerba Buena Island for military; US Light House Service established Pacific Coast depot on island. 1898, Yerba Buena Island site for first West Coast naval training school (transferred to San Diego, 1923) and island became Navy receiving station. Today, part of Yerba Buena Island site of Navy family housing; remainder of island is Coast Guard's San Francisco base, Yerba Buena Island lighthouse, and Vessel Traffic Service, which monitors movement of all ships between Golden Gate and Sacramento.

Key Contacts

COMMANDER: LCDR S D Dilks; (415) 399-3505.

PUBLIC AFFAIRS: LTjg J J Briggs; (415) 399-3504.

TRANSPORTATION: SKC A A Trias.

PERSONNEL/COMMUNITY ACTIVITIES: See Public Affairs Officer.

Services *Housing:* Located at Treasure Island facility and Hamilton AFB. *Temporary Housing:* Located at Treasure Island facility and Hamilton AFB.

TREASURE ISLAND NAVAL STATION

San Francisco, CA 94130
(415) 395-0111; Autovon 869-0111

Profile

BRANCH: Navy.

SIZE AND LOCATION: 400 acres. Treasure Island in center of entrance to San Francisco Bay connected to Yerba Buena Island and access to I-80 San Francisco Oakland Bay Bridge, with San Francisco and Oakland 5 min away.

MAJOR UNITS: Commander, Naval Base San Francisco; Naval Technical Training Center; Reserve Readiness Command Region

TREASURE ISLAND NAVAL STATION
(continued)

20; Navy Marine Corps Reserve Center; USS *Roark*; USS *Lang*; USS *Gray*; USS *Excel*; USS *Gallant* .

BASE HISTORY: Yerba Buena is a natural island. Treasure Island was built for 1939-40 Golden Gate International Exposition and was to become San Francisco's airport after the fair. 1936-37, island built atop Yerba Buena shoals, shallow sheet of rock extending N from Yerba Buena Island; publicity men dubbed it "Treasure Island." Following Golden Gate Exposition, San Francisco leased island to Navy. WWII, processed up to 12,000 men every day bound for war zones in Pacific; some spent a night, others learned to operate naval vessels; WAVES trained recruits in recognizing enemy aircraft, Marine Corps housed and equipped nearly all Marines who passed through San Francisco; German POWs housed on western shore of island; city traded island to Navy for government land that became San Francisco IAP. 1987, naval vessels once again stationed at Treasure Island. Legacy of Exposition remains in would-be airport terminal and two hangars, which remain little altered since 1940. Today, Island operates training schools, processes outbound and homecoming personnel, and provides housing for personnel stationed in Bay Area.

VISITOR ATTRACTIONS: Treasure Island Museum, History of Navy, Marine Corps, and Coast Guard in the Pacific, open daily, 10-3, except Christmas, New Year's and Easter.

Personnel and Expenditures
ACTIVE DUTY PERSONNEL: 3000
DEPENDENTS: 2000
CIVILIAN PERSONNEL: 1000
MILITARY PAYROLL EXPENDITURE: $75 mil
CONTRACT EXPENDITURE: $45 mil
Services *Housing:* Family units 725; BEQ units. *Temporary Housing:* BOQ units. *Commissary:* Base commissary; Retail store; Barber shop; Service station. *Child Care/Capacities:* Day care center. *Schools:* Kindergarten/Preschool; Elementary. *Base Library:* Yes. *Medical Facilities:* Medical clinic; Dental clinic. *Recreational Facilities:* Bowling; Movie theater; Pool; Gym; Tennis; Racquetball; Skating rink; Fitness center; Softball field; Football field; Auto shop; Officers club; NCO club; Fishing/Hunting.

US ARMY CORPS OF ENGINEERS, SOUTH PACIFIC DIVISION
630 Sansome St, San Francisco, CA 94111
(415) 556-0914
Profile
BRANCH: Army.
SIZE: Offices only.
Key Contacts
COMMANDER: Brig Gen John F Sobke; Division Engineer.

SAN LUIS OBISPO

CAMP SAN LUIS OBISPO
PO Box 8104, San Luis Obispo, CA 93403-8104
(805) 549-3800
OFFICER-OF-THE-DAY: (805) 549-3806
Profile
BRANCH: Army National Guard.
SIZE AND LOCATION: 4160 acres. 5 mi NE of San Luis Obispo on Hwy 1.
MAJOR UNITS: US Property and Fiscal Office for California (USP&FO CA); 351st Supply and Service Company (CA ARNG); Detachment 1, 649th Military Police

Company; US Coast Guard Reserve; 6222nd US Army Reserve School.
BASE HISTORY: 1928, established as Camp Merriam, named after Gov Frank F Merriam. 1940, name changed to Camp San Luis Obispo by Army. 1940-41, virtually all construction in cantonment area took place. 1946, returned to state; home of USPFO for CA, providing logistical and fiscal support for entire CANG. For a number of years, training site for 40th and 49th Infantry Divisions, CANG. 1950, Army leased camp as Class I installation and Southwest Signal Corps Training Center as Class II activity. 1965, Army returned camp to state. Made site of California Military Academy as well as Sixth US Army sponsored unit training schools.
VISITOR ATTRACTIONS: Small aircraft museum.
Key Contacts
COMMANDER: LTC John W Hageman; (805) 549-3816.
PROCUREMENT: CSM Harlan J Harris; (805) 549-3820.
PERSONNEL/COMMUNITY ACTIVITIES: (805) 549-3816.
Personnel and Expenditures
ACTIVE DUTY PERSONNEL: 150
CIVILIAN PERSONNEL: 1000
CONTRACT EXPENDITURE: $1.2 mil
Services *Housing:* BOQ cottages 5; Barracks spaces 12; Dormitory spaces 79; RV/Camper sites 12; Two person huts 101. *Temporary Housing:* VIP cottages 4; VOQ cottages 5; Apartment units 8; Dormitory units 2; Two person huts 101. *Commissary and Exchange:* Retail store. *Recreational Facilities:* Fitness center; Officers club; NCO club; Camping.

SANTA ANA

EL TORO MARINE CORPS AIR STATION
Santa Ana, CA 92709
(714) 726-3830; 726-3700; 726-3901; Autovon 997-3830; 997-3700; 997-3901
OFFICER-OF-THE-DAY: (714) 726-3901, Autovon 997-3901
Profile
BRANCH: Marines.
SIZE AND LOCATION: 4741 acres. Between cities of Irvine and El Toro; approx 1 mi from I-5, Sand Canyon Exit. S of I-5/H-55 intersection and N of I-5/H-133 intersection. John Wayne Airport approx 12 mi NW.
MAJOR UNITS: 3rd Marine Aircraft Wing Headquarters; Marine Aircraft Group (MAG)-11; Marine Air Control Group-38; Marine Wing Support Group 37; Marine Aircraft Group-46 (4th MAW); Commander Marine Corps Air Bases Western Area (HQs); Air Weapons Training Unit MWHS-3 (Det); Headquarters and Maintenance Squadron (H&MS)-11; Marine Tactical Reconnaissance Squadron (VMFP)-3; Marine Fighter Attack Squadron (VMFA)-314; Marine Fighter Attack Squadron (VMFA)-323; Marine Fighter Attack Squadron (VMFA)-531; Marine All Weather Attack Squadron (VMA)-121; Marine All Weather Attack Squadron (VMA)-242; Detachment B, 1st Force Service Support Group; Naval Air Maintenance Training Group Detachments (NAMTRAGRUDETS); Regional Automated Service Center (RASC).
BASE HISTORY: 1943, commissioned as temporary Marine Corps Air Station; built on former Irvine Ranch. 1945, made permanent West Coast Marine Corps Air Station. 1968-74, major support base for President Nixon's visits to Western White House at San Clemente. 1975, first point

of arrival for 50,000 Vietnamese refugees. 1984, one of 15 DOD "Model Installations" test sites to reduce bureaucracy and inefficiency. Today, showcase for Marine Corps Aviation and reserve mobilization site.
VISITOR ATTRACTIONS: Historical aircraft display throughout air station.
Key Contacts
COMMANDER: Commanding General, (714) 726-3622, Autovon 997-3622.
PUBLIC AFFAIRS: Director, Joint Public Affairs Office; (714) 726-2937, Autovon 997-2937.
PROCUREMENT: Director, Supply Division; (714) 726-3855, Autovon 997-3855.
TRANSPORTATION: Officer in Charge, Motor Transport Division, (714) 726-2178, Autovon 997-2178.
PERSONNEL/COMMUNITY ACTIVITIES: Community Plans and Liaison, (714) 726-3702, Autovon 997-3702.
Personnel and Expenditures
ACTIVE DUTY PERSONNEL: 11,830
DEPENDENTS: 2989
CIVILIAN PERSONNEL: 958
MILITARY PAYROLL EXPENDITURE: $216 mil
CONTRACT EXPENDITURE: $10.9 mil
Services *Housing:* Family units 1202; BOQ cottages 40; BEQ units 1238; Senior NCO units 246; RV/Camper sites 16. *Temporary Housing:* VIP cottages 4; VOQ cottages 40; BOQ units 8; Lodge units 24; Transient living quarters 970. *Commissary:* Base commissary; Retail store; Barber shop; Dry cleaners; Food shop; Florist; Banking; Service station; Thrift shop. *Child Care/Capacities:* Day care center 410; Home day care program. *Base Library:* Yes. *Medical Facilities:* Medical clinic; Dental clinic. *Recreational Facilities:* Bowling; Movie theater; Pool; Gym; Recreation center; Golf; Stables; Tennis; Racquetball; Fitness center; Softball field; Football field; Auto shop; Crafts; Officers club; NCO club; Big Bear Lake facility, 100 mi NE in the San Bernardino Mts.

SANTA MONICA

CLOVER FIELD CIVIL AIR PATROL STATION
3200 Airport Ave, Ste #7, Santa Monica, CA 90405
(213) 390-9363
OFFICER-OF-THE-DAY: (213) 390-9635
Profile
BRANCH: Air Force Civil Air Patrol.
SIZE AND LOCATION: 0.001 acres. On the Santa Monica Municipal Airport.
MAJOR UNITS: 51st Clover Field Composite Squadron.
Key Contacts
COMMANDER: Capt Richard A DeCastro.
PUBLIC AFFAIRS: John C Jay.
TRANSPORTATION: 1st Lt D R Arbeit.
PERSONNEL/COMMUNITY ACTIVITIES: Robert C Woods.
Personnel and Expenditures
CIVILIAN PERSONNEL: 1
Services *Housing:* RV/Camper sites 1. *Base Library:* Yes.

SEAL BEACH

SEAL BEACH NAVAL WEAPONS STATION
Seal Beach, CA 90740-5000
(213) 594-7011; Autovon 873-7011
OFFICER-OF-THE-DAY: (213) 594-7101, Autovon 873-7101

SEAL BEACH NAVAL WEAPONS STATION (continued)
Profile
BRANCH: Navy.
SIZE AND LOCATION: 14,000 acres (all 4 sites). Los Angeles IAP to NWSSB: take Hwy 405 S (Long Beach) to Seal Beach Blvd, make a left, head SE to NWSSB, main gate 3 blocks on left.
MAJOR UNITS: Mobile Mine Assembly Group (MOMAG Det 1); Navy Publications & Printing Service (NPPS).
BASE HISTORY: 1944, commissioned as Naval Ammunition and Net Depot, to receive, store and load ammunition for fleet. 1962, renamed Naval Weapons Station; readies approx 365 ships each year with missiles, torpedoes, and conventional ammunition for deployment. Organized into five centers: Seal Beach, Corona, Pomona, and Fallbrook. Seal Beach Navy's major southern West Coast port facility for storing weapons and loading them onto ships. Key combat systems overhaul depot; depot level repair of more than 500 vital weapon system components, surface missile and antisubmarine combat systems.
VISITOR ATTRACTIONS: Seal Beach National Wildlife Refuge (1000 acres).
Key Contacts
COMMANDER: Capt Stephen T Holl; Commanding Officer, (213) 594-7301, Autovon 873-7301.
PUBLIC AFFAIRS: Tracey Schwarze; ATTN: Code 01P, (213) 594-7215, Autovon 873-7215.
PROCUREMENT: Supply Officer, Code 11, (213) 594-7202, Autovon 873-7202.
Personnel and Expenditures
ACTIVE DUTY PERSONNEL: 300
DEPENDENTS: 200
CIVILIAN PERSONNEL: 2300
MILITARY PAYROLL EXPENDITURE: $71 mil
Services *Housing:* Handled by Long Beach Naval Station Housing Office, (213) 547-7840. *Commissary and Exchange:* Retail store; Barber shop; Food shop; Banking; Service station. *Child Care/Capacities:* Vacation day-care program. *Base Library:* Yes. *Medical Facilities:* Medical clinic. *Recreational Facilities:* Bowling; Gym; Recreation center; Tennis; Racquetball; Softball field; Auto shop; NCO club; Camping; Fishing/Hunting; Bunker 33, food/cocktail club.

SONOMA

SKAGGS ISLAND NAVAL SECURITY GROUP ACTIVITY
Sonoma, CA 95476
(707) 553-3341
Profile
BRANCH: Navy.
SIZE AND LOCATION: 4300 acres. On shore of San Pablo Bay, northern part of San Francisco Bay, near Vallejo, CA; 8 mi W of Mare Island Navy Shipyard.
MAJOR UNITS: Naval Security Group Activity.
BASE HISTORY: 1941, commissioned as Naval Radio Station, San Francisco Receivers Unit. 1962, command redesignated as Naval Security Group Activity.
Services *Housing:* Housing units 84. *Commissary:* Base commissary; Retail store. *Medical Facilities:* Nearest available at Mare Island. *Recreational Facilities:* Bowling; Movie theater; Pool; Crafts; Fishing/Hunting.

STOCKTON

STOCKTON NAVAL COMMUNICATIONS STATION
Stockton, CA 95203-5000
(209) 944-0338; Autovon 466-7338
OFFICER-OF-THE-DAY: (209) 944-0343, Autovon 466-7343
Profile
BRANCH: Navy.
SIZE AND LOCATION: 1433 acres. On Rough and Ready Island approx 10 mi from downtown Stockton; approx 3 mi from I-5 and 2 mi from Hwy 4; 10 mi from Stockton Airport.
MAJOR UNITS: Naval Communications Station; General Services Administration.
BASE HISTORY: After WWI, built. 1943, Navy acquired Rough and Ready Island and owns all of island except for two 13-acre parcels owned by Shell and Mobil. Developed into major supply annex in support of tactics for WWII. Now, major communications station for eastern Pacific Fleet.
Key Contacts
COMMANDER: Capt R A Kamrath; (209) 944-0225, Autovon 466-7225.
PUBLIC AFFAIRS: Lt D M Cicoria; (209) 944-0511, Autovon 466-7338.
PROCUREMENT: LCDR Robertson; (209) 944-0211, Autovon 466-7211.
TRANSPORTATION: CDR Moreau; (209) 944-0271, Autovon 466-7271.
PERSONNEL/COMMUNITY ACTIVITIES: Phaa Simmons; (209) 944-0338, Autovon 466-7338.
Personnel and Expenditures
ACTIVE DUTY PERSONNEL: 287
DEPENDENTS: 78
CIVILIAN PERSONNEL: 315
MILITARY PAYROLL EXPENDITURE: $8.5 mil
CONTRACT EXPENDITURE: $3.8 mil
Services *Housing:* Family units 43; BEQ units 3. *Commissary:* Base commissary (large); Retail store; Barber shop; Food shop; Florist; Banking; Service station; Convenience store/Shopette. *Base Library:* Yes. *Medical Facilities:* Medical clinic; Dental clinic. *Recreational Facilities:* Bowling; Movie theater; Pool; Gym; Recreation center; Golf; Tennis; Racquetball; Fitness center; Softball field; Football field; Auto shop; Crafts; Fishing/Hunting; Consolidated mess.

SUNNYVALE

ONIZUKA AIR FORCE BASE
1080 Lockheed Way, Sunnyvale, CA 94088-3430
(408) 752-3000; Autovon 359-3000
Profile
BRANCH: Air Force.
SIZE AND LOCATION: 23 acres. 8 mi N of San Jose; 40 mi S of San Francisco; 0.5 mi from Moffett Field NAS.
MAJOR UNITS: 6594th Air Base Group; 1004th Space Group; 2d Satellite Tracking Group; Consolidated Space Center; 1999th Communications Squadron.
BASE HISTORY: 1960, established as Satellite Test Annex. 1971, renamed Sunnyvale AFS. 1987, renamed Onizuka AFB for LTC Ellison S Onizuka who died aboard space shuttle *Challenger*.
Key Contacts
PUBLIC AFFAIRS: 1004th Space Support Group, PO Box 3430.
Personnel and Expenditures
ACTIVE DUTY PERSONNEL: 800
DEPENDENTS: 1400
CIVILIAN PERSONNEL: 2300
Services *Housing:* See Moffett Field NAS. *Temporary Housing:* See Moffett Field NAS. *Commissary and Exchange:* Large exchange at Moffett Field NAS. *Medical Facilities:*

Uses dispensary at Moffett Field NAS; Oakland Naval Hospital and Presidio of San Francisco. *Recreational Facilities:* Fitness center (weight room); Fishing/Hunting; Water sports.

TRACY

DEFENSE DEPOT TRACY
Tracy, CA 95376-5000
(209) 832-9023; Autovon 462-9023
OFFICER-OF-THE-DAY: (209) 832-9072, Autovon 462-9072
Profile
BRANCH: Defense Logistics Agency.
SIZE AND LOCATION: 448 acres. In central CA, 2.5 mi SE of Tracy, 18 mi SSW of Stockton. Served by I-5, I-580, I-205, and CA Hwy 99.
MAJOR UNITS: Defense Automatic Addressing System's Western Division; US Army General Materiel and Petroleum Center's Petroleum Field Office, West; Medical Equipment Maintenance Division, US Army Medical Materiel Agency; Sixth US Army Veterinary Food Inspection Detachment, Tracy Branch.
BASE HISTORY: 1963, established as westernmost depot in DLA system; receives, stores, and issues supplies common to all military services. Served by three interstate highways, two major railroads, deep water Port of Stockton, 20 mi N, and MAC facilities, Travis AFB, 65 mi NE; also operates warehouse, Alameda, CA, which reprovisions ships of Pacific Fleet homeported in Bay Area and supports industrial plant equipment maintenance mission at Naval Communications Station, Stockton, 20 mi NE of Tracy.
Key Contacts
COMMANDER: Col Joe C Creel; (209) 832-9001, Autovon 462-9001.
PUBLIC AFFAIRS: Fred M Greene.
PROCUREMENT: Carol Croxton; (209) 832-9103, Autovon 462-9103.
TRANSPORTATION: LTC John Miller; (209) 832-9599, Autovon 462-9599.
PERSONNEL/COMMUNITY ACTIVITIES: Frank X Hamel; Director of Personnel.
Personnel and Expenditures
ACTIVE DUTY PERSONNEL: 15
CIVILIAN PERSONNEL: 1750
MILITARY PAYROLL EXPENDITURE: $63 mil
Services *Medical Facilities:* Medical clinic. *Recreational Facilities:* Softball field.

TRAVIS AFB

TRAVIS AIR FORCE BASE
Travis AFB, CA 94535
(707) 438-4011; Autovon 837-2801
Profile
BRANCH: Air Force.
SIZE AND LOCATION: 6000 acres. Off I-80 on CA-12 within corporate limits of Fairfield; 50 mi NE of San Francisco.
MAJOR UNITS: Headquarters, 22nd Air Force; David Grant Medical Center; 60th Military Airlift Wing; 1901st Information Systems Group; 349th Military Airlift Wing (Associate).
BASE HISTORY: 1942, established as Fairfield-Suisun Army Air Field. 1951, renamed for Brig Gen Robert F Travis, killed in B-29 crash.
Personnel and Expenditures
ACTIVE DUTY PERSONNEL: 7500
DEPENDENTS: 12,500
CIVILIAN PERSONNEL: 2400
Services *Housing:* Family units 2167; Trailer spaces 50; RV/Camper sites 24. *Temporary Housing:* VIP cottages 23; VOQ cottages 231; VAQ units 197; Guesthouse units; Transient living quarters 40; Family units

TRAVIS AIR FORCE BASE (continued)
129. *Commissary:* Base commissary; Retail store. *Child Care/Capacities:* Day care center 160; Home day care program. *Schools:* Elementary. *Medical Facilities:* Hospital 350; Veterinary services. *Recreational Facilities:* Bowling; Movie theater; Pool; Gym; Golf; Stables; Tennis; Fitness center; Auto shop; Crafts; Officers club; NCO club; Camping; Fishing/Hunting; Youth center (Club); Boating; Skeet shooting; Snow sports; Aero club; Parks.

TUSTIN

TUSTIN MARINE CORPS AIR STATION
Tustin, CA 92710
(714) 726-7245; Autovon 997-7245
OFFICER-OF-THE-DAY: (714) 726-7501, Autovon 997-7501
Profile
BRANCH: Marines.
SIZE AND LOCATION: 1691 acres. In coastal alluvial plain area, elevation 54 ft. Santa Ana Mts approx 17 mi N-NW, and San Joaquin Hills 5 mi to SE. Approx 7 mi NW of El Toro MCAS.
MAJOR UNITS: Marine Aircraft Group (MAG)-16.
BASE HISTORY: 1942, commissioned as US Naval Lighter-than-Air-Base for helium-filled airships conducting anti-submarine patrols off CA coast during WWII. Two hangars, built 1942, are world's largest freestanding structures; served as blimp base until decommissioned, 1949. 1951, air station reactivated, as Marine Corps Air Facility Santa Ana, country's first activity devoted to helicopter operations. 1969, renamed Marine Corps Air Station (Helicopter) Santa Ana. 1978, annexation by city of Tustin precipitated redesignation as MCAS(H) Tustin. 1985, administratively renamed MCAS Tustin; under jurisdiction of Commander, Marine Corps Air Bases Western Area, MCAS El Toro. Station major training site for Marine transport helicopter aircrews destined for duty in Western Pacific.
Key Contacts
COMMANDER: Col Robert Wemheuer.
PUBLIC AFFAIRS: SSgt Richard Ness.
PROCUREMENT: (714) 726-3855, Autovon 997-7501.
TRANSPORTATION: (714) 726-3952, Autovon 997-3952.
PERSONNEL/COMMUNITY ACTIVITIES: Col Jack Wagner; Community Plans and Liaison, Marine Corps Air Station, El Toro, Santa Ana, CA 92709, (714) 726-3703, Autovon 997-3703.
Personnel and Expenditures
ACTIVE DUTY PERSONNEL: 3874
DEPENDENTS: 2036
CIVILIAN PERSONNEL: 269
MILITARY PAYROLL EXPENDITURE: $43.4 mil
CONTRACT EXPENDITURE: $27.4 mil
Services *Housing:* Family units 1257; BEQ units 589; Barracks spaces 2; Senior NCO units 30. *Temporary Housing:* VIP cottages 1. *Commissary and Exchange:* Retail store; Barber shop; Dry cleaners; Food shop; Florist; Banking; Service station; Book store. *Child Care/Capacities:* Day care center 75. *Base Library:* Yes. *Medical Facilities:* Medical clinic; Dental clinic. *Recreational Facilities:* Bowling; Fitness center; Softball field; Football field; Auto shop; Officers club; NCO club.

TWENTYNINE PALMS

TWENTYNINE PALMS MARINE CORPS AIR GROUND COMBAT CENTER
Twentynine Palms, CA 92278-5000
(619) 368-7200; Autovon 952-7200
OFFICER-OF-THE-DAY: (619) 368-7200, Autovon 952-7200
Profile
BRANCH: Marines.
SIZE AND LOCATION: 596,480 acres. In southern tip of Mojave Desert, 60 mi NE of Palm Springs, and 150 mi E of Los Angeles; E on I-10, exit on State Hwy 62 and continue for approx 50 mi; W on I-40, exit at Amboy Rd to Twentynine Palms (Note: no service stations between Amboy Rd and Twentynine Palms); Bus service available from San Diego and Palm Springs.
MAJOR UNITS: Marine Corps Air Ground Combat Center; 7th Marine Expeditionary Brigade; Marine Corps Communications-Electronics School.
BASE HISTORY: 1940, Army used area for training glider crews. 1943, Army switched to training fighter pilots; Navy used area for bombing and gunnery ranges until end of WWII. 1945, inactive. 1952, designated HQs, Marine Corps Training Center, Twentynine Palms and home to 120 Marines. 1957, commissioned Marine Corps Base. 1979, became Marine Corps Air Ground Combat Center. 1980, Combined Arms Command activated, provides command HQs for Fleet Marine Force, Pacific units garrisoned here; home for HQs Nucleus of 7th Marine Amphibious Brigade, Near Term Prepositioning Ships Program. 1981, 27th Marine Regiment HQs Nucleus reactivated to serve as Ground Combat Element of 7th Marine Amphibious Brigade. Exercise Support Base, formerly Camp Wilson, recently added major improvements for units participating in combined arms and other training exercises. Currently, fastest growing base in Marine Corps.
Key Contacts
COMMANDER: Maj Gen G A Deegar; (619) 368-6106, Autovon 952-6106.
PUBLIC AFFAIRS: Capt K P Murphy; (619) 368-6118, Autovon 952-6118.
PROCUREMENT: Capt J H Callahan; (619) 368-6814, Autovon 952-6814.
TRANSPORTATION: CWO-3 M Montoya; (619) 368-6356, Autovon 952-6356.
PERSONNEL/COMMUNITY ACTIVITIES: Maj Brush; (619) 368-6600, Autovon 952-6600.
Personnel and Expenditures
ACTIVE DUTY PERSONNEL: 7905
DEPENDENTS: 4028
CIVILIAN PERSONNEL: 1220
MILITARY PAYROLL EXPENDITURE: $75 mil
CONTRACT EXPENDITURE: FY 89, $83 mil
Services *Housing:* Family units 1611; Mobile home units 75; Highrise (Hotel-style Barracks) 12; Bachelor Officer Suites 31. *Temporary Housing:* VIP cottages (suites) 4; Guesthouse units 1; Temporary lodging facility 24. *Commissary:* Base commissary; Retail store; Barber shop; Dry cleaners; Food shop; Florist; Banking; Service station; Furniture store; Bakery; Book store; Package beverages. *Child Care/Capacities:* Day care center 120. *Base Library:* Yes. *Medical Facilities:* Hospital 31; Dental clinic. *Recreational Facilities:* Bowling; Movie theater; Pool; Gym; Recreation center; Golf; Stables; Tennis; Racquetball; Softball field; Football field; Auto shop; Crafts; Officers club; NCO club; Basketball courts; Volleyball courts; Skeet range; Miniature golf; Motocross; Youth activities.

VALLEJO

MARE ISLAND NAVAL COMPLEX
Naval Station Mare Island, Vallejo, CA 94592-5000
(707) 646-0111; Autovon 253-0111
OFFICER-OF-THE-DAY: (707) 646-3200, Autovon 253-3200
Profile
BRANCH: Navy.
SIZE AND LOCATION: 2956 acres. 30 mi from San Francisco and 20 mi from Oakland, directly on Hwy I-80.
MAJOR UNITS: Mare Island Naval Shipyard; Marine Corps Security Force, Battalion Pacific; Combat Systems Technical Schools Command; Explosive Ordnance Detachment, Mobile Unit Nine.
BASE HISTORY: 1852, federal government purchased Mare Island and CMDR (later Adm) David Farragut took command to build naval base; first and only docking and repair facilities for Pacific commerce including Navy's Pacific Squadron, New England whalers, Cape Horn clippers, and gold-carrying Nicaragua steamers. Civil War, included Naval Hospital, Marine Barracks, and Naval Ammunition Depot. WWII, one of world's largest ship construction and repair facilities. Oldest Naval base on West Coast; major mission today is modernization, refueling and overhaul of Navy submarines.
VISITOR ATTRACTIONS: Oldest Naval Chapel in US; California Registered Historical Landmark.
Key Contacts
COMMANDER: Capt R J Sands.
PUBLIC AFFAIRS: Deborah Franz-Anderson; (707) 646-4465, Autovon 253-4465.
PROCUREMENT: Supply Officer; (707) 646-4138, Autovon 253-4138.
PERSONNEL/COMMUNITY ACTIVITIES: Personnel Support; (707) 646-2387, Autovon 253-2387.
Personnel and Expenditures
ACTIVE DUTY PERSONNEL: 3925
DEPENDENTS: 4753
CIVILIAN PERSONNEL: 12,100
Services *Housing:* Family units 865; BEQ units 1062; Duplex units 300; Townhouse units 100; Senior NCO units 88. *Temporary Housing:* VIP cottages 2; BOQ units 46; BAQ units; Dormitory units; Transient living quarters 218. *Commissary:* Base commissary; Retail store; Barber shop; Dry cleaners; Food shop; Florist; Service station. *Child Care/Capacities:* Day care center. *Schools:* Kindergarten/Preschool; Elementary. *Base Library:* Yes. *Medical Facilities:* Medical clinic; Dental clinic. *Recreational Facilities:* Bowling; Movie theater; Pool; Gym; Recreation center; Golf; Stables; Tennis; Racquetball; Fitness center; Softball field; Football field; Auto shop; Officers club; NCO club; Fishing/Hunting; Sailing club.

VAN NUYS

VAN NUYS AIR NATIONAL GUARD BASE
Van Nuys Airport, Van Nuys, CA 91409
(213) 781-5980; Autovon 873-6310
Profile
BRANCH: Air National Guard.
SIZE AND LOCATION: 62 acres. Off I-405, W of intersection with Roscoe Blvd.
MAJOR UNITS: 146th Tactical Airlift Wing (ANG); 147th Combat Communications Squadron (Contingency).
Personnel and Expenditures
ACTIVE DUTY PERSONNEL: 1284
CIVILIAN PERSONNEL: 323
MILITARY PAYROLL EXPENDITURE: $14.9 mil

VANDENBERG AFB

VANDENBERG AIR FORCE BASE
4392nd Aerospace Support Wing,
Vandenberg AFB, CA 93437-5000
(805) 866-3050; Autovon 276-3595
OFFICER-OF-THE-DAY: (805) 866-9961,
Autovon 276-9961

Profile
BRANCH: Air Force.

SIZE AND LOCATION: 98,320 acres. 55 mi N of Santa Barbara on central coast of CA. From N, take Hwy 101 to Betteravia Exit in Santa Maria, turn left off Broadway, which turns into CA State Hwy in Orcutt, continue for approx 6 mi to Lomoc/Vandenberg Exit, following it 12 mi to main gate. From S, take Hwy 101 to Hwy 246 Exit in Buellton (Buellton Lompoc Rd), continue for approx 20 mi, exit at State Rte 1, exit for Vandenberg AFB, main gate approx 10 mi.

MAJOR UNITS: 1st Strategic Aerospace Division (1STRAD); 4392nd Aerospace Support Wing (4392d ASW); Space & Missile Test Organization (SAMTO); Western Space & Missile Center (WSMC).

BASE HISTORY: 1941, built as training center for rapid development of armored forces in Burton Mesa area; designated Camp Cooke for Maj Gen Phillip St George Cooke, pioneer cavalry officer. WWII, armored and infantry divisions trained in preparation for combat. 1944, POW camp established for German and Italian prisoners and 16 branch POW camps; maximum security Army Disciplinary Barracks (now US Penitentiary, Lompoc) constructed. 1946, deactivated. 1950, reactivated. 1953, inactivated again. 1955, finally reactivated. Mid-1957, USAF took control of northern two-thirds of site for nation's first combat-ready missile base. 1958, Cooke AFB became Vandenberg AFB, for Gen Hoyt S Vandenberg, Second Air Force Chief of Staff and early advocate of aerospace preparedness. 1958, first launch. Since then, more than 1600 launches of Atlas, Titan, Minuteman, and Peacekeeper missiles have been conducted.

VISITOR ATTRACTIONS: Hearst Castle; Little Denmark (Solvang); Los Padres National Forest; La Purisma Mission; Lake Cachuma; Mequelito Park; Jamala Beach; Ocean Beach; Najoqui Falls; Gaviota Beach.

Key Contacts
COMMANDER: Brig Gen Arlen Jameson; 1STRAD/CC, (805) 866-4101, Autovon 276-4101; Col Ronald Oliverio; 4392d ASW Commander, (805) 866-4602, Autovon 276-4602.

PUBLIC AFFAIRS: LTC Richard Hill; 4392d ASW/PA, (805) 866-3595, Autovon 276-3595.

PROCUREMENT: LTC Robert A Derr; Chief of Contracting, 4392d ASW/LG, (805) 866-5001, Autovon 276-5001.

TRANSPORTATION: LTC Charles B Bitner; Transportation Squadron Commander, 4392d ASW/LGT, (805) 866-5747, Autovon 276-5747.

PERSONNEL/COMMUNITY ACTIVITIES: LTC David W Backstrom; Director of Personnel, 4392d ASW/DP, (805) 866-6200, Autovon 276-6200.

Personnel and Expenditures
ACTIVE DUTY PERSONNEL: 3824
DEPENDENTS: 5330
CIVILIAN PERSONNEL: 1479
MILITARY PAYROLL EXPENDITURE: $76.8 mil
CONTRACT EXPENDITURE: $297.3 mil

Services *Housing:* Family units 2078; Duplex units 168; Townhouse units 100; Barracks spaces 1144; Dormitory spaces 1144; Mobile home units 172; RV/Camper sites 69. *Temporary Housing:* VIP cottages 20; VOQ cottages 389; VEQ units 70; Tent spaces 20. *Commissary:* Base commissary; Retail store; Barber shop; Dry cleaners; Food shop; Florist; Banking; Service station. *Child Care/Capacities:* Day care center 135; Home day care program; Before and after school care for 6-10 yr olds 118. *Schools:* Kindergarten/Preschool; Elementary; Intermediate/Junior high; High school 6 mi from base. *Base Library:* Yes. *Medical Facilities:* Hospital 45; Dental clinic. *Recreational Facilities:* Bowling; Movie theater; Pool; Gym; Recreation center; Golf; Stables; Tennis; Racquetball; Fitness center; Softball field; Football field; Auto shop; Crafts; Officers club; NCO club; Camping; Fishing/Hunting.

COLORADO

AURORA

BUCKLEY AIR NATIONAL GUARD BASE

18500 E 6th Ave, Aurora, CO 80011-9599
(303) 366-5363; Autovon 877-9011
OFFICER-OF-THE-DAY: (303) 340-9930,
  Autovon 877-9930
Profile
BRANCH: Air National Guard.
SIZE AND LOCATION: 3300 acres. 7 mi E of
  Denver on E-central edge of Aurora; 2.5
  mi E of intersection of I-225 and E 6th
  Ave.
MAJOR UNITS: 140th Tactical Fighter Wing;
  Detachment One, Headquarters Colorado
  Air National Guard (OL-BB); 154th Tac-
  tical Control Group; 227th Air Traffic
  Control Flight (ATCF); Detachment 3,
  Space Division (Aerospace Data Facility);
  2d Communication Squadron (Aerospace
  Data Facility); Detachment 3, 375th
  Aeromedical Airlift Wing (MAC); Detach-
  ment 29, 17th Weather Squadron (MAC);
  1987th Communications Squadron; Ma-
  rine Reserve Training Unit (Surface/Air);
  Naval Reserve Training Unit (Surface/
  Air); Colorado Army National Guard (CO
  ANG), Company A 5th Battalion, 19th
  Special Forces Group; 147th Medical
  Hospital (CO ANG); 2d Battalion, 135th
  Aviation (CO ANG); Army Aviation Support Facility (CO ANG); 104th Public Affairs Detachment (CO ANG); Organizational Maintenance Shop #9 (CO ANG).
BASE HISTORY: 1942, activated and named
  Buckley Field for 1st Lt John H Buckley,
  WWI pilot killed in Meuse-Argonne Of-
  fensive and former CO Guardsman. 1946,
  transferred from Army to CO ANG.
  1947, transferred to Navy. 1959, decom-
  missioned as NAS. 1960, CO ANG as-
  sumed command. Provides combat readi-
  ness training of tactical units of CO
  ANG; area's only military flying base,
  charged with aircraft search and rescue
  activities.
Key Contacts
COMMANDER: LTC Kenneth R Kimber; 140
  TFW/DCS, Bldg 801, Stop 21, (303) 340-
  9700, Autovon 877-9700.
PUBLIC AFFAIRS: Bruce A Collins; 140 TFW/
  PA, Bldg 27, Stop 24, (303) 340-9431,
  Autovon 877-9431.
PROCUREMENT: Art Dalton; 140 RMS/LGC,
  Bldg 27, Stop 53, (303) 340-9945, Auto-
  von 877-9945.
TRANSPORTATION: Pedro Tobias; 140 RMS/
  LGT, Bldg 940, Stop 11, (303) 340-9516,
  Autovon 877-9516.
PERSONNEL/COMMUNITY ACTIVITIES: Vacant,
  140 MSS/DPM, Bldg 801, Stop 15, (303)
  340-9422, Autovon 877-9422.

Personnel and Expenditures
ACTIVE DUTY PERSONNEL: 3600
CIVILIAN PERSONNEL: 2600
Services *Temporary Housing:* See Lowry
AFB for transient quarters. *Medical Facili-
ties:* Medical clinic. *Recreational Facilities:*
Softball field; Fishing/Hunting; Flying Club;
All-ranks Club; Rod and Gun Club.

FITZSIMONS ARMY MEDICAL CENTER

Aurora, CO 80045-5001
(303) 361-8241; Autovon 943-1101
Profile
BRANCH: Army.
SIZE AND LOCATION: 577 acres. In city of
  Aurora off I-225; approx 7 mi E of down-
  town Denver.
MAJOR UNITS: Fitzsimons Army Medical
  Center; Army Medical Equipment and
  Optical School; Office of Champus.
BASE HISTORY: 1918, ground broken. 1920,
  named after 1st Lt William Thomas Fitz-
  simons, doctor and first American officer
  killed in action in WWI.
Key Contacts
COMMANDER: Brig Gen Thomas Bowen.
PUBLIC AFFAIRS: Ralph Yoder; (303) 361-
  3192, Autovon 943-3192.
Personnel and Expenditures
ACTIVE DUTY PERSONNEL: 2600
DEPENDENTS: 2000
CIVILIAN PERSONNEL: 1000
Services *Housing:* Family units 181; BOQ
cottages 35; BEQ units 40. *Temporary Hous-
ing:* VIP cottages 10; Guesthouse units 35.
Commissary: Base commissary; Retail store;
Barber shop; Dry cleaners; Food shop; Flo-
rist; Banking; Service station. *Child Care/
Capacities:* Day care center 200; Home day
care program. *Base Library:* Yes. *Medical
Facilities:* Hospital 504; Medical clinic; Den-
tal clinic. *Recreational Facilities:* Bowling;
Movie theater; Pool; Gym; Golf; Tennis;
Racquetball; Skating rink; Softball field;
Auto shop; Crafts; Officers club; NCO club;
Fishing/Hunting; Picnicking.

COLORADO SPRINGS

CHEYENNE MOUNTAIN AIR FORCE BASE

Cheyenne Mountain Support Group, Stop
#4, Colorado Springs, CO 80914
(719) 473-2056; Autovon 834-2056
Profile
BRANCH: Joint Service Installation; Dual-Na-
  tion (US-Canada).
SIZE AND LOCATION: 4.5 acres. Approx 6 mi
  from city of Colorado Springs; 15 mi S of
  Municipal Airport of Colorado Springs;
  60 mi S of Denver. Off CO Hwy 115 to
  3.5 mi 1,000 foot paved road climb leading to underground complex. 7,200 ft
  above sea level.

MAJOR UNITS: North American Aerospace
  Defense Command; US Space Command;
  Air Force Space Command; Air Force
  Communications Command; Military Air-
  lift Command; Federal Emergency Man-
  agement Agency; 1010th Special Security
  Squadron; 1010th Civil Engineering
  Squadron.
BASE HISTORY: 1961, original construction
  begun. 1966, first opened. Cheyenne
  Mountain AFB and Cheyenne Mountain
  Complex are tightly secured, special access only, military installations just out-
  side and inside hollowed mountainside of
  CO Rocky Mountains. Inside are 15 steel
  buildings which function 24 hours a day.
  Parking for 600 vehicles outside. Operational centers keep watch on aircraft, mis-
  siles, and space systems that might pose
  threat to US and Canada.
VISITOR ATTRACTIONS: Non-military tours
  not available; military and DOD civilians
  arranged 5-6 months in advance by
  NORAD/USSPACECMD Public Affairs
  (719) 554-3733; 554-3003.
Key Contacts
COMMANDER: Col Edward M Smith, USAF.
PUBLIC AFFAIRS: Capt Leslie C Fraze; 3rd
  Space Support Wing/Public Affairs, Stop
  #15, Peterson AFB, CO 80914-5000,
  (719) 554-7825, 554-4696, Autovon 692-
  7825, 692-4696.
PROCUREMENT: 3 SSW or AFSPACECMD
  Contracting Office, S/LK3, Peterson AFB,
  CO 80914-5000, (719) 554-5250, 554-
  5251, Autovon 692-5250, 692-5251.
TRANSPORTATION: Lt Col Margaret Walsh;
  TRANS Division, Stop #42, Peterson
  AFB, CO 80914-5000, (719) 554-4719,
  Autovon 692-4719.
PERSONNEL/COMMUNITY ACTIVITIES: 1003rd
  Space Support Group/DP, Stop #48,
  Peterson AFB, CO 80914-5000, (719)
  554-4635, Autovon 692-4635.
Personnel and Expenditures
ACTIVE DUTY PERSONNEL: 1100
MILITARY PAYROLL EXPENDITURE: $117.5 mil
Services *Temporary Housing:* All facilities at
Peterson AFB. *Commissary and Exchange:*
Barber shop; Snacks. *Medical Facilities:* Hos-
pital 2; Medical Aid Station with dental of-
fice and pharmacy. *Recreational Facilities:*
Fitness center; Dining facility, Granite Inn.

DENVER

AIR RESERVE PERSONNEL CENTER

Denver, CO 80280-5000
(303) 370-4631

AIR RESERVE PERSONNEL CENTER
(continued)
Profile
BRANCH: Air Force.
SIZE: Offices only.
BASE HISTORY: 1953, established as Detachment 1, HQs Continental Air Command, to centralize custody and maintenance of master personnel records of AFRES members not on extended active duty. 1954, detachment began operations, responsible for wide variety of personnel actions, including administrative capability for mobilization of AFRES. 1957, became HQs Air Reserve Records Center, within Continental Air Command. 1965, renamed Air Reserve Personnel Center. 1968, ARPC designated separate operating agency. 1971, personnel records of ANG officers added; and airmen, 1978. 1978, status changed to named unit and organizational element of AFRES. 1983, separate operating agency status reestablished.
Key Contacts
COMMANDER: Col Joseph C Ramsey Jr.
PUBLIC AFFAIRS: HQ ARPC/PA.

FALCON AFB

FALCON AIR FORCE BASE
Falcon AFB, CO 80912-5000
(719) 550-4113; Autovon 560-1110
Profile
BRANCH: Air Force.
SIZE AND LOCATION: 640 acres. 9 mi E of Peterson AFB, Colorado Springs, on Enoch Rd; 2 mi S of State Hwy 94.
MAJOR UNITS: 2d Space Wing; National Test Facility for Strategic Defense Initiative (SDI).
BASE HISTORY: 1985, operational base activated with no base support on site.
Key Contacts
COMMANDER: Col Jimmey Morrell; 2nd Space Wing/CC, (719) 550-5000, Autovon 560-5000.
PUBLIC AFFAIRS: William Baugh; (719) 550-5040, Autovon 560-5040.
Personnel and Expenditures
ACTIVE DUTY PERSONNEL: 2000
CIVILIAN PERSONNEL: 2400
Services *Medical Facilities:* Medical clinic. *Recreational Facilities:* Racquetball; Fitness center; Softball field.

FORT CARSON

FORT CARSON AND 4TH INFANTRY DIVISION (MECHANIZED)
Fort Carson, CO 80913-5000
(719) 579-3240; Autovon 691-3240
OFFICER-OF-THE-DAY: (719) 579-3400, Autovon 691-3400
Profile
BRANCH: Army.
SIZE AND LOCATION: 137,391 acres. Bordering S side of Colorado Springs; Approx 40 mi from Pueblo. I-25, adj to Fort, runs N to Denver.
MAJOR UNITS: 4th Infantry Division (Mechanized).
BASE HISTORY: 1942, Cheyenne Valley Ranch purchased and donated to federal government for camp named for Brig Gen Christopher "Kit" Carson, frontiersman; buildings turned over to 89th Infantry Division; also constructed Camp Hale, 20 mi W of Leadville, first US training post for mountain troops. WWII, largest hospital center in US; POW camp. 1954, declared permanent fort; air operations based at Peterson Field until 1954, air operations moved to camp. 1956, operations relocated to Mesa Air Strip. 1957,

Mountain and Cold Weather Training Command transferred to Ft Greeley, AK, and Camp Hale training site for Carson ski teams. 1965, declared surplus and traded for land on Ft Carson's southern border. 1966, present facility, Butts Field completed. 1970, initial test site for modern Volunteer Army concept (VOLAR). 1983, Pinon Canyon Maneuver Site acquired (245,000 acres, about 100 air mi SE of main Fort).
VISITOR ATTRACTIONS: Listed historic site.
Key Contacts
COMMANDER: Maj Gen Dennis J Reimer; Bldg 1430, (719) 579-3406, Autovon 691-3406.
PUBLIC AFFAIRS: LTC Terry A McCann; Bldg 1544.
PROCUREMENT: Ms Stewart; Bldg 6222, (719) 579-5040, Autovon 691-5040.
TRANSPORTATION: Mr Mestas; Bldg 847, (719) 579-3126, Autovon 691-3126.
PERSONNEL/COMMUNITY ACTIVITIES: LTC R J Shooner; Bldg 1526, (719) 579-5601, Autovon 691-5601.
Personnel and Expenditures
ACTIVE DUTY PERSONNEL: 19,369
DEPENDENTS: 6396
CIVILIAN PERSONNEL: 3208
MILITARY PAYROLL EXPENDITURE: FY 88, $366 mil
CONTRACT EXPENDITURE: FY 88, $9 mil
Services *Housing:* Family units 1828; BOQ cottages 25; BEQ units 6. *Temporary Housing:* VIP cottages 5; VOQ cottages 155; VEQ units 105; Guesthouse units 1. *Commissary:* Base commissary; Retail store; Barber shop; Dry cleaners; Food shop; Florist; Banking; Service station. *Child Care/Capacities:* Day care center 554; Home day care program. *Schools:* Kindergarten/Preschool; Elementary; Intermediate/Junior high; Note: Schools not DOD schools. *Base Library:* Yes. *Medical Facilities:* Hospital 195; Medical clinic; Dental clinic; Hospital can be expanded to 300 beds. *Recreational Facilities:* Bowling; Movie theater; Pool; Gym; Recreation center; Golf; Stables; Tennis; Racquetball; Fitness center; Softball field; Football field; Auto shop; Crafts; Officers club; NCO club; Fishing/Hunting.

LA JUNTA

LA JUNTA STRATEGIC TRAINING RANGE
30800 1st Ave, La Junta, CO 81050
(719) 384-4419; Autovon 692-4126
OFFICER-OF-THE-DAY: Autovon 692-4123
Profile
BRANCH: Air Force.
SIZE AND LOCATION: 35 acres. Operations facilities on E ramp of La Junta Municipal Airport off Hwy 109, approx 5 mi N of city of La Junta, CO. Support facilities and base housing off Hwy 109 approx 2.5 mi S of city of La Junta.
MAJOR UNITS: Detachment 1, 1 CEVG (SAC).
BASE HISTORY: Small SAC installation with very limited facilities. 1960, moved from Denver. 1988-89, facilities upgraded and base housing constructed.
Key Contacts
COMMANDER: LTC James B Houston Jr; 822 Carson, Autovon 692-4125.
PUBLIC AFFAIRS: SSgt James E Walsh; Autovon 692-4126.
PROCUREMENT: SSgt Tami S Doty.
TRANSPORTATION: MSgt Daniel J Sullivan, Autovon 692-4123.
PERSONNEL/COMMUNITY ACTIVITIES: SMSgt William Miesowitz.

Personnel and Expenditures
ACTIVE DUTY PERSONNEL: 90
DEPENDENTS: 200
CIVILIAN PERSONNEL: 4
MILITARY PAYROLL EXPENDITURE: $1.5 mil
CONTRACT EXPENDITURE: $0.25 mil
Services *Housing:* Family units 40; Barracks spaces 32; Junior NCO units 30. *Temporary Housing:* Military contract motel quarters. *Commissary:* Base commissary; BX Annex store. *Medical Facilities:* Medical technician and infirmary. *Recreational Facilities:* Recreation center; Tennis; Fitness center; Softball field; Auto shop; Crafts; All Ranks Club.

LOWRY AFB

LOWRY AIR FORCE BASE
Lowry Technical Training Center, Lowry AFB, CO 80230-5000
(303) 370-1110; Autovon 926-1110
OFFICER-OF-THE-DAY: (303) 370-4171, Autovon 926-4171
Profile
BRANCH: Air Force.
SIZE AND LOCATION: 5781 acres. 5 mi E of downtown Denver; 2.5 mi S of Stapleton IAP; take Exit I-225 W on 6th Ave; main gate is approx 2 mi W of I-225.
MAJOR UNITS: Headquarters, Lowry Technical Training Center; 3400th Technical Training Wing; Deputy Commander for Resource Management; 3415th Air Base Group; USAF Clinic; 3320th Correction and Rehabilitation Squadron; Air Force Accounting and Finance Center; Air Reserve Personnel Center; Air Force Audit Agency Detachment; Air Force Trial Judiciary, 4th Circuit Detachment; 3567th Recruiting Squadron; Detachment 4, 3314th Management Engineering Squadron; Detachment 1, 2d Communications Squadron; Air Force Office of Special Investigations, District 14; 1987th Communications Squadron; Area Defense Council; Air Force Disaster Preparedness Resource Center; Detachment 5, Air Force Occupational Measurement Center; 560th Army Signal Battalion; Marine Corps Detachment; Navy Personnel Support Activity Detachment, Denver; Air Force Comptroller Management Engineering Team; Detachment 057, Air Force Technical Applications Center; Field Training Detachment 526, Operating Location A.
BASE HISTORY: 1937, Army Air Corps training base; named for Lt Francis Brown Lowry, Denver aviator killed in action in WWI; former Agnes Phipps Sanatorium, tuberculosis clinic. WWII, photography, armaments, and B-29 crew training. 1948, Lowry Field became Lowry AFB. 1953-1955, served as President Dwight D Eisenhower's "Summer White House"; presidential offices housed in old headquarters building. 1955-1958 home to USAF Academy. 1958-1965, Missile Range I used by SAC in Titan I missile program. 1966, runways closed. One of world's largest training complexes in audiovisual, avionics, logistics, munitions, and space operations.
VISITOR ATTRACTIONS: Lowry Heritage Museum.
Key Contacts
COMMANDER: Maj Gen Dale C Tabor; Senior Commander, LTTC/CC, (303) 370-3101, Autovon 926-3101.
PUBLIC AFFAIRS: LTC George W Titus; LTTC/PA, (303) 370-2161, Autovon 926-2161.
PROCUREMENT: Col Craig D Elliot; Deputy Commander for Resource Management, LTTC/LGC, (303) 370-2848, Autovon 926-2848.

LOWRY AIR FORCE BASE (continued)
TRANSPORTATION: Maj Stephen M Blackburn; 3415th ABG/LGT, (303) 370-4038, Autovon 926-4038.
PERSONNEL/COMMUNITY ACTIVITIES: LTC Lawrence M Beach; Director of Personnel, 3415th ABG/DP, (303) 370-7496, Autovon 926-7495.
Personnel and Expenditures
ACTIVE DUTY PERSONNEL: 9783
DEPENDENTS: 6000
CIVILIAN PERSONNEL: 5400
MILITARY PAYROLL EXPENDITURE: $137.1 mil
CONTRACT EXPENDITURE: $66.8 mil
Services *Housing:* Family units 340; BOQ cottages; BEQ units; BAQ units; Dormitory spaces 243; RV/Camper sites. *Temporary Housing:* VOQ cottages 328; VEQ units 1206; VAQ units 974; Dormitory units 3706; Transient living quarters 80. *Commissary:* Base commissary; Retail store; Barber shop; Dry cleaners; Food shop; Florist; Banking; Service station; Bakery; MCSS. *Child Care/Capacities:* Day care center; Home day care program. *Base Library:* Yes. *Medical Facilities:* Medical clinic; Dental clinic; Dependents treated at Fitzsimons AMC 4 mi NE of Lowry. *Recreational Facilities:* Bowling; Movie theater; Pool; Gym; Recreation center; Golf; Tennis; Racquetball; Fitness center; Softball field; Football field; Auto shop; Crafts; Officers club; NCO club; Camping; Fishing/Hunting.

PETERSON AFB

PETERSON AIR FORCE BASE
3rd Space Support Wing, Peterson AFB, CO 80914-5000
(719) 554-7321; Autovon 692-7321; 692-7011
Profile
BRANCH: Air Force.
SIZE AND LOCATION: 1196 acres. 8 mi NE of Colorado Springs and 60 mi S of Denver. Peterson AFB adj to Colorado Springs Municipal Airport. Peterson "Complex" includes military and civilian personnel at Peterson AFB, Cheyenne Mountain AFB, and Falcon AFB.
MAJOR UNITS: Headquarters North American Aerospace Defense Command (NORAD); Headquarters US Space Command; Headquarters Air Force Space Command; Headquarters Army Space Command; 3rd Space Support Wing; 1st Space Wing; 302nd Tactical Airlift Wing (Reserve); Air Force Audit Agency; Office of Special Investigations; Detachment 1, 94th Airmanship Training Squadron; Detachment 4, 1401st Military Airlift Squadron; 3423rd Technical Training Squadron; AF Special Staff Management Engineering Team; 1013th Combat Crew Training Squadron; Space Communications Division; 4th Weather Wing.
BASE HISTORY: 1925, established as civil airport for Colorado Springs. 1941, large portion of airport taken for Army air base. 1942, named Peterson Field for 1st Lt Edward J Peterson, native of Englewood, CO, photo reconnaissance pilot killed, 1942. Following WWII, city took control and dismantled barracks. 1948, flying facility for 15th Air Force established at Ent AFB, Colorado Springs. 1949, USAF portion of Peterson Field inactive status. 1951, Aerospace Defense Command reactivated Field. 1976, renamed Peterson AFB. 1979, transferred to SAC. 1983, transferred to AF Space Command, 1st Space Wing. 1986, 3rd Space Support Wing host of Peterson Complex.

VISITOR ATTRACTIONS: Edward J Peterson Space Museum, with WWII and space exhibits, open Tue-Sat, (719) 554-4915 for information.
Key Contacts
COMMANDER: Col James O Palmer; 3rd Space Support Wing/CC, (719) 554-4582, Autovon 692-4582.
PUBLIC AFFAIRS: Maj Bruce E Lewis Jr; 3rd Space Support Wing/Public Affairs, Peterson AFB, CO 80914-5000, (719) 554-7825, 554-4696, Autovon 692-7825, 692-4696.
PROCUREMENT: LTC Ronald C Pierce; 3rd Space Support Wing/PK (Contracting), Peterson AFB, CO 80914-5001, (719) 554-7597, Autovon 692-7597.
TRANSPORTATION: LTC Margaret A Walsh; 3rd Space Support Wing/LGTO, (719) 554-4718, Autovon 692-4718.
PERSONNEL/COMMUNITY ACTIVITIES: LTC Ronald A Berkshire; Chief, Morale, Welfare and Recreation, 3rd Space Support Wing/SS, (719) 554-4323, Autovon 692-4323.
Personnel and Expenditures
ACTIVE DUTY PERSONNEL: 6040
DEPENDENTS: 8188
CIVILIAN PERSONNEL: 2651
MILITARY PAYROLL EXPENDITURE: $163.7 mil
CONTRACT EXPENDITURE: $20.1 mil
Services *Housing:* Family units 491; Duplex units 6; Townhouse units 77; Barracks spaces 540; Dormitory spaces 6; Senior NCO units 78; Junior NCO units 306; Mobile home units 50; Trailer spaces 50. *Temporary Housing:* VOQ cottages 66; VEQ units 82; BOQ units 2; BAQ units 6; Dormitory units 40; DV suites 4. *Commissary:* Base commissary; Retail store; Barber shop; Dry cleaners; Food shop; Florist; Banking; Service station; Furniture store; Bakery; Book store; Beauty shop; Clothing sales. *Child Care/Capacities:* Day care center 151; Home day care program. *Base Library:* Yes. *Medical Facilities:* Medical clinic; Dental clinic. *Recreational Facilities:* Bowling; Movie theater; Pool; Gym; Recreation center; Golf; Tennis; Racquetball; Fitness center; Softball field; Football field; Auto shop; Crafts; Officers club; NCO club; Fishing/Hunting; Gun club; Family support center.

PUEBLO

PUEBLO ARMY DEPOT ACTIVITY
Bldg 1, SDSTE-PU-PA, Pueblo, CO 81001-5000
(719) 549-4141; 549-4135; Autovon 749-4141; 749-4135
Profile
BRANCH: Army.
SIZE AND LOCATION: 23,000 acres. 15 mi E of Pueblo, CO via US Hwy 50 near the Pueblo Memorial Airport.
BASE HISTORY: 1942, construction of Pueblo Ordnance Depot to receive, store and issue general supplies to support WWII. 1946, mission of maintaining and overhauling artillery, fire control, and optical equipment. 1948, renovation and demilitarization of ammunition. 1962, renamed Pueblo Army Depot. 1976, given Depot Activity status and assigned to Tooele Army Depot. Today, responsible for storing, demilitarizing and renovating ammunition, storing chemical munitions and performing maintenance on equipment and components; depot Systems Command's Center of Technical Excellence for Pershing II missile system and radiographic inspection facility; stores and maintains equipment for Rapid Deployment of Water and Petroleum Systems; disassembling and storing Pershing mis-

sile and elimination of Pershing rocket motor.
VISITOR ATTRACTIONS: "Hi-Pardner" Park just outside main gate, antique munitions on display.
Key Contacts
COMMANDER: LTC John C Rickman; Bldg 1, SDSTE-PU-CO.
PUBLIC AFFAIRS: W Allen Kenitzer.
PROCUREMENT: Roger K Bates; Bldg 6, SDSTE-PU-CO.
TRANSPORTATION: Richard Alcon; Bldg 3, SDSTE-PU-EEQ, (719) 549-4151.
PERSONNEL/COMMUNITY ACTIVITIES: Bob Knox; Bldg 2, SDSTE-PCCP-PUP, (719) 549-4252.
Personnel and Expenditures
ACTIVE DUTY PERSONNEL: 6
DEPENDENTS: 45
CIVILIAN PERSONNEL: 650
MILITARY PAYROLL EXPENDITURE: $21 mil (military and civilian)
CONTRACT EXPENDITURE: $14.4 mil
Services *Housing:* Family units. *Commissary and Exchange:* Barber shop; Convenience store/Shopette. *Medical Facilities:* Medical clinic. *Recreational Facilities:* Pool; Racquetball; Fitness center; Softball field; Auto shop; Crafts; Community club.

UNITED STATES AIR FORCE ACADEMY

US AIR FORCE ACADEMY
United States Air Force Academy, CO 80840
(719) 472-1818; Autovon 259-3110
OFFICER-OF-THE-DAY: (719) 472-2910, Autovon 259-2910
Profile
BRANCH: Air Force.
SIZE AND LOCATION: 18,000 acres. W of I-25, just N of Colorado Springs; two gates, about 5 mi apart, provide access from I-25 and are clearly marked.
MAJOR UNITS: Cadet Wing; Frank J Seiler Research Lab; DOD Medical Examination Review Board; Headquarters US Air Force Academy; 1876th Communications Group.
BASE HISTORY: 1948, board civilian and military educators planned curriculum for USAF Academy. 1954, Congress authorized USAF Academy creation. 1955, first class entered at temporary facilities, Lowry AFB, Denver. 1958, cadet wing moved into permanent home. 1959, Commission of Colleges and Universities of North Central Association of Colleges and Secondary Schools accredited academy's degree program; first graduating class of 206. 1964, expanded from 2529 to 4417 cadets. 1976, women entered academy.
VISITOR ATTRACTIONS: Barry Goldwater USAF Academy Visitor Center; The Cadet Chapel.
Key Contacts
COMMANDER: Lt Gen Charles R Hamm; Superintendent, (719) 472-4140, Autovon 259-4140.
PUBLIC AFFAIRS: Col David M Wallace; Director of Public Affairs, HQ USAFA/PAM, USAF Academy, CO 80840-5151, (719) 472-2990, Autovon 259-2990.
PROCUREMENT: Maj Lanis F Powell; HQ USAFA/LGC, PO Box 189, USAFA, CO 80840-0189, (719) 472-2075, Autovon 259-2075.
TRANSPORTATION: Ray Deimel; HQ USAFA/LGT, (719) 472-3504, Autovon 259-3504.
PERSONNEL/COMMUNITY ACTIVITIES: Maj Steven T Wacholtz; Chief, Morale, Welfare and Recreation, HQ USAFA/SS, (719) 472-4815, Autovon 259-4815.

US AIR FORCE ACADEMY *(continued)*
Personnel and Expenditures
ACTIVE DUTY PERSONNEL: 7519, plus 4417
cadets
DEPENDENTS: 2527
CIVILIAN PERSONNEL: 1761
MILITARY PAYROLL EXPENDITURE: FY 89,
$103.3 mil
CONTRACT EXPENDITURE: FY 89, $2.4 mil
Services *Housing:* Family units 1216; Dormitory spaces 202. *Temporary Housing:* VIP cottages 10; VOQ cottages 78; Guesthouse units 26; Senior enlisted suites 2. *Commissary:* Base commissary; Retail store; Barber shop; Dry cleaners; Food shop; Florist; Banking; Service station; Bakery; Credit union. *Child Care/Capacities:* Day care center 179; Home day care program. *Schools:* Kindergarten/Preschool; Elementary; High school. *Base Library:* Yes. *Medical Facilities:* Hospital 60; Medical clinic; Dental clinic. *Recreational Facilities:* Bowling; Movie theater; Pool; Gym; Recreation center; Golf; Stables; Tennis; Racquetball; Skating rink; Fitness center; Softball field; Football field; Auto shop; Crafts; Officers club; NCO club; Camping; Fishing/Hunting.

CONNECTICUT

GROTON

NEW LONDON NAVAL SUBMARINE BASE
Box 00, Groton, CT 06349-5000
(203) 449-3444; Autovon 241-3444
OFFICER-OF-THE-DAY: (203) 449-3444,
  Autovon 241-3444
Profile
BRANCH: Navy.
SIZE AND LOCATION: 1325 acres. Situated on
  the E bank of the Thames River about 6
  mi upstream from the estuary and within
  the townships of Ledyard and Groton.
  Main gate is located off I-95, Exit 86, on
  Crystal Lake Rd.
MAJOR UNITS: Submarine Group TWO; Na-
  val Submarine School; Submarine Squad-
  ron TEN; Submarine Squadron TWO;
  Submarine Development Squadron
  TWELVE; Naval Submarine Support Fa-
  cility New London/Groton; Supervisor of
  Shipbuilding, Conversion and Repair; Naval Submarine Medical Research Laboratory; Naval Undersea Medical Institute;
  Personnel Support Activity Detachment;
  Naval Security Group Activity, Groton;
  Naval Underwater Systems Center, New
  London Laboratory; Naval Legal Service
  Office, Groton; Naval Investigative Ser-
  vice.
BASE HISTORY: Birthplace of submarine force.
  1868, CT donated 112 acres. 1872, build-
  ings and pier built as Navy Yard. 1881,
  downgraded to coaling station. 1915,
  monitor *Ozark*, brought 4 submarines to
  pier. 1916, converted to submarine base.
  Between wars, schools and training facili-
  ties established.
VISITOR ATTRACTIONS: Nautilus Memorial;
  Submarine Force Library and Museum
  (located adjacent to the Main Gate).
Key Contacts
PUBLIC AFFAIRS: (203) 449-3889, Autovon
  241-3889.
Personnel and Expenditures
ACTIVE DUTY PERSONNEL: 20,000
DEPENDENTS: 25,000
CIVILIAN PERSONNEL: 1500
MILITARY PAYROLL EXPENDITURE: $184 mil
CONTRACT EXPENDITURE: $1.3 bil
Services *Housing:* Family units 2627; BOQ
cottages 3 bldgs; BEQ units 13 bldgs; Bar-
racks spaces 5135; Trailer spaces 105; BOQ
spaces 188. *Temporary Housing:* VOQ cot-
tages 4; VEQ units 2; BOQ units 141; BAQ
units (spaces) 225. *Commissary:* Base commissary; Retail store; Barber shop; Dry
cleaners; Food shop; Florist; Banking; Service station; Bakery; Video rental; Ice cream;
Personalized services. *Child Care/Capacities:*
Day care center 100; Home day care program. *Base Library:* Yes. *Medical Facilities:*
Hospital; Medical clinic; Dental clinic. *Recreational Facilities:* Bowling; Movie theater;

Pool; Gym; Recreation center; Golf; Stables;
Tennis; Racquetball; Fitness center; Softball
field; Auto shop; Officers club; NCO club;
Lake for swimming/ice skating; Marina with
boat slips.

NEW LONDON

NAVAL UNDERWATER SYSTEMS CENTER
New London Laboratory, New London, CT
06320
(203) 440-4000
Profile
BRANCH: Navy.
LOCATION: On US Naval Submarine Base,
  New London.
BASE HISTORY: 1970, result of merger be-
  tween Naval Underwater Sound Labora-
  tory, New London and Naval Underwater
  Weapons Research and Engineering Sta-
  tion, Newport (formerly NUOS). Also see
  Naval Education and Training Center,
  Newport, RI.
Key Contacts
COMMANDER: Capt Harry P Salmon Jr; Earle
  L Messere, Technical Director.
PUBLIC AFFAIRS: Kathleen P O'Beirne.
Personnel and Expenditures
ACTIVE DUTY PERSONNEL: 19
CIVILIAN PERSONNEL: 1506
MILITARY PAYROLL EXPENDITURE: $3.2 mil
CONTRACT EXPENDITURE: $245.9 mil
Services *Housing:* See US Naval Submarine
Base, New London. *Temporary Housing:* See
US Naval Submarine Base, New London.

US COAST GUARD ACADEMY
Mohegan Dr, New London, CT 06320-4195
(203) 444-8444; FTS 642-8444
OFFICER-OF-THE-DAY: (203) 444-8450, 444-
  8451; FTS 642-8450, 642-8451
Profile
BRANCH: Coast Guard.
SIZE AND LOCATION: 100 acres. 5 minutes N
  of downtown New London, across the
  Thames River from Groton, located N of
  I-95 in SE CT.
MAJOR UNITS: Research and Development
  Center, Avery Point; Central Oil Iden-
  tification Laboratory, Groton; Interna-
  tional Ice Patrol, Avery Point, Groton;
  USCGC *Vigorous*; USCGC *Eagle*;
  USCGC *Redwood*.
BASE HISTORY: 1876, founded as Revenue
  Cutter School of Instruction. 1878,
  Barque *Chase* served as seagoing Acad-
  emy until 1900. 1910, Arundel Cove,
  MD, became second land-based Academy
  site. Academy relocated to Ft Trumbull,
  former Army installation, New London,
  CT. 1915, Life Saving and Revenue Cutter Services merged as US Coast Guard,
  providing Academy with current name.
  1922, Academy moved to accommodate

increased corps size. 1932, construction of
  new facility completed.
VISITOR ATTRACTIONS: Coast Guard Museum
  located in Waesche Hall, open year round
  9-4 weekdays, 9-5 weekends and holidays
  (May-Oct); Visitors Pavilion open 9-5
  (May-Oct); Barque *Eagle*, America's Tall-
  ship, Fri, Sat, Sun 12-5 when in port;
  Dress parades are held in Spring and Fall
  on the Washington parade field.
Key Contacts
COMMANDER: Superintendent Rear Adm
  Richard P Cueroni; (203) 444-8285; FTS
  642-8285.
PUBLIC AFFAIRS: Lt Paul Preusse; (203) 444-
  8270; FTS 642-8270.
PROCUREMENT: CDR R M Acker Jr; (203)
  444-8240; FTS 642-8240.
TRANSPORTATION: CWO M E Yensz; (203)
  444-8303; FTS 642-8303.
PERSONNEL/COMMUNITY ACTIVITIES: Jerry
  Brooks; (203) 444-8475/74; FTS 642-
  8475/8474.
Personnel and Expenditures
ACTIVE DUTY PERSONNEL: 600/900 cadets
CIVILIAN PERSONNEL: 200
MILITARY PAYROLL EXPENDITURE: $21 mil
Services *Housing:* Family units 5. *Commis-
sary and Exchange:* Retail store; Barber
shop; Dry cleaners; Food shop; Florist;
Banking; Service station. *Base Library:* Yes.
Medical Facilities: Medical clinic; Dental
clinic. *Recreational Facilities:* Bowling; Pool;
Gym; Tennis; Racquetball; Softball field;
Auto shop; Officers club; NCO club.

WINDSOR LOCKS

103RD TACTICAL FIGHTER GROUP (ANG)
Bradley IAP, Windsor Locks, CT 06096
(203) 623-8291; Autovon 636-8310
Profile
BRANCH: Air National Guard.
SIZE AND LOCATION: 158 acres. 15 mi N of
  Hartford, exit 40 off I-91.
MAJOR UNITS: 103rd Tactical Fighter Group
  (ANG); Army National Guard Aviation
  Battalion.
BASE HISTORY: Named for Lt Eugene M
  Bradley, killed in aircraft crash in 1941.
Personnel and Expenditures
ACTIVE DUTY PERSONNEL: 878
CIVILIAN PERSONNEL: 197
MILITARY PAYROLL EXPENDITURE: $9.4 mil

DELAWARE

DOVER AFB

DOVER AIR FORCE BASE

HQ 436th Military Airlift Wing, Dover AFB, DE 19902
(302) 678-7011; Autovon 455-7011

Profile

BRANCH: Air Force.

SIZE AND LOCATION: 3735 acres. From Dover, DE, follow US Hwy 113-S, a few miles past Blue Hen Mall and Dover AFB on the left.

MAJOR UNITS: 436th Military Airlift Wing; 436th Aerial Port Squadron; 436th Air Base Group; 436th Avionics Maintenance Squadron; 436th Civil Engineering Squadron; 436th Comptroller Squadron; 436th Field Maintenance Squadron; 436th Organizational Maintenance Squadron; 436th Security Police Squadron; 436th Supply Squadron; 436th Transportation Squadron; 3rd Military Airlift Squadron; 9th Military Airlift Squadron; USAF Hospital; 512th Military Airlift Wing (Reserve Associate); AF Office of Special Investigations (AFOSI); AF Civil Air Patrol Liaison; AF Commissary Service; AF Logistics Management Engineering Team; Armed Forces Courier Station (Army); Army and Air Force Exchange Service; Army Escort Detachment; Civil Engineering Maintenance, Inspection, Repair and Training; Defense Reutilization/Marketing Office; Detachment 5, 15th Weather Squadron; Detachment 5, 1600th Management Engineering Squadron; Military Air Traffic Coordinating Unit; USAF Judiciary Area Defense Counsel; 21st Air Force Noncommissioned Officer Leadership School; 219th Field Training Detachment; 2016th Communications Squadron.

BASE HISTORY: 1941, newly completed Dover Municipal Airfield leased to US Army Air Corps and assigned to Eastern Defense Command as coastal patrol base. 1942, antisubmarine patrols conducted. Feb to Aug 1943, closed to complete construction on main runway. Following reopening, along with fighter pilot training, base became site for development of air launched rockets. Following WWII, became a pre-separation processing center, deactivated, and reactivated in 1951 and assigned to Air Defense Command. 1952, MATS (later MAC) assumed command and Dover become strategic airlift base.

VISITOR ATTRACTIONS: Historical Center.

Key Contacts

COMMANDER: Col F Keith Tedrow; Commander, 436th Military Airlift Wing; Col Primoli; Commander, 436th Air Base Group.

Personnel and Expenditures

ACTIVE DUTY PERSONNEL: 4400
CIVILIAN PERSONNEL: 1300
MILITARY PAYROLL EXPENDITURE: FY 88, $100.2 mil
CONTRACT EXPENDITURE: FY 88, $32.4 mil

Services *Housing:* Family units 1556; Duplex units; Townhouse units; Dormitory spaces 1860; Mobile home units. *Temporary Housing:* Transient living quarters 14; VOQ/VAQ rooms 164 (reservations for duty personnel only). *Commissary:* Base commissary; Retail store; Barber shop; Dry cleaners; Florist; Banking; Service station; Military clothing sales; Convenience store/Shopette; Snacks; Beauty shop; Laundry; Optical shop; Construction materials; Thrift shop; Credit union. *Child Care/Capacities:* Day care center. *Schools:* Elementary; Intermediate/Junior high. *Base Library:* Yes. *Medical Facilities:* Hospital; Dental clinic. *Recreational Facilities:* Bowling; Movie theater; Pool; Recreation center (and game room); Golf; Tennis; Racquetball; Fitness center (and sauna); Softball field; Crafts; Officers club; NCO club; Youth center; Arcade; Basketball; Squash; SATO; Ticket sales.

WILMINGTON

166TH TACTICAL AIRLIFT GROUP (ANG)

Greater Wilmington Airport, Wilmington, DE 19720
(302) 322-2261; Autovon 455-9000

Profile

BRANCH: Air National Guard.

SIZE AND LOCATION: 57 acres. 5 mi S of Wilmington, off I-95, exit 5 (Basin Rd).

MAJOR UNITS: 166th Tactical Airlift Group (ANG); Army National Guard Aviation Company.

Personnel and Expenditures

ACTIVE DUTY PERSONNEL: 820
CIVILIAN PERSONNEL: 171
MILITARY PAYROLL EXPENDITURE: $7.8 mil

Services *Medical Facilities:* 2-bed dispensary.

DISTRICT OF COLUMBIA

BOLLING AFB

BOLLING AIR FORCE BASE
Bolling AFB, DC 20332-5000
(202) 767-4600; Autovon 297-4600
OFFICER-OF-THE-DAY: (202) 767-5316,
Autovon 297-5316

Profile
BRANCH: Air Force.
SIZE AND LOCATION: 604 acres. SW portion of DC, on E side of Potomac River, off Rte I-295.
MAJOR UNITS: Air Force District of Washington (AFDW); 1100th Air Base Group; 1100th Resource Management Group; Air Force Honor Guard; US Air Force Band; Air Force Office of Scientific Research; Headquarters Air Force Office of Special Investigations; AF Surgeon General; AF Chaplain Service; Defense Intelligence Agency; Air Force Directorate Administration; Air Force Office of History.
BASE HISTORY: 1918, field opened and named for first high-ranking Air Service officer killed in WWI, Col Raynal C Bolling. Flying field originally located (where Anacostia NAS is today) just N of present site; moved S following severe floods in 1930s. 1927, Lindbergh's "Spirit of St Louis" returned to Bolling after transatlantic flight. 1933, Wiley Post completed round-the-world flight on Bolling's runway. 1946, became first HQs of SAC. 1948, redesignated HQ Command USAF. 1962, to decrease air congestion around National Airport, fixed-wing and later helicopter, flying activities moved to Andrews AFB and Bolling changed to support base. 1976, assigned to MAC. 1985, became official HQs AF District of Washington. Now serves as administrative and technological center of AF in Washington, DC.
VISITOR ATTRACTIONS: F-105 static display.

Key Contacts
COMMANDER: Brig Gen Ralph R Rohatsch Jr.
PUBLIC AFFAIRS: (202) 767-4781, Autovon 297-4781.

Personnel and Expenditures
ACTIVE DUTY PERSONNEL: 1116
DEPENDENTS: 3500
CIVILIAN PERSONNEL: 736
Services *Housing:* Family units 1395; Dormitory spaces; General officers' quarters. *Temporary Housing:* VOQ cottages 68; VAQ units 48; Transient living quarters 150. *Commissary:* Base commissary; Retail store; Barber shop; Dry cleaners; Food shop; Florist; Service station; Military clothing sales; Convenience store/Shopette; Beauty shop; Optical shop; Video rental; Tailor. *Child Care/Capacities:* Day care center 175; Home day care program. *Base Library:* Yes. *Medical Facilities:* Medical clinic; Dental clinic. *Recreational Facilities:* Bowling; Movie the-

ater; Pool; Gym; Recreation center; Tennis; Racquetball; Fitness center; Softball field; Auto shop; Crafts; Officers club; NCO club; Marina; Aero club; Youth activities; Picnic pavilions; MWR supply.

WASHINGTON

ANACOSTIA NAVAL STATION
Naval Military Personnel Command, Bldg 72, Washington, DC 20374
(202) 433-2235; Autovon 288-2235

Profile
BRANCH: Navy.
LOCATION: Adj to Bolling AFB; along Anacostia River.
MAJOR UNITS: Naval Military Personnel Command; Seabees; Naval & Marine Corps Reserve Center; HMX1 (USMC).

Personnel and Expenditures
ACTIVE DUTY PERSONNEL: 250
Services *Commissary and Exchange:* At Bolling AFB. *Recreational Facilities:* Gym; Racquetball; Fitness center (sauna); Softball field.

ARMED FORCES INSTITUTE OF PATHOLOGY
6925 16th St, NW (WRAMC, Bldg 54), Washington, DC 20306-6000
(206) 576-2900; Autovon 291-2900
OFFICER-OF-THE-DAY: (206) 576-2900, Autovon 291-2900

Profile
BRANCH: Joint Service Installation; Department of Defense.
LOCATION: On the grounds of the Walter Reed Army Medical Center.
BASE HISTORY: Evolved from Army Medical Museum founded in 1862 to undertake a systematic collection and study of anatomical and disease related specimens produced as a result of Civil War.
VISITOR ATTRACTIONS: National Museum of Health & Medicine of the AFIP located in the south wing of Bldg 54, WRAMC, open daily, 9:30-:30 weekdays, 11:30-4:30 weekends and holidays. Tours, lectures, and seminars can be arranged, call (202) 576-2348.

Key Contacts
COMMANDER: Capt Robert F Karnel Jr, MC, USN; Director, (206) 576-2904, Autovon 291-2904.
PUBLIC AFFAIRS: Michael E Howard; (206) 576-0233, Autovon 291-0233.
PROCUREMENT: Col Malachi B Jones, MSC, USA; (206) 576-2919, Autovon 291-2919.
PERSONNEL/COMMUNITY ACTIVITIES: Maj James Affonco; Personnel, (206) 576-2902, Autovon 291-2902.
Services *Commissary:* Base commissary. *Base Library:* Yes.

FORT LESLEY J MCNAIR
Headquarters, US Military District of Washington, Washington, DC 20319-5050
(202) 475-0856; 475-0855; Autovon 335-0856; 335-0855

Profile
BRANCH: Army.
SIZE AND LOCATION: 98 acres. Where Anacostia River empties into Potomac River in SW portion of DC; approx 6 mi from Washington National Airport.
MAJOR UNITS: Headquarters, Military District of Washington; US Army Garrison, Ft McNair; Company A, 1st Battalion, 3rd Infantry; National Defense University; Inter-American Defense College; 67th Ordnance Detachment.
BASE HISTORY: In continuous use as military reservation since 1794; known as Turkey Buzzard Point (later Greenleaf Point). During War of 1812, US Arsenal at Greenleaf's Point destroyed when powder ignited. 1826, land purchased N of Arsenal as site for first federal penitentiary; conspirators in Lincoln assassination imprisoned and executed here. 1881, became Washington Barracks, transferred to Quartermaster Department. 1898-1909, general hospital, forerunner of Walter Reed Army Hospital, located here; Maj Walter Reed did research here. 1935, name changed to Ft Humphreys. 1939, changed back to Army War College (Post), and Army War College (School). 1943, joint Army-Navy Staff College established (forerunner of National War College). 1948, renamed for commander of Army Ground Forces during WWII, Lt Gen Lesley J McNair, killed at Normandy, 1944. 1924, Industrial College of Armed Forces founded to prepare officers for top level posts in future wartime supply organization and to study problems of industrial mobilization. 1962, Inter-American Defense College opened; curriculum includes study of international situation and world blocs, and planning for hemispheric defense. Home of US Army Military District of Washington HQs since 1942.
VISITOR ATTRACTIONS: National War College building a National Historic Landmark.

Key Contacts
COMMANDER: Col Michael C Schmidtman (Acting); (202) 475-1822, Autovon 335-1822.
PUBLIC AFFAIRS: Col James D Weiskopf.
PROCUREMENT: Chester Dailey; Bldg 15, Cameron Station, Alexandria, VA 22304-5050, (202) 274-7990, Autovon 284-7992.
TRANSPORTATION: Samuel H Hermans; Bldg 17, Cameron Station, Alexandria, VA 22304-5050, (202) 274-6503, Autovon 284-6503.

FORT LESLEY J MCNAIR (continued)

PERSONNEL/COMMUNITY ACTIVITIES: Maj A Rizer (Acting); Community and Family Support Directorate, Bldg 202, Ft Myer, VA 22211-5050, (202) 696-3041.

Personnel and Expenditures

ACTIVE DUTY PERSONNEL: 820

DEPENDENTS: 63

CIVILIAN PERSONNEL: 1300

Services *Housing:* Family units 25; Duplex units 12. *Temporary Housing:* Transient living quarters 20. *Commissary:* Base commissary; Retail store; Barber shop; Dry cleaners; Service station; Book store. *Base Library:* Yes. *Medical Facilities:* Medical clinic; Dental clinic. *Recreational Facilities:* Bowling; Movie theater; Pool; Gym; Golf; Softball field; Officers club; NCO club.

MARINE BARRACKS, WASHINGTON

8th & I Sts, SE, Washington, DC 20390

(202) 433-6060; Autovon 288-6060

Profile

BRANCH: Marines.

SIZE AND LOCATION: 2 acres. SE Washington, DC, near the Washington Navy Yard.

MAJOR UNITS: Marine Band; Marine Drum and Bugle Corps; Marine Corps Institute.

BASE HISTORY: 1801, established; oldest post of Marine Corps and residence of Commandant of Marine Corps since 1805. Site chosen by President Jefferson. Arranged in quadrangle as today. Only original building Commandant's house. 1900-1971, buildings rebuilt. Trained new officers and recruits continued throughout 19th century. Location of Marine Corps HQ until 1901. 1976, designated National Historic Landmark. Home of US Marine Band, "The President's Own," since 1801. Marines at Barracks perform variety of duties: official ceremonies of State, Evening Parades, special security for President, and operate Marine Corps Institute (Corps' correspondence school founded 1920 by Maj Gen John A Lejune). 1934 Marine Drum and Bugle Corps "Commandant's Own" formed.

VISITOR ATTRACTIONS: Evening Parade, every Fri evening, May through Sept 1 at 8:20 p.m., call/write for reservations; Sunset Parade, every Tue evening, May 30 through Aug 22 at 7:00 p.m. at Marine Corps Memorial, located just N of Arlington National Cemetery; Summer Concert Series, Wed evenings, Jun through Aug at 8:00 p.m. on W steps of Capitol and Sun evenings, at Sylvan Theater, located on Washington Monument grounds; Marine Corps Museum located in Bldg 58, Washington Navy Yard.

Key Contacts

COMMANDER: Col Peter Pace; (202) 433-4073, Autovon 288-4073.

PUBLIC AFFAIRS: Capt M D Viscomage; (202) 433-4173, Autovon 288-4173.

PERSONNEL/COMMUNITY ACTIVITIES: See Public Affairs Officer.

Personnel and Expenditures

ACTIVE DUTY PERSONNEL: 1200

CIVILIAN PERSONNEL: 20

Services *Housing:* Family units 4; BEQ units 2. *Recreational Facilities:* Gym.

MILITARY DISTRICT OF WASHINGTON

Washington, DC 20319-5000

(202) 475-1822; Autovon 335-1822

Profile

BRANCH: Army.

LOCATION: Washington, DC.

MAJOR UNITS: Fort Myer; Cameron Station; Fort McNair; Davison Aviation Command; The Pentagon; Fort Belvoir; Arlington National Cemetery; US Army Band; 3rd US Infantry, The Old Guard; Tomb Guard; Fife and Drum Corps; Commander-in-Chief's Guard; Caisson Platoon; Salute Guns Platoon; Drill Team.

BASE HISTORY: 1921, began as District of WA; within Third Corps Area and included DC, Ft Washington, MD, and Ft Hunt and Ft Myer, VA. 1927, District of Washington dissolved; responsibility for military ceremonies and troops in DC assigned to Commanding General, 16th Infantry Brigade, Ft Hunt. 1939, new organization, Washington Provisional Brigade created. May 1942, brigade became MDW. 1966, HQ moved to Ft McNair. 1971, functions consolidated and performed by MDW HQ.

VISITOR ATTRACTIONS: See individual bases.

Key Contacts

PUBLIC AFFAIRS: Col David Burpee; PAO, US Army Military District of Washington, Bldg 42, Ft McNair, Washington, DC 20319, (202) 475-0856, 475-0897, Autovon 335-0856, 335-0897.

Personnel and Expenditures

ACTIVE DUTY PERSONNEL: 13,500

CIVILIAN PERSONNEL: 8900

NAVAL RESEARCH LABORATORY

4555 Overlook Ave, SW, Washington, DC 20375-5000

(202) 767-3200; Autovon 297-3200

OFFICER-OF-THE-DAY: (202) 767-2505, Autovon 297-2505

Profile

BRANCH: Navy.

SIZE AND LOCATION: 134 acres. In Washington, DC; 7 mi to Washington National Airport; 40 mi to Dulles IAP; 30 mi to Baltimore-Washington IAP.

MAJOR UNITS: Executive Directorate, NRL; Director of Research, NRL; Director of Research for Strategic Planning, NRL; Director of Technical Services, NRL; Director of General Science and Technology, NRL; Director of Warfare Systems and Sensors Research, NRL; Director of Materials Science and Components Technology, NRL; Director of Naval Center for Space Technology, NRL.

BASE HISTORY: 1923, established with two divisions-Radio and Sound. WWII, produced practical equipment, sonar sets, direction-finding devices, and first practical radar equipment built in US. 1946, placed under Office of Naval Research and is its principal in-house research laboratory. Accomplishments include Deep Ocean Search System, space investigations, 78 satellites, including Vanguard I, experiments aboard Skylab, HEAO spacecraft, and several space shuttle missions, TIMATION project, NAVSTAR Global Positioning System program. Designated major shore command.

Key Contacts

COMMANDER: Capt William G Clautice; (202) 767-3404, Autovon 297-3404.

PUBLIC AFFAIRS: James W Gately Jr; (202) 767-2541, Autovon 297-2541.

PROCUREMENT: CMDR Walter E Ralls; (202) 767-3446, Autovon 297-3446.

TRANSPORTATION: Joe Milstead; Code 2504.1, (202) 767-2548, Autovon 297-2548.

PERSONNEL/COMMUNITY ACTIVITIES: Betty A Duffield; Code 1800, (202) 767-3421, Autovon 297-3421.

Personnel and Expenditures

ACTIVE DUTY PERSONNEL: 100

CIVILIAN PERSONNEL: 3100

Services *Base Library:* Yes. *Recreational Facilities:* Pool; Gym; Recreation center.

NAVAL SECURITY STATION

3801 Nebraska Ave NW, Washington, DC 20393-5230

(202) 282-0211; Autovon 292-0211

Profile

BRANCH: Navy.

SIZE AND LOCATION: 38 acres. At Nebraska and Massachusetts Ave NW.

MAJOR UNITS: Headquarters Naval Security Group Command; Naval Telecommunication Command; Naval Electronic Systems Security Engineer Center; Marine Support Battalion.

Personnel and Expenditures

ACTIVE DUTY PERSONNEL: 750

Services *Housing:* Family units 48. *Medical Facilities:* Medical clinic; Dental clinic. *Recreational Facilities:* Tennis; Racquetball; Fitness center (weight room); Auto shop; Basketball.

SPACE & NAVAL WARFARE SYSTEMS COMMAND

Washington, DC 20363-5100

(202) 692-8954; Autovon 222-8954

Profile

BRANCH: Navy.

SIZE: Offices only.

Key Contacts

COMMANDER: Rear Adm John Weaver.

US ARMY CORPS OF ENGINEERS, HEADQUARTERS

20 Massachusetts Ave NW, Pulaski Bldg, Washington, DC 20314

(202) 272-0001

Profile

BRANCH: Army.

SIZE: Offices only.

Key Contacts

COMMANDER: Lt Gen Henry J Hatch; Commanding General.

US COAST GUARD HEADQUARTERS

2100 Second St, SW, Washington, DC 20593-0001

(202) 267-2229; FTS 8-267-2229

OFFICER-OF-THE-DAY: (202) 267-2100; FTS 8-267-2100

Profile

BRANCH: Coast Guard.

SIZE AND LOCATION: 1 city block. Six-story rented office building in SW Washington, DC.

BASE HISTORY: HQ moved here in 1982 with lease until 1992.

Key Contacts

COMMANDER: G-C; (202) 267-2390; FTS 8-267-2390.

PUBLIC AFFAIRS: G-CP; (202) 267-1587; FTS 8-267-1587.

PROCUREMENT: G-A; (202) 267-2007; FTS 8-267-2007.

TRANSPORTATION: G-CCS; (202) 267-1642; FTS 8-267-1642.

PERSONNEL/COMMUNITY ACTIVITIES: Community Activities; G-CP-3, (202) 267-0936; FTS 8-267-0936; Military Personnel; G-CAS-1, (202) 267-2320; FTS 8-267-2320; Civilian Personnel; (202) 267-2059; FTS 8-267-2059.

Personnel and Expenditures

ACTIVE DUTY PERSONNEL: 1200

CIVILIAN PERSONNEL: 1050

MILITARY PAYROLL EXPENDITURE: $35 mil

CONTRACT EXPENDITURE: $113 mil

Services *Commissary and Exchange:* Military clothing sales; Snacks. *Base Library:* Yes. *Medical Facilities:* Medical clinic; Dental clinic available elsewhere. *Recreational Facilities:* Facilities available at nearby Ft McNair.

US NAVAL OBSERVATORY

34th & Massachusetts Ave NW, Washington, DC 20392-5100
(202) 653-1507; Autovon 294-1507
Profile
BRANCH: Navy.
SIZE AND LOCATION: 72 acres. In NW Washington, DC.
MAJOR UNITS: Official Residence of the Vice President of the US; Office of the Oceanographer of the Navy.
BASE HISTORY: Founded 1830, as Depot of Charts and Instruments, one of oldest scientific agencies in US; original mission included caring for Navy's chronometers, charts, and other navigational equipment. 1844, Depot reestablished as US Naval Observatory and located on hill N of where Lincoln Memorial now stands. 1893, moved to present site. 1966, old Observatory buildings in Foggy Bottom declared National Historic Monuments. In Astrometry, Observatory uses astrographic telescopes in Washington, DC, Flagstaff, AZ, and Black Birch, New Zealand. Few institutions make such fundamental observations regularly.
VISITOR ATTRACTIONS: Public tours of Observatory, Mon night, 7:30 (winter), 8:30 (summer) except federal holidays and overcast days; One of the leading astronomical libraries in the world.
Key Contacts
COMMANDER: Capt J B Hagen, USN.
PUBLIC AFFAIRS: G Cleece.
Personnel and Expenditures
ACTIVE DUTY PERSONNEL: 6
DEPENDENTS: 3
CIVILIAN PERSONNEL: 200
MILITARY PAYROLL EXPENDITURE: $.2 mil
Services *Housing:* Family units 5; Duplex units 2. *Base Library:* Yes. *Recreational Facilities:* Tennis.

WALTER REED ARMY MEDICAL CENTER

7100 Georgia Ave NW, Washington, DC 20307-5001
(202) 576-3501; FTS 8-291-3501
OFFICER-OF-THE-DAY: (202) 576-2309; FTS 8-291-2309
Profile
BRANCH: Army.
SIZE AND LOCATION: 113 acres. The main section of WRAMC is located between Rock Creek Park and Georgia Ave near the MD-DC boundary, approx 6 mi from I-495. Ground transportation is available between WRAMC and Andrews AFB (for info contact Air Evacuation 576-1141).
MAJOR UNITS: Walter Reed Army Medical Center; Walter Reed Army Institute of Research; Armed Forces Institute of Pathology; US Army Dental Laboratory; US Army Institute of Dental Research; US Army Dental Activity; Armed Forces Pest Management Board; US Army Information Systems Command; Army Office for Defense Medical Information Systems; US Army Physical Disability Agency.
BASE HISTORY: May 1, 1909, first patients admitted. Medical center, named for Maj Walter Reed, established to integrate patient care, teaching and research. WWI, capacity grew from 80 patient beds to 2,500. 1977, new Walter Reed Army Medical Center dedicated; 5,500 rooms; 28 acres of floor space; accommodations for 1,280 patients; admissions of 22,000 a year. Outlying clinics at Ft Myer, Cameron Station, Pentagon, Ft Detrick, and Ft McNair.
VISITOR ATTRACTIONS: Armed Forces Medical Museum.

Key Contacts
COMMANDER: (202) 576-1100; FTS 8-291-1100.
PUBLIC AFFAIRS: Peter B Esker; Bldg #1, Rm 103, (202) 576-2177; FTS 8-291-2177.
PROCUREMENT: Lt Col Franklin Heim; (202) 576-2015; FTS 8-291-2015.
TRANSPORTATION: Maj Larry Slade; (202) 576-3431; FTS 8-291-3431.
PERSONNEL/COMMUNITY ACTIVITIES: Col Kenneth Damian; (202) 576-3355; FTS 8-291-3355.
Personnel and Expenditures
ACTIVE DUTY PERSONNEL: 4971
CIVILIAN PERSONNEL: 3851
MILITARY PAYROLL EXPENDITURE: $132 mil
CONTRACT EXPENDITURE: $75 mil
Services *Housing:* Family units 43; BEQ units 25; Townhouse units 85; Barracks spaces 544. *Temporary Housing:* VIP cottages 6; VOQ cottages 51; VEQ units 63; Transient living quarters 120. *Commissary:* Base commissary; Retail store; Barber shop; Dry cleaners; Food shop; Banking; Service station; Optical shop; Tailor; Beauty shop; Four Seasons store. *Child Care/Capacities:* Day care center 25. *Base Library:* Yes. *Medical Facilities:* Hospital 962; Medical clinic; Dental clinic. *Recreational Facilities:* Bowling; Pool; Gym; Recreation center; Tennis; Fitness center; Softball field; Auto shop; Crafts; Officers club; NCO club; Community center; Patient recreation center; ITT service.

WASHINGTON NAVY YARD, NAVAL DISTRICT OF WASHINGTON

Washington, DC 20374
(202) 545-6700; Autovon 288-6700
Profile
BRANCH: Navy.
SIZE AND LOCATION: 572 acres. 9th and M Sts SE.
MAJOR UNITS: Naval District of Washington; Washington Navy Yard.
VISITOR ATTRACTIONS: Navy Yard; Marine Corps Museum; Navy Memorial Museum; Combat Art Gallery; Willard Park Naval Weapons Collection.
Services *Temporary Housing:* Lodge units (at Bolling AFB) 50. *Commissary and Exchange:* Barber shop; Dry cleaners; Banking; Service station; Convenience store/Shopette; Beauty shop; Laundry; Souvenirs; Also use nearby Bolling AFB exchange. *Child Care/Capacities:* Day care center 75; Home day care program. *Medical Facilities:* Dental clinic; Dispensary. *Recreational Facilities:* Pool; Tennis; Racquetball; Fitness center; Auto shop; Officers club; NCO club; Marina; Picnicking; Recreation center at Solomons Island.

FLORIDA

ASTOR

CECIL FIELD NAVAL AIR STATION, DETACHMENT

PO Box 84, Astor, FL 32002-0084
(904) 759-2111; 778-5456; Autovon 860-5456
OFFICER-OF-THE-DAY: (904) 759-2111, 778-5456, Autovon 860-5456
Profile
BRANCH: Navy.
SIZE AND LOCATION: 124 acres. 1.5 mi S of Hwys 19 & 40; 10 mi W of Astor, FL; Approx 65 mi N of Orlando, FL.
MAJOR UNITS: NAS Cecil Field.
BASE HISTORY: Opened about 1950, served as Army, Air Force, and Naval installation. Only Navy bombing range on East Coast open for live ordnance.
Key Contacts
COMMANDER: LCDR Jeffry L McMann.
PUBLIC AFFAIRS: Lt Charles F Martin.
PROCUREMENT: SK1 Kenneth J Tompkins.
TRANSPORTATION: See Public Affairs Officer.
PERSONNEL/COMMUNITY ACTIVITIES: See Public Affairs Officer.
Personnel and Expenditures
ACTIVE DUTY PERSONNEL: 100
CIVILIAN PERSONNEL: 70
Services *Housing:* BEQ units 12. *Commissary and Exchange:* Retail store; Service station. *Base Library:* Yes. *Recreational Facilities:* Gym; Recreation center.

CLEARWATER

CLEARWATER COAST GUARD AIR STATION

Clearwater, FL 34622
(813) 535-1437; Autovon 968-4273
Profile
BRANCH: Coast Guard.
LOCATION: St Petersburg/Clearwater Airport at the intersection of 49th St & Roosevelt in Clearwater.
MAJOR UNITS: USCG Air Station; USCG Air Station Reserve.
BASE HISTORY: 1934, Albert Whitted Airport, downtown St Petersburg, became homebase for Coast Guard amphibious aircraft and helicopters. 1976, moved to St Petersburg/Clearwater Airport for longer runways and changed name to Coast Guard Air Station Clearwater. Station's motto, "Anytime, Anywhere" describes current operation. Missions in support of search and rescue, law enforcement, aids to navigation, marine environmental protection, and others are flown on daily basis. Air Station involved in Cuban Boatlift, Grenada Rescue Mission, Operation Wagonwheel and Hunter, inter-agency and international narcotics interdiction

efforts, and response to Space Shuttle *Challenger* disaster.
Key Contacts
COMMANDER: Capt Daniel Shorey.
PUBLIC AFFAIRS: Lt David Seavey; (813) 535-1437 ext 206.
PROCUREMENT: CWO Gary Lewis.
TRANSPORTATION: See Procurement Officer.
PERSONNEL/COMMUNITY ACTIVITIES: Lt Darrell Folsom.
Personnel and Expenditures
ACTIVE DUTY PERSONNEL: 350
CIVILIAN PERSONNEL: 40
Services *Commissary and Exchange:* Retail store; Barber shop. *Medical Facilities:* Medical clinic; Dental clinic. *Recreational Facilities:* Tennis; Softball field; NCO club.

COCOA BEACH

CAPE CANAVERAL AIR FORCE STATION

Cocoa Beach, FL 32925
(407) 853-1110; Autovon 467-1110
Profile
BRANCH: Air Force.
MAJOR UNITS: Cape Canaveral AFS (AFSC).

CORTEZ

CORTEZ COAST GUARD STATION

Cortez, FL 34215
(813) 794-1607
Profile
BRANCH: Coast Guard.
SIZE AND LOCATION: 1.75 acres. In Cortez, FL, on N side of Sarasota Bay.
MAJOR UNITS: USCG Station Cortez.
BASE HISTORY: Housed in building constructed in 1890 as Albion Inn. 1976, commissioned. Area of responsibility from Egmont Key to southern tip of Gasparilla Island.
Key Contacts
COMMANDER: Senior Chief Boatswain's Mate, Officer in Charge.
PUBLIC AFFAIRS: See USCG Group/Station, St Petersburg, FL.
Personnel and Expenditures
ACTIVE DUTY PERSONNEL: 29
Services *Housing:* Single personnel only. *Recreational Facilities:* Recreation center (ping pong, pool table); Fitness center (weight room); Camping; Fishing/Hunting; Boating; Volleyball.

FORT MYERS BEACH

FORT MYERS BEACH COAST GUARD STATION

Fort Myers Beach, FL 33931
(813) 463-5754

Profile
BRANCH: Coast Guard.
LOCATION: In Ft Myers Beach off State Rte 865.
MAJOR UNITS: USCGC *Point Steele*.
BASE HISTORY: 1979, remodeled and recommissioned. Southernmost station in Group St Petersburg; area of responsibility from S of Sarasota to Everglades City, FL.
Key Contacts
COMMANDER: Senior Chief Boatswain's Mate, Officer in Charge.
PUBLIC AFFAIRS: See USCG Group/Station, St Petersburg, FL.
Personnel and Expenditures
ACTIVE DUTY PERSONNEL: 30
Services *Housing:* Crew's quarters only. *Commissary and Exchange:* Small exchange. *Recreational Facilities:* Recreation center; Fishing/Hunting; Basketball.

FORT WALTON BEACH

EGLIN AIR FORCE BASE

Fort Walton Beach, FL 32542
(904) 882-3931; Autovon 872-3931
Profile
BRANCH: Air Force.
SIZE AND LOCATION: 463,704 acres. Eglin is 26 mi S of I-10, Crestview, FL. Hwy 85 runs S from Crestview and junctions with Hwy 20 at Niceville, FL; a right turn on Hwy 20 will take you to the E gate.
MAJOR UNITS: Armament Division; Tactical Air Warfare Center; 33rd Tactical Fighter Wing; 39th Special Operations Squadron; Air Force Armament Laboratory.
BASE HISTORY: 1935, established as Valparaiso Bombing and Gunnery Base. 1937, redesignated Eglin Field for LTC Frederick I Eglin, US Air Corps. 1940, Forestry Service ceded Choctawhatchee National Forest. 1941, Air Corps Proving Ground activated and Eglin site for gunnery training and major testing center for aircraft, equipment, and tactics; pioneer in missile development, First Experimental Guided Missiles Group. 1950, established Air Research and Development Command (now Air Force Systems Command). 1951, AF Armament Center brought development and testing together. 1957, Air Proving Ground Center formed and built Eglin Gulf Test Range. 1968, redesignated Armament Development and Test Center. 1975, one of four Vietnamese Refugee Processing Centers. 1979, Center renamed Armament Division. 1980, processing center for Cuban refugees.
VISITOR ATTRACTIONS: Air Force Armament Museum.

EGLIN AIR FORCE BASE (continued)
Key Contacts
COMMANDER: Col Howard J Oakes; 3201 ABG/CC, (904) 882-3333, Autovon 872-3333.
PUBLIC AFFAIRS: LTC Salvatore J Giammo; AD/PA, (904) 882-3931, Autovon 872-3931.
PROCUREMENT: Col William Todd; AD/PM, (904) 882-4398, Autovon 872-4398.
TRANSPORTATION: LTC G T Thompson; 3200 SPTW/LGT, (904) 882-4581, Autovon 872-4581.
PERSONNEL/COMMUNITY ACTIVITIES: Col Hoyt Prindle, Jr; AD/DP, (904) 882-4335, Autovon 872-4335.
Personnel and Expenditures
ACTIVE DUTY PERSONNEL: 10,000
DEPENDENTS: 13,600
CIVILIAN PERSONNEL: 4850
MILITARY PAYROLL EXPENDITURE: $208.7 mil
Services *Housing:* Family units 2359; BOQ cottages 20; Dormitory spaces 4100; Senior NCO units 21; Mobile home units 225; RV/Camper sites 15. *Temporary Housing:* VIP cottages 3; VOQ cottages 147; VAQ units 188; Transient living quarters 88. *Commissary:* Base commissary; Retail store; Barber shop; Dry cleaners; Food shop; Florist; Banking; Service station; Furniture store; Bakery. *Child Care/Capacities:* Day care center. *Schools:* Kindergarten/Preschool; Elementary. *Base Library:* Yes. *Medical Facilities:* Hospital; Medical clinic; Dental clinic. *Recreational Facilities:* Bowling; Movie theater; Pool; Gym; Recreation center; Golf; Stables; Tennis; Racquetball; Fitness center; Softball field; Football field; Auto shop; Crafts; Officers club; NCO club; Camping; Fishing/Hunting.

HOMESTEAD

HOMESTEAD AIR FORCE BASE
Homestead AFB, Homestead, FL 33039-5000
(305) 257-8396; Autovon 791-8396
Profile
BRANCH: Air Force.
SIZE AND LOCATION: 3345 acres. Approx 35 mi S of Miami, 2 mi E on Biscayne Dr from US Rte 1.
MAJOR UNITS: 31st Tactical Fighter Wing (TFW); 482nd TFW (AFRES); 301st ARRS (AFRES); 125th FIG (ANG), Det 1; 726th TCS; 3613th CCTS; Naval Security Group Activity; 1942nd CS.
BASE HISTORY: 1941, airstrip deeded to government by Pan American Airways. Maintenance stopover point for aircraft ferried to Caribbean and North Africa. Runway, Homestead Army Air Field, belonged to Caribbean Wing of Air Transport Command. 1943, home of 2nd Operational Training Unit, providing advanced training for air crews. 1945, base closed due to massive hurricane. 1955, reactivated as Homestead AFB with 823rd Air Division; growing threat from Cuba brought 31st TFW from George AFB, CA, and tent city of 10,000 Army troops. 1968, TAC took control. 1985, 31st TFW returns to host.
Key Contacts
COMMANDER: W Thomas West; (305) 257-7301, Autovon 791-7301.
PUBLIC AFFAIRS: LTC Margaret M Stanek; (305) 257-8396, Autovon 791-8396.
Personnel and Expenditures
ACTIVE DUTY PERSONNEL: 5139
DEPENDENTS: 2791
CIVILIAN PERSONNEL: 1102
MILITARY PAYROLL EXPENDITURE: $95.7 mil
CONTRACT EXPENDITURE: $134.4 mil

Services *Housing:* Family units 1614; Dormitory spaces 2503; RV/Camper sites 12. *Temporary Housing:* Dormitory units Visiting airmen/NCO temporary quarters 29; Temporary lodging quarters 56. *Commissary:* Base commissary; Retail store; Barber shop; Dry cleaners; Food shop; Florist; Banking; Service station; Furniture store; Bakery; Book store. *Child Care/Capacities:* Day care center; Home day care program. *Base Library:* Yes. *Medical Facilities:* Hospital 70; Medical clinic; Dental clinic. *Recreational Facilities:* Bowling; Movie theater; Pool; Gym; Recreation center; Golf; Tennis; Racquetball; Fitness center; Softball field; Football field; Auto shop; Crafts; Officers club; NCO club; Camping; Fishing/Hunting.

RICHMOND HEIGHTS AIR FORCE STATION
Homestead, FL 33039
Autovon 791-8124
Profile
BRANCH: Air Force.
MAJOR UNITS: Richmond Heights AFS (TAC).

HURLBURT FIELD

HURLBURT FIELD
Hurlburt Field, FL 32544
(904) 881-6668; Autovon 579-1139
Profile
BRANCH: Air Force.
SIZE AND LOCATION: 6600 acres. In panhandle of FL on US 98; 7 mi W of Ft Walton Beach on Santa Rosa Sound.
MAJOR UNITS: 1st Special Operations Wing; 2d Air Division; Air Ground Operations School; AF Special Operations School; Special Missions Operations Test and Evaluation Center; 2068th Communications Squadron; Detachment 75, 7th Weather Wing; 823rd Civil Engineering Squadron (Red Horse); 23rd AF NCO Leadership School; 4442nd Tactical Control Group; 727th Tactical Control Squadron (TEST); Detachment 8, 1361st Audiovisual Squadron.
BASE HISTORY: 1948, established as gunnery and training field, part of Eglin AFB complex; named for 1st Lt Donald W Hurlburt, killed in aircraft crash at Eglin Army Airfield.
Personnel and Expenditures
ACTIVE DUTY PERSONNEL: 4600
DEPENDENTS: 8250
CIVILIAN PERSONNEL: 400
Services *Housing:* Family units 380. *Temporary Housing:* VOQ cottages 172; VEQ units 76. *Commissary:* Base commissary; Banking. *Child Care/Capacities:* Day care center. *Schools:* Elementary. *Base Library:* Yes. *Medical Facilities:* Medical clinic; Dental clinic; Eglin Regional Hospital nearby. *Recreational Facilities:* Bowling; Movie theater; Pool; Gym; Recreation center; Golf; Tennis; Auto shop; Crafts; Officers club; NCO club; Fishing/Hunting; Marina; Picnicking.

JACKSONVILLE

CECIL FIELD NAVAL AIR STATION
Jacksonville, FL 32215-5000
(904) 778-5626; Autovon 860-5626
OFFICER-OF-THE-DAY: (904) 778-5626, Autovon 860-5626
Profile
BRANCH: Navy.
SIZE AND LOCATION: 17,607 acres. SE of Jacksonville off State Rte 228.

MAJOR UNITS: Commander, Strike-Fighter Wings Atlantic; Commander, Light Attack Wing One; Commander, Sea Strike Wing, One; Commander, Carrier Air Wing Six; Commander, Carrier Air Wing Seventeen.
Key Contacts
COMMANDER: Capt F J Herron.
PUBLIC AFFAIRS: Bert Byers; (904) 778-6055, Autovon 860-6055.
PROCUREMENT: Supply Officer; (904) 778-5770, Autovon 860-5770.
TRANSPORTATION: Transportation Officer; (904) 778-5912, Autovon 860-5912.
Services *Housing:* Family units 297; BOQ cottages (temporary) 81 (permanent) 50; BEQ units 3343; Duplex units 90; Townhouse units 200; Barracks spaces 3344; Trailer spaces 36; RV/Camper sites 4. *Commissary:* Base commissary; Retail store; Barber shop; Dry cleaners; Food shop; Florist; Service station. *Child Care/Capacities:* Day care center. *Base Library:* Yes. *Medical Facilities:* Medical clinic; Dental clinic. *Recreational Facilities:* Bowling; Pool; Gym; Golf; Tennis; Racquetball; Fitness center; Softball field; Football field; Auto shop; Officers club; NCO club.

JACKSONVILLE NAVAL AIR STATION
Jacksonville, FL 32212-5000
(904) 772-2340; Autovon 942-2340
OFFICER-OF-THE-DAY: (904) 772-2338, Autovon 942-2338
Profile
BRANCH: Navy.
SIZE AND LOCATION: 3400 acres. Approx 13 mi S of downtown Jacksonville. Take I-295 around Jacksonville to the intersection of I-295 and US 17 (Roosevelt Blvd); take US 17 N Exit (marked NAS Jacksonville) and the main gate is about 3 mi N of the intersection. Jacksonville IAP is about 35 mi.
MAJOR UNITS: Commander, Patrol Wing Eleven; Commander, Helicopter Wings Atlantic; Naval Hospital Jacksonville; Naval Supply Center; Naval Aviation Depot; Naval Air Reserve Unit; Patrol Squadron Five; Patrol Squadron Sixteen; Patrol Squadron Twenty-Four; Patrol Squadron Thirty; Patrol Squadron Forty-Five; Patrol Squadron Forty-Nine; Patrol Squadron Fifty-Six; Helicopter Antisubmarine Wing One; Helicopter Antisubmarine Squadron One; Helicopter Antisubmarine Squadron Three; Helicopter Antisubmarine Squadron Five; Helicopter Antisubmarine Squadron Nine; Helicopter Antisubmarine Squadron Eleven; Helicopter Antisubmarine Squadron Fifteen; Helicopter Antisubmarine Squadron Seventeen; Naval Air Reserve, Jacksonville; Naval Oceanography Command Facility; Marine Barracks Detachment, Jacksonville; US Army Reserve School.
BASE HISTORY: During WWI, area Camp Joseph E Johnston (Army) and later Camp Foster (National Guard). 1940, commissioned. WWII, base provided training for aviation cadets and POW camp for German soldiers. 1945, separation center and Naval Hospital. 1946, first home Navy's Flight Demonstration Team, Blue Angels. 1948, mission changed to fleet units support. 1950s, establishment of Patrol Squadrons with mission of antisubmarine warfare. Today, air station stands at forefront of antisubmarine warfare readiness.
Key Contacts
COMMANDER: Capt Kevin F Delaney.
PUBLIC AFFAIRS: Nicholas P Young; Box 2, (904) 772-2413, Autovon 942-2413.
PROCUREMENT: Supply Officer; (904) 772-5420, Autovon 942-5420.

JACKSONVILLE NAVAL AIR STATION
(continued)
TRANSPORTATION: (904) 772-2461, Autovon 942-2461.

PERSONNEL/COMMUNITY ACTIVITIES: Steve Gregg; Director of Personnel, (904) 772-3253, Autovon 942-3253.

Services *Housing:* Family units; BOQ cottages 214; BEQ units 2200; Duplex units; Barracks spaces; Senior NCO units; Junior NCO units; Trailer spaces. *Temporary Housing:* VIP cottages; BOQ units; Lodge units; Transient living quarters. *Commissary:* Base commissary; Retail store; Barber shop; Dry cleaners; Food shop; Florist; Service station; Convenience store/Shopette; Home care center; Garden center; Thrift shop; Uniform & Tailor; Beauty shop; Shoe repair; Optical shop; Ice cream; Cafeteria; Exchange equipment rental; Package beverages. *Child Care/Capacities:* Day care center. *Schools:* Kindergarten/Preschool. *Base Library:* Yes. *Medical Facilities:* Hospital 263; Medical clinic; Dental clinic. *Recreational Facilities:* Bowling; Pool; Gym; Recreation center (game room); Golf; Tennis; Racquetball; Skating rink; Fitness center; Softball field; Football field; Auto shop; Crafts; Officers club; Camping (summer day); NCO club; Fishing/Hunting; ITT office; Youth and family program; Marina; Equipment rental; Picnicking.

JACKSONVILLE NAVAL HOSPITAL
Child St, Jacksonville, FL 32214-5000
(904) 777-7300; Autovon 942-7300
OFFICER-OF-THE-DAY: (904) 777-7301, Autovon 942-7301
Profile
BRANCH: Navy.

SIZE AND LOCATION: 25 acres. On board Naval Air Station, Jacksonville, FL, off US 17.

BASE HISTORY: 1941, originally constructed for inpatient care of military personnel, gradually changed to provide care for dependents and retired personnel. 1967, present 8 story facility constructed. 1972, Naval Regional Medical Center Command established. 1983, decommissioned and Naval Hospital commissioned; Naval Regional Medical Clinic, Key West, FL, made separate entity.
Key Contacts
COMMANDER: Capt R G Relinski Jr; Medical Service Corps.

PUBLIC AFFAIRS: LTC P Denzer; Medical Service Corps, (904) 777-7317, Autovon 942-7317.

PROCUREMENT: Lt D Stratton; (904) 777-7713, Autovon 942-7713.

TRANSPORTATION: Lt J Davis; (904) 777-7593, Autovon 942-7593.
Personnel and Expenditures
ACTIVE DUTY PERSONNEL: 1100

CIVILIAN PERSONNEL: 280

MILITARY PAYROLL EXPENDITURE: $20 mil

Services *Commissary:* Base commissary; Retail store; Barber shop; Dry cleaners; Food shop; Florist; Banking; Service station. *Child Care/Capacities:* Day care center 40. *Base Library:* Yes. *Medical Facilities:* Hospital 176; Medical clinic; Dental clinic. *Recreational Facilities:* Bowling; Pool; Gym; Recreation center; Golf; Tennis; Racquetball; Softball field; Football field; Auto shop; Crafts; Officers club; NCO club; Fishing/Hunting.

JACKSONVILLE NAVAL SUPPLY CENTER
Box 97, NAS Jacksonville, Jacksonville, FL 32212-0097
(904) 772-5165; Autovon 942-5165
OFFICER-OF-THE-DAY: (904) 772-2472, Autovon 942-2472

Profile
BRANCH: Navy.

SIZE AND LOCATION: 260 acres. In Jacksonville, on NAS Jacksonville.

MAJOR UNITS: Naval Supply Center.

BASE HISTORY: 1982, established by consolidating supply departments of Naval Station Mayport and NAS Jacksonville and Jacksonville Fuel Depot. One of eight major supply centers where supplies and repairs are purchased and stored for use when needed by ships, aircraft, and shore activities. Main site on St John's River at NAS Jacksonville. 19 mi N of main site is Fuel Directorate, and 40 mi NE of main site is NSC Jacksonville Fleet Support Center, on Mayport Naval Station, providing direct support to Fleet customers.

Key Contacts
COMMANDER: Capt Ralph Parrott; Commanding Officer, (904) 772-2471, Autovon 942-2471.

PUBLIC AFFAIRS: Richard Crews; Code 01, (904) 772-5140, Autovon 942-5140.

PROCUREMENT: CDR Bill Jenkins; Code 200, (904) 772-2453, Autovon 942-2453.

TRANSPORTATION: CDR Jim Molcombe; Code 400, (904) 772-5268, Autovon 942-5268.
Personnel and Expenditures
ACTIVE DUTY PERSONNEL: 30

CIVILIAN PERSONNEL: 470

MILITARY PAYROLL EXPENDITURE: Included with NAS JAX

CONTRACT EXPENDITURE: FY 88, $80 mil

Services *Commissary and Exchange:* See Jacksonville NAS. *Recreational Facilities:* See Jacksonville NAS.

US ARMY CORPS OF ENGINEERS, JACKSONVILLE DISTRICT
400 West Bay St, Jacksonville, FL 32202-0019
(904) 791-2235
Profile
BRANCH: Army.

LOCATION: Downtown Jacksonville at the intersection of Bay and Julia Sts, approx 15 mi from Jacksonville IAP.

MAJOR UNITS: Corps of Engineers Jacksonville District.

BASE HISTORY: Jacksonville District, one of six districts in South Atlantic Division, responsible for civil works mission in peninsular FL (entire state for regulatory functions), PR, and US Virgin Islands. Current projects include navigation, flood control, beach erosion control, regulatory functions, recreation, hurricane protection, water supply, water pollution control, hydroelectric power, flood plain management services, urban studies program, environmental quality policy, and emergency operations.
Key Contacts
COMMANDER: Col Bruce A Malson; District Commander and District Engineer, (904) 791-2242.

PUBLIC AFFAIRS: Juan A Colon; Chief, District Public Affairs Office, (904) 791-2235.

PERSONNEL/COMMUNITY ACTIVITIES: See Public Affairs Officer.
Personnel and Expenditures
ACTIVE DUTY PERSONNEL: 3

CIVILIAN PERSONNEL: 400

Services *Base Library:* Yes. *Medical Facilities:* Medical clinic. *Recreational Facilities:* Fitness center.

125TH FIGHTER INTERCEPTOR GROUP, FLORIDA AIR NATIONAL GUARD
PO Box 18018, Jacksonville IAP, Jacksonville, FL 32229-0018
(904) 751-7100; Autovon 460-7100

OFFICER-OF-THE-DAY: (904) 751-7120, Autovon 460-7120
Profile
BRANCH: Air National Guard.

SIZE AND LOCATION: 303 acres. On W end of Jacksonville IAP; 3 mi W of I-95, approx 10 mi N of Jacksonville.

MAJOR UNITS: 125th Fighter Interceptor Group; 159th Fighter Interceptor Squadron.

BASE HISTORY: 1968, built to replace 1947 original unit. Expanded over past 5 years with new fuel building, and civil engineering facility.
Key Contacts
COMMANDER: Col Marion D (Don) Garrett; (904) 751-7101, Autovon 460-7101.

PUBLIC AFFAIRS: Maj William C Warner; (904) 751-7150, Autovon 460-7150.

PROCUREMENT: TSgt Charlie Wilson; Contracting, (904) 751-7441, Autovon 460-7441.

TRANSPORTATION: Capt Jessie Kinghorn; (904) 751-7410, Autovon 460-7410.

PERSONNEL/COMMUNITY ACTIVITIES: Maj William Whittaker; (904) 751-7501, Autovon 460-7501.
Personnel and Expenditures
ACTIVE DUTY PERSONNEL: 61

CIVILIAN PERSONNEL: 245

MILITARY PAYROLL EXPENDITURE: $16.3 mil

CONTRACT EXPENDITURE: $1.4 mil

Services *Medical Facilities:* Medical clinic. *Recreational Facilities:* Softball field; Officers club; NCO club.

KEY WEST

KEY WEST NAVAL AIR STATION
Key West, FL 33040-5000
(305) 292-2268; Autovon 483-2268
OFFICER-OF-THE-DAY: (305) 292-2268, Autovon 483-2268
Profile
BRANCH: Navy.

SIZE AND LOCATION: 5215 acres. Consists of 5 separate areas located throughout the Key West area. The Naval airfield is now located on Boca Chica Key at mile marker 8 on US 1 (Overseas Hwy) approx 6 mi E of the city of Key West and Key West IAP. NAS Key West also includes Trumbo Point, located in NW Key West. Truman Annex, located on the western end of Key West, is home for Commander US Forces Caribbean.

MAJOR UNITS: Fighter Squadron 45 (VF-45); Tactical Electronic Warfare Squadron 33 (VAQ-33); Fighter Squadron 101 (VF-101); PHMRON Two, Hydrofoil Squadron; Coast Guard Group, Key West.

BASE HISTORY: 1917, begun as coastal air patrol station. 1918, seaplane and blimp facility established. After WWI, caretaker status until 1939, major additions made: satellite Meacham Field (now Key West IAP), for lighter-than-air, and Boca Chica Field for land planes. 1940, Seaplane Base formally reestablished as NAS and operating and training base for fleet aircraft squadrons. 1945, satellite fields disestablished and combined into one aviation activity under current designation and maintained as training and experimental site. Country's southernmost naval base.
Key Contacts
COMMANDER: Capt John C Ensch; (305) 292-2866, Autovon 483-2866.

PUBLIC AFFAIRS: Lt Maria O S Gothard; (305) 292-2425, Autovon 483-2425.

PROCUREMENT: CDR Robert M Perkins; Supply Officer, (305) 292-2463, Autovon 483-2463.

KEY WEST NAVAL AIR STATION
(continued)
TRANSPORTATION: Don Carey; Transportation Supervisor, (305) 292-2586, Autovon 483-2586.

PERSONNEL/COMMUNITY ACTIVITIES: D K Dye; Director Welfare, Morale & Recreation, (305) 292-2112, Autovon 483-2112.

Personnel and Expenditures
ACTIVE DUTY PERSONNEL: 2663
DEPENDENTS: 2984
CIVILIAN PERSONNEL: 433
MILITARY PAYROLL EXPENDITURE: $38 mil
CONTRACT EXPENDITURE: $20 mil
Services *Housing:* Family units 1391; Barracks spaces; RV/Camper sites 26. *Temporary Housing:* VIP cottages 1; BOQ units 257; Guesthouse units 8. *Commissary:* Base commissary; Retail store; Barber shop; Food shop; Service station. *Child Care/Capacities:* Day care center; Home day care program. *Base Library:* Yes. *Medical Facilities:* Medical clinic; Dental clinic. *Recreational Facilities:* Bowling; Pool; Gym; Recreation center; Tennis; Racquetball; Fitness center; Softball field; Auto shop; Crafts; Officers club; NCO club; Fishing/Hunting.

MACDILL AFB

MACDILL AIR FORCE BASE
56th Tactical Training Wing, MacDill AFB, FL 33608-5000
(813) 830-2215; Autovon 84-968-2215
OFFICER-OF-THE-DAY: (813) 830-4621, Autovon 84-968-4621
Profile
BRANCH: Air Force.
SIZE AND LOCATION: 5700 acres. Take I-75 to I-275 S, exit at Dale Mabry Hwy (U S-92) S, 5 mi S to main gate. Tampa is 5 mi N.
MAJOR UNITS: 56th Tactical Training Wing (TTW); US Central Command; US Special Operations Command; Joint Communications Support Element.
BASE HISTORY: 1941, activated as MacDill Field, named for Col Leslie MacDill, aviation pioneer. First a SAC base, flew bombers until 1963 when it got F-4C (First Base). 1970, mission changed from replacement training to combat-ready operational. 1979, became 56th TTW and converted to F-16s. Present mission to train pilots and maintain F-16s.
Key Contacts
COMMANDER: Brig Gen James L Jamerson; 56th TTW/CC, (813) 830-4444, Autovon 84-968-4444.
PUBLIC AFFAIRS: Capt S Dian Lawhan; 56th TTW/PA, (813) 830-4444, Autovon 84-968-4444.
PROCUREMENT: Col R Pietras; 56th TTW/RM, (813) 830-3240, Autovon 84-968-3240.
TRANSPORTATION: Capt McDuff; 56th TRANS/CC, (813) 830-2031, Autovon 84-968-2031.
PERSONNEL/COMMUNITY ACTIVITIES: Capt Hubbard; Director of Personnel, 56th MSSQ/MSP, (813) 830-3618, Autovon 84-968-3618.
Personnel and Expenditures
ACTIVE DUTY PERSONNEL: 6849
DEPENDENTS: 12,489
CIVILIAN PERSONNEL: 1894
MILITARY PAYROLL EXPENDITURE: $156 mil
CONTRACT EXPENDITURE: $2.9 mil
Services *Housing:* Family units 804; Barracks spaces Barracks/Dormitories 1050; Trailer spaces with hookups 112; RV/Camper sites without hookups 20. *Temporary Housing:* VIP cottages (Quarters) 14; VOQ cottages (and BOQ) 35; VAQ units (BAQ) 124; Transient living quarters 60. *Commissary:* Base commissary; Retail store; Barber shop; Dry cleaners; Food shop; Florist;

Banking; Service station; Furniture store; Bakery; Book store; Personal items; Laundry. *Child Care/Capacities:* Day care center 180. *Schools:* Kindergarten/Preschool; Elementary. *Base Library:* Yes. *Medical Facilities:* Hospital 75; Dental clinic. *Recreational Facilities:* Bowling; Movie theater; Pool; Gym; Recreation center; Golf; Stables; Tennis; Racquetball; Fitness center; Softball field; Football field; Auto shop; Crafts; Officers club; NCO club; Camping; Fishing/Hunting.

MAYPORT

MAYPORT NAVAL STATION
Mayport, FL 32228-5000
(904) 246-5201; Autovon 960-5201
OFFICER-OF-THE-DAY: (904) 246-5401, Autovon 960-5401
Profile
BRANCH: Navy.
SIZE AND LOCATION: 3414 acres. At the mouth of the St Johns River, 18 mi E of downtown Jacksonville; accessible from Rte A1A or Rte 10-W; take the Beaches Exit from I-95 and follow Atlantic Blvd to Mayport Rd, turn left onto Mayport Rd which will dead end at the Naval Station.
MAJOR UNITS: Naval Air Station, Mayport; Commander, Cruiser Destroyer Group Twelve; Commander, Carrier Group Six; USS *Forrestal* (CV 59) & USS *Saratoga* (CV 60).
BASE HISTORY: 1942, commissioned. By 1951, more than doubled in size, serving first carrier. 1962, Cuban Missile Crisis served as advance staging area. 1982-1984, ships homeported at Mayport involved in operations off coast of Beirut, Lebanon, and Operation Urgent Fury in Grenada. 1987, USS *Stark*, struck by Iraqi missiles in Persian Gulf. Homeport to 33 ships.
VISITOR ATTRACTIONS: Weekend ship visit, (904) 241-6289.
Key Contacts
COMMANDER: Capt John B Mitchell; (904) 246-5201, Autovon 960-5201.
PUBLIC AFFAIRS: LCDR Timothy B Taylor; PO Box 205, Mayport, FL 32228-0205, (904) 246-5226, Autovon 960-5226.
PROCUREMENT: LCDR Michael B Shea; Supply Officer, PO Box M, Code N712, Mayport, FL 32228-0013, (904) 246-5255, Autovon 960-5255.
TRANSPORTATION: W E Howell; PO Box 265, Mayport, FL 32228, (904) 246-5222, Autovon 960-5222.
PERSONNEL/COMMUNITY ACTIVITIES: Julian Barrs; Morale, Welfare, and Recreation, Bldg 414, Naval Station, Mayport, FL 32228, (904) 246-5228, Autovon 960-5228.
Personnel and Expenditures
ACTIVE DUTY PERSONNEL: 18,000
DEPENDENTS: 19,000
CIVILIAN PERSONNEL: 3000
MILITARY PAYROLL EXPENDITURE: $26 mil
Services *Housing:* Family units 53; Duplex units 628; Trailer spaces 50. *Temporary Housing:* Lodge units 19. *Commissary:* Base commissary; Retail store; Barber shop; Dry cleaners; Food shop; Florist; Banking; Service station. *Child Care/Capacities:* Day care center. *Base Library:* Yes. *Medical Facilities:* Medical clinic; Dental clinic; NAVCARE, approx 5 mi at Jacksonville Beach. *Recreational Facilities:* Bowling; Pool; Gym; Recreation center; Golf; Tennis; Racquetball; Softball field; Auto shop; Crafts; Officers club; Fishing/Hunting; Chief Club; Track; EM Club; Beach; Boat rental; Car wash.

MIAMI BEACH

MIAMI BEACH COAST GUARD BASE
100 MacArthur Causeway, Miami Beach, FL 33139
(305) 535-4300; FTS 8-820-0300
OFFICER-OF-THE-DAY: (305) 535-4315, FTS 8-820-0315
Profile
BRANCH: Coast Guard.
SIZE AND LOCATION: 14 acres. On MacArthur Cswy (I-395) approx 1 mi W from Miami Beach; 4 mi E from Miami; 12 mi E from Miami IAP.
MAJOR UNITS: USCG Group Miami Beach; USCG Base Miami Beach; Patrol Boat Squadron One; ATON (Aids to Navigation) Miami; USCGC *Hudson*; USCGC *Farallon*; USCGC *Matagorda*; USCGC *Maui*; USCGC *Manitou*; USCGC *Baranof*; USCGC *Chandeleur*; USCGC *Dauntless*; Coast Guard Reserve Center Miami; Mobile Aerostat Platform Division Two.
BASE HISTORY: 1941, Coast Guard acquired man-made island to replace beach facilities previously located at Ft Lauderdale and Miami Beach. Coast Guard Depot, Causeway Island until 1946, when designated as Base Miami Beach. Current multi-mission responsibility: command and control center for Coast Guard Group Miami; serves Greater Miami area as world's busiest search and rescue; services aids to navigation; industrial plant, second largest in Coast Guard; services units throughout 7th Coast Guard District.
VISITOR ATTRACTIONS: Tours are available upon request subject to operational commitments.
Key Contacts
COMMANDER: Capt G Nelson.
PUBLIC AFFAIRS: Ltjg A O Crespo; (305) 535-4346, FTS 8-820-0346.
PROCUREMENT: CWO Bekken; (305) 535-4322, FTS 8-820-0322.
TRANSPORTATION: See Procurement Officer.
PERSONNEL/COMMUNITY ACTIVITIES: Ens E Giese; Director of Personnel, (305) 535-4342.
Personnel and Expenditures
ACTIVE DUTY PERSONNEL: 300
CIVILIAN PERSONNEL: 100
Services *Temporary Housing:* Dormitory units 6. *Commissary and Exchange:* Retail store; Barber shop; Dry cleaners; Food shop. *Medical Facilities:* Medical clinic; Dental clinic. *Recreational Facilities:* Pool; Gym; Tennis; Racquetball; Fitness center (workout room); Officers club; NCO club; Basketball; Indoor firing range.

MILTON

WHITING FIELD NAVAL AIR STATION
Milton, FL 32570
(904) 623-7437; Autovon 868-7437
OFFICER-OF-THE-DAY: (904) 623-7437, Autovon 868-7437
Profile
BRANCH: Navy.
SIZE AND LOCATION: 3973 acres. 8 mi NE of Milton, FL.
MAJOR UNITS: Naval Training Air Wing Five; Naval Oceanographic Command; Naval Air Maintenance Training; VT-2; VT-3; VT-6; HT-8; HT-18; Navy Resale; Branch Medical Clinic; Personnel Support.
BASE HISTORY: 1943, commissioned; named for Naval hero Kenneth Whiting. 1945, POW camp established with Camp Rucker, AL. After WWII, reverted to NAS

WHITING FIELD NAVAL AIR STATION
(continued)

and known as backbone of Navy's flight program. 1949-50, home of Blue Angels, precision flying team, and Navy's first jet training unit, JUT ONE, commissioned. 1972, home of Training Air Wing Five and established helicopter training at South Field and North Field home of three fixed-wing squadrons. Above includes all of NASWF's Outlying Landing Fields: Barin, Brewton, Choctow, Evergreen, Harold, Holley, Pace, Santa Rosa, Saufley, Site 6, Site 8, Silverhill, Spencer, Summerdale, and Wolf.

Key Contacts
COMMANDER: Capt Paul E Pedisich; (904) 623-7121, Autovon 868-7121.
PUBLIC AFFAIRS: Ensign Erica A Smith; (904) 623-7651, Autovon 868-7651.
PROCUREMENT: CDR Gage Woodward; Comptroller, (904) 623-7510.
TRANSPORTATION: LCDR J D Macfarquhar; Public Works Officer, (904) 623-7268.
PERSONNEL/COMMUNITY ACTIVITIES: Ed Dee; MWR Director, (904) 623-7221.

Personnel and Expenditures
ACTIVE DUTY PERSONNEL: 2560
DEPENDENTS: 5120
CIVILIAN PERSONNEL: 429
MILITARY PAYROLL EXPENDITURE: $102.4 mil
CONTRACT EXPENDITURE: $41.9 mil
Services *Housing:* Family units 412; BOQ cottages Units 232; BEQ units 305; Duplex units 100. *Temporary Housing:* VIP cottages 2; BOQ units 62; BEQ 12. *Commissary:* Base commissary; Retail store; Barber shop; Dry cleaners; Food shop; Florist; Banking; Service station. *Child Care/Capacities:* Day care center 32. *Base Library:* Yes. *Medical Facilities:* Medical clinic; Dental clinic. *Recreational Facilities:* Bowling; Movie theater; Pool; Gym; Recreation center; Golf; Tennis; Racquetball; Fitness center; Softball field; Auto shop; Crafts; Officers club; NCO club; Camping; Fishing/Hunting; Water sports.

OLD TOWN

OPERATING LOCATION ALPHA BRAVO SOUTH EAST AIR DEFENSE SECTOR
Rte 2, Box 321, Old Town, FL 32680-9710
(904) 542-7457; Autovon 460-3905
Profile
BRANCH: Air Force.
SIZE AND LOCATION: 5 acres. From Cross City, FL, US 19 turn E on County Rd 351, approx 12 mi on N side of road.
MAJOR UNITS: Federal Aviation Administration (FAA).
BASE HISTORY: Joint FAA/USAF radar site.
Key Contacts
COMMANDER: Edward S Collier; Site Chief.
PUBLIC AFFAIRS: Ernest W Muschner.
Personnel and Expenditures
CIVILIAN PERSONNEL: 7

OPA-LOCKA

MIAMI COAST GUARD AIR STATION
Opa-Locka Airport, Opa-Locka, FL 33054
(305) 953-2100; Autovon 894-1190
OFFICER-OF-THE-DAY: (305) 953-2280
Profile
BRANCH: Coast Guard.
SIZE AND LOCATION: 20 acres. Opa-Locka Airport.
MAJOR UNITS: US Coast Guard Air Station Miami.
BASE HISTORY: 1932, commissioned on Biscayne Bay, first aviation unit in Coast Guard. Today, world's busiest air/sea res-

cue unit. Now at Opa-Locka Airport, mission includes search and rescue, maritime law enforcement, and environmental protection.
VISITOR ATTRACTIONS: Air Station tours conducted by Public Affairs Office.
Key Contacts
COMMANDER: Capt Kent M Ballantyne; (305) 953-2101.
PUBLIC AFFAIRS: Ltjg Daniel P Allen; (305) 953-2151.
Personnel and Expenditures
ACTIVE DUTY PERSONNEL: 339
CIVILIAN PERSONNEL: 2
CONTRACT EXPENDITURE: $22 mil
Services *Housing:* BEQ units Two person rooms 26. *Commissary:* Base commissary; Retail store; Barber shop. *Medical Facilities:* Medical clinic; Dental clinic. *Recreational Facilities:* Pool; Gym; Tennis; Auto shop; NCO club.

ORLANDO

NAVAL RESEARCH LABORATORY, UNDERWATER SOUND REFERENCE LABORATORY
3909 S Summerlin Ave, Orlando, FL 32806-6905
(407) 857-5170
Profile
BRANCH: Navy.
LOCATION: On the edge of Orlando, FL.
MAJOR UNITS: USRD Technical Services Branch; USRD Computer Branch; USRD Electronics Branch; USRD Transducer Branch; USRD Measurements Branch; USRD Acoustics Materials Branch.
Key Contacts
COMMANDER: Dr J E Blue; Superintendent, (407) 857-5230.
PUBLIC AFFAIRS: James W Gately Jr; Information Services Br, Code 2610, Naval Research Lab, Washington, DC 20375-5000, (202) 767-2541, (297) 2541.
Services *Base Library:* Yes.

NAVAL TRAINING SYSTEMS CENTER
12350 Research Pkwy, Orlando, FL 32826-3224
(407) 380-4000; Autovon 960-4000
Profile
BRANCH: Navy.
SIZE AND LOCATION: 40 acres. In Central FL Research Park, just off Alafaya Trail, approx 1.5 mi N of State Rd 50 and approx 15 mi from downtown Orlando; approx 12 mi E of the Naval Training Center, Orlando and about 17 mi NE of Orlando IAP; adj to the Univ of Central FL.
MAJOR UNITS: Naval Training Systems Center; Army Project Manager for Training Devices (PM TRADE).
BASE HISTORY: Early 1940s, began as three-man desk in Navy's Bureau of Aeronautics; evolved into complex, multidisciplinary organization that annually procures about a billion dollars in training systems. Pioneered development of simulation devices for military training. At de Florez Building since 1988. Field activity of Naval Air Systems Command.
Key Contacts
COMMANDER: Capt C D Rowley; Commanding Officer NTSC, Col R J Lunsford; Commanding Officer PM TRADE.
PUBLIC AFFAIRS: Allen Q Collier Jr; NTSC, (407) 380-8208, Autovon 960-3208.
PROCUREMENT: CDR M L Kalapos, SC, USN; (407) 380-8386, Autovon 960-8386.
PERSONNEL/COMMUNITY ACTIVITIES: J L Bigham; Civilian Personnel Officer for the CCPO (Consolidated Civilian Person-

nel Office), (407) 380-8114, Autovon 960-8114.
Personnel and Expenditures
ACTIVE DUTY PERSONNEL: 50
CIVILIAN PERSONNEL: 1200
CONTRACT EXPENDITURE: $4.5 mil
Services *Base Library:* Yes. *Medical Facilities:* Naval Hospital, Orlando. *Recreational Facilities:* Bowling; Movie theater; Golf; Tennis; Softball field; Auto shop; Officers club; NCO club; Items only at NTC Orlando for those eligible.

ORLANDO RECRUIT TRAINING COMMAND
Naval Training Center, Orlando, FL 32813
(407) 646-5112
Profile
BRANCH: Navy.
LOCATION: NTC on N side of Orlando; Annex on S (formerly McCoy AFB).
MAJOR UNITS: Recruit Training Command.
BASE HISTORY: 1940, commissioned as Army Air Corps base. 1968, recommissioned NTC. Today, provides basic through specialized training for officer and enlisted, regular Navy and reserves.
Key Contacts
PUBLIC AFFAIRS: Recruit Affairs Office, (407) 646-4522.
Personnel and Expenditures
ACTIVE DUTY PERSONNEL: 550 staff, 8000 trainees
CIVILIAN PERSONNEL: 3500
Services *Housing:* Family units 960; Trailer spaces. *Temporary Housing:* Lodge units. *Commissary:* Base commissary; Retail store. *Child Care/Capacities:* Day care center. *Medical Facilities:* 50 bed Annex of Orlando Naval Regional Medical Center. *Recreational Facilities:* Bowling; Movie theater; Pool; Gym; Golf; Auto shop; Crafts; Officers club; NCO club; Marina; Picnic area; Beach.

PANAMA CITY

NAVAL COASTAL SYSTEMS CENTER
Panama City, FL 32407-5000
(904) 234-4011; Autovon 436-4011
OFFICER-OF-THE-DAY: (904) 234-4316, Autovon 436-4316
Profile
BRANCH: Navy.
SIZE AND LOCATION: 580 acres. 1 mi W of Panama City on US Hwy 98; 1 mi W of Gulf Coast Community College and Florida State Univ-Panama City Campus.
MAJOR UNITS: Navy Diving and Salvage Training Center; Navy Experimental Diving Unit.
BASE HISTORY: 1942, Navy established base providing safe harbor for WWII convoy ships. 1944, established training center for amphibious vessel crews, including crews in D-Day invasion. 1945, training center closed; forerunner of Naval Coastal Systems Center moved to site; equipment and personnel from deactivated US Mine Warfare Test Station, Solomons Island, MD, nucleus of new facility; station redesignated US Navy Mine Defense Laboratory. 1968, renamed Naval Ship Research and Development Laboratory, Panama City. 1972, renamed Naval Coastal Systems Laboratory. 1978, received present name.
Key Contacts
COMMANDER: Capt Michael W Gavlak; (904) 234-4201, Autovon 436-4201.
PUBLIC AFFAIRS: Michael L Jones; (904) 234-4817, Autovon 436-4817.

NAVAL COASTAL SYSTEMS CENTER
(continued)
Personnel and Expenditures
ACTIVE DUTY PERSONNEL: 1650
DEPENDENTS: 145
CIVILIAN PERSONNEL: 1350
MILITARY PAYROLL EXPENDITURE: $70 mil
CONTRACT EXPENDITURE: $107 mil
Services *Housing:* Family units 65; BOQ cottages (rooms) 6; BEQ units 13; Senior NCO units 15; Junior NCO units 15; RV/ Camper sites 14. *Temporary Housing:* VIP cottages (suites) 5; VOQ cottages 36; VEQ units 184; RV Trailer rentals 11. *Commissary and Exchange:* Retail store; Barber shop; Dry cleaners; Food shop; Florist. *Base Library:* Yes. *Medical Facilities:* Medical clinic; Dental clinic. *Recreational Facilities:* Bowling; Pool; Gym; Tennis; Racquetball; Fitness center; Softball field; Auto shop; Officers club; NCO club; Camping; Fishing/ Hunting.

PATRICK AFB

PATRICK AIR FORCE BASE
Patrick AFB, FL 32925
(305) 494-1110; Autovon 854-1110
Profile
BRANCH: Air Force.
SIZE AND LOCATION: 2342 acres. 3 mi S of Cocoa Beach on Rte A1A.
MAJOR UNITS: Eastern Space and Missile Center; Eastern Test Range; 6555th Aerospace Test Group; USAF Hospital, Patrick; 6550th Air Base Group; AF Technical Applications Center; 2d Combat Information Systems Group; 2179th Communication Group; Defense Equal Opportunity Management Institute; Detachment 15, 41st Rescue and Weather Reconnaissance Wing.
BASE HISTORY: 1940, established as Banana River NAS. 1948, USAF took over; renamed it for Maj Gen Mason M Patrick, Chief of Army Air Service, 1921-27.
Personnel and Expenditures
ACTIVE DUTY PERSONNEL: 4494
DEPENDENTS: 4826
CIVILIAN PERSONNEL: 6697
MILITARY PAYROLL EXPENDITURE: $69.5 mil
Services *Housing:* Family units 1576. *Temporary Housing:* VIP cottages 8; VOQ cottages 248; VAQ units 152; Transient living quarters 31. *Commissary:* Base commissary; Retail store; Barber shop; Dry cleaners; Food shop; Florist; Service station; Military clothing sales; Convenience store/Shopette; Furniture store; Mini-mall; Laundry; Beauty shop; Optical shop; Video rental; Car rental; Toys. *Child Care/Capacities:* Day care center 150. *Medical Facilities:* Hospital 25; Veterinary services. *Recreational Facilities:* Bowling; Movie theater; Pool; Gym; Golf; Stables; Tennis; Racquetball; Fitness center; Auto shop; Crafts; Officers club; NCO club; Camping; Fishing/Hunting; Youth center (activities); Water sports; Skeet shooting; Aero club; Beach.

PENSACOLA

CORRY STATION NAVAL TECHNICAL TRAINING CENTER
Pensacola, FL 32511-5000
(904) 452-6512; Autovon 922-6512
OFFICER-OF-THE-DAY: (904) 452-6512, Autovon 922-6512
Profile
BRANCH: Navy.
SIZE AND LOCATION: 400 acres. On the FL panhandle Gulf Coast, 5 min from Pensacola, FL. Access via New Warrington Rd (State Rd 295) and US Hwy 98.

MAJOR UNITS: Naval Technical Training Center.
BASE HISTORY: 1923, opened; originally Corry Field, named for LCDR William M Corry Jr, naval pioneer aviator; 1928, moved to present site, as aviation training command. After WWII, auxiliary air station. 1958, decommissioned. 1960, recommissioned Naval Communications Training Center. 1973, Navy electronic warfare training schools consolidated at Corry and Naval Schools of Photography detachment; renamed Naval Technical Training Center. 1989, Opticalman and Instrumentman Applied Instruction from Great Lakes, IL.
Key Contacts
COMMANDER: Capt Joseph D Burns; Commanding Officer, (904) 452-6516, Autovon 922-6516.
PUBLIC AFFAIRS: Sandra E Bansemer; (904) 452-6302, Autovon 922-6302.
PROCUREMENT: Lt Melvin Moody; Supply Officer, (904) 452-6570, Autovon 922-6570.
Personnel and Expenditures
ACTIVE DUTY PERSONNEL: 3000
DEPENDENTS: 4500
CIVILIAN PERSONNEL: 475
MILITARY PAYROLL EXPENDITURE: $76.2 mil
CONTRACT EXPENDITURE: $1.7 mil
Services *Housing:* Family units; BEQ units; Senior NCO units; Junior NCO units; RV/ Camper sites. *Commissary:* Base commissary; Retail store; Barber shop; Dry cleaners; Food shop; Florist; Banking; Service station; Furniture store; Bakery; Book store. *Base Library:* Yes. *Medical Facilities:* Hospital 342; Medical clinic; Dental clinic. *Recreational Facilities:* Bowling; Movie theater; Pool; Gym; Recreation center; Tennis; Racquetball; Fitness center; Softball field; Football field; Auto shop; Crafts; NCO club; Camping; Fishing/Hunting; Camp site on Perdido Bay.

NAVAL EDUCATION AND TRAINING PROGRAM MANAGEMENT SUPPORT ACTIVITY
Saufley Field, Pensacola, FL 32509-5000
(904) 452-1788; Autovon 922-1788
OFFICER-OF-THE-DAY: (904) 452-1628, Autovon 922-1628
Profile
BRANCH: Navy.
SIZE AND LOCATION: 900 acres. 7 mi NW of Pensacola, FL; Approx 2.5 mi W of junction of US Hwy 90 and Saufley Field Rd; Approx 8 mi W of Pensacola Municipal Airport.
MAJOR UNITS: Federal Prison Camp, Bureau of Prisons; Navy Comptroller Standard Systems Activity; Defense Activity for Nontraditional Education Support (DANTES); Navy Training Systems Center, Regional Office Atlantic; Naval Reserve Center; US Customs Service; Outlying Landing Field Saufley; Naval Aviation Depot Detachment.
BASE HISTORY: 1940, opened. 1943, commissioned Naval Auxiliary Air Station. 1968, redesignated NAS. 1976, disestablished and placed in caretaker status with airfield designated as Outlying Landing Field. 1979, reactivated; HQ Naval Education and Training Program Management Support Activity; Navy's first Federal Prison Camp, operated by Bureau of Prisons. Airfield currently used as outlying field with touch-and-go landings for pilot training by NAS Whiting Field.
Key Contacts
COMMANDER: Capt Charles E Ward; (904) 452-1310, Autovon 922-1310.
PUBLIC AFFAIRS: Margaret Flowers; (904) 452-1788, Autovon 922-1788.

PERSONNEL/COMMUNITY ACTIVITIES: See Public Affairs Officer.
Personnel and Expenditures
ACTIVE DUTY PERSONNEL: 265
CIVILIAN PERSONNEL: 992
MILITARY PAYROLL EXPENDITURE: $27.2 mil
Services *Commissary and Exchange:* Retail store; Barber shop; Banking. *Recreational Facilities:* Pool; Gym; Golf; Tennis; Racquetball; Softball field.

PENSACOLA COAST GUARD STATION
Pensacola NAS, Pensacola, FL 32508
(904) 453-8282
Profile
BRANCH: Coast Guard.
LOCATION: On NAS Pensacola.
MAJOR UNITS: Station Pensacola; Aids to Navigation Team, Pensacola; CGC Point Verde.
BASE HISTORY: Original US Life Saving Service located on Santa Rosa Island in 1885. 1979, following two hurricanes, Station relocated on Big Lagoon, W of Pensacola Pass. 1987, present site dedicated. Mission: search and rescue, law enforcement, aids to navigation, and safety and marine environment coverage extends along FL Panhandle.
Personnel and Expenditures
ACTIVE DUTY PERSONNEL: 45
Services *Housing:* Crew's quarters only. *Commissary and Exchange:* Also uses Pensacola NAS. *Recreational Facilities:* Shares facilities with Pensacola NAS.

PENSACOLA NAVAL AIR STATION
Pensacola, FL 32508-5000
(904) 452-2312; Autovon 922-2312
OFFICER-OF-THE-DAY: (904) 452-2353, Autovon 922-2353
Profile
BRANCH: Navy.
SIZE AND LOCATION: 5800 acres (16,500 acres entire complex). Approx 11 mi SW of Pensacola, FL, on Navy Blvd and about 12 mi E of the AL state line.
MAJOR UNITS: Chief of Naval Education and Training; Training Air Wing Six; Training Squadron Four; Training Squadron Ten; Training Squadron Eighty-Six; USS *Lexington*; Naval Aviation Schools Command; Naval Aviation Depot; Naval Supply Center; Navy Public Works Center (NPWC); Construction Battalion Unit 402; Helicopter Combat Support Squadron 16; Naval Aerospace Medical Institute (NAMI); US Navy Flight Demonstration Squadron; Navy Regional Data Automation Center (NARDAC); Joint Oil Analysis Program Technical Support Center (JOAP-TSC); Naval Oceanography Command Detachment; Marine Aviation Training Support Group (MATSG).
BASE HISTORY: "Cradle of Naval Aviation," established 1914, oldest NAS. 1825, Pensacola Navy yard established on original site; decommissioned 1911. WWI, "Annapolis of the Air." 1928, auxiliary base, Corry Field, constructed 5 mi N of main station. WWII, auxiliary fields added: Bronson, Barin, and Whiting, FL. 1948, Naval Air Basic Training Command HQ. 1971, Chief of Naval Education and Training.
VISITOR ATTRACTIONS: Naval Aviation Museum; Fort Barrancas; Barrancas National Cemetery; USS *Lexington*.
Key Contacts
COMMANDER: Capt Harry A Jupin; Commanding Officer, Bldg 624, (904) 452-2713, Autovon 922-2713.
PUBLIC AFFAIRS: J B McKamey; Public Affairs Office, Bldg 191, (904) 452-2312, Autovon 922-2312.

PENSACOLA NAVAL AIR STATION
(continued)
PROCUREMENT: LCDR D E Carl; Supply Officer, Supply Department, Bldg 624, (904) 452-3526, Autovon 922-3526.
TRANSPORTATION: Cindy Rodrique; FMD, Bldg 1754, (904) 452-2753, Autovon 922-2753.
PERSONNEL/COMMUNITY ACTIVITIES: See Public Affairs Officer.
Personnel and Expenditures
ACTIVE DUTY PERSONNEL: 6522
DEPENDENTS: 10,500
CIVILIAN PERSONNEL: 8169
MILITARY PAYROLL EXPENDITURE: $205.5 mil
CONTRACT EXPENDITURE: $41.2 mil
Services *Housing:* Family units 585; BEQ units 660; BAQ units 506; Mobile home units lots 52; RV/Camper sites 61; Cabin units for rent 12. *Temporary Housing:* VOQ cottages 26; Lodge units 38. *Commissary and Exchange:* Retail store; Barber shop; Dry cleaners; Food shop; Banking; Service station; Military clothing sales; Car rental; Package beverages; Fast food; Commissary located on Hwy 98 nearby; Florist at NEX Mall on Hwy 98. *Child Care/Capacities:* Day care center. *Base Library:* Yes. *Medical Facilities:* Medical clinic; Navy Hospital on Hwy 98 nearby. *Recreational Facilities:* Bowling; Movie theater; Pool; Gym; Recreation center; Golf; Tennis; Racquetball; Fitness center; Softball field; Football field; Auto shop; Crafts; Officers club; NCO club; Camping; Fishing/Hunting; Water sports.

PENSACOLA NAVAL AVIATION DEPOT
Bldg 52, Naval Air Station, Pensacola, FL 32508-5300
(904) 452-3208; Autovon 922-3208
OFFICER-OF-THE-DAY: (904) 452-3525, Autovon 922-3525
Profile
BRANCH: Navy.
SIZE AND LOCATION: 326 acres. Approx 5 mi from downtown Pensacola, 3 mi from US Hwy 98, and 10 mi from I-10. Pensacola Municipal Airport 12 mi.
MAJOR UNITS: Naval Aviation Depot.
BASE HISTORY: Oldest of Navy's six aviation depots, and largest industrial employer. Depot level maintenance activity performing complete range of rework operations on designated aircraft and associated accessories and equipment: manufacturing aircraft parts and assemblies, providing engineering services in support of assigned aircraft and components, and providing technical services on aircraft maintenance and logistics problems.
Key Contacts
COMMANDER: Capt David R Riley; Commanding Officer, (904) 452-3324, 452-3325, Autovon 922-3324, 922-3325.
PUBLIC AFFAIRS: Marge Sanders; (904) 452-3208, Autovon 922-3208.
Personnel and Expenditures
ACTIVE DUTY PERSONNEL: 35
CIVILIAN PERSONNEL: 3854
MILITARY PAYROLL EXPENDITURE: $132.2 mil
CONTRACT EXPENDITURE: $16.8 mil
Services *Housing:* See Pensacola NAS. *Temporary Housing:* See Pensacola NAS. *Commissary and Exchange:* See Pensacola NAS. *Medical Facilities:* See Pensacola NAS. *Recreational Facilities:* See Pensacola NAS.

PENSACOLA NAVAL HOSPITAL
Pensacola, FL 32507
(904) 452-6601
Profile
BRANCH: Navy.
SIZE AND LOCATION: 78 acres. On Hwy 98, between Navy Blvd and Fairfield Dr.
MAJOR UNITS: Naval Hospital.

BASE HISTORY: Since early 19th century, Navy medicine practiced in six different facilities in Pensacola area. 1976, newest, 8-story, structure dedicated. 1983, redesignated Naval Hospital Pensacola. Also, responsible for branch hospital and eight branch medical clinics in MS and FL.
Key Contacts
PUBLIC AFFAIRS: (904) 452-6413.
Services *Housing:* See Pensacola NAS. *Temporary Housing:* See Pensacola NAS. *Commissary and Exchange:* Retail store; Barber shop; Food shop; Florist; Convenience store/Shopette; Laundry; Tailor; Optical shop; Beauty shop; Video rental. *Medical Facilities:* Hospital 342; Medical clinic. *Recreational Facilities:* Tennis.

SAINT PETERSBURG

EGMONT KEY COAST GUARD LIGHT STATION
C/O USCG Station, St Petersburg, Saint Petersburg, FL 33701
(813) 823-5588
Profile
BRANCH: Coast Guard.
SIZE AND LOCATION: 1.5 acres. On island of Egmont Key, 1.5 mi W of entrance to Tampa Bay.
MAJOR UNITS: Light Station.
BASE HISTORY: 1940, land set aside for military use and established as Coast Guard Station. Primary mission upkeep of light, grounds, radiobeam, foghorn, and assisting in search and rescue around island.
VISITOR ATTRACTIONS: Remains of Spanish-American War fort; Lighthouse dating to 1858; 55 acre bird sanctuary.
Key Contacts
COMMANDER: BM1, Officer in Charge.
PUBLIC AFFAIRS: See USCG Group/Station, St Petersburg, FL.
Personnel and Expenditures
ACTIVE DUTY PERSONNEL: 4
Services *Housing:* Crew's quarters only.

ST PETERSBURG COAST GUARD STATION
600 8th Ave, SE, Saint Petersburg, FL 33701-5030
(813) 893-3454; FTS 826-3454
OFFICER-OF-THE-DAY: (813) 893-3454
Profile
BRANCH: Coast Guard.
SIZE AND LOCATION: 10 acres. Approx 20 mi from Tampa Airport; bounded by Albert Whitted Airport to the N, Univ of S FL, St Petersburg campus to the W, Bayboro Harbor to the S and separated from Tampa Bay to the E by an airport landing strip.
MAJOR UNITS: US Coast Guard Group St Petersburg.
BASE HISTORY: 1928, originally commissioned on S side of Bayboro Harbor. Air Station relocated to Clearwater. 1976, Station moved to vacated Air Station facilities across harbor. Old site, still part of station, serves as South Moorings for USCGC *Steadfast*, USCGC *Decisive*, USCGC *White Sumas*, and USCGC *Vise*. Old Station office building serves as Reserve training facility. Group Offices co located at Station. Missions: search and rescue, law enforcement, and industrial support.
Key Contacts
COMMANDER: Capt B C Sonner.
PUBLIC AFFAIRS: Lt Patterson; (813) 893-3454 ext 535.
PROCUREMENT: CWO Waechter.
TRANSPORTATION: See Procurement Officer.

Personnel and Expenditures
ACTIVE DUTY PERSONNEL: 120
CIVILIAN PERSONNEL: 6
Services *Commissary and Exchange:* Retail store; Barber shop; Food shop. *Medical Facilities:* Medical clinic; Dental clinic. *Recreational Facilities:* Pool; NCO club.

STARKE

CAMP BLANDING TRAINING SITE
Rte 1, Box 465, Starke, FL 32091-9703
(904) 533-2268; Autovon 960-3100
OFFICER-OF-THE-DAY: (904) 533-3356, Autovon 960-3356
Profile
BRANCH: Army National Guard.
SIZE AND LOCATION: 30,000 acres. In N central FL, off State Rd 16, 5 mi E of Starke, on Kingsley Lake.
MAJOR UNITS: 653rd Engineer Detachment (Utilities); 107th Public Affairs Detachment; 221st Ordnance Detachment; Florida National Guard Military Academy (FNGMA); 202nd Civil Engineering Squadron (CES), Florida Air National Guard; Headquarters and Headquarters Detachment, 3rd Battalion, 20th Special Forces Group (Airborne); Support Company, 3rd Battalion; 20th Special Forces Group (Airborne); Health Services Liaison Detachment (HSLD); 253rd Medical Detachment; 853rd Supply and Service Company; US Property and Fiscal Office (USPFO) Warehouse; State Maintenance Office (SMO); Combined Support Maintenance Shop (CSMS); Mobilization and Training Equipment Site (MATES).
BASE HISTORY: Site already location of FL NGs, Camp Foster. 1939, named for Lt Gen Albert H Blanding, distinguished FL soldier. 1940, leased to Army as active duty training center. During WWII, served as infantry replacement training center, induction center, POW compound, and separation center. Following WWII, 30,000 acres returned to armory board. 1950-70, limited use by military. 1970s, expansion began. 1981, redesignated as Class A military installation. Parachute drop zone and airfield expanded training capacity; Navy uses bombing and strafing target in southern portion of post. E I DuPont de Nemours and Co mines restricted area on western edge of post where ilmenite and other heavy minerals found.
VISITOR ATTRACTIONS: Camp Blanding Museum of World War II (Under construction, opening date Nov 1990).
Key Contacts
COMMANDER: Col James E Rogers.
PUBLIC AFFAIRS: Maj Douglass F Wiles; 601 Peggy Pl, St Augustine, FL 32086, (904) 829-2201, Autovon 797-3210.
PROCUREMENT: Maj Drexel Bullivant; (904) 533-3507, Autovon 960-3507.
PERSONNEL/COMMUNITY ACTIVITIES: LTC Samuel Smithers; (904) 533-3378, Autovon 960-3378.
Personnel and Expenditures
ACTIVE DUTY PERSONNEL: 75
CIVILIAN PERSONNEL: 50
Services *Temporary Housing:* VIP cottages 3; Officer/enlisted quarters for temporary use during training 80. *Commissary and Exchange:* Retail store; Barber shop; Tailor. *Medical Facilities:* Medical clinic. *Recreational Facilities:* Tennis; Racquetball; Softball field; Football field; Officers club; NCO club; Camping; Fishing/Hunting; Water sports; Picnicking.

SUGARLOAF SHORES

CUDJOE KEY AIR FORCE STATION
PO Box 800, Sugarloaf Shores, FL 33044-0046
(305) 292-3121
Profile
BRANCH: Air Force.
SIZE AND LOCATION: 65 acres. Off US Rte 1 on FL Keys approx 30 mi N of Key West; 130 mi S of Homestead AFB; at end of State Rd 5 (unmarked) on N side of US 1 by mile marker 21.5.
MAJOR UNITS: Detachment 3, Southeast Air Defense Sector.
BASE HISTORY: 1959, activated as missile tracking station for Eglin Test Range. 1960, designated Cudjoe Key AFS. 1967, transferred to AF Security Service. 1971, reassigned to Aerospace Defense Command for testing of medium range balloon-borne radar surveillance system, Seek Skyhook. 1980, fully operational continuous air defense radar surveillance. 1982, Project Seek Skyhook redesignated Tethered Aerostat Radar System (TARS). Detachment 3, Operation Location AM, 20th Air Defense Squadron went through several redesignations until receiving current designation, 1987.
Key Contacts
COMMANDER: Capt Norman D Potter.
PUBLIC AFFAIRS: SSgt Edwin R Hernandez Sr; Information Specialist.
Personnel and Expenditures
CIVILIAN PERSONNEL: 42
CONTRACT EXPENDITURE: $3.7 mil

TALLAHASSEE

NAVAL & MARINE CORPS RESERVE CENTER, TALLAHASSEE
2910 Roberts Ave, Tallahassee, FL 32310-5098
(904) 576-6194
Profile
BRANCH: Marines; Naval Reserve.
SIZE AND LOCATION: 2.71 acres. Downtown Tallahassee.
MAJOR UNITS: Naval Reserve; Marine Corps Reserve.
Key Contacts
COMMANDER: G A Dacosta.
PROCUREMENT: SK2 D O Green.
Personnel and Expenditures
ACTIVE DUTY PERSONNEL: 14
Services *Recreational Facilities:* Gym.

TAMPA

TAMPA COAST GUARD MARINE SAFETY OFFICE
155 Columbia Dr, Tampa, FL 33606
(813) 228-2191
Profile
BRANCH: Coast Guard.
SIZE AND LOCATION: Offices only. In city of Tampa.
MAJOR UNITS: Marine Safety Office, Tampa.
BASE HISTORY: Jurisdiction encompasses almost entire W coast of FL from Stake Point in N to Everglades City on S and extending inland generally to center of state.
Personnel and Expenditures
ACTIVE DUTY PERSONNEL: 36
CIVILIAN PERSONNEL: 2

TYNDALL AFB

TYNDALL AIR FORCE BASE
Tyndall AFB, FL 32403-5000
(904) 283-1110; Autovon 523-1110
OFFICER-OF-THE-DAY: (904) 283-1110, Autovon 523-1110
Profile
BRANCH: Air Force.
SIZE AND LOCATION: 29,000 acres. 12 mi E of Panama City, FL on US Hwy 98; Bay Co/Panama City Municipal Airport approx 15 mi.
MAJOR UNITS: USAF Air Defense Weapons Center (Tactical Air Command Unit); Southeast Air Defense Sector (TAC); Air Force Engineering and Services Center (SOA); 3625th Technical Training Squadron (ATC).
BASE HISTORY: 1941, commissioned as Air Corps' first flexible gunnery school named for Lt Frank B Tyndall, native of FL and WWI flying ace. 1946, home of Air University's Air Tactical School. 1950, training all weather jet interceptor pilots and air weapons controllers. 1957, transferred to Air Defense Command shifting mission to weapons center. 1968, Air Defense Weapons Center activated. 1979, transferred to TAC. 1981, 325th Fighter Weapons Wing (later renamed 325th Tactical Training Wing) activated. Home of Air Force Air-to-Air Weapons Meet, William Tell, since 1958. 1983, TAC's first Region Operations Control Center (ROCC) established. Today, Tyndall continues its training role.
VISITOR ATTRACTIONS: Located in a resort area with unlimited fresh and salt water activities available.
Key Contacts
COMMANDER: Maj Gen Richard M Pascoe, USAF; Commander USAF ADWC/CC, (904) 283-4271, Autovon 523-4271.
PUBLIC AFFAIRS: Maj Charles G Merlo; USAF ADWC/PA, (904) 283-2983, Autovon 523-2983.
PROCUREMENT: Capt Victor H Burke, Contracting Officer; USAF ADWC/LGC, (904) 283-3266, Autovon 523-3266.
TRANSPORTATION: Maj Mark D Moncure; USAF ADWC/LGT, (904) 283-2304, Autovon 523-2304.
PERSONNEL/COMMUNITY ACTIVITIES: LTC Leslie M Dula; Director of Personnel, 325 MSSQ/CC, (904) 283-3241, Autovon 523-3241, (Community Activities see Public Affairs).
Personnel and Expenditures
ACTIVE DUTY PERSONNEL: 4600
DEPENDENTS: 3500
CIVILIAN PERSONNEL: 1900
MILITARY PAYROLL EXPENDITURE: $147 mil
CONTRACT EXPENDITURE: $40 mil
Services *Housing:* Family units 1070; Duplex units; Townhouse units; RV/Camper sites 24. *Temporary Housing:* VOQ cottages 239; VAQ units 694; BAQ units 48; Guesthouse units 40. *Commissary:* Base commissary; Retail store; Barber shop; Dry cleaners; Food shop; Florist; Service station; Bakery. *Child Care/Capacities:* Day care center 178; Home day care program. *Schools:* Kindergarten/Preschool; Elementary. *Base Library:* Yes. *Medical Facilities:* Hospital 40; Medical clinic; Dental clinic. *Recreational Facilities:* Bowling; Movie theater; Pool; Gym; Recreation center; Golf; Stables; Tennis; Racquetball; Fitness center; Softball field; Football field; Auto shop; Crafts; Officers club; NCO club; Camping; Fishing/Hunting.

YANKEETOWN

YANKEETOWN COAST GUARD STATION
Yankeetown, FL 32698
(904) 447-2657
Profile
BRANCH: Coast Guard.
LOCATION: Houseboat on Withalachoochee River, approx 3.5 mi from Gulf of Mexico; approx 3 mi from US Hwy 19.
MAJOR UNITS: USCG Station, Yankeetown.
BASE HISTORY: 1963, houseboat (61 ft long and 28 ft beam) built and commissioned CG Lifeboat Station Islamorada, FL. 1975, houseboat refurbished and recommissioned Station Yankeetown; responsible for search and rescue, law enforcement, and aids to navigation from Bayport to Fenholloway River, FL. Permanent station being built to replace houseboat.
Key Contacts
COMMANDER: Chief Boatswain's Mate, Officer in Charge.
PUBLIC AFFAIRS: See USCG Group/Station, St Petersburg, FL.
Personnel and Expenditures
ACTIVE DUTY PERSONNEL: 22
Services *Housing:* Crew's quarters only. *Recreational Facilities:* Recreation center (ping pong); Fishing/Hunting; Basketball; Volleyball.

GEORGIA

ALBANY

ALBANY MARINE CORPS LOGISTICS BASE

MCLB, Albany, GA 31704-5000
(912) 439-5202; Autovon 567-5202
OFFICER-OF-THE-DAY: (912) 439-5206,
Autovon 567-5206
Profile
BRANCH: Marines.
SIZE AND LOCATION: 3330 acres. In the SE
corner of Albany; accessible from US
Hwy 19; road signs mark the way to the
base; the Albany/Dougherty County Air-
port is approx 12 mi SW of Albany.
MAJOR UNITS: Headquarters Battalion; Morale, Welfare and Recreation Division;
Facilities and Services Division; Comptroller Directorate; Executive Director for
Logistics Operations; Integrated Logistics
Support Directorate; Storage and Distribution Directorate; Contracts Directorate;
Maintenance Directorate; Information Resources Management Directorate.
BASE HISTORY: 1952, commissioned as Marine Corps Depot of Supplies. 1954, large
depot repair facility completed; command
renamed Marine Corps Supply Center.
1954-1967, managed and controlled supplies at storage and issue locations in
eastern half of US, Atlantic, Caribbean
and Mediterranean areas. 1976, renamed
Marine Corps Logistics Support Base, Atlantic. 1978, given present name. Serves
as Inventory Control Point of Marine
Corps.
VISITOR ATTRACTIONS: Indian Lake Wildlife
Refuge is dedicated to the American Indian, who used the area as a hunting
ground. Deer, bobcat, raccoon, opossum,
and waterfowl are protected inside the
refuge, however, fishing and boating are
permitted. The refuge is open year-round
to MCLB personnel and tour groups on
request.
Key Contacts
COMMANDER: Maj Gen J E Cassity; Commanding General (Code 1), (912) 439-
5201, Autovon 567-5201.
PUBLIC AFFAIRS: CWO-2 T R Bennett; Public
Affairs Officer (Code 130), (912) 439-
5215, Autovon 567-5215.
PROCUREMENT: Charles Nobes; Principal Director, Contracts Directorate (Code 90),
(912) 439-6735, Autovon 567-6735.
TRANSPORTATION: Linda Weaver; Housing
and Transportation Officer (Code 873/
2A), (912) 439-5823, 439-5824, 439-5817,
Autovon 567-5823, 567-5824, 567-5817.
PERSONNEL/COMMUNITY ACTIVITIES: See Pub-
lic Affairs Officer.
Personnel and Expenditures
ACTIVE DUTY PERSONNEL: 1200
DEPENDENTS: 1217
CIVILIAN PERSONNEL: 2800

MILITARY PAYROLL EXPENDITURE: $25.3 mil
CONTRACT EXPENDITURE: $133 mil
Services *Housing:* Family units 685; BOQ
cottages 13; Barracks spaces 522; Senior
NCO units 43; Trailer spaces 20. *Temporary
Housing:* VIP cottages 3; BOQ units 6; BAQ
units 4; Transient living quarters 4. *Commissary:* Base commissary; Retail store; Bar-
ber shop; Dry cleaners; Food shop; Banking;
Service station. *Child Care/Capacities:* Day
care center 3 centers, 130 children; Home
day care program. *Schools:* Kindergarten/
Preschool. *Base Library:* Yes. *Medical Facilities:* Medical clinic; Dental clinic; Local civilian hospitals provide in-patient care. *Recreational Facilities:* Bowling; Movie theater;
Pool; Gym; Recreation center; Golf; Tennis;
Racquetball; Fitness center; Softball field;
Football field; Auto shop; Officers club;
NCO club; Fishing/Hunting; Soccer.

ATHENS

NAVY SUPPLY CORPS SCHOOL

Athens, GA 30606-5000
(404) 354-1500; Autovon 588-7305
OFFICER-OF-THE-DAY: (404) 354-1500,
Autovon 588-7305
Profile
BRANCH: Navy.
SIZE AND LOCATION: 58 acres. Corner of
Prince and Oglethorpe Aves, Athens GA;
65 mi NE of Atlanta.
MAJOR UNITS: Navy Supply Corps School.
BASE HISTORY: Located in Athens since 1954,
sole training location where Navy Supply
Corps officers receive basic supply corps
qualification training. In addition, 17 oth-
er courses of instruction taught at school
including US Marine Corps Aviation Sup-
ply Officer Qualification Course.
VISITOR ATTRACTIONS: Navy Supply Corps
Museum.
Key Contacts
COMMANDER: Capt L J Sapera; (404) 354-
7200, Autovon 588-7200.
PUBLIC AFFAIRS: Lt S H Powell; Code 61,
(404) 354-7316, Autovon 588-7316.
PROCUREMENT: CWO3 J Roth; Code 62,
(404) 354-7329, Autovon 588-7329.
TRANSPORTATION: See Procurement Officer.
PERSONNEL/COMMUNITY ACTIVITIES: R
White; Director of Civilian Personnel,
Code 04, (404) 354-7308, Autovon 588-
7308.
Personnel and Expenditures
ACTIVE DUTY PERSONNEL: 120 staff, 300 stu-
dents
DEPENDENTS: 500
CIVILIAN PERSONNEL: 150
MILITARY PAYROLL EXPENDITURE: $9 mil
CONTRACT EXPENDITURE: $3 mil

Services *Housing:* Family units 56; BEQ
units 25. *Temporary Housing:* BOQ units
150. *Commissary:* Base commissary; Retail
store; Barber shop; Service station. *Child
Care/Capacities:* Day care center 25. *Base
Library:* Yes. *Medical Facilities:* Medical
clinic; Dental clinic. *Recreational Facilities:*
Pool; Gym; Tennis; Racquetball; Fitness center; Softball field; Officers club; Enlisted
Club.

ATLANTA

GEORGIA DEPARTMENT OF DEFENSE, MILITARY DIVISION

PO Box 17965, Office of the Adjutant
General, Atlanta, GA 30316-0965
(404) 624-6000
Profile
BRANCH: Air National Guard; Army National
Guard.
SIZE: Offices only.
Key Contacts
COMMANDER: Maj Gen Joseph W Griffin.

US ARMY CORPS OF ENGINEERS, SOUTH ATLANTIC DIVISION

510 Title Bldg, Atlanta, GA 30303
(404) 221-6711
Profile
BRANCH: Army.
SIZE: Offices only.
Key Contacts
COMMANDER: Maj Gen Robert M Bunker;
Division Engineer.

DOBBINS AFB

DOBBINS AIR FORCE BASE

HQ 94 Tactical Airlift Wing, Dobbins AFB,
GA 30069-5000
(404) 421-5055; Autovon 925-5055
Profile
BRANCH: Air Force; Air National Guard.
SIZE AND LOCATION: 1800 acres. In Marietta,
GA, 16 mi NW of Atlanta.
MAJOR UNITS: 94th Tactical Airlift Wing;
14th Air Force; 94th Combat Support
Group; 128th Tactical Fighter Squadron
of the 116th Tactical Fighter Wing; Geor-
gia Army Reserve; Georgia National
Guard; Naval Air Station Atlanta; Naval
Attack Squadron VA-205; Marine Air
Group 46, Detachment; 700th Tactical
Airlift Squadron; 94th Consolidated
Maintenance Squadron; Air Force Re-
serve Transportation Proficiency Center;
The Heavy Equipment School; Prime
Ribs (a portable field kitchen training de-
tachment); 79th APS; 80th MAPS; 94th
CES; 94th CS (DDMS); 94th SPF; 94th
MSF; 94th TAC Hosp; 64th AEF; 2185
Com Group.

DOBBINS AIR FORCE BASE *(continued)*

BASE HISTORY: 1943, built as Rickenbacker Field. 1950, named for Capt Charles Dobbins, flyer from Marietta killed, 1943. Hosts 94th Combat Support Group which maintains facilities; busiest Air Reserve training base in world; owned by Air Force Reserve; supports more than 5000 Air National Guardsmen and Reservists from Army, Navy, Air Force, and Marines; Lockheed-Georgia Co shares runways, control tower, and weather facilities.

VISITOR ATTRACTIONS: Closed to public.

Key Contacts

COMMANDER: Col William F Haber, USAFR; 94 CSG/CC.

PUBLIC AFFAIRS: Capt Robert D Coffman, Jr; 94 CSG/PA.

Personnel and Expenditures

ACTIVE DUTY PERSONNEL: 66 active duty, 5000 Guardsmen and Reservists

CIVILIAN PERSONNEL: 2000

Services *Housing:* BOQ cottages; BAQ units; RV/Camper sites. *Temporary Housing:* VOQ cottages 1; VAQ units 1. *Commissary and Exchange:* Retail store; Barber shop; Banking. *Medical Facilities:* Navy Medical and Dental Clinics. *Recreational Facilities:* Gym; Recreation center; Tennis; Racquetball; Softball field; Camping.

FOREST PARK

FORT GILLEM

Forest Park, GA 30050-5000
(404) 362-7311; Autovon 797-7311
OFFICER-OF-THE-DAY: (404) 752-2980, Autovon 572-2980

Profile

BRANCH: Army.

SIZE AND LOCATION: 1500 acres. 15 min S of downtown Atlanta off I-75 and I-85. - Hartsfield IAP is 15 min W; installation is just outside Exchange 285 which goes around Atlanta and just off Bypass 675 which connects I-75 to 285 and I-85.

MAJOR UNITS: Second US Army; HQ, US Army Criminal Investigation Laboratory; 3rd Region US Army Criminal Investigation Division Command; 2d Recruiting Bde; HQ, 547th Explosive Ordnance Disposal Control Center; 13th Explosive Ordnance Disposal Detachment; Army and Air Force Exchange System Distribution Center; Atlanta Readiness Group; US Army Troop Support Agency.

BASE HISTORY: 1941, began Atlanta General Army Depot moved Candler Warehouse to what is now Ft Gillem. Depot saw many name changes as it served as trainer and supplier. 1973, responsibility transferred from Army Materiel Command to Forces Command; renamed Ft Gillem; subpost of Ft McPherson; named for Lt Gen Alvan C Gillem Jr, who began as private at Ft McPherson in 1910 and retired as commanding general 3rd US Army, now headquartered at Ft McPherson. Serves as staging area for Red Cross Disaster Action Team and storage space for federally-owned house trailers to be used as temporary homes in national emergency.

Key Contacts

COMMANDER: Col Gerald Lord; HQ Ft McPherson, Garrison Commander, Bldg 65, Ft McPherson, GA 30330-5000, (404) 752-2206, Autovon 572-2206; LTC Michael R Stewart; Deputy Garrison Commander, Ft Gillem.

PUBLIC AFFAIRS: Robert Bolia; Bldg 65, Ft McPherson, GA 30330-5000, (404) 752-2204, Autovon 572-2204.

Personnel and Expenditures

ACTIVE DUTY PERSONNEL: 737

CIVILIAN PERSONNEL: 3317

MILITARY PAYROLL EXPENDITURE: $77 mil (includes Ft McPherson)

CONTRACT EXPENDITURE: $98 mil (includes Ft McPherson)

Services *Housing:* Family units (Officer and NCO sets) 10; BOQ cottages 18; Barracks spaces 70; Senior NCO units 48. *Temporary Housing:* VIP cottages 1; Transient living quarters Officer or enlisted 6. *Commissary:* Base commissary; Retail store; Barber shop; Dry cleaners; Food shop; Banking; Personal items; Credit union. *Medical Facilities:* Branch pharmacy. *Recreational Facilities:* Pool; Gym; Tennis; Racquetball; Fitness center; Softball field; Officers club; NCO club; Camping; Fishing/Hunting; Recreation area at Lake Lanier; Marchman and Stevens recreational lakes with picnicking; Soccer field (formerly Morris Airfield); Skeet shooting.

FORT BENNING

FORT BENNING

HQ, US Army Infantry Center, Fort Benning, GA 31905
(404) 544-2011; Autovon 784-2011
OFFICER-OF-THE-DAY: (404) 545-2218, Autovon 835-2218

Profile

BRANCH: Army.

SIZE AND LOCATION: 182,000 acres. I-85 S runs into Ft Benning less than 1 mi S of Columbus, GA.

MAJOR UNITS: 197th Infantry Brigade; 1st Infantry Engineering Brigade; 2d Infantry Engineering Brigade; 29th Infantry Regiment; 30th Adjutant Battalion; 36th Engineering Group; 34th Medical Battalion.

BASE HISTORY: 1918, began with move of School of Musketry (later, Infantry School of Arms) from Ft Sill, OK, to Camp Benning; known as "Home of the Infantry," named for Confederate Maj Gen Henry Lewis Benning; original site proved unsuitable; Bussey Plantation, S of Columbus, purchased. Following WWI, camp abandoned. 1922, camp renamed Ft Benning; permanent construction of Infantry School began. 1930s, Public Works Administration, Works Progress Administration, and Civilian Conservation Corps built new buildings; Tank School moved from Ft Meade; Officer Candidate Program; and Parachute School. 1950, Ranger Training Command organized. 1958, Martin Army Hospital opened. 1961, airborne training consolidated at Infantry School. 1970, Army Training School closed; HQ, US Army Infantry Center, reorganized under CONUS Installation Management Study (CIMS). Following Vietnam Conflict, activities phased down; emphasis shifted to more conventional warfare, especially VOLAR concept (Volunteer Army).

VISITOR ATTRACTIONS: Infantry Museum; Airborne and Ranger shows.

Key Contacts

COMMANDER: Maj Gen K C Leuer; (404) 545-5111, Autovon 835-5111.

PUBLIC AFFAIRS: R S Moore; ATZB-PAO, Ft Benning, GA 31905-5065, (404) 545-2236, Autovon 835-2236.

PROCUREMENT: R Bollinger; (404) 545-1716, Autovon 835-1716.

TRANSPORTATION: W Wilson; (404) 545-4788, Autovon 835-4788.

PERSONNEL/COMMUNITY ACTIVITIES: Col C Boterweg; (404) 545-1511, Autovon 835-1511.

Personnel and Expenditures

ACTIVE DUTY PERSONNEL: 27,090

DEPENDENTS: 11,339

CIVILIAN PERSONNEL: 9815

MILITARY PAYROLL EXPENDITURE: $409 mil

CONTRACT EXPENDITURE: $130 mil

Services *Housing:* Family units 4082; Barracks spaces 25,005; RV/Camper sites 40. *Temporary Housing:* VIP cottages 16; VOQ cottages 1319; VEQ units 273; BOQ units 48; Guesthouse units 34. *Commissary:* Base commissary; Retail store; Barber shop; Food shop; Banking; Service station; Book store. *Child Care/Capacities:* Day care center 244. *Schools:* Elementary; Intermediate/Junior high; High school. *Base Library:* Yes. *Medical Facilities:* Hospital 347; Medical clinic; Dental clinic. *Recreational Facilities:* Bowling; Movie theater; Pool; Gym; Recreation center; Golf; Stables; Racquetball; Fitness center; Auto shop; Crafts; Officers club; NCO club; Camping; Fishing/Hunting.

FORT GORDON

FORT GORDON

US Army Signal Center & Fort Gordon, Fort Gordon, GA 30905-5000
(404) 791-0110; Autovon 780-4517
OFFICER-OF-THE-DAY: (404) 791-4517, Autovon 780-4517

Profile

BRANCH: Army.

SIZE AND LOCATION: 55,588 acres. 15 mi SW of Augusta, GA.

MAJOR UNITS: US Army Signal Center; Eisenhower Army Medical Center.

BASE HISTORY: 1941, Camp Gordon, named for Confederate Lt Gen John Brown Gordon, activated for infantry and armor training. WWII, divisional training base for 4th and 26th Infantry Divisions and 10th Armored Division, US Disciplinary Barracks and POW camp for German and Italian captives. Almost deserted after WWII. 1948, Signal Corps Training Center, Military Police School, and Engineer Aviation Unit Training Center. 1950s, Military Government Training, Army Criminal Investigation Laboratory, Rehabilitation Training Center, and US Disciplinary Barracks added. 1953, Basic Replacement Training Center and Advanced Leader's School established. 1956, made permanent Army installation and designated Ft Gordon. 1957-58, US Army Training Center (Basic) and Civil Affairs School activated. During Vietnam War, infantry, military police and signal soldiers trained. 1962, Signal Corps Training Center reorganized under US Army Southeastern Signal School. 1974, communications training consolidated at Ft Gordon with relocation of Signal School from Ft Monmouth, NJ. Presently world's largest communications electronics facility.

VISITOR ATTRACTIONS: Signal Museum.

Key Contacts

COMMANDER: Maj Gen Leo M Childs; (404) 791-4588, Autovon 780-4588.

PUBLIC AFFAIRS: Maj Harry S Ritter; Public Affairs Office, Ft Gordon, GA 30905-5283, (404) 791-7003, Autovon 780-7003.

PROCUREMENT: Patricia D Wallace, Acting Director; (404) 791-2249, Autovon 780-2249.

TRANSPORTATION: Maj Winton W Hunter; (404) 791-5186, Autovon 780-5186.

PERSONNEL/COMMUNITY ACTIVITIES: Col Kenneth C Griffith; (404) 791-4140, Autovon 780-4140.

Personnel and Expenditures

ACTIVE DUTY PERSONNEL: 14,451

DEPENDENTS: 2746

CIVILIAN PERSONNEL: 4409

FORT GORDON *(continued)*
MILITARY PAYROLL EXPENDITURE: $324 mil
CONTRACT EXPENDITURE: $32 mil
Services *Housing:* Family units 877; Barracks spaces 10,746. *Temporary Housing:* VIP cottages 5; VOQ cottages 371; VEQ units 170; Guesthouse units 91. *Commissary:* Base commissary; Retail store; Barber shop; Dry cleaners; Food shop; Florist; Banking (not part of exchange); Service station; Bakery. *Child Care/Capacities:* Day care center 324; Home day care program. *Base Library:* Yes. *Medical Facilities:* Hospital 465; Medical clinic; Dental clinic. *Recreational Facilities:* Bowling; Movie theater; Pool; Gym; Recreation center; Golf; Stables; Tennis; Racquetball; Fitness center; Softball field; Football field; Auto shop; Crafts; Officers club; NCO club; Camping; Fishing/Hunting; Recreation area at Lake Thurmond; Dinner theater.

FORT MCPHERSON

FORT MCPHERSON
Fort McPherson, GA 30330
(404) 752-2980; Autovon 572-1110
OFFICER-OF-THE-DAY: (404) 752-3602,
  Autovon 572-3602
Profile
BRANCH: Army.
SIZE AND LOCATION: 483 acres. Borders the southern portion of the city of Atlanta and is about 10 min from downtown and 10 min from the airport.
MAJOR UNITS: US Forces Command Headquarters; 3rd US Army Headquarters.
BASE HISTORY: Named after Civil War Gen James Birdseye McPherson, who died nearby. 1889, permanent Army station. Spanish-American War, served as General Hospital, jail for spies, Spanish POWs, and recruit training center. 1914, troop garrison ordered to TX and post nearly abandoned. WWI, again served as General Hospital and War Prison Barracks. 1920-1923 and 1927-1934, HQ for IV Corps Area and 8th Infantry Brigade and 22nd Infantry Regiment, last major troop regiment stationed at post. Along southern boundary of post, Camp Jessup, automobile depot, established (1927, incorporated into Fort). 1930s, hospital expanded and post known as rehabilitation center. WWII, served as hospital center, general supply depot and reception center for processing recruits (later major separation center). 1947, home of Third US Army. 1973, reorganization brought US Army Forces Command (FORSCOM). 1974, Ft Gillem, GA, designated subinstallation and in 1977, Ft Buchanan, PR. 1982, Third US Army reactivated Army component headquarters for US Central Command.
VISITOR ATTRACTIONS: The post historic district features 40 buildings on the National Register of Historic Places which date from 1887-1910.
Key Contacts
COMMANDER: Col Gerald Lord; (404) 752-2206, Autovon 572-2206.
PUBLIC AFFAIRS: Robert Bolia; (404) 752-2204, Autovon 572-2204.
PROCUREMENT: T W Corley; Director of Contracting, (404) 752-3316, Autovon 572-3316.
TRANSPORTATION: LTC G A Sirois; Director of Logistics, (404) 752-2802, Autovon 572-2802.
PERSONNEL/COMMUNITY ACTIVITIES: LTC H T Williams; (404) 752-3915, Autovon 572-3915.

Personnel and Expenditures
ACTIVE DUTY PERSONNEL: 2649 (includes Ft Gillem)
DEPENDENTS: 8386 (includes Ft Gillem)
CIVILIAN PERSONNEL: 9018 (includes Ft Gillem)
MILITARY PAYROLL EXPENDITURE: $77 mil (includes Ft Gillem)
CONTRACT EXPENDITURE: $98 mil (includes Ft Gillem)
Services *Housing:* Family units 99. *Temporary Housing:* VIP cottages (suites) 6; Guesthouse units 51. *Commissary:* Base commissary; Retail store; Barber shop; Dry cleaners; Florist; Banking; Service station. *Child Care/Capacities:* Day care center 116. *Base Library:* Yes. *Medical Facilities:* Medical clinic. *Recreational Facilities:* Bowling; Pool; Gym; Recreation center; Golf; Tennis; Racquetball; Fitness center; Softball field; Football field; Auto shop; Crafts; Officers club; NCO club.

GARDEN CITY

TRAVIS FIELD
PO Box 7568, Savannah International Airport, Garden City, GA 31498
(912) 964-1941; Autovon 860-8210
OFFICER-OF-THE-DAY: (912) 964-1941
Profile
BRANCH: Air National Guard.
LOCATION: At Savannah IAP, Garden City, GA, approx 2 mi N of Savannah.
MAJOR UNITS: Headquarters Georgia Air National Guard; 165th Tactical Airlift Group; 117th Tactical Control Squadron; 283rd Combat Communications Squadron.
BASE HISTORY: 1946, 165th Tactical Airlift Group began at Travis Field (Chatham Field at that time) as 158th Fighter Squadron. 1949, 158th moved to Hunter Field until activated during Korean Conflict, 1950; stationed at Misawa AFB, Japan. 1952, returned to Travis Field and placed on Air Guard status. 1962, became 158th Air Transport Squadron assigned to 165th Air Transport Group. 1967, assigned to MAC. 1975, unit designated 165th TAG.
Key Contacts
COMMANDER: Col Douglas M Padgett.
PUBLIC AFFAIRS: Maj Sylvester Brown.
PERSONNEL/COMMUNITY ACTIVITIES: See Public Affairs Officer.
Personnel and Expenditures
ACTIVE DUTY PERSONNEL: 1470
CIVILIAN PERSONNEL: 30
Services *Housing:* Field Training Site. *Temporary Housing:* VIP cottages 2; Field Training Site. *Commissary and Exchange:* Retail store. *Medical Facilities:* Clinic only on weekends.

HINESVILLE

FORT STEWART
Fort Stewart, Hinesville, GA 31314-5000
(921) 767-1411, Avutovon 870-1110
OFFICER-OF-THE-DAY: (912) 767-8666,
  Autovon 870-8666
Profile
BRANCH: Army.
SIZE AND LOCATION: 279,270. 41 mi SW of Savannah; near US 17, I-16, and I-95; bisected by GA hwy 144, 119, and US 17; Savannah and Jessup are served by Amtrak; Hinesville is 1 mi from main gate; Claxton is 37 mi NW; Glenville is 19 mi; Pembroke is 18 mi N; Richmond Hill is midway between post and Savannah; Ludowici is 13 mi SW of post.

MAJOR UNITS: 24th Infantry Division (Mechanized); 1st Battalion, 75th Ranger Division; Victory Brigade; 92nd Engineer Battalion; 260th Quartermaster Battalion; 224th Military Intelligence Battalion (Aerial Exploitation).
BASE HISTORY: Camp Stewart activated June 1940 as Anti-aircraft Artillery Center. After WWII, separation center of redeployed troops and later inactive. 1950, reopened as Third Army Anti-aircraft Artillery Training Center; 1953, tank training added; 1956, became permanent military installation, Ft Stewart Anti-aircraft Artillery and Tank Training Center. 1966, Army Aviation School relocated from Ft Rucker, AL; new mission, helicopter gunnery courses and helicopter pilot. 1971, designation changed to US Army Garrison, Ft Stewart. 1974, home to infantry units; 1975, 24th Infantry Division, the Victory Division, officially activated at Stewart's Donovan Field, motto "First to Fight." The heavy element of 18th Airborne, of Rapid Deployment Forces (RDF). Largest Army installation E of Mississippi River.
VISITOR ATTRACTIONS: 24th Infantry Division and Ft Stewart Museum
Key Contacts
COMMANDER: Maj Gen H G Taylor; Commander, 24th Inf Div (Mech), ATTN AFZP-CG, (912) 767-5606, Autovon 870-5606.
PUBLIC AFFAIRS: Maj Donald W Keeling; Commander, 24th Inf Div (Mech), ATTN AFZP-PO, (912) 767-7833, Autovon 870-8666.
PROCUREMENT: Nolan E Purcell; Director of Contracting, Commander, 24th Inf Div (Mech), ATTN AFZP-DC, (912) 767-8420, Autovon 870-8420.
TRANSPORTATION: Harry E Scott; Chief of Transportation Division, Commander, 24th Inf Div (Mech), ATTN AFZP-DLT, (912) 767-3377, Autovon 870-3377.
PERSONNEL/COMMUNITY ACTIVITIES: LTC Gregory W Dyson; Commander, 24th Inf Div (Mech), ATTN AFZP-PA, (912) 767-5065; 767-2401, Autovon 870-5065; 870-2401.
Personnel and Expenditures
ACTIVE DUTY PERSONNEL: 15,000
DEPENDENTS: 14,000
MILITARY PAYROLL EXPENDITURE: $347.8 mil
CONTRACT EXPENDITURE: $50.8 mil
Services *Housing:* Family units 227; BOQ cottages 2700; Duplex units; Townhouse units; Barracks spaces 9591; Trailer spaces 109. *Temporary Housing:* VIP cottages 4; Guesthouse units 70; Transient living quarters 75; Temporary duty personnel without families at Hunter AAF 13. *Commissary:* Base commissary; Retail store; Barber shop; Dry cleaners; Food shop; Florist; Banking; Service station; Bakery; Book store; Military clothing sales; Car rental; Ice cream parlor; Optical shop; Tailor shop; Photo store; Video rental; Watch repair shop. *Child Care/Capacities:* Day care center 300; Home day care program. *Schools:* Kindergarten/Preschool; Elementary. *Base Library:* Yes. *Medical Facilities:* Hospital 109. *Recreational Facilities:* Bowling; Movie theater; Pool; Gym; Recreation center; Golf; Stables; Tennis; Softball field; Fitness center; Softball field; Football field; Auto shop; Crafts; Officers club; NCO club; Camping; Fishing/Hunting; Enlisted club Performing arts center; Track; Skeet and trap ranges; Garden plots; Youth activities.

KENNESAW

129TH TACTICAL CONTROL SQUADRON

McColum Airport, Kennesaw, GA 30144
(404) 422-2500; Autovon 925-2474
Profile
BRANCH: Air National Guard.
SIZE AND LOCATION: 13 acres. 27 mi N of Atlanta; 10 mi from Dobbins AFB; off I-75.
MAJOR UNITS: 129th Tactical Control Squadron.
Personnel and Expenditures
ACTIVE DUTY PERSONNEL: 299
CIVILIAN PERSONNEL: 48

KINGS BAY

KINGS BAY NAVAL SUBMARINE BASE

Kings Bay, GA 31547-5000
(912) 673-2000; Autovon 860-2111
OFFICER-OF-THE-DAY: (912) 673-2020, Autovon 860-2020
Profile
BRANCH: Navy.
SIZE AND LOCATION: 16,000 acres. On the outskirts of St Marys, GA, about 5 mi E of I-95, Exits 1, 2, and 2A; nearby towns are Kingsland, about 8 mi W, and Woodbine, 18 mi N; nearest cities are Brunswick, GA, about 35 mi N and Jacksonville, FL, about 35 mi S.
MAJOR UNITS: Naval Submarine Base; TRIDENT Refit Facility; TRIDENT Training Facility; Strategic Weapons Facility, Atlantic; Submarine Squadron 16; Submarine Squadron 20; USS *Canopus* (AS34); USS *Oak Ridge* (ARDM 1).
BASE HISTORY: 1954-58, acquired by Army for military ocean terminal. Following completion placed in inactive ready status; Army base never activated. Used twice: 1964, shelter from Hurricane Dora; and, during Cuban Missile Crisis. Following withdrawal of Fleet Ballistic Missile Submarine Squadron from Rota, Spain, Kings Bay selected for relocation. 1978, base transferred from Army to Navy. 1982, name changed from Naval Submarine Support Base to Naval Submarine Base. Today, originally planned submarine support base nearly completed. Current facilities being expanded to serve as homeport, refit site, and training facility for next generation of strategic submarines.
Key Contacts
COMMANDER: Capt William F Ramsey.
PUBLIC AFFAIRS: (912) 673-4714, Autovon 860-4714.
Personnel and Expenditures
ACTIVE DUTY PERSONNEL: 2880
CIVILIAN PERSONNEL: 4599
CONTRACT EXPENDITURE: $20 mil
Services *Housing:* Family units 415; BEQ units 180; Barracks spaces 461. *Temporary Housing:* BOQ units 34; Lodge units 26. *Commissary:* Base commissary; Retail store; Barber shop; Dry cleaners; Food shop; Florist; Banking; Service station; Beauty shop; Post office. *Child Care/Capacities:* Day care center 99. *Base Library:* Yes. *Medical Facilities:* Medical clinic; Dental clinic. *Recreational Facilities:* Bowling; Movie theater; Pool; Gym; Tennis; Racquetball; Fitness center; Softball field; Football field; Auto shop; Crafts; Officers club; NCO club.

MARIETTA

ATLANTA NAVAL AIR STATION

Marietta, GA 30188
(404) 421-5392; Autovon 925-5392
OFFICER-OF-THE-DAY: (404) 421-5392, Autovon 925-5392
Profile
BRANCH: Naval Reserve.
SIZE AND LOCATION: 184 acres. In Marietta, GA, on Hwy 75, about 20 mi N of Atlanta between Marietta and Smyrna, adj to Dobbins AFB.
MAJOR UNITS: Naval Attack Squadron VA-205; Fleet Logistics Support Squadron VR-46; Marine Air Group 46, Detachment C; Marine Observation Squadron (VMO) Four; Marine Attack Helicopter Squadron (HMA) 773.
BASE HISTORY: Training center for Navy and Marine Corps Reservists; air station provides services, training and support for drilling reservists; NAS Atlanta adjacent to, but not part of, Dobbins AFB; shares runways with Dobbins AFB and Lockheed.
Key Contacts
COMMANDER: Capt Peter C Hunt; (404) 421-5413, Autovon 925-5413.
PUBLIC AFFAIRS: LTjg Morelan; (404) 421-5420, Autovon 925-5420.
PROCUREMENT: ATTN Supply Officer; (404) 421-5533, Autovon 925-5533.
TRANSPORTATION: Public Works Officer; (404) 421-5512, Autovon 925-5512.
PERSONNEL/COMMUNITY ACTIVITIES: Administration Officer; (404) 421-5418, Autovon 925-5418.
Personnel and Expenditures
ACTIVE DUTY PERSONNEL: 811
DEPENDENTS: 20
CIVILIAN PERSONNEL: 191
MILITARY PAYROLL EXPENDITURE: $20 mil
CONTRACT EXPENDITURE: $10 mil
Services *Housing:* Family units 10; Barracks spaces (bldgs) 2. *Temporary Housing:* VIP cottages 4; BOQ units (bldg) 1. *Commissary and Exchange:* Retail store; Barber shop; Food shop; Florist; Service station. *Child Care/Capacities:* Day care center 20. *Medical Facilities:* Medical clinic; Dental clinic. *Recreational Facilities:* Bowling; Pool; Recreation center; Tennis; Racquetball; Fitness center; Auto shop; Officers club; NCO club; Camping; Fishing/Hunting; Lakeside recreation site with cabins.

MOODY AFB

MOODY AIR FORCE BASE

347th Tactical Fighter Wing, Moody AFB, GA 31699-5000
(912) 333-4211; Autovon 460-4211
Profile
BRANCH: Air Force.
SIZE AND LOCATION: 5039 acres. 10 mi NE of Valdosta, GA, on GA-125. S on I-75, take Exit 7 to GA-122, travel E on GA-122 through Hahira, GA toward Lakeland, GA, turn right (S) onto GA-125 and travel 4 mi to base. N on I 75, take Exit 4 to US-84, travel east on US-84 (Hill Ave) to downtown Valdosta, turn left (N) onto GA-7 (Ashley St), follow Ashley St N to GA-125 (Bemiss Rd), stay in the extreme right-hand lane, 9 mi to base.
MAJOR UNITS: 347th Tactical Fighter Wing; 1878th Communications Squadron; 3751st Field Training Squadron, Detachment 322; 3rd Weather Squadron, Detachment 23; 4400th Management Engineering Squadron, Detachment 23; 4400th Management Engineering Squadron, Detachment 8; Air Force Office of Special Investigations.

BASE HISTORY: 1942, established as Moody Field Advanced Pilot Training School; named for Maj George Putnam Moody, early Air Force pioneer. 1946, placed on inactive status. 1951, reactivated for Korean conflict; Air Force Pilot Instrument School and Instrument Flying School. 1958, under Air Training Command training all weather interceptor pilots. 1960, pilot training combined into one element as 3550th Pilot Training Wing, later 38th Flying Training Wing. 1975, 347th TFW activated from Thailand.
Key Contacts
COMMANDER: Col Raymond Trusz; 347Combat Support Group/CC, (912) 333-3479, Autovon 460-3479.
PUBLIC AFFAIRS: Capt Cynthia M Nelson; 347TFW/PA, (912) 333-3395, Autovon 460-3395.
PROCUREMENT: 347TFW/LGC; (912) 333-3453, Autovon 460-3453.
TRANSPORTATION: 347TFW/LGT; (912) 333-3448, Autovon 460-3448.
PERSONNEL/COMMUNITY ACTIVITIES: 347TFW/PA; (912) 333-3282, Autovon 460-3395.
Personnel and Expenditures
ACTIVE DUTY PERSONNEL: 3326
DEPENDENTS: 4437
CIVILIAN PERSONNEL: 486
MILITARY PAYROLL EXPENDITURE: $71 mil
CONTRACT EXPENDITURE: $4 mil
Services *Housing:* Family units 34; Dormitory spaces 662; Senior NCO units 40; Junior NCO units 230; Trailer spaces 39. *Temporary Housing:* VOQ cottages 31; VEQ units 3; VAQ units 33; BOQ units 3; Apartment units 12; Transient living quarters 12. *Commissary:* Base commissary; Retail store; Barber shop; Dry cleaners; Food shop; Florist; Banking; Service station. *Child Care/Capacities:* Day care center 105. *Schools:* Preschool for 3 & 4 year olds only. *Base Library:* Yes. *Medical Facilities:* Hospital; Medical clinic; Dental clinic. *Recreational Facilities:* Bowling; Movie theater; Pool; Gym; Recreation center; Golf; Tennis; Racquetball; Fitness center; Softball field; Football field; Auto shop; Crafts; Officers club; NCO club; Camping; Fishing/Hunting.

ROBINS AFB

ROBINS AIR FORCE BASE

2853 ABG/CC, Robins AFB, GA 31098
(912) 926-1113; Autovon 468-1001
Profile
BRANCH: Air Force.
SIZE AND LOCATION: 8700 acres. Adj to Warner Robins, GA; 15 mi SE of Macon on Hwy GA 247.
MAJOR UNITS: Warner Robins Air Logistics Center; 2853 ABG; 19th Air Refueling Wing; Headquarters Air Force Reserve; 5th CCG; 9th MWS; 2955th CLSS.
BASE HISTORY: Early 1941, Army Air Corps established maintenance and supply depot. 1942, original construction completed and air depot named Wellston Air Depot. City of Wellston changed name to Warner Robins for Brig Gen Augustine Warner Robins, native of VA and chief of Materiel Division of Army Air Corps. 1942, depot redesignated Warner Robins Army Air Depot. Depot underwent other name changes: Warner Robins Air Depot Control Air Command; Warner Robins Air Service; Warner Robins Air Technical Service Command; and Warner Robins Air Materiel Area; and, current name Warner Robins Air Logistics Center, 1974. Installation remained Robins Field until 1948 when renamed Robins AFB.
VISITOR ATTRACTIONS: Museum of Aviation adjacent to the base.

HAWAII NATIONAL PARK

KILAUEA MILITARY CAMP, ARMED FORCES RECREATION CENTER
Hawaii National Park, HI 96718-5000
(808) 967-7315
Profile
BRANCH: Joint Service Installation.
SIZE AND LOCATION: 20 acres. At 4000 ft atop Kilauea Summit approx 30 mi from Hilo, HI, heading due S along Hwy 11.
BASE HISTORY: Started out as business venture by group of Hilo businessmen, investing to create maneuvering ground for NG and vacation spot for HI's Army. 1916, opened and offered officer's building, eating and cooking facilities, latrines, and tents for sleeping; military members received special rates. KMC, however, was not profitable and Army took over management, 1921. 1936, received 20-year lease for major projects and expansion, and operated under special use permit from National Park Service. Also used as POW camp, facility for mentally depressed, and bombing site.
VISITOR ATTRACTIONS: Located on edge of Kilauea Caldera, home of Madame Pele, world's most active volcano; tours to all parts of island.
Key Contacts
COMMANDER: Capt Randy A Hart.
PUBLIC AFFAIRS: 1st Lt Elaine Waters.
PROCUREMENT: Marc L Swanson.
Personnel and Expenditures
ACTIVE DUTY PERSONNEL: 15
DEPENDENTS: 7
CIVILIAN PERSONNEL: 100
Services *Housing:* Family units 3; Barracks spaces 50. *Temporary Housing:* VIP cottages 1; Guest cottages 56; Dormitory units 1. *Commissary and Exchange:* Service station; Cafeteria; Laundry; General store. *Base Library:* Yes. *Medical Facilities:* Dispensary. *Recreational Facilities:* Bowling; Gym; Recreation center; Golf; Tennis; Softball field; Lounge; Rental equipment; Nature walks.

HICKAM AFB

HICKAM AIR FORCE BASE
15th Air Base Wing, Hickam AFB, HI 96853-5000
(808) 471-7100; Autovon 471-7100
Profile
BRANCH: Air Force.
SIZE AND LOCATION: 2700 acres. 9 mi from downtown Honolulu, between Pearl Harbor Naval Base and the Honolulu IAP; 12 mi from Waikiki.
MAJOR UNITS: 15th Air Base Wing; Headquarters Pacific Air Forces; 834th Airlift Division.
BASE HISTORY: 1934, Quartermaster Corps hacked airfield from tangled brush and sugar cane fields; Hickam Field named for LTC Horace Meek Hickam, killed in aircraft accident, 1934. Japanese attack, Dec 7, 1941, resulted in 124 killed, 37 missing, 274 wounded at Hickam. WWII, hub of Pacific aerial network. Hawaiian Air Depot supported transient aircraft ferrying troops and supplies to forward areas; also played major role in training and staging, and supply center for both air and ground troops. After WWII, represented almost exclusively by Air Transport Command and its successor, MATS (today's MAC), until 1957, when HQs Far East Air Forces moved from Japan to Hawaii, redesignated Pacific Air Forces. 1985, Hickam designated National Historic Landmark.

Key Contacts
COMMANDER: 15 ABW/CC; (808) 449-6341, Autovon 449-6341.
PUBLIC AFFAIRS: 15 ABW/PA; (808) 449-2490, Autovon 449-2490.
PROCUREMENT: 15 ABW/LGC; (808) 449-6860, Autovon 449-6860.
TRANSPORTATION: 15 ABW/LGT; (808) 449-6570, Autovon 449-6570.
PERSONNEL/COMMUNITY ACTIVITIES: Director of Personnel, 15 ABW/MS; (808) 449-5696, Autovon 449-5696.
Personnel and Expenditures
ACTIVE DUTY PERSONNEL: 6000
DEPENDENTS: 6813
CIVILIAN PERSONNEL: 2000
MILITARY PAYROLL EXPENDITURE: $174.2 mil
CONTRACT EXPENDITURE: $25.8 mil
Services *Housing:* Family units 2946; BOQ cottages 24; BEQ units 546; Dormitory spaces 988; Senior NCO units 50. *Temporary Housing:* VIP cottages 12; VOQ cottages 156; VEQ units 172. *Commissary:* Base commissary; Retail store; Barber shop; Dry cleaners; Food shop; Florist; Banking; Service station; Furniture store. *Child Care/Capacities:* Day care center; Home day care program. *Schools:* Kindergarten/Preschool; Elementary. *Base Library:* Yes. *Medical Facilities:* Medical clinic; Dental clinic. *Recreational Facilities:* Bowling; Movie theater; Pool; Gym; Recreation center; Golf; Tennis; Racquetball; Skating rink; Fitness center; Softball field; Football field; Auto shop; Crafts; Officers club; NCO club; Fishing/Hunting.

HILO

POHAKULOA TRAINING AREA
US Army, Hilo, HI 96556
(808) 969-2400
Profile
BRANCH: Army.
LOCATION: Approx halfway between Hilo and Kona on Island of HI; Off Saddle Rd at 7000 ft level on S flank of Mauna Kea (13,976 ft).
BASE HISTORY: Currently training site in mountain area; approx 27,000 troops train here a year.
Key Contacts
COMMANDER: Col Teixeira; (808) 536-2294.
PUBLIC AFFAIRS: Russell Park; USACSH-Island of Oahu, Ft Shafter, HI 96858, (808) 438-1086, Autovon 438-1086.
PROCUREMENT: DOL; US Army Support Command Hawaii, Ft Shafter, HI 96858, (808) 438-2201.
PERSONNEL/COMMUNITY ACTIVITIES: US Army Support Command Hawaii, Ft Shafter, HI 96858, (808) 438-2333.
Services *Housing:* BEQ units 5; Barracks spaces 20. *Temporary Housing:* VIP cottages 1. *Commissary and Exchange:* Barber shop; Food shop; Service station. *Medical Facilities:* Medical clinic; Dental clinic. *Recreational Facilities:* Movie theater; Tennis; Fitness center; Softball field; Officers club; NCO club; Camping.

HONOLULU

FORT DERUSSY
Honolulu, HI 96815
(808) 438-1818
Profile
BRANCH: Army.
SIZE AND LOCATION: 72 acres. On the beach at Waikiki, 10 mi from Honolulu Airport.
MAJOR UNITS: US Army Pacific Reserves Headquarters; Armed Forces Recreation Center.

BASE HISTORY: Built on land once duck ponds for Hawaiian royalty; open post, park, and beach area; enjoyed by Hawaiian residents, tourists, and all service personnel. An estimated 2 million people visit each year.
VISITOR ATTRACTIONS: Army Museum of the Pacific; Hale Koa Hotel a first-class resort reserved exclusively for active duty and retired military personnel of all services. Has more than 400 rooms, restaurants, shows, and white sand beach on Waikiki. Room rates depend on pay grade, present status, and room's location. Reservations accepted up to year in advance (recommended) with active duty personnel given priority.
Key Contacts
COMMANDER: Capt Rothwell.
PUBLIC AFFAIRS: Russell Park; US Army Support Command, Hawaii (USASCH), Ft Shafter, HI 96858-5000, (808) 438-1086, Autovon 438-1086.
PROCUREMENT: See Ft Shafter.
TRANSPORTATION: See Ft Shafter.
PERSONNEL/COMMUNITY ACTIVITIES: See Ft Shafter.
Services *Temporary Housing:* 420 room, 14-story hotel, reserve 6 months to 1 year in advance. *Commissary and Exchange:* Retail store; Barber shop; Dry cleaners; Florist; Beauty shop; Laundry; Car rental. *Recreational Facilities:* Recreation equipment storage.

FORT KAMEHAMEHA
Honolulu, HI 96853
(808) 438-2227
Profile
BRANCH: Army.
LOCATION: At Hickam Air Force Base next to Honolulu IAP.
MAJOR UNITS: Hawaii Air National Guard.
BASE HISTORY: Primarily a housing area located with Hickam AFB.
Key Contacts
PUBLIC AFFAIRS: Russell Park; US Army Support Command, Hawaii (USASCH), Ft Shafter, HI 96858-5000, (808) 438-1086, Autovon 438-1086.
PROCUREMENT: See Ft Shafter.
TRANSPORTATION: See Ft Shafter.
PERSONNEL/COMMUNITY ACTIVITIES: See Ft Shafter.
Personnel and Expenditures
ACTIVE DUTY PERSONNEL: 506
Services *Recreational Facilities:* Tennis.

FORT RUGER
Honolulu, HI 96816
(808) 737-5996
Profile
BRANCH: Army.
LOCATION: On southern coast of Oahu off H-1, near Diamond Head.
MAJOR UNITS: Headquarters, Hawaii Army and Air National Guard.
BASE HISTORY: Originally a coastal defense post built, 1908-1911.
VISITOR ATTRACTIONS: Officer's Club, Mon-Tue, Private Parties only; Wed-Sat, 6-9pm; Sun, Brunch 10am-1pm.

SAND ISLAND COAST GUARD STATION
Honolulu, HI 96819
Profile
BRANCH: Coast Guard.
LOCATION: On Honolulu Harbor across from Aloha Tower.
MAJOR UNITS: Coast Guard Station.
BASE HISTORY: 1926, Sand Island's mud flats fortified with coral and mud dredged from harbor channel; first buildings medical treatment stations for victims of leprosy. Currently, station's helicopters op-

SAND ISLAND COAST GUARD STATION
(continued)

erate out of Barbers Point NAS. Sand Island also called Anuenue (Rainbow) Island.
Personnel and Expenditures
ACTIVE DUTY PERSONNEL: 200 (including civilians)
Services *Housing:* Barracks spaces; Housing at USCG Red Hill. *Commissary and Exchange:* Barber shop; Service station; Package beverages. *Recreational Facilities:* Pool; Gym; Tennis; Racquetball; Fitness center; Auto shop; Marina; Boating; All hands club.

US ARMY CORPS OF ENGINEERS, PACIFIC OCEAN DIVISION
Bldg 230, Ft Shafter, Honolulu, HI 96858
(808) 438-1500
Profile
BRANCH: Army.
SIZE: Offices only.
Key Contacts
COMMANDER: Brig Gen Arthur E Williams; Division Engineer.

KANEOHE BAY

KANEOHE BAY MARINE CORPS AIR STATION
Kaneohe Bay, HI 96863-5001
(808) 257-2378; Autovon 457-2378
OFFICER-OF-THE-DAY: (808) 257-1824, Autovon 457-1824
Profile
BRANCH: Marines.
SIZE AND LOCATION: 2951 acres. 11 mi from Honolulu on the N shore of Oahu on Mokapu Peninsula.
MAJOR UNITS: 1st Marine Expeditionary Brigade; Marine Air Group-24; 3rd Marine Regiment.
BASE HISTORY: 1918, Ft Hase commissioned and known as Kuwaaohe Military Reservation. 1939, Navy constructed small seaplane base and as NAS role expanded to administration of Kaneohe Bay Naval Defense Sea Area. 1941, Army artillery moved in. Dec 7, 1941, NAS Kaneohe Bay attacked first. After WWII, NAS limited to small air operations, small security detachment, and federal communications center. 1951, combined air-ground team with Marines assuming control of NAS activities when operations moved to Barbers Point NAS. Location ideal for deployment to Far East as well as intermediate refueling and maintenance stop for tactical and support aircraft during transpacific flights.
VISITOR ATTRACTIONS: Hawaiian Burial Grounds; Site of first attack on Dec 7, 1941.
Key Contacts
COMMANDER: Col W E Daniell.
PUBLIC AFFAIRS: Maj K K Gershaneck; (808) 257-1347, Autovon 457-1347.
PROCUREMENT: Fred Tester; Procurement Officer, MCAS Kaneohe Bay, HI 96783, (808) 257-0092, Autovon 457-0092.
PERSONNEL/COMMUNITY ACTIVITIES: Bill Buck; (808) 257-5743, Autovon 457-5743.
Personnel and Expenditures
ACTIVE DUTY PERSONNEL: 15,000
DEPENDENTS: 4844
CIVILIAN PERSONNEL: 1400
MILITARY PAYROLL EXPENDITURE: $119.5 mil
CONTRACT EXPENDITURE: $10.8 mil
Services *Housing:* Family units 1800. *Temporary Housing:* VIP cottages 1; Guesthouse units 12. *Commissary:* Base commissary; Retail store; Barber shop; Dry cleaners; Food shop; Florist; Banking; Service station; Furniture store. *Child Care/Capacities:* Day care center. *Schools:* Kindergarten/Preschool; Ele-

mentary. *Base Library:* Yes. *Medical Facilities:* Medical clinic; Dental clinic. *Recreational Facilities:* Bowling; Movie theater; Pool; Gym; Recreation center; Golf; Tennis; Racquetball; Fitness center; Softball field; Football field; Auto shop; Crafts; Officers club; NCO club; Fishing/Hunting; Surfing; Boating.

KEKAHA, KAUAI

PACIFIC MISSILE RANGE FACILITY, HAWAIIAN AREA
PO Box 128, Kekaha, Kauai, HI 96752-0128
(808) 335-4234; Autovon 471-6234
OFFICER-OF-THE-DAY: (808) 335-4254, Autovon 471-6254
Profile
BRANCH: Navy.
SIZE AND LOCATION: 1885 acres. On W side of island of Kauai, off Hwy 50, approx 26 mi from nearest commercial airport, 6 mi W of Kekaha on Kaumualii Hwy; Kukui Grove Ctr primary mall area in Lihue approx 30 mi.
MAJOR UNITS: 154th Composite Group; Hawaii Air National Guard; 150th Aircraft Warning Squadron; National Bureau of Standards; Naval Undersea Warfare Engineering Station; Sandia National Laboratories.
BASE HISTORY: 1940, Army acquired and named airfield Mana Airport. During WWII, heavily used by military. 1941-1948, used by Hawaiian Airlines and Pan American Clippers going westward. 1954, established as Bonham Airfield under USAF. 1958, transferred to Navy, and first PMRF instrumentation vans positioned near airstrip. 1965, transferred within Navy Department from Commanding Officer, NAS, Barbers Point to Commander, Pacific Missile Range and renamed PMRF, Barking Sands. Today, trains fleet under realistic open ocean war-at-sea scenarios.
VISITOR ATTRACTIONS: Barking Sands sand dunes.
Key Contacts
COMMANDER: Capt Thomas E McFeely; (808) 335-4251, Autovon 471-6251.
PUBLIC AFFAIRS: Vida N Mossman; (808) 335-4374, Autovon 471-6374.
PROCUREMENT: Lt Ricky Dennis; (808) 335-4211, Autovon 471-6211.
TRANSPORTATION: Lt Ed Von Hagel; (808) 335-4635, Autovon 471-6635.
PERSONNEL/COMMUNITY ACTIVITIES: Mike Greenwood; (808) 335-4446, Autovon 471-6446.
Personnel and Expenditures
ACTIVE DUTY PERSONNEL: 130
DEPENDENTS: 128
CIVILIAN PERSONNEL: 551
MILITARY PAYROLL EXPENDITURE: $1 mil
CONTRACT EXPENDITURE: $26.1 mil
Services *Housing:* Family units 56; BOQ cottages 1; BEQ units 23. *Temporary Housing:* VIP cottages 1; Guest cottages 4; Transient living quarters 15. *Commissary and Exchange:* Retail store; Barber shop; Dry cleaners; Food shop; Service station; Furniture store. *Child Care/Capacities:* Day care center 25; Home day care program. *Schools:* Kindergarten/Preschool. *Medical Facilities:* medical dispensary (for military only). *Recreational Facilities:* Bowling; Movie theater; Pool; Gym; Recreation center; Tennis; Racquetball; Fitness center; Softball field; Auto shop; Crafts; Officers club; NCO club; Camping; Miniature golf; All hands club.

PEARL HARBOR

MARINE BARRACKS, HAWAII
Pearl Harbor, HI 96860-5440
(808) 471-0672; Autovon 471-0672
OFFICER-OF-THE-DAY: Autovon 471-3626
Profile
BRANCH: Marines.
SIZE AND LOCATION: 49 acres. On Naval Base, Pearl Harbor.
MAJOR UNITS: Marine Barracks, HI; Headquarters and Service Company; Guard Company Pearl Harbor.
BASE HISTORY: 1904, detachment of Marines arrived in Honolulu for duty as guard force; quartered in empty coal shed fitted for temporary use for four years before moving into tents on a site, now covered by Fort Armstrong. 1914, moved from Honolulu to Pearl Harbor. Through the years improved to include over 50 buildings; one of largest in Marine Corps. 1976, three Marine barracks (Pearl Harbor, Barbers Point, and Lualualei) consolidated into one named Marine Barracks Hawaii. 1976, reorganization to include deactivation of Guard Company Barbers Point, Guard Company Lualualei, and turning over security responsibilities for gates at Naval Station, Pearl Harbor.
VISITOR ATTRACTIONS: See Naval Base, Pearl Harbor.
Key Contacts
COMMANDER: Col W C Bartels; Autovon 471-0672.
PUBLIC AFFAIRS: 1st Lt C C Berget; Autovon 474-0370.
PROCUREMENT: CWO W O Urdy; Autovon 474-8189.
TRANSPORTATION: CWO T M Coleman; Autovon 474-6287.
Personnel and Expenditures
ACTIVE DUTY PERSONNEL: 450
Services *Housing:* See Pearl Harbor Navy Station. *Temporary Housing:* See Pearl Harbor Naval Station.

PEARL HARBOR FLEET TRAINING GROUP
Pearl Harbor, HI 96860-7600
(808) 472-8881; Autovon 430-0111, ask for 472-8881
OFFICER-OF-THE-DAY: (808) 472-8881, Autovon 430-0111, ask for 472-8881
Profile
BRANCH: Navy.
LOCATION: On Ford Island in the center of Pearl Harbor; must take ferry/small boat to get on or off island.
MAJOR UNITS: Fleet Training Group (COMFLETRAGRU).
BASE HISTORY: Mission to provide education and training support service ashore and afloat to over 100 Navy, Marine, and USCG commands in HI, and more than 30 Navy and USCG ships homeported at Pearl Harbor, Guam, and AK. Average of 1500 students graduate monthly from Basic Damage Control to Advanced Transistor and Solid State Theory. Operates antisubmarine warfare attack trainer, mobile multi-threat environmental control trainer, along with complete firefighting complex, near Dry Dock No 4.
Key Contacts
COMMANDER: Capt Jerry R Bailey; (808) 472-8881, ext 304.
PUBLIC AFFAIRS: Lt Linda L Muth; (808) 472-8881, ext 317.
PROCUREMENT: (808) 472-8881, ext 344.
Personnel and Expenditures
ACTIVE DUTY PERSONNEL: 200
CIVILIAN PERSONNEL: 3

PEARL HARBOR FLEET TRAINING GROUP
(continued)
Services *Housing:* Family units; BEQ units. *Commissary:* Base commissary; Retail store; Barber shop; Dry cleaners; Food shop; Banking. *Medical Facilities:* Medical clinic; Dental clinic. *Recreational Facilities:* Pool; Gym; Recreation center; Golf; Tennis; Racquetball; Softball field.

PEARL HARBOR NAVAL STATION
Pearl Harbor, HI 96860
(808) 474-6249; Autovon 474-6249
OFFICER-OF-THE-DAY: (808) 474-6249, Autovon 474-6249
Profile
BRANCH: Navy.
SIZE AND LOCATION: 830 acres (plus 4960 acres of submerged land). 2 mi W of Honolulu IAP; 9 mi from downtown Honolulu; 12 mi from downtown Waikiki; From H-1 Fwy, follow segment passing next to Honolulu Airport, exit at 15B to Nimitz Gate.
MAJOR UNITS: Naval Station, Pearl Harbor (NAVSTA); Naval Base Pearl Harbor (COMNAVBASE); HQ Commander in Chief, US Pacific Fleet (CINCPACFLT); Commander Third Fleet (COMTHIRDFLT); Pearl Harbor Naval Shipyard (NAVSHIPYD PEARL); Pearl Harbor Submarine Base (SUBASE); Marine Barracks; Naval Submarine Training Center, Pacific (NAVSUBTRACNEPAC); Commander, Naval Logistics Command (COMNAVLOGPAC); Naval Surface Group, Middle Pacific (COMNAVSURFGRU MIDPAC); Naval Supply Center, Pearl Harbor (NSC Pearl); Naval Legal Service Office; Naval and Marine Corps Reserve Center, Honolulu; Fleet Training Group, Pearl Harbor (COMFLETRAGRU); Fleet Intelligence Center (FICPAC); Naval Investigative Service Regional Office Pacific (NSIROPAC); Intelligence Center Pacific (IPAC); Naval Security Group Activity (NAVSECGRUACT); Navy Data Automation Facility (NAVDAF); Shore Intermediate Maintenance Activity (SIMA); Naval Publications and Printing Service Detachment Office, Pearl Harbor (NPPSDO); Officer in Charge of Construction Mid-Pacific (OICC MIDPAC); Naval Electronics Engineering Activity, Pacific (NEEACT PAC).
BASE HISTORY: 1908, Congress authorized establishment of naval station at Pearl Harbor, named from pearl oysters that thrived in its waters. 1912, began as Receiving Ship at Hospital Point. 1916, 14th Naval District established. 1937, NAVSTA Pearl transferred to small barge near Submarine Base; remained until 1940; renamed Receiving Station and moved to present HQs, Bldg 150. Dec 7, 1941, Japanese attack resulted in sinking of four battleships, badly damaged four more and put other warships permanently or temporarily out of commission; in addition, 2113 Navy men and Marines died, another 987 wounded. By 1954, nearly 90 percent of Navy's personnel en route to or from duty in Pacific processed through Receiving Station. 1955, Naval Station established, absorbing functions of Receiving Station and coming under Commander, Naval Logistics, Pacific Fleet. Today, Navy's most important base in Pacific.
VISITOR ATTRACTIONS: *Arizona* Memorial; USS *Bowfin Park*; Pacific Submarine Museum; Ship open-house.

Key Contacts
COMMANDER: Capt Dennis C Blair; (808) 474-2152, Autovon 474-2152.
PUBLIC AFFAIRS: Frank A DeSilva; Code 93, MWR Marketing, Naval Station Box 20, Pearl Harbor, HI 96860-6000, (808) 474-0818.
PROCUREMENT: Lt Richard B Drehoff, SC; Code 40, Supply Officer, Naval Station Box 23, Pearl Harbor, HI 96860, (808) 471-1220, Autovon 474-9187.
TRANSPORTATION: Chief Yusuf Abdul-Rashad; Code 22, Transportation Officer, Naval Station Box 21, Pearl Harbor, HI 96860, (808) 474-4084.
PERSONNEL/COMMUNITY ACTIVITIES: Lawrence Warnken; MWR, Code 90, Naval Station Box 20, Pearl Harbor, HI 96860-6000, (808) 474-0787.
Personnel and Expenditures
ACTIVE DUTY PERSONNEL: 32,705
DEPENDENTS: 35,360
CIVILIAN PERSONNEL: 15,794
MILITARY PAYROLL EXPENDITURE: $34.2 mil
CONTRACT EXPENDITURE: $118.1 mil
Services *Housing:* BOQ cottages 3; BEQ units 9; Barracks spaces 9 bldgs; Dormitory spaces 9 bldgs; Senior NCO units 62. *Temporary Housing:* Transient living quarters 207. *Commissary:* Base commissary; Retail store; Barber shop; Dry cleaners; Food shop; Florist; Banking; Service station; Furniture store. *Child Care/Capacities:* Day care center 200. *Schools:* Various satellite colleges. *Base Library:* Yes. *Medical Facilities:* Medical clinic; Dental clinic. *Recreational Facilities:* Bowling; Pool; Gym; Recreation center; Golf; Tennis; Racquetball; Fitness center; Softball field; Football field; Auto shop; Officers club; NCO club; Fishing/Hunting.

PEARL HARBOR NAVAL SUBMARINE BASE
Pearl Harbor, HI 96860-6500
(808) 471-2770; Autovon 471-2770
OFFICER-OF-THE-DAY: (808) 471-2770
Profile
BRANCH: Navy.
SIZE AND LOCATION: 104 acres. On the Nimitz Hwy, between Aiea and the airport; 5 mi W of Honolulu.
MAJOR UNITS: Commander Submarine Squadron One (COMSUBRON ONE); Commander Submarine Squadron Seven (COMSUBRON SEVEN); Naval Submarine Training Center Pacific (NSTCP); Commander Submarine Force, US Pacific Fleet (COMSUBPAC).
BASE HISTORY: 1914, submarines operated from Pier 5 across from old Naval Station, downtown Honolulu. 1915, submarines assigned to operate out of Pearl Harbor using temporary submarine base on Kuahua Island, site of today's Naval Supply Center. 1919, Submarine Division Fourteen arrived and moored at Quarry Point, site of present base. 1923, first permanent building constructed. 1932, Escape Training Tank completed. 1985, last diesel submarine transferred out.
VISITOR ATTRACTIONS: Submarine Memorial; Dive Tower.
Key Contacts
COMMANDER: Capt Richard E Fast; (808) 471-0702.
PUBLIC AFFAIRS: Joe DeMattos; (808) 471-2728.
PROCUREMENT: LCDR R G Poston; (808) 471-0980.
TRANSPORTATION: LTjg D L Pointon; (808) 471-2445.
PERSONNEL/COMMUNITY ACTIVITIES: Al Worley; (808) 471-9183.
Personnel and Expenditures
ACTIVE DUTY PERSONNEL: 3904
CIVILIAN PERSONNEL: 387

Services *Housing:* BOQ cottages 143; BEQ units 890. *Commissary and Exchange:* Retail store; Barber shop; Dry cleaners; Food shop; Service station. *Child Care/Capacities:* Day care center 70. *Medical Facilities:* Mental health clinic. *Recreational Facilities:* Bowling; Movie theater; Pool; Gym; Tennis; Racquetball; Fitness center; Softball field; Auto shop; Crafts; Officers club; NCO club; Enlisted club.

PEARL HARBOR NAVY PUBLIC WORKS CENTER
Pearl Harbor, HI 96860-5470
(808) 471-7300; Autovon 471-7300
OFFICER-OF-THE-DAY: (808) 471-8481, Autovon 471-8481
Profile
BRANCH: Navy.
SIZE AND LOCATION: 71 acres. Above Kamehameha Hwy and Makalapa Gate to Pearl Harbor Naval Base, on Radford Dr, about 15 mi from downtown Honolulu.
MAJOR UNITS: Public Works Center, Pearl Harbor.
BASE HISTORY: 1933, general services shop established for Submarine Base, Pearl Harbor. WWII, served Shipyard and other Naval activities. 1946, moved to present site. 1954, officially established under control of Commander, US Naval Base, Pearl Harbor. 1967, came under Commander, Pacific Division, Naval Facilities Engineering Command. 1960-83, underwent several consolidations, extended area of responsibility from Pearl Harbor to many other major Oahu-based Navy commands; also provided public works support to other Pacific commands. Only PWC to provide direct support to Navy shipyard. 1987, again reported to COMNAVBASE PEARL. As a Navy Industrial Fund activity, Center provided services on basis of set rates and payment received for services used to pay employees' salaries and for materials used.
Key Contacts
COMMANDER: Capt David J Nash; (808) 471-3926, Autovon 471-3926.
PUBLIC AFFAIRS: Leslie S Ozawa.
PROCUREMENT: See Commander.
PERSONNEL/COMMUNITY ACTIVITIES: David Gibbons; Director of Personnel, (808) 474-3586.
Personnel and Expenditures
ACTIVE DUTY PERSONNEL: 15
CIVILIAN PERSONNEL: 1380
MILITARY PAYROLL EXPENDITURE: FY 88, $0.5 mil
CONTRACT EXPENDITURE: FY 89, $50 mil
Services *Housing:* Available in the Pearl Harbor Naval Complex. *Temporary Housing:* Available in the Pearl Harbor Naval Complex. *Commissary and Exchange:* Retail store; Barber shop; Dry cleaners; Food shop; Florist; Banking; Service station; Furniture store; Credit union; Commissary and Exchange directly across the street from command. *Recreational Facilities:* Tennis; Softball field; Picnic area.

SCHOFIELD BARRACKS

SCHOFIELD BARRACKS
Schofield Barracks, HI 96786
(808) 655-4930; Autovon 455-4930
Profile
BRANCH: Army.
SIZE AND LOCATION: 13,777 acres. In center of Oahu off H-2 Fwy.
MAJOR UNITS: 25th Infantry Division (Light); 45th Support Group; Field Station Kunia.
BASE HISTORY: Home of 25th Infantry Division since establishment, Oct 1941.
VISITOR ATTRACTIONS: Post Museum.

SCHOFIELD BARRACKS (continued)
Personnel and Expenditures
ACTIVE DUTY PERSONNEL: 15,000
DEPENDENTS: 10,000
CIVILIAN PERSONNEL: 1100
CONTRACT EXPENDITURE: $56 mil
Services *Housing:* Family units 3600; BOQ cottages 36. *Temporary Housing:* VIP cottages 1; Guesthouse units 63. *Commissary:* Base commissary; Retail store; Barber shop; Dry cleaners; Food shop; Florist; Banking; Service station; Furniture store; Bakery; Convenience store/Shopette; Credit union; Beauty shop; Toys; Car center; Package beverages; Car rental; Clothing sales; Laundry; Thrift shop; Shoe repair; Optical shop. *Child Care/Capacities:* Day care center 75. *Schools:* Elementary. *Base Library:* Yes. *Medical Facilities:* Medical clinic; Dental clinic; Veterinary services. *Recreational Facilities:* Bowling; Movie theater; Pool; Gym; Recreation center; Golf; Tennis; Racquetball; Fitness center (spa); Softball field; Football field; Auto shop; Crafts; Officers club; NCO club; Youth center (activities); Equipment rentals.

TRIPLER AMC

TRIPLER ARMY MEDICAL CENTER
Tripler AMC, HI 96859-5000
(808) 433-6661; Autovon 433-6661
Profile
BRANCH: Army.
LOCATION: On island of Oahu, top of Moanalua Ridge overlooking S shore; approx 7 mi from Waikiki and 5 mi from downtown Honolulu; approx 3 mi to Honolulu IAP and Pearl Harbor.
MAJOR UNITS: Tenant activity of the US Army Support Command, Hawaii.
BASE HISTORY: 1907, several wooden structures at Ft Shafter used as hospital. 1920, named for Brevet Brig Gen Charles Stuart Tripler, for contributions to Army medicine during Civil War. WWII, 450 bed capacity, expanded to 1000 beds. 1942, plans for new Tripler drawn and construction completed in 1948. Architecturally distinctive coral pink structure atop Moanalua Ridge, a familiar landmark on S side of Oahu ever since. 1985, three new wings adjoining original facility dedicated. Currently, renovation project expected to be completed in 1990; largest military medical treatment facility in Pacific; only Army medical center not located on US Mainland; major teaching center for graduate training; operates Army Health Clinic at Schofield Barracks, Troop Medical Clinic at Armed Forces Recreation Center, Kilauea Military Camp, and Troop Medical Clinic, Pohakuloa Training Area; administrative and logistical support to US Army Dental Activity, HI, headquartered on Moanalua Ridge near medical center; veterinary support; and, sanitary inspection program throughout Pacific Basin.
Key Contacts
COMMANDER: Brig Gen Girard Seitter III.
PUBLIC AFFAIRS: George A Vidis.
Personnel and Expenditures
ACTIVE DUTY PERSONNEL: 1700
CIVILIAN PERSONNEL: 1000
Services *Housing:* See Ft Shafter. *Temporary Housing:* See Ft Shafter. *Base Library:* Yes. *Medical Facilities:* Hospital 537. *Recreational Facilities:* Bowling; Pool; Gym; Tennis; Fitness center; Softball field; Football field; Officers club; NCO club; These come under USASCH Ft Shafter.

WAHIAWA

WAHIAWA NAVAL COMMUNICATIONS AREA MASTER STATION, EASTERN PACIFIC
Wahiawa, HI 96786-5000
(808) 653-5383
OFFICER-OF-THE-DAY: (808) 653-5385
Profile
BRANCH: Navy.
SIZE AND LOCATION: 800 acres. 20 mi N of Pearl Harbor and Pearl City at Kamehameha Hwy and Whitmore Village.
MAJOR UNITS: Communications Security Group; US Coast Guard Detachment; Marine Detachment.
BASE HISTORY: Dec 7, 1941, Naval radio stations proved to be highly vulnerable to attack; all equipment was moved to Wahiawa, an excellent and protected receiving site. Shortly thereafter, Security Group Unit moved from Heeia. 1943, Communications Security Unit established at Wahiawa under Chief of Naval Operations, to assist in cryptographic security, traffic control, and analysis. Following WWII, central radio station returned to Pearl Harbor and Wahiawa relegated to receiver site. 1956, central station relocated to Wahiawa site. 1959, radio station at Heeia turned over to Marine Corps Air Station, Kaneohe, and Haiku station was placed in non-operational status. 1967, consolidation with message centers at Pearl Harbor (NAVSHIPYD), Makalapa (CINCPACFLT), Camp Smith (CINCPAC), Moanalua (FLEWEACEN), Secure Voice Pearl Harbor, and Consolidated Maintenance under NAVCOMMACTS Honolulu. 1977, NAVCOMMACTS Pearl Harbor disestablished. 1974, Naval Communications Processing and Routing System (NAVCOMPARS) at Wahiawa activated with dual access to AUTODIN switches at Wahiawa and Norton AFB, CA. 1976, Common User Digital Information Exchange System (CUDIXS), automated communication system using satellites, became operational.
Key Contacts
COMMANDER: Capt Davis; (808) 653-5345.
PUBLIC AFFAIRS: Lt Debra Roemisch; (808) 653-5571.
PROCUREMENT: LCDR Eastlund; (808) 653-5287.
TRANSPORTATION: Lt Ludivici; (808) 653-5473.
PERSONNEL/COMMUNITY ACTIVITIES: Mr Abatello; Director of Personnel, (808) 653-5337.
Personnel and Expenditures
ACTIVE DUTY PERSONNEL: 1200
DEPENDENTS: 200
CIVILIAN PERSONNEL: 300
Services *Housing:* Family units 141; BEQ units 3; Senior NCO units 15. *Commissary and Exchange:* Retail store; Barber shop; Dry cleaners; Food shop; Banking; Service station. *Child Care/Capacities:* Day care center 30; Home day care program. *Base Library:* Yes. *Medical Facilities:* Medical clinic; Dental clinic. *Recreational Facilities:* Bowling; Movie theater; Pool; Gym; Tennis; Racquetball; Fitness center; Softball field; Football field; Auto shop; Crafts; Officers club; NCO club.

WAIANAE

NAVMAG LUALUALEI
Waianae, HI 96792
Profile
BRANCH: Navy.
LOCATION: In Lualualei Valley approx 38 mi from Honolulu.
MAJOR UNITS: NAVMAG Lualualei; Mobile Mine Assembly Group (MOMAG); Naval Undersea Warfare Engineering Station Detachment (NUWES); MK48 Torpedo Division (SUBASE Weapons); US Army Support Command Hawaii, Director of Logistics, Munitions Branch (USASCH, DOL); EOD Group One; EOD Training Unit One; EOD Mobile Unit One.
BASE HISTORY: 1934, originally commissioned as Naval Ammunition Depot, Oahu. NAVMAG Lualualei receives, renovates, maintains, stores and issues ammunition, explosives, expendable ordnance items and weapons and technical ordnance materiels. Command composed of HQs at Lualualei and West Loch and Waikele branches.
Personnel and Expenditures
ACTIVE DUTY PERSONNEL: 200
CIVILIAN PERSONNEL: 120
Services *Commissary:* Base commissary; Service station. *Medical Facilities:* Medical clinic; Dental clinic. *Recreational Facilities:* Movie theater; Pool; Gym; Tennis; Fitness center; Softball field; Football field; Auto shop; Morale, welfare, & recreation services.

WAIANAE ARMY RECREATION CENTER
85-010 Army St, Waianac, HI 96792
(808) 696-2494
Profile
BRANCH: Army.
LOCATION: W coast of Oahu, 35 mi from Waikiki.
BASE HISTORY: A beach vacation camp constructed during WWII to provide soldiers rest and recreation.
VISITOR ATTRACTIONS: Operated primarily for enjoyment of Army members and their families, other service members, retired military personnel, and DOD civilians also welcome on space available basis. Cabin charges modest and vary according to cabin type and individual's rank; 14-day stay limit for each visit. Maid service not provided and pets not allowed.
Services *Temporary Housing:* Guest cottages 33. *Commissary and Exchange:* Food shop; Package beverages; Laundry. *Medical Facilities:* First aid station. *Recreational Facilities:* Fishing/Hunting; Water sports equipment rental; Beach; All ranks club; Water sports.

WAIMANALO

BELLOWS AIR FORCE STATION
PO Box 1010, Waimanalo, HI 96795
(808) 259-5941
OFFICER-OF-THE-DAY: (808) 259-5955
Profile
BRANCH: Air Force.
SIZE AND LOCATION: 1500 acres. On SE coast of Oahu on windward side of island approx 16 mi from business district of Honolulu and 19 mi from downtown Waikiki with access from Kalanianaole Hwy; 25 mi from Hickam AFB.
MAJOR UNITS: Detachment 1, 15th Air Base Wing; 1957th Communications Group/Operating Location-A; Hawaii Army National Guard Military Academy; 1st Marine Expeditionary Brigade Training Area.

BELLOWS AIR FORCE STATION (continued)
BASE HISTORY: 1917, established by presidential order as Waimanalo Military Reservation. Later named Bellows Field after 2nd Lt F B Bellows, aviator killed in WWI. Credited for capturing first POW of WWII. 1958, flying activities terminated. Presently, recreational facility for military; interference-free site for AF Communications Command Transmitter Complex; training area for Marine Corps; and, site of HI Army NG Military Academy.
VISITOR ATTRACTIONS: Beach.

Key Contacts
COMMANDER: Capt Charles R Carr.
PUBLIC AFFAIRS: MSgt Jackie Rhodes; (808) 259-5955.
PERSONNEL/COMMUNITY ACTIVITIES: Richard Coupe; (808) 259-5947.

Personnel and Expenditures
ACTIVE DUTY PERSONNEL: 43
DEPENDENTS: 5
CIVILIAN PERSONNEL: 75

Services *Housing:* Family units 6; Barracks spaces 19. *Temporary Housing:* VIP cottages 3; Guest cottages 102. *Commissary and Exchange:* Food shop; Service station; Convenience store/Shopette. *Recreational Facilities:* Recreation center; Tennis; Softball field; Camping; All ranks club; Beach cottages; Golf driving range; Sailboat rentals.

WHEELER AFB

WHEELER AIR FORCE BASE
Wheeler AFB, HI 96854
(808) 655-1414; Autovon 455-7411
Profile
BRANCH: Air Force.
SIZE AND LOCATION: 1391 acres. 22 mi from Honolulu, near Wahiawa; off Rte 99, next to Schofield Barracks.
MAJOR UNITS: 15th Air Base Squadron; 22nd Tactical Air Support Squadron; 326th Air Division.
BASE HISTORY: 1922, established as part of Schofield Barracks; named after Maj Sheldon H Wheeler, killed in aircraft accident that year. 1941, sustained extensive damage during attack on Pearl Harbor. During WWII and until 1949, under command of 7th Air Force and successor commands. 1949-51, inactivated on minimum caretaker status. During Korean Conflict reactivated. Army responsible for airfield operations; Navy for crash and rescue operations.

Personnel and Expenditures
ACTIVE DUTY PERSONNEL: 970
DEPENDENTS: 1300
CIVILIAN PERSONNEL: 500
CONTRACT EXPENDITURE: $7.7 mil

Services *Housing:* Family units 491; Barracks spaces. *Commissary and Exchange:* Barber shop; Credit union. *Child Care/Capacities:* Day care center 86. *Schools:* Kindergarten/Preschool; Elementary; Intermediate/Junior high. *Base Library:* Yes. *Medical Facilities:* Medical clinic; Dental clinic; Veterinary services. *Recreational Facilities:* Bowling; Movie theater; Pool; Gym; Recreation center; Golf; Tennis; Racquetball; Fitness center; Softball field; Football field; Auto shop; Crafts; Officers club; NCO club; Camping; Youth center (activities); Aero Club; Skeet shooting.

IDAHO

BOISE

GOWEN FIELD
PO Box 45, Boise, ID 83707
(208) 389-5011; Autovon 941-5011
OFFICER-OF-THE-DAY: (208) 389-5011,
Autovon 941-5011
Profile
BRANCH: Air National Guard; Army National
Guard.
SIZE AND LOCATION: 138,000 acres. On S side
of Boise Municipal Airport, approx 3 mi
from downtown Boise.
MAJOR UNITS: Headquarters, Idaho Army
National Guard; Headquarters, Idaho Air
National Guard; 124th Tactical Recon-
naissance Group; Headquarters, 116th
Cavalry Brigade.
BASE HISTORY: 1940, Army Air Corps se-
lected site as operations and training cen-
ter for medium bombardment wing, Boise
Air Field. 1941, name changed to Gowen
Field, to honor Lt Paul Gowen, Army
aviator killed in aircraft accident in Panama. 1946, ID ANG formed here and
home of first annual training site in
1950s. 240 sq mi range area is military
training site; desert maneuver area S of
Gowen Field contains 20 live-fire ranges
(99,000 acres) and Army NG conducts
training for M60A3 tanks.
Key Contacts
COMMANDER: Col Don Troyer; (208) 389-
5830, Autovon 941-5830.
PUBLIC AFFAIRS: Maj James Ball; (208) 389-
5268, Autovon 941-5268.
PROCUREMENT: LTC Gene Klefman; (208)
389-5253, Autovon 941-5253.
TRANSPORTATION: Col Leroy Hiner; (208)
389-5211, Autovon 941-5211.
PERSONNEL/COMMUNITY ACTIVITIES: Col Kris
Larsen; (208) 389-5094, Autovon 941-
5094.
Personnel and Expenditures
ACTIVE DUTY PERSONNEL: 1365
CIVILIAN PERSONNEL: 150
MILITARY PAYROLL EXPENDITURE: $52 mil
CONTRACT EXPENDITURE: $5 mil
Services *Housing:* Barracks spaces 2820.
Temporary Housing: BOQ units 297;
Guesthouse units 17. *Commissary:* Base
commissary; Retail store; Barber shop; Dry
cleaners. *Medical Facilities:* Medical clinic.
Recreational Facilities: Movie theater; Pool;
Tennis; Fitness center; Softball field; Officers
club; NCO club.

IDAHO FALLS

IDAHO FALLS NAVAL ADMINISTRATIVE UNIT
550 1st St, Idaho Falls, ID 83401-3998
(208) 526-0366
Profile
BRANCH: Navy.
SIZE AND LOCATION: 2 acres. In Idaho Falls,
E of Snake River; Approx 3 mi E from I-
15; Approx 4 mi from Idaho Falls Mu-
nicipal Airport; Approx 50 mi E of Naval
Nuclear Power Training Unit; Nearest
military base, Hill AFB in Odgen, UT.
MAJOR UNITS: Personnel Support Activity
Detachment; Naval Administrative Unit.
BASE HISTORY: 1965, established to provide
administrative and logistic support, not
training, to Naval Nuclear Power Train-
ing Unit, Idaho Falls. Due to limited mis-
sion, Navy did not establish base in Ida-
ho Falls.
Key Contacts
COMMANDER: LCDR Margaret D Jamieson,
USN; Officer in Charge, Naval Admin-
istrative Unit, (208) 526-0144.
PROCUREMENT: Lt James B Latham, SC,
USNR; (208) 526-0444.
TRANSPORTATION: Marilee Fitzwater; (208)
526-0425.
Personnel and Expenditures
ACTIVE DUTY PERSONNEL: 11
CIVILIAN PERSONNEL: 17
MILITARY PAYROLL EXPENDITURE: $0.25 mil
Services *Medical Facilities:* Medical clinic;
Dental clinic. *Recreational Facilities:* Gym;
Softball field; Camping; Fishing/Hunting.

IDAHO FALLS NAVAL NUCLEAR POWER TRAINING UNIT
Idaho Falls, ID 83401
(208) 526-5334
Profile
BRANCH: Navy.
LOCATION: 65 mi W of Idaho Falls off Rte
20 in Department of Energy Federal Res-
ervation.
MAJOR UNITS: Nuclear Power Training Unit;
Naval Reactors Facility.
VISITOR ATTRACTIONS: Access restricted to
staff and students.
Personnel and Expenditures
ACTIVE DUTY PERSONNEL: 1500
DEPENDENTS: 2000

MOUNTAIN HOME AFB

MOUNTAIN HOME AIR FORCE BASE
366th Tactical Fighter Wing, Mountain
Home AFB, ID 83648-5000
(208) 828-2111; Autovon 857-2111
Profile
BRANCH: Air Force.
SIZE AND LOCATION: 9112 acres. 10 mi SW
of town of Mountain Home; 13 mi from
I-84 between Boise and Twin Falls.
MAJOR UNITS: 366th Tactical Fighter Wing
(TFW); 777th Radar Squadron; 2036th
Communications Squadron.
BASE HISTORY: 1943, opened with 396th
Bombardment Group. 1944, designated
Mountain Home Army Air Field, replace-
ment training unit for B-24s (later B-29s).
1945, deactivated. 1948, SAC reactivated
base 311th Air Division, Reconnaissance.
1949, again deactivated. 1951, MATS as-
sumed control. 1953, SAC returned.
1962, 3 Titan I ICBM launch complexes
constructed. 1966, TAC assumed jurisdic-
tion. 1972, 366th TFW replaced 347th, to
train aircrews and maintain aircraft. Also
responsible for Saylor Creek Bombing and
Electronic Combat Range (110,000 acres),
Owyhee County approx 20 mi SE of base.
VISITOR ATTRACTIONS: F-111 Monument in-
side front gate; Heritage Park near Wing
HQ.
Key Contacts
COMMANDER: Col Victor C Andrews; 366
TFW Commander, (208) 828-2366, Auto-
von 857-2366.
PUBLIC AFFAIRS: Capt Steven M Solmonson;
Chief of Public Affairs, 366 TFW/PA,
Mountain Home AFB, ID 83648-5428,
(208) 828-6800, Autovon 857-6800.
PROCUREMENT: Col Jeffrey L Beran; Deputy
Commander of Resource Management,
366 TFW/RM, (208) 828-6122, Autovon
857-6122.
TRANSPORTATION: Capt Terry J Kinney; 366
Transportation Commander, 366 TFW/
LGT, (208) 828-2088, Autovon 857-2088.
PERSONNEL/COMMUNITY ACTIVITIES: Col
Danny D Howard; 366 Combat Support
Group Commander, 366 CSG/CC, (208)
828-6366, Autovon 857-6366.
Personnel and Expenditures
ACTIVE DUTY PERSONNEL: 3890
DEPENDENTS: 4900
CIVILIAN PERSONNEL: 513
MILITARY PAYROLL EXPENDITURE: FY 88,
$73.6 mil
CONTRACT EXPENDITURE: FY 88, $38 mil
Services *Housing:* Family units 1521; Dor-
mitory spaces 1405; Senior NCO units 187;
Junior NCO units; RV/Camper sites 12.
Temporary Housing: VIP cottages 10; VOQ
cottages 53; VEQ units 38; Transient living
quarters 16. *Commissary:* Base commissary;
Retail store; Barber shop; Dry cleaners;
Food shop; Florist; Banking; Service station;
Fast food; Alterations; Laundry; Video rent-
al; Optical shop; Beauty shop. *Child Care/
Capacities:* Day care center 91. *Schools:*
Kindergarten/Preschool; Elementary;
Intermediate/Junior high. *Base Library:* Yes.
Medical Facilities: Hospital 31; Medical clin-
ic; Dental clinic. *Recreational Facilities:*
Bowling; Movie theater; Pool; Gym; Recrea-
tion center; Golf; Stables; Tennis; Racquet-
ball; Fitness center; Softball field; Football
field; Auto shop; Crafts; Officers club; NCO
club; Camping; Theater; Skateboard ramp.

WILDER

WILDER AIR FORCE STATION
General Delivery, Wilder, ID 83676
(208) 482-6215; Autovon 857-2216
Profile
BRANCH: Air Force.
SIZE AND LOCATION: 10 acres. 3 mi W of
Wilder town center on Peckham Rd.
MAJOR UNITS: Detachment 5, 1 CEVG.
Key Contacts
COMMANDER: LTC Max D Lunt.
PUBLIC AFFAIRS: Capt Steven M Solmonson;
Chief of Public Affairs, 366 TFW/PA,
Mountain Home AFB, ID 83648-5428,
(208) 828-6800, Autovon 857-6800.
Personnel and Expenditures
ACTIVE DUTY PERSONNEL: 55
CIVILIAN PERSONNEL: 1
Services *Commissary and Exchange:* Retail
store. *Base Library:* Yes. *Medical Facilities:*
IDMT. *Recreational Facilities:* Recreation
center; Racquetball; Fitness center; Auto
shop; Crafts; All Ranks Club.

ILLINOIS

CHANUTE AFB

CHANUTE AIR FORCE BASE

Chanute AFB, IL 61868-5000
(217) 495-1110; Autovon 862-1110
OFFICER-OF-THE-DAY: (217) 495-3866,
  Autovon 862-3866
Profile
BRANCH: Air Force.
SIZE AND LOCATION: 2485 acres. At Rantoul,
  IL, approx 2 mi E of I-57, Exit 250,
  approx 20 mi N of Champaign-Urbana,
  IL. Serviced by Univ of IL-Willard Air-
  port, Savoy, IL, approx 45 min from
  base.
MAJOR UNITS: Chanute Technical Training
  Center; 3330th Technical Training Wing;
  3345th Air Base Group; HQ 3505th
  USAF Recruiting Group; 1963rd Communications Squadron.
BASE HISTORY: Third oldest AFB in US and
  oldest technical training center. May
  1917, activated; pilot training base. 1921,
  Air Service Mechanics School moved to
  base, and, until, 1938, only technical
  training center for Army Air Corps. Today, provides training in missile, automotive, and aircraft mechanics; aerospace
  ground equipment and weather equipment maintenance; life support; metallur-
  gy and nondestructive inspection; weather
  observation and forecasting; fuels; and,
  fire protection and rescue. Currently, approx 400 Army, Navy, and Marine Corps
  students attend courses.
VISITOR ATTRACTIONS: Air Park with aircraft
  from WWII to present; Thunderbird Circle; Display Center.
Key Contacts
COMMANDER: Installation Commander,
  3345th Air Base Group/CC.
PUBLIC AFFAIRS: CTTC/PA, (217) 495-4566,
  Autovon 862-4566.
Personnel and Expenditures
ACTIVE DUTY PERSONNEL: 2154 active; 2700
  students
DEPENDENTS: 6448
CIVILIAN PERSONNEL: 2627
MILITARY PAYROLL EXPENDITURE: $102 mil
CONTRACT EXPENDITURE: $83.8 mil
Services *Housing:* Family units 1322; BOQ
cottages 8; BAQ units 416; Duplex units
488; Townhouse units 742; Dormitory
spaces 4086; Senior NCO units 140; Junior
NCO units 1028; Trailer spaces 95; RV/
Camper sites 30. *Temporary Housing:* VIP
cottages 4; VOQ cottages 186; VAQ units
944; Transient living quarters 32; Tent
spaces, 4. *Commissary:* Base commissary;
Retail store; Barber shop; Dry cleaners; Florist; Service station; 2 branch exchanges.
Child Care/Capacities: Day care center 183;
Home day care program. *Schools:* Preschool
during school year. *Base Library:* Yes. *Medical Facilities:* Hospital 35; Medical clinic;
Dental clinic. *Recreational Facilities:* Bowl-

ing; Movie theater; Pool; Gym; Recreation
center; Golf; Tennis; Racquetball; Fitness
center; Softball field; Football field; Auto
shop; Crafts; Officers club; NCO club;
Camping; Fishing/Hunting.

CHICAGO

US ARMY CORPS OF ENGINEERS, CHICAGO DISTRICT

111 N Canal St, River Center Bldg, Chicago,
IL 60606
Profile
BRANCH: Army.
SIZE: Offices only.

US ARMY CORPS OF ENGINEERS, NORTH CENTRAL DIVISION

5365 Clark St, Chicago, IL 60605
(312) 353-6310
Profile
BRANCH: Army.
SIZE: Offices only.
Key Contacts
COMMANDER: Brig Gen Theodore Vander
  Els; Division Engineer.

FORT SHERIDAN

FORT SHERIDAN

US Army Garrison, Bldg 140, Fort Sheridan,
IL 60037-5000
(312) 926-4111; Autovon 459-4111
OFFICER-OF-THE-DAY: (312) 926-3058, 926-
  3098, Autovon 459-3058, 459-3098
Profile
BRANCH: Army.
SIZE AND LOCATION: 695 acres. On shore of
  Lake Michigan between Highland Park on
  S and Lake Forest on N and adj to village
  of Highwood. 28 mi N of Chicago loop, 8
  mi S of Great Lakes NTC, 12 mi S of
  Waukegan, IL, and approx 60 mi S of
  Milwaukee. Main gate 1.5 mi E of US
  Rte 41 from Old Elm Rd exit in Lake
  Forest. 22 mi NE of O'Hare IAP.
MAJOR UNITS: Fourth US Army Headquar-
  ters; US Army Recruiting Command; US
  Army Readiness Group-Sheridan; Fourth
  Recruiting Brigade (MW); 85th Maneuver
  Training Command (USAR); 425th
  Transportation Brigade; 30th Hospital
  Center; Fourth US Army Band; 2d ROTC
  Brigade; US Army Information Systems
  Command; 51st Explosive Ordnance Dis-
  posal Detachment; Fort Sheridan Field
  Office Criminal Investigation Command.
BASE HISTORY: 1888, camp officially named
  Ft Sheridan for Lt Gen Philip H Sheri-
  dan, first living general to have post
  named in his honor. 1913-16, active in
  Mexican border disturbances. WWI, mid-
  west training center for recruits. WWII,
  administrative HQs for 46 POW camps

in MI, IL, and WI. Following WWII, separation and rehabilitation center and
  Sixth Service Command Training Center,
  which reeducated and returned to duty
  first offenders of Army disciplinary regu-
  lations. 1960s-1970s, home of 5th Region
  US Army Air Defense Command, 45th
  Artillery Brigade, and 22nd Artillery
  Group. 1967, HQ, Fifth Army relocated
  from Old Chicago Beach Hotel until
  merged with Fourth Army and moved to
  Ft Sam Houston, TX. 1973, HQ, US
  Army Recruiting Command established;
  managed worldwide recruiting operations.
  1984, HQ, Fourth US Army activated.
VISITOR ATTRACTIONS: About 240 acres Na-
  tional Historic Landmarks, based on de-
  sign and structure of 93 buildings con-
  structed, 1890-1900. Museum includes
  military equipment and artifacts dating to
  Civil War.
Key Contacts
COMMANDER: Col William N Johnson; (312)
  926-3095, Autovon 459-3095.
PUBLIC AFFAIRS: Daniel R Trew; Public Af-
  fairs Office, AFKE-ZO-PO, (312) 926-
  6385, Autovon 459-6385.
PROCUREMENT: Ken Nale; Directorate of
  Contracting, Bldg 142, (312) 926-3326,
  Autovon 459-3326.
TRANSPORTATION: Marvin Vieth; Transporta-
  tion Officer, Bldg 142, (312) 926-3560,
  Autovon 459-3560.
PERSONNEL/COMMUNITY ACTIVITIES: LTC
  Ralph Eldridge; DPCA, Bldg 142, (312)
  926-2225, Autovon 459-2225.
Personnel and Expenditures
ACTIVE DUTY PERSONNEL: 1550
DEPENDENTS: 1500
CIVILIAN PERSONNEL: 1720
Services *Housing:* Family units 496; BOQ
cottages 42 rooms 6 apts; BEQ units 45;
Duplex units 60; Townhouse units 335; Bar-
racks spaces for RC billets/training 3475;
Dormitory spaces 600; Senior NCO units 35;
Junior NCO units 249; RV/Camper sites
(storage only 50). *Temporary Housing:* BOQ
units 6; Guesthouse units 16; Guesthouses,
substandard 59. *Commissary:* Base commis-
sary; Retail store; Barber shop; Dry cleaners;
Food shop; Service station; Optical shop;
Snacks. *Child Care/Capacities:* Day care center; Home day care program. *Schools:*
Kindergarten/Preschool. *Base Library:* Yes.
Medical Facilities: Medical clinic; Dental
clinic. *Recreational Facilities:* Bowling; Pool;
Gym; Recreation center; Golf; Tennis; Racquetball; Fitness center; Softball field; Football field; Auto shop; Crafts; All Ranks Club;
Tower Club (E1-E9); Equipment rental center; SATO travel office; ITT office.

GLENVIEW

GLENVIEW NAVAL AIR STATION

Glenview, IL 60026
(312) 657-1000; Autovon 932-1000

Profile

BRANCH: Navy.

SIZE AND LOCATION: 1200 acres. 20 mi N of Chicago between I-294 and I-94 at Lake Ave and Shermer Rd; 10 mi from O'Hare IAP.

MAJOR UNITS: VP-90; VP-60; VR-51; Coast Guard Air Station, Chicago; Ft Sheridan Flight Detachment; Marine Air Control Group 48; Reserve units.

BASE HISTORY: 1937, begun as Curtiss-Reynolds Airport. 1942, construction began on then Naval Reserve Aviation Base. During WWII, provided primary flight training for naval and Marine Corps pilots.

Personnel and Expenditures

ACTIVE DUTY PERSONNEL: 1000
DEPENDENTS: 2500
CIVILIAN PERSONNEL: 300

Services *Housing:* Family units 16; BOQ cottages 1; BEQ units 4; Trailer spaces 65; Units for officers/enlisted 263. *Temporary Housing:* VIP cottages 5; VOQ cottages 124; VEQ units 230; BOQ units; Transient living quarters 130; CPO units 88; Family rooms (PCS) 6; Private rooms 14. *Commissary and Exchange:* Retail store. *Child Care/Capacities:* Day care center 20. *Medical Facilities:* Medical clinic; Veterinary services. *Recreational Facilities:* Bowling; Movie theater; Pool; Gym; Golf; Tennis; Racquetball; Fitness center; Auto shop; Crafts; Camping; Youth center (activities); Aero Club; Skeet shooting.

GRANITE CITY

CHARLES MELVIN PRICE SUPPORT CENTER, US ARMY

SAVAS-G, Granite City, IL 62040-1801
(618) 452-4212; Autovon 892-4212

Profile

BRANCH: Army.

SIZE AND LOCATION: 930 acres. On IL Hwy 3 at Niedring Ave in Granite City, IL, approx 15 min from downtown St Louis.

BASE HISTORY: WWI site selected. 1942, construction began and Granite City Engineer Depot opened. Except Korean War, two postwar decades saw sharp drop in activity. 1962, became Granite City Army Depot and control from Corps of Engineers to Army Materiel Command. Mission remained until 1966, when it assumed support missions for Greater St Louis area from deactivated Army Support Center. 1971, depot proper closed and merged with various Army Aviation Systems Command support services to become Headquarters and Installation Support Activity. 1975, Granite City element changed again, became St Louis Area Support Center (SLASC). Currently, supports approx 55 military and federal agencies in St Louis area. Named for late Congressman Price. Subordinate command of US Army Aviation Systems Command, St Louis, MO.

Key Contacts

COMMANDER: LTC John J Magrosky Jr.

PUBLIC AFFAIRS: Howard DeMere; US Army AVSCOM, 4300 Goodfellow Blvd, St Louis, MO 63120-1798, (314) 263-1164, Autovon 693-1164.

PROCUREMENT: Jack A Sockoch; AMSAV-PDS-2, (618) 452-4482, Autovon 892-4482.

TRANSPORTATION: Vernon Shelby (COR); SAVAS-L, (618) 452-4407, Autovon 892-4407.

PERSONNEL/COMMUNITY ACTIVITIES: Capt Walter Krupco; AMSAV-T, (618) 452-4577, Autovon 892-4577.

Personnel and Expenditures

ACTIVE DUTY PERSONNEL: 10 assigned; 282 attached
CIVILIAN PERSONNEL: 900
CONTRACT EXPENDITURE: $9.6 mil

Services *Housing:* Family units 158; BEQ units 64; Duplex units 26; Townhouse units 128; Barracks spaces 195; Enlisted units 128; Single family dwellings 4. *Temporary Housing:* BOQ units 8; Guesthouse units 7. *Commissary:* Base commissary; Retail store; Barber shop; Dry cleaners; Service station. *Child Care/Capacities:* Day care center. *Base Library:* Yes. *Medical Facilities:* Army medical clinic in downtown St Louis; Hospital at Scott AFB, IL. *Recreational Facilities:* Bowling; Pool; Gym; Golf; Tennis; Racquetball; Fitness center; Softball field; Auto shop; Crafts; Community Club; Picnicking.

GREAT LAKES

GREAT LAKES NAVAL TRAINING CENTER

Commander, NTC, Bldg 1, Great Lakes, IL 60088-5000
(312) 688-3400; Autovon 792-3400
OFFICER-OF-THE-DAY: (312) 688-3939, Autovon 792-3939

Profile

BRANCH: Navy.

SIZE AND LOCATION: 1760 acres. On Lake Michigan approx 35 mi N of Chicago on I-94, Exit Rte 137; 40 mi S of Milwaukee; serviced by O'Hare IAP 25 mi SW.

MAJOR UNITS: Recruit Training Command; Service School Command; Military In-Processing Command; Naval Dental Research Institute; Naval Medical Command, Northeast Region; Naval Reserve Readiness Command; Naval Training Station; Public Works Center; Navy Recruiting Area Five; Naval Data Automation Facility; Navy Regional Finance Center; Naval Investigative Service; Navy Publishing and Printing Service Detachment Office; Defense Reutilization and Marketing Office; Naval Legal Service Office; Naval Telecommunications Center; NJROTC, Area Nine; Naval Reserve Readiness Command, Region Thirteen; Region III HQ, Selective Service System; Navy Drug Screening Laboratory; Marine Corps Absentee Collection Unit; Naval Reserve Force Recruiting, Region II; US Military Entrance Processing; Naval Hospital; Naval Dental Clinic; Naval Hospital Corps School.

BASE HISTORY: 1911, dedicated by President Taft; Navy's largest training facility; site divided by 4 natural plateaus: main training camp; receiving camp; Naval hospital; and Marine barracks. During WWI, Seabees originated with 12th Regiment, "Fighting Tradesmen." John Philip Sousa, age 62, commissioned a lieutenant, USNR as commanding officer of band and formed 14 regimental bands. Following WWI, baseball team included major leaguers. 1918, football team undefeated against major college opponents and wins 1919 Rose Bowl game. WWI, aviation school, Great Lakes Aeronautical Society, nicknamed "The Millionaire Squadron," with members from wealthy Chicago families who built their own hangar. 1918, official NAS and Commandant Moffett became known as "Father of Naval Aviation." 1923, Naval Reserve Air Base established. 1933-1935, reduced to maintenance status. 1937, operations transferred to Glenview NAS. 1942, first WAVE (Women Accepted for Volunteer Emergency Service) unit established. 1944, changed from Station to Center. 1948, first recruit school for women "regulars." Currently, Service School Command largest single command in Navy.

VISITOR ATTRACTIONS: Recruit graduation review held each Friday afternoon.

Key Contacts

COMMANDER: Rear Adm John F Calhoun.

PUBLIC AFFAIRS: Lt Nancy Slivka; Bldg 1, Rm B-25, (312) 688-2201, Autovon 792-2201.

PROCUREMENT: Lt Daniel Downey; NTC Comptroller, Bldg 3200, (312) 688-3371, Autovon 792-3371.

TRANSPORTATION: Capt Stephen Quigley; Public Works Center, Bldg 1H, (312) 688-6895, Autovon 792-6895.

PERSONNEL/COMMUNITY ACTIVITIES: CDR Caroline Argall; Personnel Support Activity, Bldg 122, (312) 688-3301, Autovon 792-3301.

Personnel and Expenditures

ACTIVE DUTY PERSONNEL: 21,000
DEPENDENTS: 5500
CIVILIAN PERSONNEL: 3500
MILITARY PAYROLL EXPENDITURE: $15.3 mil
CONTRACT EXPENDITURE: $88.8 mil

Services *Housing:* BOQ cottages 171; BEQ units 754; Barracks spaces 1243; Senior NCO units 41; Junior NCO units 41. *Temporary Housing:* BOQ units 112; Lodge units 50. *Commissary:* Base commissary; Retail store; Barber shop; Dry cleaners; Food shop; Florist; Banking; Service station; Bakery; Optical shop; Computer shop; Ice cream. *Child Care/Capacities:* Day care center 225; Home day care program; Infant care center. *Schools:* Elementary. *Base Library:* Yes. *Medical Facilities:* Hospital 717; Medical clinic; Dental clinic. *Recreational Facilities:* Bowling; Movie theater; Pool; Gym; Recreation center; Golf; Tennis; Racquetball; Fitness center; Softball field; Football field; Auto shop; Crafts; Officers club; NCO club; Fishing/Hunting; Sailing.

RECRUIT TRAINING COMMAND, GREAT LAKES

Great Lakes, IL 60088
(312) 688-5670; Autovon 792-5670
OFFICER-OF-THE-DAY: (312) 688-4962, 688-4963, Autovon 792-4962, 792-4963

Profile

BRANCH: Navy.

SIZE AND LOCATION: 140 acres. Take I-94 N to Rte 137, E 3 mi RTC will be on the right. From WI, exit I-94 at the IL State Line, take Rte 41 S to Rte 137, Buckley Rd, go left 1.5 mi, RTC will be on right.

MAJOR UNITS: Recruit Training Command.

BASE HISTORY: See Great Lakes Naval Training Center.

VISITOR ATTRACTIONS: RTC is a restricted base and general visitation is not permitted. However, there is a recruit graduation review held every Fri (except Christmas week) that is open to the public and visitors are welcome.

Key Contacts

COMMANDER: Capt David L O'Neill; Commanding Officer, Bldg 1127, RTC Great Lakes, IL 60088-5300.

PUBLIC AFFAIRS: AECS(AW) Jack G Stiteley; Bldg 1311, (312) 688-5670, Autovon 792-5670.

PERSONNEL/COMMUNITY ACTIVITIES: LCDR E A Bowles; Administration Officer, Bldg 1127, (312) 688-4962, Autovon 792-4962.

Personnel and Expenditures

ACTIVE DUTY PERSONNEL: 632
CIVILIAN PERSONNEL: 6

Services *Housing:* See Great Lakes Naval Training Center.

JOLIET

JOLIET ARMY AMMUNITION PLANT
Joliet, IL 60436-5000
(815) 424-2031; Autovon 696-2031
Profile
BRANCH: Army.
SIZE AND LOCATION: 23,500 acres. In the Des Plaines River Valley, approx 10 mi S of Joliet, IL, on IL Rte 53.
BASE HISTORY: 1940, construction began on Kankakee Ordnance Works (KOW) and Elwood Ordnance Plant (EOP) and completed during WWII. Combined, one of nation's largest producers of munitions. Sanderson and Porter Co built and operated ammunition loading line at EOP until 1945. E I DuPont built and operated high explosive line at KOW until 1942 when US Rubber Co was retained as contractor. 1945, KOW and EOP consolidated and redesignated as Joliet Arsenal. 1945-65, federal government operated plant. 1965, Elwood unit inactivated and standby status; US Rubber Co responsible for all Joliet AAP. 1966-76, reactivated and in production. 1976, inactive status with Uniroyal, Inc (formerly US Rubber Co) as contractor. 1973, MUCOM, APSA (a tenant at Joliet AAP), and WECOM merged to form ARMCOM.
Key Contacts
COMMANDER: LTC Jack D Conway; Iowa Army Ammunition Plant, Middletown, IA 52638, (319) 753-7200, Autovon 585-7200.
PUBLIC AFFAIRS: Douglas J Thompson; (815) 424-2001, Autovon 696-2001.
Personnel and Expenditures
ACTIVE DUTY PERSONNEL: 60 (Not assigned to mission of installation)
DEPENDENTS: 140
CIVILIAN PERSONNEL: 400
CONTRACT EXPENDITURE: $1.5 mil
Services *Housing:* Family units 45.

O'HARE ARFF

O'HARE AIR RESERVE FORCES FACILITY
928th Tactical Airlift Group, O'Hare ARFF, IL 60666-5000
(312) 694-6823; Autovon 930-6823
Profile
BRANCH: Air Force Reserve.
SIZE AND LOCATION: 400 acres. Military side of O'Hare IAP at corner of Mannheim & Higgins off Northwest Tollway.
MAJOR UNITS: 928th Tactical Airlift Group; 928th Consolidated Aircraft Maintenance Squadron; 28th Mobile Aerial Port Squadron; 928th Combat Support Squadron; 928th Communications Squadron; 928th Mobility Support Flight; 928th Tactical Clinic; 928th Security Police Flight; 64th Tactical Airlift Squadron; 928th Civil Engineering Squadron; 36th Medical Services Evacuation Squadron; 91st Aerial Port Squadron; 63rd Aeromedical Evacuation Squadron; 912th Civil Engineering Squadron; Operating Location Alpha; HQ, Illinois Air National Guard; 126th Air Refueling Wing (ILANG); 217th Engineering Installation Squadron (ILANG); 264th Combat Communications Squadron (ILANG); 566th Air Force Band (ILANG); Aeronautical System Division; Civil Air Patrol; Defense Contract Administrative Services; US Army Reserve, Ft Dearborn, IL.
BASE HISTORY: This AF Reserve complex can be traced back to 141st AFBU(RT) at Douglas-Orchard Airport, Park Ridge, IL, former name for O'Hare IAP. 1963,

928th TAG activated, component of 64th TAS. Holds Air Force's top record, 40 years accident-free flying. Major activity hosting VIPs. Since Eisenhower, unit received every American president and vice-president, the Pope, royalty, and foreign presidents and government officials visiting Chicago area.
Key Contacts
COMMANDER: Col Grant R Mulder; Group Commander, 928th TAG/CC, (312) 694-6050, Autovon 930-6050.
PUBLIC AFFAIRS: Capt Belinda L Clearmen; 928th TAG/PA, (312) 694-6823, Autovon 930-6823.
Personnel and Expenditures
CIVILIAN PERSONNEL: 2000
MILITARY PAYROLL EXPENDITURE: $56 mil
Services *Housing:* A reserve base no facilities available.

PEORIA

182ND TACTICAL AIR SUPPORT GROUP
Greater Peoria Airport, Peoria, IL 61607-1498
(309) 633-3000; Autovon 724-9210
Profile
BRANCH: Air National Guard.
SIZE AND LOCATION: 136 acres. Co-located with Greater Peoria Airport; Main gate on Airport Rd heading into Bartonville, IL.
MAJOR UNITS: 182nd Tactical Air Support Group; 169th Tactical Air Support Group; 182nd Civil Engineering; 182nd Communications Electronics Maintenance; 182nd Consolidated Aircraft Maintenance; 182nd Tactical Clinic; 182nd Weapons System Security Flight; 182nd Resource Management Squadron.
BASE HISTORY: 1946, 169th Fighter Squadron created. 1958, redesignated 169th FIG. 1961-62, active duty during Berlin Crisis. 1962, reorganized as 182nd TFG with 169th as subordinated squadron. Changed missions and aircraft, fighter group to Tactical Air Support Group. Unit building new base on other side of present flightline. 1993-94, move and Army Guard helicopter unit taking over current installation.
Key Contacts
COMMANDER: Col Kenneth D Peterson; (309) 633-3000, Autovon 724-3200.
PUBLIC AFFAIRS: Maj Robert G Arnett; (309) 633-3000, Autovon 724-3200.
PERSONNEL/COMMUNITY ACTIVITIES: LTC V Sandy Cain; (309) 633-3260, Autovon 724-3260.
Personnel and Expenditures
ACTIVE DUTY PERSONNEL: 45; 1000 total guard force
CIVILIAN PERSONNEL: 150
Services *Base Library:* Yes. *Medical Facilities:* Medical clinic available only on unit training assembly weekend. *Recreational Facilities:* NCO club.

ROCK ISLAND

ROCK ISLAND ARSENAL
Rock Island, IL 61299-5000
(309) 786-6001; Autovon 793-6001
OFFICER-OF-THE-DAY: (309) 782-5621, Autovon 793-5621
Profile
BRANCH: Army.
SIZE AND LOCATION: 946 acres. Metropolitan area of Moline and Rock Island, IL, and Davenport and Bettendorf, IA, off I-74 and I-80; served by Quad City Airport, Moline.

MAJOR UNITS: Headquarters, US Army Armament, Munitions & Chemical Command; US Army Corps of Engineers; US Army Industrial Engineering Activity.
BASE HISTORY: Authorized in 1862. Civil War site for Confederate prison. Produced military equipment almost since inception. Today, M-119 and M-198 howitzers primary production items. Island a National Historic Landmark.
VISITOR ATTRACTIONS: Rock Island Arsenal Museum; Ft Armstrong; the Bridge Monument; Clock Tower Building; Arsenal sun dial; National and Confederate Cemeteries.
Key Contacts
COMMANDER: Col David T Morgan; (309) 782-6035, Autovon 793-6035.
PUBLIC AFFAIRS: Alvin Schwartz; (309) 782-4793, Autovon 793-4793.
PROCUREMENT: Gary Wagler; (309) 782-3041, Autovon 793-3041.
TRANSPORTATION: Les Black; (309) 782-1587, Autovon 793-1587.
PERSONNEL/COMMUNITY ACTIVITIES: Pat Broderick; (309) 782-1212, Autovon 793-1212.
Personnel and Expenditures
ACTIVE DUTY PERSONNEL: 22
CIVILIAN PERSONNEL: 2
CONTRACT EXPENDITURE: FY 88, $112.2 mil
Services *Housing:* Family units 58; BEQ units 20; Senior NCO units 2. *Temporary Housing:* Apartment units 1. *Commissary:* Base commissary; Retail store; Barber shop; Food shop. *Child Care/Capacities:* Day care center 70; Home day care program; Summer camp. *Base Library:* Yes. *Medical Facilities:* Medical clinic. *Recreational Facilities:* Softball field; Crafts; Officers club.

US ARMY CORPS OF ENGINEERS, ROCK ISLAND DISTRICT
PO Box 2004, Clock Tower Bldg, Rock Island, IL 61204-2004
(309) 788-6361
OFFICER-OF-THE-DAY: (309) 788-6361
Profile
BRANCH: Army.
LOCATION: HQ building in Rock Island, IL, W end of Arsenal Island.
BASE HISTORY: 1866, established to improve shallow upper Mississippi River into major inland waterway capable of handling rapidly increasing river traffic following Civil War. 1930, District outgrew its location in federal building in Rock Island, above post office; one office moved to Liberty Building, another, Safety Building. 1931, HQ moved into Clock Tower. Operates and maintains 25 public recreation areas along 314 mi stretch of Mississippi River from Guttenberg, IA, to Saverton, MO. Covers 78,000 sq mi in portions of five states (IA, IL, MO, MN, and WI).
VISITOR ATTRACTIONS: Headquarters located in Clock Tower Building, completed in 1867 and on National Register of Historic Places. Two visitors centers at Lock and Dam 15 in Quad Cities at Mississippi River and at Starved Rock Lock and Dam on Illinois River. Also visitors centers at three reservoirs.
Key Contacts
COMMANDER: Col Neil A Smart.
PUBLIC AFFAIRS: Robert Faletti; (309) 788-6361 ext 274.
PROCUREMENT: Don Phillips.
TRANSPORTATION: Mary Strassberger.
PERSONNEL/COMMUNITY ACTIVITIES: Christine Roberts.
Personnel and Expenditures
ACTIVE DUTY PERSONNEL: 3
DEPENDENTS: 8
CIVILIAN PERSONNEL: 700-800

US ARMY CORPS OF ENGINEERS, ROCK ISLAND DISTRICT (continued)
Services *Housing:* Family units 1. *Commissary:* Base commissary; Retail store; Barber shop; Dry cleaners. *Recreational Facilities:* Rock Island Arsenal, nearby, has many recreational facilities.

SAVANNA

SAVANNA ARMY DEPOT ACTIVITY
Savanna, IL 61074-9636
(815) 273-8700; Autovon 585-8700
OFFICER-OF-THE-DAY: (815) 273-8832, Autovon 585-8832
Profile
BRANCH: Army.
SIZE AND LOCATION: 13,172 acres. 150 mi W of Chicago; 60 mi N of the Quad Cities.
MAJOR UNITS: Defense Ammunition Center & School; ASQNC-SAV; Defense Reutilization & Marketing Office; Occupational Health Nursing Office; 300th Supply Company USAR; 339th Military Police Company USAR.
BASE HISTORY: 1918, opened. 1919-20, building expansion; 18 warehouses built then still in use. 1920-WWII, 52nd Ordnance Ammunition Company assigned to Savanna. 1921, Savanna Ordnance Depot independent of Rock Island Arsenal. WWII, manufacturing and storage facilities were greatly expanded; loaded special bombs for Gen James Doolittle's historic Tokyo raid. 1941, designated to study and develop safe and adequate loading, bracing, and staying of all types of ammunition and explosives for shipment. Since then, associated functions added to require development of outloading and storage procedures for all ammunition within Army Ammunition Supply System.
Key Contacts
COMMANDER: LTC Jerald E Kleager.
PUBLIC AFFAIRS: Jean R Kean.
PROCUREMENT: M J Hanson; (815) 273-8351, Autovon 585-8351.
TRANSPORTATION: K T Sproule; (815) 273-8649, Autovon 585-8649.
Personnel and Expenditures
ACTIVE DUTY PERSONNEL: 4
DEPENDENTS: 12
CIVILIAN PERSONNEL: 554
MILITARY PAYROLL EXPENDITURE: $92,000
CONTRACT EXPENDITURE: $0.8 mil
Services *Housing:* Family units 4; BEQ units 4. *Medical Facilities:* Occupational Health Nursing Office. *Recreational Facilities:* Pool; Gym; Tennis; Softball field; Camping; Fishing/Hunting.

SCOTT AFB

SCOTT AIR FORCE BASE
Scott AFB, IL 62225-0000
(618) 256-1110; Autovon 576-1110
OFFICER-OF-THE-DAY: (618) 256-5891, Autovon 576-5891
Profile
BRANCH: Air Force.
SIZE AND LOCATION: 3297 acres. S of I-64 off IL-158 and IL-161, approx 20 mi E of St Louis, MO; commercial service through Lambert Airport, St Louis.
MAJOR UNITS: HQ US Transportation Command (joint service); HQ Military Airlift Command; HQ Air Force Communications Command; HQ Air Weather Service; HQ Aerospace Rescue and Recovery Service; 375th Aeromedical Airlift Wing; Defense Commercial Communications Office; 932nd Aeromedical Airlift Group.
BASE HISTORY: Active installation since 1917, named after Army Cpl Frank S Scott, killed in Wright biplane crash, 1912.

WWI and WWII training base; once housed dirigibles. Now, home to three major commands with worldwide commitment, C-9 medical aircraft, C-12 and C-21 support aircraft, C-140 flight checking aircraft, and H-60 Army (Reserve) helicopters.
VISITOR ATTRACTIONS: Tours on request.
Key Contacts
COMMANDER: 375 ABG/CC, Scott AFB, IL 62225-5001, (618) 256-3283, Autovon 576-3283.
PUBLIC AFFAIRS: 375 AAW/PA, Scott AFB, IL 62225-5154, (618) 256-4241, Autovon 576-4241.
PROCUREMENT: 375 AAW/LGC, Scott AFB, IL 62225-5001, (618) 256-3036, Autovon 576-3036.
TRANSPORTATION: 375 AAW/LGT, Scott AFB, IL 62225-5001, (618) 256-2004, Autovon 576-2004.
PERSONNEL/COMMUNITY ACTIVITIES: Director of Personnel, 375 ABG/DP, Scott AFB, IL 62225-5001, (618) 256-2126, Autovon 576-2126.
Personnel and Expenditures
ACTIVE DUTY PERSONNEL: 8000
DEPENDENTS: 5000
CIVILIAN PERSONNEL: 3000
MILITARY PAYROLL EXPENDITURE: $210 mil
CONTRACT EXPENDITURE: $114 mil
Services *Housing:* Family units 1778; Mobile home units 193; Dorms 6. *Temporary Housing:* VOQ cottages 10; VAQ units 5; Transient living quarters (bldgs) 2. *Commissary:* Base commissary; Retail store; Barber shop; Dry cleaners; Florist; Banking; Service station. *Child Care/Capacities:* Day care center 100; Home day care program. *Base Library:* Yes. *Medical Facilities:* Regional AF Medical Ctr 150 beds. *Recreational Facilities:* Bowling; Movie theater; Pool; Gym; Recreation center; Golf; Stables; Tennis; Racquetball; Fitness center; Softball field; Auto shop; Crafts; Officers club; NCO club; Camping; Fishing/Hunting.

SPRINGFIELD

CAMP LINCOLN
1301 N MacArthur Blvd, Springfield, IL 62702-2399
(217) 785-3500; Autovon 555-3500
Profile
BRANCH: Army National Guard.
SIZE AND LOCATION: 160 acres. On N side of Springfield, bordering Rte 29, 0.5 mi from airport; almost in the shadow of Lincoln's Monument.
MAJOR UNITS: 204th MED; 1144th TRANS; 232nd S&S; 3637th Maintenance; State Area Command; 139th PAD; 233rd Military Police; 114th Army Band.
BASE HISTORY: 1886, Camp Lincoln first used; rifle range considered finest in the West and equal to any in country. Currently, used by IL NG for encampment during annual training.
VISITOR ATTRACTIONS: Military Civil War museum on post.
Key Contacts
COMMANDER: Maj Gen Harold Holesinger.
PUBLIC AFFAIRS: LTC Donald Kunzweiler; (217) 785-3569, Autovon 555-3643.
PROCUREMENT: (217) 785-3500.
TRANSPORTATION: LTC Daniel Cedusky; (217) 785-3597, Autovon 555-3597.
PERSONNEL/COMMUNITY ACTIVITIES: LTC Thomas Nevill; (217) 785-3558.
Personnel and Expenditures
ACTIVE DUTY PERSONNEL: Army Guard members
CIVILIAN PERSONNEL: 25

183RD TACTICAL FIGHTER GROUP (ANG)
Capitol Airport, Springfield, IL 62707
(217) 753-8850; Autovon 631-8210
Profile
BRANCH: Air National Guard.
SIZE AND LOCATION: 70 acres. In the NW section of Springfield off State Rte 29.
MAJOR UNITS: 183rd Tactical Fighter Group (ANG).
Personnel and Expenditures
ACTIVE DUTY PERSONNEL: 1014
CIVILIAN PERSONNEL: 253
MILITARY PAYROLL EXPENDITURE: $10.5 mil
Services *Medical Facilities:* Dispensary.

INDIANA

CRANE

NAVAL WEAPONS SUPPORT CENTER CRANE

Crane, IN 47522
(812) 854-1394; Autovon 482-1394
OFFICER-OF-THE-DAY: (812) 854-1222,
Autovon 482-1222

Profile

BRANCH: Navy.

SIZE AND LOCATION: 62,000 acres. In S-central IN, 75 mi SW of Indianapolis, 71 mi NW of Louisville; IN Hwy 558 and 158 lead into the center and Hwy 45 goes to the gate.

MAJOR UNITS: Naval Weapons Support Center; Crane Army Ammunition Activity.

BASE HISTORY: 1941, commissioned as Naval Ammunition Depot, Burns City, to supply ammunition. 1943, renamed Crane for Commodore William Montgomery Crane, first Chief of Naval Ordnance; mission expanded to include applied sciences, weapons engineering, and quality evaluation. 1975, renamed Naval Weapons Support Center Crane and production and storage transferred to Crane Army Ammunition Activity. Center comprises area larger than DC. 400 mi of roads and trails, 170 mi of railroad, 800 acre lake and 3000 buildings.

Key Contacts

COMMANDER: Capt Charles E Johnson; (812) 854-1210, Autovon 482-1210.

PUBLIC AFFAIRS: Richard McGarvey; Code B2, (812) 854-1640, Autovon 482-1640.

PROCUREMENT: CDR R J Gallitz; Code 11, (812) 854-1122, Autovon 482-1122.

TRANSPORTATION: CDR M L Frey; Code 09, (812) 854-1344, Autovon 482-1344.

PERSONNEL/COMMUNITY ACTIVITIES: Rose Queen; Director of Personnel, Code 06, (812) 854-1602, Autovon 482-1602.

Personnel and Expenditures

ACTIVE DUTY PERSONNEL: 50
DEPENDENTS: 100
CIVILIAN PERSONNEL: 4600
CONTRACT EXPENDITURE: $18.5 mil

Services *Housing:* Family units 6; BEQ units 25. *Temporary Housing:* VIP cottages 1; BOQ units 15; Apartment units 3. *Commissary:* Base commissary; Retail store; Barber shop; Banking; Service station. *Child Care/Capacities:* Day camp. *Base Library:* Yes. *Medical Facilities:* Medical clinic. *Recreational Facilities:* Bowling; Pool; Gym; Golf; Tennis; Racquetball; Fitness center; Softball field; Crafts; Officers club; NCO club; Camping; Fishing/Hunting; Marina; Picnicking.

FORT BENJAMIN HARRISON

FORT BENJAMIN HARRISON

Fort Benjamin Harrison, IN 46216
(317) 546-9211
OFFICER-OF-THE-DAY: (317) 542-4541

Profile

BRANCH: Army.

SIZE AND LOCATION: 2500 acres. NE of Indianapolis, off I-465; served by the Indianapolis IAP.

MAJOR UNITS: US Army Soldier Support Center; US Army Finance & Accounting Center; US Army Enlisted Records & Evaluation Center; Defense Information School.

BASE HISTORY: 1903, established, remained nameless until 1906 when President Theodore Roosevelt named it after predecessor and friend. Originally intended as station for one infantry regiment. WWI, officers' training camp. WWI-WWII, infantry post, housing at one time or another 10th, 11th, 20th, 23rd, 40th, 45th, and 46th Infantry Regiments. WWII, reception center, Finance Replacement Training Center, part of Army Finance School, Army Chaplains' School, Cook and Bakers School, Military Police Disciplinary Barracks, and POW camp for German and Italian prisoners. 1947, placed on inactive list. 1948, Indiana Military District HQs; Army released control to Air Force, name changed to Benjamin Harrison AFB; 10th Air Force HQ. 1950, Army regained control. 1951, Army Finance Center. 1957, Adjutant General and Finance Schools. 1965, Defense Information School. 1973, placed under Army Training and Doctrine Command (TRADOC), designed Army Administration Center; Adjutant General and Finance Schools were merged as Army Institute of Administration. 1980, post reorganized and renamed Army Soldier Support Center; Institute of Administration became Institute of Personnel and Resource Management. 1984, Institute renamed Army Soldier Support Institute.

VISITOR ATTRACTIONS: Finance Museum.

Key Contacts

COMMANDER: Maj Gen Stephen R Woods Jr.

PUBLIC AFFAIRS: Sally L Spriggs; Bldg 600, Ft Benjamin Harrison, IN 46216-5040, (317) 542-4198, Autovon 699-4198.

PROCUREMENT: (317) 549-5806.

TRANSPORTATION: (317) 549-5728.

PERSONNEL/COMMUNITY ACTIVITIES: (317) 542-4513.

Personnel and Expenditures

ACTIVE DUTY PERSONNEL: 1900
DEPENDENTS: 864
CIVILIAN PERSONNEL: 4200
MILITARY PAYROLL EXPENDITURE: $72 mil

CONTRACT EXPENDITURE: $52 mil

Services *Housing:* Family units 283; BOQ cottages 17; BEQ units 116; Senior NCO units 42; Mobile home units 100; RV/Camper sites. *Temporary Housing:* VIP cottages 7; VOQ cottages 377; VEQ units 166; Guesthouse units 16. *Commissary:* Base commissary; Retail store; Barber shop; Dry cleaners; Food shop; Banking; Service station. *Child Care/Capacities:* Day care center. *Base Library:* Yes. *Medical Facilities:* Hospital 25; Medical clinic; Dental clinic. *Recreational Facilities:* Bowling; Movie theater; Pool; Gym; Recreation center; Golf; Stables; Tennis; Racquetball; Fitness center; Softball field; Auto shop; Crafts; Officers club; NCO club; Camping; Fishing/Hunting.

FORT WAYNE

122ND TACTICAL FIGHTER WING (ANG)

Fort Wayne Municipal Airport, Fort Wayne, IN 46809
(219) 747-4141; Autovon 889-1550

Profile

BRANCH: Air National Guard.

SIZE AND LOCATION: 87 acres. 5 mi SSW of Fort Wayne.

MAJOR UNITS: 122nd Tactical Fighter Wing (ANG).

Personnel and Expenditures

ACTIVE DUTY PERSONNEL: 1006
CIVILIAN PERSONNEL: 248
MILITARY PAYROLL EXPENDITURE: $9.9 mil

GRISSOM AFB

GRISSOM AIR FORCE BASE

Grissom AFB, IN 46971
(317) 689-2104; Autovon 928-2104

Profile

BRANCH: Air Force.

SIZE AND LOCATION: 3100 acres. On Hwy 31 approx 15 mi N of Kokomo, IN, 50 mi N of Indianapolis.

MAJOR UNITS: 305th Air Refueling Wing (ARW); 434th Air Refueling Wing (ARW); 930th Tactical Fighter Group (TFG).

BASE HISTORY: 1943, began as Bunker Hill Naval Station, named after nearby hamlet of Bunker Hill, IN. 1954, redesignated Bunker Hill AFB. May 1968, renamed for LTC Virgil I Grissom, IN native and one of three astronauts who died in *Apollo* spacecraft tragedy, Jan 1967.

VISITOR ATTRACTIONS: Aircraft museum located just outside main gate.

GRISSOM AIR FORCE BASE (continued)
Key Contacts
COMMANDER: Col Robert J Beck; 305 CSG/
CC, (317) 689-3344, Autovon 928-3344.
PUBLIC AFFAIRS: Capt Ronald N McGee; 305
AREFW/PA, (317) 689-2104, Autovon
928-2104.
PROCUREMENT: Capt Bud Campbell; 305
ARW/LGC, (317) 689-3101, Autovon
928-3101.
TRANSPORTATION: Maj Larry Spence; 305
TRNSS/CC, (317) 689-3136, Autovon
928-3136.
PERSONNEL/COMMUNITY ACTIVITIES: Maj
John Earl Collier; Personnel Director, 305
MSSQ/CC, (317) 689-2265, Autovon 928-
2265; Community Activities see Public
Affairs Officer.
Personnel and Expenditures
ACTIVE DUTY PERSONNEL: 2800
DEPENDENTS: 4114
CIVILIAN PERSONNEL: 1255
MILITARY PAYROLL EXPENDITURE: FY 88,
$56.3 mil
CONTRACT EXPENDITURE: FY 88, $60 mil
Services *Housing:* Family units 1116; BOQ
cottages 12; BEQ units 1059; BAQ units 83;
Duplex units 744; Townhouse units 200;
Barracks spaces 1059; Dormitory spaces
1059; Senior NCO units 8; Junior NCO
units 1051. *Temporary Housing:* VIP cot-
tages 4; VOQ cottages 33; VAQ units 88;
BOQ units 16; BAQ units 67; Guesthouse
units 12; Apartment units 12; Dormitory
units 1059; Transient living quarters 12.
Commissary: Base commissary; Retail store;
Barber shop; Dry cleaners; Food shop; Florist; Banking; Service station; Bakery. *Child
Care/Capacities:* Day care center. *Schools:*
Kindergarten/Preschool; Elementary. *Base
Library:* Yes. *Medical Facilities:* Medical
clinic; Dental clinic; Veterinary services. *Recreational Facilities:* Bowling; Movie theater;
Pool; Gym; Recreation center; Golf; Stables;
Tennis; Racquetball; Fitness center; Softball
field; Football field; Auto shop; Crafts; Of-
ficers club; NCO club.

INDIANAPOLIS

NAVAL AVIONICS CENTER, INDIANAPOLIS
6000 E 21st St, Indianapolis, IN 46219-2189
(317) 353-7000; Autovon 369-7000
OFFICER-OF-THE-DAY: (317) 353-3104,
Autovon 369-3104
Profile
BRANCH: Navy.
SIZE AND LOCATION: 163 acres. On the NE
side of Indianapolis close to I-465 and I-
70. Take the Shadeland Ave Exit to 21st
St; 20 min from Indianapolis IAP and in
walking distance to hotels.
MAJOR UNITS: Navy Avionics Center.
BASE HISTORY: 1942, originated as Naval
Ordnance Plant, GOCO facility. Produced
Norden Bombsight and support for avion-
ics systems such as LAMPS MK III Heli-
copter, A-6 Intruder, F-14 Tomcat, Space
Shuttle, F/A-18 Hornet, and E-2
Hawkeye.
Key Contacts
COMMANDER: Capt Russell Henry; (317) 353-
7000, Autovon 369-7000.
PUBLIC AFFAIRS: Diana K Hogue; (317) 353-
7076, Autovon 369-7076.
PROCUREMENT: (317) 353-7600, Autovon
369-7600.
TRANSPORTATION: LCDR William McIntyre;
(317) 353-7730, Autovon 369-7730.
PERSONNEL/COMMUNITY ACTIVITIES: David
Fogleman; (317) 353-7500, Autovon 369-
7500.

Personnel and Expenditures
ACTIVE DUTY PERSONNEL: 14
CIVILIAN PERSONNEL: 3200
CONTRACT EXPENDITURE: $385 mil
Services *Housing:* Family units 5. *Base Li-
brary:* Yes. *Recreational Facilities:* Softball
field.

MADISON

JEFFERSON PROVING GROUND
US 421 S, Madison, IN 47250-5100
(812) 273-7211; Autovon 480-7211
OFFICER-OF-THE-DAY: (812) 273-7149,
Autovon 480-1491
Profile
BRANCH: Army.
SIZE AND LOCATION: 55,264 acres. 3 mi N of
Madison, IN, on US 421 S; area served
by the Greater Cincinnati Airport, 60 mi
and Standiford Field, Louisville, KY, 50
mi.
Key Contacts
COMMANDER: Col Carl V Glover; (812) 273-
7201, Autovon 480-7201.
PUBLIC AFFAIRS: Gary Stegner; (812) 273-
7345, Autovon 480-7345.
PROCUREMENT: Mary N Gassert; (812) 273-
7281, Autovon 480-7281.
TRANSPORTATION: Robert Stacey; (812) 273-
7232, Autovon 480-7232.
PERSONNEL/COMMUNITY ACTIVITIES: Russell
Shorten; (812) 273-7416, Autovon 480-
7416.
Personnel and Expenditures
ACTIVE DUTY PERSONNEL: 3
DEPENDENTS: 40
CIVILIAN PERSONNEL: 450
Services *Housing:* Family units 13. *Recrea-
tional Facilities:* Tennis; Softball field;
Camping; Fishing/Hunting.

TERRE HAUTE

181ST TACTICAL FIGHTER GROUP (ANG)
Hulman Regional Airport, Terre Haute, IN
47803
(812) 877-5210; Autovon 724-1210
Profile
BRANCH: Air National Guard.
SIZE AND LOCATION: 279 acres. 5 mi E of
Terre Haute; S of US-40, off State Rte
42.
MAJOR UNITS: 181st Tactical Fighter Group
(ANG).
Personnel and Expenditures
ACTIVE DUTY PERSONNEL: 874
CIVILIAN PERSONNEL: 222
MILITARY PAYROLL EXPENDITURE: $9.3 mil
Services *Medical Facilities:* 5-bed dispen-
sary.

IOWA

DES MOINES

IOWA AIR NATIONAL GUARD
3100 McKinley Ave, Des Moines, IA 50321-2799
(515) 287-9210; Autovon 939-8210
OFFICER-OF-THE-DAY: (515) 287-9220, Autovon 939-8220
Profile
BRANCH: Air National Guard.
SIZE AND LOCATION: 113 acres. In SW quadrant of Des Moines. Des Moines IAP adj to base. Army Post Rd (Hwy 5) intersects with Fleur Dr at SE corner of airport, approx 5 mi from downtown Des Moines.
MAJOR UNITS: 132nd Tactical Fighter Wing; 124th Tactical Fighter Squadron.
BASE HISTORY: 1941, origin of IA ANG and 132nd TFW traced back to 1941 with 124th Observation Squadron at Des Moines Municipal Airport. Korean Conflict, called to active duty; served 21 months. 1988, 132nd TFW first ANG unit deployed to Far East and participated in multi-national exercise.
Key Contacts
COMMANDER: Brig Gen Gerald W Swartzbaugh; (515) 287-9200, Autovon 939-8200.
PUBLIC AFFAIRS: 1Lt Robert Young; (515) 287-9214, Autovon 939-8214.
PROCUREMENT: MSgt Elmer Riggle; (515) 287-9461, Autovon 939-8461.
TRANSPORTATION: SMSgt Kenneth Croat; (515) 287-9445, Autovon 939-8445.
PERSONNEL/COMMUNITY ACTIVITIES: Capt Frank Sarcone; (515) 287-9525, Autovon 939-8525.
Personnel and Expenditures
ACTIVE DUTY PERSONNEL: 55
CIVILIAN PERSONNEL: 250
MILITARY PAYROLL EXPENDITURE: $18 mil
CONTRACT EXPENDITURE: $16 mil
Services *Commissary and Exchange:* Retail store.

JOHNSTON

CAMP DODGE IOWA
7700 NW Beaver Dr, Johnston, IA 50131-1902
(515) 242-5011; Autovon 946-2011
Profile
BRANCH: Army National Guard.
SIZE AND LOCATION: 2300 acres. 5 mi N of Des Moines; 2 mi N of Johnston, IA; Take Hwy 401, 4 mi N off I-80 exchange.
MAJOR UNITS: HQ Iowa Army National Guard; 134th S&S Battalion; 34th Military Police Battalion; 34th RAOC; Regional Training Center (Maintenance); Iowa Military Academy.
BASE HISTORY: 1907, site purchased for training of state militia; named Camp Dodge for Maj Gen Grenville M Dodge, from

Council Bluffs, IA, active in organizing early IA militia. federal government used Camp during WWI and II, during interim periods, leased portions to state. 1955, title conveyed to IA State. Currently, Annual Training Site and weekend training of IA NG, and Logistical Support Center for IA. Terrain flat to rolling. one battalion-sized infantry, artillery, engineer or combat type service type unit conducting non-live fire exercises, can be accommodated at one time. Usually three to four large annual training periods. Used by Army and Navy Reserve, ANG, ROTC, and USMC Reserve.
VISITOR ATTRACTIONS: Military Museum (open Mon-Wed-Fri, 1330-1630); Adjacent to Saylorville Recreation Area; 11th largest wildlife refuge in state. One of world's largest outdoor filtered swimming pools.
Key Contacts
COMMANDER: Maj Gen Warren G Lawson.
PUBLIC AFFAIRS: LTC James E Brown; (515) 242-5305, Autovon 946-2305.
PROCUREMENT: CW3 Jim Huyck; (515) 242-5248, Autovon 946-2248.
TRANSPORTATION: Maj John Rice; (515) 242-5271, Autovon 946-2271.
PERSONNEL/COMMUNITY ACTIVITIES: Col James McCullough; (515) 242-5360, Autovon 946-2360.
Personnel and Expenditures
ACTIVE DUTY PERSONNEL: 1500
MILITARY PAYROLL EXPENDITURE: $33.8 mil
CONTRACT EXPENDITURE: $4.4 mil
Services *Temporary Housing:* VIP cottages 1; VEQ units 28; BOQ units 46. *Commissary and Exchange:* Retail store. *Medical Facilities:* Medical clinic. *Recreational Facilities:* Pool; Softball field; Fishing/Hunting.

MIDDLETOWN

IOWA ARMY AMMUNITION PLANT
ATTN: SMCIO-CO, Middletown, IA 52638-5000
(319) 753-7200; Autovon 585-7200
Profile
BRANCH: Army.
SIZE AND LOCATION: 19,000 acres. 8 mi W of Burlington, IA.
BASE HISTORY: A GOCO military industrial installation under jurisdiction of Army Armament, Munitions and Chemical Command. Original plant constructed Feb 1942. Employment ranged from 12,200 in 1941 to low of 923 in 1983.
Key Contacts
COMMANDER: LTC Jack D Conway.
PUBLIC AFFAIRS: Darlene I Norton.
TRANSPORTATION: Thomas Hauck.

Personnel and Expenditures
ACTIVE DUTY PERSONNEL: 14
DEPENDENTS: 87
CIVILIAN PERSONNEL: 1400
CONTRACT EXPENDITURE: $50.7 mil
Services *Housing:* Family units 52. *Medical Facilities:* Hospital 1; Numerous examining tables. *Recreational Facilities:* Tennis; Fitness center; Softball field; Fishing/Hunting.

SERGEANT BLUFF

185TH TACTICAL FIGHTER GROUP (ANG)
PO Box 278A, Sioux Gateway Airport, Sergeant Bluff, IA 51054-1002
(712) 279-7500
Profile
BRANCH: Air National Guard.
SIZE AND LOCATION: 90 acres. In W IA; approx 5 mi S of Sioux City, IA; off I-29 at the Sioux Gateway Airport.
MAJOR UNITS: Headquarters 185th Tactical Fighter Group; 174th Tactical Fighter Squadron; 8185th Security Force.
BASE HISTORY: Began as 174th Fighter Squadron, federally recognized 1946, as unit of Iowa ANG. 1951, called to active duty and moved to Dow AFB, Bangor, ME, reactivated to that base. 1952, released from active duty and returned to state control. 1968, after series of reorganizations and redesignations, 185th recalled to active duty as result of Pueblo Crisis. 1969, returned to Sioux City and released from active duty.
Key Contacts
COMMANDER: Col Dennis Swanstrom.
PUBLIC AFFAIRS: Capt Bruce Scheid.
Personnel and Expenditures
ACTIVE DUTY PERSONNEL: 900 (full & part time)
CIVILIAN PERSONNEL: 40
MILITARY PAYROLL EXPENDITURE: $3.9 mil
CONTRACT EXPENDITURE: $2.9 mil
Services *Housing:* Barracks spaces; Dormitory spaces. *Medical Facilities:* Medical clinic.

KANSAS

ATCHISON

DEFENSE INDUSTRIAL PLANT EQUIPMENT FACILITY

RR 1, PO Box 532, Atchison, KS 66002
(913) 367-4300; Autovon 886-1520
Profile
BRANCH: Army.
SIZE AND LOCATION: 125 acres. 1 mi S of Atchison, KS, on old Hwy 73.
MAJOR UNITS: AMCCOM Vaults 1 & 2; Industrial Plant Equipment Machines; Clothing & Medical Supplies.
BASE HISTORY: 1944, War Food Administration leased a limestone mine and developed it for perishable foods. 1952-63, Army took over operation for storage of industrial plant equipment. Currently, GOCO industrial activity under Defense Industrial Plant Equipment Center, Memphis, TN; also off-site storage facility for Defense Reutilization and Marketing Offices (DRMOs) at Ft Leavenworth, and Ft Riley, KS.
Key Contacts
COMMANDER: A B Kocour.
PUBLIC AFFAIRS: William Lopez.
PROCUREMENT: Ruthann Meyer.
TRANSPORTATION: Catherine Kovan.
Personnel and Expenditures
CIVILIAN PERSONNEL: 30
CONTRACT EXPENDITURE: $1.2 mil
Services *Medical Facilities:* First aid room.

FORT LEAVENWORTH

FORT LEAVENWORTH

US Army Combined Arms Center & Fort Leavenworth, Fort Leavenworth, KS 66027
(913) 684-4021; Autovon 552-4021
OFFICER-OF-THE-DAY: (913) 684-4154, Autovon 552-4154
Profile
BRANCH: Army.
SIZE AND LOCATION: 5600 acres. Adj to Leavenworth, KS, on US Hwy 73 and KS Rte 92, approx 30 mi NW of Kansas City, MO.
MAJOR UNITS: Command and General Staff College; Combined Arms Combat Developments Activity; Combined Arms Training Activity; US Disciplinary Barracks; HQs TRADOC Analysis Command; HQ 35th Infantry Division (M)(ANG).
BASE HISTORY: 1827, established by Col Henry Leavenworth. 1830s-1840s branches of Santa Fe and Oregon Trails traversed post carrying settlers west. Mexican War (1846-48), important Army HQs. Mid-1850s saved from abandonment by US Secretary of War, Jefferson Davis. George A Custer and his brother Tom, first man to earn two Medals of Honor, served here and Tom buried in National Cemetery

here. May 1881, what is today US Army Command and General Staff College established.
VISITOR ATTRACTIONS: Ft Leavenworth is a National Historic Landmark; Frontier Army Museum (open 10-4, Mon-Sat, 12-4, Sun & Holidays, except New Year's, Christmas, Thanksgiving, and Easter).
Key Contacts
COMMANDER: Lt Gen Leonard P Wishart III.
PUBLIC AFFAIRS: LTC John C Garlinger; Bldg 198, Ft Leavenworth, KS 66027-5050, (913) 684-5604, Autovon 552-5604.
PROCUREMENT: Robert Bristow; Bldg 198, (913) 684-3383, Autovon 552-3383.
TRANSPORTATION: Capt Billy Mathews; Bldg 198, (913) 684-5631, Autovon 552-5631.
PERSONNEL/COMMUNITY ACTIVITIES: LTC Walter Kazor; Bldg 198, (913) 684-3719, Autovon 552-3719.
Personnel and Expenditures
ACTIVE DUTY PERSONNEL: 5600
DEPENDENTS: 7000
CIVILIAN PERSONNEL: 3100
MILITARY PAYROLL EXPENDITURE: FY 88, $100 mil
CONTRACT EXPENDITURE: FY 88, $150 mil
Services *Housing:* Family units 1574; BOQ cottages 4; BEQ units 8; Trailer spaces 30. *Temporary Housing:* VIP cottages 23; VOQ cottages 735; Guesthouse units 16. *Commissary:* Base commissary; Retail store; Barber shop; Dry cleaners; Food shop; Banking; Service station; Book store; Computer shop; Clothing sales; Beauty shop; Optical shop; Video rental. *Child Care/Capacities:* Day care center 279; Home day care program. *Schools:* Elementary; Intermediate/Junior high. *Base Library:* Yes. *Medical Facilities:* Hospital 38; Dental clinic. *Recreational Facilities:* Bowling; Movie theater; Pool; Gym; Recreation center; Golf; Stables; Tennis; Racquetball; Fitness center; Softball field; Football field; Auto shop; Crafts; Officers club; NCO club; Camping; Fishing/Hunting; Picnic areas; Museum.

FORT RILEY

FORT RILEY

HQs, 1st Infantry Division (Mechanized), Bldg 500, Huebner Rd, Fort Riley, KS 66535
(913) 239-3524; Autovon 856-3032
OFFICER-OF-THE-DAY: (913) 239-2222, Autovon 856-2222
Profile
BRANCH: Army.
SIZE AND LOCATION: 100,752 acres. Between Manhattan & Junction, KS; Manhattan is 15 mi E and Junction City at W gate; Ogden at E gate.

MAJOR UNITS: 1st Infantry Division; Third Region ROTC: US Army Correctional Activity/1st, 2d & 7th Brigades; 937th Engineer Corps.
BASE HISTORY: Since 1917, 1st Infantry Division, "No Mission Too Difficult, No Sacrifice Too Great, Duty First," has been fighting and serving. 1955-65, "Big Red One" stationed here; first division to go to Vietnam. 1970, 1st Infantry Division returned.
VISITOR ATTRACTIONS: US Cavalry Museum; Custer House; 1st Territorial Capital of KS; Buffalo herd.
Key Contacts
COMMANDER: Maj Gen Gordon Sullivan; (913) 239-3516, Autovon 856-3516.
PUBLIC AFFAIRS: Maj Bill Ackerly; Bldg 511, (913) 239-3032, Autovon 856-3032.
PROCUREMENT: LTC Allard; Bldg 200, (913) 239-6458, Autovon 856-6458.
TRANSPORTATION: Maj Taborosi; Director of Logistics, Patton Hall, Ft Riley, KS 66442-5016, (913) 239-3041, Autovon 856-3041.
PERSONNEL/COMMUNITY ACTIVITIES: LTC Hugharty; Bldg 403, (913) 239-3467, Autovon 856-3467.
Personnel and Expenditures
ACTIVE DUTY PERSONNEL: 15,700
DEPENDENTS: 31,700
CIVILIAN PERSONNEL: 4200
MILITARY PAYROLL EXPENDITURE: $432 mil
Services *Housing:* Family units 3180; BEQ units; BAQ units; Barracks spaces. *Temporary Housing:* Guesthouse units. *Commissary:* Base commissary; Retail store; Barber shop; Dry cleaners; Food shop; Florist; Banking; Book store. *Child Care/Capacities:* Day care center; Home day care program. *Schools:* Kindergarten/Preschool; Elementary; Intermediate/Junior high; Child care facilities. *Base Library:* Yes. *Medical Facilities:* Hospital; Medical clinic; Dental clinic. *Recreational Facilities:* Bowling; Movie theater; Pool; Gym; Recreation center; Golf; Stables; Tennis; Racquetball; Skating rink; Fitness center; Softball field; Football field; Auto shop; Crafts; Officers club; NCO club; Fishing/Hunting; Camping at nearby State Lake.

MCCONNELL AFB

MCCONNELL AIR FORCE BASE

384th BMW, McConnell AFB, KS 67221
(316) 652-6100; Autovon 743-6100
OFFICER-OF-THE-DAY: (316) 652-3250, Autovon 743-3250
Profile
BRANCH: Air Force.
SIZE AND LOCATION: 3066 acres. On S edge of Wichita. From N on KS Tpke, use E Wichita exit and go W 0.5 mi on US Hwy 54 (Kellogg Ave) and turn left at

MCCONNELL AIR FORCE BASE (continued)
Rock Rd. From S on KS Tpke, take K-15 exit, turn right, and W gate approx 1 mi straight ahead. If arriving on I-35, take Kellogg E to Rock Rd and drive S to base's E gate.

MAJOR UNITS: 384th Bombardment Wing (SAC); 184th Tactical Fighter Group (KS ANG).

BASE HISTORY: 1972, 384th Air Refueling Wing (Heavy) activated at McConnell assigned to 12th Strategic Missile Division and HQs 15th Air Force. 384th aircraft have supported many TAC and ANG fighter deployments all over the world. 1987, 384th AREFW redesignated 384th BMW (SAC), making McConnell fourth base to host B-1B bomber. 384th reports to HQ SAC, Offutt AFB, NE, through HQ 8th Air Force, Barksdale AFB, LA, and its intermediary, 19th Air Division, Carswell AFB, TX.

Key Contacts
COMMANDER: Col Phillip J Ford; 384 BMW/CC, (316) 652-3100, Autovon 743-3100.

PUBLIC AFFAIRS: LTC Paul E Muehring; 384 BMW/PA, (316) 652-3141, Autovon 743-3141.

PROCUREMENT: Capt John E Potts; Contracting, 384 BMW/DPC, (316) 652-3275, Autovon 743-3275.

TRANSPORTATION: LTC James J Boni Jr; 384 TRNS/CC, (316) 652-5249, Autovon 743-5249.

PERSONNEL/COMMUNITY ACTIVITIES: Maj Darrell D Jones; Director of Personnel, 384 CSG/DP, (316) 652-3730, Autovon 743-3730.

Personnel and Expenditures
ACTIVE DUTY PERSONNEL: 3259
DEPENDENTS: 7136
CIVILIAN PERSONNEL: 415
MILITARY PAYROLL EXPENDITURE: $76.8 mil
CONTRACT EXPENDITURE: $13.9 mil

Services *Housing:* Family units 589; BOQ cottages 1; Dormitory spaces 968. *Temporary Housing:* VOQ cottages 27; VAQ units 36; BOQ units 2; Transient living quarters 25. *Commissary:* Base commissary; Retail store; Barber shop; Dry cleaners; Food shop; Banking; Service station. *Child Care/Capacities:* Day care center; Home day care program. *Schools:* Elementary; K-6 in McConnell Manor, base housing area. *Base Library:* Yes. *Medical Facilities:* Hospital 7; Dental clinic. *Recreational Facilities:* Bowling; Movie theater; Pool; Gym; Recreation center; Golf; Tennis; Racquetball; Fitness center; Softball field; Football field; Auto shop; Crafts; Officers club; NCO club; Fishing/Hunting.

OVERLAND PARK

US MARINE CORPS RESERVE SUPPORT CENTER
10950 El Monte, Overland Park, KS 66211
(913) 481-7500; Autovon 465-3101; 465-3102 plus ext
OFFICER-OF-THE-DAY: (913) 491-7500, Autovon 465-3101, ext 7500

Profile
BRANCH: Marines.

SIZE AND LOCATION: Office bldg with annex. In SW section of Kansas City Metro area, off I-435, first exit W of State Line Rd (KS/MO border); Take Roe exit S to 109th (immediate left) in Fox Hill Office complex and follow into El Monte, sign on parking lot clearly marks facility.

BASE HISTORY: 1965, originally established as Reserve Records Branch (Class III), under USMC Reserve Data Services Center, administrative support center for Reserve of USMC. 1972, redesignated Marine Corps Reserve Forces Records Branch (Class III), subordinate branch of Division of Reserve under Reserve Automated Systems Manpower Branch for Systems Management. 1973, redesignated Marine Corps Reserve Forces Administrative Activity (MCRFAA). 1976, again redesignated Marine Corps Reserve Forces Administrative Center (MCRFAC). Basic mission remained constant until 1981; Marine Corps Reserve Forces Administration Center amalgamated into administrative and management complex designated MCRSC. 1982, moved into current facility. Provides Marine Corps with pretrained individual manpower, consisting of IRR, Standby Reserve, Fleet Marine Corps Reserve not on active duty, regular and retired Reservists, and Individual Mobilization Augmentees (IMAs). Additionally, recruits prior service Marines for drilling SMCR units within 4th Marine Division/4th Marine Aircraft Wing team (4th DWT).

Key Contacts
COMMANDER: Brig Gen John F Cronin; Director, (913) 491-7502, Autovon 465-3101, ext 7502.

PUBLIC AFFAIRS: Capt Lerae S Stanton; (913) 491-7905, 491-7910, Autovon 465-3101, ext 7905.

PROCUREMENT: Maj Dante L Petrizzo; (913) 491-7900, Autovon 465-3101, ext 7900.

PERSONNEL/COMMUNITY ACTIVITIES: Capt Karen F Hubbard; Personnel, Head, HQ Division, (913) 491-7710, Autovon 465-3101, ext 7710; Community Activities see Public Affairs Officer.

Personnel and Expenditures
ACTIVE DUTY PERSONNEL: 312
CIVILIAN PERSONNEL: 90

Services *Housing:* Facilities located at Richards-Gebaur AFB. Housing is maintained by the Marine Corps Finance Ctr, Kansas City, MO.

PARSONS

KANSAS ARMY AMMUNITION PLANT
Parsons, KS 67357-9107
(316) 421-7456; Autovon 956-1456

Profile
BRANCH: Army.

SIZE AND LOCATION: 13,838 acres. In SE KS on US-160; 4 mi E of Parsons, KS; 6 mi W of Strauss.

Key Contacts
COMMANDER: Samuel E Cantey Jr.
PUBLIC AFFAIRS: Virginia A Lane.
PROCUREMENT: Jerry Riley.
TRANSPORTATION: Sharon Allen.

Personnel and Expenditures
ACTIVE DUTY PERSONNEL: 2
CIVILIAN PERSONNEL: 32

Services *Base Library:* Yes. *Medical Facilities:* First aid facility.

TOPEKA

190TH AIR REFUELING GROUP, FORBES FIELD
Forbes Field ANG, Topeka, KS 66619-5000
(913) 862-1234; Autovon 720-4791
OFFICER-OF-THE-DAY: (913) 231-4663, Autovon 720-4663

Profile
BRANCH: Air National Guard.

SIZE AND LOCATION: 140 acres. Adj to US Hwy 75; adjoins Pauline, KS, to the E; 3 mi S of Topeka, KS; adjoins Topeka's Airport (MTAA).

MAJOR UNITS: 190th Air Refueling Group; 117th Refueling Squadron; 127th Weather Flight; 190th USAF Clinic.

BASE HISTORY: 1942, opened as Topeka Army Air Corps Base. End of WWII, closed. 1948, reopened; renamed after Maj Daniel H Forbes, native Topekan, killed 1948, test flying Northrup YB-49, "Flying Wing." 1949-51, closed. 1961, Atlas E missiles, deactivated 4 years later, and TAC base until deactivation, 1973. Most of base turned over to city of Topeka for municipal airport; Forbes ANGB licensed to state of KS. 190th Air Refueling Group began as 440th Bombardment Squadron, Light, 1942; deactivated following WWII and reorganized as 117th Bombardment Squadron, Light, PA NG; Korean War activated as training unit, Langley AFB, VA. Came to Hutchinson, KS 1957 as 117th FIS. 1967, 190th TRG transferred to Forbes as tactical bombardment unit.

VISITOR ATTRACTIONS: Restored EB-57 on display at new base gate.

Key Contacts
COMMANDER: Col Charles M "Mick" Baier; (913) 231-4791, Autovon 720-4791.

PUBLIC AFFAIRS: 1st Lt Phillip C Blahut; (913) 231-4195, Autovon 720-4195.

PROCUREMENT: LTC David K Pitman; (913) 231-4490, Autovon 720-4490.

TRANSPORTATION: 2nd Lt Donna Shockley; (913) 231-4618, Autovon 720-4618.

PERSONNEL/COMMUNITY ACTIVITIES: Capt William Mulich; (913) 231-4134, Autovon 720-4134.

Personnel and Expenditures
ACTIVE DUTY PERSONNEL: 1000
CIVILIAN PERSONNEL: 75

Services *Housing:* Local motels for UTA drill. *Temporary Housing:* Local motels for weekend guests. *Commissary and Exchange:* Retail store. *Medical Facilities:* Medical clinic. *Recreational Facilities:* Fitness center; Softball field; Recreation Center for Alert Crews only.

KENTUCKY

FORT CAMPBELL

FORT CAMPBELL
Fort Campbell, KY 42223-5000
(502) 798-2151; Autovon 635-2151
OFFICER-OF-THE-DAY: (502) 798-8722,
Autovon 635-8722
Profile
BRANCH: Army.
SIZE AND LOCATION: 104,793 acres. On Rte
41A between Clarksville, TN, and Hop-
kinsville, KY, on the KY/TN border. Approx 60 mi NW of Nashville.
MAJOR UNITS: 101st Airborne Division (Air
Assault); 5th Special Forces Group
(Airborne).
BASE HISTORY: 1942, Camp Campbell constructed, named for William Campbell,
army veteran of Seminole, FL and Mexican Wars, TN congressman, and governor. Base two-thirds in TN, Post office in
KY; TN first designated official address;
6 months later, without explanation, KY
named permanent address. WWII, training ground for 8th, 12th, 14th, 20th, and
26th Armored Divisions and HQs for
XXII Corps and IV Armored Corps. Following WWII, center for assembly and
redeployment of troops. 1950, became
Fort Campbell, permanent military status.
1951-1953, under 2nd Army. 1953, transferred to Third Army. 1956, 101st Airborne Division moved from Ft Jackson,
SC. 1966-72, Army Training Center.
1972, 101st Airborne Division
"Screaming Eagles" returned.
VISITOR ATTRACTIONS: 101st Airborne Di-
vision Museum.
Key Contacts
COMMANDER: Maj Gen Teddy G Allen; Di-
vision Headquarters, (502) 798-8515,
Autovon 635-8515.
PUBLIC AFFAIRS: Maj Randy Schoel; Public
Affairs Office, (502) 798-3025, 798-3427,
Autovon 635-3025; 635-3427.
PROCUREMENT: L Carroll; DOC, (502) 798-
7126, Autovon 635-7126.
TRANSPORTATION: Maj C W Glover; Divi-
sion Transportation Officer, (502) 798-
5720, Autovon 635-5720.
PERSONNEL/COMMUNITY ACTIVITIES: LTC W
B Crawford; DPCA, (502) 798-8551,
Autovon 635-8551.
Personnel and Expenditures
ACTIVE DUTY PERSONNEL: 21,500
DEPENDENTS: 27,800
CIVILIAN PERSONNEL: 3900
MILITARY PAYROLL EXPENDITURE: FY 88,
$384.9 mil
CONTRACT EXPENDITURE: FY 88, $239.5 mil
Services *Housing:* Family units 4040; BOQ
cottages 140; BEQ units 74; Barracks spaces
12,039. *Temporary Housing:* VIP cottages 3;
VOQ cottages 24; Guesthouse units 74;
DVQ suite 1. *Commissary:* Base commis-
sary; Retail store; Barber shop; Dry cleaners;

Food shop; Florist; Banking; Service station;
Bakery; Fast food; Ice cream. *Child Care/
Capacities:* Day care center. *Schools:*
Kindergarten/Preschool; Elementary;
Intermediate/Junior high; High school; College representative on Post teaching graduate
and undergraduate courses. *Base Library:*
Yes. *Medical Facilities:* Hospital 241; Medical clinic; Dental clinic. *Recreational Facilities:* Bowling; Movie theater; Pool; Gym; Recreation center; Golf; Stables; Tennis; Racquetball; Fitness center; Softball field; Football field; Auto shop; Crafts; Officers club;
NCO club; Camping; Fishing/Hunting.

FORT KNOX

FORT KNOX
US Army Armor Center & Fort Knox, Fort
Knox, KY 40121-5000
(502) 624-3351; 624-7451; Autovon 464-
3351; 464-7451
OFFICER-OF-THE-DAY: (502) 624-6450,
Autovon 464-6450
Profile
BRANCH: Army.
SIZE AND LOCATION: 110,000 acres. From the
N take I-65 to Gen Snyder Expy, S on
31W/US 60 to Ft Knox. From the S take
I-65 to Elizabethtown, N on 31W to Ft
Knox. 45 min drive from Louisville; 40
min from Standiford Field Louisville Air-
port.
MAJOR UNITS: US Army Armor School; 1st
Army Training Brigade; 4th Training Bri-
gade; 194th Armored Brigade (Separate);
HQ US Army 2d ROTC Region; US
Army MEDDAC (Ireland Army Commu-
nity Hospital); US Armor and Engineer
Board; US Army NCO Academy/Drill
Sergeant School; 113th Army Band
(Dragoons); The US Bullion Depository.
BASE HISTORY: 1918, established as Camp
Henry Knox, field artillery training cen-
ter, named for Maj Gen Henry Knox,
Chief of Artillery Continental Army,
American Revolution and first Secretary
of War. 1922, closed as permanent in-
stallation. 1922-32, served as training cen-
ter for 5th Corps area, Citizens Military
Training Camps and National Guard.
1925-28, designated Camp Henry Knox
National Forest. 1932, designated perma-
nent garrison and name changed to Ft
Knox. 1930s, center for cavalry mecha-
nization. 1937, Gold Vault opened
(during WWII, stored Constitution, Bill of
Rights, Declaration of Independence,
British Crown Jewels, Magna Carta, and
gold reserves of several occupied European nations). 1940, Armored Force
School and Armored Force Replacement
Center established. Home of Armor and
Cavalry to this day. Every soldier in Ar-

mored Force serves here at least once
during term of service.
VISITOR ATTRACTIONS: Patton Museum of
Cavalry and Armor; No visitors are per-
mitted at the US Bullion Depository.
Key Contacts
COMMANDER: Maj Gen Thomas H Tait; In-
stallation Commander, (502) 624-2121,
Autovon 464-2121.
PUBLIC AFFAIRS: Maj John Eagles; PO Box
995, (502) 624-3351, Autovon 464-3351.
PROCUREMENT: J L Berthold; Director of
Contracting, (502) 624-5454, Autovon
464-5454.
TRANSPORTATION: W Shipley; (502) 624-
2149, Autovon 464-2149.
PERSONNEL/COMMUNITY ACTIVITIES: Col J W
Ritter; (502) 624-7948, Autovon 464-
7948.
Personnel and Expenditures
ACTIVE DUTY PERSONNEL: 21,000
DEPENDENTS: 5000
CIVILIAN PERSONNEL: 8000
MILITARY PAYROLL EXPENDITURE: $331.9 mil
CONTRACT EXPENDITURE: $342.2 mil
Services *Housing:* Nonfamily housing bldgs
1976; Family housing bldgs 4370. *Commis-
sary:* Base commissary; Retail store; Barber
shop; Dry cleaners; Food shop; Florist;
Banking; Service station; Fast food; Ice
cream. *Child Care/Capacities:* Day care cen-
ter; Home day care program. *Schools:*
Kindergarten/Preschool; Elementary;
Intermediate/Junior high; High school. *Base
Library:* Yes. *Medical Facilities:* Hospital
168; Medical clinic; Dental clinic. *Recreational Facilities:* Bowling; Movie theater;
Pool; Gym; Recreation center; Golf; Stables;
Tennis; Racquetball; Fitness center; Softball
field; Football field; Auto shop; Crafts; Officers club; NCO club; Camping; Fishing/
Hunting; Skeet shooting; Camp Carlson outdoor recreation area; Equipment rental center; Tioga Falls National Recreational Trail.

LEXINGTON

LEXINGTON-BLUE GRASS ARMY DEPOT
Lexington, KY 40511
(606) 293-3011; Autovon 745-3011
Profile
BRANCH: Army.
SIZE AND LOCATION: 782 acres, Lexington;
15,499 acres, Blue Grass. Lexington facility is 10 mi E of Lexington, I-64 is 2
mi from the depot's main gate, with easy
access to I-75. The Blue Grass facility is 4
mi S of Richmond, KY, on US 421 off
US 25; the facility can be reached from I-
75 by taking the Eastern KY Univ bypass . Located on portion of Richmond
Civil War Battle Site.

LEXINGTON-BLUE GRASS ARMY DEPOT
(continued)

MAJOR UNITS: Materiel Readiness Support Activity (MRSA); Central Test, Measurement, & Diagnostic Equipment (TMDE) Activity; DESCOM Quality Systems and Engineering Center; Defense Reutilization and Marketing Office; Army Calibration Repair Center; Ionizing Radiation Dosimetry Center; Detachment 8, 1st Combat Evaluation Group, Strategic Air Command; Federal Emergency Management Agency.

BASE HISTORY: 1941-42, created as two separate installations, Lexington Signal Depot and Blue Grass Ordnance Depot. 1964, merged. 1966, under Army Materiel Command. 1977, change in mission and function and assigned as depot activity under Red River Army Depot, TX. 1980, transferred to Anniston Army Depot, AL. 1985, full depot status; one of 13 depots under Depot System Command, Chambersburg, PA.

VISITOR ATTRACTIONS: Closed to the public.

Key Contacts

COMMANDER: Col Ross I Sanders; (606) 293-3911, Autovon 745-3911.

PUBLIC AFFAIRS: Richard R Dyer; (606) 293-3039, Autovon 745-3039.

PROCUREMENT: (606) 293-3866, Autovon 745-3866.

TRANSPORTATION: Ronald G Trinkle; (606) 293-3217, Autovon 745-3217.

PERSONNEL/COMMUNITY ACTIVITIES: Barbara Kirkpatrick; (606) 293-3126, Autovon 745-3126.

Personnel and Expenditures

ACTIVE DUTY PERSONNEL: 50 Army; 65 Air Force

DEPENDENTS: 20

CIVILIAN PERSONNEL: 2100

MILITARY PAYROLL EXPENDITURE: FY 88, $60.3 mil

CONTRACT EXPENDITURE: FY 88, $3.3 mil

Services *Housing:* Family units 15; BEQ units 6. *Temporary Housing:* Guesthouse units 1. *Commissary:* Base commissary; Retail store; Barber shop; Credit union at both facilities. *Medical Facilities:* Medical clinic. *Recreational Facilities:* Recreation center; Golf; Softball field; Officers club; Fishing/Hunting; Small game hunting at Blue Grass.

LOUISVILLE

LOUISVILLE NAVAL ORDNANCE STATION

Southside Dr, Louisville, KY 40214-5001
(502) 364-5011; Autovon 989-5011
OFFICER-OF-THE-DAY: (502) 364-5205, Autovon 989-5205

Profile

BRANCH: Navy.

SIZE AND LOCATION: 147 acres. 6 mi S of downtown Louisville and 3 mi W of Louisville Airport; 2 mi S of Watterson Expy, Exit 3rd St/Southern Pkwy, I-264, and 3 mi W of I-65.

BASE HISTORY: 1941, commissioned as Naval Ordnance Plant Louisville, GOCO, operated by Westinghouse Electric Co until after WWII. 1946, Station became Navy-operated/owned. 1950, standby/reactivation by Korean Conflict. Today, only government-owned, government-operated facility working to overhaul and maintain naval gun systems, missile launchers, and gun control radars and computers; operates under Naval Sea Systems Command, Washington, DC.

Key Contacts

COMMANDER: Capt J B Brady.

PUBLIC AFFAIRS: W J Meers; (502) 364-5456, Autovon 989-5456.

PROCUREMENT: LCDR David Porter; (502) 364-5828, Autovon 989-5828.

PERSONNEL/COMMUNITY ACTIVITIES: Sylvia Parish; Director of Personnel, (502) 364-5501, Autovon 989-5501.

Personnel and Expenditures

ACTIVE DUTY PERSONNEL: 11

DEPENDENTS: 15

CIVILIAN PERSONNEL: 2300

CONTRACT EXPENDITURE: $75 mil

Services *Housing:* Family units 8. *Medical Facilities:* Medical clinic. *Recreational Facilities:* Pool; Tennis; Softball field.

123RD TACTICAL AIRLIFT WING/ KENTUCKY AIR NATIONAL GUARD

Standiford Field ANGB, Louisville, KY 40213-2678
(502) 364-9400; Autovon 989-9400

Profile

BRANCH: Air National Guard.

SIZE AND LOCATION: 36 acres. In the heart of Louisville near I-65 and I-64.

MAJOR UNITS: 123rd Tactical Airlift Wing; 123rd WSSF; 123rd CES; 165th Tactical Airlift Squadron; 123rd Tactical Airlift Command Hospital; 123rd MSS.

BASE HISTORY: 1946, 359th Fighter Group and 368th Fighter Squadron, Army Air Corps designated 123rd Fighter Group and 165th Fighter Squadron, and allotted to KY State. 1950, activated for Korean Conflict; moved from Standiford Field to Godman Field, Ft Knox, KY. 1951, Wing ordered to Manston RAF Station, Margate, England. 1952, deactivated and returned to ANG status. 1968-69, Pueblo Crisis precipitated recall to federal service; part of Tactical Air Command. 123rd TAC Reconnaissance Wing, renamed 123rd Tactical Airlift Wing, 1989, with subordinate tactical units in AR (123rd RTS), ID (124th TRG), and NV (152nd TRG). Only Air Force installation in KY.

Key Contacts

COMMANDER: Brig Gen John L Smith; (502) 364-9404, Autovon 989-9404.

PUBLIC AFFAIRS: Maj Jeffrey K Butcher; (502) 364-9404, Autovon 989-9404.

PROCUREMENT: Maj Robert Jordan; (502) 364-9404, Autovon 989-9404.

Personnel and Expenditures

ACTIVE DUTY PERSONNEL: 350

CIVILIAN PERSONNEL: 14

Services *Commissary and Exchange:* Retail store; Food shop; Banking. *Medical Facilities:* Hospital 3; Medical clinic; Dental clinic.

LOUISIANA

ALEXANDRIA

ENGLAND AIR FORCE BASE
23rd Tactical Fighter Wing, Alexandria, LA 71311-5004
(318) 448-2100; Autovon 683-2100
Profile
BRANCH: Air Force.
SIZE AND LOCATION: 2435 acres. In central LA, off US-1; 8 mi SE of Boyce, LA; 7 mi NW of Alexandria.
MAJOR UNITS: 23rd Tactical Fighter Wing; 23rd Combat Support Group; Area Defense Council; Defense Investigative Service; Defense R&M Office; Detachment 4, 4400th Management Engineering Squadron (TAC); Detachment 5, 3rd Weather Squadron (MAC); Detachment 31, 5th Weather Squadron (MAC); Detachment 210, Air Force Commissary Services; Detachment 309, 3752nd Field Training Squadron; Detachment 810, Air Force Office of Special Investigations; 1908th Communications Squadron; Navy Construction Office.
BASE HISTORY: 1939, served as emergency airstrip for Esler Army Airfield. WWII, Army Air Corps expanded facilities to train B-17 and B-29 pilots as Alexandria Army Air Base. 1946, deactivated/standby status, used as Municipal Airport. 1950, reactivated and assigned to TAC to train tactical fighter units. 1955, named England AFB for LTC John B England, squadron commander, who died in crash in France. Since 1972, 23rd TFW, WWII's "Flying Tigers" host unit. Today, flies A-10A Thunderbolt II.
VISITOR ATTRACTIONS: Air park of historic aircraft.
Key Contacts
COMMANDER: Col Harry W Brooks; 23CSG/CC, (318) 448-5815, Autovon 683-5815.
PUBLIC AFFAIRS: Capt David C Talley; 23TFW/PA, (318) 448-2401, Autovon 683-2401.
PROCUREMENT: Capt Goebel A Johnson; 23CPTS/LGC, (318) 448-2333, Autovon 683-2333.
TRANSPORTATION: Capt Edward T Fox; 23TFW/LGT, (318) 448-2351, Autovon 683-2351.
PERSONNEL/COMMUNITY ACTIVITIES: LTC Gerald Rolwes; 23CSG/DP, (318) 448-2211, Autovon 683-2211.
Personnel and Expenditures
ACTIVE DUTY PERSONNEL: 3137
DEPENDENTS: 1899
CIVILIAN PERSONNEL: 969
MILITARY PAYROLL EXPENDITURE: $61.9 mil
CONTRACT EXPENDITURE: $16.6 mil
Services *Housing:* Family units 598; Duplex units 148; Townhouse units 240; Senior NCO units 80; Junior NCO units 430; Trailer spaces 48. *Temporary Housing:* VIP cottages 5; VOQ cottages 34; VAQ units 1; BOQ units 2; BAQ units 7. *Commissary:* Base commissary; Retail store; Barber shop; Dry cleaners; Food shop; Florist; Banking; Service station; Bakery. *Child Care/Capacities:* Day care center. *Schools:* Kindergarten/ Preschool; Elementary. *Base Library:* Yes. *Medical Facilities:* Hospital 20; Medical clinic; Dental clinic. *Recreational Facilities:* Bowling; Movie theater; Pool; Gym; Recreation center; Golf; Stables; Tennis; Racquetball; Fitness center; Softball field; Football field; Auto shop; Crafts; Officers club; NCO club; Camping and fishing at recreation area off base.

BARKSDALE AFB

BARKSDALE AIR FORCE BASE
Barksdale AFB, LA 71110
(318) 456-2252; Autovon 781-2252
Profile
BRANCH: Air Force.
LOCATION: 4 mi E of Shreveport, in corporate limits of Bossier City off I-20.
MAJOR UNITS: Headquarters, 8th Air Force; 2d Bombardment Wing; 917th Tactical Fighter Wing; 2d Combat Support Group; 8th Air Force NCO Leadership School; Strategic Air Command NCO Academy; 1st Combat Evaluation Group.
BASE HISTORY: Feb 1933, established; named for Lt Eugene H Barksdale, killed in flight test, 1926.
Personnel and Expenditures
ACTIVE DUTY PERSONNEL: 7800
DEPENDENTS: 7873
CIVILIAN PERSONNEL: 1334
MILITARY PAYROLL EXPENDITURE: $137.3 mil
Services *Housing:* Family units 1062; RV/ Camper sites 12. *Temporary Housing:* Transient living quarters 33; Double rooms 16; Single rooms 8; VOQ/VAQ 125. *Commissary:* Base commissary; Convenience store/ Shopette. *Child Care/Capacities:* Day care center 170; Home day care program. *Medical Facilities:* Hospital 65; Dental clinic; Veterinary services. *Recreational Facilities:* Bowling; Movie theater; Pool; Gym; Golf; Tennis; Racquetball; Fitness center; Softball field; Auto shop; Crafts; Camping (Famcamp); Fishing/Hunting; Youth center (activities); Aero club; Picnicking; Water sports; Skeet shooting.

BELLE CHASSE

NEW ORLEANS NAVAL AIR STATION
Belle Chasse, LA 70143-5000
(504) 393-3260; Autovon 363-3260
OFFICER-OF-THE-DAY: (504) 581-8822
Profile
BRANCH: Navy.
SIZE AND LOCATION: 4883 acres. On LA Hwy 23, approx 15 mi SW of New Orleans; Take Greater New Orleans Bridge to W bank, exit on Terry Pkwy, turn left on Belle Chasse Hwy, base approx 4 mi on right.
MAJOR UNITS: Naval Air Station, New Orleans; VA-204; VP-94; 926th Tactical Fighter Group (AFRES); Marine Air Group, Detachment 46 (Marine Reserve); 159th Tactical Fighter Group (LA ANG); US Coast Guard Air Station, New Orleans.
BASE HISTORY: 1941, Naval Air Reserve Air Base, on shores of Lake Pontchartrain, commissioned. 1942, designated NAS, as primary training base for student aviators. 1946, mission training Naval Air Reservists. 1957, first Naval contingent assigned to new field. 1958, installation dedicated to Alvin Andrew Callender, native of New Orleans, killed in WWI. Since then, known to public as Alvin Callender Field. Unique facility with each branch of military represented.
VISITOR ATTRACTIONS: Air Show every Nov.
Key Contacts
COMMANDER: Capt Joseph L Harford, USN; (504) 393-3201, Autovon 363-3201.
PUBLIC AFFAIRS: Lt Jim Doak.
PROCUREMENT: CDR William R Walls; (504) 393-3589, Autovon 363-3589.
TRANSPORTATION: Ens Susanne M Clautice; (504) 393-3250, Autovon 363-3250.
Personnel and Expenditures
ACTIVE DUTY PERSONNEL: 1000
DEPENDENTS: 1000
CIVILIAN PERSONNEL: 920
Services *Housing:* Family units 224; BOQ cottages 40; BEQ units 40; Barracks spaces 40; RV/Camper sites 15. *Commissary and Exchange:* Retail store; Barber shop; Dry cleaners; Food shop; Banking; Service station. *Child Care/Capacities:* Day care center 65. *Base Library:* Yes. *Medical Facilities:* Medical clinic; Dental clinic. *Recreational Facilities:* Bowling; Pool; Gym; Recreation center; Golf; Tennis; Racquetball; Fitness center; Softball field; Football field; Auto shop; Officers club; NCO club; Camping; Fishing/Hunting.

926TH TACTICAL FIGHTER GROUP, HEADQUARTERS
HQ 926th Tactical Fighter Group, Belle Chasse, LA 70143-5400
(504) 393-3293; Autovon 363-3293
OFFICER-OF-THE-DAY: (504) 393-3177, Autovon 363-3177
Profile
BRANCH: Navy.
LOCATION: See New Orleans Naval Air Station.

926TH TACTICAL FIGHTER GROUP, HEADQUARTERS (continued)

MAJOR UNITS: Naval Air Station, New Orleans; VA-204; VP-94; 926th Tactical Fighter Group (AFRES); Marine Air Group, Detachment 46 (Marine Reserve); 159th Tactical Fighter Group (LA ANG); US Coast Guard Air Station, New Orleans.

BASE HISTORY: 926th TFG a completely self-supporting tenant unit of NAS New Orleans. 1958, 357th Troop Carrier Squadron first AFRES unit at NAS. 1961, 706th Troop Carrier Squadron moved from Barksdale AFB, LA. 1963, assigned to 926th Troop Carrier Group, TAC. 1976, designation changed to 926th TAG. 1977, converted to combat mission and 926th TFG. Parent wing, 917th TFW, Barksdale AFB. Also see New Orleans Naval Air Station for history of Naval Station.

Key Contacts

COMMANDER: Col Bob L Efferson, USAF; Mail Stop CC/926TFG.

PUBLIC AFFAIRS: 2 Lt Anna Pilutti; 926TFG/PA, (504) 393-3493, Autovon 363-3493.

PROCUREMENT: Phil Lysiak; 926TFG/LGS.

TRANSPORTATION: Jim Savoie; 926TFG/LGT, (504) 393-3748, Autovon 363-3748.

PERSONNEL/COMMUNITY ACTIVITIES: Lovie Smith; 926TFG/DPC, (504) 393-3482, Autovon 363-3482.

Personnel and Expenditures

ACTIVE DUTY PERSONNEL: 360 Reservists
CIVILIAN PERSONNEL: 135
MILITARY PAYROLL EXPENDITURE: $4.5 mil
CONTRACT EXPENDITURE: $7.5 mil
Services *Base Library:* Yes.

FORT POLK

FORT POLK

5th Infantry Division and Fort Polk, Fort Polk, LA 71459-5000
(318) 535-2606; Autovon 863-2606
OFFICER-OF-THE-DAY: (318) 535-2228, Autovon 863-2228

Profile

BRANCH: Army.

SIZE AND LOCATION: 198,000 acres. In W-central LA, 9 mi S of Leesville, off Hwy 171. Nearest cities include Alexandria, 50 mi, Lake Charles, 70 mi, and DeRidder, 20 mi.

MAJOR UNITS: 5th Infantry Division; US Army Garrison, Devil Troop Brigade; 588th Engineer Battalion; Company C, 34th Engineer Battalion (Combat Heavy); 5th Finance Support Unit; 5th Personnel Service Company; 84th Chemical Company (Smoke); 565th Medical Company (Ambulance); 539th Maintenance Company; 603rd Transportation Company; 5th Replacement Detachment; 261st Maintenance Detachment; 36th Medical Detachment; 585th Transportation Detachment; 5th Infantry Division (Mechanized) NCO Academy; US Army Information Systems Command (USAISC); 5th Military Police Company; 258th Military Police Company; Company A, USAG (MP).

BASE HISTORY: 1941, camp built; named after Confederate General and Episcopal Bishop Leonidas Polk; established to support famous LA Maneuvers prior to WWII. Following WWII until 1960s, series of closings and reopenings; opened only in summer for reserve training. Active Army units stationed on temporary basis during Korean War and Berlin Crisis. 1962-74, Infantry Training Center. Vietnam years, trained soldiers in basic and advanced infantry skills. Has varying terrain, from jungle-type vegetation to broad, rolling plains. Since 1974, permanent home of 5th Infantry Division (Red Devils) and recipient of largest military construction bill ever for single installation.

VISITOR ATTRACTIONS: Museum.

Key Contacts

COMMANDER: Maj Gen James R Taylor.

PUBLIC AFFAIRS: Maj Terrance Hall; (318) 535-4033, 535-2714, Autovon 863-4033, 863-2714.

PROCUREMENT: Maj Al Weinnig; Directorate of Contracting, (318) 535-6510, Autovon 863-6510.

TRANSPORTATION: David Wiggins; Directorate of Logistics-Transportation Division, (318) 535-4315, Autovon 863-4315.

PERSONNEL/COMMUNITY ACTIVITIES: LTC Rodney Nutt; DPCA, (318) 535-2101, Autovon 863-2101.

Personnel and Expenditures

ACTIVE DUTY PERSONNEL: 14,787
DEPENDENTS: 9975
CIVILIAN PERSONNEL: 4558
MILITARY PAYROLL EXPENDITURE: $317 mil
CONTRACT EXPENDITURE: $52 mil
Services *Housing:* Family units 3942; BOQ cottages 168; BEQ units 265; Barracks spaces 7000; Trailer spaces 398; Family units under construction 312. *Temporary Housing:* VIP cottages 7; VOQ cottages 50; VEQ units 31; Guesthouse units 70. *Commissary:* Base commissary; Retail store; Barber shop; Dry cleaners; Florist; Banking; Service station; Bakery; Book store; Car rental; Optical shop; Video rental. *Child Care/Capacities:* Day care center 315; Home day care program; Child care readily available. *Schools:* Kindergarten/Preschool; Elementary; Students are bused to off-post intermediate and high schools. *Base Library:* Yes. *Medical Facilities:* Hospital 169; Medical clinic; Dental clinic. *Recreational Facilities:* Bowling; Movie theater; Pool; Gym; Recreation center; Golf; Tennis; Racquetball; Fitness center; Softball field; Football field; Auto shop; Crafts; Officers club; NCO club; Camping; Fishing/Hunting; Playhouse; Music center; ITT; Travel agency; Youth center; 2 lakes with picnic sites, beach, boat rental and water skiing at Toledo Bend Lake Recreation Area; Skeet range.

HAMMOND

HAMMOND AIR NATIONAL GUARD STATION

PO Box 1438, Hammond MAP, Hammond, LA 70404
(504) 345-1837; Autovon 363-1416

Profile

BRANCH: Air National Guard.

SIZE AND LOCATION: 22 acres. In SE LA, 1 mi E of Hammond, LA, off Hwy 190.

MAJOR UNITS: 236th Combat Communications Squadron, LA ANG.

BASE HISTORY: A former WWII auxiliary field.

Key Contacts

COMMANDER: LTC Rufus L Warren III.

PUBLIC AFFAIRS: See Base Commander.

Personnel and Expenditures

ACTIVE DUTY PERSONNEL: 4 active; 200 ANG
CIVILIAN PERSONNEL: 26
MILITARY PAYROLL EXPENDITURE: $1.3 mil
CONTRACT EXPENDITURE: $0.1 mil

NEW ORLEANS

EIGHTH COAST GUARD DISTRICT

Hale Boggs Bldg, 500 Camp St, New Orleans, LA 70130-3396
(504) 589-6198

Profile

BRANCH: Coast Guard.

SIZE AND LOCATION: Offices only. In downtown New Orleans; top three floors of Hale Boggs Federal Bldg.

BASE HISTORY: Administrative command for Coast Guard District 8.

Key Contacts

COMMANDER: Adm William F Merlin; (504) 589-6298.

PUBLIC AFFAIRS: Lt Philbin.

JACKSON BARRACKS

LA National Guard, Office of the AG, Jackson Barracks, New Orleans, LA 70146-0330
(504) 271-6262; Autovon 312-485-8215
OFFICER-OF-THE-DAY: Staff duty officer changes daily

Profile

BRANCH: Air National Guard; Army National Guard.

SIZE AND LOCATION: 200 acres. Divides St Bernard and Orleans Parish. Sprawls across 3 city streets (Dauphine, St Claude, & Claiborne) and runs from Mississippi River to Florida Ave; bounded by Delery & Angela streets. Approx 15 min from downtown New Orleans and about 30 min from New Orleans IAP.

MAJOR UNITS: HQ STARC; 159th MASH; 209th Pers Svc Co; 204th Area Support Group; 773rd Maintenance Battalion; 3673rd Maintenance Company; 39th Military Police Company; 1st Battalion, 141st Field Artillery; HQ LA Air National Guard; 214th Engineering Installation Squadron.

BASE HISTORY: 1834-35, constructed as training post for troops of forts along Mississippi. Initially named New Orleans Barracks and referred to as "US Barracks." 1866, renamed Jackson Barracks for Andrew Jackson, hero of Battle of New Orleans and President. Mexican War, embarkation point for troops bound for Mexico. 1847, made general hospital for wounded returning from Mexico and forerunner to veterans hospitals. 1861-62, occupied by Confederate troops. 1866-81, accepted by infantry units. 1881-1914, Third Artillery. WWI, active processing and training center. 1922, turned over to LANG. 1930s, renovation by WPA. Shortly before WWII, federal government repossessed Jackson Barracks and operated as part of New Orleans Port of Embarkation. After WWII, returned to state control. 1955, full ownership vested in LA State.

VISITOR ATTRACTIONS: Military museum housed in old powder magazine, circa 1837; Residential plantation homes; HQ buildings date back to 1830s and 1940s.

Key Contacts

COMMANDER: Maj Gen Ansel M Stroud Jr; Adj Gen, (504) 278-6212, Autovon 312-485-8212.

PUBLIC AFFAIRS: 2nd Lt Maria L Jonkers; LA National Guard, Office of the AG, LANG-PAO (ATTN: 2LT Jonkers), Jackson Barracks, New Orleans, LA 70146-0330, (504) 278-6281, Autovon 312-485-8281.

PROCUREMENT: LTC Louis May; LA National Guard, Office of the AG, ATTN: LANG-DLS-P, Jackson Barracks, New Orleans, LA 70146-0330, (504) 278-6412, Autovon 312-485-8412.

TRANSPORTATION: WO Jody L Moore; LA National Guard, Office of the AG, ATTN: LANG-DLS-T, Jackson Barracks, New Orleans, LA 70146-0330, (504) 278-6442, Autovon 312-485-8442.

JACKSON BARRACKS (continued)

PERSONNEL/COMMUNITY ACTIVITIES: Col Urban M Martinez; LA National Guard, Office of the AG, LANG-DPA (ATTN: Col Martinez), Jackson Barracks, New Orleans, LA 70146-0330, (504) 278-6300, Autovon 312-485-8300.

Personnel and Expenditures
ACTIVE DUTY PERSONNEL: 248
DEPENDENTS: 118
CIVILIAN PERSONNEL: 30
MILITARY PAYROLL EXPENDITURE: $16.1 mil
CONTRACT EXPENDITURE: $1.3 mil
Services *Housing:* Family units 37; BOQ cottages 2; BEQ units 5; Townhouse units 7; Senior NCO units 3; Trailer spaces 30; Senior officer apartments 2. *Temporary Housing:* VIP cottages 2; BOQ units 30; BAQ units 25; Apartment units 5; Dormitory units 80. *Commissary and Exchange:* Retail store; Barber shop; Banking; Military clothing sales. *Base Library:* Yes. *Recreational Facilities:* Gym; Tennis; Officers club; NCO club.

NEW ORLEANS NAVAL SUPPORT ACTIVITY

New Orleans, LA 70142-5000
(504) 361-2507; Autovon 485-2507
OFFICER-OF-THE-DAY: (504) 361-2655, Autovon 485-2655
Profile
BRANCH: Army.
SIZE AND LOCATION: 228 acres. On W bank of Mississippi River approx 2 mi from downtown New Orleans and 13 mi from Moisant IAP. Main gate at intersection of Gen Meyer Ave and Shirley Dr in Algiers section of New Orleans.
MAJOR UNITS: Commander Naval Reserve Force; Commander Naval Air Reserve Force; Commander Naval Surface Reserve Force; Enlisted Personnel Management Center; Fourth Marine Aircraft Wing; Fourth Marine Division; Headquarters 8th Marine Corps District; Military Traffic Management Command Gulf Outport; Naval Reserve Personnel Center; Naval Reserve Readiness Command Region Ten; Special Boat Unit 22.
BASE HISTORY: 1849, Naval Support Activity on land purchased for intended Navy yard. 1901, Naval Dry Dock (YFD #2) arrived and Naval Station established. 1911-1915, closed. 1915, reopened as industrial Navy yard for repair of vessels. 1933, placed in maintenance status. 1939, reactivated to handle transient naval personnel. WWII, provided general naval indoctrination, firefighting, anti-aircraft gunnery, and other special courses. 1944, designated Naval Repair Base. 1947, redesignated Naval Station. 1962, HQ, Support Activity, New Orleans, Eighth Naval District. 1960s, HQ disestablished for Naval Support Activity. 1966, New Orleans Army Base (18.64 acres on E bank) transferred to Navy. Today, Naval Support Activity provides logistical support for activities and tenant commands on both sides of Mississippi.
Key Contacts
COMMANDER: Capt A H Lawrence, USNR; (504) 361-2104, Autovon 485-2104.
PUBLIC AFFAIRS: A R Foucha; (504) 361-2540, Autovon 485-2540.
PROCUREMENT: LCDR R E Williams, USN; (504) 361-2655, Autovon 485-2655.
TRANSPORTATION: LCDR R E Schenk, USN; (504) 361-2500, Autovon 485-2500.
PERSONNEL/COMMUNITY ACTIVITIES: W P Fried; Morale, Welfare, & Recreation Director, (504) 361-2269, Autovon 485-2269.

Personnel and Expenditures
ACTIVE DUTY PERSONNEL: 2815
DEPENDENTS: 858
CIVILIAN PERSONNEL: 1569
MILITARY PAYROLL EXPENDITURE: $112.5 mil
CONTRACT EXPENDITURE: $712.9 mil
Services *Housing:* Family units 286; BOQ cottages 14; BEQ units 5 rooms, 387; Barracks spaces 232; Senior NCO units 32; Junior NCO units 60; RV/Camper sites 16; Substandard enlisted family units 82. *Temporary Housing:* VEQ units 5; rooms 306; BOQ units 62; Transient living quarters 92. *Commissary:* Base commissary; Retail store; Barber shop; Dry cleaners; Food shop; Service station; Military clothing sales; Beauty shop; Optical shop. *Child Care/Capacities:* Day care center 62. *Base Library:* Yes. *Medical Facilities:* Medical clinic; Dental clinic. *Recreational Facilities:* Bowling; Movie theater; Pool; Gym; Recreation center; Tennis; Racquetball; Fitness center; Softball field; Football field; Auto shop; Crafts; Officers club; NCO club; Camping; Leisure travel office; ITT office.

PINEVILLE

CAMP BEAUREGARD

ARNG Training Site, 409 F St, Pineville, LA 71360-3737
(318) 640-2080
Profile
BRANCH: Air National Guard; Army National Guard.
SIZE AND LOCATION: 700 acres. 6 mi N of Alexandria, LA, on Hwy 165 N.
MAJOR UNITS: Combined Support and Maintenance Shop; USP&FO Warehouse Facility for LA; Louisiana Military Academy (NCOA & OCS); HQ & HHC 225th Engineer Group; Company A, 527th Engineer Battalion; 3671st Heavy Equipment Maintenance Company; HHD 165th Transportation Battalion; 399th Medical Detachment; 935th Engineer Detachment; Detachment 1, 3673rd Maintenance Company; Detachment 1, 1086th Transportation Company; Detachment 1, 225th Engineer Group (Aviation); Detachment 256th Infantry Brigade (Aviation); Branch HQ State Civil Defense.
BASE HISTORY: 1917, designated one of 16 original camp sites training troops in WWI; named for Pierre Gustav Toutant Beauregard, LA's "Napoleon in Gray," Confederate commander and later Adj Gen of LA. 1919, deactivated. 1940, reactivated with 3rd Armored Division formed; Camps Livingston, Clairborne, and Polk established; Esler Field, Alexandria Air Base, and Pollock Air Field constructed within 10 mile radius; Camp Beauregard and satellite camps deactivated and allowed to deteriorate following WWII. 1948, Camp Beauregard became State Military Reservation. 1972, NG Bureau funded expansion of facilities. Maintained with inmate trainees from Work Training Facility-North, LA Department of Corrections, camp major training center for Army NG.
VISITOR ATTRACTIONS: Stafford House.
Key Contacts
COMMANDER: Col Richard G Brown; Post Commander, LA ARNG.
Personnel and Expenditures
CIVILIAN PERSONNEL: 451
Services *Housing:* Family units 79; BOQ cottages; BEQ units; Barracks spaces; Male soldiers 720; Female soldiers 40. *Commissary and Exchange:* Small exchange. *Medical Facilities:* Dispensary. *Recreational Facilities:* Movie theater; Pool; Gym; Tennis; Softball field; Officers club; NCO club; Basketball; Volleyball.

SHREVEPORT

LOUISIANA ARMY AMMUNITION PLANT

PO Box 30058, Shreveport, LA 71130-0058
(318) 459-5501
Profile
BRANCH: Army.
SIZE AND LOCATION: 15,000 acres. On US-80; 6 mi E of Fillmore; 3 mi W of Dixie Inn.
BASE HISTORY: 1941, site acquired by federal government; facility constructed and operated by Silas Mason Company. WWII, 65 different ammunition items produced. 1945, placed in standby status. 1951, Remington Rand assumed GOCO contract for reactivation in support of Korean Conflict. 1958, production ceased with Sperry Rand Corporation preserving LAAP facilities. 1961, reactivated to support Vietnam War. 1975, Thiokol Corp (later Morton Thiokol Inc) assumed operation.
Key Contacts
PUBLIC AFFAIRS: (318) 459-5144.
TRANSPORTATION: ATTN: SMCLA-TM.
Personnel and Expenditures
ACTIVE DUTY PERSONNEL: 2
CIVILIAN PERSONNEL: 1400
Services *Housing:* Small housing area.

MAINE

BANGOR

BANGOR AIR NATIONAL GUARD BASE

Bangor International Airport, Bangor, ME 04401-3099
(207) 941-0710; Autovon 476-6225
Profile
BRANCH: Air National Guard.
SIZE AND LOCATION: 299 acres. City of Bangor at airport.
MAJOR UNITS: HQ 101st Air Refueling Wing; 101st Civil Engineering Squadron; 101st Consolidated Aircraft Maintenance Squadron; 101st Mission Support Squadron; 101st Mission Support Flight; 101st Resource Management Squadron; 101st Security Police Flight; 101st USAF Clinic; 132nd Air Refueling Squadron; OTH-B (Over-the-Horizon Backscatter) Program.
BASE HISTORY: Feb 1947, 101st Fighter Group and 132nd Fighter Squadron allotted to ME State and received federal recognition at Camp Keyes, Augusta, and Dow AFB, Bangor, respectively. 1976, group converted from fighter interceptor mission to air refueling.
Key Contacts
COMMANDER: Gen Nicholas Eremita, Autovon 476-6224.
PUBLIC AFFAIRS: 1st Lt Mark Tuck, Autovon 476-6408.
PROCUREMENT: MSgt Robert Busch, Autovon 476-6419.
TRANSPORTATION: MSgt Colby Gordon, Autovon 476-6259.
PERSONNEL/COMMUNITY ACTIVITIES: Lt Col Robert Trefethen, Autovon 476-6389.
Personnel and Expenditures
ACTIVE DUTY PERSONNEL: 300
CIVILIAN PERSONNEL: 264
MILITARY PAYROLL EXPENDITURE: $8 mil
CONTRACT EXPENDITURE: $1.1 mil
Services *Commissary:* Base commissary; Retail store; Food shop. *Medical Facilities:* Medical clinic. *Recreational Facilities:* Gym; Softball field; NCO club.

BATH

BATH SUPERVISOR OF SHIPBUILDING, CONVERSION AND REPAIR

574 Washington St, Bath, ME 04530-0998
(207) 443-6611
Profile
BRANCH: Navy.
LOCATION: Off US-1 near the Bath Iron Works, within the corporate limits of Bath, ME.
BASE HISTORY: Field office of Naval Sea Systems Command (NAVSEA), Washington, DC; mission to ensure that Navy receives complete and fully operational ships on

time and within cost and design constraints of contract.
Key Contacts
COMMANDER: Capt Paul M Robinson.
PUBLIC AFFAIRS: Patricia Gross; (207) 443-6611, ext 2946.
PERSONNEL/COMMUNITY ACTIVITIES: Steven Baranowski; (207) 443-6611, ext 3547 (Code 120).
Personnel and Expenditures
ACTIVE DUTY PERSONNEL: 30
CIVILIAN PERSONNEL: 300

BRUNSWICK

BRUNSWICK NAVAL AIR STATION

NASB, Brunswick, ME 04011-5000
(207) 921-1110; Autovon 476-1110
OFFICER-OF-THE-DAY: (207) 921-2214, Autovon 476-2214
Profile
BRANCH: Navy.
SIZE AND LOCATION: 3087 acres. I-95 Exit 9, follow 95 N Thru Traffic-Brunswick, continue on Rte 95 for approx 18 mi to Exit Coastal Rte 1, Brunswick, get off at exit "Cooks Corner-NAS" and turn right at the light, after .2 mi turn left into NASB's main gate.
MAJOR UNITS: VP-8; VP-10; VP-11; VP-23; VP-26; VP-44; Patrol Wings Atlantic (Topsham Annex).
BASE HISTORY: April 1943, commissioned; trained Royal Canadian Air Force Pilots in formal flying, gunnery procedures and carrier landings. Satellite landing fields at Sanford, Rockland, Portsmouth, Bar Harbor, Augusta, and sea plane ramp in Casco Bay. 1947, deactivated. 1951, reactivated antisubmarine warfare and Fleet Air Wing THREE (later Patrol Wing FIVE). 1971, Commander Patrol Wings, US Atlantic Fleet established HQ. 1970, acquisition of former Topsham AFB. Support to over 30 off-station and tenant activities: Naval Communications Unit Cutler, East Machias; Naval Survival School, Rangeley; and Department of Naval Sciences, Maine Maritime Academy, Castine. Under operational control of Commander Naval Air Force, US Atlantic Fleet, Norfolk, VA.
Key Contacts
COMMANDER: Capt Bruce E Darsey; (207) 921-2203, Autovon 476-2203.
PUBLIC AFFAIRS: Lt William A Sandgren; (207) 921-2527 921-2327, Autovon 476-2527 476-2327.
PROCUREMENT: Supply Officer; (207) 921-2520, Autovon 476-2520.
TRANSPORTATION: Transportation/Dispatcher; (207) 921-2667, Autovon 476-2667.
PERSONNEL/COMMUNITY ACTIVITIES: Morale, Welfare, and Recreational Department; (207) 921-2364, Autovon 476-2364.

Personnel and Expenditures
ACTIVE DUTY PERSONNEL: 3428
CIVILIAN PERSONNEL: 610
MILITARY PAYROLL EXPENDITURE: $85.3 mil (total payroll)
CONTRACT EXPENDITURE: $5.5 mil
Services *Housing:* Family units; BEQ units; Barracks spaces; Mobile home units. *Temporary Housing:* BOQ units; Lodge units; Transient living quarters. *Commissary:* Base commissary; Retail store; Barber shop; Dry cleaners; Food shop; Florist; Banking; Service station; Main cafeteria; Beauty shop; Laundry; Optical shop. *Child Care/Capacities:* Day care center. *Schools:* New Hampshire College. *Base Library:* Yes. *Medical Facilities:* Medical clinic; Dental clinic. *Recreational Facilities:* Bowling; Movie theater; Pool; Gym; Recreation center; Golf; Tennis; Racquetball; Skating rink; Fitness center; Softball field; Football field; Auto shop; Crafts; Officers club; NCO club; Picnic grounds; Hobby center; Woodworking shop; Metal shop; Ski shop.

EAST MACHIAS

CUTLER NAVAL COMMUNICATIONS UNIT

East Machias, ME 04630-1000
(207) 259-8203; Autovon 476-7203
OFFICER-OF-THE-DAY: (207) 259-8229, Autovon 476-7229
Profile
BRANCH: Navy.
SIZE AND LOCATION: 3000 acres. Approx 90 mi E of Bangor, ME on Rte 191; Within corporate limits of Cutler.
BASE HISTORY: Late 1940s site chosen for very high powered, low frequency transmitter which could broadcast to North Atlantic and Arctic Oceans. 1958-1961, constructed. Home of world's most powerful transmitter, over 2 million watts, provides link between high level command authority ashore and ships, planes, and submarines operating in northern latitudes. Also operates primary High Frequency Transmitter site in NE.
VISITOR ATTRACTIONS: The "Downeast" area of ME famous for its beautiful scenery.
Key Contacts
COMMANDER: Commanding Officer; (207) 259-8211, Autovon 476-7211.
PUBLIC AFFAIRS: (207) 259-8203, Autovon 476-7203.
PROCUREMENT: Supply Officer; (207) 259-8215, Autovon 476-7215.
TRANSPORTATION: See Procurement.
PERSONNEL/COMMUNITY ACTIVITIES: See Public Affairs Officer.
Personnel and Expenditures
ACTIVE DUTY PERSONNEL: 120
DEPENDENTS: 115
CIVILIAN PERSONNEL: 105

CUTLER NAVAL COMMUNICATIONS UNIT
(continued)

MILITARY PAYROLL EXPENDITURE: $3.7 mil
CONTRACT EXPENDITURE: $871,000
Services *Housing:* Family units 60; BEQ
units 19; RV/Camper sites 4. *Commissary:*
Base commissary; Retail store; Barber shop;
Dry cleaners; Florist; Service station. *Child
Care/Capacities:* Home day care program.
Base Library: Yes. *Medical Facilities:* Medical clinic. *Recreational Facilities:* Bowling;
Gym; Tennis; Racquetball; Skating rink;
Softball field; Auto shop; NCO club; Camping; Fishing/Hunting.

LORING AFB

LORING AIR FORCE BASE

42nd Bombardment Wing, Loring AFB, ME
04751-5000
(207) 999-1110; Autovon 920-1110
Profile
BRANCH: Air Force.
SIZE AND LOCATION: 11,000 acres. In NE ME
5 mi from Canadian border; Take I-95 N
through Houlton, ME, at Mars Hill take
Alternate 1A through Fort Fairfield and
Limestone, route to base marked. Flights
to Presque Isle from Boston daily, USAF
transportation available to Loring.
MAJOR UNITS: 42nd Bombardment Wing;
42nd Air Refueling Squadron; 407th Air
Refueling Squadron; 69th Bomb Squadron; 42nd Avionics Maintenance Squadron; 42nd Field Maintenance Squadron;
42nd Organizational Maintenance Squadron; 42nd Munitions Maintenance Squadron; 42nd Combat Support Group; 42nd
Transportation Squadron; 42nd Supply
Squadron; 42nd Civil Engineering Squadron; 42nd Consolidated Headquarters
Squadron; 42nd Security Police Squadron; Detachment 1, 102nd Fighter Interceptor Wing, Massachusetts Air National
Guard; Area Defense Council; 2192nd
Communications Squadron; Detachment
2, 1000th Satellite Operations Group; Detachment 7, 1st Combat Evaluation
Group; Detachment 204, 3753rd Field
Training Squadron; 71st Flying Training
Wing; Office of Special Investigations;
SAC Management Engineering Teams;
Detachment 4, 26th Weather Squadron
(MAC).
BASE HISTORY: First air base different in layout from older converted Army posts.
1947-53, constructed out of virgin forest.
1953, Limestone AFB operational, unit of
Eighth Air Force and 42nd BMW activated. 1954, renamed for Maj Charles J
Loring Jr, Portland, ME native killed on
mission in Korean Conflict. 1955, 42nd
Air Refueling Squadron activated. 1983,
arrival of first Harpoon missile modified
aircraft and joint operations with Navy
and United Kingdom. 1984, wing
achieved B-52 Harpoon Integration Initial
Operational Capability.
VISITOR ATTRACTIONS: Base is minutes away
from Canada; beautiful scenery especially
in the fall.
Key Contacts
COMMANDER: Col Terry A Burke; 42nd
BMW/CC, (207) 999-2273, 999-2275,
Autovon 920-2273, 920-2275.
PUBLIC AFFAIRS: Capt Kellie B Rebscher;
42nd BMW/PA, (207) 999-2170, 999-
3179, Autovon 920-2170, 920-3179.
PROCUREMENT: LTC Earl A Small Jr; Resource Management, (207) 999-2133, 999-
2171, Autovon 920-2133, 920-2171.
TRANSPORTATION: LTC John J Fox; (207)
999-2575, Autovon 920-2575.
PERSONNEL/COMMUNITY ACTIVITIES: Capt
Rowley; Director of Personnel, (207) 999-
7178, Autovon 920-7178.

Personnel and Expenditures
ACTIVE DUTY PERSONNEL: 3000
DEPENDENTS: 5500
CIVILIAN PERSONNEL: 500
CONTRACT EXPENDITURE: $20.2 mil
Services *Housing:* Family units 1744; BOQ
cottages 52; Dormitory spaces 1083; Senior
NCO units 11; RV/Camper sites 16. *Temporary Housing:* VIP cottages 4; BOQ units
40; BAQ units 38; Transient living quarters
24. *Commissary:* Base commissary; Barber
shop; Dry cleaners; Food shop; Florist;
Banking; Service station; Furniture store;
Video rental. *Child Care/Capacities:* Day
care center 150-180. *Schools:* Elementary.
Base Library: Yes. *Medical Facilities:* Hospital 23. *Recreational Facilities:* Bowling;
Movie theater; Pool; Gym; Recreation center; Golf; Tennis; Racquetball; Skating rink;
Fitness center; Softball field; Football field;
Auto shop; Crafts; Officers club; NCO club;
Camping; Fishing/Hunting; Youth center;
Snow sports.

PORTLAND

NAVAL RESERVE READINESS CENTER PORTLAND

350 Commercial St, Portland, ME 04101-
4620
(207) 775-6555
Profile
BRANCH: Navy.
SIZE AND LOCATION: 8 acres. On the waterfront in downtown Portland, approx 2 mi
from US Rte 295.
MAJOR UNITS: NR AE-343401; NR 4MDY
25; NR NSY PORTS NH 408; NR
BRUN NDCL 101; NR NH BETH 101;
NR MED IMA 2801; NR SIMA NORVA
201; NR AS-11 DET 301; NR
MBDVSVUT2 DET 101; NR NCSO N
ENG 301; NR SUPSHIP 101.
BASE HISTORY: Sept 1973, commissioned to
train naval reservists in southern ME
area.
Key Contacts
COMMANDER: LCDR Gary L Piepkorn,
USNR.
PUBLIC AFFAIRS: YN1 W R Perry.
PERSONNEL/COMMUNITY ACTIVITIES: RMCS
A W Herricks.
Personnel and Expenditures
ACTIVE DUTY PERSONNEL: 9
CIVILIAN PERSONNEL: 1

WINTER HARBOR

WINTER HARBOR NAVAL SECURITY GROUP ACTIVITY

Winter Harbor, ME 04693-0900
(207) 963-5534; Autovon 476-9211
OFFICER-OF-THE-DAY: (207) 963-5534,
Autovon 476-9211
Profile
BRANCH: Navy.
SIZE AND LOCATION: 110 acres. In Acadia
National Park, approx 280 mi NE of Boston and about 60 mi S of Bangor, ME.
MAJOR UNITS: US Naval Security Group.
BASE HISTORY: Aug 1917, began as Otter
Cliffs Radio Station on Mt Desert Island,
approx 5 mi from present site. 1935, station closed due to deterioration of buildings; moved to Winter Harbor as Navy
Radio and Direction Finding Station.
WWII, expanded including land near
Corea, ME and addition of cryptologic
operations. Name changes: Supplementary
Navy Radio Station, Winter Harbor; Naval Radio Station (R), Winter Harbor;
and finally NSGA, Winter Harbor in
1958.
VISITOR ATTRACTIONS: Schoodic Point Section of Acadia National Park.

Key Contacts
COMMANDER: Capt J T Mitchell.
PUBLIC AFFAIRS: Lt F O MacVane; PAO,
(207) 963-7502, ext 205.
Personnel and Expenditures
ACTIVE DUTY PERSONNEL: 300
DEPENDENTS: 350
Services *Housing:* RV/Camper sites 10.
Temporary Housing: BOQ units 4. *Commissary:* Base commissary; Retail store; Barber
shop; Food shop; Service station. *Child
Care/Capacities:* Home day care program.
Base Library: Yes. *Medical Facilities:* Medical clinic; Dental clinic. *Recreational Facilities:* Bowling; Gym; Tennis; Racquetball;
Skating rink; Fitness center; Softball field;
Auto shop; Camping; COM.

MARYLAND

ABERDEEN PROVING GROUND

ABERDEEN PROVING GROUND
Aberdeen Proving Ground, MD 21005
(301) 278-5201; Autovon 298-5201
OFFICER-OF-THE-DAY: (301) 278-4500,
Autovon 298-4500
Profile
BRANCH: Army.
SIZE AND LOCATION: 72,518 acres. 25 mi NE
of Baltimore; 3 mi E from Aberdeen Exit
85 on I-95; 1 mi E from US Rte 40 in
Aberdeen, MD.
MAJOR UNITS: US Army Test and Evaluation
Command; US Army Ordnance Center &
School; US Army Chemical Research, De-
velopment & Engineering Center; Human
Engineering Laboratory; Ballistics Re-
search Laboratory; Army Environmental
Hygiene Agency; Toxic and Hazardous
Materials Agency.
BASE HISTORY: 1917, established; home of
US Army Ordnance. July 1971, former
Edgewood Arsenal merged with APG;
that section of post referred to as Ed-
gewood Area, remaining section referred
to as Aberdeen Area.
VISITOR ATTRACTIONS: US Army Ordnance
Museum.
Key Contacts
COMMANDER: Col Wilson R Rutherford III;
Aberdeen Proving Ground Support Activ-
ity, (301) 278-4006, Autovon 298-4006.
PUBLIC AFFAIRS: Gary A Holloway; US Army
Test and Evaluation Command, (301)
278-3251, Autovon 298-3251.
PROCUREMENT: T Douglass; Aberdeen Prov-
ing Ground Support Activity, (301) 278-
3497, Autovon 298-3497.
TRANSPORTATION: B Higdon; Aberdeen
Proving Ground Support Activity, (301)
278-3896, Autovon 298-3896.
PERSONNEL/COMMUNITY ACTIVITIES: T Jes-
sup; Aberdeen Proving Ground Support
Activity, (301) 278-5793, Autovon 298-
5793.
Personnel and Expenditures
ACTIVE DUTY PERSONNEL: 6000
DEPENDENTS: 3847
CIVILIAN PERSONNEL: 8000
MILITARY PAYROLL EXPENDITURE: $107.9 mil
CONTRACT EXPENDITURE: $260 mil
Services *Housing:* Family units 1184; BOQ
cottages 83; BEQ units 32; Duplex units
252; Townhouse units 407; Barracks spaces
4775; Trailer spaces 44. *Temporary Housing:*
VIP cottages 8; VOQ cottages 285; VEQ
units 73; Guesthouse units 37. *Commissary:*
Base commissary; Retail store; Barber shop;
Dry cleaners; Food shop; Florist; Service sta-
tion. *Child Care/Capacities:* Day care center
102; Home day care program. *Base Library:*
Yes. *Medical Facilities:* Medical clinic; Dental clinic. *Recreational Facilities:* Bowling;
Movie theater; Pool; Gym; Recreation center; Golf; Stables; Tennis; Racquetball; Softball field; Football field; Auto shop; Crafts;
Officers club; NCO club.

ADELPHI

ADELPHI LABORATORY CENTER
2800 Powder Mill Rd, Adelphi, MD 20783-
1145
(301) 394-2515; Autovon 290-2515
OFFICER-OF-THE-DAY: (301) 394-4476,
Autovon 290-4476
Profile
BRANCH: Army.
SIZE AND LOCATION: 137 acres. Off New
Hampshire Ave, just outside I-495
(Capital Beltway) on Powder Mill Rd; Accessible to I-95, Baltimore/Washington
Pkwy, Baltimore/Washington IAP, Washington National Airport, Dulles Airport.
MAJOR UNITS: US Army Laboratory Command (LABCOM); Harry Diamond Laboratories; US Army Information Systems
Command; US Army Test, Measurement,
and Diagnostic Equipment (TMDE) Sup-
port Operations (Woodbridge).
BASE HISTORY: 1989, Adelphi Laboratory
Center officially established. Harry Diamond Laboratories (HDL) occupied research facility since 1975. HDL shared
site with HQs, Electronics Research and
Development Command (ERADCOM),
1978-1985 when ERADCOM disestablished and US Army Laboratory Command activated. Adelphi Laboratory Center provides identity for site of LABC-
OM, HDL, and Installation Support Activity, which supports both organizations.
New name of installation reflects LAB-
COM's Army-wide responsibility for development of technology base. Location
for Aurora, world's largest full-threat gam-
ma radiation simulator, operated by HDL
under Defense Nuclear Agency. HDL
controls test range, Blossom Point, MD,
and research facilities, Woodbridge, VA.
Key Contacts
COMMANDER: Col Stephen H Young; Instal-
lation Commander, (301) 394-3137, Auto-
von 290-3137.
PUBLIC AFFAIRS: Marian K Singleton; LAB-
COM Public Affairs Officer, (301) 394-
3590, Autovon 290-3590.
PROCUREMENT: R Tomko; (301) 394-3690,
Autovon 290-3690.
PERSONNEL/COMMUNITY ACTIVITIES: L John-
son; Director of Personnel, (301) 394-
3310, Autovon 290-3310.
Personnel and Expenditures
ACTIVE DUTY PERSONNEL: 30
CIVILIAN PERSONNEL: 1200
MILITARY PAYROLL EXPENDITURE: $1.2 mil
CONTRACT EXPENDITURE: $43.7 mil

Services *Medical Facilities:* Nurse's clinic
during duty hrs.

ANDREWS AFB

ANDREWS AIR FORCE BASE
Andrews AFB, MD 20331
(301) 981-1110; Autovon 858-1110
OFFICER-OF-THE-DAY: (301) 981-5058,
Autovon 858-5058
Profile
BRANCH: Air Force.
SIZE AND LOCATION: 4332 acres. Approx 12
mi E of Washington, DC, Exit 9
(Allentown Rd, Andrews AFB) State Rte
337 off Rte I-95. Approx 50 mi S of
Baltimore, MD.
MAJOR UNITS: 1776th Air Base Wing; 89th
Military Airlift Wing; Malcolm Grow
USAF Medical Center; Headquarters Air
Force Systems Command; 10th Aeromed-
ical Staging Flight; 2045th Communica-
tions Group; Headquarters Research and
Acquisition Communications Division;
1402d Military Airlift Squadron; 459th
Military Airlift Wing (AFRES); 113th
Tactical Fighter Group (ANG); Naval Air
Facility; Marine Aircraft Group 41.
BASE HISTORY: Aug 25, 1942, established as
Camp Springs Army Airfield. May 1943,
became operational. Named for Lt Gen
Frank M Andrews, European commander
operations for Army Air Forces. Served
largely as headquarters base in post-
WWII; home of Continental Air Command, SAC, and MATS and AF Systems
Command. Korean War, combat readiness training for B-25 medium bomber
crews; main port of entry for foreign military and government officials. 1963, Naval Air Facility, Anacostia, moved headquarters to E side of base. July 1961,
established as home of official presidential aircraft, *Air Force One.* Historic visits:
body of assassinated President Kennedy,
1963; US prisoners of war returning from
Vietnam, 1973; Pope John Paul II, 1979;
return of US hostages from Iran, 1981;
and, arrival of most foreign dignitaries.
Key Contacts
COMMANDER: Col William R Phillips; (301)
981-2456, Autovon 858-2456.
PUBLIC AFFAIRS: Maj Valerie A Elbow; (301)
981-4511, Autovon 858-4511.
PROCUREMENT: Col John Santamaria; (301)
981-2601, Autovon 858-2601.
TRANSPORTATION: Lt Col J L Prather; (301)
981-2611, Autovon 858-2611.
PERSONNEL/COMMUNITY ACTIVITIES: Maj
Dean D Sandmire; Director of Personnel,
(301) 981-4407, Autovon 858-4407; Maj
Larry Flowers; Director of Community
Activities, (301) 981-4944, Autovon 858-
4944.

ANDREWS AIR FORCE BASE (continued)
Personnel and Expenditures
ACTIVE DUTY PERSONNEL: 14,039
DEPENDENTS: 11,351
CIVILIAN PERSONNEL: 2620
MILITARY PAYROLL EXPENDITURE: $202 mil
CONTRACT EXPENDITURE: $87 mil
Services *Housing:* Family units 2083; Dormitory spaces 2366; Trailer spaces 212. *Temporary Housing:* VOQ cottages 23; VAQ units 2; BOQ units 1; Transient living quarters 6. *Commissary:* Base commissary; Barber shop; Dry cleaners; Food shop; Florist; Banking; Service station; Bakery. *Child Care/Capacities:* Day care center. *Base Library:* Yes. *Medical Facilities:* Hospital 350; Medical clinic; Dental clinic. *Recreational Facilities:* Bowling; Movie theater; Pool; Gym; Recreation center; Golf; Tennis; Racquetball; Fitness center; Softball field; Auto shop; Crafts; Officers club; NCO club.

WASHINGTON, DC, NAVAL AIR FACILITY
Washington, DC, Andrews AFB, MD 20396-5130
(301) 981-4880; Autovon 858-4880
OFFICER-OF-THE-DAY: (301) 981-4880, 981-3779, Autovon 858-4880
Profile
BRANCH: Naval Reserve.
SIZE AND LOCATION: 119 acres. Immediately off I-95 at Camp Springs, MD; a tenant command on Andrews AFB, MD; approx 10 mi S/SE of Washington, DC.
MAJOR UNITS: VP-68; VR-48; MAG-41; FLELOGSUPWINGDET; VAQ-209; VMFA-321; MALS-41; VR-48; MASD Andrews; FLSW Detachment.
BASE HISTORY: 1958-61, functions of Anacostia NAS moved to Andrews AFB, concurrent with commissioning of new Naval Air Facility at Andrews. 1972, Naval Air Reserve Training Unit, Washington (NARTU) became Naval Air Reserve Unit (NARU) Washington. Since 1976, support mission of NAF Washington included administrative and transport flight operations and transient service to fleet and logistics aircraft. 1978, NAF Washington transferred to Chief of Naval Reserve.
Key Contacts
COMMANDER: Capt Thomas L Sanderson; (301) 981-3783, 981-3779, Autovon 858-3783.
PUBLIC AFFAIRS: Lt Gordon J Delcambre Jr; (301) 981-2892, Autovon 858-2892.
PROCUREMENT: LCDR Dixie Lindley; Supply Officer, (301) 981-3726, 981-3727, Autovon 858-3726, 858-3727.
TRANSPORTATION: Lt Brad Beisswanger; Public Works Officer, (301) 981-3867, Autovon 858-3867.
PERSONNEL/COMMUNITY ACTIVITIES: Anita Carol; Civilian Personnel Resources, (301) 981-5705, Autovon 858-5705.
Personnel and Expenditures
ACTIVE DUTY PERSONNEL: 700
CIVILIAN PERSONNEL: 136
Services *Housing:* Family units; BEQ units. *Temporary Housing:* BOQ units; Transient living quarters. *Commissary:* Base commissary; Retail store; Barber shop; Dry cleaners; Food shop; Florist; Banking; Service station; Bakery; Book store; Andrews AFB facilities. *Child Care/Capacities:* Day care center. *Base Library:* Yes. *Medical Facilities:* Hospital 200; Medical clinic; Dental clinic. *Recreational Facilities:* Bowling; Movie theater; Pool; Gym; Recreation center; Golf; Tennis; Racquetball; Fitness center; Softball field; Football field; Auto shop; Crafts; Officers club; NCO club; Camping; Fishing/Hunting; Andrews AFB facilities.

ANNAPOLIS

ANNAPOLIS NAVAL STATION
Annapolis, MD 21402-5054
(301) 267-2385; 267-2386; Autovon 281-2385
OFFICER-OF-THE-DAY: Rotates
Profile
BRANCH: Navy.
SIZE AND LOCATION: 275.5 acres. On Severn River, adj to US Naval Academy; western border Rte 50/301 and southern border runs down Annapolis Neck Peninsula area just S of Forest Dr; 27 mi from both Washington, DC and Baltimore, MD.
MAJOR UNITS: Naval Station Annapolis; Naval Construction Battalion Unit 403; Marine Barracks.
BASE HISTORY: 1851, 6 years after founding of US Naval Academy, first midshipmen training ship USS *Preble* arrived at what was then Ft Severn. 1911, completion of NAS, Greenbury Point, home of Naval Aviation, first NAS. 1939, first Yard Patrol Craft arrived. 1941, Severn River Naval Command established; Naval Air Facility reestablished. 1947, Severn River Command expanded to include Naval Small Craft Facility, Naval Air Facility, Naval Station, and Naval Barracks. 1962, Severn River Naval Command disestablished and all missions transferred to Naval Station.
Key Contacts
COMMANDER: Capt Robert V Gamba; (301) 267-2387, Autovon 281-2387.
PUBLIC AFFAIRS: Ginger Thomas; (301) 267-2385, 267-2386, Autovon 281-2385.
PROCUREMENT: Lt Jeffrey McKinless; (301) 267-2227, Autovon 281-2227.
TRANSPORTATION: BUC Douglas Smith; (301) 267-3142, Autovon 281-3142.
PERSONNEL/COMMUNITY ACTIVITIES: MWR Director; (301) 267-2518, Autovon 281-2518.
Personnel and Expenditures
ACTIVE DUTY PERSONNEL: 322
CIVILIAN PERSONNEL: 86
Services *Housing:* Family units 413; BEQ units 91; Mobile home units 16; RV/Camper sites 10. *Temporary Housing:* BOQ units 16. *Commissary:* Base commissary; Retail store; Barber shop; Dry cleaners; Florist; Banking; Service station; Fast food. *Child Care/Capacities:* Day care center 97; Home day care program. *Schools:* Kindergarten/Preschool. *Base Library:* Yes. *Medical Facilities:* Medical clinic; Dental clinic. *Recreational Facilities:* Bowling; Pool; Gym; Recreation center; Golf; Tennis; Racquetball; Fitness center; Softball field; Auto shop; Crafts; Officers club; NCO club; Camping; Fishing/Hunting (and crabbing); Water sports.

DAVID TAYLOR RESEARCH CENTER, ANNAPOLIS LABORATORY
Annapolis, MD 21402-5067
(301) 267-3160
Profile
BRANCH: Navy.
LOCATION: On Severn River directly opposite Naval Academy.
MAJOR UNITS: Propulsion and Auxiliary Systems Department; Ship Materiels Engineering Department.
BASE HISTORY: Former US Naval Engineering Experiment Station, established in 1908 under guidance of Rear Adm George W Melville. 1963, original mission to develop and test machinery prior to fleet use expanded; renamed Marine Engineering Laboratory. 1967, site became part of Center.

Key Contacts
COMMANDER: Capt C Graham.
PUBLIC AFFAIRS: James M Scott; (301) 267-3160.
Personnel and Expenditures
ACTIVE DUTY PERSONNEL: 950 (military & civilians)

US NAVAL ACADEMY
Annapolis, MD 21402
(301) 267-6100; Autovon 281-6100
Profile
BRANCH: Navy.
SIZE AND LOCATION: 1747 acres. Near downtown Annapolis on S bank of Severn River; 30 mi S of Baltimore; 40 mi E of Washington, DC; follow signs off US Rte 50.
MAJOR UNITS: Brigade of Midshipmen.
BASE HISTORY: 1845, established as undergraduate college of US Navy, as Naval School, Fort Severn in Annapolis; initially, instruction required 5 years, first and last at Annapolis and middle years at sea. 1850, Naval School became US Naval Academy. 1851, adopted current course of instruction which includes 4 consecutive years at Annapolis with at-sea training during summers. During Civil War, Academy moved to Newport, RI. 1865, reestablished at Annapolis. During WWI (until 1921) and WWII, courses shortened to 3 years and reserve officers also trained here. July 1976, first women midshipmen entered. Naval Academy and Naval Station (separate commands) share many personnel support and recreational facilities.
VISITOR ATTRACTIONS: A national tourist attraction; many buildings, statues and monuments, represent highlights in Navy history. Several buildings and most of Academy grounds (the Yard) open to visitors from 9-sunset. Academic buildings and residences closed to general public except special occasions. Marine Barracks, quartered across Severn River, provide honor guard for superintendent, tomb of John Paul Jones, and Naval Academy Museum, Preble Hall. Visitors center in Ricketts Hall.
Key Contacts
COMMANDER: Adm Virgil Hill; Office of Superintendent.
PUBLIC AFFAIRS: CDR Stephen Becker.
Personnel and Expenditures
ACTIVE DUTY PERSONNEL: 1134; 4500 Midshipmen
DEPENDENTS: 2700
Services *Housing:* Family units 413; BEQ units 247; Trailer spaces 16. *Temporary Housing:* VIP cottages 1; VOQ cottages 15. *Commissary:* Base commissary; Retail store; Barber shop; Dry cleaners; Military clothing sales; Beauty shop; Shoe repair; Computer store; Laundry; Midshipmen store; Tailor; Personal services shop; Travel agency; All other services at Annapolis Naval Station and Naval Hospital. *Child Care/Capacities:* Day care center. *Schools:* See Annapolis Naval Station. *Base Library:* Yes. *Medical Facilities:* Medical clinic; Dental clinic; See Annapolis Naval Station. *Recreational Facilities:* Bowling; Movie theater; Pool; Gym; Recreation center; Golf; Tennis; Racquetball; Fitness center; Softball field; Football field; Auto shop; Crafts; Officers club; NCO club; Camping; Fishing/Hunting; Sailing marina; Archery range; Equipment checkout; Soccer field; Picnic areas; Youth activities center.

BALTIMORE

ARMY PUBLICATIONS DISTRIBUTION CENTER
2800 Eastern Blvd, Baltimore, MD 21220-2896
(301) 682-8500; Autovon 584-3887
Profile
BRANCH: Army.
SIZE: Offices only.

US ARMY CORPS OF ENGINEERS, BALTIMORE DISTRICT
PO Box 1715, Baltimore, MD 21203-1715
(301) 962-7608
Profile
BRANCH: Army.
SIZE AND LOCATION: Offices only. Federal Bldg downtown Baltimore, 2 blocks from Inner Harbor; approx 12 mi from Baltimore-Washington IAP.
MAJOR UNITS: Corps of Engineers.
Key Contacts
COMMANDER: Col Bernard E Stalmann; (301) 962-4545.
PUBLIC AFFAIRS: Harold K Kanarek (Acting Chief); ATTN: CENAB-PA, (301) 962-4616, 962-4617.
PROCUREMENT: C J Dow; ATTN: CENAB-CT, (301) 962-2196.
TRANSPORTATION: Patrick Dockery; Chief, Logistics Management Office, ATTN: CENAB-LO, (301) 962-2023.
PERSONNEL/COMMUNITY ACTIVITIES: Joseph Levy; ATTN: CENAB-PE, (301) 962-2100.
Personnel and Expenditures
ACTIVE DUTY PERSONNEL: 12
CIVILIAN PERSONNEL: 700
Services Base Library: Yes.

175TH TACTICAL AIRLIFT GROUP (ANG)
Glenn L Martin State Airport, Baltimore, MD 21220
(301) 687-6270; Autovon 235-9210
Profile
BRANCH: Air National Guard.
SIZE AND LOCATION: 75 acres. 8 mi E of Baltimore; 1 mi NE of Middle River.
MAJOR UNITS: 175th Tactical Airlift Group (ANG).
Personnel and Expenditures
ACTIVE DUTY PERSONNEL: 1600
CIVILIAN PERSONNEL: 308
MILITARY PAYROLL EXPENDITURE: $10.6 mil

BETHESDA

NATIONAL NAVAL MEDICAL CENTER
8901 Wisconsin Ave, Bethesda, MD 20814-5000
(301) 295-5385; Autovon 295-5385
OFFICER-OF-THE-DAY: (301) 295-4611, Autovon 295-4611
Profile
BRANCH: Navy.
SIZE AND LOCATION: 250 acres. On Wisconsin Ave, just inside I-495 and across from National Institutes of Health (NIH) and Medical Center Metrorail stop.
MAJOR UNITS: Naval Medical Command National Capital Region; Naval Hospital; Naval Health Sciences Education and Training Command; Naval Dental Clinic; Naval Medical Research Institute.
BASE HISTORY: Naval Medical Command National Capital Region (formerly National Naval Medical Center) at present suburban MD site since 1942. Originally established, 1935, at 23rd and E Sts, NW, Washington, DC, present site of Naval Medical Command, Washington. The

Command can be traced to 1802 when first naval medical facility in Washington area was established in rented building near Washington Navy Yard. Present site chosen personally by President Franklin D Roosevelt, 1938; personally sketched elevation and ground plan which became architect's guide; dedicated by him, 1942. Capacity increased during war; WWII, 2464 beds; Korean Conflict, 1167; and, Vietnam Conflict, 1122. 1973, Naval Hospital and National Naval Medical Center consolidated into one command, National Naval Medical Center. 1980, replacement hospital dedicated. 1982, Naval Medical Command National Capital Region established, Naval Hospital, Bethesda, reestablished as regional activity and Naval Dental Clinic reorganized, both under Naval Medical Command.
Key Contacts
COMMANDER: Rear Adm Donald F Hagen; (301) 295-5800, Autovon 295-5800.
PUBLIC AFFAIRS: LCDR Thomas A Hatcher; Public Affairs Office, (301) 295-5727, Autovon 295-5727.
PROCUREMENT: Lt Abeya; (301) 295-0503, Autovon 295-0503.
TRANSPORTATION: LCDR A Bertsche; (301) 295-1114, Autovon 295-1114.
Personnel and Expenditures
ACTIVE DUTY PERSONNEL: 12,000
MILITARY PAYROLL EXPENDITURE: $95 mil
Services Housing: Family units 8; BOQ cottages 107; BEQ units 319. Temporary Housing: Lodge units 22. Commissary and Exchange: Retail store; Barber shop; Dry cleaners; Food shop; Banking; Service station; Optical shop; Beauty shop; Tailor. Child Care/Capacities: Day care center 30. Base Library: Yes. Medical Facilities: Hospital 500; Dental clinic. Recreational Facilities: Bowling; Pool; Gym; Tennis; Officers club; NCO club.

DAVID TAYLOR RESEARCH CENTER
Bethesda, MD 20084-5000
(202) 227-1142; Autovon 287-1142
Profile
BRANCH: Navy.
LOCATION: Just outside the Capital Beltway, I-495, on MacArthur Blvd.
MAJOR UNITS: Ship Systems Integration Department; Ship Hydromechanics Department; Aviation Department; Ship Electromagnetic Signatures Department; Ship Structures and Protection Department; Ship Acoustics Department; Computation, Mathematics and Logistics Department.
BASE HISTORY: 1898, original model basin built at Washington Navy Yard and used for 40 years; named for Rear Adm David W Taylor, who urged Congress to establish towing tanks to study scale models of ships before construction. Navy's first wind tunnels occupied same site. 1940, operations at Carderock began with complex of towing tanks still used today. With seven technical departments, laboratory remains largest facility of its kind in western world. Detachments provide environment for both model and full-scale trials: include Acoustic Research Detachment, Bayview, ID; Acoustic Trials Detachment, Cape Canaveral, FL; Puget Sound Detachment, Bremerton, WA; Underwater Explosions Research Division, Portsmouth, VA; and Surface Effects Ship Support Office, NAS, Patuxent River, MD.

Key Contacts
COMMANDER: Capt C Graham; (202) 227-1221, Autovon 287-1221.
PUBLIC AFFAIRS: Ellen Shapiro; (202) 227-1142, Autovon 287-1142.
Personnel and Expenditures
ACTIVE DUTY PERSONNEL: 70
CIVILIAN PERSONNEL: 2800
Services Base Library: Yes.

CHELTENHAM

NAVAL COMMUNICATION UNIT, WASHINGTON
Washington, DC 20390, Cheltenham, MD 20623
(301) 238-2380; Autovon 251-2380
OFFICER-OF-THE-DAY: (301) 238-2380, Autovon 251-2380
Profile
BRANCH: Navy.
SIZE AND LOCATION: 434 acres. In suburban MD, adj to community of Cheltenham, 3 mi from Andrews AFB; Take Exit 7A from I-95, turn left onto MD 223 (Woodward Rd), then abrupt right onto Dangerfield Rd, NCU approx 12 mi from Washington, DC.
MAJOR UNITS: Navy-Marine Corps Military Affiliate Radio System (HQ, MARS); Naval Telecommunications Automation Support Center (NAVTASC); Naval Telecommunications Center (NTSIC).
BASE HISTORY: 1938, commissioned. Preceding WWII, steadily grew to handle mounting communications requirements in and out of Washington, DC area. Following WWII, continued to grow, but encroaching population density reduced effectiveness as receiving site. 1975, designated as Naval Communication Unit. Of original land, 125 acres transferred to county and 17 acres leased to county for a firefighter training academy. Today, provides communications support to over 300 military, DOD, and federal government agencies throughout Washington, DC area, as well as military installations in Newport, RI, and Great Lakes, IL. Under operational control of Commander, Naval Telecommunications Command.
Key Contacts
COMMANDER: CDR S C Arey; (301) 238-2228, Autovon 251-2228.
PUBLIC AFFAIRS: MACM (SW) M J Hof; (301) 238-2414, Autovon 251-2414.
PROCUREMENT: S V Shoop; (301) 238-2211, Autovon 251-2211.
PERSONNEL/COMMUNITY ACTIVITIES: J D Alsop; (301) 238-2444, Autovon 251-2444.
Personnel and Expenditures
ACTIVE DUTY PERSONNEL: 116
DEPENDENTS: 78
CIVILIAN PERSONNEL: 216
MILITARY PAYROLL EXPENDITURE: $3.1 mil
Services Housing: Family units 39; Duplex units 32. Commissary and Exchange: Convenience store/Shopette; Package beverages. Recreational Facilities: Bowling; Movie theater; Gym; Softball field; Auto shop; Crafts.

CUMBERLAND

CUMBERLAND NAVAL RESERVE CENTER
No 1 Navy Way, Cumberland, MD 21502-2598
(301) 777-3141
OFFICER-OF-THE-DAY: See Base Commander
Profile
BRANCH: Naval Reserve.
SIZE AND LOCATION: 13 acres. In city limits of Cumberland, MD; From Rte 40/48 use Willowbrook Rd exit.

CUMBERLAND NAVAL RESERVE CENTER
(continued)
MAJOR UNITS: RNMCB-23 Detachment 0623;
NR AD-41 Yellowstone Detachment
0966; NR FF-1084 McCandless Detachment 8406; NR NH Bethesda Detachment 2606; NR CHB-10 Detachment D-106; NR VTU Detachment 0605.
BASE HISTORY: 1946, Director of Naval Reserve for Fifth Naval District visited Cumberland to secure site for Naval Armory; arrangements made to use training facilities at Fort Hill High School until Armory completed. Nov 20, 1946, division activated.

Key Contacts
COMMANDER: Lt John S Runyon.
PUBLIC AFFAIRS: HMC Gerald R Batesole.
PROCUREMENT: See Base Commander.
TRANSPORTATION: See Base Commander.
PERSONNEL/COMMUNITY ACTIVITIES: See Base
Commander.

Personnel and Expenditures
ACTIVE DUTY PERSONNEL: 11
MILITARY PAYROLL EXPENDITURE: $223,000
CONTRACT EXPENDITURE: $56,000
Services *Recreational Facilities:* Softball
field.

CURTIS BAY

US COAST GUARD YARD
Curtis Bay, MD 21226-1797
(301) 789-1600
OFFICER-OF-THE-DAY: (301) 789-1600, ext
370
Profile
BRANCH: Coast Guard.
SIZE AND LOCATION: 112 acres. On Curtis
Creek 2 mi E of Baltimore; 5 mi from
Baltimore-Washington IAP.
MAJOR UNITS: US Coast Guard Yard; US
Coast Guard Group Baltimore; Curtis
Bay Station; CGC *Sledge*; CGC *Red
Birch*.
BASE HISTORY: Founded in 1899, only shipbuilding and repair facility of USCG. Until 1910, Yard first permanent home of
Coast Guard Academy, now New London, CT. Today, Coast Guard's largest,
most modern industrial plant, responsible
for construction, repairs, and renovation
of vessel and various aids to navigation,
and manufacturing of miscellaneous Coast
Guard peculiar equipment; provides logistics support to Coast Guard Fleet as ships
Inventory Control Point; also storage facility for decommissioned vessels.

Key Contacts
COMMANDER: Capt Hugh L Thomas; (301)
789-1600, ext 227.
PUBLIC AFFAIRS: Dorothy Mitchell; (301)
789-1600, ext 250.
PROCUREMENT: CDR Ken Kruetter; (301)
789-1600, ext 250.
TRANSPORTATION: Eileen Stiltner; (301) 789-
1600, ext 263.
PERSONNEL/COMMUNITY ACTIVITIES: Don
Harvey; Chief, Civilian Personnel Office,
(301) 789-1600, ext 213.

Personnel and Expenditures
ACTIVE DUTY PERSONNEL: 250
CIVILIAN PERSONNEL: 830
MILITARY PAYROLL EXPENDITURE: $70 mil
budget
Services *Housing:* BOQ cottages 7; BEQ
units 144; Trailer spaces 4. *Temporary Housing:* Transient living quarters 5. *Commissary
and Exchange:* Retail store; Barber shop;
Food shop. *Medical Facilities:* Medical clinic; Dental clinic. *Recreational Facilities:*
Bowling; Pool; Gym; Recreation center; Tennis; Racquetball; Softball field; Auto shop;
Officers club; NCO club.

FORT MEADE

FORT GEORGE G MEADE
Fort Meade, MD 20755-5000
(301) 677-6261; Autovon 923-6261
OFFICER-OF-THE-DAY: (301) 677-7723, 677-
6667, Autovon 923-7723, 923-6667
Profile
BRANCH: Air Force; Army; Marines; Navy.
SIZE AND LOCATION: 13,000 acres. Almost
midway between Baltimore and Washington, DC; Several miles from I-95 and
Baltimore-Washington Pkwy, just off MD
State Rte 175 and 198.
MAJOR UNITS: Headquarters Command Battalion; 85th Medical Battalion; 519th
Military Police Battalion; National Security Agency; Headquarters, First US
Army; 97th Army Reserve Command;
11th Special Forces Group; Kimborough
Army Medical Center.
BASE HISTORY: 1917, built for troops drafted
for WWI; originally named Camp Meade
for Maj Gen George Gordon Meade, Civil War general. 1928, renamed Ft Leonard
Wood, Pennsylvanians registered protest
resulting in change to Ft Meade. WWII,
training center. 1947, Second US Army
HQ arrived. 1966, Second Army merged
with First Army and HQs moved in from
Ft Jay, NJ. 1973, Army reorganization
provided for transition from Active Army
organization to Reserve Components.
Mission includes command and supervision of all Reserve units and Army NG in
First US Army area.
VISITOR ATTRACTIONS: Ft Meade Museum.

Key Contacts
COMMANDER: Col Gorham L Black III; Garrison Commander, (301) 677-2131, Autovon 923-2131.
PUBLIC AFFAIRS: Julius L Simms; Garrison
Public Affairs, Bldg 2718, Ft Meade, MD
20755-5025, (301) 677-6361, 677-6362,
677-6388, Autovon 923-6361, 923-6362,
923-6388.
PROCUREMENT: (301) 677-4570, Autovon
457-2131.
TRANSPORTATION: (301) 677-2111, 677-2112,
677-2113, Autovon 923-2111, 923-2112,
923-2113.
PERSONNEL/COMMUNITY ACTIVITIES: (301)
677-6111, 677-6112, Autovon 923-6111,
923-6112.

Personnel and Expenditures
ACTIVE DUTY PERSONNEL: 11,000
DEPENDENTS: 8500
CIVILIAN PERSONNEL: 5550
MILITARY PAYROLL EXPENDITURE: $158 mil
CONTRACT EXPENDITURE: $68 mil
Services *Housing:* Family units 3125; BOQ
cottages 62. *Temporary Housing:* VOQ cottages 69; Guesthouse units 1. *Commissary:*
Base commissary; Retail store; Barber shop;
Dry cleaners; Food shop; Florist; Banking;
Service station; Bakery. *Child Care/Capacities:* Day care center; Home day care program. *Schools:* Kindergarten/Preschool; Elementary; Intermediate/Junior high; High
school. *Base Library:* Yes. *Medical Facilities:*
Hospital; Dental clinic. *Recreational Facilities:* Bowling; Movie theater; Pool; Gym; Recreation center; Golf; Stables; Tennis; Racquetball; Fitness center; Softball field; Football field; Auto shop; Crafts; Officers club;
NCO club; Fishing/Hunting; Small arms
range.

FORT RITCHIE

ALTERNATE JOINT
COMMUNICATIONS CENTER/SITE R
c/o Fort Ritchie, Fort Ritchie, MD 21719-
5010

Profile
BRANCH: Joint Service Installation.
LOCATION: 6 mi NE of Ft Ritchie, MD.
MAJOR UNITS: Alternate National Military
Command Center (ANMCC); 1111th Signal Battalion.
BASE HISTORY: 1950, construction began of
AJCC, also called Site R, and became
operational, 1954. Tenants represent each
of military departments and Joint Chiefs
of Staff. Housekeeping, logistical and engineering support responsibility of HQ,
US Army Garrison, Ft Ritchie. Scheduled
buses provide daily transportation from
post to Site R. Most military personnel
working at site live on Ft Ritchie.

Key Contacts
COMMANDER: See Fort Ritchie, MD.
Services *Housing:* See Ft Ritchie, MD.
Temporary Housing: See Ft Ritchie, MD.
Commissary and Exchange: Barber shop;
Dining hall; Cafeteria; Snacks; Chapel; Post
office; Additional facilities at Ft Ritchie,
MD. *Medical Facilities:* Medical clinic; Dental clinic. *Recreational Facilities:* See Ft
Ritchie, MD.

FORT RITCHIE
7th Signal Command and Ft Ritchie, Fort
Ritchie, MD 21719-5010
(301) 878-1300; Autovon 277-1300
OFFICER-OF-THE-DAY: (301) 878-5626,
Autovon 277-5626
Profile
BRANCH: Army.
SIZE AND LOCATION: 648 acres. Near the PA
border approx 80 mi from Washington,
DC; 80 mi from Baltimore, MD; and 80
mi from Harrisburg, PA. Take I-270 N
from Washington, DC, to Frederick, MD,
then take Rte 15 N to Thurmont, then
MD Rte 550 to Ft Ritchie's main gate.
Washington County Regional Airport is
approx 12 mi.
MAJOR UNITS: Headquarters, 7th Signal Command; 1107th US Army Signal Brigade;
1108th US Army Signal Brigade; Headquarters, US Army Garrison; Army Information Systems Engineering Command; Alternate Joint Communications
Center (AJCC).
BASE HISTORY: 1926, Ft Ritchie area chosen
as training site for MDNG and facilities
built; HQs building built to resemble castle on Army Corps of Engineers insignia;
named Camp Albert C Ritchie for governor of MD. WWII, Army leased Camp
to become centralized Military Intelligence Training Center and name shortened to Camp Ritchie; German and Japanese POWs used for training purposes;
soldiers trained as interrogators, military
interpreters, translators, aerial photography interpreters, and order of battle specialists. By 1944, all Counter Intelligence
Corps personnel trained here. 1946, center moved to Ft Riley, KS, and Camp
Ritchie returned to state. 1946-50, used
for state's Chronic Disease Hospital.
1948, Army needed post for support of
Alternate Joint Communications Center
(AJCC), known as Site R. 1964, redesignated Class II Installation under US
Army Strategic Communications Command. 1971, USASTRATCOM-CONUS
HQs relocated from Alexandria, VA.
1973, command's name changed to US
Army Communications Command. 1975,
renamed to current 7th Signal Command.
VISITOR ATTRACTIONS: Post Historical Collection, Ft Ritchie Museum.

FORT RITCHIE (continued)
Key Contacts
COMMANDER: Col Robert E Wynn; (301) 878-5666, Autovon 277-5666.
PUBLIC AFFAIRS: Steven B Blizard; (301) 878-5306, 878-5874, Autovon 277-5306, 277-5874.
PROCUREMENT: Jerry Lowell; Chief, Office of Acquisition, (301) 878-4301, Autovon 277-4301.
TRANSPORTATION: CWO3 Dan Ringquist; (301) 878-4392, Autovon 277-4392.
PERSONNEL/COMMUNITY ACTIVITIES: LTC Robert Siepielski; (301) 878-5233, Autovon 277-5233.
Personnel and Expenditures
ACTIVE DUTY PERSONNEL: 1181
DEPENDENTS: 1497
CIVILIAN PERSONNEL: 1145
MILITARY PAYROLL EXPENDITURE: $18.6 mil
CONTRACT EXPENDITURE: $46.2 mil
Services *Housing:* Family units 341; BOQ cottages 18; BEQ units 25; Duplex units; Barracks spaces 347; RV/Camper sites off-post. *Temporary Housing:* VIP cottages 1; VOQ cottages 12; VEQ units 1; BOQ units 18; Guesthouse units 30; Apartment units 2; Lodge units 10. *Commissary:* Base commissary; Retail store; Barber shop; Dry cleaners; Food shop; Banking; Service station; Military clothing sales; Convenience store/Shopette; Credit union; Package beverages; Thrift shop. *Child Care/Capacities:* Day care center 94; Home day care program. *Schools:* Kindergarten/Preschool. *Base Library:* Yes. *Medical Facilities:* Medical clinic; Dental clinic; Veterinary clinic. *Recreational Facilities:* Bowling; Movie theater; Pool; Gym; Recreation center; Golf; Tennis; Racquetball; Skating rink; Softball field; Auto shop; Crafts; Fishing/Hunting; Consolidated Community Club; Lake Royer, Upper and Lower.

FREDERICK

FORT DETRICK
Frederick, MD 21701-5000
(301) 663-8000; Autovon 343-8000
Profile
BRANCH: Army.
SIZE AND LOCATION: 1200 acres. Off US-15 within the city limits of Frederick, MD; 50 mi from Washington, DC and Baltimore, MD.
MAJOR UNITS: US Army Garrison; Health Services Command; 1110th Signal Battalion; Headquarters Medical Research and Development.
BASE HISTORY: US Army Health Services Command installation traces its roots to small municipal airport, Detrick Field, in 1930s; 104th Observation Squadron, MDNG, set up summer camp; Ft Detrick, named after Army medical officer, Maj Frederick L Detrick. 1969, biological warfare laboratories closed. Today, multi-mission installation providing space for offices, laboratories, and advanced communication facilities; Army Medical Department's leading microbiological containment research campus.
VISITOR ATTRACTIONS: Historical buildings.
Key Contacts
COMMANDER: Col Richard W Haver Jr; (301) 663-7314, Autovon 343-8000.
PUBLIC AFFAIRS: Norman M Covert; (301) 663-2018, Autovon 343-8000.
PROCUREMENT: LTC James H Ostrander; (301) 663-2183, Autovon 343-8000.
TRANSPORTATION: Ralph L Barkley Jr; (301) 663-2708, Autovon 343-8000.
PERSONNEL/COMMUNITY ACTIVITIES: Edward J O'Hearn; (301) 663-7323, Autovon 343-8000.

Personnel and Expenditures
ACTIVE DUTY PERSONNEL: 1100
DEPENDENTS: 381
CIVILIAN PERSONNEL: 3000
MILITARY PAYROLL EXPENDITURE: $23.8 mil
CONTRACT EXPENDITURE: $10 mil
Services *Housing:* Family units 155; Barracks spaces. *Temporary Housing:* BOQ units 2; Guesthouse units 4. *Commissary and Exchange:* Retail store; Barber shop; Dry cleaners; Food shop; Service station. *Child Care/Capacities:* Day care center. *Base Library:* Yes. *Medical Facilities:* Medical clinic; Dental clinic. *Recreational Facilities:* Bowling; Pool; Gym; Tennis; Racquetball; Fitness center; Softball field; Football field; Auto shop; Crafts; Fishing/Hunting; Community Club.

INDIAN HEAD

INDIAN HEAD NAVAL ORDNANCE STATION
Indian Head, MD 20640
(301) 743-4000; Autovon 364-4000
Profile
BRANCH: Navy.
SIZE AND LOCATION: 3401 acres. 20 mi S of Washington, DC, on the Potomac River, at the end of Rte 210.
MAJOR UNITS: Naval School of Explosive Ordnance Disposal; Naval Explosive Ordnance Disposal Technology Center; Naval Sea Systems Command Automated Data Systems Activity.
Key Contacts
COMMANDER: Capt E P Nicholson.
Personnel and Expenditures
ACTIVE DUTY PERSONNEL: 500
DEPENDENTS: 700
Services *Housing:* Family units 20; BOQ cottages 1; BEQ units 2; Trailer spaces; Apartment units 206. *Commissary and Exchange:* Small exchange. *Child Care/Capacities:* Day care center 100. *Medical Facilities:* Medical clinic; Dental clinic. *Recreational Facilities:* Bowling; Pool; Gym; Golf; Tennis; Racquetball; Fitness center; Auto shop; Crafts; Fishing/Hunting; Picnicking.

PATUXENT RIVER

PATUXENT RIVER NAVAL AIR STATION
Patuxent River, MD 20670-5409
(301) 863-3000; Autovon 356-3000
OFFICER-OF-THE-DAY: (301) 863-1095, 863-1096, 863-1097, Autovon 356-1095, 356-1096, 356-1097
Profile
BRANCH: Navy.
SIZE AND LOCATION: 6400 acres. On the Chesapeake Bay, 60 mi SE of Washington, DC, and about 35 mi S of Waldorf, MD just off Rte 235.
MAJOR UNITS: Naval Air Station; Naval Air Test Center; Fleet Air Reconnaissance Squadron FOUR (VQ-4); Air Test and Evaluation Squadron ONE (VX-1); Oceanographic Development Squadron EIGHT (VXN-8); Naval Aviation Maintenance Office; Naval Research Laboratory Flight Support Detachment; Surface Effect Ship Support Office; Naval Oceanography Command Detachment; Board of Inspection and Survey, Aviation Board; Marine Aviation Detachment; Naval Aviation Depot Operations Center; Navy Recreational Services Unit; NAS Patuxent River Solomons Annex.
BASE HISTORY: 1942, established to centralize air testing facilities. 1944, first US all jet-powered airplane, XP-59A, flight-tested. 1945, Naval Air Test Center. 1958, Naval Test Pilot School established. 1975, reorganized; principal site for development

testing, comprised of Strike Aircraft, Antisubmarine Aircraft, Rotary Wing Aircraft, and Systems Engineering Test with Computer Services, Technical Support and Naval Test Pilot School.
VISITOR ATTRACTIONS: Naval Air Test & Evaluation Museum, outside main gate.
Key Contacts
COMMANDER: Capt Donald A Wright III; Commanding Officer, NAS, (301) 863-1020, Autovon 356-1020; Rear Adm Donald V Boecker; Commander NATC, (301) 863-1111, Autovon 356-1111.
PUBLIC AFFAIRS: Lola Hilton; (301) 862-7513, Autovon 356-7513.
PROCUREMENT: F Carl Raley; Procurement, NATC Patuxent River, MD 20670-5304, (301) 863-1824, Autovon 356-1824.
TRANSPORTATION: Don Goddard; (301) 863-3288, Autovon 356-3288.
PERSONNEL/COMMUNITY ACTIVITIES: Bill Wagoner; (301) 863-3330, Autovon 356-3330.
Personnel and Expenditures
ACTIVE DUTY PERSONNEL: 3599
DEPENDENTS: 2222
CIVILIAN PERSONNEL: 3807
CONTRACT EXPENDITURE: $96 mil
Services *Housing:* Family units 857; BOQ cottages 11; BEQ units 11; Barracks spaces 1038. *Temporary Housing:* VIP cottages 1; BOQ units 1; Transient living quarters BEQ 17; CPO 20. *Commissary:* Base commissary; Retail store; Barber shop; Food shop; Florist; Service station; Furniture store. *Child Care/Capacities:* Day care center 110; Annex 60-70; Preschool, Aug-May, 85; Before & after school 50; Mattapany Day Camp 135. *Base Library:* Yes. *Medical Facilities:* Hospital 13; Medical clinic; Dental clinic. *Recreational Facilities:* Bowling; Movie theater; Pool; Gym; Recreation center; Golf; Stables; Tennis; Racquetball; Skating rink; Fitness center; Softball field; Football field; Auto shop; Crafts; Officers club; NCO club; Camping; Fishing/Hunting.

SOLOMONS

NAVY RECREATION CENTER
PO Box 147, Solomons, MD 20688
(301) 326-4217; 326-4216; Autovon 356-3566
Profile
BRANCH: Navy.
SIZE AND LOCATION: 295 acres. Off MD Rte 2 and 4, 65 mi SE of Washington, DC.
BASE HISTORY: Component command of Naval District Washington, DC, a destination recreation area established to provide affordable recreational programs and facilities for Navy personnel in Washington, DC metro area. 1983, placed under custodianship of NAS Patuxent River.
Key Contacts
COMMANDER: Christine Davis; Director.
PUBLIC AFFAIRS: Melinda Simmons; Publicity Clerk.
PERSONNEL/COMMUNITY ACTIVITIES: Karen Clements; Recreation Director.
Personnel and Expenditures
ACTIVE DUTY PERSONNEL: 13
CIVILIAN PERSONNEL: 100
CONTRACT EXPENDITURE: Primarily funded by non-appropriated funds
Services *Temporary Housing:* Guesthouse units 21; Guest cottages 17; Apartment units 15; Campsites 350. *Recreational Facilities:* Bowling; Movie theater; Pool; Recreation center; Golf (driving range, miniature); Tennis; Racquetball; Skating rink; Fitness center; Softball field; Camping; Fishing/Hunting (and crabbing); Marina/Boat rentals; Playgrounds; Picnicking; Beach; Water sports.

MASSACHUSETTS

BEDFORD

HANSCOM AIR FORCE BASE
Bedford, MA 01731
(617) 377-4441; Autovon 478-5980
OFFICER-OF-THE-DAY: (617) 377-5144,
Autovon 478-5144
Profile
BRANCH: Air Force.
SIZE AND LOCATION: 790 acres. 20 mi NW of
Boston within the boundaries of the
towns of Bedford, Concord, Lexington,
and Lincoln. Take I-95 to the Rte 2A W
Exit, 1 mi towards Concord to the Han-
scom exit, turn right about .5 mi on the
right.
MAJOR UNITS: HQ Electronic Systems Di-
vision; Air Force Geophysics Laboratory;
3501st USAF Recruiting Group; 2014th
Information Systems Squadron; 2d
Weather Squadron; Aerial Port Squad-
rons; Air Force Computer Acquisition
Center; Audit Agency; Air Force Office of
Special Investigations DET 102; Civil Air
Patrol; 94th Army Reserve Command.
BASE HISTORY: WWII, built; turned over to
Commonwealth of MA; named for
Laurence G Hanscom, civil aviation en-
thusiast and political editor of Worcester
Telegram; Hanscom Field operated as Re-
serve Training Center and Test Support
Wing. All active squadrons left 1973.
After WWII, leader in electronics. 1951,
Air Force Cambridge Research Center
(AFCRC); MIT's Lincoln Laboratory.
1957, Air Defense Systems Management
Office (ADSMO) established. All systems
development/acquisition activities merged
into Air Force Systems Command, An-
drews AFB, MD. Electronic Systems Di-
vision formed at Hanscom.
VISITOR ATTRACTIONS: Hanscom is located in
the Boston metro area, near the city,
ocean, and mountains.
Key Contacts
COMMANDER: Col Charles Seifert; 3245
ABG/CC, (617) 377-2301, Autovon 478-
2301.
PUBLIC AFFAIRS: Lt Col Bruce Fagaley; ESD/
PA, (617) 377-5191, Autovon 478-5191.
TRANSPORTATION: Transportation Officer;
3245 ABG/LGT, (617) 377-2588, Auto-
von 478-2588.
PERSONNEL/COMMUNITY ACTIVITIES: Director
of Personnel/Community Activities; 3245
ABG/MWR, (617) 377-3901, Autovon
478-3901.
Personnel and Expenditures
ACTIVE DUTY PERSONNEL: 2000
DEPENDENTS: 2500
CIVILIAN PERSONNEL: 8000
MILITARY PAYROLL EXPENDITURE: $382 mil
CONTRACT EXPENDITURE: $2 bil

Services *Housing:* Family units 859; BOQ
cottages; BEQ units; Townhouse units; Bar-
racks spaces; Dormitory spaces; Senior NCO
units; Junior NCO units; Mobile home units;
Trailer spaces; RV/Camper sites. *Temporary
Housing:* VIP cottages; VOQ cottages; VEQ
units; VAQ units; BOQ units; BAQ units;
Guesthouse units; Guest cottages; Apartment
units; Transient living quarters. *Commissary:*
Base commissary; Retail store; Barber shop;
Dry cleaners; Food shop; Florist; Banking;
Service station; Bakery; Optical shop; Beauty
shop; Garden center; Lunch bar. *Child Care/
Capacities:* Day care center; Home day care
program. *Schools:* Kindergarten/Preschool;
Elementary; Intermediate/Junior high. *Base
Library:* Yes. *Medical Facilities:* Medical
clinic; Dental clinic. *Recreational Facilities:*
Bowling; Movie theater; Pool; Gym; Recrea-
tion center; Golf; Tennis; Racquetball; Fit-
ness center; Softball field; Auto shop; Crafts;
Officers club; NCO club; Camping.

BOSTON

NAVY RECRUITING DISTRICT
BOSTON
495 Summer St, Boston, MA 02210-2103
(617) 451-4683
Profile
BRANCH: Navy.
LOCATION: Downtown Boston.
BASE HISTORY: Headquarters for all Navy
Recruiting Stations in ME, NH, VT, RI,
and central and eastern MA.
Key Contacts
COMMANDER: CDR John G Horan.
PUBLIC AFFAIRS: JOC(SW) Timothy M Sig-
gia; (617) 451-4793.
Personnel and Expenditures
ACTIVE DUTY PERSONNEL: 200
CIVILIAN PERSONNEL: 9

CAMP EDWARDS

CAMP EDWARDS, ARNG TRAINING
SITE
Massachusetts Army National Guard
Training Site, Camp Edwards, MA 02542-
5003
(508) 968-5885; Autovon 557-5902
OFFICER-OF-THE-DAY: DOD Police (508) 968-
5208
Profile
BRANCH: Army National Guard.
SIZE AND LOCATION: 11,000 acres. On upper
Cape Code, MA, 4 mi S of the Bourne
Bridge between the towns of Falmouth (7
mi S), Sandwich (5 mi NE), and Mashpee, MA. Nearest airport is Hyannis, MA,
located 20 mi E of base, served by commuter airlines only. Logan Airport in Boston is 80 mi. I-495 connects the cape with
western and central MA and I-95 points

S. Coastal Rte 3 connects to the Boston
Express & Beltways and I-95 to/from
points N.
MAJOR UNITS: 26th Infantry Division; 26th
Aviation Battalion; 2d Battalion, US Ma-
rine Corp Reserve; 25th Marines; co-lo-
cated with Otis Air National Guard Base
and the Coast Guard Air Station, Cape
Cod (also see Massachusetts Military
Reservation/Otis Air National Guard
Base).
BASE HISTORY: Originally acquired 1935,
from Swawme Crowell State Forest.
Named for Maj Gen Clarence R Edwards,
WWI commander, 26th "Yankee" Infan-
try Div of MA. Only artillery ranges in
New England and largest maneuver area
in region. Multi-service facility, units
from ARNG, ANG, USAR, USMCR,
USNR, USCGR, and USAFR perform
IDT and AT training; several state and
federal law enforcement agencies use
small arms ranges.
Key Contacts
COMMANDER: Col William Labrie; (508) 968-
5885, Autovon 557-5902.
PUBLIC AFFAIRS: WO James M Girard; Lt
Colleen Hammond; ATTN PAO, (508)
968-5975, Autovon 577-5902, ext 5975.
PROCUREMENT: Maj Kevin Killeen; ATTN
DOL, (508) 968-5909, Autovon 557-5909.
TRANSPORTATION: See Procurement Officer.
PERSONNEL/COMMUNITY ACTIVITIES: Lt Col
Anthony J Cimino; (508) 968-5883, Auto-
von 557-5902.
Personnel and Expenditures
ACTIVE DUTY PERSONNEL: 167 full time,
1039 part time in FY 88
DEPENDENTS: None
CIVILIAN PERSONNEL: 500
MILITARY PAYROLL EXPENDITURE: $3.7 mil,
FY 87
Services *Housing:* BEQ units 500; Barracks
spaces 2500. *Temporary Housing:* Units con-
trolled by USCG 630. *Commissary:* Base
commissary; Retail store; Barber shop; Dry
cleaners; Food shop; Banking; Service sta-
tion; Furniture store. *Child Care/Capacities:*
Day care center 50. *Schools:* Kindergarten/
Preschool; Elementary; Intermediate/Junior
high. *Base Library:* Yes. *Medical Facilities:*
Medical clinic; Dental clinic. *Recreational
Facilities:* Bowling; Golf; Stables; Tennis;
Racquetball; Fitness center; Softball field;
Football field; Auto shop; Crafts; Fishing/
Hunting; All services/rank activities center
(limited hrs).

CAPE COD

MASSACHUSETTS MILITARY
RESERVATION/OTIS AIR NATIONAL
GUARD BASE
Otis ANGB, Cape Cod, MA 02542

MASSACHUSETTS MILITARY RESERVATION/OTIS AIR NATIONAL GUARD BASE *(continued)*

OFFICER-OF-THE-DAY: CGAS Cape Cod: (508) 968-5306 (Weekdays), (508) 968-5330 (all other)

Profile

BRANCH: Air Force; Marines; Coast Guard; Air National Guard; Army National Guard.

SIZE AND LOCATION: 15,000 acres. On upper Cape Code, MA, 4 mi S of the Bourne Bridge between the towns of Falmouth (7 mi S), Sandwich (5 mi NE), and Mashpee, MA. Nearest airport is Hyannis, MA, located 20 mi E of base, served by commuter airlines only; major airports in Boston and Providence, RI are about 1.5 hrs away. I-495 connects the Cape with western and central MA and I-95 points S. Coastal Rte 3 connects to the Boston Expy & Beltways and I-95 to/from points N.

MAJOR UNITS: US Coast Guard Air Station Cape Cod; 102nd Fighter Interceptor Wing, Massachusetts Air National Guard; 26th Aviation Brigade; Army Aviation Support Group, Massachusetts Army National Guard; Camp Edwards Army National Guard Training Site; 1st Battalion, 25th Marines; Cape Cod Air Force Station.

BASE HISTORY: 1940, established as state Army NG training site; named Camp Edwards for Maj Gen Clarence Edwards, commander, 26th "Yankee" Infantry Division, WWI. Intense activity WWII and Korean War. Convalescent facilities for troops, 1945. Otis Field, completed 1938, for Boston City Hospital surgeon Lt Frank Jesse Otis, Jr. 1953, Air Force took over most of base; Camp Edwards reduced to small area northern corner Otis AFB. 1970, Coast Guard consolidated Salem, MA and Quonset Point, RI to USCG Air Station Cape Cod, Otis. Otis AFB deactivated 1973, control of airfield to 102nd FIW. Later, Cape Cod AFS (Flat Rock area of Camp Edwards) added. 1980, Otis AFB renamed Otis ANGB. Installation designated MMR with all commands operating independently (shared responsibilities and maintenance) and none designated as senior.

Key Contacts

COMMANDER: CGAS Cape Cod: Capt R F Powers, USCG; (508) 968-5300, Autovon 557-5300; 102nd FIW: Col D W Shepperd; (508) 968-4667; Army Post Commander, Col W Labrie; (508) 968-5885, Autovon 557-5902.

PUBLIC AFFAIRS: CGAS Cape Cod PAO: (508) 968-5316, Autovon 557-5316; 102nd FIW, PAO: D Karson; (508) 968-4003; Camp Edwards PAO: (508) 968-5975.

TRANSPORTATION: CGAS Cape Cod: CWO Fortin; (508) 968-5504, Autovon 557-5504.

Personnel and Expenditures

ACTIVE DUTY PERSONNEL: Coast Guard 313; Air National Guard 388 full time, 1200 part time; Camp Edwards 167 full time, 1039 part time

DEPENDENTS: 1200 Coast Guard

CIVILIAN PERSONNEL: Coast Guard 195; Air National Guard 300; Camp Edwards 65

MILITARY PAYROLL EXPENDITURE: Coast Guard FY 88, $10.5 mil; Air National Guard FY 88, $23.4 mil; Camp Edwards FY 87, $3.7 mil

CONTRACT EXPENDITURE: N/A

Services *Housing:* Family units 150; Duplex units 74; Townhouse units 408. *Temporary Housing:* Guest cottages 4; Apartment units 4; Lodge units 14; hotel-style rooms, 7.

Commissary: Base commissary; Retail store; Barber shop; Dry cleaners; Food shop; Florist; Banking; Service station; Bakery. *Child Care/Capacities:* Day care center 50. *Schools:* Elementary; Intermediate/Junior high. *Base Library:* Yes. *Medical Facilities:* Medical clinic; Dental clinic. *Recreational Facilities:* Movie theater; Golf; Stables; Tennis; Racquetball; Softball field; Auto shop; Crafts; Fishing/Hunting; Enlisted club All services/rank activities center (limited hrs).

FORT DEVENS

FORT DEVENS

PO Box 3, Fort Devens, MA 01433-5030
(508) 796-3307; 796-2159; Autovon 256-3307; 256-2159
OFFICER-OF-THE-DAY: (508) 796-3711, Autovon 256-3711

Profile

BRANCH: Army.

SIZE AND LOCATION: 10,000 acres. Just off Rte 2, 35 mi NW of Boston, adj to Ayer, MA.

MAJOR UNITS: 10th Special Forces; US Army Intelligence School.

BASE HISTORY: Sept 1917, established as infantry training center. Named for Maj Gen Charles Devens, Union Army general and attorney general during presidency of Rutherford B Hayes.

VISITOR ATTRACTIONS: Museum and self-guided tours of historic sites on post, also the 3rd weekend in May is Armed Forces Weekend celebration open to the public.

Key Contacts

COMMANDER: Maj Gen Joseph J Skaff; Post Headquarters, Ft Devens, MA 01433-5000, (508) 796-2601, Autovon 256-2601.

PUBLIC AFFAIRS: John R Rasmuson; Public Affairs Office, Ft Devens, MA 01433-5030, (508) 796-3307, 796-2159, Autovon 256-3307, 256-2159.

PROCUREMENT: Penny Waltner; Contracting Office, Ft Devens, MA 01433-5340, (508) 796-2430, Autovon 256-2430.

TRANSPORTATION: Mark Steetle; Transportation Division, Ft Devens, MA 01433-5060, (508) 796-3027, Autovon 256-3027.

PERSONNEL/COMMUNITY ACTIVITIES: Col John Andrle; DPCA, Ft Devens, MA 01433-5110, (508) 796-2444, Autovon 256-2444.

Personnel and Expenditures

ACTIVE DUTY PERSONNEL: 5735
DEPENDENTS: 6404 (4826 on post)
CIVILIAN PERSONNEL: 2364
MILITARY PAYROLL EXPENDITURE: $174 mil
CONTRACT EXPENDITURE: $38 mil

Services *Housing:* Family units 1170; BEQ units; BAQ units; Barracks spaces; Junior NCO units 994; Mobile home units 30. *Temporary Housing:* VIP cottages 3; BOQ units; Guesthouse units 60. *Commissary:* Base commissary; Retail store; Barber shop; Dry cleaners; Food shop; Florist; Banking; Service station; Bakery. *Child Care/Capacities:* Day care center 400; Home day care program. *Schools:* Kindergarten/Preschool; Elementary. *Base Library:* Yes. *Medical Facilities:* Dental clinic; Cutler Army Hospital. *Recreational Facilities:* Fishing/Hunting; Sports; Parachute Club; Amateur Radio Club.

NATICK

ARMY NATICK RESEARCH, DEVELOPMENT & ENGINEERING CENTER

Kansas St, Natick, MA 01760-5000
(508) 651-4300; Autovon 256-4300
OFFICER-OF-THE-DAY: (508) 651-4214, Autovon 256-4214

Profile

BRANCH: Army.

SIZE AND LOCATION: 78 acres. Approx 20 mi W of Boston in Natick, MA, situated just off Rte 9, less than 1 mi from Exit 13 of the MA Tpke, Rte 27 S (Natick), turn right onto Kansas St to the entrance to the center; 22 mi from Logan IAP.

MAJOR UNITS: Directorate for Resource Management; Science and Advanced Technology Directorate; Individual Protection Directorate; Food Engineering Directorate; Services and Facilities Directorate; Personnel Administrative Directorate; Directorate for Engineering Programs Management; Information Management Directorate; Advanced Systems Concepts Directorate; Aero-Mechanical Engineering Directorate.

BASE HISTORY: WWI and WWII, mission scattered under Army Quartermaster Corps. 1952, operational centers (IN, VA, MA, DC, and PA) moved to Natick. 1963, Quartermaster Research and Engineering Center at Natick changed to US Army Natick Laboratories. Today, four separate directorates and four major support activities. 1983, renamed US Army Natick Research and Development Center, subordinate command of US Army Troop Support Command (TROSCOM), St Louis, MO and subsequently redesignated as USANRDEC.

VISITOR ATTRACTIONS: Located in the Boston metro area.

Key Contacts

COMMANDER: Clinton A Hodder; (508) 651-4206, Autovon 256-4206.

PUBLIC AFFAIRS: Harvey Keene; (508) 651-4300, 651-5340, Autovon 256-4300, 256-5340.

Personnel and Expenditures

ACTIVE DUTY PERSONNEL: 181
CIVILIAN PERSONNEL: 1340

Services *Housing:* Family units. *Commissary and Exchange:* Barber shop. *Base Library:* Yes. *Medical Facilities:* Medical clinic. *Recreational Facilities:* Officers club; NCO club; Recreation center; Officers' open mess.

NAVAL CLOTHING AND TEXTILE RESEARCH FACILITY

21 Strathmore Rd, Natick, MA 01760-2490
(508) 651-4172; Autovon 256-4172

Profile

BRANCH: Navy.

SIZE AND LOCATION: 1 acre. NCTRF is a small, government R&D laboratory located about 20 mi W of Boston in Natick, MA; situated just off Rte 9, less than 1 mi from Exit 13 of the MA Tpke. The laboratory building is located 3 mi E on the grounds of the US Army Natick Research, Development and Engineering Center.

MAJOR UNITS: Materials Research Division; Clothing Development Division; Environmental Sciences Division; Standardization & Specifications Division.

BASE HISTORY: 1879, began as Clothing Manufacturing Department of Naval Clothing Depot, Brooklyn. 1943, Textile and Clothing R&D Department formed. 1947, research arm of Clothing Supply Office (CSO). 1958, CSO reorganized; Clothing and Textile Research and Development Division remained in Brooklyn as division of Naval Supply Research and Development Facility, Bayonne, NJ. 1962, moved to Bayonne. 1967, closed; renamed Navy Clothing and Textile Research Unit and relocated in Natick, MA. March 1976, unit received current title.

**NAVAL CLOTHING AND TEXTILE RE-
SEARCH FACILITY** *(continued)*
Key Contacts
COMMANDER: Officer in Charge, CDR William E Johnson, SC, USN.
PUBLIC AFFAIRS: John A Mylotte; (508) 651-4680, Autovon 256-4680.
PROCUREMENT: Zander Krowitz; (508) 651-4196, Autovon 256-4196.
TRANSPORTATION: See Procurement Officer.
PERSONNEL/COMMUNITY ACTIVITIES: Joan Lunney.
Personnel and Expenditures
ACTIVE DUTY PERSONNEL: 1
CIVILIAN PERSONNEL: 54
MILITARY PAYROLL EXPENDITURE: FY 88, $3.5 mil
CONTRACT EXPENDITURE: $806,000
Services *Base Library:* Yes.

NEW BEDFORD

**FORT RODMAN, US ARMY
RESERVE CENTER**
Fort Rodman, New Bedford, MA 02744-1237
(508) 994-4677
Profile
BRANCH: Army Reserve.
SIZE AND LOCATION: 11.71 acres. At the southernmost tip of New Bedford, MA, within 5 mi of I-195 E.
MAJOR UNITS: 1114th MI Gp (RTU); HQ 483d Engineer Battalion (C)(C); HHC 483d Engineer Battalion (C)(C); Co C 483d Engineer Battalion (C)(C); Co D 483d Engineer Battalion (C)(C).
Key Contacts
COMMANDER: Lt Col John J Alfano.
PUBLIC AFFAIRS: Capt David G Quimby; (508) 993-6893.
PROCUREMENT: CW3 Dwight J Doane; (508) 994-4427.
TRANSPORTATION: See Procurement Officer.
Personnel and Expenditures
ACTIVE DUTY PERSONNEL: 8
CIVILIAN PERSONNEL: 8

NORTH TRURO

**NORTH TRURO AIR FORCE
STATION**
North Truro, MA 02652
(617) 487-1248
Profile
BRANCH: Air Force.
MAJOR UNITS: North Truro AFS (AAC).

SOUTH WEYMOUTH

**SOUTH WEYMOUTH NAVAL AIR
STATION**
Commanding Officer, Naval Air Station, South Weymouth, MA 02190-5000
(617) 786-2933; Autovon 955-2933
OFFICER-OF-THE-DAY: (617) 786-2933, Autovon 955-2933
Profile
BRANCH: Naval Reserve.
SIZE AND LOCATION: 1443 acres. Approx 15 mi SE of Boston on Rte 18; Within corporate limits on S Weymouth on White St.
MAJOR UNITS: VP-92; HSL-74; MAG 49-DET A.
BASE HISTORY: 1941, commissioned. July 1946, turned over to Naval Air Reserve Training Command. June 1949, deactivated. Dec 1953, recommissioned. Today, only Naval Reserve Air Station in New England; supports about 2000 Naval and Marine Corps reservists.

Key Contacts
COMMANDER: Capt Charles E Long, USNR; (617) 786-2963, Autovon 955-2963.
PUBLIC AFFAIRS: Ens Ed Matlak; (617) 786-2607, Autovon 955-2607.
PROCUREMENT: LCDR George Herning; (617) 786-2641, Autovon 955-2641.
TRANSPORTATION: LCDR Thomas W Nielsen; (617) 786-2655, Autovon 955-2655.
PERSONNEL/COMMUNITY ACTIVITIES: Dodds Cupit; (617) 786-2931, Autovon 955-2931.
Personnel and Expenditures
ACTIVE DUTY PERSONNEL: 800
DEPENDENTS: 500
CIVILIAN PERSONNEL: 300
MILITARY PAYROLL EXPENDITURE: $20 mil
CONTRACT EXPENDITURE: $5.5 mil
Services *Housing:* Family units; Duplex units; Barracks spaces 235; Family units NAS SOWEY 165; Squantum 105; Otis AFB 95. *Temporary Housing:* BOQ units 102. *Commissary and Exchange:* Retail store; Barber shop; Dry cleaners; Food shop; Florist; Service station; Military clothing sales; Package beverages; Credit union; Navy relief; Galley; Personnel Support Detachment; Family service center; Thrift shop. *Child Care/Capacities:* Day care center 30. *Medical Facilities:* Medical clinic; Dental clinic. *Recreational Facilities:* Bowling; Pool; Gym; Recreation center; Tennis; Racquetball; Fitness center; Softball field; Football field; Auto shop; Crafts; Officers club; NCO club; Youth center; Rental center for camping & skiing gear.

WALTHAM

**US ARMY CORPS OF ENGINEERS,
NEW ENGLAND DIVISION**
424 Trapelo Rd, Waltham, MA 02154
(617) 894-2400
Profile
BRANCH: Army.
SIZE: Offices only.
Key Contacts
COMMANDER: Col Daniel M Wilson; Division Engineer.

WATERTOWN

**ARMY MATERIELS TECHNOLOGY
LABORATORY**
US Army Laboratory Command, Watertown, MA 02172-0001
(617) 923-5158; Autovon 955-5158
Profile
BRANCH: Army.
SIZE AND LOCATION: 32 acres. On banks of Charles River, in Boston suburb of Watertown.
MAJOR UNITS: Materiels Technology Laboratory.
BASE HISTORY: 1816, founded as Watertown Arsenal; MTL still occupies same buildings of famous predecessor. 1816-1967, Watertown Arsenal, second oldest arsenal, noted for innovative achievements in armament production, from Rodman method of casting cannon during Civil War, to Skysweeper anti-aircraft gun of Korean Conflict and first atomic cannon. 1967, ceased production, but facilities and employees of Army Materiels Research Agency (AMRA) remained to carry on R&D. 1968, AMRA redesignated Army Materiels and Mechanics Research Center which became MTL, 1985. American Society of Civil Engineers designated MTL historic landmark.
Key Contacts
PUBLIC AFFAIRS: (617) 923-5277, Autovon 955-5277.

Personnel and Expenditures
CIVILIAN PERSONNEL: 550

WESTFIELD

**104TH TACTICAL FIGHTER GROUP
(ANG)**
Barnes Municipal Airport, Westfield, MA 01085
(413) 568-9151; Autovon 636-1210; 636-1211
Profile
BRANCH: Air National Guard.
SIZE AND LOCATION: 133 acres. 3 mi N of Westfield; N of I-90, off exit 3, Southampton Rd.
MAJOR UNITS: 104th Tactical Fighter Group (ANG).
Personnel and Expenditures
ACTIVE DUTY PERSONNEL: 873
CIVILIAN PERSONNEL: 191
MILITARY PAYROLL EXPENDITURE: $9.7 mil

WESTOVER AFB

WESTOVER AIR FORCE BASE
Westover AFB, MA 01022-5000
(413) 557-1110; Autovon 589-1110
Profile
BRANCH: Air Force Reserve.
SIZE AND LOCATION: 2500 acres. Exit 5 off I-90 (Massachusetts Tpke) in Chicopee, Westover AFB on MA-33, N of I-90, signs mark way to base. Nearest major city Springfield, 8 mi S. Bradley IAP approx 30 mi SW.
MAJOR UNITS: 439th Military Airlift Wing.
BASE HISTORY: 1940, activated and served as bomber training site and transition station for overseas missions; named for Maj Gen Oscar Westover, then top-ranking US military pilot and first Chief of Air Corps. 1946-55, freight and passenger terminal for Military Transport Service. 1955-74, SAC in operation; HQ Eighth Air Force tenant until 1970. 1974, Air Force Reserve base with 439th MAW.
VISITOR ATTRACTIONS: Public Affairs Office offers tours of the C-5A Galaxy aircraft, base fire station, weather station, etc.
Key Contacts
COMMANDER: Col Thomas G Hargis; 439th ABG/CC, (413) 557-3044, Autovon 589-3044.
PUBLIC AFFAIRS: Gordon A Newell; 439th ABG/PA, (413) 557-3500, Autovon 589-3500.
PROCUREMENT: Michael LaFortune; 439th ABG/LGC, (413) 557-3508, Autovon 589-3508.
TRANSPORTATION: Howard Altman; 439th ABG/LGT, (413) 557-2544, Autovon 589-2544.
PERSONNEL/COMMUNITY ACTIVITIES: Robert Gibson; 439th ABG/DPC, (413) 557-2871, Autovon 589-2871.
Personnel and Expenditures
ACTIVE DUTY PERSONNEL: 1
CIVILIAN PERSONNEL: 1000
MILITARY PAYROLL EXPENDITURE: $13 mil
CONTRACT EXPENDITURE: FY 88, $10.3 mil
Services *Housing:* Family units 11; Duplex units (Junior grade 34; Enlisted 258). *Temporary Housing:* VOQ cottages 72; VAQ units 523. *Commissary and Exchange:* Retail store; Barber shop; Food shop; Service station. *Medical Facilities:* USAF clinic available only to reservists on active-duty status and civilian employees for work-related emergencies. *Recreational Facilities:* Bowling; Movie theater; Pool; Gym; Recreation center; Tennis; Racquetball; Fitness center; Softball field.

WOODS HOLE

WOODS HOLE COAST GUARD GROUP

Little Harbor Rd, Woods Hole, MA 02543-1099
(508) 548-1700; FTS 829-8220
OFFICER-OF-THE-DAY: (508) 548-1700, ext 210, FTS 829-8221

Profile
BRANCH: Coast Guard.
SIZE AND LOCATION: 2 acres. In the Village of Woods Hole which is in the town of Falmouth. From the center of Falmouth, follow Woods Hole Rd approx 4 mi and as you enter Woods Hole you will see the facility on your left.
MAJOR UNITS: Coast Guard Aids to Navigation Team Woods Hole; Coast Guard Station Woods Hole; USCGC *Bittersweet*; USCGC *Sanibel*; USCGC *Monomoy*; USCGC *Cape Henlopen*; USCGC *Point Jackson*.
BASE HISTORY: 1966, established as "Supergroup." One of largest units in Coast Guard and covers over 600 mi of coastline from Plymouth, MA to RI/CT border. Mission is Search and Rescue, Maritime Law Enforcement, and Aids to Navigation. Woods Hole is administrative and operational center.
VISITOR ATTRACTIONS: This is strictly a working facility with no berthing or recreational facilities. The public can tour the facility after the work day and on weekends. Larger groups can request a guided tour by contacting the Public Affairs Officer.

Key Contacts
COMMANDER: Capt Anthony J Pettit; (508) 548-1700 ext 220; FTS 829-8220.
PUBLIC AFFAIRS: Lt Hank Leeper; (508) 548-1700 ext 227; FTS 829-8227.
PROCUREMENT: CWO3 Patrick Flynn; (508) 548-1700 ext 240; FTS 829-8240.
TRANSPORTATION: SSC Michael Leathe; (508) 548-1700 ext 247; FTS 829-8247.
PERSONNEL/COMMUNITY ACTIVITIES: CWO3 Ronald Eslick; Director of Personnel, (508) 548-1700 ext 226; FTS 829-8226.

Personnel and Expenditures
ACTIVE DUTY PERSONNEL: 200
CIVILIAN PERSONNEL: 20
Services *Medical Facilities:* Corpsman assigned.

MICHIGAN

ALPENA

PHELPS COLLINS AIR NATIONAL GUARD BASE
HQ, ANG Field Training Site, Alpena, MI 49707
(517) 354-4141; Autovon 722-3760
Profile
BRANCH: Air National Guard.
SIZE AND LOCATION: 2711 acres. 7 mi W of Alpena, MI, off State Rte 32.
MAJOR UNITS: HQ, ANG Field Training Site.
BASE HISTORY: Named for Capt W H Phelps Collins, American Flying Corps, killed in France in 1918. Facilities used by ANG and AFRES units for annual field training and ARNG and Marine Reserve for special training.
Personnel and Expenditures
ACTIVE DUTY PERSONNEL: 52
Services *Medical Facilities:* Hospital 14; Dispensary.

BATTLE CREEK

BATTLE CREEK AIR NATIONAL GUARD BASE
3367 W Dickman Rd, 110th Tactical Air Support Group, Battle Creek, MI 98571
(616) 963-1596; Autovon 580-3221
Profile
BRANCH: Air National Guard.
SIZE AND LOCATION: 315 acres. At the W K Kellogg Regional Airport off of US Business 94.
MAJOR UNITS: 110th Tactical Air Support Group; 110th Communications Electronics Maintenance Squadron; 110th Consolidated Aircraft Maintenance Squadron; 110th Direct Air Support Center Squadron; 172nd Tactical Air Support Squadron; 110th Resource Management Squadron; 110th Mission Support Squadron; 110th Engineering Squadron; 110th Tactical Clinic.
BASE HISTORY: 1928, Kellogg Regional Airport, largest municipally-owned airport in MI, built. 1942, civilian flying banned when Army Air Corps needed field to train pilots and crews for combat. 1946, Battle Creek NG Air Corps began. 1947, Governor designated Kellogg Regional Airport as HQs with federal recognition.
Key Contacts
COMMANDER: Col Ronald L Seely; Group Commander.
PUBLIC AFFAIRS: Maj David W Lubbers.
Personnel and Expenditures
ACTIVE DUTY PERSONNEL: 48
CIVILIAN PERSONNEL: 155
MILITARY PAYROLL EXPENDITURE: FY 88, $3.9 mil
CONTRACT EXPENDITURE: FY 88, $10 mil
Services *Medical Facilities:* Clinic.

DEFENSE REUTILIZATION AND MARKETING SERVICE
74 N Washington, Federal Center, Battle Creek, MI 49017-3092
(616) 961-5974; Autovon 932-5974
Profile
BRANCH: Defense Logistics Agency.
SIZE AND LOCATION: Offices only. In Battle Creek.
MAJOR UNITS: Defense Reutilization and Marketing Service.

CALUMET

CALUMET AIR FORCE STATION
Calumet, MI 49913
(906) 337-4200
Profile
BRANCH: Air Force.
MAJOR UNITS: Calumet AFS (TAC).

DETROIT

DETROIT COAST GUARD GROUP/ BASE
Ft of Mt Elliott Ave, Detroit, MI 48207-4380
(313) 568-9525; FTS 374-9525
OFFICER-OF-THE-DAY: (313) 568-9525, FTS 374-9525
Profile
BRANCH: Coast Guard.
SIZE AND LOCATION: 1 acre. Downtown Detroit, facing Detroit River, directly N of western tip of Belle Isle, approx 1 mi E of Renaissance Center.
MAJOR UNITS: USCGC *Mariposa* (WLB 397); USCGC *Bristol Bay* (WTGB 102); USCG Aids to Navigation Team, Detroit; Marine Safety Office Detroit (Captain of the Port); US Coast Guard Air Station Detroit.
BASE HISTORY: 1859, first obtained by Lighthouse Service. Base passed to USCG; most buildings replaced with single multipurpose building. Missions include: supply and logistics support; maintenance/repair aids-to-navigation; and communication with all vessels in Group's area; parent command for 12 search and rescue stations, support base, 2 aids-to-navigation teams, 2 electronics support facilities, and 2 icebreakers; responsible for all US waters in lower two-thirds of Lake Huron, including Saginaw Bay, St Clair River, Lake St Clair, Detroit River, and approx western two-thirds of Lake Erie; helicopters housed at Selfridge ANG Base.
Key Contacts
COMMANDER: Capt Jan F Smith; (313) 568-9600, FTS 374-9600.
PUBLIC AFFAIRS: Lt Christine D Balboni; (313) 568-9521, FTS 374-9521.

PROCUREMENT: CWO2 (F&S) Charles P Landeau; (313) 568-9513, FTS 374-9513.
TRANSPORTATION: See Procurement Officer.
PERSONNEL/COMMUNITY ACTIVITIES: CWO2 (PERS) Peter F Sommer; (313) 568-9470, FTS 374-9470.
Personnel and Expenditures
ACTIVE DUTY PERSONNEL: 73
CIVILIAN PERSONNEL: 11
Services *Commissary and Exchange:* Small exchange. *Base Library:* Yes. *Medical Facilities:* Small clinic. *Recreational Facilities:* Bowling; Movie theater; Pool; Gym; Recreation center; Golf; Tennis; Racquetball; Skating rink; Fitness center; Softball field; Football field; Auto shop; Crafts; Officers club; NCO club; Camping; Fishing/Hunting; Marina; Rod and Gun Club; Parks; Picnicking.

US ARMY CORPS OF ENGINEERS, DETROIT DISTRICT
PO Box 1027, 477 Michigan Ave, Detroit, MI 48231
(313) 226-6413
Profile
BRANCH: Army.
SIZE AND LOCATION: 2 floors. HQs are downtown Detroit at 477 Michigan Ave at Cass Ave.
MAJOR UNITS: Engineering Division; Planning Division; Construction Operations Division; Program Management and Information Management.
BASE HISTORY: Detroit District conducts federal water resources activities throughout Great Lakes Region.
VISITOR ATTRACTIONS: Soo Locks at Sault Ste. Marie, MI; Canal Park Museum at Duluth, MN.
Key Contacts
COMMANDER: Col John D Glass; (313) 226-6762.
PUBLIC AFFAIRS: Michael J Perrini; (313) 226-4680.
PROCUREMENT: Wanda Carter Davis; (313) 226-5148.
TRANSPORTATION: Glen Cunningham; (313) 226-7236.
PERSONNEL/COMMUNITY ACTIVITIES: Thomas Harper; (313) 226-6423.
Personnel and Expenditures
ACTIVE DUTY PERSONNEL: 3
CIVILIAN PERSONNEL: 200
Services *Base Library:* Yes.

EMPIRE AFS

EMPIRE AIR FORCE STATION
Empire AFS, MI 49630
(616) 326-6211
Profile
BRANCH: Air Force.
MAJOR UNITS: Empire AFS (TAC).

GRAYLING

CAMP GRAYLING ARMY AND AIR NATIONAL GUARD TRAINING CENTER

Camp Grayling, Grayling, MI 49739-0001
(517) 348-7621; Autovon 722-8200
Profile
BRANCH: Air National Guard; Army National Guard.
SIZE AND LOCATION: 147,000 acres. On I-75, 3 mi SW of Grayling, MI, 200 mi NW of Detroit.
MAJOR UNITS: Installation Support Unit; 1071st Maintenance Co; 1438th Engineering Detachment; 1439th Engineering Detachment; 1440th Engineering Detachment; 745th Ordnance Detachment (EOD); Detachment 2, 207th Evacuation Hospital.
BASE HISTORY: 1913, originated, with 14,000-acre grant of private land to MI State. Continuously used as military training site, now encompassing wooded and rolling terrain; all conventional Army weapons can be fired on ranges, with maneuver space for entire division, including infantry, armor, artillery, and aerial gunnery; largest National Guard training center in US.
VISITOR ATTRACTIONS: Hartwick Pines State Park, a 93-acre stand of virgin pines; Heart of Michigan's vacation land; Trout fishing on nearby rivers.
Key Contacts
COMMANDER: Col David "Skip" Hanson; (517) 348-3601, Autovon 722-8601.
PUBLIC AFFAIRS: Maj Jerold E Foehl; (517) 348-7621, Autovon 722-8432.
Personnel and Expenditures
ACTIVE DUTY PERSONNEL: 36
CIVILIAN PERSONNEL: 140
MILITARY PAYROLL EXPENDITURE: $6 mil
CONTRACT EXPENDITURE: $18.1 mil
Services *Housing:* BOQ cottages 3; Barracks spaces 7500; Mobile home units 2; Trailer spaces 30. *Temporary Housing:* VIP cottages 5; VOQ cottages (guest rooms) 6; BOQ units 650. *Commissary and Exchange:* Retail store; Barber shop; Food shop; Military clothing sales. *Medical Facilities:* Troop medical clinic is open during major encampments. *Recreational Facilities:* Tennis; Softball field; Officers club; NCO club; Fishing/Hunting; EP Club.

MICHIGAN NATIONAL GUARD MOBILIZATION AND TRAINING EQUIPMENT SITE

Bldg 1400, North Down River Rd, Grayling, MI 49738-9802
(517) 348-3651; Autovon 722-8351
Profile
BRANCH: Army National Guard.
SIZE AND LOCATION: 9 acres. Take I-75 N to Exit 254, Grayling, MI, Business Loop I-75, 2 mi N to North Down River Rd, 3 mi E to the MATES.
MAJOR UNITS: Michigan National Guard.
BASE HISTORY: 1948, on-site maintenance for tracked vehicles at Camp Grayling began with one-bay shop. 1960, construction of three-bay structure completed, named Field Training Equipment Concentration Site. 1968, ten-bay building was constructed; name changed to Annual Training Equipment Pool. 1976, name changed to current MATES. 1988, construction of present installation completed with 34 work bays. Equipment pooled from units of MI, OH, and IN, National Guard and two US Army Reserve units.

Key Contacts
COMMANDER: Col Michael P McNamara; (517) 348-3620, Autovon 722-8620.
PROCUREMENT: CW3 James R Failing; (517) 348-3652, Autovon 722-8652.
TRANSPORTATION: MSG Martin Nieman; (517) 348-3653, Autovon 722-8653.
Personnel and Expenditures
ACTIVE DUTY PERSONNEL: 1
CIVILIAN PERSONNEL: 95 National Guard Technicians
Services *Base Library:* Yes. *Recreational Facilities:* Running.

K I SAWYER

K I SAWYER AIR FORCE BASE

410th BMW, K I Sawyer, MI 49843-5000
(906) 346-2010; Autovon 472-1038; 472-2010
Profile
BRANCH: Air Force.
SIZE AND LOCATION: 5202 acres. 23 mi SE of Marquette, MI, off of H-553.
MAJOR UNITS: 410th Bombardment Wing (Heavy); 410th Combat support Group; 410th Strategic Hospital; 2001st Communications Squadron; 46th Air Refueling Squadron; 307th Air Refueling Squadron; 644th Bomb Squadron; 71st Flying Training Wing.
BASE HISTORY: Through efforts of Kenneth I Sawyer, Marquette County Road Commissioner, first airport built at site of present base, early 1940s. 1955, K I Sawyer County Airport became AFB. 1956, activated. 1959, runway opened; first host 56th Fighter Wing. 1958, Sault Ste Marie Air Defense Sector (Semi-Automatic-Ground Environment operation), and 402nd Strategic Wing (SAC) moved to base. 1963, 402nd, redesignated 410th Bombardment Wing (Heavy), phased out, 56th deactivated, control passed to 410th. 1971, 87th FIS transferred from Duluth, MN. Controlled by Eighth Air Force, Barksdale AFB, LA, and SAC, Offutt AFB, NE.
VISITOR ATTRACTIONS: Aircraft static displays, B-52 and F-101 Voodoo.
Key Contacts
COMMANDER: Col Michael Lock; 410 CSG/CC, (906) 346-2851, Autovon 472-2851.
PUBLIC AFFAIRS: Capt Paul Bicking; 410 BMW/PA, (906) 346-2010, Autovon 472-2010.
PROCUREMENT: Col Michael Howayeck; 410 BMW/RM, (906) 346-2185, Autovon 472-2485.
TRANSPORTATION: Maj Gregory Thomas; 410 BMW LG/CC, (906) 346-1209, Autovon 472-1209.
PERSONNEL/COMMUNITY ACTIVITIES: Lt Col Thomas Starkavich; 410 BMW/DPM, (906) 346-2094, Autovon 472-2094.
Personnel and Expenditures
ACTIVE DUTY PERSONNEL: 3800
DEPENDENTS: 5000
CIVILIAN PERSONNEL: 600
MILITARY PAYROLL EXPENDITURE: $92 mil
CONTRACT EXPENDITURE: $25 mil
Services *Housing:* Family units 1693; Duplex units 772; Townhouse units 788; Barracks spaces 770; Senior NCO units 192; Junior NCO units 1222; Mobile home units 199. *Temporary Housing:* VIP cottages 3; VOQ cottages 16; VAQ units 22; BOQ units 16; BAQ units 10; Guest cottages 23. *Commissary:* Base commissary; Retail store; Barber shop; Dry cleaners; Food shop; Florist; Banking; Service station; Furniture store; Book store. *Child Care/Capacities:* Day care center 86; Home day care program. *Schools:* Elementary. *Base Library:* Yes. *Medical Facilities:* Hospital 15; Medical clinic; Dental clinic. *Recreational Facilities:* Bowling; Mov-

ie theater; Gym; Recreation center; Golf; Tennis; Racquetball; Fitness center; Softball field; Football field; Auto shop; Crafts; Officers club; NCO club; Camping; Fishing/Hunting.

PORT AUSTIN

PORT AUSTIN AIR FORCE STATION, OPERATING LOCATION ALPHA NANCY, NORTHEAST AIR DIVISION SECTOR

8195 N Van Dyke, Port Austin, MI 48467-8195
(517) 738-5111
Profile
BRANCH: Air Force.
SIZE AND LOCATION: 59 acres. One mi S of village of Port Austin on MI-25, on "Tip of the Thumb" region of MI on Lake Huron.
MAJOR UNITS: Caretaker Force.
BASE HISTORY: 1950-51, constructed as manual Aircraft Control and Warning Squadron under central NORAD Region. 1959, converted to Long Range Radar station under 34th Air Division, HQ Battle Creek, MI. 1965, Back Up Intercept Control (BUIC) II mission. 1968, BUIC III, computerized system of air defense, installed. 1970, reverted solely to Long Range Radar under 23rd Air Division, Duluth, MN. Dec 15, 1988, closed. Currently on caretaker status.
Key Contacts
COMMANDER: Doyle E Evins; Site Chief.
Personnel and Expenditures
CIVILIAN PERSONNEL: 5
Services *Housing:* Family units 9; Dormitory spaces 76; Before site closure. *Temporary Housing:* BOQ units 1; BAQ units 10; Before site closure. *Commissary and Exchange:* Prior to closing had commissary and base exchange. *Medical Facilities:* Had medical and dental clinic prior to closing. *Recreational Facilities:* Bowling; Pool; Gym; Tennis; Racquetball; Fitness center; Softball field; Auto shop; Crafts; NCO club; All prior to closing.

SAULT STE MARIE

SAULT STE MARIE COAST GUARD BASE

337 Water St, Sault Ste Marie, MI 49783
(906) 635-3217
OFFICER-OF-THE-DAY: (906) 635-3228
Profile
BRANCH: Coast Guard.
SIZE AND LOCATION: 5 acres. Eastern Upper Peninsula of MI on the St Mary's River, bordering Canada. Take I-75 as far N as you can and get off just before the Canadian border.
MAJOR UNITS: Coast Guard Group Sault; Coast Guard Base Sault; USCGC *Katmai Bay*; USCGC *Buckthorn*; Coast Guard Station Sault; Coast Guard Aid to Navigation Team Sault.
Key Contacts
COMMANDER: Capt Jimmie H Hobaugh.
PUBLIC AFFAIRS: LTjg William P Green; (906) 635-3241.
PROCUREMENT: CWO Jim Cropper; (906) 635-3240.
TRANSPORTATION: See Procurement Officer.
PERSONNEL/COMMUNITY ACTIVITIES: See Public Affairs Officer.
Personnel and Expenditures
ACTIVE DUTY PERSONNEL: 148
CIVILIAN PERSONNEL: 6
MILITARY PAYROLL EXPENDITURE: $2.8 mil
CONTRACT EXPENDITURE: $.5 mil

SAULT STE MARIE COAST GUARD BASE
(continued)
Services *Housing:* Barracks spaces 8. *Commissary and Exchange:* Retail store. *Medical Facilities:* Medical clinic.

SELFRIDGE ANG BASE

DETROIT NAVAL AIR FACILITY
Selfridge ANG Base, MI 48043
(313) 466-4420; Autovon 273-4420
OFFICER-OF-THE-DAY: (313) 466-4420,
Autovon 273-4420
Profile
BRANCH: Navy.
SIZE AND LOCATION: 300 acres. On the Selfridge ANG Base, approx 1.5 mi E of junction I-94 and MI 59. 25 mi NE of Detroit; nearest city is Mount Clemens, 2.5 mi W.
MAJOR UNITS: Naval Air Facility Detroit; VP-93; VR-62.
BASE HISTORY: 1970, Navy joined Selfridge. Tenant command, Selfridge ANG Base; facilities under control of Automotive Tank Command (TACOM) USA.
Key Contacts
COMMANDER: Capt John T Williams; (313) 466-4420, Autovon 273-4420.
PUBLIC AFFAIRS: Lt Janie L Leo; (313) 466-4557, Autovon 273-4557.
PROCUREMENT: Lt Christian; (313) 466-5515, Autovon 273-5515.
TRANSPORTATION: Lt L E Mault Jr; (313) 466-4742, Autovon 273-4742.
Personnel and Expenditures
ACTIVE DUTY PERSONNEL: 500
CIVILIAN PERSONNEL: 70
Services *Housing:* BEQ units 75. *Temporary Housing:* BOQ units 75. *Medical Facilities:* Medical clinic; Dental clinic. *Recreational Facilities:* Softball field; NCO club.

SELFRIDGE AIR NATIONAL GUARD BASE
Selfridge ANG Base, MI 48045-5004
(313) 466-4011; Autovon 273-4011
OFFICER-OF-THE-DAY: (313) 466-4011,
Autovon 273-4011
Profile
BRANCH: Air National Guard.
SIZE AND LOCATION: 3700 acres. Main gate approx 1.5 mi E of junction I-94 and MI 59; 25 mi NE of Detroit; nearest city Mount Clemens, 2.5 mi W.
MAJOR UNITS: Michigan Air National Guard; 127th Tactical Fighter Wing (TFW); 191st Fighter Interceptor Group (FIG); 927th Tactical Airlift Group (AFRES); 305th Aerospace Rescue & Recovery Squadron; Naval Air Facility Detroit; US Coast Guard Air Station Detroit; Marine Wing Support Group 47; US Army Tank Automotive Support Group-Selfridge; Army Readiness Group.
BASE HISTORY: Originally built as Joy Aviation Field; later used by Packard Motor Co as test field. 1917, leased by government; named Selfridge Field for 1st Lt Thomas E Selfridge, first person to die from aircraft accident. 1921, named permanent installation. 1920s, first night landing. WWII, training of many units including 332nd Fighter Group, all-black unit commanded by Col Benjamin O Davis Jr. 1946, 56th Fighter Group reactivated. 1947, became Selfridge AFB. 1950s, HQ 10th Air Force in charge of training, recall, and records of all Air Reservists, 13-state area. 1960s, Coast Guard Station, Detroit and Marine Air Reserve Training Detachment added; 5th Air Force Reserve Region transferred; SAC refueling tankers and NIKE missiles removed. Nicknamed "Home of the

Generals." 1970, Naval Air Facility, Detroit. 1970, MIANG. 1971, became Selfridge ANG Base.
VISITOR ATTRACTIONS: Selfridge Military Air Museum (open every Sun except Easter, 1-5pm).
Key Contacts
COMMANDER: Col Sam R Smith; Deputy Commander for Support, 127TFW/DS, (313) 466-5545, Autovon 273-5545.
PUBLIC AFFAIRS: Donald E Odell; 127TFW/PA, (313) 466-5576, Autovon 273-5576.
PROCUREMENT: George Harris; 127TFW/PK, (313) 466-5508, Autovon 273-5508.
TRANSPORTATION: Maj Dennis Gamble; 127TFW/LGT, (313) 466-5260, Autovon 273-5260.
PERSONNEL/COMMUNITY ACTIVITIES: Jerome Kurtz; Director of Personnel, Civilian, 127TFW/DPC, (313) 466-4791, Autovon 273-4791.
Personnel and Expenditures
ACTIVE DUTY PERSONNEL: 998
DEPENDENTS: 2000
CIVILIAN PERSONNEL: 2283
MILITARY PAYROLL EXPENDITURE: $57.4 mil
Services *Housing:* Family units 974; Barracks spaces 36. *Temporary Housing:* Guesthouse units 14; VOQ/VEQ 26. *Commissary:* Base commissary; Retail store; Barber shop; Dry cleaners; Food shop; Florist; Banking; Service station; Package beverages; Thrift shop. *Child Care/Capacities:* Day care center 145; Home day care program. *Base Library:* Yes. *Medical Facilities:* Medical clinic; Dental clinic. *Recreational Facilities:* Bowling; Movie theater; Pool; Gym; Recreation center; Golf; Tennis; Racquetball; Skating rink; Fitness center; Softball field; Football field; Auto shop; Crafts; Officers club; NCO club; Camping; Fishing/Hunting; Marina berthing; Rod and Gun Club; Parks; Picnicking.

TRAVERSE CITY

TRAVERSE CITY COAST GUARD AIR STATION
Airport Access Rd, Traverse City, MI 49684-3586
(616) 922-8214; Autovon 722-3470
OFFICER-OF-THE-DAY: (616) 922-8214
Profile
BRANCH: Coast Guard.
SIZE AND LOCATION: 100 acres. Within Traverse City city limits. Adj to the Cherry Capital Airport on Airport Access Rd which crosses Parsons Rd and meets Hwy 31 and 72.
MAJOR UNITS: Coast Guard Air Station.
BASE HISTORY: 1938, established as one plane detachment to provide search and rescue service for Great Lakes. 1948, formally founded. Station now HH-3F only air station, operating three helicopters and providing operational response from Duluth, MN, on Lake Superior to Lake Michigan, Lake Huron, Lake Erie and, on occasion Lake Ontario.
Key Contacts
COMMANDER: CDR Andrew L Gerfin; (616) 922-8222.
PUBLIC AFFAIRS: Capt Michael B Jarvis, USAF; (616) 922-8218.
PROCUREMENT: CWO3 Michael E Yense; (616) 922-8320.
TRANSPORTATION: See Procurement Officer.
PERSONNEL/COMMUNITY ACTIVITIES: LCDR Richard M Wright; (616) 922-8224.
Personnel and Expenditures
ACTIVE DUTY PERSONNEL: 130
CIVILIAN PERSONNEL: 5

Services *Commissary:* Base commissary; Food shop; Furniture store. *Medical Facilities:* Medical clinic; Dental clinic. *Recreational Facilities:* Tennis; Softball field; Football field; NCO club; Picnicking.

WARREN

ARMY TANK-AUTOMOTIVE COMMAND
Warren, MI 48397-5000
(313) 574-5000
Profile
BRANCH: Army.
SIZE AND LOCATION: 350 acres. At Detroit Arsenal in Warren, MI.
MAJOR UNITS: Army Tank-Automotive Command (TACOM); Louisville Engineering District, Detachment of Resident Officer; 902nd Military Intelligence Group, SANG; Army Health Services Command; Army MEDDAC, Ft Leonard Wood-Health Clinic (SANGB); Army Occupational Health Clinic; Human Engineering Laboratory, Detachment; Army Special Security Detachment, Warren Detachment Commander; NCOIC; Army Commissary, Selfridge ANG Base; Detachment Branch Office, CID (Gen Crimes Div); Detroit Fraud Team; Army & Air Force Exchange Service; Army TMDE Support Operation; Army Explosive Ordnance Disposal, 75th Ordnance Detachment (EOD).
BASE HISTORY: Currently responsible for wheeled and tracked vehicles and associated automotive equipment used by all military services. Mission involves research, development, procurement, distribution, repair parts supply, preparation of maintenance doctrine and operational training. Foreign military sales program lists more than 60 friendly nations as customers. National inventory control and maintenance point for 1.2 million vehicles. Most of TACOM's facilities, including contractor operated tank plant, housed at Detroit Arsenal, Warren, MI.
Key Contacts
COMMANDER: Maj Gen Leo J Pigaty.
PUBLIC AFFAIRS: Arthur E Volpe; AMSTA-CT.
Personnel and Expenditures
ACTIVE DUTY PERSONNEL: 400
CIVILIAN PERSONNEL: 5500
CONTRACT EXPENDITURE: $4.9 bil
Services *Commissary:* Base commissary. *Medical Facilities:* Medical clinic.

DETROIT ARSENAL
Warren, MI 48397
Profile
BASE HISTORY: See US Army Tank-Automotive Command

WURTSMITH AFB

WURTSMITH AIR FORCE BASE
379th Bombardment Wing, Wurtsmith AFB, MI 48753-5000
(517) 739-2011; Autovon 623-1110
Profile
BRANCH: Air Force.
SIZE AND LOCATION: 5221 acres. From S, take I-75 N from Bay City to Standish (US-23) Exit, stay on US-23 N until passing through Oscoda, turn left onto F-41, gate about 2 mi. From N, follow I-75 S to Grayling interchange, follow M-72 to Harrisville, turn S, follow US-23 to Oscoda, turning right onto F-41 to main gate. Nearest commercial airline Tri-Cities Airport (Saginaw), approx 100 mi S. Make arrangements through sponsor or

WURTSMITH AIR FORCE BASE *(continued)*
vehicle management taxis dispatcher (517) 747 6544, Autovon 623-6544, before you arrive in Saginaw.
MAJOR UNITS: 379th Bombardment Wing.
BASE HISTORY: 1924, first named for Capt Burt E Skeel, WWI pilot, killed in air race; 1942, renamed Oscoda Army Air Field. 1943, home of 100th Pursuit Squadron, famous all-black fighter unit, "Black Panthers." 1953, renamed for Detroit native Maj Gen Paul Bernard Wurtsmith, WWII hero, killed in training flight in NC. 1960, turned over to Strategic Air Command. 1961, 379th BMW arrived. 1969, aircrews flew combat missions, SE Asia.

Key Contacts
COMMANDER: Col Albert H Sauter II; Wing Commander, (517) 747-6416, Autovon 623-6416.
PUBLIC AFFAIRS: Capt Roger L Davis; 379 BMW/PA, (517) 747-5103, Autovon 623-5103.
PROCUREMENT: Capt Michael Krites; 379 BMW/LGC, (517) 747-6482, Autovon 623-6482.
TRANSPORTATION: Maj Paul Paris; 379 BMW/LGT, (517) 747-6351, Autovon 623-6351.
PERSONNEL/COMMUNITY ACTIVITIES: Capt James Haugen; 379 BMW/DP, (517) 747-6231, Autovon 623-6231.

Personnel and Expenditures
ACTIVE DUTY PERSONNEL: 3225
DEPENDENTS: 4319
CIVILIAN PERSONNEL: 691
MILITARY PAYROLL EXPENDITURE: $81 mil (military and civilian)
CONTRACT EXPENDITURE: $16.5 mil

Services *Housing:* Family units 1342; BOQ cottages 20; Dormitory spaces 936; RV/Camper sites 2. *Temporary Housing:* VOQ cottages 20; VAQ units 34; Transient living quarters 7. *Commissary:* Base commissary; Retail store; Barber shop; Food shop; Florist; Service station; Optical store; Card shop; Beauty shop. *Child Care/Capacities:* Day care center. *Base Library:* Yes. *Medical Facilities:* Hospital 20; Dental clinic. *Recreational Facilities:* Bowling; Movie theater; Gym; Recreation center; Tennis; Racquetball; Skating rink; Fitness center; Softball field; Football field; Auto shop; Crafts; Officers club; NCO club; Camping; Fishing/Hunting.

MINNESOTA

DULUTH

148TH TACTICAL RECONNAISSANCE GROUP (ANG)
Duluth IAP, Duluth, MN 55814
(218) 727-6886; Autovon 825-7210
Profile
BRANCH: Air National Guard.
SIZE AND LOCATION: 152 acres. 5 mi NW of Duluth, off US-53.
MAJOR UNITS: 148th Tactical Reconnaissance Group (ANG); 148th Fighter Interceptor Group (FIG).
Personnel and Expenditures
ACTIVE DUTY PERSONNEL: 972
CIVILIAN PERSONNEL: 233
MILITARY PAYROLL EXPENDITURE: $10.2 mil

MINNEAPOLIS-SAINT PAUL IAP

133RD TACTICAL AIRLIFT WING
Minneapolis-Saint Paul IAP, MN 55111-4098
(612) 296-4673
Profile
BRANCH: Air National Guard.
SIZE AND LOCATION: 150 acres. Off of I-494 in S Minneapolis on the Minneapolis-St Paul IAP.
MAJOR UNITS: Headquarters 133rd Tactical Airlift Wing (MAC); 133rd Civil Engineering Squadron; 133rd Consolidated Aircraft Maintenance Squadron; 133rd Mission Support Squadron; 133rd Mobile Aerial Port Squadron; 133rd Resource Management Squadron; 133rd Tactical Hospital; 133rd Field Training Flight; 133rd Mission Support Flight; 133rd Security Police Flight; 133rd Services Flight; 133rd Students Flight; 109th Aeromedical Evacuation Flight; 109th Tactical Airlift Squadron; 208th Weather Flight; 210th Engineering and Installation Squadron; 237th Air Traffic Control Flight.
BASE HISTORY: Minnesota ANG considered nation's oldest federally recognized ANG unit. 1921, established by Brig Gen Ray S Miller, 109th Observation Squadron assigned to Army NG; first airfield at what is now Larpenteur and Snelling Avenues, St Paul. Later, state rented airfield near Fort Snelling called Speedway Field, current Minneapolis-St Paul IAP. 1930, moved to Holman Field, downtown St Paul. After WWII, unit returned to St Paul as 109th Fighter Squadron. 1957, ANG took over former USAF site at IAP. 1960s, Wing carried cargo to Vietnam.
Key Contacts
COMMANDER: Col John Broman.
PUBLIC AFFAIRS: Capt Clinton C Collins.

Personnel and Expenditures
ACTIVE DUTY PERSONNEL: 1400
MILITARY PAYROLL EXPENDITURE: $8.1 mil
CONTRACT EXPENDITURE: $3.8 mil
Services *Temporary Housing:* Temporary quarters are provided by the 934th TAG, Air Force Reserve.

SAINT PAUL

US ARMY CORPS OF ENGINEERS, ST PAUL DISTRICT
1135 US Post Office & Custom House, Saint Paul, MN 55101-1479
(612) 220-0200
Profile
BRANCH: Army.
SIZE: Offices only.

MISSISSIPPI

BILOXI

KEESLER AIR FORCE BASE
Biloxi, MS 39534
(601) 377-1110; Autovon 868-1110
OFFICER-OF-THE-DAY: Base Command Post, (601) 377-4330, Autovon 868-4330
Profile
BRANCH: Air Force.
SIZE AND LOCATION: 3600 acres. Within the city limits of Biloxi, between I-10 and US Hwy 90. Signs direct visitors driving on I-10, US 90, and I-110. Transportation is available from New Orleans and Gulfport Airports. It is approx 90 mi W of Mobile, AL and 100 mi E of New Orleans.
MAJOR UNITS: Keesler Technical Training Center; 3300th Technical Training Wing; 3380th Air Base Group; US Air Force Medical Center; 403rd Tactical Airlift Wing; 53rd Weather Reconnaissance Squadron (Military Airlift Command); 7th Airborne Command & Control Squadron (Tactical Air Command); 1839th Engineering Installation Group; Detachment 212, Air Force Commissary; Air Force Communications Command; 2052nd Communications Group; 1872nd School Squadron; Air Force Communication Computer System Doctrine; Detachment 2, 3314th Management Engineering Squadron (Air Training Command); Detachment 514, Air Force Audit Agency; Detachment 812, Air Force Office of Special Investigations; US Army Detachment; US Navy Detachment.
BASE HISTORY: 1941, founded; named for 2nd Lt Samuel Reeves Keesler, aerial observer from Greenwood, MS, killed in action in France, WWI. During WWII, Air-Sea Rescue School, Chemical Warfare School, first Rotary Wing School. 1943, women and foreign nationals began training. 1947, "Electronics Center of the Air Force" with addition of radar school. 1967-73, flying training. 1968, Personnel, Administration, Astronautics, and Space Systems courses added. Currently five technical groups: avionics, computer systems, radio systems, radar systems, and administration and personnel systems operation.
VISITOR ATTRACTIONS: Guided tours and self-guided, drive-through tours are available by calling the Community Relations Office (601) 377-2254, Autovon 868-2254. The 24-hour arrival point is Muse Manor or Shaw House. The Air Force First Sergeant Academy is located at KAFB. The 53rd WRS, "Hurricane Hunters," are best know for flying into hurricanes for the National Hurricane Center. Second largest Medical Center in the USAF.

Key Contacts
COMMANDER: Col George E Long; 3380 ABG/CC, (601) 377-2510, Autovon 868-2510.
PUBLIC AFFAIRS: Maj Kenneth L Garrett; KTTC/PA, (601) 377-3901, Autovon 868-3901.
PROCUREMENT: Maj Robert C Macky; Chief of Base Contracts, KTTC/LGC, (601) 377-4610, Autovon 868-4610.
TRANSPORTATION: Lt Col Francia Sullivan; KTTC/LGT, (601) 377-2525, Autovon 868-2525.
PERSONNEL/COMMUNITY ACTIVITIES: Lt Col James M Spain; Chief of Military Personnel Office, 3380 MSSQ/CC, (601) 377-3185, Autovon 868-3185.
Personnel and Expenditures
ACTIVE DUTY PERSONNEL: 10,000
DEPENDENTS: 11,000
CIVILIAN PERSONNEL: 2100
MILITARY PAYROLL EXPENDITURE: $170 mil
CONTRACT EXPENDITURE: $16.5 mil
Services *Housing:* Family units 1953; Duplex units 1058; Townhouse units 400; Dormitory spaces 2786; Trailer spaces 51. *Temporary Housing:* VIP cottages 1; VOQ cottages 6; VAQ units 16; BOQ units 600; BAQ units 1100; Transient living quarters 40. *Commissary:* Base commissary; Retail store; Barber shop; Dry cleaners; Food shop; Banking; Service station; Bakery. *Child Care/Capacities:* Day care center 180. *Schools:* Kindergarten/Preschool. *Base Library:* Yes. *Medical Facilities:* Hospital 335; Medical clinic; Dental clinic. *Recreational Facilities:* Bowling; Movie theater; Pool; Gym; Recreation center; Golf; Tennis; Racquetball; Fitness center; Softball field; Football field; Auto shop; Crafts; Officers club; NCO club; Camping; Fishing/Hunting; Marina with boat rentals.

CAMP SHELBY

CAMP SHELBY TRAINING SITE
ARNG Training Site, Camp Shelby, MS 39407-5500
(601) 584-2000; Autovon 921-2000
Profile
BRANCH: Army National Guard.
SIZE AND LOCATION: 136,000 acres. 12 mi S of Hattiesburg, MS, off Hwy 49, on the N edge of the De Soto National Forest.
MAJOR UNITS: NGB Regional Schools; Mississippi Military Academy; 40th ORD Detachment (EOD); Mobilization and Training Equipment Site (MATES); Combined Support Maintenance Shop (CSMS); USAR Equipment Pool (ECS).
BASE HISTORY: 1917, Camp Shelby established; named for Isaac Shelby, Indian Fighter, Revolutionary War hero, and first Gov of KY. Following WWI, demobilized and deactivated. 1934, state acquired site for summer camp by National Guard. 1940, reopened as federal installation. WWII, site of largest tent city in world; Japanese American 442nd Regimental Combat Team trained here. Post contained convalescent hospital and POW camp for German Africa Corps. After WWII, closed. Korean Conflict, developed as Emergency Railhead Facility. 1956, Continental Army Command designated it as Permanent Training Site, directed by 3rd Army HQ; also site of Hagler Army Air Field. A State Operated Mobilization Site (SOMS); approx 110,000 National Guard and USAR troops train here each year.
VISITOR ATTRACTIONS: Historical Holding Facility (museum).
Key Contacts
COMMANDER: Col Garland Boleware; (601) 584-2764, Autovon 921-2764.
PUBLIC AFFAIRS: Maj Jimmy F Zdenek; (601) 584-2219, Autovon 921-2219.
PROCUREMENT: CW4 Louis F Pace; (601) 584-2691, Autovon 921-2691.
TRANSPORTATION: Lt David Williams; (601) 584-2698, Autovon 921-2698.
PERSONNEL/COMMUNITY ACTIVITIES: Lt Mark Thomas; (601) 584-2655, Autovon 921-2655.
Personnel and Expenditures
ACTIVE DUTY PERSONNEL: 300
CIVILIAN PERSONNEL: 500
MILITARY PAYROLL EXPENDITURE: $52 mil
CONTRACT EXPENDITURE: $7.7 mil
Services *Housing:* Barracks spaces 9722; Senior NCO units (bed spaces) 80; RV/Camper sites 25. *Temporary Housing:* VIP cottages 8; BOQ units (bed spaces) 166. *Commissary and Exchange:* Retail store; Barber shop; Food shop. *Medical Facilities:* Medical clinic; Dental clinic. *Recreational Facilities:* Movie theater; Pool; Recreation center; Tennis; Softball field; Officers club; NCO club; Camping; Fishing/Hunting.

COLUMBUS

COLUMBUS AIR FORCE BASE
Columbus, MS 39701
(601) 434-7322; Autovon 742-7322
Profile
BRANCH: Air Force.
SIZE AND LOCATION: 4933 acres. 10 mi N of the city of Columbus on US Hwy 45 N.
MAJOR UNITS: 14th Flying Training Wing; 37th Flying Training Squadron; 50th Flying Training Squadron; 14th Student Squadron; USAF Hospital; 14th Air Base Group.
BASE HISTORY: Began as training facility for fighter and bomber crews. 1942, pilot training. After WWII closed. 1951, reopened as contract flying school providing flight training for pilots during Korean

COLUMBUS AIR FORCE BASE (continued)

War. 1955-69, Strategic Air Command Base. 1970, returned to Air Training Command. Primary mission to provide undergraduate pilot training to qualified AF officers and ANG, AF Reserve, and foreign officers.

Key Contacts
COMMANDER: Col John A Marr; 14ABG/CC, (601) 434-7093, Autovon 742-7093.
PUBLIC AFFAIRS: Capt Margaret C Durrett; 14FTW/PA, (601) 434-7065, Autovon 742-7065.

Personnel and Expenditures
ACTIVE DUTY PERSONNEL: 1968
DEPENDENTS: 2500
CIVILIAN PERSONNEL: 958
MILITARY PAYROLL EXPENDITURE: $77.2 mil
CONTRACT EXPENDITURE: $19.3 mil

Services *Housing:* Family units 820; BOQ cottages Units 120; BEQ units 576; Duplex units 447; NCO quarters 103. *Temporary Housing:* VOQ cottages 18; VAQ units 38; Transient living quarters 20. *Commissary:* Base commissary; Retail store; Barber shop; Dry cleaners; Food shop; Banking; Service station. *Child Care/Capacities:* Day care center 100; Home day care program. *Schools:* Kindergarten/Preschool. *Base Library:* Yes. *Medical Facilities:* Hospital 15; Dental clinic. *Recreational Facilities:* Bowling; Movie theater; Pool; Gym; Recreation center; Golf; Stables; Tennis; Racquetball; Fitness center; Softball field; Football field; Auto shop; Crafts; Officers club; NCO club; Fishing/Hunting.

GULFPORT

GULFPORT NAVAL CONSTRUCTION BATTALION CENTER

Gulfport, MS 39501-5000
(601) 865-2121; Autovon 363-2121
OFFICER-OF-THE-DAY: (601) 865-2555, Autovon 363-2555

Profile
BRANCH: Navy.
SIZE AND LOCATION: 1100 acres. Off I-10 in Gulfport, MS, 70 mi E of New Orleans and 60 mi W of Mobile, AL.
MAJOR UNITS: Naval Mobile Construction Battalion (1st, 7th, 62nd, and 133rd Battalions); 20th Naval Construction Regiment; Navigational Support Unit; Naval Construction Training Center.
BASE HISTORY: 1942, Advanced Base Depot established: Armed Guard School, Cooks and Bakers School, Advanced Base Receiving Barracks added. 1944, Naval Training Center established. 1945, depot became US Naval Storehouse. 1946, training center decommissioned. 1948, national stockpile: bauxite, tin, copper, sisal, and abaca. 1952, Naval Storehouse disestablished; US Naval Construction Battalion Center established. Since 1969, center in constant state of construction.
VISITOR ATTRACTIONS: Seabee Museum.

Key Contacts
COMMANDER: Capt Herbert H Lewis Jr; (601) 865-2201, Autovon 363-2201.
PUBLIC AFFAIRS: Nancy C Brooks; Public Affairs Office, Code 15, (601) 865 2393, Autovon 363-2393.

Personnel and Expenditures
ACTIVE DUTY PERSONNEL: 4800
CIVILIAN PERSONNEL: 800
MILITARY PAYROLL EXPENDITURE: $126 mil (military and civilian)
CONTRACT EXPENDITURE: $182.8 mil

Services *Housing:* Family units 107; BOQ cottages 25; BEQ units 1000; Trailer spaces 25; Navy lodge. *Temporary Housing:* Lodge units 13. *Commissary:* Base commissary; Retail store; Barber shop; Dry cleaners; Food shop; Florist; Banking; Service station; Fam-

ily service center. *Child Care/Capacities:* Day care center 100. *Base Library:* Yes. *Medical Facilities:* Medical clinic; Dental clinic. *Recreational Facilities:* Bowling; Movie theater; Pool; Gym; Recreation center; Golf; Tennis; Racquetball; Fitness center; Softball field; Auto shop; Crafts; Officers club; NCO club; Fishing/Hunting.

MISSISSIPPI AIR NATIONAL GUARD FIELD TRAINING SITE, HEADQUARTERS

Gulfport-Biloxi Airport, Gulfport, MS 39501
(601) 863-8624; Autovon 363-8210

Profile
BRANCH: Air National Guard.
SIZE AND LOCATION: 211 acres. Within city limits of Gulfport, off US-90 at Hewes Rd.
MAJOR UNITS: HQ, Mississippi Air National Guard Field Training Site; 255th Combat Communications Squadron; Army National Guard Transportation Repair Shop.
BASE HISTORY: An air-to-ground gunnery range, 70 mi due N.

Personnel and Expenditures
ACTIVE DUTY PERSONNEL: 348
CIVILIAN PERSONNEL: 18

Services *Medical Facilities:* 2-bed dispensary.

JACKSON

US PROPERTY & FISCAL OFFICE FOR MISSISSIPPI

PO Box 4447, Jackson, MS 39296-4447
(601) 936-8500; Autovon 731-9500

Profile
BRANCH: Army.
SIZE AND LOCATION: 40 acres. On Foxhall Rd, off MS Hwy 475 at Thompson Field, just N of Jackson Municipal Airport.

Key Contacts
COMMANDER: Col James E Williamson; USPFO for Mississippi.
PROCUREMENT: CW3 Jesse C Spence; (601) 936-8502, Autovon 731-9502.
TRANSPORTATION: 2nd Lt Estus T Blair; (601) 936-8548, Autovon 731-9548.

Personnel and Expenditures
ACTIVE DUTY PERSONNEL: 1

Services *Commissary and Exchange:* Retail store.

172ND TACTICAL AIRLIFT GROUP (ANG)

Allen C Thompson Field, Jackson Municipal Airport, Jackson, MS 39208
(601) 939-3633; Autovon 731-9310

Profile
BRANCH: Air National Guard.
SIZE AND LOCATION: 84 acres. 7 mi E of Jackson, off I-20.
MAJOR UNITS: 172nd Tactical Airlift Group (ANG).

Personnel and Expenditures
ACTIVE DUTY PERSONNEL: 807
CIVILIAN PERSONNEL: 183
MILITARY PAYROLL EXPENDITURE: $9.2 mil

Services *Medical Facilities:* 6-bed dispensary.

MERIDIAN

MERIDIAN NAVAL AIR STATION

Meridian, MS 39301-5000
(601) 679-2602; 679-2340; Autovon 446-2602; 446-2340
OFFICER-OF-THE-DAY: (601) 679-2528, Autovon 446-2528

Profile
BRANCH: Navy.
SIZE AND LOCATION: 8064 acres; plus 5000 acres outlying fields. Approx 89 mi from Jackson, MS, 12 mi NE of Meridian, MS, on Hwy 39 N, clearly marked access road leads to main gate.
MAJOR UNITS: Commander Training Air Wing One; Naval Technical Training Center (NTTC); Training Squadron 7 (VT-7); Training Squadron 19 (VT-19); Naval Air Station; Marine Aviation Training Support Group.
BASE HISTORY: 1961, commissioned Naval Auxiliary Air Station (NAAS). 1968, became full NAS. 1982, upgraded to Major Shore Command. Main base largely undeveloped forest land. Improved area: Administration Area; Family Housing Area; and air operations area (Centroid Area). Outlying sites: Outlying Landing Field (OLF) Bravo in NW Kemper County, 18 mi NW of station and OLF Alpha, in S-central Noxubee County, 22 mi N of main base (currently leased to Air Force under host-tenant agreement, signed 1978.) Multipurpose Target Range, in W-central Noxubee County, 33 mi NW of main base.
VISITOR ATTRACTIONS: Model Installation Program Initiative (MIPI), Base designee.

Key Contacts
COMMANDER: Capt Robert A Maier; (601) 679-2111, 679-3400, Autovon 446-2111, 446-3400.
PUBLIC AFFAIRS: Ens K Riddle; (601) 679-2602, 679-2340, Autovon 446-2602, 446-2340.
PROCUREMENT: NASMER Supply Officer; (601) 679-2165, 679-2594, Autovon 446-2165, 446-2594.
TRANSPORTATION: See Procurement Officer.
PERSONNEL/COMMUNITY ACTIVITIES: (601) 679-2602, 679-2340, Autovon 446-2602, 446-2340.

Personnel and Expenditures
ACTIVE DUTY PERSONNEL: 2502
DEPENDENTS: 1715
CIVILIAN PERSONNEL: 1238
MILITARY PAYROLL EXPENDITURE: $33.2 mil
CONTRACT EXPENDITURE: $63.6 mil

Services *Housing:* Family units 520; BEQ units Perm 368; Trans 1466; Townhouse units 382; Barracks spaces 48; Junior NCO units 432. *Temporary Housing:* VOQ cottages 8; VEQ units 2; BOQ units 46; Transient living quarters 25. *Commissary:* Base commissary; Retail store; Barber shop; Dry cleaners; Food shop; Florist; Banking; Service station; Book store. *Child Care/Capacities:* Day care center 50; Home day care program. *Schools:* Kindergarten/Preschool. *Base Library:* Yes. *Medical Facilities:* Medical clinic; Dental clinic. *Recreational Facilities:* Bowling; Movie theater; Pool; Gym; Recreation center; Golf; Stables; Tennis; Racquetball; Skating rink; Fitness center; Softball field; Football field; Auto shop; Crafts; Officers club; NCO club; Camping; Fishing/Hunting; Youth/Community center; Sportsman's lodge; Child development center; ITT; Athletic retail sales; Enlisted club.

186TH TACTICAL RECONNAISSANCE GROUP (ANG)

Key Field, Meridian, MS 39301
(601) 693-5031; Autovon 363-9210

Profile
BRANCH: Air National Guard.
SIZE AND LOCATION: 74 acres. Within city limits of Meridian, between I-59 and US-11.
MAJOR UNITS: 186th Tactical Reconnaissance Group (ANG).

**186TH TACTICAL RECONNAISSANCE
GROUP (ANG)** *(continued)*
Personnel and Expenditures
ACTIVE DUTY PERSONNEL: 1148
CIVILIAN PERSONNEL: 242
MILITARY PAYROLL EXPENDITURE: $10.3 mil
Services *Medical Facilities:* 2-bed dispensary.

PASCAGOULA

PASCAGOULA SUPERVISOR OF SHIPBUILDING, CONVERSION AND REPAIR
Pascagoula, MS 39568-2210
(601) 769-6160; Autovon 457-4999
OFFICER-OF-THE-DAY: (601) 769-4628,
Autovon 457-4628
Profile
BRANCH: Navy.
BASE HISTORY: Navy activity housed in contractor facility with responsibility for administering Navy shipbuilding contracts of local contractors. Navy owns property at Lakeside Manor which supports ships' crews when in port for overhaul and repair of naval vessels at contractor's facilities.
Key Contacts
COMMANDER: Capt M G Simpson; Supervisor of Shipbuilding, (601) 769-4242, Autovon 457-4242.
PUBLIC AFFAIRS: Joan C Lee; (601) 769-4254, Autovon 457-4254.
PROCUREMENT: CDR James H Sillman; Materiel Officer, (601) 769-4189, Autovon 457-4189.
TRANSPORTATION: John Flemming; (601) 769-4809, Autovon 457-4809.
PERSONNEL/COMMUNITY ACTIVITIES: Lyle Graham; (601) 769-4186, Autovon 457-4186.
Personnel and Expenditures
ACTIVE DUTY PERSONNEL: 64
CIVILIAN PERSONNEL: 440
MILITARY PAYROLL EXPENDITURE: $2.7 mil
CONTRACT EXPENDITURE: $1 bil
Services *Housing:* BEQ units 84. *Commissary and Exchange:* Retail store. *Medical Facilities:* Medical clinic; Dental clinic. *Recreational Facilities:* Softball field.

STENNIS SPACE CENTER

MISSISSIPPI ARMY AMMUNITION PLANT
Stennis Space Center, MS 39529
(601) 467-8902; Autovon 446-8902
Profile
BRANCH: Army.
SIZE AND LOCATION: 5000 acres. In the Stennis Space Ctr, 15 mi from Picayune, MS; 40 mi from Gulfport, MS; 60 mi from New Orleans.
BASE HISTORY: 1978, established as GOCO ammunition plant as part of NASA space complex which includes other Navy, contractor, and NASA installations.
VISITOR ATTRACTIONS: NASA visitors center.
Key Contacts
COMMANDER: LTC Stephen C Zakrzewski.
PUBLIC AFFAIRS: Capt Jason R Annitto.
Personnel and Expenditures
ACTIVE DUTY PERSONNEL: 2
CIVILIAN PERSONNEL: 1700
Services *Child Care/Capacities:* Day care center.

NAVAL OCEANOGRAPHY COMMAND
Stennis Space Center, MS 39529-5000
(601) 688-2211
Profile
BRANCH: Navy.
SIZE: Offices only.
MAJOR UNITS: Headquarters, Naval Oceanography Command.
Key Contacts
PUBLIC AFFAIRS: T V Fredian.

VICKSBURG

US ARMY CORPS OF ENGINEERS, LOWER MISSISSIPPI VALLEY DIVISION
Box 80, Vicksburg, MS 39180
(601) 634-5750
Profile
BRANCH: Army.
SIZE: Offices only.
Key Contacts
COMMANDER: Maj Gen Thomas A Sands; Division Engineer.

US ARMY CORPS OF ENGINEERS WATERWAYS EXPERIMENT STATION
PO Box 631, 3909 Halls Ferry Rd, Vicksburg, MS 39181-0631
(601) 636-3111
Profile
BRANCH: Army.
SIZE AND LOCATION: 700 acres. Main entrance 2 mi S of I-20 on Halls Ferry Rd.
BASE HISTORY: 1929, established as hydraulics laboratory to help control floods in lower MS Valley. Today, principal research and development facility of Corps of Engineers. Six laboratory complex: Coastal Engineering Research Center, Environmental, Geotechnical, Hydraulics, Information Technology and Structures laboratories. Solves engineering and scientific problems for federal, state, and local government, industry or individuals on a reimbursable basis.
VISITOR ATTRACTIONS: Water resources demonstration model; nature trail; Niagara River and Falls model; landing mat and membrane display and experimental vehicles; Special services are provided for the reception of official and casual visitors; Guided tours are conducted twice daily on weekdays for the general public, special tours are conducted for professional and civic groups.
Key Contacts
COMMANDER: Col Dwayne G Lee; Commander and Director, (601) 634-2513.
PUBLIC AFFAIRS: Billy C Bridges; Chief, Public Affairs Office, PO Box 631, Bldg 1000, (601) 634-2504.
PROCUREMENT: Jo Ann H O'Connor; Chief, Logistics Office, PO Box 631, Bldg 3287, (601) 634-2509.
TRANSPORTATION: Walter L Luster; Chief, Transportation and Travel Management Branch, PO Box 631, Bldg 2059, (601) 634-2933.
PERSONNEL/COMMUNITY ACTIVITIES: Leon R Johnson; Chief, Vicksburg Area Engineer Consolidated Civilian Personnel Office, PO Box 80, (601) 634-5133.
Personnel and Expenditures
ACTIVE DUTY PERSONNEL: 25
CIVILIAN PERSONNEL: 1575
MILITARY PAYROLL EXPENDITURE: $.5 mil
CONTRACT EXPENDITURE: $64 mil
Services *Housing:* Family units 12. *Commissary and Exchange:* Retail store; Two concession areas. *Base Library:* Yes. *Medical Facilities:* Health and safety services, First aid center. *Recreational Facilities:* Tennis; Racquetball; Softball field; Fishing/Hunting; Soccer field; Jogging track.

MISSOURI

BRIDGETON

NAVY AND MARINE CORP RESERVE READINESS CENTER
10810 Natural Bridge Rd, Bridgeton, MO 63044-2314
(314) 263-6490; Autovon 693-6490
Profile
BRANCH: Naval Reserve.
SIZE AND LOCATION: 9 acres. On MO ANG base at Lambert Field.
MAJOR UNITS: 136th Engineering Brigade; Army Training Center Engineers; 3rd BT Brigade; 1st Engineers Batallion; 132nd Engineering Brigade; General Leonard Wood Army Community Hospital; Medical Activity..
BASE HISTORY: Naval reserves in St Louis date back to 1904. Present building constructed on site of old naval air station, 1961.
Key Contacts
COMMANDER: Capt John A Fears, USN.
PUBLIC AFFAIRS: Lt David F Winkler, USNR.
Personnel and Expenditures
ACTIVE DUTY PERSONNEL: 35
CIVILIAN PERSONNEL: 5
Services *Base Library:* Yes.

FORT LEONARD WOOD

FORT LEONARD WOOD
US Army Engineer Center & Fort Leonard Wood, Fort Leonard Wood, MO 65473-5000
(314) 596-0131; Autovon 581-0131
OFFICER-OF-THE-DAY: (314) 596-1515, Autovon 581-1515
Profile
BRANCH: Army.
SIZE AND LOCATION: 62,910 acres. 125 mi SW of St Louis, MO, off I-44 at the Waynesville/St Robert exit.
MAJOR UNITS: 136th Engineering Brigade; Army Training Center Engineers; 3rd BT Brigade; 1st Engineers Batallion; 132nd Engineering Brigade; General Leonard Wood Army Community Hospital; Medical Activity
BASE HISTORY: 1940, Seventh Corps Area Training Center completed. 1941, renamed for Maj Gen Leonard Wood, an Army surgeon, Rough Rider, Military Gov of Cuba and the Philippines, and Medal of Honor recipient. 1941, HQs designation changed to Engineer Replacement Training Center (ERTC). 1943, POW camp. 1946, inactivated; used for summer training of NG. 1950, reactivated under 6th Armored Division (Training). 1953, Army Reception Station established. 1955, 5th Army training camp. 1956, redesignated US Army Training Center, Engineer and, although only temporary post until that

time (original Orders designated it "Fort"), made permanent military installation. 1965, Gen Leonard Wood Army Hospital built. Mission of Engineer School is to train Army Engineer Officers. School began with US Military Academy, West Point. 1866, Essayons Club founded at Willets Point, NY, and out of that Engineer School of Application, recognized by War Dept, 1885. 1901, school moved to Washington Barracks, DC, and after WWII, moved to Camp Humphreys (later Ft Belvoir), VA; 1988, transferred to Ft Leonard Wood.
VISITOR ATTRACTIONS: World War II museum.
Key Contacts
COMMANDER: Maj Gen Daniel R Schroeder.
PUBLIC AFFAIRS: Virginia M Mahan; (314) 596-1514, Autovon 581-1514.
PROCUREMENT: M Spears; (314) 596-3914, Autovon 581-3914.
TRANSPORTATION: Mr Porter; (314) 596-7114, Autovon 581-7114.
PERSONNEL/COMMUNITY ACTIVITIES: Col William Pennell; (314) 596-1121, Autovon 581-1121.
Personnel and Expenditures
ACTIVE DUTY PERSONNEL: 13,431
DEPENDENTS: 7158
CIVILIAN PERSONNEL: 4812
MILITARY PAYROLL EXPENDITURE: $180.1 mil
CONTRACT EXPENDITURE: $48.7 mil
Services *Housing:* Family units; BOQ cottages; BEQ units; Barracks spaces; Senior NCO units; Junior NCO units. *Temporary Housing:* BOQ units; Guesthouse units; Guest cottages. *Commissary:* Base commissary; Retail store; Barber shop; Dry cleaners; Food shop; Florist; Banking; Service station; Bakery. *Child Care/Capacities:* Day care center. *Schools:* Kindergarten/Preschool; Elementary; Intermediate/Junior high. *Base Library:* Yes. *Medical Facilities:* Hospital; Dental clinic. *Recreational Facilities:* Bowling; Movie theater; Pool; Gym; Recreation center; Golf; Stables; Tennis; Racquetball; Softball field; Auto shop; Crafts; Officers club; NCO club; Camping; Fishing/Hunting.

KANSAS CITY

US ARMY CORPS OF ENGINEERS, KANSAS CITY DISTRICT
601 E 12th St, 700 Federal Bldg, Kansas City, MO 64106
Profile
BRANCH: Army.
SIZE: Offices only.

RICHARDS-GEBAUR AFB

RICHARDS-GEBAUR AIR FORCE BASE
Richards-Gebaur AFB, MO 64030-5000
(816) 348-2000; Autovon 463-2000

Profile
BRANCH: Air Force.
SIZE AND LOCATION: 200 acres. 17 mi S of downtown Kansas City, MO, at the junction of US-71 and MO-150.
MAJOR UNITS: 442nd Tactical Fighter Wing.
BASE HISTORY: 1941, used as auxiliary airport. During WWII, President Truman used what was then Grandview Airport for trips home. 1952, Aerospace Defense Command leased airport from Kansas City for air defense operations. 1955, Grandview AFB permanent AF installation. 1957, redesignated Richards-Gebaur AFB for two native Kansas City airmen, 1st Lt John F Richards, killed Argonne offensive WWI, and LTC Arthur W Gebaur Jr, killed in Korean War combat. 1970, AF Communication Command assumed command. 1977, 1607th ABG (later Squadron) host as MAC base. 1980, AFRES assumed operational control with 442nd Combat Support Squadron. 1984, 442nd Combat Support Group took over. 1985, joint-use agreement between AF and Kansas City, allowing continued joint use of airport facilities; excess base property returned to Kansas City; renamed Richards-Gebaur Airport.
Key Contacts
COMMANDER: Col Gary Reeves.
PUBLIC AFFAIRS: Bill Barber; (816) 348-2228, Autovon 463-2228.
PROCUREMENT: Contracting Officer, (816) 348-2073, Autovon 463-2073.
Personnel and Expenditures
ACTIVE DUTY PERSONNEL: 5
CIVILIAN PERSONNEL: 300
Services *Temporary Housing:* VOQ/VEQ combined 100. *Commissary and Exchange:* Retail store. *Medical Facilities:* Reserve facility only. *Recreational Facilities:* Pool; Recreation center; Fitness center; Consolidated club.

SAINT JOSEPH

139TH TACTICAL AIRLIFT GROUP (ANG)
Rosecrans Memorial Airport, Saint Joseph, MO 64503
(816) 271-1300; Autovon 720-9210
Profile
BRANCH: Air National Guard.
SIZE AND LOCATION: 298 acres. 4 mi W of St Joseph.
MAJOR UNITS: 139th Tactical Airlift Group (ANG).
Personnel and Expenditures
ACTIVE DUTY PERSONNEL: 687
CIVILIAN PERSONNEL: 173
MILITARY PAYROLL EXPENDITURE: $7.7 mil

SAINT LOUIS

ARMY RESERVE PERSONNEL CENTER
9700 Page Blvd, Saint Louis, MO 63132-5200
(314) 263-7828; Autovon 693-7828
Profile
BRANCH: Army.
SIZE AND LOCATION: 85 acres. From Hwy 270 and Page Blvd, 2 mi E on Page; From Hwy I-270 and Page Blvd, 0.25 mi W on Page; Served by St Louis IAP, 10 mi.
MAJOR UNITS: Officer Personnel Management Directorate; Enlisted Personnel Management Directorate; Mobilization, Operations and Training Directorate; Information Management Directorate; Personal Actions Directorate; Personnel Records Management Directorate; Resource Management Directorate.
BASE HISTORY: 1919, Adjutant General established agency to maintain records of soldiers; demobilized after WWI. After WWII, moved to St Louis. 1956, moved to current building. 1971, named Reserve Components Personnel and Administration Center (RCPAC), including Army Reserve; first central nationwide administrative agency for Army Reserve soldiers, including Individual Ready Reserve (IRR). 1983, ARPERCEN established as field operating agency of Chief Army Reserve. 1985, RCPAC mission assumed by ARPERCEN, to provide life cycle personnel management services for US Army Reserve soldiers to support defined readiness requirements, focus on mobilization.
Key Contacts
COMMANDER: Col Bobby R Sanders; Acting Commander.
PUBLIC AFFAIRS: Maj Arthur E House; (314) 263-7828, Autovon 693-7828.
Personnel and Expenditures
ACTIVE DUTY PERSONNEL: 700
CIVILIAN PERSONNEL: 1600
Services *Commissary and Exchange:* Barber shop. *Recreational Facilities:* Softball field; Officers club; NCO club.

ARMY TROOP SUPPORT COMMAND
4300 Goodfellow Blvd, Saint Louis, MO 63120-1798
(314) 263-9075; Autovon 693-9075
Profile
BRANCH: Army.
LOCATION: In St Louis, MO.
MAJOR UNITS: HQ US Army Troop Support Command.
BASE HISTORY: Mission: management of equipment and support items to sustain soldiers in field. Army Program Executive Office for Troop Support located with Command's HQs and responsible for management oversight. TROSCOM has two research and engineering centers: Natick and Belvoir. Philadelphia facility manages stocks of such items as clothing, footwear, flags, insignia, medals, and ribbons. Command's other activities include: US Army Fuels and Lubricants Laboratory, TX; Petroleum Field Office-West, CA; Charleston Storage Facility, SC; mobile repair shops, PA, TX, and UT; and, major rail overhaul facility, UT. Also, storage and overhaul missions at Sharpe, Red River, New Cumberland, Tobyhanna, Letterkenny, Tooele Army Depots, and Pueblo Depot Activity. Logistics Assistance Representatives serve with units in US and critical areas overseas to solve problems and provide feed-

back to TROSCOM and parent command, US Army Materiel Command.
Key Contacts
COMMANDER: Maj Gen John E Long; (314) 263-2201, Autovon 693-2201.
PUBLIC AFFAIRS: Paul E Powell Jr; (314) 263-9075, Autovon 693-9075.
Services *Base Library:* Yes. *Recreational Facilities:* Gym; Fitness center.

DEFENSE MAPPING AGENCY AEROSPACE CENTER
3200 S 2nd St, Saint Louis, MO 63118-3399
(314) 263-4142; Autovon 693-4142
Profile
BRANCH: Department of Defense.
SIZE: Offices only.
MAJOR UNITS: Defense Mapping Agency.
Key Contacts
PUBLIC AFFAIRS: ATTN: PA.

ST LOUIS COAST GUARD BASE
Foot of Iron St, Saint Louis, MO 63111-2536
(314) 425-6800
OFFICER-OF-THE-DAY: (314) 425-6800
Profile
BRANCH: Coast Guard.
SIZE AND LOCATION: 4.5 acres. On the Mississippi Riverfront in S St Louis on the 4500 block of S Broadway between Loughborough and Bates Sts.
MAJOR UNITS: USCG Base St Louis; USCGC *Sumac*; USCGC *Cheyenne*; USCGC *Obion*; 2d Coast Guard District Armory; Coast Guard Reserve Unit A; Coast Guard Reserve Unit B.
BASE HISTORY: 1942-44, small buildings constructed to support naval vessels. Since WWII, primarily involved in search and rescue, aids to navigation, logistics, and industrial support.
VISITOR ATTRACTIONS: Weekend tours of base and moored Coast Guard river tender (Cutter).
Personnel and Expenditures
ACTIVE DUTY PERSONNEL: 55
CIVILIAN PERSONNEL: 7
Services *Housing:* Barracks spaces 25. *Temporary Housing:* Transient living quarters 1. *Commissary and Exchange:* Retail store; Package beverages. *Recreational Facilities:* Pool; Officers club; NCO club; Equipment rental; Base Service Club and Function Hall available to military.

US ARMY CORPS OF ENGINEERS, ST LOUIS DISTRICT
210 N 12th St, Saint Louis, MO 63101
Profile
BRANCH: Army.
SIZE: Offices only.

131ST TACTICAL FIGHTER WING (ANG)
St Louis IAP, Lambert Field, Saint Louis, MO 63145
(314) 263-6356; Autovon 693-6356
Profile
BRANCH: Air National Guard.
SIZE AND LOCATION: 50 acres. In NW St Louis, near the intersection of I-70 and US-67.
MAJOR UNITS: 131st Tactical Fighter Wing (ANG).
Personnel and Expenditures
ACTIVE DUTY PERSONNEL: 1235
CIVILIAN PERSONNEL: 306
MILITARY PAYROLL EXPENDITURE: $15.4 mil

3545TH US AIR FORCE RECRUITING SQUADRON
Federal Mart Bldg, 405 S Tucker Blvd, Saint Louis, MO 63102-1134

(314) 263-0330; Autovon 693-0330
OFFICER-OF-THE-DAY: (314) 263-0311, Autovon 693-0311
Profile
BRANCH: Air Force.
SIZE AND LOCATION: 1 city block. In downtown St Louis, 2 mi from I-70, I-55, I-44, and I-64; St Louis Lambert Field 15 mi; Scott AFB, IL (MAC) 20 mi.
MAJOR UNITS: 3545th USAF Recruiting Squadron; USA Recruiting Squadron; USN Recruiting Squadron; USMC Recruiting Squadron.
BASE HISTORY: One of 7 squadrons in 3504th USAF Recruiting Group, Lackland AFB, TX. Responsible for AF recruiting over southern and central IL and eastern MO. Approx 30 geographically separated USAF recruiting offices manned by active duty sergeants/master sergeants.
VISITOR ATTRACTIONS: Federal Mart Building on National Register of Historic Places. Currently undergoing 3-year, renovation.
Key Contacts
COMMANDER: LTC Barry L Slaughenhaupt, USAF; 3545 USAFRSq/CC, 405 S Tucker Blvd, St Louis, MO 63102-1132, (314) 263-0474, Autovon 693-0474.
PUBLIC AFFAIRS: Capt Arthur F Hebbeler III, USAF; 3545 USAFRSq/RSA, (314) 263-0330, Autovon 693-0330.
PROCUREMENT: Capt Darrell W Vickers, USAF; 3545 USAFRSq/RSR, (314) 263-0311, Autovon 693-0311.
TRANSPORTATION: SSgt Allen Garner, USAF; 3545 USAFRSq/RSRL, (314) 263-0312, Autovon 693-0312.
PERSONNEL/COMMUNITY ACTIVITIES: TSgt Dana Smith, USAF; Personnel, 3545 USAFRSq/RSRP, (314) 263-0312, Autovon 693-0312; Community Activities, See Base Commander.
Personnel and Expenditures
ACTIVE DUTY PERSONNEL: 79
CIVILIAN PERSONNEL: 8

WHITEMAN AFB

WHITEMAN AIR FORCE BASE
351 SMW, Whiteman AFB, MO 65305-5000
(816) 687-3727; Autovon 975-3727
Profile
BRANCH: Air Force.
SIZE AND LOCATION: 4700 acres. 60 mi SE of Kansas City, MO, near US Hwy 50, near Knob Noster, MO; From E take I-70 to Sedalia exit onto US-65 S, turn right on US-50 W in Sedalia, drive approx 20 mi to Knob Noster exit, Rte J, turn left on Rte J (State St) and go approx 2 mi S to main gate. From W take I-70 to Warrensburg exit onto State Hwy 13 S, approaching Warrensburg turn left onto US Hwy 50 E, just at end of Hwy 13 overpass, and drive approx 10 mi to State Hwy 132 exit and turn right onto State Hwy 132 S for approx 2 mi to Warrensburg entrance.
MAJOR UNITS: 351st Strategic Missile Wing.
BASE HISTORY: 1942, site selected for Sedalia Army Air Field; training base for WACO glider pilots. 1947, inactivated. 1951, SAC reactivated base to support B-47 bomber and KC-47 aerial refueling tanker. 1952, 340th BMW activated at redesignated Sedalia AFB. 1955, renamed Whiteman AFB for 2nd Lt George A Whiteman, Sedalia native who died in attack on Pearl Harbor. 1962, 351st Strategic Missile Wing activated. Currently responsible for 150 Minutemen II ICBMs. Early 1990s, will receive B-2 Bomber.
VISITOR ATTRACTIONS: Heritage Center, exhibits of base's history; Peace Park, B-47 Stratojet and Minuteman I missile on display.

WHITEMAN AIR FORCE BASE *(continued)*
Key Contacts
COMMANDER: Col Tom Goslin; 351 CSG/
CC, (816) 687-3897, Autovon 975-3897.
PUBLIC AFFAIRS: Capt Thomas Boneparte;
351 SMW/PA, (816) 687-3727, Autovon
975-3727.
PROCUREMENT: Capt Joseph L Stanley; Con-
tracting Officer, 351 SMW/LGC, (816)
687-3641, Autovon 975-3641.
TRANSPORTATION: MSgt Donald Wood; Ve-
hicle Operations Superintendent, 351
TRANS/LGTO, (816) 687-3518, Autovon
975-3518.
PERSONNEL/COMMUNITY ACTIVITIES: Maj
Douglas L Hammerstrom; Director of
Personnel, 351 CSG/DP, (816) 687-3659,
Autovon 975-3659.
Personnel and Expenditures
ACTIVE DUTY PERSONNEL: 3000
DEPENDENTS: 1200
CIVILIAN PERSONNEL: 500
MILITARY PAYROLL EXPENDITURE: $66 mil
CONTRACT EXPENDITURE: $18 mil
Services *Housing:* Family units 990; Dor-
mitory spaces 902; Senior NCO units 109;
Junior NCO units 681; UNCOQ 19. *Tem-
porary Housing:* VIP cottages 1; VOQ cot-
tages 19; VAQ units 40; Guesthouse units 4.
Commissary: Base commissary; Retail store;
Barber shop; Dry cleaners; Food shop; Ser-
vice station; Video rental; Ice cream. *Child
Care/Capacities:* Day care center; Home day
care program. *Schools:* Kindergarten/Pre-
school; Elementary; Elementary grades 1-3.
Base Library: Yes. *Medical Facilities:* Hospital 30; Dental clinic. *Recreational Facilities:* Bowling; Movie theater; Pool; Gym; Recreation center; Golf; Tennis; Racquetball;
Fitness center; Softball field; Football field;
Auto shop; Officers club; NCO club; Fishing/
Hunting; Knob Noster State Park just outside gate.

MONTANA

FORSYTH

1ST COMBAT EVALUATION GROUP, DETACHMENT 18 (SAC)
PO Box 5026, Forsyth, MT 59327-5026
(406) 346-5216; Autovon 675-5212
Profile
BRANCH: Air Force.
SIZE AND LOCATION: Housing area, 53 acres; Operational area, 5.3 acres. SE Montana, in Forsyth; Housing area on E side of town; Operations area: 22 mi NW on US Hwy 12, near ghost town of Vananda; 281 mi from support base, Ellsworth AFB, SD.
MAJOR UNITS: Detachment 18, 1st Combat Evaluation Group.
BASE HISTORY: Mar 15, 1986, Detachment 18 activated. Jun 4, 1986, began full scoring operations.
Key Contacts
COMMANDER: LTC Alvin E Krebs Jr.
Personnel and Expenditures
ACTIVE DUTY PERSONNEL: 57
DEPENDENTS: 85
CIVILIAN PERSONNEL: 2
Services *Housing:* Duplex units 24; Dormitory spaces 25; Single family houses 2. *Commissary:* Base commissary; Snacks. *Recreational Facilities:* Gym; Recreation center; Weight room.

GREAT FALLS

MALMSTROM AIR FORCE BASE
Great Falls, MT 59402-5000
(406) 731-1110; Autovon 632-1110
Profile
BRANCH: Air Force.
SIZE AND LOCATION: 29,067 acres. E of Great Falls, MT, off of Hwy 89 Bypass; Great Falls is in N-central MT about 75 mi E of the Rockies.
MAJOR UNITS: 40th Air Division; 341st Strategic Missile Wing (SMW); 301st Air Refueling Wing.
BASE HISTORY: May 1942, construction began on East Base, assigned to 2nd Air Force with bombardment groups training here. 1943, Station 5, Alaskan Wing, Air Transport Command organized and transferred to Air Service Command and moved from Gore Field (Great Falls Municipal Airport) to base. 1944, reassigned to Air Transport Command to ferrying lend-lease aircraft to USSR and Station 5 deactivated to 1455th Army Air Force Base Unit. Following WWII, mission of support for personnel assigned to Alaskan air bases. 1948, training site for Operation Vittles, Berlin Air-Lift. 1954, SAC replaced MATS. 1956, dedicated for Col Einar Axel Malmstrom, vice wing commander who died in air crash. Activation

of 341st Strategic Missile Wing, America's "Ace in the Hole," dubbed by President Kennedy during Cuban Missile Crisis. 341st SMW has 200 Minuteman missiles spread out across MT. 1988, first flying wing since 1961, 301st Air Refueling Wing responsible for KC-135 stratotankers, which refuel fighter, bomber, and transport aircraft.
VISITOR ATTRACTIONS: Malmstrom AFB Museum and Park, just inside Main Gate and sponsored by the Malmstrom Historical Foundation (open noon to 3, Mon-Sat, summer, get pass at gate); display of aircraft and missiles previously deployed.
Key Contacts
COMMANDER: Col Dennis Abbey; 341st CSG/CC.
PUBLIC AFFAIRS: Capt Don Planalp; 341st AD/PA.
PROCUREMENT: Capt Gabriela Reitz; 341st SMW/LGC.
TRANSPORTATION: LTC Robert Warrick; 840th TRANS/LGT.
Personnel and Expenditures
ACTIVE DUTY PERSONNEL: 4500
DEPENDENTS: 5338
CIVILIAN PERSONNEL: 547
MILITARY PAYROLL EXPENDITURE: $65.3 mil
CONTRACT EXPENDITURE: $10.4 mil
Services *Housing:* Family units 1406; BEQ units; BAQ units; Duplex units; Dormitory spaces; Senior NCO units; Junior NCO units; Mobile home units 98; RV/Camper sites. *Temporary Housing:* VOQ cottages; VAQ units; BOQ units; Transient living quarters. *Commissary:* Base commissary; Dry cleaners; Food shop; Florist; Banking; Service station; Beauty shop. *Child Care/Capacities:* Day care center; Home day care program. *Base Library:* Yes. *Medical Facilities:* Medical clinic; Dental clinic. *Recreational Facilities:* Bowling; Movie theater; Pool; Gym; Recreation center; Stables; Tennis; Racquetball; Softball field; Football field; Auto shop; Crafts; Officers club; NCO club; Camping; Fishing/Hunting.

120TH FIGHTER INTERCEPTOR GROUP AIR NATIONAL GUARD BASE
Great Falls, Great Falls, MT 59401-5000
(406) 791-6628; Autovon 279-2228
Profile
BRANCH: Air National Guard.
SIZE AND LOCATION: 139 acres. Co-located with the Great Falls IAP, W of Great Falls, MT.
MAJOR UNITS: 120th Fighter Interceptor Group.
BASE HISTORY: 1947, 186th Fighter Squadron formed and equipped with P-51 Mustang aircraft. When unit returned from Korean Conflict, reformed at Great Falls IAP. 1953, first Air Guard unit assigned F-86 Sabrejet; unit entered Air Defense role it

still performs today. 1956, 120th Fighter Group established. 1984, mission expanded; assigned operation of alert detachment permanently stationed at Davis-Monthan AFB, Tucson, AZ.
Key Contacts
COMMANDER: LTC Don Stevlingson; (406) 791-6285, Autovon 279-2285.
PUBLIC AFFAIRS: Maj Lynn Hebert; (406) 791-6628, Autovon 279-2228.
PROCUREMENT: MSgt Paul Stashi; (406) 791-6246, Autovon 279-2246.
TRANSPORTATION: Lt Jim Oehmcke; (406) 791-6315, Autovon 279-2315.
PERSONNEL/COMMUNITY ACTIVITIES: Capt Joanna Shumaker; (406) 791-6281, Autovon 279-2281.
Personnel and Expenditures
ACTIVE DUTY PERSONNEL: 1100 guardsmen
MILITARY PAYROLL EXPENDITURE: $10.4 mil
CONTRACT EXPENDITURE: $27.7 mil
Services *Medical Facilities:* Clinic on guard drill weekends. *Recreational Facilities:* Fitness center.

HELENA

FORT WILLIAM HENRY HARRISON
PO Box 1157, Helena, MT 59624-1157
(406) 444-6907; Autovon 857-3007
Profile
BRANCH: Army National Guard.
SIZE AND LOCATION: 2912 acres. On W city limits of Helena, adj to Veterans Administration Hospital. Follow US Hwy 12 W, exit at sign marked Veterans Administration Hospital and National Guard Facilities.
MAJOR UNITS: STARC HQ; 1049th EN plt (FFTG); 103d PAD; Montana Military Academy; 210th PERS SVC CO; HQ & SVC CO; 189th AVN CO; 189th AHC 1-189th AVN CO, CO "A"; 189th AHC 1-189th AVN CO, CO "B"; 189th AHC 1-189th AVN CO, CO "C"; CO "C" 163d CAV; CO "B" MAINT 143D SPT BN.
BASE HISTORY: Late 1800s, established for MT volunteers. 1942, Special Forces Brigade (Devil's Brigade) training. 1980s, begun to modernize, replacing many pre-WWII structures; many small arms ranges. Ideal post for winter and mountain terrain training.
Key Contacts
COMMANDER: Brig Gen Gary C Blair; The Adjutant General, PO Box 4789, Helena, MT 59604-4789, (406) 444-6910, Autovon 857-3010.
PUBLIC AFFAIRS: Col Richard R Mooney; Dept of Military Affairs, State of Montana, PO Box 4789, Helena, MT 59604-4789, (406) 444-6995, Autovon 857-3095.
PROCUREMENT: Maj Gary R Heidle; USPFO, (406) 444-7920, Autovon 857-3120.

FORT WILLIAM HENRY HARRISON
(continued)

TRANSPORTATION: 1st Lt Robert A Sparing; USPFO, (406) 444-7927, Autovon 857-3127.

PERSONNEL/COMMUNITY ACTIVITIES: CWO Michael Day; Family Program Specialist, PO Box 4789, Helena, MT 59604-4789, (406) 444-6930, Autovon 857-3030.

Personnel and Expenditures

ACTIVE DUTY PERSONNEL: 38

MILITARY PAYROLL EXPENDITURE: $26.3 mil

CONTRACT EXPENDITURE: $2.9 mil

Services *Housing:* Barracks spaces. *Commissary:* Base commissary. *Medical Facilities:* Medical clinic. *Recreational Facilities:* Officers club; NCO club.

LAKESIDE

KALLSPELL AIR FORCE STATION
Lakeside, MT 59922
(406) 844-3351
Profile
BRANCH: Air Force.
MAJOR UNITS: Kallspell AFS (TAC).

NEBRASKA

GRAND ISLAND

CORNHUSKER ARMY AMMUNITION PLANT
Grand Island, NE 68801-2041
(308) 389-2100; Autovon 939-3690
Profile
BRANCH: Army.
SIZE AND LOCATION: 12,000 acres. Grand Island, NE, near I-80 and NE-281.
BASE HISTORY: WWII ammunition plant built in 1942. Active production, 1942-1945; Korean Conflict, 1950-1957; and Vietnam War, 1965-1973. Current status inactive/standby.
Key Contacts
COMMANDER: Thomas L Jameson; Contracting Officer's Representative.
PUBLIC AFFAIRS: See Base Commander.
Personnel and Expenditures
CIVILIAN PERSONNEL: 50
CONTRACT EXPENDITURE: $2.1 mil
Services *Housing:* Family units 10.

HASTINGS

1ST COMBAT EVALUATION GROUP, DETACHMENT 10 (SAC)
RR 2, Box 174K, Hastings, NE 68901
(402) 463-1990; Autovon 271-6300; 271-7747
Profile
BRANCH: Air Force.
SIZE AND LOCATION: 10 acres. 3 mi E of Hastings, NE, to Central Community College of Hastings on Hwy 6, turn left and follow road for approx 4 mi, look for old school house.
MAJOR UNITS: Detachment 10, 1st Combat Evaluation Group (SAC).
Key Contacts
COMMANDER: Maj M Wayne Roe.
PUBLIC AFFAIRS: SSgt Wesley Brown.
Personnel and Expenditures
ACTIVE DUTY PERSONNEL: 40
DEPENDENTS: 80
CIVILIAN PERSONNEL: 5
Services *Commissary and Exchange:* Retail store. *Recreational Facilities:* Gym; NCO club.

LINCOLN

LINCOLN AIR NATIONAL GUARD BASE
Lincoln Municipal Airport, 2301 W Adams St, Lincoln, NE 68524-1897
(402) 471-3241; Autovon 720-1210
OFFICER-OF-THE-DAY: (402) 471-1266, Autovon 720-1266

Profile
BRANCH: Air National Guard.
SIZE AND LOCATION: 163 acres. NW corner of city of Lincoln, approx 3 mi from downtown; adj to city airport and parallels I-80.
MAJOR UNITS: 155th Tactical Reconnaissance Group.
BASE HISTORY: Second oldest ANG unit in nation. 1943, began as 401st Fighter Squadron at Westover Field, MA. 1948, NEANG held first summer field training in Lincoln. Korean Conflict, active service at Dow AFB, Bangor, ME, and completed service at Alexandria AFB, LA. 1954, squadron redesignated 173rd FIS, Air Defense Command. 1956, moved to present facilities as SAC base. 1964, mission changed from air defense to tactical photo-reconnaissance; 155th TRG, motto, "Alone, Unarmed, and Unafraid," under command of TAC.
VISITOR ATTRACTIONS: T-33, F-86, and RF-84 static aircraft display.
Key Contacts
COMMANDER: Col Bruce Schantz; (402) 471-1233, Autovon 720-1233.
PUBLIC AFFAIRS: Capt Pat McGrane; (402) 471-1350, Autovon 720-1350, UTA weekends only.
PROCUREMENT: (402) 471-1214, Autovon 720-1214.
TRANSPORTATION: (402) 471-1280, Autovon 720-1280.
PERSONNEL/COMMUNITY ACTIVITIES: Capt Dennis Gries; (402) 471-1324, Autovon 720-1324.
Personnel and Expenditures
ACTIVE DUTY PERSONNEL: 1100 Guard
CIVILIAN PERSONNEL: 225
CONTRACT EXPENDITURE: $0.9 mil
Services *Commissary and Exchange:* Retail store; Food shop. *Recreational Facilities:* Softball field; Officers club; NCO club; Running track.

OFFUTT AFB

OFFUTT AIR FORCE
Offutt AFB, NE 68113-5000
(402) 294-3663; Autovon 271-3663
Profile
BRANCH: Air Force.
SIZE AND LOCATION: 4100 acres. 10 mi S of Omaha off Rte 75; 1 mi S of Fort Crook; 3 mi N of La Platte on US-75.
MAJOR UNITS: Headquarters, Strategic Air Command; 55th Strategic Reconnaissance Wing; 55th Combat Support Group; National Emergency Airborne Command Post; 544th Strategic Intelligence Wing; Air Force Global Weather Central; 6949th Electronic Security Squadron; Strategic Communications Division; 1st Aerospace Communications Wing; 1000th Satellite Operations Group; Strategic Air Command Band; Ehrling Bergquist Strategic Hospital.
BASE HISTORY: 1896, originally intended to replace Ft Omaha, began as Ft Crook, named for Gen George Crook. WWI, first air unit, 61st Balloon Company, assigned to post. 1920, first flying field. 1924, field dedicated for Omaha's first air casualty during WWI, Lt Jarvis J Offutt. Following WWI, used mostly for training air reservists. 1930s, aircraft manufacturing plant, Glenn L Martin Nebraska Bomber Assembly Plant, constructed at Offutt Field. WWII, Italian POW camp established. After WWII, reverted to training facility for Army Reservists. 1948, Offutt Field and Ft Crook designated Offutt AFB; redesignation of units to 3902nd ABW. 1948, SAC HQs moved from Andrews AFB, MD. 1959-65, served as Atlas D missile site; later, Atlas missile plants, and operating locations for USAF, Army and Navy units. 1986, 55th Strategic Reconnaissance Wing host unit.
Key Contacts
COMMANDER: Col Daniel R Peterson; 55 SRW/CC, (402) 294-5533, Autovon 271-5533.
PUBLIC AFFAIRS: LTC Ralph J Tosti; Chief 55 SRW/PA, (402) 294-3663, Autovon 271-3663.
PROCUREMENT: 55 SRW/LGC, Bldg 323C, (402) 294-2455, Autovon 271-2455.
TRANSPORTATION: 55 SRW/LGT, Bldg 301D, (402) 294-5533, Autovon 271-5533.
PERSONNEL/COMMUNITY ACTIVITIES: 55 CSG/CC, Bldg 323C, (402) 294-3663, Autovon 271-3663.
Personnel and Expenditures
ACTIVE DUTY PERSONNEL: 12,500
DEPENDENTS: 31,000
CIVILIAN PERSONNEL: 1900
MILITARY PAYROLL EXPENDITURE: $322.9 mil
CONTRACT EXPENDITURE: $87.1 mil
Services *Commissary:* Base commissary; Retail store; Barber shop; Dry cleaners; Food shop; Florist; Banking; Service station; Furniture store; Bakery. *Child Care/Capacities:* Day care center; Home day care program. *Schools:* Kindergarten/Preschool; Elementary; Intermediate/Junior high; High school. *Base Library:* Yes. *Medical Facilities:* Hospital; Medical clinic; Dental clinic. *Recreational Facilities:* Bowling; Movie theater; Pool; Gym; Recreation center; Golf; Stables; Tennis; Racquetball; Fitness center; Softball field; Football field; Auto shop; Crafts; Officers club; NCO club; Camping; Fishing/Hunting.

OMAHA

US ARMY CORPS OF ENGINEERS, MISSOURI RIVER DIVISION

12565 West Center Rd, Omaha, NE 68144
(402) 221-7208

Profile

BRANCH: Army.

SIZE AND LOCATION: 0.5 acre. In the western portion of the city of Omaha.

MAJOR UNITS: US Army Corps of Engineers.

BASE HISTORY: 1933, established; division office, Kansas City, MO, was responsible for improvement of Missouri River and tributaries from Hermann, MO, to headwater arising on eastern slopes of Rocky Mts. Previously, work on Missouri River accomplished by old Kansas City District, dating from 1907. With formation of Missouri River District, 1933, Omaha District and Fort Peck District established. 1942, Division headquarters moved to Omaha.

Key Contacts

COMMANDER: Brig Gen Robert H Ryan; (402) 221-7200.

PUBLIC AFFAIRS: Paul Johnston.

Personnel and Expenditures

ACTIVE DUTY PERSONNEL: 4

CIVILIAN PERSONNEL: 280

US ARMY CORPS OF ENGINEERS, OMAHA DISTRICT

215 N 17th St, Omaha, NE 68102-4978
(402) 221-3900

Profile

BRANCH: Army.

SIZE AND LOCATION: Offices only. In downtown Omaha.

MAJOR UNITS: US Army Corps of Engineers.

Key Contacts

COMMANDER: Col Donald E Hazen.

PUBLIC AFFAIRS: Betty M White; (402) 221-3916.

PROCUREMENT: Donald Robinson; (402) 221-4100.

TRANSPORTATION: Norma I Kolbe; (402) 221-3241.

PERSONNEL/COMMUNITY ACTIVITIES: Frances Watson; (402) 221-4071.

NEVADA

CARSON CITY

NEVADA NATIONAL GUARD HEADQUARTERS

2525 S Carson St, Carson City, NV 89701-5502
(702) 887-7331; Autovon 830-5331
OFFICER-OF-THE-DAY: (702) 887-7297, Autovon 830-5297

Profile

BRANCH: Air National Guard; Army National Guard.
SIZE AND LOCATION: 30 acres. In the center of Carson City, NV.
MAJOR UNITS: Headquarters STARC; Headquarters Nevada Army National Guard; Headquarters Nevada Air National Guard; 150th Maintenance Company; US Property and Fiscal Office.
BASE HISTORY: State HQs for NV National Guard.

Key Contacts

COMMANDER: Maj Gen Drennan A Clark; The Adjutant General, (702) 887-7302, Autovon 830-5302.
PUBLIC AFFAIRS: Maj Chris A Anastassatos; (702) 887-7256, Autovon 830-5256.
PROCUREMENT: WO1 Shirley A Dobbie; 2601 S Carson St, Carson City, NV 89701-5596, (702) 887-7205, Autovon 830-5205.
TRANSPORTATION: SFC Larry W Miller; 2601 S Carson St, Carson City, NV 89701-5596, (702) 887-7220, Autovon 830-5220.

Personnel and Expenditures

ACTIVE DUTY PERSONNEL: 80
CIVILIAN PERSONNEL: 60
MILITARY PAYROLL EXPENDITURE: $5.3 mil
CONTRACT EXPENDITURE: $0.8 mil

FALLON

FALLON NAVAL AIR STATION

Fallon, NV 89406-5000
(702) 426-2714; 426-5161; Autovon 830-2714; 830-2110

Profile

BRANCH: Navy.
SIZE AND LOCATION: 57,584 acres. 65 mi E of Reno, NV; 8 mi S of Fallon, NV.
MAJOR UNITS: Naval Air Station; Explosive Ordnance Disposal, Group 1, Detachment, Fallon; Naval Oceanography Command Detachment (NOCD); Naval Strike Warfare Center (NSWC); Naval Weapons Station, Seal Beach Detachment Fallon (FLTAC); ROICC; VFA-127; VFA-106 Detachment, Fallon; VFA-125 Detachment, Fallon.
BASE HISTORY: 1942, Army Air Corps built four air bases on eastern side of Sierras for defensive facilities. When threat of Japanese invasion ended, facility at Fallon offered to Navy for training torpedo, attack and fighter pilots. Designated as Naval Auxiliary Air Station for aircraft operating out of Naval Air Center Alameda. WWII, placed in caretaker status until Korean War; redesignated Auxiliary Landing Field for NAS Alameda. 1953, reestablished as Naval Auxiliary Air Station under Fleet Air Alameda. 1958, landing field named for LCDR Bruce Van Voorhis, Fallon native killed in Battle of Solomon Islands. 1960s, expansion and associated Bombing and Electronic Warfare Ranges (Ranges B-16, B-17, B-19, and B-20) to prepare air crews for Vietnam. 1972, designated major NAS. 1984, Naval Strike Warfare Center established and expansion of Carrier Battle Groups.

Personnel and Expenditures

ACTIVE DUTY PERSONNEL: 950
DEPENDENTS: 1177
CONTRACT EXPENDITURE: $71.1 mil
Services *Housing:* Family units 301; BOQ cottages; BEQ units 9. *Temporary Housing:* Lodge units 6. *Commissary:* Base commissary; Retail store; Barber shop; Service station; Military clothing sales; Convenience store/Shopette; Beauty shop; Car rental; Snacks; Credit union; Tailor. *Child Care/ Capacities:* Day care center 70. *Base Library:* Yes. *Medical Facilities:* Medical clinic; Dental clinic. *Recreational Facilities:* Bowling; Movie theater; Pool; Gym; Golf (mini); Stables; Tennis; Softball field; Football field; Auto shop; Crafts; Officers club; NCO club; Camping; Fishing/Hunting; Picnicking; Go-cart track; Ski equipment rental; Skeet shooting.

HAWTHORNE

HAWTHORNE ARMY AMMUNITION PLANT

Bldg 1, Hawthorne, NV 89415-5000
(702) 945-7001; Autovon 830-7001

Profile

BRANCH: Army.
SIZE AND LOCATION: 147,000 acres. 135 mi SE of Reno, NV, on Hwy 95, 1 mi from Hawthorne; US 95 and State Hwy 359 divide the plant into three separate ammunition storage and production areas, plus an industrial area.
MAJOR UNITS: Day & Zimmerman/Basil Inc.
BASE HISTORY: 1926, following fire at Navy ammunition depot, Lake Denmark, NJ, Hawthorne selected as ammunition storage site, because of arid climate and close proximity to West Coast. 1930, Naval Ammunition Depot (NAD) Hawthorne commissioned. 1977, Army designated as Single Manager for Conventional Ammunition and NAD Hawthorne transferred to Army Armament, Munitions and Chemical Command (AMCCOM) and renamed Hawthorne Army Ammunition Plant (HWAAP). 1980, converted to GOCO installation. Today, claims to be "World's Largest Ammunition Depot."

Key Contacts

COMMANDER: LTC John D Nelson.
PUBLIC AFFAIRS: Capt Gary A Baratta; Executive Officer, (702) 945-7018, Autovon 830-7018.
PROCUREMENT: Florentino (Tiny) Cardenas; (702) 945-7341, Autovon 830-7341.
TRANSPORTATION: Sharon Lininger; (702) 945-7118, Autovon 830-7118.
PERSONNEL/COMMUNITY ACTIVITIES: Madeline Davis; (702) 945-7013, Autovon 830-7013.

Personnel and Expenditures

ACTIVE DUTY PERSONNEL: 8
DEPENDENTS: 12
CIVILIAN PERSONNEL: 810
CONTRACT EXPENDITURE: $21 mil
Services *Housing:* Family units 30; BEQ units 16; BAQ units; Duplex units 50. *Medical Facilities:* Medical clinic. *Recreational Facilities:* Bowling; Recreation center; Golf; Softball field; Football field; Fishing/Hunting.

LAS VEGAS

NELLIS AIR FORCE BASE

Las Vegas, NV 89191-5000
(702) 652-1110; 652-2446; Autovon 682-1110; 682-1110
OFFICER-OF-THE-DAY: (702) 652-2446, Autovon 682-2446

Profile

BRANCH: Air Force.
SIZE AND LOCATION: 11,000 acres; ranges 3,000,000. Take Craig Rd Exit off I-15 and follow signs approx 8 mi NE of Las Vegas.
MAJOR UNITS: Tactical Fighter Weapons Center; 57th Fighter Weapons Wing; 474th Tactical Fighter Wing; 554th Operations Support Wing; 4450th Tactical Group; USAF Fighter Weapons School; 4440th Tactical Fighter Training Group; USAF Air Demonstration Squadron, "Thunderbirds"; 64th Aggressor Squadron; 65th Aggressor Squadron; Tactics and Test Deputate; Adversary Tactics Deputate; 4513th Adversary Threat Training Group; 2069th Communications Group; 820th Civil Engineering Squadron (Red Horse); Detachment 3, 1365th Audiovisual Squadron; Detachment 3, Air Force Operational Test and Evaluation Center; Detachment 13, 4400th Management Engineering Squadron; Detachment 16, 25th Weather Squadron; Field Training Detachment 523; 3096th Aviation Depot Squadron; USAF Area Defense Counsel; Defense Reutilization and Marketing Office; Detachment 1812, Air Force Office of Special Investigations.

NELLIS AIR FORCE BASE *(continued)*

BASE HISTORY: 1941, began as Army Air Corps Flexible Gunnery School training B-17 gunners. 1945, crew training for B-29. Following WWII, temporary standby status, finally closing, 1947. 1949, re-opened. 1950, renamed for Lt William Harrell Nellis, NV resident killed in action over Luxembourg. Korean War, virtually every fighter pilot trained here. 1958, assigned to TAC. Today, provides training for composite strike forces that includes every type of aircraft in USAF inventory, along with air and ground units of Army, Navy, Marines, and NATO and allied air units. 4440th Tactical Fighter Training Group provides realistic simulated combat training for US and allied crews in exercises called "Red Flag, Green Flag."

VISITOR ATTRACTIONS: USAF Demonstration Squadron (Thunderbird) Museum.

Key Contacts

COMMANDER: Maj Gen Joseph W Ashy; Commander, Tactical Fighter Weapons Center (TFWC).

PUBLIC AFFAIRS: Maj Victor J Andrijauskas; (702) 652-2750, Autovon 682-2750.

PROCUREMENT: 554 OSW/LGC, (702) 652-4002, Autovon 682-4002.

TRANSPORTATION: 554 OSW/LGT, (702) 652-4713, Autovon 682-4713.

PERSONNEL/COMMUNITY ACTIVITIES: Director of Personnel, 554 MSSQ/MSP, (702) 652-5210, Autovon 682-5210.

Personnel and Expenditures

ACTIVE DUTY PERSONNEL: 11,400

DEPENDENTS: 34,000

CIVILIAN PERSONNEL: 1040

MILITARY PAYROLL EXPENDITURE: $444 mil

CONTRACT EXPENDITURE: $29.3 mil

Services *Housing:* Family units 1382; Duplex units; Dormitory spaces 1661; Trailer spaces 100; RV/Camper sites 20. *Temporary Housing:* VOQ cottages 134; VAQ units 550; Transient living quarters 60; DV quarters, 18. *Commissary:* Base commissary; Retail store; Barber shop; Dry cleaners; Food shop; Florist; Banking; Service station. *Child Care/Capacities:* Day care center 220; Home day care program. *Schools:* Kindergarten/Preschool; Elementary. *Base Library:* Yes. *Medical Facilities:* Hospital 40; Medical clinic; Dental clinic; Veterinary services. *Recreational Facilities:* Bowling; Movie theater; Pool; Gym; Recreation center; Golf; Stables; Tennis; Racquetball; Fitness center; Softball field; Football field; Auto shop; Crafts; Officers club; NCO club.

RENO

MAY AIR NATIONAL GUARD BASE

Cannon IAP, Reno, NV 89502

(702) 323-1011; Autovon 830-8310

Profile

BRANCH: Air National Guard.

SIZE AND LOCATION: 123 acres. 5 mi SE of Reno, off of I-580.

MAJOR UNITS: 152nd Tactical Reconnaissance Group (ANG).

BASE HISTORY: Named for Maj Gen James A May, state Adjutant General.

Personnel and Expenditures

ACTIVE DUTY PERSONNEL: 916

CIVILIAN PERSONNEL: 224

MILITARY PAYROLL EXPENDITURE: $9.1 mil

Services *Medical Facilities:* Dispensary.

NEW HAMPSHIRE

HANOVER

ARMY COLD REGIONS RESEARCH AND ENGINEERING LABORATORY

72 Lyme Rd, Hanover, NH 03755-1290
(603) 646-4100; Autovon 684-4100
Profile
BRANCH: Army.
SIZE AND LOCATION: 20 acres. 2 mi N of Hanover, NH.
BASE HISTORY: Feb 1961, established; combining of Snow, Ice, and Permafrost Research Establishment (SIPRE) and Arctic Construction and Frost Effects Laboratory (ACFEL). 1962, transferred from Corps of Engineers to Army Materiel Command. 1963, laboratory fully operational. 1968, redesignated Army Terrestrial Sciences Center (TSC). 1970, Photographic Interpretation Research Division transferred to Army Materiel Command. 1970-85, Ice Engineering Facility and Frost Effects Research Facility added.
Key Contacts
COMMANDER: Col Charles S Nichols.
PUBLIC AFFAIRS: Benjamin S Yamashita.
PROCUREMENT: Raymond F May.
TRANSPORTATION: Thomas B Ladd.
PERSONNEL/COMMUNITY ACTIVITIES: David B Wilber.
Personnel and Expenditures
ACTIVE DUTY PERSONNEL: 4
CIVILIAN PERSONNEL: 240
MILITARY PAYROLL EXPENDITURE: $10.3 mil
CONTRACT EXPENDITURE: $4.7 mil

PEASE AFB

PEASE AIR FORCE BASE

509th Bombardment Wing, Pease AFB, NH 03803-5270
(603) 430-0100; Autovon 852-0100
Profile
BRANCH: Air Force.
SIZE AND LOCATION: 4300 acres. Located 3 mi NW of downtown Portsmouth, NH and 50 mi NE of Boston. Take I-95 to Spaulding Tpke to maingate.
MAJOR UNITS: 509th Bombardment Wing; 393rd & 715th Bombardment Squadrons; 509th Air Refueling Squadron.
BASE HISTORY: June 1956, opened. Sep 1957, renamed Pease for Capt Harl Pease, Jr, NH native and graduate of Univ of NH. All but 2 of 33 years shared with 509th Bombardment Wing. Pease initially home of 100th Bombardment Wing, inactivated 1966.
VISITOR ATTRACTIONS: Airpark near main gate for viewing.
Key Contacts
COMMANDER: Col James R Wilson; 509 CSG/CC, (603) 430-3303, Autovon 852-3303.

PUBLIC AFFAIRS: Capt Bruce Alexander; 509 BMW/PA, (603) 430-3577, Autovon 852-3577.
PROCUREMENT: Maj Augustus Mays, Jr; 509 SUP/CC, (603) 430-3434, Autovon 852-3434.
TRANSPORTATION: Maj Jesse Echord; 509 TRANS/CC, (603) 430-2107, Autovon 852-2107.
PERSONNEL/COMMUNITY ACTIVITIES: Director of Personnel, Maj Robert A Seymour; 509 CSG/DP, (603) 430-3314, Autovon 852-3314.
Personnel and Expenditures
ACTIVE DUTY PERSONNEL: 3600
DEPENDENTS: 5500
CIVILIAN PERSONNEL: 650
MILITARY PAYROLL EXPENDITURE: $97 mil
CONTRACT EXPENDITURE: $29 mil
Services *Housing:* Family units 1209; Dormitory spaces 1675; Mobile home units 50. *Temporary Housing:* VOQ cottages 42; VAQ units 55; Transient living quarters 20. *Commissary:* Base commissary; Retail store; Barber shop; Dry cleaners; Food shop; Florist; Banking; Service station. *Child Care/Capacities:* Day care center 159; Home day care program. *Schools:* Kindergarten/Preschool; Elementary. *Base Library:* Yes. *Medical Facilities:* Hospital 70; Medical clinic; Dental clinic. *Recreational Facilities:* Bowling; Movie theater; Gym; Recreation center; Golf; Tennis; Racquetball; Fitness center; Softball field; Football field; Auto shop; Crafts; Officers club; NCO club; Fishing/Hunting.

PORTSMOUTH

PORTSMOUTH NAVAL SHIPYARD

Portsmouth, NH 03801
(207) 438-1000; Autovon 684-1000
Profile
BRANCH: Navy.
SIZE AND LOCATION: 1309 acres. On Seavey's Island at mouth of Piscataqua River on border of ME (telephone exchange) and NH (ZIP Code); 1 mi off I-95; 50 mi N of Boston.
MAJOR UNITS: Portsmouth Naval Shipyard.
VISITOR ATTRACTIONS: Closed to the public.
Personnel and Expenditures
ACTIVE DUTY PERSONNEL: 100
DEPENDENTS: 300
Services *Housing:* Family units 234; BOQ cottages 34; BEQ units 211. *Temporary Housing:* Enlisted family rooms 5. *Commissary and Exchange:* Retail store. *Child Care/Capacities:* Day care center 40. *Base Library:* Yes. *Medical Facilities:* Use Pease AFB, 3 mi away. *Recreational Facilities:* Bowling; Gym; Tennis; Racquetball; Fitness center; Auto shop; Crafts; Officers club; NCO club; Camping; Fishing/Hunting; Water sports.

NEW JERSEY

BAYONNE

BAYONNE MILITARY OCEAN TERMINAL

Foot of 32nd St, Bayonne, NJ 07002-5302
(201) 823-5111; Autovon 247-5111
OFFICER-OF-THE-DAY: Staff Duty Officer
(201) 823-7207, Autovon 247-7207

Profile

BRANCH: Army.

SIZE AND LOCATION: 432 acres. The city of Bayonne lies right outside the terminal's main gate. Bayonne has 9 mi of waterfront; Newark Bay lies W of the city and Upper New York Bay lies to the E, Staten Island lies to the S. 1.5 mi to the Statue of Liberty and approx 8 mi to Newark IAP.

MAJOR UNITS: Military Traffic Management Command, Eastern Area; Military Sealift Command, Atlantic.

BASE HISTORY: 1942, commissioned US Naval Supply Depot, Bayonne. WWII, principal transshipment point, including Pacific Theater. 1959, designated as Naval Supply Center. 1965, MOTBY established under Military Traffic Management and Terminal Service (MTMTS); 1965 operational as tenant of Naval Supply Center, Bayonne. Assumed operations from MOT Brooklyn. 1967, Naval Supply Center disestablished and title transferred to Army and officially designated MOTBY; world's largest military water terminal in physical area/facilities. 1974-75, HQ, MTMTS, Eastern Area moved from Brooklyn Army Terminal to MOTBY. Commands terminals and regional storage offices in 26 states E of Mississippi River, IA, DC, Azores, Panama, and PR.

VISITOR ATTRACTIONS: Ready access to a rich diversity of activities, cultural events, sports, and attractions.

Key Contacts

COMMANDER: Col Ralph Stocker; (201) 823-6321, Autovon 247-6321.

PUBLIC AFFAIRS: June M Pagan; (201) 823-6351, Autovon 247-6351.

PERSONNEL/COMMUNITY ACTIVITIES: Glen Perlakowski; (Chief), Director Personnel, Community, and Family Activities Division, (201) 823-5566 823-5690, Autovon 247-5566 247-5690.

Personnel and Expenditures

ACTIVE DUTY PERSONNEL: 250

DEPENDENTS: 320

CIVILIAN PERSONNEL: 1800

Services *Housing:* Family units 124; BOQ cottages 3; Barracks spaces 66. *Temporary Housing:* VIP cottages 1; VOQ cottages 1; Guesthouse units scheduled for opening in 1991 40. *Commissary and Exchange:* Retail store; Barber shop; Dry cleaners; Food shop; Service station. *Child Care/Capacities:* Day care center 46; Home day care program;

School-age latchkey program available through youth activities center. *Base Library:* Yes. *Medical Facilities:* Medical clinic. *Recreational Facilities:* Bowling; Movie theater; Pool; Gym; Tennis; Racquetball; Fitness center; Softball field; Auto shop; Crafts; Community club; Woodworking shop; Bocce courts; Miniature golf course.

CAPE MAY

CAPE MAY COAST GUARD TRAINING CENTER

Commanding Officer: USCG Training Center, Cape May, NJ 08204
(609) 884-6900
OFFICER-OF-THE-DAY: (609) 884-6915

Profile

BRANCH: Coast Guard.

SIZE AND LOCATION: 500 acres. At Cape May on NJ's southernmost point at the end of the Garden State Pkwy over the bridge on Rte 109 and follow the signs. From the Lewes, DE, ferry take a right on Rte 109 for approx 5 mi.

MAJOR UNITS: USCG Training Center/Group; USCG Air Station; USCG Small Boat Station; CGC *Alert*; CGC *Matinicus*; CGC *Hornbeam*; CGC *Point Batan*; CGC *Point Franklin*.

BASE HISTORY: May 1948, commissioned. Current mission to provide recruits with basic skills. 8-week curriculum embraces military customs and courtesies, Coast Guard organization and history, training in small arms marksmanship, seamanship, physical conditioning, fire fighting, and lifesaving techniques.

VISITOR ATTRACTIONS: Recruit graduation every Fri morning at 11; Occasional sunset parades in the summer.

Key Contacts

COMMANDER: Capt Michael K Cain; (609) 884-6901.

PUBLIC AFFAIRS: PA2 Glenn Rasenholm; (609) 884-6914.

PROCUREMENT: Mrs Clymer & Mrs Smith; (609) 884-6930 884-6306.

TRANSPORTATION: Mr Hodsen; (609) 884-6931.

PERSONNEL/COMMUNITY ACTIVITIES: See Commanding Officer.

Personnel and Expenditures

ACTIVE DUTY PERSONNEL: 800

DEPENDENTS: 500

CIVILIAN PERSONNEL: 50

MILITARY PAYROLL EXPENDITURE: $25 mil

CONTRACT EXPENDITURE: $6.8 mil

Services *Housing:* Family units 173; Duplex units 5; Townhouse units; Barracks spaces 12; Senior NCO units; Junior NCO units. *Temporary Housing:* VOQ cottages; VEQ units 6; Apartment units 173; Transient living quarters 6; VOQ/VEQ combined. *Commissary:* Base commissary; Retail store; Bar-

ber shop; Dry cleaners; Food shop; Tailor. *Child Care/Capacities:* Day care center 30. *Medical Facilities:* Hospital 46; Medical clinic; Dental clinic. *Recreational Facilities:* Movie theater; Pool; Gym; Recreation center; Racquetball; Fitness center; Softball field; Football field; Auto shop; Officers club; NCO club; Fishing/Hunting.

FORT DIX

FORT DIX

US Army Training Center & Fort Dix, Fort Dix, NJ 08640-5000
(609) 562-4034; Autovon 944-1110
OFFICER-OF-THE-DAY: Staff Duty Officer, (609) 562-2643, Autovon 944-2643

Profile

BRANCH: Army.

SIZE AND LOCATION: 32,000 acres. 15 mi E of the NJ Tpke Exit 7; 25 mi SE of Trenton and 50 mi E of Philadelphia; on NJ-68, 1 mi SE of intersection of NJ-68 and Burlington Co-528 spur or 1 mi SW of intersection of NJ-68 and Burlington Co-545; near Wrightstown off Rte 528 spur.

MAJOR UNITS: Headquarters Command; Walson Army Hospital; 3d Basic Training Brigade; 5th Training Brigade.

BASE HISTORY: 1917, established; named after Maj Gen John Adams Dix, 19th century soldier-statesman. During WWI, served as training post. 1939, designated permanent installation, Fort Dix. Largest military installation in NE; shares common boundaries with McGuire AFB and Lakehurst NAS.

VISITOR ATTRACTIONS: Ft Dix Museum.

Key Contacts

COMMANDER: Maj Gen James W Wurman.

PUBLIC AFFAIRS: Richard V Dowling; PAO.

PROCUREMENT: M Kastberg; DOC, (609) 562-4252, Autovon 944-4252.

TRANSPORTATION: R Guyton; ATZD-GDT, (609) 562-4451, Autovon 944-4451.

PERSONNEL/COMMUNITY ACTIVITIES: Col W Sawczyn; DPCA, (609) 562-3353, Autovon 944-3353.

Personnel and Expenditures

ACTIVE DUTY PERSONNEL: 11,000

DEPENDENTS: 6800

CIVILIAN PERSONNEL: 3317

MILITARY PAYROLL EXPENDITURE: FY 89, $2.1 bil

CONTRACT EXPENDITURE: FY 89, $50 mil

Services *Housing:* Family units 2180; BOQ cottages 72; SBEQ units 212. *Temporary Housing:* VIP cottages 16; VOQ cottages 10; VEQ units 90; Guesthouse units 2; Dormitory units 169. *Commissary:* Base commissary; Retail store; Barber shop; Dry cleaners; Food shop; Florist; Banking; Service station; Bakery. *Child Care/Capacities:* Day care center; Home day care program. *Schools:* Elementary; 1 Elem on post, all students bus-

FORT DIX (continued)
sed. *Base Library:* Yes. *Medical Facilities:* Hospital 464; Medical clinic; Dental clinic. *Recreational Facilities:* Bowling; Movie theater; Pool; Gym; Recreation center; Golf; Tennis; Racquetball; Fitness center; Softball field; Football field; Auto shop; Crafts; Officers club; NCO club; Fishing/Hunting; Bridle Lake camping and picnic area; Skeet and trap ranges; Driving range.

FORT MONMOUTH

FORT MONMOUTH
Fort Monmouth, NJ 07703-5000
(201) 532-9000; Autovon 922-9000
OFFICER-OF-THE-DAY: (201) 532-2110,
Autovon 992-2110
Profile
BRANCH: Army.
SIZE AND LOCATION: 1560 acres. NJ Tpke to I-95; E to Garden State Pkwy; N to Exit 105 for Eatontown & Fort Monmouth; nearest city, New Brunswick, 23 mi NW; 10 min from Atlantic Ocean beaches; nearby Monmouth Park Race Track; 1.5 hrs S of New York City.
MAJOR UNITS: Communications-Electronics Command; 513th Military Intelligence Brigade; US Military Academy Preparatory School; US Army Chaplain Center and School; Information Systems Engineering Command; 235th Signal Detachment; 535th Engineering Detachment; 54th Explosive Ordnance Detachment; Army Recruiting Battalion; 389th Army Band; Joint Tactical C3 Agency; Army Aviation R&D Activity; Army Electronics Technology and Devices Laboratory.
BASE HISTORY: July 20, 1917, Army established reserve officers training battalion at Signal Corps Camp, Little Silver. Sept 1917, renamed Camp Alfred Vail. Aug 1925, made permanent military post, Fort Monmouth, in honor of soldiers of American Revolution who fought in nearby fields. Leading military technological and logistics center.
VISITOR ATTRACTIONS: Communications-Electronics Museum has equipment and documents that trace the development of Army communications from 1860 to the present; US Army Chaplains Museum; Post Chapel.
Key Contacts
COMMANDER: Maj Gen Billy M Thomas; Commander Communications-Electronics Command and Fort Monmouth, (201) 532-1515, Autovon 922-1515.
PUBLIC AFFAIRS: Alvin M Schwartz; Public Affairs Office (AMSEL-IO), (201) 532-1258, Autovon 992-1258.
PROCUREMENT: J Levanson; (201) 532-5601, Autovon 992-5601.
TRANSPORTATION: L Wilson; (201) 532-3545, Autovon 992-3545.
PERSONNEL/COMMUNITY ACTIVITIES: Lt Col Lynn Fleury; (201) 532-7810, Autovon 992-7810.
Personnel and Expenditures
ACTIVE DUTY PERSONNEL: 2535
DEPENDENTS: 5200
CIVILIAN PERSONNEL: 8143
MILITARY PAYROLL EXPENDITURE: $47.2 mil
CONTRACT EXPENDITURE: $4.5 bil
Services *Housing:* Family units 881; Duplex units 186; Senior NCO units 100; Trailer spaces 24. *Temporary Housing:* VIP cottages 6; VOQ cottages 60; Guesthouse units 70; off-base hotel/motel rooms w/year round rates 135. *Commissary:* Base commissary; Retail store; Barber shop; Dry cleaners; Food shop; Banking; Service station; Military clothing sales; Jewelry/watch sales and repair; Cafeteria; Optical shop; Tailor; Laundry; Credit union. *Child

Care/Capacities: Day care center 250; Home day care program; Certified child care homes 57. *Base Library:* Yes. *Medical Facilities:* Hospital 49; Medical clinic; Dental clinic. *Recreational Facilities:* Bowling; Movie theater; Pool; Gym; Recreation center; Golf; Tennis; Racquetball; Fitness center; Softball field; Football field; Auto shop; Crafts; Officers club; NCO club; Fishing/Hunting; Marina.

GIBBSBORO

GIBBSBORO AIR FORCE STATION
OLAJ NE AD Sector, Gibbsboro, NJ 08026-1299
(609) 783-1449; 783-1533; Autovon 440-2898
Profile
BRANCH: Air Force.
SIZE AND LOCATION: 21.8 acres. On Rte 561 approx 14 mi E of Camden, NJ; 2 mi W of Berlin, NJ; 50 mi W of Atlantic City, NJ; 33 mi S of McGurie AFB, NJ.
MAJOR UNITS: Operating Location AJ, Northeast Air Defense Sector.
Key Contacts
COMMANDER: TSgt Michael S Race; Site Chief.
PUBLIC AFFAIRS: Louise "Lou" Griest; Secretary/Information Management Specialists.
Personnel and Expenditures
ACTIVE DUTY PERSONNEL: 2
CIVILIAN PERSONNEL: 2

LAKEHURST

NAVAL AIR ENGINEERING CENTER
Lakehurst, NJ 08733-5000
(201) 323-2308; Autovon (624) 323-2308
OFFICER-OF-THE-DAY: (201) 323-2308, Autovon 624-2308
Profile
BRANCH: Navy.
SIZE AND LOCATION: 7400 acres. Approx 60 mi from Philadelphia and Atlantic City; 70 mi from NYC. From NJ Tpke take either Rte 70 E or Rte 524 E to Rte 539 E to NAEC. From the Garden State Pky take Exit 11 (Shore Areas) W to NAEC.
MAJOR UNITS: Naval Air Technical Training Center; Marine Aviation Training Support Group; Personnel Support Activity Detachment; Branch Commissary Store; Naval Hospital Philadelphia Branch Clinic Lakehurst; Naval Dental Clinic Branch Lakehurst; CECOM Airborne Electronics Research Activity; Naval Oceanography Command.
BASE HISTORY: 1917, founded. Mission to ensure effectiveness of Navy's air arm by researching, developing, and testing innovative technologies and equipment needed to support sophisticated aircraft. One of Navy's largest research, engineering, development, test, and evaluation complexes.
VISITOR ATTRACTIONS: Hindenburg Memorial; Hangar 1, Registered National Historic Landmark.
Key Contacts
COMMANDER: Capt James R MacDonald; (201) 323-2380, Autovon 624-2380.
PUBLIC AFFAIRS: Frank Montarelli; Public Affairs Office, Naval Air Engineering Center, Lakehurst, NJ 08733-5041, (201) 323-2620, Autovon 624-2620.
PROCUREMENT: Carmen DeCinque; Quality Management, Engineering and Procurement Division, NAEC, Lakehurst, NJ 08733-5130, (201) 323-2760, Autovon 624-2760.

TRANSPORTATION: Murray Chipps; Transportation Division, NAEC, Lakehurst, NJ 08733-5071, (201) 323-2511, Autovon 624-2511.
PERSONNEL/COMMUNITY ACTIVITIES: Frederick Olson; Civilian Personnel Dept, NAEC, Lakehurst, NJ 08733-5055, (201) 323-2423, Autovon 624-2423.
Personnel and Expenditures
ACTIVE DUTY PERSONNEL: 1327
CIVILIAN PERSONNEL: 3169
MILITARY PAYROLL EXPENDITURE: $98.8 mil (military & civilian)
CONTRACT EXPENDITURE: $16 mil
Services *Housing:* Family units 223; Barracks spaces 255; Dormitory spaces 938; Mobile home units 52; Trailer spaces 52. *Temporary Housing:* VIP cottages 1; BOQ units 28. *Commissary:* Base commissary; Retail store; Barber shop; Food shop; Banking; Service station. *Child Care/Capacities:* Day care center; Home day care program. *Schools:* Kindergarten/Preschool. *Base Library:* Yes. *Medical Facilities:* Medical clinic; Dental clinic. *Recreational Facilities:* Bowling; Movie theater; Pool; Gym; Recreation center; Golf; Tennis; Racquetball; Fitness center; Softball field; Auto shop; Crafts; Fishing/Hunting.

MCGUIRE AFB

MCGUIRE AIR FORCE BASE
438th Military Airlift Wing, McGuire AFB, NJ 08641-5154
(609) 724-4111 724-1100; Autovon 440-4111 440-1100
Profile
BRANCH: Air Force.
SIZE AND LOCATION: 3597 acres. 45 mi NE of Philadelphia; 20 mi SE of Trenton, NJ; Exit 7 NJ Tpke.
MAJOR UNITS: 438th Military Airlift Wing (MAW); Headquarters 21st Air Force; 514th Military Airlift Wing (MAW) (Associate); 108th Tactical Fighter Group; 170th Air Refueling Group; 21st Air Force; 30th Military Airlift Squadron; 18th Military Airlift Squadron; 6th Military Airlift Squadron; 438th Air Base Group; 438th Headquarters Squadron; 438th Civil Engineering Squadron; 438th Security Police Squadron; 1998th Communications Group; Military Airlift Command Noncommissioned Officers Academy-East; 590th Air Force Band; 3515th Recruiting Squadron; 15th Weather Squadron; Detachment 10, 15th Weather Squadron; New Jersey Air National Guard; 177th Fighter Interceptor Group; Field Training Detachment 203; USAF-Civil Air Patrol, Northeast Liaison Region.
BASE HISTORY: Largest Military Airlift Command port of embarkation/debarkation on East Coast. Named for Maj Thomas B McGuire, native of Ridgewood, NJ, second leading WWII flying ace. 1937, began as Rudd Field, under control of Ft Dix. WWII, antisubmarine patrols flown and aircraft shuttled to Europe. 1945, reception center for returning forces. 1949, became McGuire AFB. 1966, MATS redesignated Military Airlift Command and 438th Military Airlift Wing activated and host.
Key Contacts
COMMANDER: 438th Air Base Group.
Personnel and Expenditures
ACTIVE DUTY PERSONNEL: 9116
CIVILIAN PERSONNEL: 2900
MILITARY PAYROLL EXPENDITURE: $196 mil
CONTRACT EXPENDITURE: $53 mil

MCGUIRE AIR FORCE BASE *(continued)*
Services *Housing:* Family units 1753; Dormitory spaces 2570; Mobile home units 177 lots. *Temporary Housing:* VOQ cottages 237; VEQ units 626; Transient living quarters 64. *Commissary:* Base commissary; Retail store; Barber shop; Dry cleaners; Food shop; Florist; Banking; Service station; Bakery. *Child Care/Capacities:* Day care center. *Schools:* Kindergarten/Preschool; Elementary. *Base Library:* Yes. *Medical Facilities:* Medical clinic; Dental clinic; use Ft Dix Hospital. *Recreational Facilities:* Bowling; Movie theater; Pool; Gym; Recreation center; Golf; Tennis; Racquetball; Fitness center; Softball field; Auto shop; Crafts; Officers club; NCO club; Aero club.

PLEASANTVILLE

177TH FIGHTER INTERCEPTOR GROUP, NJANG
400 Langley Rd, ANGB ACY IAP,
Pleasantville, NJ 08232-9500
(609) 645-6000; Autovon 445-6000
OFFICER-OF-THE-DAY: (609) 645-6000, Autovon 445-6000
Profile
BRANCH: Air National Guard.
SIZE AND LOCATION: 286 acres. 12 mi NW of Atlantic City, NJ on Tilton Rd; Exit 9 off Atlantic Expy; Exit 36 N off Garden State Pky, Exit 37 S.
MAJOR UNITS: 177th Fighter Interceptor Group; 119th Fighter Interceptor Squadron, NJANG.
BASE HISTORY: Sept 1917, 119th Aero Squadron, Langley Field VA. Inactivated until 1928, reorganized as 119th Observation Squadron, NJNG, at Metropolitan Airport, Newark, NJ, part of 44th Division Aviation. 1930, federal recognition. Sept 1940, active service as 490th Fighter Squadron. 1945, redesignated 119th Fighter Squadron (SE). 1946, redesignated ANG Newark. 1958, moved to former Atlantic City Naval Air Station, now Federal Aviation Administration Technical Center. Berlin Crisis 1961, rotated to Chaumont AB, France. "Pueblo Crisis", assigned to 113th TFW, Myrtle Beach AFB, SC. 1969, returned to Atlantic City. 1972, reorganized as 177th FIG and 119th FIS.
VISITOR ATTRACTIONS: A base tour is available for groups making advanced reservations.
Key Contacts
COMMANDER: Col Richard C Cosgrave; 117FIG/CC, (609) 645-6011, Autovon 445-6011.
PUBLIC AFFAIRS: Capt Joseph E Murphy; 177MSF/ISO, (609) 645-6180, Autovon 445-6180.
PROCUREMENT: MSgt Wharton C Brown; 177RMS/LGC, (609) 645-6095, Autovon 445-6095.
TRANSPORTATION: MSgt Edward C O'Reilly; 177RMS/LGTM, (609) 645-6090, Autovon 445-6090.
PERSONNEL/COMMUNITY ACTIVITIES: Capt Joan F Searfoss; 177MSS/DPMU, (609) 645-6213, Autovon 445-6213.
Personnel and Expenditures
ACTIVE DUTY PERSONNEL: 52
CIVILIAN PERSONNEL: 265
Services *Commissary and Exchange:* Retail store.

TRENTON

NAVAL AIR PROPULSION CENTER
PO Box 7176, Trenton, NJ 08628-0176
Profile
BRANCH: Navy.
SIZE AND LOCATION: 67 acres. E of I-95 at Bear Tavern Rd, off of Upper Ferry Rd; NW of Trenton, NJ; Within corporate limits of Ewing Township.
BASE HISTORY: Begun in 1917. One of world's premier facilities for research, development, test, and evaluation of air-breathing propulsion systems. Test facilities can simulate any atmospheric condition an aircraft may encounter in flight. Off-site facility for power plant testing maintained at Naval Air Engineering Center, Lakehurst, NJ. NAPC houses fully instrumented chemistry lab for analysis of aviation fuels and lubricants.
Key Contacts
COMMANDER: Capt Carl S Park Jr; (609) 896-5602, Autovon 442-7602.
PUBLIC AFFAIRS: David B Polish; Code A3, (609) 896-5633, Autovon 442-7633.
PROCUREMENT: LCDR Michael Simcich.
PERSONNEL/COMMUNITY ACTIVITIES: William Hoffman; Personnel.
Personnel and Expenditures
ACTIVE DUTY PERSONNEL: 7
CIVILIAN PERSONNEL: 720
MILITARY PAYROLL EXPENDITURE: $386,000
CONTRACT EXPENDITURE: $15.2 mil
Services *Base Library:* Yes. *Medical Facilities:* Nurse. *Recreational Facilities:* Tennis; Softball field.

NEW MEXICO

ALBUQUERQUE

KIRTLAND AIR FORCE BASE
Albuquerque, NM 87117-5000
(505) 844-0011; Autovon 244-0011
OFFICER-OF-THE-DAY: (505) 844-4676,
Autovon 244-4676

Profile

BRANCH: Air Force; Army; Navy; Department of Energy.

SIZE AND LOCATION: 52,000 acres. In Albuquerque on SE side of US-66. From I-40/US-66 turn S on Wyoming Blvd; from I-25 turn E on Gibson Blvd to main gate.

MAJOR UNITS: Sandia National Laboratories; Naval Weapons Evaluation Facility; Air Force Weapons Laboratory; Field Command, Defense Nuclear Agency; Air Force Contract Management Division; Air Force Test and Evaluation Center; Air Force Space Technology Center; 1606th Air Base Wing; 1550th Aircrew Training and Test Wing.

BASE HISTORY: 1939, began servicing transient military aircraft; large bomber crew training base; and, named for Col Roy C Kirtland, military aviation pioneer; also established training depot for aircraft mechanics to E of Kirtland Field, near original private airport, Oxnard Field, Sandia Base (later used as convalescent center for wounded air crewmen and storage and dismantling facility for surplus aircraft); units of Z Division moved to Sandia Base (predecessor of Sandia Corporation, which became and remains, as Sandia National Laboratories), largest tenant on Kirtland; Armed Forces Special Weapons Project (later Defense Atomic Support Agency, then Defense Nuclear Agency) operated Sandia Base. 1949, AF Special Weapons Command established at Kirtland; Navy established weapons test detachments that evolved into Naval Weapons Evaluation Facility. 1952, AF Special Weapons Command redesignated AF Special Weapons Center. 1960s, AF Weapons Laboratory created. Late 1970s, the Trestle, largest simulation facility ever built, completed. 1971, Kirtland and Sandia merged, under control of USAF and replaced Field Command, Defense Nuclear Agency, as host unit. 1976, Special Weapons Center disestablished and Contract Management Division and 4900th ABW, became host. 1977, 1606th ABW created when MAC took over operation. 1982, AF Space Technology Center activated, under AF Systems Command's Space Division, HQ, Los Angeles.

VISITOR ATTRACTIONS: National Atomic Museum.

Key Contacts

COMMANDER: (505) 844-1606, Autovon 244-1606.

PUBLIC AFFAIRS: (505) 844-5991, Autovon 244-5991.

Personnel and Expenditures

ACTIVE DUTY PERSONNEL: 5891

DEPENDENTS: 7000

CIVILIAN PERSONNEL: 15,109

MILITARY PAYROLL EXPENDITURE: $177.7 mil

CONTRACT EXPENDITURE: $625.4 mil

Services *Housing:* Family units 1599; RV/Camper sites 40; General's quarters 4. *Temporary Housing:* VOQ cottages 238; VAQ units 249; Dormitory units 16; Transient living quarters 40. *Commissary:* Base commissary; Retail store; Barber shop; Dry cleaners; Food shop; Florist; Banking; Service station. *Child Care/Capacities:* Day care center; Home day care program. *Schools:* Kindergarten/Preschool; Elementary. *Base Library:* Yes. *Medical Facilities:* Hospital; Medical clinic; Dental clinic. *Recreational Facilities:* Bowling; Movie theater; Pool; Gym; Recreation center; Golf; Stables; Tennis; Racquetball; Skating rink; Fitness center; Softball field; Football field; Auto shop; Crafts; Officers club; NCO club.

CANNON AFB

CANNON AIR FORCE BASE
27th CSG, Cannon AFB, NM 88103
(505) 784-2761; Autovon 681-2761
OFFICER-OF-THE-DAY: (505) 784-2253,
Autovon 681-2253

Profile

BRANCH: Air Force.

SIZE AND LOCATION: 26,642 acres. In High Plains of eastern NM near TX Panhandle. 7 mi W of Clovis, NM, on US Hwy 60-84; 17 mi SW of Clovis Airport; altitude 4,295 ft.

MAJOR UNITS: 27th Tactical Fighter Wing; 27th CSG; 522nd Tactical Fighter Squadron; 523rd Tactical Fighter Squadron; 524th Tactical Fighter Training Squadron; 27th AGS; 27th EMS; 27th CRS; 27th SPS; 2040th CS; 27th Tactical Fighter Wing Hospital.

BASE HISTORY: Late 1920s, civilian passenger facility for commercial transcontinental flights, Portair Field, established. 1930s, Portair renamed Clovis Municipal Airport. WWII, Clovis Army Air Base and glider detachment took over. 1943, 16th Bombardment Operational Wing arrived and trained B-24, B-17, and B-29 heavy bombers; renamed Clovis Army Air Field. 1947, inactivated. 1951, reassigned to TAC, with 140th Fighter-Bomber Wing, and airfield renamed Clovis AFB. 1957, renamed Cannon AFB for Gen John K Cannon, former commander of TAC. 1959, 312th Fighter Bomber Group deactivated and replaced by 27th TFW. 1965, mission changed to replacement training unit, largest such unit in TAC.

VISITOR ATTRACTIONS: Apollo Park with vintage planes flown at Cannon.

Key Contacts

COMMANDER: Col David E Benson.

PUBLIC AFFAIRS: Capt Marie K Yancey; 27 TFW/PA, (505) 784-4131, Autovon 681-4131.

PROCUREMENT: Capt Charles Buckman; 27 TFW/LGC, (505) 784-2321, Autovon 681-2321.

TRANSPORTATION: Capt Gary Gibbs; 27 TRANS, (505) 784-2683, Autovon 681-2683.

PERSONNEL/COMMUNITY ACTIVITIES: Capt Guerillmo Birmingham; Director of Morale, Welfare and Recreation, 27 CSG/SS, (505) 784-4138, Autovon 681-4138.

Personnel and Expenditures

ACTIVE DUTY PERSONNEL: 3511

DEPENDENTS: 5260

CIVILIAN PERSONNEL: 450

MILITARY PAYROLL EXPENDITURE: $68.9 mil

CONTRACT EXPENDITURE: $19 mil

Services *Housing:* Family units 1011; Dormitory spaces 1244; Trailer spaces 56. *Temporary Housing:* VOQ cottages 29; VAQ units 21; Transient living quarters 31. *Commissary:* Base commissary; Retail store; Barber shop; Dry cleaners; Food shop; Florist; Banking; Service station; Video rental. *Child Care/Capacities:* Day care center 97. *Base Library:* Yes. *Medical Facilities:* Hospital 40; Medical clinic; Dental clinic. *Recreational Facilities:* Bowling; Movie theater; Pool; Gym; Recreation center; Golf; Tennis; Racquetball; Fitness center; Softball field; Football field; Auto shop; Officers club; NCO club; Arcade.

GALLUP

FORT WINGATE DEPOT ACTIVITY
Gallup, NM 87301
(505) 488-5411; Autovon 488-6411
OFFICER-OF-THE-DAY: (505) 488-5411,
Autovon 790-5411

Profile

BRANCH: Army.

SIZE AND LOCATION: 22,120 acres. Near town of Gallup, NM.

BASE HISTORY: 1862, began as garrison post; key location during Indian wars; stockade remains of first fort, now known as Old Fort Wingate, adjacent to today's depot. 1928, ammunition mission began with renovation, receipt, packing, storage, and shipment (sole mission today). 1976, reassigned to Tooele Army Complex. Listed for closing in Base Realignments and Closure Law as Fort Wingate Ammunition Storage Depot.

FORT WINGATE DEPOT ACTIVITY
(continued)
VISITOR ATTRACTIONS: Old Ft Wingate; An-
astazi Indian site.
Key Contacts
PUBLIC AFFAIRS: Susan Broadbent; SDSTE-
PAO, Tooele Army Depot, UT 84074-
5000, (801) 833-3216, Autovon 790-3216.
PROCUREMENT: Robert Corrigan; SDSTE-
CD, Tooele Army Depot, UT 84074-
5000, (801) 833-2616, Autovon 790-2616.
TRANSPORTATION: Deroy Burt; Tooele Army
Depot, UT 84074-5000, (801) 833-2914,
Autovon 790-2914.
PERSONNEL/COMMUNITY ACTIVITIES: V Blaine
Kelley; SDSTE-PC, Tooele Army Depot,
UT 84074-5000, (801) 833-2412, Auto-
von 790-2412.
Personnel and Expenditures
ACTIVE DUTY PERSONNEL: 2
CIVILIAN PERSONNEL: 80
MILITARY PAYROLL EXPENDITURE: $2 mil
Services *Housing:* Family units. *Medical Fa-
cilities:* Health clinic. *Recreational Facilities:*
Tennis.

HOLLOMAN AFB

HOLLOMAN AIR FORCE BASE
Hwy 70, Holloman AFB, NM 88330-5000
(505) 479-1110; Autovon 867-1110
OFFICER-OF-THE-DAY: Command Post, (505)
479-7575, Autovon 867-7575
Profile
BRANCH: Air Force.
SIZE AND LOCATION: 50,000 acres. Approx 10
mi from Alamogordo Municipal Airport.
El Paso approx 85 mi S on Hwy 54; Las
Cruces approx 60 mi SW on Hwy 70;
Junction of Hwys 70 and 54 approx 5 mi
from base gate. Shuttle service from El
Paso airport; no public transportation
with Alamorgordo.
MAJOR UNITS: 833rd Air Division (TAC);
49th Tactical Fighter Wing; 479th Tactical Training Wing; 6585th Test Group.
BASE HISTORY: 1942, Alamogordo Army Airfield began to train heavy bombardment
groups. 1944, became Combat Crew
Training Center, training replacement
crews for bombardment groups. 1945,
first atomic bomb detonated in NW corner of airfield's bombing range, known as
Trinity Site. Following WWII, inactivated
until 1946; reactivated by AMC. 1948,
renamed Holloman AFB for Col George
V Holloman, pioneer in guided missile
research. 1952, became Holloman Air Development Center and designated permanent USAF installation; Holloman test
range integrated with White Sands Proving Grounds, under Army. 1968, 49th
TFW assigned. 1970, Missile Development Center deactivated and 49th TFW
assumed host responsibilities. 1971, TAC
assumed command. 1977, Tactical Training Center. 1980, renamed 833rd Air Division. Since 1981, provides contingency
support for Space Shuttle at White Sands
Space Harbor.
Key Contacts
COMMANDER: Brig Gen James S Allen; 833
AD/CC, (505) 479-5571, Autovon 867-
5571.
PUBLIC AFFAIRS: Capt Betsy L Well; 833 AD/
PA, (505) 479-5406, Autovon 867-5406.
PROCUREMENT: Capt Ronnie E Nickel; Contracting Office, 833 AD/LGC, (505) 479-
3040, Autovon 867-3040.
TRANSPORTATION: LTC George Bussing; 833
TRNSP SQ, (505) 479-5527, Autovon
867-5527.
PERSONNEL/COMMUNITY ACTIVITIES: Capt
Marjorie Bradley; 833 CSG/SS, (505)
479-5537, Autovon 867-5537.

Personnel and Expenditures
ACTIVE DUTY PERSONNEL: 6530
DEPENDENTS: 8096
CIVILIAN PERSONNEL: 2997
MILITARY PAYROLL EXPENDITURE: $126.4 mil
CONTRACT EXPENDITURE: $14.6 mil
Services *Housing:* Family units 1551; Dor-
mitory spaces 15. *Temporary Housing:* VIP
cottages 6; VOQ cottages 5; VAQ units 2;
BAQ units 7; Transient living quarters 2.
Commissary: Base commissary; Retail store;
Barber shop; Dry cleaners; Food shop; Flo-
rist; Banking; Service station; Convenience
store/Shopette; Video rental; Beauty shop;
Optical shop. *Child Care/Capacities:* Day
care center. *Schools:* Kindergarten/Preschool;
Elementary; Intermediate/Junior high. *Base
Library:* Yes. *Medical Facilities:* Hospital 30;
Dental clinic. *Recreational Facilities:* Bowl-
ing; Movie theater; Pool; Gym; Recreation
center; Golf; Stables; Tennis; Racquetball;
Softball field; Auto shop; Crafts; Officers
club; NCO club; Camping (supplies);
Fishing/Hunting (supplies); Water sports.

SANTA FE

NEW MEXICO NATIONAL GUARD STATE HEADQUARTERS
2600 Cerrillos Rd, Santa Fe, NM 87502
(505) 473-2402; Autovon 867-9402
Profile
BRANCH: Air National Guard; Army National
Guard.
SIZE AND LOCATION: 22 acres. 5 mi N of
Hwy I-25 in city limits of Santa Fe; take
Cerrillos Rd Exit off I-25.
MAJOR UNITS: State Headquarters New Mexico National Guard; Troop Command;
515th Maintenance Battalion.
BASE HISTORY: Origin of New Mexico Army
NG can be traced back to 1606, local
militia, the "Neighbors," took over home
defense. 1851, Territorial Legislature created Office of Adjutant General for central control of local militia units during
peacetime. NMNG served in every war
since Civil War with commanders such as
Kit Carson and Teddy Roosevelt. 111th
Air Defense Brigade in Albuquerque and
five Chaparral air defense battalions
headquartered in Belen, Las Cruces,
Roswell, Clovis, and Springer; two missile
battalions, Hawk battalion at Albuquerque's West Mesa and Roland battalion at
McGregor Range E of Las Cruces. Other
units in Santa Fe, Las Cruces, and Las
Vegas, NM, have maintenance, aviation,
and transportation missions.
Key Contacts
COMMANDER: Maj Gen Edward D Baca;
(505) 473-2402, Autovon 867-9402.
PUBLIC AFFAIRS: Thomas O Koch; 204 Front-
age Rd, Rio Rancho, NM 87124, (505)
891-2472.
PROCUREMENT: Col Antonio Gabaldon;
USPFO, 2600 Cerrillos Rd, Santa Fe,
NM 87502, (505) 473-2428, Autovon
867-9428.
TRANSPORTATION: See Procurement Officer.
PERSONNEL/COMMUNITY ACTIVITIES: Maj
Danny Isaacs; USPFO, 2600 Cerrillos Rd,
Santa Fe, NM 87502, (505) 473-2453,
Autovon 867-9453.
Personnel and Expenditures
ACTIVE DUTY PERSONNEL: 225
CIVILIAN PERSONNEL: 22
MILITARY PAYROLL EXPENDITURE: $51.4 mil

WHITE SANDS MISSILE RANGE

WHITE SANDS MISSILE RANGE
US Army White Sands Missile Range, White
Sands Missile Range, NM 88002
(505) 678-2121; Autovon 258-2121
OFFICER-OF-THE-DAY: (505) 678-2031,
Autovon 258-2031
Profile
BRANCH: Army.
SIZE AND LOCATION: 2,000,000 acres. In
Tularosa Basin between Sacramento
Mountains on E and San Andres and Or-
gan Mountains on W. From El Paso: take
Alamogordo/Hwy 54 Exit off I-10, as you
leave off-ramp you will be on Gateway N,
continue through NE part of city until
Gateway N becomes War Hwy, WSMR
straight ahead approx 40 mi. From Las
Cruces: take Hwy 70082 E Exit from I-10
or I-25 and proceed through city about 25
mi to missile range exit. From Al-
amogordo: take Hwy 70 W, proceed ap-
prox 47 mi to Post HQ.
MAJOR UNITS: National Range; Instrumenta-
tion Directorate; Army Materiel Test and
Evaluation Directorate (ARMTE); Direct-
ed Energy Directorate; Ground Based
Free Electron Laser Technical Integration
Experiment (GBFEL-TIE); Headquarters
Support Troops; Army Air Operations Di-
rectorate (AAOD); Analysis Command
(TRADOC); Vulnerability Assessment
Laboratory (VAL) (LABCOM); Defense
Mapping Agency; Atmospheric Sciences
Laboratory (ASL); Information Systems
Command (USAISC); Armament Divi-
sion, Air Force Systems Command; Naval
Ordnance Missile Test Station; National
Aeronautics and Space Administration
White Sands Test Facility.
BASE HISTORY: Much of WSMR once part of
San Augustin Ranch, owned by Cox family since late 1800s and who still occupy
house a few miles W of main post. 1945,
opened to test feasibility of using missiles
in warfare; world's first atomic bomb detonated in area known as Trinity Site;
missile testing with Tiny Tim firings.
Army airfield is Condron Field, SE of
main post in dry lake bed. Designated as
national test range, largest over land test
facility in US. Test bed of Army, Navy,
Air Force, other government agencies,
some foreign governments, and private
companies. White Sands Space Harbor an
alternate landing site for space shuttle and
training site for NASA shuttle pilots. Mar
30, 1982, Space Shuttle *Columbia* ended
third mission at WSMR.
VISITOR ATTRACTIONS: Visitors center; Outdoor missile display (open 8-3:30, Mon-
Fri); Trinity Site, first atomic explosion
(open 1st Sat in Apr and Oct), call (505)
678-1134 for info; Launch Site 33, a National Historic Landmark (visits on special occasions).
Key Contacts
COMMANDER: Maj Gen Thomas J P Jones;
Commanding General, (505) 678-1101,
Autovon 258-1101.
PUBLIC AFFAIRS: Public Affairs Office, White
Sands Missile Range, NM 88002-5047,
(505) 678-1134, Autovon 258-1134.
PROCUREMENT: Richard W Kaheny; Con-
tracting Directorate, (505) 678-1215,
Autovon 258-1215.
TRANSPORTATION: Col Milton L Howell Jr;
Engineering, Housing and Logistics Direc-
torate, (505) 678-5924, Autovon 258-
5924.

WHITE SANDS MISSILE RANGE *(continued)*
PERSONNEL/COMMUNITY ACTIVITIES: Col
John Sherburn; Directorate of Personnel
and Community Activities, (505) 678-
6103, Autovon 258-6103.
Personnel and Expenditures
ACTIVE DUTY PERSONNEL: 1178
DEPENDENTS: 1424
CIVILIAN PERSONNEL: 8382
MILITARY PAYROLL EXPENDITURE: $22.3 mil
CONTRACT EXPENDITURE: $437 mil
Services *Housing:* Family units 848; BOQ
cottages 16; Duplex units (SEQ) 10; Barracks
spaces 492; RV/Camper sites; SEQ apart-
ments 20; OQ apartments 16. *Temporary
Housing:* VIP cottages 3; VOQ cottages 32;
VEQ units 16; Guesthouse units 15; DVQ 3.
Commissary: Base commissary; Retail store;
Barber shop; Dry cleaners; Florist; Banking;
Service station. *Child Care/Capacities:* Day
care center 125. *Schools:* Kindergarten/Pre-
school; Elementary; Intermediate/Junior
high; Army education center. *Base Library:*
Yes. *Medical Facilities:* Medical clinic; Dental clinic. *Recreational Facilities:* Bowling;
Movie theater; Pool; Gym; Recreation center; Golf; Stables; Tennis; Racquetball; Skating rink; Softball field; Football field; Auto
shop; Crafts; Officers club; NCO club; Youth
center.

NEW YORK

BALLSTON SPA

BALLSTON SPA NUCLEAR POWER TRAINING UNIT
PO Box 300, Ballston Spa, NY 12020-0300
(518) 884-1260
Profile
BRANCH: Navy.
LOCATION: 42 mi NE of Soctia, NY, near the town of West Milton, approx 3 mi from NY Rte 29.
MAJOR UNITS: Nuclear Power Training Unit.
BASE HISTORY: Department of Energy facility operated by General Electric to train Navy personnel in safe operation and maintenance of nuclear reactors.
Key Contacts
COMMANDER: CDR W S Borkin; (518) 884-1260.
PUBLIC AFFAIRS: LCDR W O Hawn; (518) 884-1260.
Personnel and Expenditures
ACTIVE DUTY PERSONNEL: 3000
Services *Housing:* Family units 100. *Medical Facilities:* Navy branch clinic located within 10 mi.

BROOKLYN

BROOKLYN COAST GUARD AIR STATION
Floyd Bennett Field, Brooklyn, NY 11234
(718) 615-2422
Profile
BRANCH: Coast Guard.
LOCATION: On Jamaica Bay across from JFK IAP; off I-278 at Flatbush Ave.
MAJOR UNITS: USCG Air Station Brooklyn.
BASE HISTORY: 1938, established at New York Municipal Airport, Floyd Bennett Field, on property granted to federal government by Mayor LaGuardia. Noted for early work with helicopters and first helicopter training school, 1943, where all Allied helicopter pilots trained. Developed early rescue equipment including rescue hoist.
VISITOR ATTRACTIONS: Tours (contact PAO).
Key Contacts
PUBLIC AFFAIRS: (718) 615-2406.
Personnel and Expenditures
ACTIVE DUTY PERSONNEL: 107
Services *Housing:* BEQ units. *Commissary and Exchange:* Retail store. *Recreational Facilities:* Pool; Gym; Softball field; Auto shop; Crafts.

BROOKLYN COAST GUARD SUPPLY CENTER
830 Third Ave, Brooklyn, NY 11232-1596
(718) 965-5091
OFFICER-OF-THE-DAY: Customer Service Branch (718) 965-5386

Profile
BRANCH: Coast Guard.
SIZE AND LOCATION: 2 warehouse buildings. In Brooklyn on corner of Third Ave and 30th St; 1 mi W of Hamilton (3rd) Ave Exit of US 278, Brooklyn-Queens Expy.
MAJOR UNITS: Coast Guard Electronics/General Materiel Inventory Control Point (E/GICP).
BASE HISTORY: 1921, established at US Army base, 58th St, Brooklyn. 1930, command moved to present location. 1942, "Coast Guard Store" relocated to Jersey City, NJ, until 1955 when it returned to present location. 1950, designated Coast Guard Supply Center. Today, an inventory control point, warehousing, light industrial facility. Open only during working hours, 0630-1700, weekdays.
Key Contacts
COMMANDER: Capt Thomas E Omri; (718) 965-5234.
PUBLIC AFFAIRS: LCDR Fredrick A Adams.
PROCUREMENT: Anne Perisano; (718) 965-5757.
TRANSPORTATION: Edward Mactutis; (718) 965-5793.
PERSONNEL/COMMUNITY ACTIVITIES: ENS D S Coard; (718) 965-5734.
Personnel and Expenditures
ACTIVE DUTY PERSONNEL: 130
CIVILIAN PERSONNEL: 130
CONTRACT EXPENDITURE: $2 mil

FORT HAMILTON
New York Area Command & Fort Hamilton, Brooklyn, NY 11252-5330
(718) 630-1110; Autovon 232-1110
OFFICER-OF-THE-DAY: Staff Duty Officer (after 4 pm), (718) 630-4565, Autovon 8-232-4565
Profile
BRANCH: Army.
SIZE AND LOCATION: 177 acres. Residential area; SW tip of the Borough of Brooklyn at the base of the Verrazano-Narrows Bridge; approx 8 mi to NYC (midtown); JFK and LGA airports approx 7-8 mi; Hwy 278.
MAJOR UNITS: New York City Recruiting Battalion; Military Enlistment Processing Station; 8th Medical Brigade.
BASE HISTORY: June 1925, cornerstone laid; named after first Secretary of Treasury, Alexander Hamilton. Original fort is Officers Club; one of few Army saluting stations with salutes fired by Ceremonial Platoon for visiting warships; provides facilities and support for Army and DOD in NY metro area, more than 300 reserve and NG units; only active Army post in NY metro area.
VISITOR ATTRACTIONS: Harbor Defense Museum, part of the original fort.

Key Contacts
COMMANDER: Col James E Bigelow II; (718) 630-4706, Autovon 8-232-4706.
PUBLIC AFFAIRS: Betsy B McDonald; (718) 630-4927, Autovon 8-232-4927.
TRANSPORTATION: Dina Piacente; (718) 630-4077, Autovon 8-232-4077.
PERSONNEL/COMMUNITY ACTIVITIES: Howard J Hurst; (718) 630-4040, Autovon 8-232-4040.
Personnel and Expenditures
ACTIVE DUTY PERSONNEL: 2100
Services *Housing:* Family units 800+; BOQ cottages; BEQ units; Barracks spaces; VOQ-VIP. *Temporary Housing:* VIP cottages 7; VOQ cottages 19; VEQ units 19; BOQ units 40; Guesthouse units 35; BEQ units 106. *Commissary:* Base commissary; Barber shop; Dry cleaners; Banking; Service station; Snacks; Package beverages. *Child Care/Capacities:* Day care center 75; Home day care program. *Base Library:* Yes. *Medical Facilities:* Medical clinic; Dental clinic. *Recreational Facilities:* Bowling; Movie theater; Pool; Gym; Recreation center; Tennis; Racquetball; Fitness center; Softball field; Auto shop; Crafts; Officers club; NCO club; Community Club.

NAVAL STATION NEW YORK (BROOKLYN)
207 Flushing Ave, Brooklyn, NY 11251
(718) 834-2000; Autovon 456-2000
Profile
BRANCH: Navy.
LOCATION: E shore of East River; N of Brooklyn Bridge on site of former Brooklyn Naval Shipyard.
MAJOR UNITS: Seabees; Regular Navy.
BASE HISTORY: Primary mission to provide administrative, supply, medical, and recreational support to activities at Staten Island and logistical support for Navy tenants. Scheduled for closure; functions to move to NS New York (Staten Island).
Personnel and Expenditures
ACTIVE DUTY PERSONNEL: 900
DEPENDENTS: 1261
Services *Housing:* Additional housing at Mitchel Field & Floyd Bennett Field. *Medical Facilities:* Medical clinic. *Recreational Facilities:* Gym; Fitness center.

BUFFALO

BUFFALO COAST GUARD GROUP
1 Fuhrmann Blvd, Buffalo, NY 14203
(716) 846-4155
OFFICER-OF-THE-DAY: (716) 846-4152
Profile
BRANCH: Coast Guard.
SIZE AND LOCATION: 10 acres. City of Buffalo; N end of Fuhrmann Blvd.
MAJOR UNITS: US Coast Guard Station, Buffalo; ANT Buffalo; ESMT Buffalo.

BUFFALO COAST GUARD GROUP
(continued)
VISITOR ATTRACTIONS: Buffalo lighthouse.
Key Contacts
COMMANDER: CDR S J Cornell.
PUBLIC AFFAIRS: Lt H T Chelpon; (716) 846-4184.
PROCUREMENT: CWO D M Brockes; (716) 846-5823.
TRANSPORTATION: SK1 C J Smith; (716) 846-5823.
PERSONNEL/COMMUNITY ACTIVITIES: YNC W B Weller.
Personnel and Expenditures
ACTIVE DUTY PERSONNEL: 75
CIVILIAN PERSONNEL: 2
Services *Housing:* Barracks spaces 8. *Commissary and Exchange:* Retail store. *Recreational Facilities:* Tennis; Softball field; Football field; Basketball.

US ARMY CORPS OF ENGINEERS, BUFFALO DISTRICT
1776 Niagara St, Buffalo, NY 14207
(716) 876-5454
Profile
BRANCH: Army.
SIZE AND LOCATION: 6 acres. On NY State Thruway, Niagara Exit in Buffalo at NY Rte 198; also at Black Rock Lock on Niagara River.
BASE HISTORY: 1824, Corps began serving lower lakes region. 1857, Buffalo District began. District boundaries have changed somewhat over the years but there has been a Buffalo District since mid-19th century. District stretches from St Lawrence Valley in northern NY to lowlands W of Toledo, OH.
VISITOR ATTRACTIONS: Lock.
Key Contacts
COMMANDER: Col Hugh F Boyd III.
PUBLIC AFFAIRS: John E Derbyshire.
PROCUREMENT: Mary Price.
TRANSPORTATION: Dennis Bermingham.
PERSONNEL/COMMUNITY ACTIVITIES: James Howard.
Personnel and Expenditures
ACTIVE DUTY PERSONNEL: 3
CIVILIAN PERSONNEL: 350
MILITARY PAYROLL EXPENDITURE: $150,000
CONTRACT EXPENDITURE: $35 mil
Services *Base Library:* Yes. *Recreational Facilities:* Horseshoe pits.

FORT DRUM

FORT DRUM
Headquarters, 10th Mountain Division (Light Infantry) and Fort Drum, Fort Drum, NY 13602-5000
(315) 772-5565; Autovon 341-5565
OFFICER-OF-THE-DAY: (315) 772-5647, Autovon 341-5647
Profile
BRANCH: Army.
SIZE AND LOCATION: 107,265 acres. Off of Rte 81, Exit 48; approx 75 mi N of Syracuse and 30 mi S of Canadian border. Watertown, nearest city, 12 mi.
MAJOR UNITS: 1st/2nd Brigade, 41st Engineer Battalion; Division Artillery; 10th Division Support Command; 10th Combat Aviation Brigade; 10th Signal Battalion; 514th Maintenance Battalion; 10th Mountain Division (Light).
BASE HISTORY: Named for Lt Gen Hugh A Drum, Commander of First US Army during early years of WWII. Training facility for Army National Guard and Reserve units.
VISITOR ATTRACTIONS: Close to Thousand Islands resorts and ski areas.

Key Contacts
COMMANDER: Maj Gen Peter J Boylan; (315) 772-5565, Autovon 341-5565.
PUBLIC AFFAIRS: Capt Robert C DesRosiers; (315) 772-5461, Autovon 341-5461.
PROCUREMENT: Charles Hamlin; (315) 772-5406, Autovon 341-5406.
TRANSPORTATION: Janet Pisula; (315) 772-5266, Autovon 341-5266.
PERSONNEL/COMMUNITY ACTIVITIES: Lt Col Michael Miller; (315) 772-5685, Autovon 341-5685.
Personnel and Expenditures
ACTIVE DUTY PERSONNEL: FY 88, 8200; FY 89, 10,500
DEPENDENTS: FY 88, 11,400; FY 89, 14,300
CIVILIAN PERSONNEL: FY 88, 3400; FY 89, 3600
MILITARY PAYROLL EXPENDITURE: $262.4 mil
CONTRACT EXPENDITURE: $45 mil
Services *Housing:* Family units 1350; BEQ units; Barracks spaces; RV/Camper sites 10. *Temporary Housing:* VIP cottages 1; VOQ cottages; VEQ units; BOQ units; BAQ units; Guesthouse units; Guest cottages; Lodge units; Hotel 110 rooms. *Commissary:* Base commissary; Retail store; Barber shop; Food shop; Florist; Banking; Service station; Bakery; Beauty shop; Optical shop; Video rental; Garden center. *Child Care/Capacities:* Day care center 150 (300 under construction). *Base Library:* Yes. *Medical Facilities:* Medical clinic; Dental clinic; Ambulatory health care center under construction. *Recreational Facilities:* Bowling; Movie theater; Pool; Gym; Recreation center; Tennis; Racquetball; Skating rink; Fitness center; Softball field; Football field; Auto shop; Crafts; Officers club; NCO club; Camping; Fishing/Hunting; Youth center; Sports equipmental rental.

FORT TILDEN

FORT TILDEN
Fort Tilden US Army Reserve Center, Fort Tilden, NY 11695-0513
(718) 945-4900; HHB 945-4972; A 945-5134; B 945-4197; C 945-6882; Service Battery 945-4902
OFFICER-OF-THE-DAY: (718) 945-4900
Profile
BRANCH: Army.
SIZE AND LOCATION: 9 acres. 5 mi W of Rockaway, NY; 1 mi E of Breezy Point Retirement Community; JFK IAP 15 mi; 2.5 mi from Exit 11 S Belt Pkwy; 12 mi from Ft Hamilton, NY.
MAJOR UNITS: HQs, 5th BN (105mm)(T), 5th Field Artillery; HHB, A, B, C, & Service Battery.
BASE HISTORY: Formally a Nike missile base with two 16" gun emplacements for coastal defense during WWII.
Key Contacts
COMMANDER: Lt Col Richard S Colt.
PUBLIC AFFAIRS: Lt Mark Weiss; (718) 945-4197.
PROCUREMENT: Lt Michael Lee; (718) 945-4902.
TRANSPORTATION: See Procurement Officer.
PERSONNEL/COMMUNITY ACTIVITIES: See Public Affairs Officer.
Personnel and Expenditures
ACTIVE DUTY PERSONNEL: 21
CIVILIAN PERSONNEL: 3
Services *Base Library:* Yes.

GOVERNORS ISLAND

GOVERNORS ISLAND COAST GUARD SUPPORT CENTER
Governors Island, NY 10004
(212) 668-7298; Autovon 664-7298

Profile
BRANCH: Coast Guard.
LOCATION: On Governors Island off S tip of Manhattan.
MAJOR UNITS: Commander, CG Atlantic Area; Commander, Maintenance and Logistics Command, New York; CG Training Center, New York; CG Support Center, New York.
Personnel and Expenditures
ACTIVE DUTY PERSONNEL: 3500
DEPENDENTS: 2300
Services *Housing:* Family units 714; BOQ cottages 145; BEQ units 470; Student units 250. *Temporary Housing:* VIP cottages 2. *Commissary:* Base commissary; Small exchange. *Child Care/Capacities:* Day care center 35; Home day care program. *Schools:* Kindergarten/Preschool; Elementary. *Medical Facilities:* Medical clinic. *Recreational Facilities:* Bowling; Movie theater; Pool; Gym; Golf; Tennis; Racquetball; Auto shop; Crafts.

GRIFFISS AFB

GRIFFISS AIR FORCE BASE
Griffiss AFB, NY 13441
(315) 330-1110; Autovon 587-1110
Profile
BRANCH: Air Force.
SIZE AND LOCATION: 5836 acres. In Rome, NY. NY State Thruway, I-90, provides access. Traveling W, take Exit 31 at Utica and follow Rte 49 W, or take Exit 32 and follow Rte 233 N. If traveling E, take Exit 33 to Rte 365 E. Each route has signs that will lead you to the Skyline Gate. By air, use Handcock IAP at Syracuse, about 45 mi, or Oneida County which is 6 mi from base.
MAJOR UNITS: 416th Bombardment Wing; 668th Bombardment Squadron; 41st Air Refueling Squadron; 24th Air Division; Northeast Air Defense Sector; Rome Air Development Center; Field Training Detachment 211; US Army 10th Aviation Brigade; 2019th Communications Squadron; Detachment 8, 26th Weather Squadron; 485th Engineering Installation Group.
BASE HISTORY: Feb 1942, operations began. 13 name changes. 1948, named for Army AF pilot Lt Col Townsend E Griffiss, Buffalo native and first American flyer killed in European operations, WWII. 1st FIG first flying unit assigned. Air Materiel Command, later AF Logistics Command, host until 1951, when Air Research and Development Command took over with Watson Laboratories, Rome Air Development Center. 1954, returned to Air Materiel Command. 1983, HQ 24th North American Defense Region. 1987, mission shifted to reserve forces. Mission of 416th BMW is immediate and sustained, long range strategic bombardment and aerial refueling.
Personnel and Expenditures
ACTIVE DUTY PERSONNEL: 4291
CIVILIAN PERSONNEL: 2777
CONTRACT EXPENDITURE: $37.5 mil
Services *Housing:* Family units 730; Dormitory spaces 6 units; Trailer spaces 50; Capehart units, Skyline Terrace 460; Woodhaven Park 270. *Commissary:* Base commissary; Retail store; Barber shop; Food shop; Service station; Military clothing sales; Convenience store/Shopette; Package beverages; Beauty shop. *Child Care/Capacities:* Day care center; Home day care program; Prekindergarten. *Schools:* Kindergarten/Preschool. *Base Library:* Yes. *Medical Facilities:* Hospital 20; Medical clinic; Dental clinic. *Recreational Facilities:* Movie theater; Pool; Gym; Recreation center; Golf; Tennis; Rac-

GRIFFISS AIR FORCE BASE *(continued)*
quetball; Fitness center; Softball field; Auto shop; Crafts; Officers club; NCO club; Camping; Fishing/Hunting; Youth center; Garden plots; Picnicking; Ski chalet; Aero Club.

LAKE SENECA

LAKE SENECA NAVAL UNDERWATER SYSTEMS CENTER DETACHMENT
Lake Seneca, NY 14441
Profile
BRANCH: Navy.
LOCATION: Dresden, NY.
BASE HISTORY: Part of Naval Underwater Systems Center HQ, Newport, RI.
Key Contacts
COMMANDER: Capt Harry P Salmon Jr; Naval Underwater Systems Center, New London, CT 06320.
PUBLIC AFFAIRS: Kathleen P O'Beirne.

LONG ISLAND

1ST MARINE CORPS DISTRICT HEADQUARTERS
605 Stewart Ave, Garden City, Long Island, NY 11530-4761
(516) 228-5641, 228-5642; Autovon 994-5641, 994-5642
Profile
BRANCH: Marines.
SIZE AND LOCATION: 4 acres. Long Island, NY.
MAJOR UNITS: Recruiters for 8 states; 2d Battalion 25th Marines; DCASMA.
Key Contacts
COMMANDER: Col George M Brooke III.
PUBLIC AFFAIRS: Capt Steve G Manuel.
Personnel and Expenditures
ACTIVE DUTY PERSONNEL: 100
DEPENDENTS: 300
CIVILIAN PERSONNEL: 150
Services *Housing:* Family units 300. *Commissary:* Base commissary; Retail store; Barber shop; Dry cleaners; Food shop; Service station. *Child Care/Capacities:* Day care center 40. *Recreational Facilities:* Movie theater; Pool; Gym; Softball field; NCO club.

NEW YORK

US ARMY CORPS OF ENGINEERS, NORTH ATLANTIC DIVISION
90 Church St, New York, NY 10007
(212) 264-7101
Profile
BRANCH: Army.
SIZE: Offices only.
Key Contacts
COMMANDER: Maj Gen James van Loben Sels; Division Engineer.

NEWBURGH

STEWART AIR NATIONAL GUARD BASE
One Militia Way, Newburgh, NY 12550-5043
(914) 563-2000; Autovon 247-2000
OFFICER-OF-THE-DAY: (914) 563-2286, Autovon 247-2286
Profile
BRANCH: Air Force; Marines; Air National Guard.
SIZE AND LOCATION: 250 acres. Entrance on Rte 17K one mi from intersection of I-84 & I-87, 4 mi W of Newburgh, adj to Stewart IAP and Stewart Army Subpost

of US Military Academy; 60 mi N of NYC.
MAJOR UNITS: 105th Military Airlift Group; Marine Air Transport Refueler Group (VMGR-452); Headquarters NY Air National Guard.
BASE HISTORY: Named for Lachian Stewart, Scottish sea captain 1850-70s. 1941, made part of West Point and dedicated as "Wings of West Point." 1947, became AFB. 1949, became air defense base. 1960s, Air Force and AF Academy Aircrew and Examining Center. 1970, released back to civilian control late 1970s, ANG unit began. Currently nation's 2nd largest airport in total area.
VISITOR ATTRACTIONS: Historic Mid-Hudson Valley; West Point Military Academy.
Key Contacts
COMMANDER: Col Paul A Weaver Jr; (914) 563-2001, Autovon 247-2001.
PUBLIC AFFAIRS: Lt Col F A Adinolfi Jr; (914) 563-2040, Autovon 247-2040.
PROCUREMENT: SMSgt Patsy DiMartino; (914) 563-2831, Autovon 247-2831.
TRANSPORTATION: MSgt Gregory Sullivan; (914) 563-2839, Autovon 247-2839.
PERSONNEL/COMMUNITY ACTIVITIES: Maj Edward A Harding Jr; (914) 563-2011, Autovon 247-2011.
Personnel and Expenditures
ACTIVE DUTY PERSONNEL: 550
CIVILIAN PERSONNEL: 400
MILITARY PAYROLL EXPENDITURE: $27 mil
Services *Commissary:* Base commissary; Retail store; Barber shop; Dry cleaners; Banking. *Child Care/Capacities:* Day care center. *Base Library:* Yes. *Medical Facilities:* Medical clinic; Dental clinic; Major hospital at West Point. *Recreational Facilities:* Bowling; Pool; Gym; Tennis; Racquetball; Softball field; Auto shop; Crafts; Officers club; NCO club.

NIAGARA FALLS

914TH TACTICAL AIRLIFT GROUP
Niagara Falls International Airport, Niagara Falls, NY 14304-5000
(716) 236-2000; Autovon 489-2000
Profile
BRANCH: Air Force Reserve.
SIZE AND LOCATION: 979 acres. 6 mi E of Niagara Falls, adj to the Niagara Falls IAP.
MAJOR UNITS: 914th Tactical Airlift Group; 328th Tactical Airlift Squadron; 70th Aeromedical Evacuation Unit; 30th Mobile Aerial Port Squadron; 23rd Medical Services Squadron.
BASE HISTORY: 1963, activated as 914th Troop Carrier Group (Medium) at Niagara Falls IAP, assigned to 512th Troop Carrier Wing (Medium). Active from Oct 28 to Nov 28, 1962 (Cuban Missile Crisis). 1967, redesignated tactical airlift group. 1971, assumed command Niagara Falls Air Reserve Base. Supports C-130 Hercules transport and is assigned to 439th MAW, Westover AFB, MA. On mobilization it will be assigned to MAC.
Key Contacts
COMMANDER: Lt Col Paul R Cooper, USAFR; (716) 236-2121, Autovon 489-2121.
PUBLIC AFFAIRS: Neil E Nolf; (716) 236-2138, Autovon 489-2138.
PROCUREMENT: Dennis Pasiak; LGC, (716) 236-2177, Autovon 489-2177.
TRANSPORTATION: Fred Wohlander; LGT, (716) 236-2220, Autovon 489-2220.
PERSONNEL/COMMUNITY ACTIVITIES: See Public Affairs Office.

Personnel and Expenditures
ACTIVE DUTY PERSONNEL: 986 Reservists
CIVILIAN PERSONNEL: 237
MILITARY PAYROLL EXPENDITURE: $13.6 mil
CONTRACT EXPENDITURE: $6.5 mil
Services *Temporary Housing:* VOQ cottages 1; Dormitory units. *Commissary and Exchange:* Retail store; Food shop. *Medical Facilities:* Medical clinic. *Recreational Facilities:* Bowling; Pool; Gym; Recreation center; Tennis; Racquetball; Fitness center; Softball field; Officers club; NCO club.

PEEKSKILL

CAMP SMITH TRAINING SITE
Rte 202, Peekskill, NY 10566
(914) 739-7703
OFFICER-OF-THE-DAY: (914) 739-7703, ext 506
Profile
BRANCH: Army National Guard.
SIZE AND LOCATION: 1970 acres. In NW corner of Westchester Co on Rte 202 and Rte 6; 1 mi from Peekskill; 8 mi from USMA, West Point; 40 mi N of NTC; Situated in NY highlands.
MAJOR UNITS: Empire State Military Academy; 199th Army Band; 102nd Engineering Battalion (CBT); 102nd Medical Battalion; 369th Transportation Battalion; Detachment 2, STARC-NY (Camp Smith Training Site).
BASE HISTORY: NG base which serves weekend training needs of local, state, and USAR. Occasionally houses transients in BOQ if room. No families unless justified to post commander. Occasionally supports boy/girl scouts troops in transit.
Key Contacts
COMMANDER: Col Patrick J Garvey (Ret); State Commander; Col Dennis J Fagan; Federal; (914) 739-2111.
PUBLIC AFFAIRS: SFC Alexander F Contini; (914) 739-7703, ext 517.
PROCUREMENT: CWO John C Kelleher; (914) 739-7703, ext 615.
TRANSPORTATION: CWO Paul V Hurtt; (914) 739-7703, ext 614.
PERSONNEL/COMMUNITY ACTIVITIES: Maj Arnold T Oftedal; Director of Personnel; (914) 739-7703, ext 518; Community Activities see Public Affairs Officer.
Personnel and Expenditures
ACTIVE DUTY PERSONNEL: 5
CIVILIAN PERSONNEL: 190
Services *Housing:* BOQ cottages 4; BEQ units 25; BAQ units 156; Barracks spaces 1680; Dormitory spaces; All temporary 30 day maximum, no weekends. *Temporary Housing:* VIP cottages 4; VOQ cottages 156; VEQ units; BOQ units 4; BAQ units 156; VIP/VOQ/VEQ weekdays only; BOQ/BAQ weekends if not scheduled for troops. *Medical Facilities:* National Guard physical exam facility. *Recreational Facilities:* Gym; Softball field; Officers club; NCO club; Camping.

PLATTSBURGH

PLATTSBURGH AIR FORCE BASE
380th Bombardment Wing, Plattsburgh, NY 12903-5000
(518) 565-5000; Autovon 689-5000
Profile
BRANCH: Air Force.
SIZE AND LOCATION: 1600 acres. On shore of Lake Champlain in North Country region of NY; 15 min from Plattsburgh Airport; 1 hr S of Montreal; 1 hr W of Burlington, VT by ferry; 2 hrs N of Albany, NY.
MAJOR UNITS: 380th Bombardment Wing; 530th Combat Crew Training Squadron.

PLATTSBURGH AIR FORCE BASE
(continued)

BASE HISTORY: 1839, construction of stone barracks began (1 remains) on Plattsburgh Barracks, oldest active combat installation in US. 1956, Plattsburgh AFB became operational with 380th BMW. 1960s, Atlas missile and 12 sites established within 50-mile radius; phase out began 1965. Plattsburgh AFB 2 bases in 1: Plattsburgh Barracks comprised of what was an Army installation until end of WWII; and Main Base, including flightline and center of present AF community.

VISITOR ATTRACTIONS: With 2-week notification, in writing, tour can be arranged, including flightline and/or different organizations.

Key Contacts

COMMANDER: Col Richard N Goddard; (518) 565-5000, Autovon 689-5000.
PUBLIC AFFAIRS: 1st Lt Cara Mason; (518) 565-7006, Autovon 689-7006.
PROCUREMENT: LGCS; (518) 565-7345, Autovon 689-7345.
TRANSPORTATION: LGTT; (518) 565-7185, Autovon 689-7185.
PERSONNEL/COMMUNITY ACTIVITIES: DPM; (518) 565-5524, Autovon 689-5524.

Personnel and Expenditures

ACTIVE DUTY PERSONNEL: 4700
DEPENDENTS: 6000
CIVILIAN PERSONNEL: 552
MILITARY PAYROLL EXPENDITURE: $71.8 mil
CONTRACT EXPENDITURE: $24.2 mil

Services *Housing:* Family units 1638; Dormitory spaces 1897; Efficiency apts 15. *Temporary Housing:* VOQ cottages 51; VAQ units 58. *Commissary:* Base commissary; Retail store; Barber shop; Dry cleaners; Food shop; Florist; Banking; Service station. *Child Care/Capacities:* Day care center; Home day care program. *Schools:* Kindergarten/Preschool; Elementary. *Base Library:* Yes. *Medical Facilities:* Hospital 20; Medical clinic; Dental clinic. *Recreational Facilities:* Bowling; Movie theater; Pool; Gym; Recreation center; Golf; Tennis; Racquetball; Skating rink; Fitness center; Softball field; Football field; Auto shop; Crafts; Officers club; NCO club; Fishing/Hunting.

QUEENS

FORT TOTTEN
Queens, NY 11359-1016
(718) 352-5700; Autovon 456-0700
Profile
BRANCH: Air Force Reserve.
LOCATION: Flushing, Queens at the Throgs Neck Bridge off of the Cross Island Expy.
MAJOR UNITS: HQ 77th US Army Reserve Command (USARCOM).
BASE HISTORY: 1967, 77th USARCOM, "Statue of Liberty" Division, one of 5 Army Reserve Commands in 1st US Army and one of 20 in continental US formed at Ft Wadsworth, June 1968, moved to Ft Totten. With assigned strength of 15,000 citizen-soldiers, largest Army Reserve Command.
VISITOR ATTRACTIONS: Tours of Old Fort Totten.
Key Contacts
COMMANDER: Maj Gen George E Barker.
PUBLIC AFFAIRS: Lt Col William T Harris III; PAO, (718) 352-5657, Autovon 456-0657.
Services *Housing:* Family units; BAQ units. *Commissary and Exchange:* Retail store; Barber shop. *Child Care/Capacities:* Day care center. *Recreational Facilities:* Pool; Gym; Tennis; Fitness center; Softball field.

ROCHESTER

US PROPERTY AND FISCAL OFFICE-NY, ROCHESTER WAREHOUSE
1500 E Henrietta Rd, Rochester, NY 14623-3181
(716) 424-3457
Profile
BRANCH: Army National Guard.
SIZE AND LOCATION: 35 acres. 2 mi S of Rochester in Henrietta, NY, at intersection of E Henrietta Rd and Jefferson Rd.
MAJOR UNITS: USP&FO-NY, ROCH. WHSE.; CSMS C; 134th Maint. Co DAS-3 unit.
BASE HISTORY: 1959, built as a supply support facility for NY Army NG handling supplies such as service stock and repair parts. Currently used as transportation terminal for Western NY State and property turn-in facility.
Key Contacts
COMMANDER: Col Ferguson; (716) 424-2165.
TRANSPORTATION: Patricia Ornt.
Personnel and Expenditures
ACTIVE DUTY PERSONNEL: 8
CIVILIAN PERSONNEL: 50

ROMULUS

SENECA ARMY DEPOT
Romulus, NY 14541
(607) 869-1110; Autovon 489-5110
Profile
BRANCH: Army.
SIZE AND LOCATION: 11,000 acres. On NY Rte 96 & 96A; 16 mi SE of Geneva, NY; 55 mi SE of Rochester; 50 mi SW of Syracuse; 35 mi N of Ithaca; 17 mi S of NY State Thruway.
MAJOR UNITS: 295th Military Police Company; 833rd Ordnance Company; Headquarters & Headquarters Company; US Army Readiness Group-Seneca; US Coast Guard LORAN-C Station, Seneca.
BASE HISTORY: 1941, established records for speed of construction broken. 1956, expansion included Sampson Air Force Base and development of special weapons site (North Depot Activity). 1963, transferred from Chief of Ordnance to US Army Supply and Maintenance Command; renamed Seneca Army Depot. 1966, reassigned to US Army Materiel Command (later DARCOM). 1976, DESCOM activated with command and control over all DARCOM depots.
Key Contacts
COMMANDER: Col William B Holmes; (607) 869-1206, Autovon 489-5206.
PUBLIC AFFAIRS: Robert S Zemanek Jr; (607) 869-1235, Autovon 489-5235.
PROCUREMENT: Shirley Kaufman; (607) 869-1317, Autovon 489-5317.
TRANSPORTATION: Maj J Baker; (607) 869-1350, Autovon 489-5350.
PERSONNEL/COMMUNITY ACTIVITIES: Bruce Johnson; (607) 869-0447, Autovon 489-8447.
Personnel and Expenditures
ACTIVE DUTY PERSONNEL: 600
DEPENDENTS: 375
CIVILIAN PERSONNEL: 1100
MILITARY PAYROLL EXPENDITURE: $16 mil
CONTRACT EXPENDITURE: $14 mil
Services *Housing:* Family units 180; Barracks spaces 300. *Temporary Housing:* Mobile home units 12; Camper spaces 6. *Commissary:* Base commissary; Retail store; Barber shop. *Child Care/Capacities:* Day care center 60. *Base Library:* Yes. *Medical Facilities:* Medical clinic; Dental clinic. *Recreational Facilities:* Bowling; Movie theater; Pool; Gym; Recreation center; Tennis; Racquetball; Fitness center; Softball field; Football field; Auto shop; Crafts; Officers club; NCO club; Camping; Fishing/Hunting.

ROSLYN

ROSLYN AIR NATIONAL GUARD STATION
Roslyn, NY 11576
(516) 299-5201; Autovon 456-5201
Profile
BRANCH: Air National Guard.
SIZE AND LOCATION: 50.3 acres. 27 mi E of New York City, on Long Island.
MAJOR UNITS: 152nd Tactical Control Group; 213th Engineering Installation Squadron; Army National Guard.
Personnel and Expenditures
ACTIVE DUTY PERSONNEL: 499
CIVILIAN PERSONNEL: 43

SCHENECTADY

109TH TACTICAL AIRLIFT GROUP (ANG)
Schenectady County Airport, Schenectady, NY 12302
(518) 372-5621; Autovon 974-9221
Profile
BRANCH: Air National Guard.
SIZE AND LOCATION: 106 acres. 2 mi N of Schenectady, off State Rte 50.
MAJOR UNITS: 109th Tactical Airlift Group (ANG).
Personnel and Expenditures
ACTIVE DUTY PERSONNEL: 782
CIVILIAN PERSONNEL: 182
MILITARY PAYROLL EXPENDITURE: $7.8 mil
Services *Medical Facilities:* Dispensary.

SOCTIA

SOCTIA NAVAL ADMINISTRATIVE UNIT
Soctia, NY 12302
(518) 374-0124
Profile
BRANCH: Navy.
LOCATION: 3 mi W of Schenectady, NY, on Rte 5.
MAJOR UNITS: Navy Recruiting Area One; Navy Readiness Command Region Two; Personnel Support Detachment.
Personnel and Expenditures
ACTIVE DUTY PERSONNEL: 2500
DEPENDENTS: 3000
Services *Commissary:* Base commissary; Small exchange. *Medical Facilities:* Medical clinic; Dental clinic.

STATEN ISLAND

NAVAL STATION NEW YORK (STATEN ISLAND)
Staten Island, NY 10305
Profile
BRANCH: Navy.
LOCATION: 20 city driving miles across Verrazano Narrows Bridge from NS NY, Brooklyn.
MAJOR UNITS: Homeport Northeast Battleship Battlegroup.
BASE HISTORY: Scheduled to take over functions of NS NY (Brooklyn).
Personnel and Expenditures
ACTIVE DUTY PERSONNEL: 900
DEPENDENTS: 1261
Services *Housing:* Family units 440; Additional housing at Mitchel Field & Floyd Bennett Field. *Temporary Housing:* VIP cottages 4; Guesthouse units 1. *Commissary and Exchange:* Military clothing sales; Small ex-

NAVAL STATION NEW YORK (STATEN IS-LAND) *(continued)*
change. *Child Care/Capacities:* At Mitchel Field. *Medical Facilities:* Medical clinic. *Recreational Facilities:* Gym; Fitness center.

SYRACUSE

174TH TACTICAL FIGHTER WING (ANG)
Hancock Field, Syracuse, NY 13211
(315) 458-5500; Autovon 587-9110
Profile
BRANCH: Air National Guard.
SIZE AND LOCATION: 443 acres. 5 mi NE of Syracuse, exit 27, off I-81.
MAJOR UNITS: 174th Tactical Fighter Wing (ANG); Base Operations for Hancock AFB, NORAD site.
Personnel and Expenditures
ACTIVE DUTY PERSONNEL: 968
CIVILIAN PERSONNEL: 258
MILITARY PAYROLL EXPENDITURE: $9.5 mil
Services *Medical Facilities:* Dispensary.

WATERVLIET

WATERVLIET ARSENAL
Watervliet, NY 12189-4050
(518) 266-5111; Autovon 974-5111
Profile
BRANCH: Army.
SIZE AND LOCATION: 140 acres. 7 mi N of Albany, NY, across Hudson River from Troy, NY, 6 mi from Albany Co. Airport.
MAJOR UNITS: Watervliet Arsenal; Benet Laboratories.
VISITOR ATTRACTIONS: Watervliet Arsenal Museum: history of cannon development; Arsenal on National Historic Register; Site of Erie Canal; 19th Century manufacturing buildings.
Key Contacts
COMMANDER: Col Joseph H Mayton Jr; (518) 266-4294, Autovon 974-4294.
PUBLIC AFFAIRS: John Swantek; (518) 266-5090 266-5418, Autovon 974-5090 974-5418.
Personnel and Expenditures
ACTIVE DUTY PERSONNEL: 22
DEPENDENTS: 60
CIVILIAN PERSONNEL: 2500
CONTRACT EXPENDITURE: $100 mil
Services *Housing:* Family units 24. *Commissary and Exchange:* Retail store. *Base Library:* Yes. *Medical Facilities:* Medical clinic. *Recreational Facilities:* Pool; Gym; Golf; Tennis; Racquetball; Fitness center; Softball field; Crafts; Officers club.

WEST POINT

UNITED STATES MILITARY ACADEMY
West Point, NY 10996-5000
(914) 938-4011; Autovon 688-1110
OFFICER-OF-THE-DAY: (914) 938-3500, Autovon 688-3500
Profile
BRANCH: Army.
SIZE AND LOCATION: 16,625 acres. Approx 50 mi from New York City; take New York Thruway N Exit 16 and follow US-6 E to Rte 293, signs to Academy clearly marked.
MAJOR UNITS: United States Corps of Cadets; 1st Battalion, 1st Infantry; Keller Army Hospital.
BASE HISTORY: Since 1802, West Point and US Military Academy have become synonymous titles. Nation's oldest service academy operated at historic site of nation's oldest military post in continuous

operation. 1778, permanent garrison of Revolutionary troops stationed here on Hudson River. Mar 16, 1802, marks birth of Military Academy; opened with 10 cadets. US Corps of Cadets, approx 4400, organized as brigade of four regiments. Cadets members of Regular Army; receive about half of basic pay of 2 Lt; pay for uniforms, textbooks, and incidentals; quarters, rations, and medical care provided. Training includes: field and classroom instruction in military skills, an intensive physical education program, and practical and classroom training in leadership. During academic year, formal military instruction limited to 2 hours per week and devoted primarily to theory and classroom work; practical, field type military training conducted in summer.
VISITOR ATTRACTIONS: National Monument; New Museum; Dress Parades, dates and times change by season, for info (914) 938-2638; New Visitors Information Center.
Key Contacts
COMMANDER: Lt Gen Dave R Palmer; Superintendent, (914) 938-2610, Autovon 688-2610.
PUBLIC AFFAIRS: Col James N Hawthorne; Directorate of Academy Relations, Bldg 600, Rm A, West Point, NY 10996-1788, (914) 938-2006, Autovon 688-2006.
PROCUREMENT: Maj Randolph Barta; Director of Purchasing and Contracting, Bldg 667A, (914) 938-3417, Autovon 688-3417.
TRANSPORTATION: LTC Ernest Poland; Bldg 626, (914) 938-2900, Autovon 688-2900.
PERSONNEL/COMMUNITY ACTIVITIES: LTC James Flowers; Bldg 622, (914) 938-2022, Autovon 688-2022.
Personnel and Expenditures
ACTIVE DUTY PERSONNEL: 1303
DEPENDENTS: 3500
CIVILIAN PERSONNEL: 2246
Services *Housing:* Family units 1530; BOQ cottages 121; Barracks spaces; Data for both West Point and Stewart Army Sub-post. *Temporary Housing:* VIP cottages (West Point Hotel Thayer; suites 8; rooms 196); Stewart Army Sub-Post 5-Star Inn 52 rooms. *Commissary:* Base commissary; Retail store; Barber shop; Dry cleaners; Food shop; Florist; Banking; Service station; Book store; Ice cream; Shoe repair. *Child Care/Capacities:* Day care center; Home day care program. *Schools:* Kindergarten/Preschool; Elementary. *Base Library:* Yes. *Medical Facilities:* Hospital; Medical clinic; Dental clinic. *Recreational Facilities:* Bowling; Movie theater; Pool; Gym; Golf; Stables; Tennis; Racquetball; Skating rink; Softball field; Football field; Auto shop; Crafts; Officers club; NCO club; Camping; Fishing/Hunting; Picnicking; Snow sports; Rod and Gun Club; Equipment rental.

WESTHAMPTON BEACH

106TH AEROSPACE RESCUE AND RECOVERY GROUP (ANG)
Suffolk County Airport, Westhampton Beach, NY 11978
(516) 288-4200; Autovon 456-7210
Profile
BRANCH: Air National Guard.
SIZE AND LOCATION: 70 acres. Within corporate limits of Westhampton Beach, on Long Island, off State Rte 31.
MAJOR UNITS: 106th Aerospace Rescue and Recovery Group (ANG).
Personnel and Expenditures
ACTIVE DUTY PERSONNEL: 743
CIVILIAN PERSONNEL: 171
MILITARY PAYROLL EXPENDITURE: $7.1 mil

WHITE PLAINS

105TH TACTICAL AIR SUPPORT GROUP (ANG)
Westchester County Airport, White Plains, NY 10604
(914) 946-9511; Autovon 456-9210
Profile
BRANCH: Air National Guard.
SIZE AND LOCATION: 692 acres. 8 mi NE of White Plains, off I-684 at the NY-CT state line.
MAJOR UNITS: 105th Tactical Air Support Group (ANG).
Personnel and Expenditures
ACTIVE DUTY PERSONNEL: 611
CIVILIAN PERSONNEL: 166
MILITARY PAYROLL EXPENDITURE: $9.3 mil
Services *Medical Facilities:* Dispensary.

NORTH CAROLINA

CAMP LEJEUNE

CAMP LEJEUNE MARINE CORPS BASE
Camp Lejeune, NC 28542
(919) 451-1113; Autovon 484-1113
OFFICER-OF-THE-DAY: (919) 451-2528, Autovon 484-2528
Profile
BRANCH: Marines.
SIZE AND LOCATION: 110,000 acres. Off Hwy 24, E of Jacksonville, NC.
MAJOR UNITS: II Marine Expeditionary Force (MEF); 2d Marine Division; 6th Marine Expeditionary Brigade; 2d Force Service Support Group (REIN); Marine Corps Support Schools (Staff NCO Academy, NCO School, Instructional Management School); Marine Corps Engineer School; School of Infantry; Field Medical Service School; MCAS New River; Naval Hospital, Camp Lejeune; Naval Dental Clinic.
BASE HISTORY: 1930s, selection board decided on New River area of NC as ideal location for new Marine training base. 1941, construction of Marine Barracks, New River. 1942, renamed for 13th Commandant of Marine Corps, Lt Gen John A Lejeune. The Camp Lejeune/New River complex, known as "The World's Most Complete Amphibious Training Base," is largest concentration of Marines and Sailors.
VISITOR ATTRACTIONS: Beirut Memorial; Grenada Memorial.
Key Contacts
COMMANDER: Brig Gen Donald Gardner; (919) 451-2526, Autovon 484-2526.
PUBLIC AFFAIRS: Maj Stu Wagner; Joint Public Affairs Office, PO Box 8438, (919) 451-1607, Autovon 484-1607.
PROCUREMENT: Contracting Officer; (919) 451-5520, Autovon 484-5520.
TRANSPORTATION: (919) 451-5019, Autovon 484-5019.
PERSONNEL/COMMUNITY ACTIVITIES: See Public Affairs Officer.
Personnel and Expenditures
ACTIVE DUTY PERSONNEL: 41,200
DEPENDENTS: 12,000
CIVILIAN PERSONNEL: 5000
MILITARY PAYROLL EXPENDITURE: FY 88, $433 mil
CONTRACT EXPENDITURE: FY 88, $102 mil
Services *Housing:* Family units 4453; BOQ cottages 19; BEQ units 233; Trailer spaces 112. *Temporary Housing:* VOQ cottages 193; Apartment units 90; Transient living quarters 1392. *Commissary:* Base commissary; Retail store; Barber shop; Dry cleaners; Food shop; Florist; Banking; Service station; Bakery. *Child Care/Capacities:* Day care center 360. *Schools:* Elementary; Intermediate/Junior high; High school. *Base Library:* Yes. *Medical Facilities:* Hospital 265; Dental clinic. *Recreational Facilities:* Bowling; Movie theater; Pool; Gym; Recreation center; Golf; Stables; Tennis; Racquetball; Fitness center; Softball field; Football field; Auto shop; Crafts; Officers club; NCO club; Camping; Fishing/Hunting.

CHARLOTTE

145TH TACTICAL AIRLIFT GROUP
5225 Morris Field Dr, Charlotte, NC 28208-5797
(704) 391-4100; Autovon 583-4100
Profile
BRANCH: Air National Guard.
LOCATION: At the Charlotte/Douglas IAP.
MAJOR UNITS: 145th Tactical Airlift Group.
Key Contacts
COMMANDER: Col William D Lackey; (704) 391-4145, Autovon 583-4145.
PUBLIC AFFAIRS: 1st Lt Robert M "Mike" Lee; (704) 391-4141, Autovon 583-4141.
PERSONNEL/COMMUNITY ACTIVITIES: LTC Allen E Massey; (704) 391-4170, Autovon 583-4170.

145TH TACTICAL AIRLIFT GROUP (ANG)
Douglas Municipal Airport, Charlotte, NC 28219
(704) 399-6363; Autovon 583-9210
Profile
BRANCH: Air National Guard.
SIZE AND LOCATION: 49 acres. SW of the intersection of I-85 and Billy Graham Pkwy.
MAJOR UNITS: 145th Tactical Airlift Group (ANG).
Personnel and Expenditures
ACTIVE DUTY PERSONNEL: 952
CIVILIAN PERSONNEL: 184
MILITARY PAYROLL EXPENDITURE: $9.4 mil
Services *Medical Facilities:* 4-bed dispensary.

CHERRY POINT

CHERRY POINT MARINE CORPS AIR STATION
Cherry Point, NC 28533
(919) 466-5236; Autovon 582-5236
OFFICER-OF-THE-DAY: (919) 466-5236, Autovon 582-5236
Profile
BRANCH: Marines.
SIZE AND LOCATION: 11,717 acres (plus 15,980 acres support locations). Midway between New Bern and Morehead City, NC. Main gate off NC Hwy 101, connects with US-70. Adj to city of Havelock and Simmons-Nott Airport, Newbern.
MAJOR UNITS: 2d Marine Aircraft Wing (MAW); Marine Aircraft Group 14; Marine Aircraft Group 32; Marine Wing Support Group 27; Marine Air Control Group 28; 2d Marine Aircraft Wing Band; Naval Aviation Depot; Naval Hospital Cherry Point; Marine Aviation Logistics Squadron 41, Detachment C; Marine Wing Support Squadron 474, Detachment B; Fleet Aviation Specialized Operational Training Group Atlantic (FASO).
BASE HISTORY: 1941, clearing of site began with extensive drainage and malaria control work. 1942, air station commissioned as Cunningham Field, for Marine Corps' first aviator, Lt Alfred A Cunningham. 1946, 2nd Marine Aircraft Wing replaced 9th MAW. 1950, became more active with reservists reporting for duty, schooling, refresher courses and training. Currently, world's largest Marine Corps Air Station and all-weather jet base.
Key Contacts
COMMANDER: Brig Gen C L Vermilyea; (919) 466-2847, Autovon 582-2847.
PUBLIC AFFAIRS: Capt Keith Oliver; Joint Public Affairs Office MCAS, Cherry Point, NC 28533-5001, (919) 466-4241, Autovon 582-4241.
PROCUREMENT: Wesley Morris; (919) 466-5959, Autovon 582-5959.
TRANSPORTATION: Roaimie D Garner; (919) 466-2301, 466-2643, Autovon 582-2301, 582-2643.
PERSONNEL/COMMUNITY ACTIVITIES: Ann Govgen; (919) 466-2301, 466-2643, Autovon 582-2301, 582-2643.
Personnel and Expenditures
ACTIVE DUTY PERSONNEL: 11,000
DEPENDENTS: 32,323
CIVILIAN PERSONNEL: 4839
MILITARY PAYROLL EXPENDITURE: $123 mil
CONTRACT EXPENDITURE: $183 mil
Services *Housing:* Family units 2690; Mobile home units 76. *Temporary Housing:* VIP cottages 4; BOQ units 78; Guesthouse units 1; Transient living quarters 79. *Commissary:* Base commissary; Retail store; Barber shop; Dry cleaners; Food shop; Florist; Banking; Service station; Video rental; Photo finishing; Package beverages; Optical shop; Ice cream. *Child Care/Capacities:* Day care center. *Base Library:* Yes. *Medical Facilities:* Hospital 43; Dental clinic; Veterinary clinic. *Recreational Facilities:* Bowling; Movie theater; Pool; Gym; Golf; Stables; Tennis; Fitness center; Softball field; Auto shop; Crafts; Officers club; Fishing/Hunting.

ELIZABETH CITY

ELIZABETH CITY COAST GUARD AIR STATION
Elizabeth City, NC 27909
(919) 335-6332; Autovon 723-6540
OFFICER-OF-THE-DAY: (919) 335-6332, Autovon 723-6540

ELIZABETH CITY COAST GUARD AIR STATION (continued)
Profile
BRANCH: Coast Guard.

SIZE AND LOCATION: 800 acres. Follow Hwy 34 from US-17 S; approx 6 mi E of Elizabeth City, NC.

MAJOR UNITS: Coast Guard Air Station; Aviation Repair and Supply Center; Support Center; Aviation Technical Training Command.

Key Contacts
COMMANDER: Capt William W Barker; (919) 335-6360.

PUBLIC AFFAIRS: LTjg Paul Lange; (919) 335-6361.

PROCUREMENT: Lt Sig Kirchner; (919) 335-6576.

TRANSPORTATION: LTjg Norm O'Melia; (919) 335-6326.

PERSONNEL/COMMUNITY ACTIVITIES: LTjg Randy Moseng; (919) 335-6468.

Personnel and Expenditures
ACTIVE DUTY PERSONNEL: 800

DEPENDENTS: 20

CIVILIAN PERSONNEL: 200

Services *Housing:* Family units; BEQ units; Mobile home units; Trailer spaces. *Commissary and Exchange:* Retail store; Barber shop; Banking; Service station. *Base Library:* Yes. *Medical Facilities:* Medical clinic; Dental clinic. *Recreational Facilities:* Pool; Gym; Tennis; Softball field; Football field; Officers club; NCO club; Fishing/Hunting.

ELIZABETH CITY COAST GUARD AIRCRAFT REPAIR & SUPPLY CENTER
Elizabeth City, NC 27909-5001

(919) 335-6212; Autovon 723-3390

OFFICER-OF-THE-DAY: (919) 335-6289

Profile
BRANCH: Coast Guard.

SIZE AND LOCATION: 55 acres. Follow Hwy 34 from US-17 S; approx 6 mi E of Elizabeth City, NC.

MAJOR UNITS: Aircraft Repair and Supply Center.

BASE HISTORY: 1946, established along Pasquotank River as tenant activity of Coast Guard Support Center, Elizabeth City, NC. AR&SC originally envisioned as central supply activity and overhaul unit for USCG aviation; now assigned responsibility for overhaul, major repair, modification of aircraft and aeronautical equipment, technical assistance including field repair team visits, and performs engineering studies prototype, kit design and installation.

Key Contacts
COMMANDER: Capt Joseph P Coleman; (919) 335-6191, Autovon 723-3390.

PUBLIC AFFAIRS: LCDR Melville B Guttormsen; (919) 335-6292, Autovon 723-3390.

PROCUREMENT: Rogelio Ramirez; (919) 335-6436, Autovon 723-3390.

TRANSPORTATION: SKCS Albilo M Lansangan; (919) 335-6485, Autovon 723-3390.

PERSONNEL/COMMUNITY ACTIVITIES: See Public Affairs Officer.

Personnel and Expenditures
ACTIVE DUTY PERSONNEL: 123

CIVILIAN PERSONNEL: 377

Services *Housing:* See Elizabeth City Coast Guard Air Station. *Commissary and Exchange:* Retail store; Barber shop; Banking; Service station. *Base Library:* Yes. *Medical Facilities:* Medical clinic; Dental clinic. *Recreational Facilities:* Pool; Gym; Tennis; Softball field; Football field; Officers club; NCO club; Fishing/Hunting.

FORT BRAGG

FORT BRAGG
XVIII Airborne Corps and Fort Bragg, Fort Bragg, NC 28307

(919) 396-0011; Autovon 236-0011

OFFICER-OF-THE-DAY: (919) 396-6100, Autovon 236-6100

Profile
BRANCH: Army.

SIZE AND LOCATION: 148,618 acres. On NC Rte 24, approx 10 mi W of Fayetteville, NC; 60 mi S of Raleigh, NC.

MAJOR UNITS: XVIII Airborne Corps; First Special Operations Command; John F Kennedy Special Warfare Center and School; First Corps Support Command; 16th Military Police Brigade; Womack Army Community Hospital; XVIII Airborne Corps Artillery; US Army Parachute Team (Golden Knights); 20th Engineer Brigade; 35th Signal Brigade; US Army First Region, ROTC Cadet Command; Readiness Group Bragg; Airborne Board; US Army Information Systems Command; 525th Military Intelligence Brigade; Dragon Brigade; 18th Aviation Brigade; 18th Corps Finance Group; Central Command; 1st Reserve Officers Training Corps Support Command; 18th Field Artillery Brigade.

BASE HISTORY: 1918, designated as Camp Bragg, field artillery site, named for Confederate Gen Braxton Bragg, artillery officer and North Carolinian. 1922, made permanent Army post and redesignated Ft Bragg. 1934, first military parachute jump. 1942, all five WWII airborne divisions trained in Ft Bragg-Camp Mackall area. Nearby Camp Mackall, established 1943, major training facility until 1948. 1946, 82nd Airborne assigned. 1951, XVIII Airborne Corps reactivated and fort became known as "Home of the Airborne." 1952, Psychological Warfare Center (now 1st Special Operations Command) established and fort became HQs for special forces. 1973, came under US Army Forces Command HQ at Ft McPherson, GA. Ft Bragg and neighboring Pope AFB form one of world's largest military complexes.

VISITOR ATTRACTIONS: 82nd Airborne Division Museum; JFK Special Warfare Museum.

Key Contacts
COMMANDER: Lt Gen Carl W Stiner; Commander, XVIII Airborne Corps and Ft Bragg, (919) 396-6100, Autovon 236-6100.

PUBLIC AFFAIRS: Maj N Baxter Ennis; ATTN: AFZA-PAO, Ft Bragg, (919) 396-2920, Autovon 236-2920.

PROCUREMENT: R Lawing; ATTN: AFZA-DC, Ft Bragg, (919) 396-2703, Autovon 236-2703.

TRANSPORTATION: M Truelove; ATTN: AFZA-DL, Ft Bragg, (919) 396-5212, Autovon 236-5212.

PERSONNEL/COMMUNITY ACTIVITIES: Col J W Loffert; ATTN: AFZA-PA, Ft Bragg, (919) 396-2407, Autovon 236-2407.

Personnel and Expenditures
ACTIVE DUTY PERSONNEL: 37,747

DEPENDENTS: 11,318

CIVILIAN PERSONNEL: 4296

MILITARY PAYROLL EXPENDITURE: $779.5 mil

CONTRACT EXPENDITURE: $158.9 mil

Services *Housing:* Family units 4842; BOQ cottages 148; Duplex units 966; Townhouse units 2868; Barracks spaces 18,186; Senior NCO units 32. *Temporary Housing:* VIP cottages 3; Guesthouse units 119; Guest cottages 14; VOQ, VEQ, VAQ, BOQ, BAQ, 547. *Commissary:* Base commissary; Retail store; Barber shop; Dry cleaners; Food shop;

Florist; Banking; Service station; Bakery. *Child Care/Capacities:* Day care center; Home day care program. *Schools:* Kindergarten/Preschool; Elementary; Intermediate/Junior high. *Base Library:* Yes. *Medical Facilities:* Hospital 310; Medical clinic; Dental clinic. *Recreational Facilities:* Bowling; Movie theater; Pool; Gym; Recreation center; Golf; Stables; Tennis; Racquetball; Skating rink; Fitness center; Softball field; Football field; Auto shop; Crafts; Officers club; NCO club; Camping; Fishing/Hunting.

GOLDSBORO

SEYMOUR JOHNSON AIR FORCE BASE
Goldsboro, NC 27531-5000

(919) 736-5400; Autovon 488-5400

Profile
BRANCH: Air Force.

SIZE AND LOCATION: 4113 acres. Right off Hwy 70, in the corporate limits of Goldsboro, NC; approx 26 mi W of Kinston, NC Airport; approx 60 mi E of Raleigh, NC.

MAJOR UNITS: 4th Tactical Fighter Wing; 68th Air Refueling Wing; 916th Air Refueling Group (AFRES); 2012th Communication Squadron.

BASE HISTORY: 1942, Seymour Johnson Field, activated as HQ, Technical School, Army Air Forces Technical Training Command; named for Navy Lt Seymour Andrew Johnson, native of Goldsboro, killed in aircraft crash. 1943, Provisional Overseas Replacement Training Center added to prepare troops for overseas duty; Aviation Cadet Pre-Training School established for basic military training of cadets. Near end WWII, designated Central Assembly Station for processing and training troops reassigned. 1945, Army Air Force Separation Center. 1946-52, inactive. 1952, city transferred base to federal government. 1956, Seymour Johnson AFB reactivated as TAC base. 1957, 4th Fighter-Day Wing (redesignated 4th TFW) replaced 83rd Fighter-Day Wing.

Key Contacts
COMMANDER: Col John O McFalls III; Wing Commander, 4TFW/CC, (919) 736-6481, Autovon 488-6481.

PUBLIC AFFAIRS: Capt Paul R Wilson; 4TFW/PA, Seymour Johnson AFB, NC 27531-5004, (919) 736-5411, Autovon 488-5411.

TRANSPORTATION: Capt James Rainey; 4LGT/CC, (919) 736-5237, Autovon 488-5237.

PERSONNEL/COMMUNITY ACTIVITIES: Col Linda Barnes; Director of Personnel, 4MSS/CC, (919) 736-6492, Autovon 488-6492.

Personnel and Expenditures
ACTIVE DUTY PERSONNEL: 4832

DEPENDENTS: 7035

CIVILIAN PERSONNEL: 1007

MILITARY PAYROLL EXPENDITURE: $106.7 mil

CONTRACT EXPENDITURE: $26 mil

Services *Housing:* Family units 1697; Dormitory spaces 1515. *Temporary Housing:* VOQ cottages 44; VAQ units 83; Transient living quarters 37. *Commissary:* Base commissary; Retail store; Barber shop; Dry cleaners; Food shop; Florist; Service station. *Child Care/Capacities:* Day care center. *Schools:* Before and after school program. *Base Library:* Yes. *Medical Facilities:* Hospital 20; Dental clinic. *Recreational Facilities:* Bowling; Movie theater; Pool; Gym; Recreation center; Golf; Tennis; Racquetball; Fitness center; Softball field; Auto shop; Crafts; Officers club; NCO club.

JACKSONVILLE

NEW RIVER MARINE CORPS AIR STATION
Jacksonville, NC 28545
(919) 451-6197; 451-6198; 451-6196;
Autovon 484-6197; 484-6198; 484-6196
OFFICER-OF-THE-DAY: (919) 451-6524,
Autovon 484-6524
Profile
BRANCH: Marines.
SIZE AND LOCATION: 4000 acres. Adj to Hwy US-17, S of Jacksonville, NC.
MAJOR UNITS: Marine Air Group (MAG)-29; Marine Air Group (MAG)-26.
BASE HISTORY: 1944, initially commissioned as Peterfield Point. End of WWII, closed. 1951, reactivated as air facility. Under concurrent jurisdiction of station is outlying field at Camp Davis, Holly Ridge. 1972, airfield named McCutcheon Field for Gen Keith Barr McCutcheon. Since 1974, many support functions, including transportation and maintenance consolidated with and under control of Camp Lejeune. 1985, MCAS (Helicopter), New River redesignated as Air Station.
VISITOR ATTRACTIONS: The last UH-34 "Sea Horse" helicopter, used in Vietnam War, on display at main gate.
Key Contacts
COMMANDER: Col D W Nelson.
PUBLIC AFFAIRS: Capt Scott B Jack.
Personnel and Expenditures
ACTIVE DUTY PERSONNEL: 5143
DEPENDENTS: 7572
CIVILIAN PERSONNEL: 238
Services *Housing:* Family units 435; BEQ units; BAQ units; Duplex units; Barracks spaces; Senior NCO units 51; Junior NCO units. *Temporary Housing:* BOQ units 44; Transient living quarters. *Commissary:* Base commissary; Retail store; Barber shop; Dry cleaners; Food shop; Florist; Banking; Service station. *Child Care/Capacities:* Day care center. *Schools:* Elementary. *Base Library:* Yes. *Medical Facilities:* Medical clinic; Dental clinic. *Recreational Facilities:* Bowling; Movie theater; Pool; Gym; Tennis; Racquetball; Fitness center; Softball field; Football field; Auto shop; Crafts; Officers club; NCO club; Camping; Fishing/Hunting.

KURE BEACH

FORT FISHER AIR FORCE STATION
Kure Beach, NC 28449
(919) 458-8251
Profile
BRANCH: Air Force.
MAJOR UNITS: Fort Fisher AFS (TAC).

FORT FISHER RECREATION AREA
PO Box 380, Kure Beach, NC 28449
(919) 458-6549; Autovon 488-3011; Ft Fisher 488-6549
Profile
BRANCH: Air Force.
SIZE AND LOCATION: 58 acres. 20 mi S of Wilmington, NC on Hwy US-421.
MAJOR UNITS: Outdoor Recreation; MWR Division.
BASE HISTORY: Constructed at beginning of Civil War. Located at mouth of Cape Fear River, kept Wilmington Port secure until last month of Civil War. 1953, Ft Fisher AFB opened. 1988, deactivated and converted to outdoor recreation area of Myrtle Beach AFB, SC.
VISITOR ATTRACTIONS: Ft Fisher Civil War Museum; Battleship *North Carolina*; NC State Aquarium; Beach activities; Several area golf courses; Special off-season rates in effect from Nov 1 thru Mar 31.

Key Contacts
COMMANDER: Larry L Day; MWR Site Manager, (919) 458-6723, 458-6742, Autovon 488-3011, Ft Fisher 488-6723.
Personnel and Expenditures
CIVILIAN PERSONNEL: 15-30
Services *Temporary Housing:* Guest cottages 25; Apartment units 8; Lodge units 56; Famcamp spaces 23. *Commissary and Exchange:* General store. *Recreational Facilities:* Pool; Recreation center; Tennis; Racquetball; Fitness center; Softball field; Camping; Fishing/Hunting; River Front Cafe; Recreation equipment rental; Volleyball; Basketball.

POPE AFB

POPE AIR FORCE BASE
Pope AFB, NC 28308-5000
(919) 394-0001; Autovon 486-1110
OFFICER-OF-THE-DAY: (919) 394-4804, Autovon 486-4804
Profile
BRANCH: Air Force.
SIZE AND LOCATION: 1800 acres. Adj to Ft Bragg; 12 mi NW of Fayetteville, NC. From I-95 S, take Business I-95/US-310 exit into Fayetteville, then take right on NC-24 (Bragg Blvd) to Ft Bragg and Pope. From I-95 N, take Business I-95/US-301 exit onto Fayetteville, take left on Owen Dr to All American Expy to Reilly Rd exit which goes to Reilly Rd gate.
MAJOR UNITS: 317th Tactical Airlift Wing; 317th Combat Support Group; USAF Airlift Center; 1943rd Communications Squadron (AFCC); 1721st Combat Control Squadron; OLC 1361st Audiovisual Squadron; 1st Aeromedical Evacuation Squadron; Detachment 3 MACOS (Combat Control School); 215th Field Training Detachment; Detachment 21, 15th Weather Wing; Detachment 12, 1600th Management Engineering Squadron; Area Defense Counsel (HQ USAF); Detachment 2101, AFOSI; Detachment 1, TAIRCW (USA); 1724th Combat Control Squadron; 53rd Mobile Aerial Port Squadron (Reserve); 915th Civil Engineering Squadron (Reserve).
BASE HISTORY: 1918, Pope Field began flights. 1919, Pope Field established (one of oldest installations in USAF) and named after 1st Lt Harley Halbert Pope killed in air crash near Fayetteville. WWII, air and ground crews trained for troop carrier and aerial resupply duty. Korean Conflict, 464th Troop Carrier Wing moved from Lawson AFB, GA. Vietnam Conflict, 317th TAW pioneered development of Adverse Weather Aerial Delivery System (AWADS). 1974, Pope transferred from TAC to MAC and US Airlift Center established. 1983, provided bulk of AF effort in Grenada and served as primary staging site for operation.
VISITOR ATTRACTIONS: Closed to the public.
Key Contacts
COMMANDER: Col Richard R Heinzman; 317th Combat Support Group Commander; (919) 394-2304, Autovon 486-2304.
PUBLIC AFFAIRS: Capt Brian Irving; Chief of Public Affairs, (919) 394-4183, Autovon 486-4183.
PROCUREMENT: Capt Mary Quinn; Contracting Division, (919) 394-2161, Autovon 486-2161.
TRANSPORTATION: LTC Richard Kells; (919) 394-2546, Autovon 486-2546.
PERSONNEL/COMMUNITY ACTIVITIES: LTC Douglas Bishop; Director of Personnel, (919) 394-4748, Autovon 486-4748.
Personnel and Expenditures
ACTIVE DUTY PERSONNEL: 4350
DEPENDENTS: 6000
CIVILIAN PERSONNEL: 700

MILITARY PAYROLL EXPENDITURE: $92 mil
CONTRACT EXPENDITURE: $10 mil
Services *Housing:* Family units 459; BOQ cottages 6; Dormitory spaces 1348. *Temporary Housing:* VOQ cottages 176; VAQ units 140. *Commissary:* Base commissary; Retail store; Barber shop; Dry cleaners; Banking; Service station. *Child Care/Capacities:* Day care center. *Schools:* Elementary. *Base Library:* Yes. *Medical Facilities:* Medical clinic; Dental clinic. *Recreational Facilities:* Bowling; Movie theater; Pool; Gym; Recreation center; Golf; Tennis; Racquetball; Fitness center; Softball field; Auto shop; Crafts; Officers club; NCO club.

RALEIGH

NAVAL & MARINE CORPS RESERVE CENTER
2725 Western Blvd, Raleigh, NC 27606-2127
(919) 834-6461
Profile
BRANCH: Navy.
SIZE AND LOCATION: 4.5 acres. Across from NC State Univ on Western Blvd which runs approx 2 mi off exit US-1 (Raleigh Beltline).
Key Contacts
COMMANDER: CDR Fred L Cohrs.
PUBLIC AFFAIRS: Lt Phillip B McGuinn.
PROCUREMENT: SK1 Donald A Harvey.
PERSONNEL/COMMUNITY ACTIVITIES: EMC Steven E Lehner.
Personnel and Expenditures
ACTIVE DUTY PERSONNEL: 35
CIVILIAN PERSONNEL: 2
Services *Temporary Housing:* Several commercial hotels in the area. *Medical Facilities:* Use: Seymour Johnson AFB, Womack Army Hospital, Camp Lejeune, NRMC.

RESEARCH TRIANGLE PARK

ARMY RESEARCH OFFICE
PO Box 12211, Research Triangle Park, NC 27709-2211
(919) 549-0641; Autovon 935-3331
Profile
BRANCH: Army.
SIZE AND LOCATION: 1 acre. Off I-40 at 4300 S Miami Blvd, exit 282; approx 14 mi equidistant from Raleigh, Durham, and Chapel Hill, NC; approx 5 mi E to Raleigh-Durham Airport.
MAJOR UNITS: Army Research Office.
BASE HISTORY: Evolved from US Army Office of Ordnance Research (OOR), Class II military installation established, 1951, Duke University. 1958, Research and Development Field Office, Ft Belvoir, redesignated US Army Research Office and moved to Arlington Hall Station, Arlington, VA. 1961, OOR transferred from Chief of Ordnance to Chief of Research and Development and redesignated US Army Research Office-Durham (AROD). AROD expanded to monitor programs in physical sciences Army-wide. 1973, ARO in Arlington discontinued and Office-Durham designated Army Research Office (ARO); 1974, transferred to AMC as separate reporting activity. 1975, ARO moved from Duke to Research Triangle Park. 1984, moved to present location. 1985, emergence of US Army Laboratory Command (LABCOM).
Key Contacts
COMMANDER: Dr George A Neece; Acting Director.
PUBLIC AFFAIRS: William W Roberts.
PROCUREMENT: Jack L Harless.

ARMY RESEARCH OFFICE *(continued)*
TRANSPORTATION: Frances H Harris.
PERSONNEL/COMMUNITY ACTIVITIES: Gerri
Rouse.
Personnel and Expenditures
ACTIVE DUTY PERSONNEL: 2
CIVILIAN PERSONNEL: 105
MILITARY PAYROLL EXPENDITURE: $56,000
CONTRACT EXPENDITURE: $78 mil

SOUTHPORT

**SUNNY POINT MILITARY OCEAN
TERMINAL**
Southport, NC 28461-5000
(919) 457-8230; Autovon 488-8230
Profile
BRANCH: Army.
SIZE AND LOCATION: 16,000 acres. 5 mi N of
Southport, NC, at the junction of NC Rte
87/133.
MAJOR UNITS: Military Traffic Management
Command Headquarters, Military Ocean
Terminal, Sunny Point; TRANS Brigade.
BASE HISTORY: 1955, activated with major
modifications completed in 1982 for con-
tainer movement and handling. Three
wharfs with two berths each; approx 100
mi of rail track, 50 mi of paved roads,
and 195,000 sq ft of building space.
VISITOR ATTRACTIONS: Closed to the public
except for official business.
Key Contacts
PUBLIC AFFAIRS: Myrtle D Meade.
Personnel and Expenditures
ACTIVE DUTY PERSONNEL: 13
CIVILIAN PERSONNEL: 253
MILITARY PAYROLL EXPENDITURE: $7.5 mil
CONTRACT EXPENDITURE: $3.5 mil
Services *Housing:* Family units 5. *Medical
Facilities:* Occupational health clinic.

NORTH DAKOTA

CAVALIER

CAVALIER AIR FORCE STATION
10 Missile Warning Squadron, Cavalier, ND 58220-5000
(701) 993-3292; Autovon 330-3292
Profile
BRANCH: Air Force.
SIZE AND LOCATION: 278 acres. In NE ND, approx 15 mi to W of Cavalier on Hwy 5; 100 mi N of Grand Forks, ND.
MAJOR UNITS: 10th Missile Warning Squadron.
BASE HISTORY: Originally acquisition radar portion of only operational anti-ballistic missile system, SAFEGUARD. 1976, all components of SAFEGUARD complex, with exception of PARCS radar, deactivated, due to 1972 Anti-Ballistic Missile Treaty. 1977, forerunner of present 10th Missile Warning Squadron began passing tactical warning and attack assessment data to Cheyenne Mountain. 1979, unit transferred to SAC. 1983, unit joined Air Force Space Command, first as Detachment 5, 1st Space Wing, and redesignated as 10th Missile Warning Squadron, 1st Space Wing, 1986.
Key Contacts
COMMANDER: LTC John H "Jack" Harris Jr; (701) 993-3297, Autovon 330-3297.
PUBLIC AFFAIRS: Lt John R Bystroff; (701) 993-3292, Autovon 330-3292.
PROCUREMENT: Capt Bitsky; 42nd AD/LGC, Grand Forks AFB, ND 58205, (701) 747-5252, Autovon 330-5252.
TRANSPORTATION: TSgt Roger Bence; (701) 993-3687, Autovon 330-3687.
PERSONNEL/COMMUNITY ACTIVITIES: TSgt Anthony Urban; (701) 993-3201, Autovon 330-3201.
Personnel and Expenditures
ACTIVE DUTY PERSONNEL: 27
DEPENDENTS: 31
CIVILIAN PERSONNEL: 151
Services *Housing:* Duplex units 6. *Temporary Housing:* BOQ units 12; BAQ units 14. *Commissary and Exchange:* Retail store; Dry cleaners; Food shop. *Base Library:* Yes. *Recreational Facilities:* Bowling; Gym; Recreation center; Racquetball; Softball field; Auto shop.

CONCRETE

CONCRETE MEWS
Concrete, ND 58221
Autovon 330-3297
Profile
BRANCH: Air Force.
MAJOR UNITS: Concrete MEWS.

FARGO

119TH FIGHTER INTERCEPTOR GROUP
Box 5536, Fargo, ND 58105-5536
(701) 237-6030; Autovon 362-8110
Profile
BRANCH: Air National Guard.
SIZE AND LOCATION: 140 acres. On NW edge of Fargo, ND; just N of corner of 19th Ave N and Univ Dr N, on 23rd Ave N.
MAJOR UNITS: 119th Fighter Interceptor Group; 119 CAMS; 119 USAF Clinic; 119 MSSQ; 119 CES; 119 SPF; 178 FIS; 119 RMS; 119 MSF; State Headquarters.
BASE HISTORY: 1947, organized. Assigned F-51 tactical aircraft during Korean Conflict and in Air Defense mission early 1950s. 1954, first jet fighter, F-94. 1959, assigned F-89J with nuclear weapons. Since then the "Happy Hooligans" progressed from F-102, F-101B, to present F-4D. Scheduled to receive F-16 in 1990.
Key Contacts
COMMANDER: Col Gary E Kaiser; Box 5536 NDANG/CC, (701) 241-7200, 241-7201, Autovon 362-8200, 362-8201.
PUBLIC AFFAIRS: Capt Dennis A Aune; 124 N Terrace c/o Oak Grove High School, Fargo, ND 58102, (701) 237-0210 (weekdays), Autovon 362-8125 (weekends).
PROCUREMENT: MSgt Dwight A Murphy; Box 5536, NDANG/LGC, (701) 241-7332, Autovon 362-8332.
TRANSPORTATION: MSgt DeLyle C Ishaug; Box 5536, NDANG/LGTT, (701) 241-7304, Autovon 362-8304.
PERSONNEL/COMMUNITY ACTIVITIES: Maj Conrad W Krabbenhoft; Box 5536, NDANG/DPM, (701) 241-7240, Autovon 362-8240.
Personnel and Expenditures
ACTIVE DUTY PERSONNEL: 2; 62 AGR, Title 32
CIVILIAN PERSONNEL: 279
MILITARY PAYROLL EXPENDITURE: $5.5 mil
CONTRACT EXPENDITURE: $0.1 mil
Services *Temporary Housing:* VIP cottages 1. *Commissary and Exchange:* Retail store. *Medical Facilities:* Medical clinic. *Recreational Facilities:* Fitness center; Softball field; Officers club; NCO club.

FINLEY

FINLEY AIR FORCE STATION
OLAC, 25NW ADS/DE, Finley, ND 58230-9791
Profile
BRANCH: Air Force.
LOCATION: In E ND.
BASE HISTORY: Operating Location Alpha Charlie, 25 North West Air Defense Sector/DE closed and in caretaker status. No military personnel stationed here currently.
Key Contacts
COMMANDER: Ralph E Bayman, Civ, USAF; Station Foreman.

FORTUNA AFS

FORTUNA AIR FORCE STATION
Fortuna AFS, ND 58844
(701) 834-2251
Profile
BRANCH: Air Force.
MAJOR UNITS: Fortuna AFS (TAC).

GRAND FORKS AFB

GRAND FORKS AIR FORCE BASE
42nd Air Division, Grand Forks AFB, ND 58205
(701) 747-3000; Autovon 362-3000
OFFICER-OF-THE-DAY: (701) 747-6711, Autovon 362-6711
Profile
BRANCH: Air Force.
SIZE AND LOCATION: 5422 acres. 16 mi W of Grand Forks, off Hwy 2.
MAJOR UNITS: 42nd Air Division; 842nd Combat Support Group; 842nd Security Police Group; 842nd Strategic Hospital; 319th Bombardment Wing; 321st Strategic Missile Wing; Area Defense Counsel, 4th Circuit; Defense Investigative Service; Defense Reutilization and Marketing Office; Detachment 3, 37th Aerospace Rescue and Recovery Squadron; Detachment 15, 26th Weather Squadron; Detachment 18, 3904th Management Engineering Squadron; Detachment 419, 3753rd Field Training Squadron; Detachment 506, AF Commissary Service; Detachment 228, AF Audit Agency; Detachment 1313, Office of Special Investigations; Operating Location C, 64th Flying Training Wing; 2152nd Communications Squadron; Operating Location FX, Rivet Mile; Operating Location EI, B1B SATAF.
BASE HISTORY: 1956, construction began for Air Defense Command (ADC) base. 1960, operations started with 18th FIS. 1963, SAC assumed control. 1964, home of first Minuteman II Wing. 1970, placed under operational control of 15th Air Force.

GRAND FORKS AIR FORCE BASE
(continued)

1988, following number of organizational changes, 42nd Air Division, under 8th Air Force, took operational control.

Key Contacts

COMMANDER: Brig Gen Patrick Caruana; 42nd Air Division Commander, (701) 747-4155, Autovon 362-4155.

PUBLIC AFFAIRS: Capt Thomas Pander III; 42nd AD/PA, (701) 747-5016, Autovon 362-5016.

PROCUREMENT: Capt Ken Bitsky; 42 AD/Contracting, (701) 747-5252, Autovon 362-5252.

TRANSPORTATION: LTC David Strom; 842nd TRANS/CC, (701) 747-3477, Autovon 362-3477.

PERSONNEL/COMMUNITY ACTIVITIES: Capt Robert Bronson; 842nd CSG/SS, (701) 747-3219, Autovon 362-3219.

Personnel and Expenditures

ACTIVE DUTY PERSONNEL: 5500
DEPENDENTS: 6000
CIVILIAN PERSONNEL: 1100
MILITARY PAYROLL EXPENDITURE: $162 mil
CONTRACT EXPENDITURE: $225 mil
Services *Housing:* Duplex units; Dormitory spaces; Trailer spaces; RV/Camper sites. *Temporary Housing:* VIP cottages; Dormitory units 1; Transient living quarters 2. *Commissary:* Base commissary; Retail store; Barber shop; Dry cleaners; Food shop; Florist; Banking; Service station; Book store. *Child Care/Capacities:* Day care center; Home day care program. *Schools:* Kindergarten/Preschool; Elementary; Intermediate/Junior high. *Base Library:* Yes. *Medical Facilities:* Hospital 50; Medical clinic; Dental clinic. *Recreational Facilities:* Bowling; Movie theater; Pool; Gym; Recreation center; Golf; Stables; Tennis; Racquetball; Skating rink; Fitness center; Softball field; Football field; Auto shop; Crafts; Officers club; NCO club.

MINOT AFB

MINOT AIR FORCE BASE

Minot AFB, ND 58705-5000
(701) 723-1110; Autovon 344-1110

Profile

BRANCH: Air Force.

SIZE AND LOCATION: 24,420 acres. 13 mi N of Minot, ND, on US Hwy 83.

MAJOR UNITS: 57th Air Division; 91st Strategic Missile Wing (SMW); 5th Bombardment Wing.

BASE HISTORY: 1957, opened as Air Defense Command installation; 4136th Strategic Wing first SAC unit provided aerial refueling for northern air defense operations. 1962, selected for Minuteman I ICBM complex; 4136th SW deactivated and 455th Strategic Missile Wing and 450th BMW activated. 1968, 91st Strategic Missile Wing replaced 455th SMW and 5th BMW replaced 450th BMW. 1970, 91st SMW converted to Minuteman III ICBM. 1988, 5th BMW received air launched Cruise missile. Today, part of 57th Air Division.

VISITOR ATTRACTIONS: Ft Lincoln State Park; Lake Metigoshe State Park; International Peace Garden; Lake Sakakawea State Park; Turtle River State Park; Icelandic State Park; Lewis and Clark State Park; Theodore Roosevelt National Park; Bottineau Winter Park; North Dakota State Fair.

Key Contacts

COMMANDER: Brig Gen Raymund E O'Mara; 57 AD/CC, (701) 723-3353, Autovon 344-3353.

PUBLIC AFFAIRS: Capt Oscar P Seara; 57 AD/PAO, (701) 723-6212, Autovon 344-6212.

PROCUREMENT: Capt Janice A Kinard; 857 CPTS/LGC, (701) 723-2261, Autovon 344-2261.

TRANSPORTATION: LTC Dan E King; 857 TRANS/CC, (701) 723-3148, Autovon 344-3148.

PERSONNEL/COMMUNITY ACTIVITIES: LTC J C McLeroy; 857 MSSQ/CC, (701) 723-2215, Autovon 344-2215.

Personnel and Expenditures

ACTIVE DUTY PERSONNEL: 5979
DEPENDENTS: 7549
CIVILIAN PERSONNEL: 737
MILITARY PAYROLL EXPENDITURE: $106.5 mil
CONTRACT EXPENDITURE: $11.1 mil
Services *Housing:* Family units 2461; Duplex units 1045; Townhouse units 1334; Dormitory spaces 1639; Senior NCO units 242; Junior NCO units 1739; Trailer spaces 163; Single units 82. *Temporary Housing:* VIP cottages 10; VOQ cottages 24; VAQ units 54; BOQ units 66; BAQ units 30; Transient living quarters 40. *Commissary:* Base commissary; Retail store; Barber shop; Dry cleaners; Food shop; Florist; Banking; Service station. *Child Care/Capacities:* Day care center 177; Home day care program. *Schools:* Kindergarten/Preschool; Elementary; Intermediate/Junior high. *Base Library:* Yes. *Medical Facilities:* Hospital 47; Dental clinic. *Recreational Facilities:* Bowling; Movie theater; Pool; Gym; Recreation center; Golf; Stables; Tennis; Racquetball; Fitness center; Softball field; Auto shop; Crafts; Officers club; NCO club.

OHIO

CINCINNATI

US ARMY CORPS OF ENGINEERS, OHIO RIVER DIVISION
Box 1159, Cincinnati, OH 45201
(513) 684-3002
Profile
BRANCH: Army.
SIZE: Offices only.
Key Contacts
COMMANDER: Col Paul Y Chinen; Division Engineer.

CLEVELAND

NAVY FINANCE CENTER
A J Celebrezze Federal Bldg, 1240 E 9th St, Cleveland, OH 44199
(216) 522-5630; Autovon 580-5630
OFFICER-OF-THE-DAY: (216) 522-5630, Autovon 580-5630
Profile
BRANCH: Navy.
SIZE AND LOCATION: 35 acres. Downtown Cleveland, Anthony J Celebrezze Federal Bldg, two blocks from lakefront/inner harbor foot of 9th St. Adj to Cleveland Stadium and Burke Lakefront Airport. Main computer facility, Consolidated Data Center, 4 mi E on Rte 90 in village of Bratenahl, OH.
MAJOR UNITS: Navy Finance Center Headquarters; Rear Admiral Isaac Campbell Kidd Consolidated Data Center (Bratenahl); Personnel Support Activity; Navy Family Allowance Activity (NFAA).
BASE HISTORY: Navy Finance Center and predecessor, Field Branch, Bureau of Supplies and Accounts, in Cleveland since 1942. Primary mission to plan, design, develop, implement and manage Navy-wide pay systems for active duty, retired, and reserve personnel. Isaac Campbell Kidd Computer Center, Bratenahl, OH, located on site formerly occupied by NIKE missile facility operated. 1974, NAVFINCEN "Bratenahl Annex" home to Navy Finance Center's communications facility and mainframe computer operations.
Key Contacts
COMMANDER: (216) 522-5511, Autovon 580-5511.
PUBLIC AFFAIRS: (216) 522-5620, Autovon 580-5620.
PROCUREMENT: (216) 522-6600, Autovon 580-6600.
TRANSPORTATION: Personal Property/Incoming Shipments, (216) 522-5616, Autovon 580-5616.
PERSONNEL/COMMUNITY ACTIVITIES: (216) 522-5597, Autovon 580-5597.

Personnel and Expenditures
ACTIVE DUTY PERSONNEL: 93
CIVILIAN PERSONNEL: 1400
MILITARY PAYROLL EXPENDITURE: $5.8 mil
CONTRACT EXPENDITURE: $18.4 mil
Services *Housing:* BEQ units 17 (off-base). *Child Care/Capacities:* Day care center 70. *Medical Facilities:* Medical clinic. *Recreational Facilities:* Fitness center by lease with downtown health club.

COLUMBUS

DEFENSE CONSTRUCTION SUPPLY CENTER
PO Box 3990, 3990 E Broad St, Columbus, OH 43216-5000
(614) 238-2328; Autovon 850-2328
Profile
BRANCH: Joint Service Installation; Defense Logistics Agency.
SIZE AND LOCATION: 570 acres. On US 16, Broad St, approx 7 mi ENE of downtown Columbus.
MAJOR UNITS: Defense Construction Supply Center (DLA); DLA Systems Automation Center; Defense Depot Columbus (DLA); Defense Revitalization and Marketing Office (DLA); Industrial Plant Equipment Operations (DLA); 83rd Army Reserve Command; USAF Occupational Medicine Clinic; Defense Industrial Security Clearance Office.
BASE HISTORY: 1918, established as Columbus Quartermaster Reserve Depot, charged with routing materiel for overseas shipment. 1930s, district headquarters for Civilian Conservation Corps; military function diminished. 1942, Quartermaster General assumed responsibility of Columbus Quartermaster Depot. During Korean Conflict, activated. 1963, assigned to Defense Supply Agency (later Defense Logistics Agency); combined with Defense Construction Supply Center located at another site in Columbus.
Key Contacts
COMMANDER: Maj Gen John P Dreska, USA; (614) 238-2166, Autovon 850-2166.
PUBLIC AFFAIRS: Forrest L Flewellen; (614) 238-2328, Autovon 850-2328.
PROCUREMENT: Col Aurther L Glassman, USA; (614) 238-2191, Autovon 850-2191.
PERSONNEL/COMMUNITY ACTIVITIES: Mary Ann Skocik; Director of Personnel, (614) 238-2236, Autovon 850-2236.
Personnel and Expenditures
ACTIVE DUTY PERSONNEL: 40
CIVILIAN PERSONNEL: 5000
CONTRACT EXPENDITURE: $1.1 bil

Services *Temporary Housing:* VOQ cottages 1; Guesthouse units 2; Guest cottages 1. *Medical Facilities:* Medical clinic. *Recreational Facilities:* Gym; Recreation center; Golf; Tennis; Racquetball; Fitness center; Softball field; Officers club; NCO club.

RICKENBACKER AIR NATIONAL GUARD BASE
Columbus, OH 43217
(614) 492-8211 ("0" Assist); Autovon 950-8211
Profile
BRANCH: Air National Guard.
SIZE AND LOCATION: 2200 acres. Approx 10 mi S-SE of Columbus, OH; 4 mi S of I-270 at Exit 49, Alum Creek Dr, at the intersection of Alum Creek Dr and Ohio State Rte 317.
MAJOR UNITS: 121st Tactical Fighter Wing; 160th Air Refueling Group (ANG); 907th Tactical Airlift Group (AFRES).
BASE HISTORY: 1942, began as Lockbourne Army Air Base, known as nation's Southwest Training Center; first used Army Air Force Glider Pilot Training School replaced by B-17 school. 1943, class of Women Air Force Service Pilots (WASP) trained as engineering test pilots. Following WWII, developed and tested equipment for all-weather flight operations. 1947, 332nd Fighter Group and 477th Composite Group formed 332nd Fighter Wing, Air Force's first all-black operational flying unit, one of first units to commence total integration in AF. 1949, Lockbourne deactivated and operational control turned over to OH NG. 1951, Lockbourne reactivated; SAC aerial refueling and aircrew training facility. 301st BMW host until 1964, redesignated 301st Air Refueling Wing (ARW). 1974, Lockbourne AFB officially renamed Rickenbacker AFB for Capt Edward "Eddie" Rickenbacker, Ace of Aces of WWI, a Columbus native. 1979, included in President Carter's base closing program; 301st ARW deactivated. 1980, transferred to OH ANG. 1986, 121st TFW OH ANG host. 1988, joined by 160th Air Refueling Group, operate as Consolidated Operating Support staff.
VISITOR ATTRACTIONS: Aircraft on static display, F-100, F-84F, F-84E, T-33; Base tour of major air command units, TAC, SAC, MAC.
Key Contacts
COMMANDER: LTC William L Howland; 121st TFW/DS, (614) 492-3385, Autovon 950-3385, Col Gordon M Campbell; Air Commander, 121st TFW/CC.
PUBLIC AFFAIRS: Thomas B Foley; 121st TFW/COS-PA, (614) 492-3400, Autovon 950-3400.

RICKENBACKER AIR NATIONAL GUARD BASE *(continued)*

PROCUREMENT: George Megimose; 121st TFW/COS-LGC, (614) 492-4233, Autovon 950-4233.

TRANSPORTATION: Darryl Miller; 121st TFW/COS-LGT, (614) 492-4516, Autovon 950-4516.

Personnel and Expenditures
ACTIVE DUTY PERSONNEL: 10; 4000 reservists
CIVILIAN PERSONNEL: 1000
MILITARY PAYROLL EXPENDITURE: $45 mil
CONTRACT EXPENDITURE: $8 mil
Services *Housing:* BOQ cottages; BEQ units; BAQ units; Above for joint use for approx 300 bed spaces for military units AFRES. *Temporary Housing:* BOQ units; BAQ units; BEQ units; Above for joint use for approx 300 bed spaces for military units AFRES. *Commissary and Exchange:* Retail store; Barber shop; Dry cleaners; Service station. *Medical Facilities:* First aid station for military units only. *Recreational Facilities:* Pool; Gym; Tennis; Racquetball; Fitness center; Softball field; Consolidated Club.

DAYTON

GENTILE AIR FORCE STATION
1507 Wilmington Pike, Dayton, OH 45444
(513) 296-5111; Autovon 986-5111
Profile
BRANCH: Joint Service Installation.
SIZE AND LOCATION: 162 acres. Near Wright-Patterson AFB.
MAJOR UNITS: Defense Electronics Supply Center; Air Force Orientation Group.
Key Contacts
COMMANDER: Brig Gen R A Tiebout, USMC.
PUBLIC AFFAIRS: Stephen A Stromp; (513) 296-6421, Autovon 986-6421.
Personnel and Expenditures
ACTIVE DUTY PERSONNEL: 200
CIVILIAN PERSONNEL: 3200
CONTRACT EXPENDITURE: $600 mil
Services *Commissary and Exchange:* Retail store; Barber shop. *Recreational Facilities:* Pool; Gym; Tennis; Racquetball; Fitness center; Softball field; Football field; Officers club; NCO club.

GREENSBURG

ARMY AVIATION SUPPORT FACILITY #1
Akron-Canton Airport, Greensburg, OH 44232
(216) 494-3191; Autovon 580-6102
Profile
BRANCH: Army.
SIZE AND LOCATION: 92 acres. Just off I-77 at Akron-Canton Airport, 10 mi to Akron and 6 mi to Canton, OH.
MAJOR UNITS: 107th Armed Calvary Regiment; HHT 4/107; CON 4/107; O TRP 4/107; P TRP 4/17; Q TRP 4/107; Detachment 1, Company D, 137th AMB; 416th Engineering Group AVN SEC.
BASE HISTORY: Fall 1986, flight facility completed. Consists of over 63,000 sq ft of office and hangar space and helicopter maintenance shops. 1988, new armory constructed for HQ aviation, ground squadron, aircraft maintenance company.
Key Contacts
COMMANDER: LTC Fred A Leistiko; 6652 Amblewood St, NW, Canton, OH 44718, (216) 494-6949.
PUBLIC AFFAIRS: Maj Thomas P Luczynski.
Personnel and Expenditures
ACTIVE DUTY PERSONNEL: 75
CIVILIAN PERSONNEL: 1

LIMA

LIMA ARMY TANK PLANT
1155 Buckeye Rd, Lima, OH 45804-1898
(419) 227-0029; Autovon 786-6223
Profile
BRANCH: Army.
SIZE AND LOCATION: 400 acres. 5 mi from downtown Lima, OH; 1 mi W of intersection I-75 and OH-65; nearest military support installation Wright-Patterson AFB, Dayton, OH, 78 mi S.
MAJOR UNITS: Tank Automotive Command (TACOM); Corps of Engineers (Louisville District); Defense Audit Agency; Communications and Electronics Command (CECOM); General Dynamics Land Systems (operating contractor).
BASE HISTORY: 1941, construction began for manufacturing plant designed to produce centrifugally cast gun tubes; improved technique for production discovered before facility completed; used for intermediate depot by Army Ordnance Corps. During WWII, depot processed over 40 types of combat vehicles. 1945, became Class III Ordnance Depot; thousands of combat vehicles placed in storage until Korean Conflict. After Korean Conflict, became inactive, renamed Lima Army Modification Center. 1961, began storing Industrial Plant Equipment and records holding area for several commands. 1976-1979, tested and rehabilitated coding plant equipment. 1976, received, inspected, and processed light utility trucks for Army; chosen as initial production site for XM1 tank. Chrysler Corp, Defense Division awarded contract. 1979, renamed Lima Army Tank Center. 1982, General Dynamics Land Systems bought out Chrysler Defense, including tank center, renamed Lima Army Tank Plant. 1985, last M1 built and production of M1A1 Abrams tank began, only item currently produced.
Key Contacts
COMMANDER: LTC Raymond Pawlicki, Commander; Charles M Hall, Plant Manager.
PUBLIC AFFAIRS: (419) 227-0029, ext 203.
Personnel and Expenditures
ACTIVE DUTY PERSONNEL: 7
CIVILIAN PERSONNEL: 2700

MANSFIELD

179TH TACTICAL AIRLIFT GROUP (ANG)
Mansfield Lahm Airport, Mansfield, OH 44901
(419) 522-9355; Autovon 696-6210
Profile
BRANCH: Air National Guard.
SIZE AND LOCATION: 210 acres. 3 mi N of Mansfield, off State Rte 13.
MAJOR UNITS: 179th Tactical Airlift Group (ANG).
BASE HISTORY: Named for aviation pioneer Brig Gen Frank P Lahm.
Personnel and Expenditures
ACTIVE DUTY PERSONNEL: 813
CIVILIAN PERSONNEL: 177
MILITARY PAYROLL EXPENDITURE: $7.3 mil
Services *Medical Facilities:* Dispensary.

NEWARK AFB

NEWARK AIR FORCE BASE
2803 ABG, Newark AFB, OH 43057-5000
(614) 522-7281; Autovon 346-7281
Profile
BRANCH: Air Force.
SIZE AND LOCATION: 70 acres. In Heath, OH, 3 mi S of Newark, OH, off of Hwy 79.

MAJOR UNITS: Aerospace Guidance and Metrology Center (AGMC).
BASE HISTORY: Early 1950s, built; part of AF Heavy Press Program. 1952, Kaiser Aluminum and Chemical Corp contracted to construct and operate aluminum presses. 1953, program curtailed. 1954, designated AF Industrial Plant 48; used as industrial equipment storage facility. 1959, redesignated Heath Maintenance Annex of Dayton AF Depot and modified; 2802nd Inertial Guidance and Calibration Group organized. 1962, Annex redesignated Newark AFS. 1968, Aerospace Guidance and Metrology Center. 1973, 2803rd ABG established. 1987, Newark AFB designated. Mission: single point repair of inertial guidance and navigations systems; providing engineering consultant and support services; performing overall technical and management direction of AF Metrology and Calibration Program; and, operating AF Measurement Standards Laboratories.
Key Contacts
PUBLIC AFFAIRS: Capt Jim Sahi; (614) 522-7779, Autovon 346-7779.
Personnel and Expenditures
ACTIVE DUTY PERSONNEL: 40
CIVILIAN PERSONNEL: 2500
MILITARY PAYROLL EXPENDITURE: $81 mil
Services *Temporary Housing:* Nearest facilities in Columbus at Defense Construction Supply Center. *Commissary and Exchange:* Retail store; Barber shop; Cafeteria; Credit union. *Medical Facilities:* Dispensary. *Recreational Facilities:* Recreation center; Racquetball; Consolidated mess; Boating at Buckeye Lake, 11 mi S.

NEWTON FALLS

OHIO NATIONAL GUARD, UNIT TRAINING EQUIPMENT SITE #1
RD #2, PO Box 390A, Newton Falls, OH 44444-9519
(216) 872-0055
OFFICER-OF-THE-DAY: (216) 872-0055
Profile
BRANCH: Army National Guard.
SIZE AND LOCATION: 920 acres. 2 mi W of Ohio Tpke, Exit 14, off of Rte 5. Approx 20 mi away from Youngstown or Ravenna, OH. Nearest airport 30 mi.
MAJOR UNITS: Ohio National Guard.
BASE HISTORY: Established to provide maintenance support for OH Army NG units; weekend training.
Key Contacts
COMMANDER: CW4 Raymond D Conti.
PUBLIC AFFAIRS: See Base Commander.
Personnel and Expenditures
CIVILIAN PERSONNEL: 13
Services *Base Library:* Yes.

SPRINGFIELD

178TH TACTICAL FIGHTER GROUP (ANG)
Springfield Municipal Airport, Springfield, OH 45501
(513) 323-8653; Autovon 346-2210
Profile
BRANCH: Air National Guard.
SIZE AND LOCATION: 113 acres. 5 mi S of Springfield, off US-68.
MAJOR UNITS: 178th Tactical Fighter Group (ANG).
Personnel and Expenditures
ACTIVE DUTY PERSONNEL: 1106
CIVILIAN PERSONNEL: 231
MILITARY PAYROLL EXPENDITURE: $10.8 mil
Services *Medical Facilities:* 6-bed dispensary.

SWANTON

180TH TACTICAL FIGHTER GROUP

Toledo Express Airport, Swanton, OH
43558-5005
(419) 866-2078; Autovon 580-2110
Profile
BRANCH: Air National Guard.
SIZE AND LOCATION: 79 acres. At Toledo
Express Airport, Swanton, OH, approx 10
mi W of Toledo.
MAJOR UNITS: 180th Tactical Fighter Group;
112th Tactical Fighter Squadron.
Key Contacts
COMMANDER: Col John Smith; (419) 866-
2030, Autovon 580-2030.
PUBLIC AFFAIRS: Maj Nancy August; (419)
866-2014, Autovon 580-2014.
Personnel and Expenditures
ACTIVE DUTY PERSONNEL: 985 ANG
CIVILIAN PERSONNEL: 35
MILITARY PAYROLL EXPENDITURE: $2.6 mil
Services *Commissary and Exchange:* Retail
store. *Medical Facilities:* Medical clinic;
Dental clinic.

VIENNA

910TH TACTICAL AIRLIFT GROUP (AFRES)

Youngstown Municipal Airport, Vienna, OH
44473
(216) 856-1645; Autovon 346-9211
Profile
BRANCH: Air National Guard.
SIZE AND LOCATION: 226 acres. 16 mi N of
Youngstown, between State Rte 11 and
193.
MAJOR UNITS: 910th Tactical Airlift Group
(AFRES); 757th Tactical Airlift Squadron
(AFRES).
BASE HISTORY: 1952, base activated.
Personnel and Expenditures
ACTIVE DUTY PERSONNEL: 909 Reservists
CIVILIAN PERSONNEL: 230
MILITARY PAYROLL EXPENDITURE: $10.5 mil

WRIGHT-PATTERSON AFB

WRIGHT-PATTERSON AIR FORCE BASE

Wright-Patterson AFB, OH 45433
(513) 257-1110; Autovon 787-1110
Profile
BRANCH: Air Force.
SIZE AND LOCATION: 8145 acres. 10 mi NE of
Dayton, OH, off Rte 444.
MAJOR UNITS: Air Force Logistics Command
(AFLC); AF Acquisition Logistics Center
(AFALC); International Logistics Center
(ILC); AF Contract Maintenance Center
(AFCMC); Logistics Operations Center
(LOC); Logistics Management Systems
Center (LMSC); AF Contract Law Center
(AFCLC); Wright-Patterson Contracting
Center (WPCC); USAF Museum; USAF
Medical Center; 2750th Air Base Wing;
Aeronautical Systems Division (ASD);
4950th Test Wing; AF Wright Aeronau-
tical Laboratories (AFWAL); Harry G
Armstrong Aerospace Medical Research
Laboratory (AAMRL); Foreign Technol-
ogy Division (FTD); AF Institute of Tech-
nology (AFIT); Defense Institute of Secu-
rity Assistance Management (DISAM);
906th Tactical Fighter Group.
BASE HISTORY: Established in 1917 as
McCook Field and renamed Wilbur
Wright Field in 1924, then Patterson
Field, for Lt Frank Patterson killed in
airplane crash, 1931. Finally designated
Wright-Patterson in 1948.

VISITOR ATTRACTIONS: USAF Museum
(largest and oldest aviation museum), free
admission.
Key Contacts
PUBLIC AFFAIRS: 2750 ABW/PA; (513) 257-
4248, Autovon 787-4248.
Personnel and Expenditures
ACTIVE DUTY PERSONNEL: 11,000
DEPENDENTS: 7500
CIVILIAN PERSONNEL: 24,000
CONTRACT EXPENDITURE: $279 mil
Services *Housing:* Family units 2366. *Tem-
porary Housing:* VIP cottages 13; VOQ cot-
tages 611; VAQ units 115; Apartment units
40; Transient living quarters. *Commissary:*
Base commissary; Retail store; Barber shop;
Dry cleaners; Food shop; Banking; Service
station; Beauty shop; Laundry; Optical shop.
Child Care/Capacities: Day care center 278.
Base Library: Yes. *Medical Facilities:* Hos-
pital 301. *Recreational Facilities:* Bowling;
Movie theater; Pool; Gym; Recreation center; Golf; Stables; Tennis; Racquetball; Fitness center; Auto shop; Crafts; Officers club;
NCO club; Camping; Fishing/Hunting; Hunt-
ing lodge; Aero Club; Rod and Gun Club;
Family camp; Park, 65 acres; Lakes, 4.

OKLAHOMA

ALTUS AFB

ALTUS AIR FORCE BASE
Altus AFB, OK 73523-5000
(405) 482-8100; Autovon 866-8100
OFFICER-OF-THE-DAY: (405) 482-8100,
  Autovon 866-8100
Profile
BRANCH: Air Force.
SIZE AND LOCATION: 4401 acres. In corporate
  city limits of city of Altus; 139 mi SW of
  Oklahoma City; Hwys 62 & 283 run
  through city.
MAJOR UNITS: 443rd Military Airlift Wing
  (Host); 340th Air Refueling Wing.
BASE HISTORY: 1943, first opened; mission to
  train multi-engine aircraft pilots for Eu-
  ropean Theater. 1945, deactivated. 1953,
  reactivated under TAC, then SAC. 1960s,
  operated 12 Atlas ICBM sites in SW OK.
  1965, deactivated. 1943, 443rd MAW be-
  gan at Sedalia Army Airfield, MO, when
  parent 443rd Troop Carrier Group ac-
  tivated. During WWII, served in China-
  Burma-India Theater. 1967, became
  MAC's Airlift Training Center; training
  mission of wing remained unchanged
  since inception.
VISITOR ATTRACTIONS: Museum of Western
  Prairie in Altus.
Key Contacts
COMMANDER: Col Gary L Thompson; 443
  ABG/CC, (405) 481-6410, Autovon 866-
  6410.
PUBLIC AFFAIRS: Don L Johnson; 443 MAW/
  PA, (405) 481-7700, Autovon 866-7700.
PROCUREMENT: Col John E Polk; 443 MAW/
  RM, (405) 481-6442, Autovon 866-6442.
Personnel and Expenditures
ACTIVE DUTY PERSONNEL: 3500
DEPENDENTS: 4800
CIVILIAN PERSONNEL: 814
MILITARY PAYROLL EXPENDITURE: $125 mil
CONTRACT EXPENDITURE: $9 mil
Services *Housing:* Family units 800; BOQ
cottages; Dormitory spaces 1132; Senior
NCO units 36; RV/Camper sites 7. *Tem-
porary Housing:* VIP cottages 4; VOQ cot-
tages 158; VEQ units 424; Transient living
quarters 8. *Commissary:* Base commissary;
Retail store; Barber shop; Dry cleaners;
Food shop; Florist; Banking; Service station;
Bakery. *Child Care/Capacities:* Day care cen-
ter. *Schools:* Kindergarten/Preschool; Elementary. *Base Library:* Yes. *Medical Facilities:* Hospital 25; Dental clinic. *Recreational
Facilities:* Bowling; Movie theater; Pool;
Gym; Recreation center; Golf; Tennis; Racquetball; Fitness center; Softball field; Football field; Auto shop; Crafts; Officers club;
Enlisted club; Camping and fishing 18 mi N
of base.

BRAGGS

CAMP GRUBER TRAINING SITE
PO Box 577, Braggs, OK 74423-0577
(918) 487-6001
Profile
BRANCH: Army National Guard.
SIZE AND LOCATION: 32,000 acres. Approx 12
  mi SE of Muskogee, OK, on State Hwy
  10, near town of Braggs. Davis Field 5 mi
  S of Muskogee on US Hwy 64; Port on
  Arkansas River, 3 mi W of Braggs; I-40
  runs approx 12 mi S of Camp.
MAJOR UNITS: Oklahoma Air Assault School;
  Camp Gruber Training Site (HQ STARC,
  OKARNG).
BASE HISTORY: 1942, opened with a 3,000
  man German POW camp; major training
  facility; 42nd Rainbow, 88th Blue Devil,
  and 86th Black Hawk Divisions activated
  here. 1947, deactivated and used very little until 1968 when OK Army NG started
  annual training. Today, classified as Class
  A Training Facility, used by Armed
  Forces, as well as local and state law en-
  forcement agencies. Facilities: weapons
  ranges; only Air Assault School for NG;
  Davis Field, capable of handling aircraft
  up to Galaxy C-5; and, port on Arkansas
  River capable of accommodating barge
  traffic.
VISITOR ATTRACTIONS: WWII POW Camp
  memorabilia.
Key Contacts
COMMANDER: Col Charles W Wootten.
PUBLIC AFFAIRS: WO1 Ron Petty; (918) 487-
  6051.
PROCUREMENT: CW4 Henry C Stone; (918)
  487-6061.
PERSONNEL/COMMUNITY ACTIVITIES: See Base
  Commander.
Personnel and Expenditures
ACTIVE DUTY PERSONNEL: 1
CIVILIAN PERSONNEL: 91
Services *Housing:* Townhouse units 1; Bar-
racks spaces 480; Mobile home units 30.
Temporary Housing: VIP cottages 3. *Com-
missary and Exchange:* Retail store. *Medical
Facilities:* Medical clinic. *Recreational Facili-
ties:* Movie theater; Recreation center; Fit-
ness center; Softball field; Officers club;
NCO club; Camping; Fishing/Hunting; Lake.

FORT SILL

FORT SILL
US Army Field Artillery Center & Fort Sill,
Fort Sill, OK 73503-5000
(405) 351-8111; Autovon 639-8111
OFFICER-OF-THE-DAY: (405) 351-4912,
  Autovon 639-4912

Profile
BRANCH: Army.
SIZE AND LOCATION: 94,220 acres. Approx 70
  mi S of Oklahoma City on H E Bailey
  Tpke (I-44); borders city of Lawton on N.
MAJOR UNITS: III Corps Artillery; US Army
  Field Artillery Training Center; US Army
  Field Artillery School.
BASE HISTORY: 1869, established by Gen
  Phillip Sheridan as frontier post for paci-
  fying Comanche and Kiowa Indian tribes
  of Southern Great Plains. 1911, School of
  Fire of Field Artillery (today, US Army
  Field Artillery School) established. Trains
  more than 15,000 officer and enlisted stu-
  dents annually. III Corps Artillery Army's
  largest, most diverse field artillery organi-
  zation; three brigades combat-ready. Field
  Artillery Board oldest test agency in
  Army. Army's Tactical Missile System
  (ATCMS) now under development.
  Verification/inspection site for INF Trea-
  ty.
VISITOR ATTRACTIONS: Cabaret Supper The-
  ater; Fort Sill Museum; Geronimo's
  Grave Site; Artillery and Military History
  exhibits in Hamilton and McLain Halls.
Key Contacts
COMMANDER: Maj Gen Raphael J Hallada;
  ATZR-C, Ft Sill, OK 73503-5001, (405)
  351-3006, Autovon 639-3006.
PUBLIC AFFAIRS: LTC John R Dobbs; ATZR-
  A, Ft Sill, OK 73503-5100, (405) 351-
  4500, Autovon 639-4500.
PROCUREMENT: B Watts; ATZR-P, Ft Sill,
  OK 73503-5100, (405) 351-4810, Auto-
  von 639-4810.
TRANSPORTATION: G Thomson; ATZR-LST,
  Ft Sill, OK 73503-5100, (405) 351-2403,
  Autovon 639-2403.
PERSONNEL/COMMUNITY ACTIVITIES: Col J C
  Tincher; ATZR-P, Ft Sill, OK 73503-
  5100, (405) 351-3001, Autovon 639-3001.
Personnel and Expenditures
ACTIVE DUTY PERSONNEL: 19,234
DEPENDENTS: 3803
CIVILIAN PERSONNEL: 6433
MILITARY PAYROLL EXPENDITURE: $94.5 mil
CONTRACT EXPENDITURE: $217.8 mil
Services *Housing:* Family units 1409. *Tem-
porary Housing:* Guesthouse units 75; Tran-
sient living quarters 931. *Commissary:* Base
commissary; Retail store; Barber shop; Dry
cleaners; Food shop; Florist; Banking; Service station; Beauty shop. *Child Care/Capac-
ities:* Day care center 162; Home day care
program. *Schools:* Kindergarten/Preschool;
Elementary. *Base Library:* Yes. *Medical Facilities:* Hospital 214; Medical clinic; Dental
clinic. *Recreational Facilities:* Bowling; Movie theater; Pool; Gym; Recreation center;
Golf; Stables; Tennis; Racquetball; Fitness
center; Softball field; Football field; Auto
shop; Crafts; Officers club; NCO club;
Camping; Fishing/Hunting.

MCALESTER

MCALESTER ARMY AMMUNITION PLANT

McAlester, OK 74501
(918) 421-2011; Autovon 956-6011
OFFICER-OF-THE-DAY: (918) 421-2642,
Autovon 956-6642

Profile

BRANCH: Army.
SIZE AND LOCATION: 45,000. Approx 9 mi S of McAlester, OK, adj to Savanna, OK on Hwy 69; approx 6 mi S of McAlester Municipal Airport; 5 mi S of intersection of Hwy 69 and Indian Nations Tnpk.
MAJOR UNITS: McAlester Army Ammunition Plant.
BASE HISTORY: Commissioned as McAlester Naval Ammunition Depto, 1943. Transferred to Army Materiel Command's single manager for conventional ammunition, 1977. Currently, 2nd largest installation of this type in US. Produces, stores, issues and receives conventional ammunition for all military branches.
VISITOR ATTRACTIONS: Wildlife tours

Key Contacts

COMMANDER: Col Walter J Shelton; (918) 421-2211, Autovon 956-6211.
PUBLIC AFFAIRS: Clare Thomas; (918) 421-2591, Autovon 956-6591.
PROCUREMENT: Neil Caldwell; (918) 421-2479, Autovon 956-6479.
TRANSPORTATION: Don Shields; (918) 421-2418, Autovon 956-6418.
PERSONNEL/COMMUNITY ACTIVITIES: Ed Southwick; (918) 421-2529, Autovon 956-6529.

Personnel and Expenditures

ACTIVE DUTY PERSONNEL: 23
DEPENDENTS: 70
CIVILIAN PERSONNEL: 1000
CONTRACT EXPENDITURE: FY 89, $13 mil
Services *Housing:* Family units 18; BOQ cottages 18; Barracks spaces 81; RV/Camper sites 1. *Temporary Housing:* BOQ units 12. *Commissary and Exchange:* Retail store; Food shop; Banking. *Child Care/Capacities:* Day care center 20. *Medical Facilities:* Medical clinic. *Recreational Facilities:* Bowling; Pool; Gym; Recreation center; Stables; Tennis; Racquetball; Fitness center; Softball field; Auto shop; Crafts; Camping; Fishing/Hunting; Enlisted club; Lakeview Community Club (military & civilian).

OKLAHOMA CITY

137TH TACTICAL AIRLIFT WING (ANG)

Will Rogers World Airport, Oklahoma City, OK 73179
(405) 681-7551; Autovon 956-8210

Profile

BRANCH: Air National Guard.
SIZE AND LOCATION: 71 acres. 7 mi SW of Oklahoma City, off I-44.
MAJOR UNITS: 137th Tactical Airlift Wing (ANG).

Personnel and Expenditures

ACTIVE DUTY PERSONNEL: 980
CIVILIAN PERSONNEL: 213
MILITARY PAYROLL EXPENDITURE: $9.2 mil

OKLAHOMA CITY AFS

OKLAHOMA CITY AIR FORCE STATION

Oklahoma City AFS, OK 73145
Autovon 735-9011

Profile

BRANCH: Air Force.
MAJOR UNITS: Oklahoma City AFS (AFLC).

TINKER AFB

TINKER AIR FORCE BASE

HQ 2854th Air Base Group (AFLC), Tinker AFB, OK 73145
(405) 732-7321; Autovon 884-1110

Profile

BRANCH: Air Force.
SIZE AND LOCATION: 1440 acres. 9 mi SE of Oklahoma City off I-40; use Gate 1 off Air Depot Blvd.
MAJOR UNITS: Oklahoma City Air Logistics Center (AFLC); Directorate of Maintenance; Directorate of Materiel Management; Directorate of Distribution; Directorate of Contracting and Manufacturing; Directorate of Competition Advocacy; Environmental Management Directorate; Comptroller; AFLC Management Engineering Team, Detachment 2, 3025 MES; 2953rd Combat Logistics Support Squadron (CLSS); 2854th Air Base Group; 28th Air Division; 552nd Airborne Warning and Control Wing; Engineering Installation Division; 3rd Combat Communications Group; 1985th Information Systems Squadron; Command and Control Systems Office; Detachment 1, 17th Weather Squadron; Detachment 15, 1365th Audiovisual Squadron; 507th Tactical Fighter Group; Detachment 1, 60th Military Airlift Wing; Defense Reutilization and Marketing Office.
BASE HISTORY: 1942, named for Maj Gen Clarence L Tinker, Oklahoman killed on Wake Island. 1943, Douglas Aircraft began production of cargo planes immediately E of base. WWII, Tinker workers repaired B-17 and B-24 bombers and outfitted B-29 bombers for combat. Following WWII, expanded to include Douglas facility and named Oklahoma City Air Materiel Area (OCAMA). Korean War, OCAMA gave materiel support. 1960s, OCAMA supported Berlin Crisis, Cuban Missile Crisis, and logistics support for B-52 bombers in Vietnam. 1967, designated inland aerial port of embarkation for Southeast Asia. 1974, renamed Oklahoma City Air Logistics Center (OC-ALC). 1980s, B-1 bomber added to management responsibilities.

Key Contacts

COMMANDER: Col Anthony E Mras; Bldg 460.
PUBLIC AFFAIRS: Gene R Pickett; Bldg 3001.
TRANSPORTATION: Eddie Allen; Bldg 2101.
PERSONNEL/COMMUNITY ACTIVITIES: LTC Carle Hall; Bldg 3001.

Personnel and Expenditures

ACTIVE DUTY PERSONNEL: 7287
Services *Housing:* Family units 730. *Temporary Housing:* VIP cottages 6; VOQ cottages 122; VAQ units 110; 40. *Commissary:* Base commissary; Retail store; Barber shop; Dry cleaners; Food shop; Florist; Banking; Service station; Military clothing sales; Convenience store/Shopette; Credit union; Jewelry/watch sales and repair; Beauty shop; Laundry; Video rental; Thrift shop; Optical shop; Package beverages. *Child Care/Capacities:* Day care center 200. *Schools:* Elementary. *Base Library:* Yes. *Medical Facilities:* Hospital 30; Medical clinic; Dental clinic; Veterinary clinic. *Recreational Facilities:* Bowling; Movie theater; Pool; Gym; Recreation center; Golf; Stables; Tennis; Racquetball; Fitness center; Auto shop; Crafts; Officers club; Camping; NCO club; Camping; Fishing/Hunting; Youth center; Rod and Gun Club; Equipment rental; Picnicking; South 40 Recreation Area with 29 RV sites.

TULSA

US ARMY CORPS OF ENGINEERS, TULSA DISTRICT

PO Box 61, Tulsa, OK 74121-0061
(918) 581-7307

Profile

BRANCH: Army.
LOCATION: Downtown Federal Building, corner of 3rd & Boulder.

Key Contacts

COMMANDER: Col F Lee Smith Jr; District Engineer, (918) 581-7311.
PUBLIC AFFAIRS: Ross Adkins; CESWT-PA.
PROCUREMENT: P Chronister; CESWT-CT-P, (918) 581-7318.
PERSONNEL/COMMUNITY ACTIVITIES: Joe Jones; CESWT-EP, (918) 581-7269.

Personnel and Expenditures

ACTIVE DUTY PERSONNEL: 2
CIVILIAN PERSONNEL: 800
CONTRACT EXPENDITURE: $160 mil
Services *Base Library:* Yes. *Recreational Facilities:* Camping and fishing at all 39 lake projects in OK, northern TX, and southern KS.

138TH TACTICAL FIGHTER GROUP (ANG)

Tulsa IAP, Tulsa, OK 74115
(918) 836-0381; Autovon 956-5297

Profile

BRANCH: Air National Guard.
SIZE AND LOCATION: 78 acres. Off Gilcrease Dr, N from I-244 within the corporate limits of Tulsa.
MAJOR UNITS: 138th Tactical Fighter Group (ANG); 219th Electronic Installation Squadron.

Personnel and Expenditures

ACTIVE DUTY PERSONNEL: 888
CIVILIAN PERSONNEL: 210
MILITARY PAYROLL EXPENDITURE: $8.3 mil

VANCE AFB

VANCE AIR FORCE BASE

71 Fly TNG WG, Vance AFB, OK 73705-5000
(405) 237-2121; Autovon 962-7110

Profile

BRANCH: Air Force.
SIZE AND LOCATION: 4000 acres. 2 mi S of Enid, OK on US Hwy 81; US Hwy 64 runs E and W through city; Woodring Municipal Airport, city airport; Vance 80 mi N of Oklahoma City.
MAJOR UNITS: 71st Flying Training Wing; 2110th Communications Squadron; Detachment 15, 24th Weather Squadron.
BASE HISTORY: 1941, Enid Army Air Field established. 1947, deactivated. 1948, reactivated as Enid Air Force Base. 1949, renamed for LTC Leon Robert Vance Jr, WWII hero and Medal of Honor winner. 1961, converted to consolidated pilot training base. 1972, Northrop Worldwide Aircraft Services, Inc assumed support contract from Serv Air Inc; 71st FTW activated; northernmost pilot training base in Air Training Command. Kegelman Auxiliary Field included in 4000 acres.
VISITOR ATTRACTIONS: Base tours, static aircraft displays, flightline and Undergraduate Pilot Training (UPT) program.

Key Contacts

COMMANDER: Col Lloyd W Newton; Air Base Commander, 71st Air Base Group, (405) 249-7519, Autovon 962-7519, Col Ronald G Shamblin; Wing Commander, 71st Flying Training Wing, (405) 249-7101, Autovon 962-7101.

VANCE AIR FORCE BASE *(continued)*
PUBLIC AFFAIRS: 1st Lt Brent B Boller; Wing
Public Affairs Officer, 71 FTW/PA, Public Affairs Division, (405) 249-7476,
Autovon 962-7476.
PROCUREMENT: Richard W Hoepner; Northrop Worldwide Aircraft Services, Inc,
NW-STP, (405) 249-7487, Autovon 962-7487.
TRANSPORTATION: Capt James R Rosewall;
71st ABG/LGT, (405) 249-7470, Autovon
962-7470.
PERSONNEL/COMMUNITY ACTIVITIES: Maj
John M Gwinnip; Chief, Personnel Division, 71st ABG/DP, (405) 249-7661,
Autovon 962-7661.
Personnel and Expenditures
ACTIVE DUTY PERSONNEL: 1200
DEPENDENTS: 1380
CIVILIAN PERSONNEL: 1367
MILITARY PAYROLL EXPENDITURE: $78.1 mil
CONTRACT EXPENDITURE: $44.1 mil
Services *Housing:* Family units 230; Senior
NCO units 18; Junior NCO units 80. *Temporary Housing:* VOQ cottages 34; Dormitory units 266; Unaccompanied Officers
Quarters UOQ 230; Temporary Lodging Facilities 10. *Commissary:* Base commissary;
Retail store; Barber shop; Dry cleaners;
Food shop; Florist; Banking; Service station;
Credit union. *Child Care/Capacities:* Day
care center 66. *Schools:* Public elementary
school just outside main gate. *Base Library:*
Yes. *Medical Facilities:* Medical clinic; Dental clinic. *Recreational Facilities:* Bowling;
Pool; Gym; Recreation center; Tennis; Racquetball; Softball field; Football field; Auto
shop; Crafts; Officers club; NCO club; Driving range.

OREGON

CHARLESTON

WHIDBEY ISLAND NAVAL FACILITY, DETACHMENT COOS HEAD
PO Box 5660, Charleston, OR 97420-0630
(503) 888-3221
Profile
BRANCH: Navy.
SIZE AND LOCATION: 2.5 acres. Remotely located, approx 10 mi S of the cities of Coos Bay and North Bend, OR; 2 mi W of Charleston, OR.
MAJOR UNITS: Navy Detachment; 104th Tactical Control Squadron (TCS), Oregon ANG.
BASE HISTORY: 1958, established and disestablished as operational command effective Dec 1, 1987. Only Officer in Charge is billeted at facility, detachment of Naval Facility, Whidbey Island, WA.
Key Contacts
COMMANDER: Lt Robert W Barnes; Officer in Charge; LTC LeCours; 104th TCS.
PUBLIC AFFAIRS: See Base Commander.
Personnel and Expenditures
ACTIVE DUTY PERSONNEL: 1
CIVILIAN PERSONNEL: 5
MILITARY PAYROLL EXPENDITURE: $1.5 mil
Services *Recreational Facilities:* Gym; Tennis; Softball field; Outside fitness trail.

DALLAS AFS

DALLAS AIR FORCE STATION
Dallas AFS, OR 97338
(503) 787-3336
Profile
BRANCH: Air Force.
MAJOR UNITS: Dallas AFS (TAC).

HEBO

MOUNT HEBO AIR FORCE STATION
Hebo, OR 97122
(503) 392-3111
Profile
BRANCH: Air Force.
MAJOR UNITS: Mt Hebo AFS (TAC).

HERMISTON

UMATILLA ARMY DEPOT ACTIVITY
Hermiston, OR 97838-9544
(503) 567-6421; Autovon 890-5421
OFFICER-OF-THE-DAY: (503) 567-5202, Autovon 890-5202
Profile
BRANCH: Army.
SIZE AND LOCATION: 19,727 acres. In High Desert in NE OR, 10 mi W of Hermiston; along main line of Union Pacific Railroad at intersections of I-82 and I-84 approx 175 mi E of Portland.
MAJOR UNITS: Army Occupational Health Clinic; Defense Reutilization and Marketing Office; Army Information Systems Command.
BASE HISTORY: 1940, site selected for new arsenal. 1941, constructed and named Umatilla Army Depot (UMD) for territorial Indian tribe. Following WWII, huge stocks of munitions returned from overseas routed to UMDA for renovation, maintenance, and storage; unserviceable ammunition demilitarized; salvage of reusable parts. Similar activities repeated for Korean and Vietnam Conflicts. 1976, changed to present name; Activity within Tooele Army Depot (TEAD) Complex.
VISITOR ATTRACTIONS: Closed to the public.
Personnel and Expenditures
ACTIVE DUTY PERSONNEL: 46
Services *Housing:* Family units 24; BEQ units 13; Housing primarily for Navy families at US Naval Training Facility, Boardman, OR. *Temporary Housing:* Arrangements made by Administrative Specialist for official visitors. *Commissary and Exchange:* Limited. *Recreational Facilities:* Movie theater; Pool; Recreation center; Golf; Tennis; Racquetball; Fitness center; Crafts; Camping; Fishing/Hunting; Skiing; Parks; Rod and gun club; Basketball; Area is bordered by the Columbia River with an abundance of recreation.

KLAMATH FALLS

114TH TACTICAL FIGHTER TRAINING SQUADRON
Kingsley Field, Klamath Falls, OR 97603
Profile
BRANCH: Air National Guard.
SIZE: 405 acres.
MAJOR UNITS: 114th Tactical Fighter Training Squadron.
Key Contacts
COMMANDER: Col Stephen Harper.
PUBLIC AFFAIRS: See 142nd Fighter Interceptor Group, Portland IAP.
Personnel and Expenditures
ACTIVE DUTY PERSONNEL: 127
CIVILIAN PERSONNEL: 52
MILITARY PAYROLL EXPENDITURE: $8.4 mil
CONTRACT EXPENDITURE: $440,000

NORTH BEND AFS

NORTH BEND AIR FORCE STATION
North Bend AFS, OR 97459
(503) 756-4146
Profile
BRANCH: Air Force.
MAJOR UNITS: North Bend AFS (TAC).

PORTLAND

US ARMY CORPS OF ENGINEERS, NORTH PACIFIC DIVISION
220 NW 8th Ave, Portland, OR 97209
(503) 221-3700
Profile
BRANCH: Army.
SIZE: Offices only.
Key Contacts
COMMANDER: Col Pat M Stevens IV; Division Engineer.

US ARMY CORPS OF ENGINEERS, PORTLAND DISTRICT
PO Box 2946, 319 SW Pine, Portland, OR 97208-2946
(503) 221-6005
Profile
BRANCH: Army.
SIZE AND LOCATION: Offices only. In the city of Portland.
MAJOR UNITS: District Headquarters.
BASE HISTORY: One of largest and most diversified programs of any district in Corps. Mission to protect and develop water resources of 79,405 sq mi in western and central OR and 8740 sq mi in southwestern WA. Major responsibilities include providing safe entrance to OR coastal and inland harbors and generating hydroelectric power for region at Bonneville, The Dalles and John Day dams on Columbia River. Lake projects in Willamette and Rogue River valleys provide flood control, some hydropower, recreation and improved water quality for areas downstream. Most recently completed project is Bonneville Second Powerhouse on WA shore of Columbia River. Only Corps district with responsibilities relating to an active volcano. Today, work continues to solve long-term problems caused by eruption of Mt St Helens.
Key Contacts
COMMANDER: Col Charles E Cowan; (503) 221-6000.
PUBLIC AFFAIRS: Alene J Jacques.
PROCUREMENT: Brian Fennemore.
PERSONNEL/COMMUNITY ACTIVITIES: Vance Boelts; Director of Personnel.
Personnel and Expenditures
ACTIVE DUTY PERSONNEL: 5
CIVILIAN PERSONNEL: 1250
MILITARY PAYROLL EXPENDITURE: $0.5 mil
CONTRACT EXPENDITURE: $100 mil
Services *Base Library:* Yes.

142ND FIGHTER INTERCEPTOR GROUP (ANG)
Portland IAP, Portland, OR 97218
(503) 335-4104; Autovon 891-1701

142ND FIGHTER INTERCEPTOR GROUP (ANG) *(continued)*
Profile
BRANCH: Air National Guard.
SIZE AND LOCATION: 273 acres. Within corporate limits of Portland, between I-205 and I-5 along Columbia River.
MAJOR UNITS: 142nd Fighter Interceptor Group (ANG); 244th Combat Communications Squadron (ANG); 244th Combat Communications Flight (ANG); 116th Tactical Control Squadron (ANG); Detachment 5, 2036th Communications Squadron (AFCC); 12th Special Forces Group (USAR); Oregon Wing (CAP); 304th Aerospace Rescue and Recovery Squadron (AFRES); 83rd Aerial Port Squadron (AFRES).
Personnel and Expenditures
ACTIVE DUTY PERSONNEL: 1681
CIVILIAN PERSONNEL: 389
MILITARY PAYROLL EXPENDITURE: $16.6 mil

WARRENTON

CAMP RILEA, OREGON NATIONAL GUARD TRAINING SITE
Rte 1, Box 497E, Warrenton, OR 97146-9711
(503) 861-4000; 861-3835; Autovon 355-3972
Profile
BRANCH: Army National Guard.
SIZE AND LOCATION: 2000 acres (plus 400,000 acres available). Immediately W of US-101 between Astoria and Seaside; 90 mi W of Portland.
MAJOR UNITS: Detachment 3, HQ STARC ORARNG; 442nd Engineer Detachment (Utilities); 549th Medical Detachment (Veterinary Services); Company D, 1249th Engineer Battalion; Company E, 1st Battalion, 413th Regiment, 1st Training Brigade, 104th Division (Training); Army National Guard Recruiters; 116th Tactical Control Squadron.
BASE HISTORY: 1927, state-owned training site founded and originally called Camp Clatsop. Prior to WWII, used as mobilization site for 249th Coast Artillery. June 21, 1942, fired on by Japanese submarine. 1959, name changed for Maj Gen Thomas E Rilea, Adj Gen of OR, 1941-59. 1975, major revitalization.
Key Contacts
COMMANDER: Maj Gen Raymond F Rees; Adj Gen OR National Guard.
PROCUREMENT: Billeting Info & Supply; (503) 861-4051.
Personnel and Expenditures
ACTIVE DUTY PERSONNEL: 72
MILITARY PAYROLL EXPENDITURE: $2.7 mil
Services *Housing:* Barracks spaces 800; RV/Camper sites 10; Troop Hutments 600. *Temporary Housing:* VQ 7; Huts for rental individual/family. *Commissary and Exchange:* Laundry. *Medical Facilities:* Dispensary. *Recreational Facilities:* Movie theater; Gym; Recreation center; Fishing/Hunting; Part of Neacoxie Lake complex; Beach; Water sports.

PENNSYLVANIA

ANNVILLE

FORT INDIANTOWN GAP
USAG, Annville, PA 17003-5011
(717) 865-5444; Autovon 235-1110
OFFICER-OF-THE-DAY: (717) 865-2362
Profile
BRANCH: Army.
SIZE AND LOCATION: 18,000 acres. Approx 20 mi NE of Harrisburg, PA, just off I-81 & Rte 443. Bus service is available from downtown Harrisburg to a restaurant off post.
MAJOR UNITS: US Army Readiness Group; 56th Explosive Ordnance Detachment; FTIG Senior Army Advisor; US Army Reserve Center; First US Army NCO Academy; Region One NCO Academy; Logistics Support Center; Pennsylvania Department of Military Affairs; Pennsylvania Army National Guard Army Aviation Support Facility.
BASE HISTORY: Named from Indian communities that flourished in area; as defense measure, many forts and blockhouses built; Swatara Fort, located N of present site. 1930, PA National Guard used Mount Gretna as training area; field training for horse cavalry. WWII, staging area for NY Port of Embarkation and later separation center. 1946, inactivated. 1951-53, reactivated 5th Infantry Division. 1953-1957, under PA Military District. 1957-1968, XXI US Army Corps, administered Army Reserve program (PA, MD, DE, VA, and DC). 1968, mission transferred to First US Army, Ft George G Meade, MD. Resettlement camp, (1975, 22,228 Vietnamese and Cambodian refugees; 1980, 19,094 Cubans). Oct 1983, became subpost of Ft Meade, MD. Mission: training Army Reserve and National Guardsmen; FTIG leased by federal government from PA State.
VISITOR ATTRACTIONS: Hunting and fishing with post permit.
Key Contacts
COMMANDER: Col David G Bell; (717) 865-2666, Autovon 235-2666.
PUBLIC AFFAIRS: James M Danley; (717) 865-2315, Autovon 235-2315.
PROCUREMENT: Mr Garvey; (717) 865-2131.
TRANSPORTATION: R Zimmerman; (717) 865-2537.
PERSONNEL/COMMUNITY ACTIVITIES: See Public Affairs Officer (Acting); (717) 865-2296, Autovon 235- 2296.
Personnel and Expenditures
ACTIVE DUTY PERSONNEL: 20,000 in summer training
CIVILIAN PERSONNEL: 500
MILITARY PAYROLL EXPENDITURE: Paid by Ft Meade
CONTRACT EXPENDITURE: $8.6 mil

Services *Housing:* Family units 5; Barracks spaces 150; Mobile home units 26. *Temporary Housing:* VIP cottages 2; Guest cottages 11; VOQ/VEQ combined 1288. *Commissary and Exchange:* Retail store; Barber shop; Banking; Service station. *Base Library:* Yes. *Medical Facilities:* Medical clinic; Dental clinic. *Recreational Facilities:* Bowling; Pool; Gym; Recreation center; Tennis; Racquetball; Fitness center; Softball field; Auto shop; Officers club; Fishing/Hunting; Officers club (summers only); Community club.

CARLISLE BARRACKS

CARLISLE BARRACKS
Headquarters Carlisle Barracks, Carlisle Barracks, PA 17013-5002
(717) 245-3232; Autovon 8-242-3232
OFFICER-OF-THE-DAY: (717) 245-4342, Autovon 8-242-4342
Profile
BRANCH: Army.
SIZE AND LOCATION: 403 acres. Approx 18 mi W of Harrisburg, PA on US-11. Maingate is on Ashburn Dr 2 mi off Exit 16 of PA Tpke.
MAJOR UNITS: Dunham US Army Health/Dental Clinic; US Army Garrison; US Army Information Systems Command; US Army War College; US Army Military History Institute.
BASE HISTORY: Second oldest active military post in US, established May 30, 1757. French and Indian War, served as supply base and jumping-off point to west. 1777, site of Ordnance Magazine and first American Artillery School. 1794, Whiskey Rebellion, President Washington's troops assembled here; Cavalry School of Practice established. 1879, transferred to Dept of Interior as Indian School. 1918, Army reclaimed post for hospital, Medical Field Service School. 1946-1951, temporary home of School of Government of Occupied Area, Adjutant General's School, Army Chaplain School, Military Police School, Army Security Agency School, and Army Information School (later Armed Forces Information School). 1951, Army War College established. Main post 217 acres; detached areas, Stanwix Area (family housing) and Farm 2 (golf course, heliport, and stables).
VISITOR ATTRACTIONS: Omar N Bradley Museum; Hessian Powder Magazine Museum; Indian Cemetery; Military History Institute; Indian Industrial School Sites; Revolutionary War Forge; Schools Monument; Army War College Alumni Weekend (May each year).

Key Contacts
COMMANDER: Maj Gen Howard D Graves; Commanding General, Carlisle Barracks, PA 17013-5050, (717) 245-4400, Autovon 8-242-4400.
PUBLIC AFFAIRS: Lt Col John C Myers; Public Affairs Office, Carlisle Barracks, PA 17013-5050, (717) 245-4101, Autovon 8-242-4101.
PROCUREMENT: Kathy M Zeigler; Director of Contracting, ATZE-DOC, Carlisle Barracks, PA 17013-5002, (717) 245-4816, Autovon 8-242-4816.
TRANSPORTATION: James H Tapscott; Transportation Officer, ATZE-DIS-L-T, Carlisle Barracks, PA 17013-5002, (717) 245-3172, Autovon 8-242-3172.
PERSONNEL/COMMUNITY ACTIVITIES: Lt Col Charles K Rosenberry; Director of Personnel and Community Activities, ATZE-PA, Carlisle Barracks, PA 17013-5002, (717) 245-4332, Autovon 8-242-4332.
Personnel and Expenditures
ACTIVE DUTY PERSONNEL: 615
DEPENDENTS: 778
CIVILIAN PERSONNEL: 616
MILITARY PAYROLL EXPENDITURE: $27.8 mil
CONTRACT EXPENDITURE: $6.1 mil
Services *Housing:* Family units 321; BOQ cottages 3; BEQ units 2; Duplex units 101; Townhouse units 50; Barracks spaces 63; Senior NCO units 25; Junior NCO units 68. *Temporary Housing:* Guesthouse units 2. *Commissary:* Base commissary; Retail store; Barber shop; Dry cleaners; Food shop; Banking; Service station; Convenience store/Shopette; Book store; Garden center; Beauty shop; Candy/Ice cream; Laundry; Tailor; Credit union; Thrift shop. *Child Care/Capacities:* Day care center 52. *Base Library:* Yes. *Medical Facilities:* Medical clinic; Dental clinic. *Recreational Facilities:* Bowling; Movie theater; Pool; Gym; Recreation center (squash); Golf; Stables; Tennis; Racquetball; Fitness center; Softball field; Football field; Auto shop; Crafts; Officers club; NCO club; Fishing/Hunting; Riding and Hunt Club; Ski Club.

CHAMBERSBURG

LETTERKENNY ARMY DEPOT
Chambersburg, PA 17201-4150
(717) 267-8300; Autovon 570-8300
Profile
BRANCH: Army.
SIZE AND LOCATION: 19,000 acres. In S central PA, about 5 mi N of Chambersburg and 8 mi SW of Shippensburg. Main road serving the area is I-81, use Exit 5 & 6 (Chambersburg) and 8 (Scotland). Air service is provided through Hagerstown Regional and Harrisburg IAP. Hagerstown is 25 mi from the depot; Harrisburg 50 mi.

LETTERKENNY ARMY DEPOT (continued)
MAJOR UNITS: US Army Depot System Command; US AMC Central Systems Design Activity-East; US AMC Area Calibration & Repair Center; Defense Reutilization and Marketing Office.
BASE HISTORY: Sept 1942, received first shipment of ammunition. 1948, depot began reworking guns fire control equipment, and combat and general service vehicles. Korean War, construction boom. 1950s, overhauled Nike ground-to-air missile components. 1960s, developed automatic data processing systems for Army depots. Vietnam period, rebuilt artillery recoil mechanisms and stored/maintained Air Force missiles. 1976, established Major Item Supply Management Agency; later US Army Depot System Command, headquartered here.

Key Contacts
COMMANDER: Col Stephen L Etzel.
PUBLIC AFFAIRS: Raymond F David; (717) 267-5102, Autovon 570-5102.
PROCUREMENT: Ruth Massey; SDSLE-P, (717) 267-9007, Autovon 570-9007.
TRANSPORTATION: John Richardson; SDSLE-TT, (717) 267-9017, Autovon 570-9017.
PERSONNEL/COMMUNITY ACTIVITIES: Timothy Banks; SDSLE-BA, (717) 267-8410, Autovon 570-8410.

Personnel and Expenditures
ACTIVE DUTY PERSONNEL: 160
DEPENDENTS: 261
CIVILIAN PERSONNEL: 5000
CONTRACT EXPENDITURE: $3.4 mil
Services *Housing:* Family units 39; BEQ units 20; Duplex units 7; Townhouse units 2; Senior NCO units 2; Junior NCO units all enlisted grade compete equally; RV/Camper sites 8. *Temporary Housing:* Guesthouse units 3. *Commissary and Exchange:* Retail store; Banking; Credit union; Package beverages. *Child Care/Capacities:* Day care center. *Base Library:* Yes. *Medical Facilities:* Medical clinic. *Recreational Facilities:* Pool; Gym; Recreation center; Golf; Tennis; Racquetball; Fitness center; Softball field; Auto shop; Crafts; Officers club; NCO club; Camping; Fishing/Hunting; Rod and Gun Club.

MECHANICSBURG

MECHANICSBURG DEFENSE DEPOT
PO Box 2030, 5450 Carlisle Pike, Mechanicsburg, PA 17055-0789
(717) 790-2000; Autovon 430-2000
Profile
BRANCH: Department of Defense; Defense Logistics Agency.
SIZE AND LOCATION: 825 acres. On US Rte 11; US Rte 15 & 11 cross approx 3 mi to the E at Camp Hill, PA; Harrisburg 8 mi E; Harrisburg IAP 18 mi E.
MAJOR UNITS: DDMP is a tenant activity of the Navy Ships Parts Control Center.
BASE HISTORY: 1962, established. 1963, became integral part of Defense Logistics Agency; began operations from scratch from functional transferees from Army, Navy, and Air Force depots. Primary responsibility of providing common supplies and services to all branches of armed forces and elements of DOD.

Key Contacts
COMMANDER: Col Robert C Zschoche; (717) 790-2324; Code 00, Autovon 430-2324.
PUBLIC AFFAIRS: Pat Bettinger; (717) 790-2456, Autovon 430-2456.
TRANSPORTATION: Lt Col Samuel J Woolf; (717) 790-5715, Autovon 430-5715.
PERSONNEL/COMMUNITY ACTIVITIES: Personnel Director, Navy Ships Parts Control Center, Mechanicsburg.

Personnel and Expenditures
ACTIVE DUTY PERSONNEL: 17
CIVILIAN PERSONNEL: 1500
Services *Commissary and Exchange:* Barber shop; Banking; Package beverages. *Child Care/Capacities:* Day care center. *Medical Facilities:* Medical clinic.

NAVY SHIPS PARTS CONTROL CENTER
PO Box 2020, 5450 Carlisle Pike, Mechanicsburg, PA 17055-0788
(717) 790-2000; Autovon 430-2000
OFFICER-OF-THE-DAY: (717) 790-4444, Autovon 430-4444
Profile
BRANCH: Navy.
SIZE AND LOCATION: 825 acres. On US Rte 11; US Rte 15 & 11 cross approx 3 mi to the E at Camp Hill, PA; Harrisburg 8 mi E; Harrisburg IAP 18 mi E.
MAJOR UNITS: Navy Fleet Materiel Support Office; Defense Depot Mechanicsburg; Naval Sea Logistics Support Engineering Center; Navy Resale and Services Support Office, Field Support Office, Mechanicsburg; Personnel Support Activity Detachment, Mechanicsburg; Navy Publications and Printing Service Detachment Office.
BASE HISTORY: July 16, 1945, established as master control center for ships parts under Naval Supply Depot Mechanicsburg. 1953, commissioned as independent command as inventory manager of hull and machinery and diesel engine parts. July 1970, decommissioned. Installation changed to Navy SPCC, responsible for inventory control and weapons systems support for all Navy ships and 950 ships of 55 foreign navies.

Key Contacts
COMMANDER: (717) 790-3701; Code 00, Autovon 430-3701.
PUBLIC AFFAIRS: James F Nieb Jr; Code 003, (717) 790-3338, Autovon 430-3338.

Personnel and Expenditures
ACTIVE DUTY PERSONNEL: 140
CIVILIAN PERSONNEL: 8000
CONTRACT EXPENDITURE: $1.4 bil
Services *Housing:* Family units 92. *Temporary Housing:* Guesthouse units. *Commissary and Exchange:* Barber shop; Banking; Package beverages. *Child Care/Capacities:* Day care center. *Base Library:* Yes. *Medical Facilities:* Medical clinic. *Recreational Facilities:* Bowling; Pool; Gym; Golf; Tennis; Racquetball; Fitness center; Softball field; Auto shop; Officers club; NCO club.

MIDDLETOWN

193RD ELECTRONIC COMBAT GROUP (ANG)
Harrisburg IAP, Middletown, PA 17057
(717) 948-2201; Autovon 454-9201
Profile
BRANCH: Air National Guard.
SIZE AND LOCATION: 72 acres. 10 mi E of Harrisburg; S of I-76, off State Rte 230.
MAJOR UNITS: 193rd Electronic Combat Group (ANG).
Personnel and Expenditures
ACTIVE DUTY PERSONNEL: 987
CIVILIAN PERSONNEL: 217
MILITARY PAYROLL EXPENDITURE: $13.5 mil

NEW CUMBERLAND

NEW CUMBERLAND ARMY DEPOT
New Cumberland, PA 17070-5001
(717) 770-6011; Autovon 977-6011
Profile
BRANCH: Army.
SIZE AND LOCATION: 850 acres. Foothills of the Cumberland Mountains 5 mi S of Harrisburg, 4 mi from intersection of US 83 and PA Tpke (I-76).
MAJOR UNITS: Army Security Affairs Command; Army Logistics Evaluation Agency; Army General Materiel & Petroleum Activity; Military Entrance Processing Station; Army Materiel Command Catalog Data Activity (AMC CDA); 315th Engineer Group; 3518th Air Force Recruiting Squadron; Mobile Rail Repair Shop No 1; Marine Corps Recruiting Station; Army Recruiting Battalion.
BASE HISTORY: Oldest and busiest depot in continuous operation in Army Depot Command. 1917, built by Corps of Engineers in as Marsh Run Storage Depot; later redesignated Army Reserve Depot for storage of Quartermaster, Signal, Ordnance, Medical, Engineer and Chemical Warfare items. Jan 1948, became separate installation under Quartermaster General. Reorganized several times since. Part of Army Materiel Command (AMC), responsible for insuring weapon, equipment and logistics readiness of Army.

Key Contacts
COMMANDER: Col Paul A Fleming; (717) 770-7401, Autovon 977-7401.
PUBLIC AFFAIRS: James J Williams; (717) 770-7902, Autovon 977-7902.
PROCUREMENT: Pat Ebersole; (717) 770-7186, Autovon 977-7186.
TRANSPORTATION: Karen E Brinton; (717) 770-6091, Autovon 977-6091.
PERSONNEL/COMMUNITY ACTIVITIES: Maj E Rouse III; (717) 770-6322, Autovon 977-6322.

Personnel and Expenditures
ACTIVE DUTY PERSONNEL: 500
DEPENDENTS: 300
CIVILIAN PERSONNEL: 3650
MILITARY PAYROLL EXPENDITURE: $119 mil
CONTRACT EXPENDITURE: $19 mil
Services *Housing:* Family units 143; BEQ units 26; Duplex units 40; Townhouse units 93; Senior NCO units 24; Junior NCO units 93; Detached units 10. *Temporary Housing:* VOQ cottages 21; BOQ units 2. *Commissary:* Base commissary; Retail store; Service station; Thrift shop; Package beverages; Airline ticket office; Credit union. *Child Care/Capacities:* Day care center 60; Home day care program; School age/latch key program, 6-12yrs 75. *Base Library:* Yes. *Medical Facilities:* Medical clinic. *Recreational Facilities:* Bowling; Movie theater; Pool; Gym; Golf; Tennis; Racquetball; Fitness center; Softball field; Auto shop; Crafts; Fishing/Hunting.

OAKDALE

CHARLES E KELLY SUPPORT FACILITY
Oakdale, PA 15071-5000
(412) 777-1173; Autovon 277-1173
Profile
BRANCH: Army.
SIZE AND LOCATION: 201 acres. 11 mi from Pittsburgh, PA, and 12 mi from the Greater Pittsburgh IAP.
MAJOR UNITS: 99th US Army Reserve Command; US Army Readiness Group Pittsburgh.

CHARLES E KELLY SUPPORT FACILITY
(continued)
BASE HISTORY: 1961, HQs, US Army Support Detachment, Oakdale moved from South Park, county park of Allegheny County, PA, to present location; first occupied by HQ and HQ Battery, 18th Artillery Group (AD) and 662nd Radar Squadron (USAF). 1962, FAA assumed radar mission from USAF. 1974, US Army Support Detachment and FAA remaining activities at Oakdale; land released to Department of Interior for Legacy of Parks program. 1977, FORSCOM implements one-post concept, deactivating HQ, US Army Support Detachment; post redesignated as Oakdale Support Element and support activities remaining transferred to existing Directorships, Ft Indiantown Gap, Annville, PA. 1983, Oakdale Support Element became subinstallation of Ft George G Meade, MD. 1987, received current name.
Key Contacts
COMMANDER: Col Robert P Hodor; Garrison Commander, ATTN: AFKA-CK-GC.
PUBLIC AFFAIRS: 1Lt Daniel E Bohr; Headquarters, ATTN: AFKA-CK-ADJ, (412) 777-1336, Autovon 277-1336.
PROCUREMENT: Diane Bogan (Acting); Headquarters, ATTN: AFKA-CK-C, (412) 777-1228, Autovon 277-1228.
TRANSPORTATION: Frederick Barbieri; Headquarters, ATTN: AFKA-CK-DL-TO, (412) 777-1202, Autovon 277-1202.
PERSONNEL/COMMUNITY ACTIVITIES: Janet E Glasser; Headquarters, ATTN: AFKA-CK-PA, (412) 777-1177, Autovon 277-1177.
Personnel and Expenditures
ACTIVE DUTY PERSONNEL: 120
CIVILIAN PERSONNEL: 150
CONTRACT EXPENDITURE: $3 mil
Services *Housing:* Family housing units are to be phased out in 1990-91. *Commissary:* Base commissary; Retail store; Barber shop; MCSS; Personal items. *Recreational Facilities:* Gym; Recreation center; Consolidated Club.

PHILADELPHIA

AVIATION SUPPLY OFFICE COMPOUND
700 Robbins Ave, Philadelphia, PA 19111-5098
(215) 697-2000; Autovon 442-2000
OFFICER-OF-THE-DAY: ASO (215) 697-2207, Autovon 442-2207; DISC (215) 697-2319, Autovon 442-2319
Profile
BRANCH: Navy.
SIZE AND LOCATION: 137 acres. NE Philadelphia, 15 mi N of Philadelphia IAP.
MAJOR UNITS: Aviation Supply Office; Defense Industrial Supply Center (DISC); Navy Publications and Forms Center (NPFC); Naval Air Technical Services Facility (NATSF); Navy Publishing & Printing Service, Northern Div (NPPS).
Key Contacts
COMMANDER: Rear Adm James E Eckelberger, SC, USN; (215) 697-2101, Autovon 442-2101.
PUBLIC AFFAIRS: Philip Sheridan; (215) 697-3131, Autovon 442-3131.
PROCUREMENT: Capt John Mullen, SC, USN; (215) 697-2848, Autovon 442-2848.
TRANSPORTATION: Carl Wright; (215) 697-4871, Autovon 442-4871.
PERSONNEL/COMMUNITY ACTIVITIES: Michael Abbott; (215) 697-2634, Autovon 442-2634.

Personnel and Expenditures
ACTIVE DUTY PERSONNEL: 150
CIVILIAN PERSONNEL: 6500
CONTRACT EXPENDITURE: $1.8 bil (ASO)
Services *Housing:* Family units; 15 total. *Temporary Housing:* VIP cottages 1. *Commissary and Exchange:* Branch of main exchange at NAVBASE, Philadelphia. *Medical Facilities:* Medical clinic. *Recreational Facilities:* Pool; Gym; Tennis; Fitness center; Softball field; Football field; Crafts; Officers club.

DEFENSE PERSONNEL SUPPORT CENTER
2800 S 20th Street, Philadelphia, PA 19101-8419
(215) 952-2000; Autovon 444-2000
Profile
BRANCH: Department of Defense; Defense Logistics Agency.
SIZE AND LOCATION: 86 acres. In S Philadelphia, right off I-76, 3 mi from airport, 6 mi from downtown.
MAJOR UNITS: Office of Commander Subsistence Field Activities and Director, Subsistence; Directorate of Clothing and Textiles; Directorate of Medical Materiel; Directorate of Manufacturing; Office of Telecommunications and Informations Systems.
BASE HISTORY: 1800, began as Philadelphia Arsenal, warehouse for supplies and ammunition. 1941, expansion with new warehouses, today's headquarters building, and clothing factory. 1965, DPSC established when Defense Subsistence Supply of Chicago and Defense Medical Supply of Brooklyn consolidated with Clothing and Textiles Supply Center in Philadelphia. Buys food, clothing, textiles, medicines, and medical equipment for members of Army, Navy, Air Force, Marines, and Coast Guard.
VISITOR ATTRACTIONS: Flag room.
Key Contacts
COMMANDER: Maj Gen John H Voorhees, USAF; (215) 952-2300, Autovon 444-2300.
PUBLIC AFFAIRS: Frank I Johnson Jr; (215) 952-2311, Autovon 444-2311.
PROCUREMENT: John Kitchenmann; (215) 952-2600, Autovon 444-2600.
TRANSPORTATION: Lt Col Barbaro Giorgianni; (215) 952-2651, Autovon 444-2651.
PERSONNEL/COMMUNITY ACTIVITIES: Jimmy Ownes; (215) 952-2320, Autovon 444-2320.
Personnel and Expenditures
ACTIVE DUTY PERSONNEL: 150
CIVILIAN PERSONNEL: 8000
CONTRACT EXPENDITURE: $4.3 bil
Services *Temporary Housing:* Apartment units 4. *Commissary and Exchange:* Barber shop; Food shop. *Base Library:* Yes. *Medical Facilities:* Medical clinic. *Recreational Facilities:* Bowling; Gym; Recreation center; Racquetball; Fitness center; Auto shop; Officers club.

PHILADELPHIA COAST GUARD MARINE SAFETY OFFICE AND GROUP
1 Washington Ave, Philadelphia, PA 19147-4395
(215) 271-4800
OFFICER-OF-THE-DAY: (215) 271-4800
Profile
BRANCH: Coast Guard.
SIZE AND LOCATION: 2 acres. At the intersection of Washington and Delaware Ave approx 1 mi N of the Walt Whitman Bridge.
MAJOR UNITS: Coast Guard Cutter *Red Oak.*

BASE HISTORY: June 7, 1988, commissioned with merger of Marine Inspection Office, Philadelphia and Base Gloucester City, NJ. Combined all USCG assets and missions under a single command. Colocation with tenant marine units of Philadelphia Police and Fire Departments. Search and rescue from falls in Trenton, NJ, in N to Ship John Shoal light in S and tributaries of Delaware River.
Key Contacts
COMMANDER: Capt Edward K Roe, USCG; (215) 271-4800, ext 804.
PUBLIC AFFAIRS: Lt James H I Weakley; (215) 271-4800, ext 889.
PROCUREMENT: CWO Robert F Vanderslice; (215) 271-4800, ext 810.
TRANSPORTATION: CWO Ronald Dinlocker; (215) 271-4800, ext 855.
PERSONNEL/COMMUNITY ACTIVITIES: CWO Connie H Bailey; (215) 271-4800, ext 806.
Personnel and Expenditures
ACTIVE DUTY PERSONNEL: 140
CIVILIAN PERSONNEL: 20
MILITARY PAYROLL EXPENDITURE: $960,000
CONTRACT EXPENDITURE: $400,000
Services *Housing:* Barracks spaces 9. *Commissary and Exchange:* Retail store.

PHILADELPHIA NAVAL BASE
Philadelphia, PA 19112
(215) 897-5000; Autovon 443-5000
OFFICER-OF-THE-DAY: (215) 897-5120, Autovon 443-5120
Profile
BRANCH: Navy.
SIZE AND LOCATION: 1000 acres. In SE Philadelphia, approx 10 min from Philadelphia IAP; Broad St Exit from I-95 or I-76, take Broad St S to main gate.
MAJOR UNITS: Commander, Naval Base Philadelphia; Defense Contract Administration Services Region Philadelphia; Defense Personnel Support Center; Fourth Marine Corps District; USS *Patterson*; USS *Oliver Hazard Perry*; USS *Clark*; USS *Estocin*; USS *Clifton Sprague*; Marine Corps Recruiting Station-Philadelphia; Marine Wing Support Squadron 474(-) Fourth Marine Aircraft Wing, Philadelphia; Naval Aviation Service Unit; Naval Damage Control Training Center; Naval Dental Clinic; Naval Facilities Engineering Command Northern Division; Naval Hospital; Naval Industrial Resources Support Activity; Naval Investigative Service Resident Agency; Naval Legal Service Office; Naval Regional Contracting Center; Naval Reserve Readiness Center; Naval Reserve Readiness Command Region Four; Naval Sea Systems Command Detachment Inactive Ship Maintenance Facility; Naval Ship Systems Engineering Station; Naval Station Philadelphia; Command Support Department; Correctional Custody Unit; Naval Brig Philadelphia; Staff Civil Engineer's Office; Supply Department; Navy Publishing and Printing Service; Navy Resale Activity; Office of Civilian Personnel Management, Northeast Region; Personnel Support Activity, Philadelphia; Philadelphia Naval Shipyard; Shore Intermediate Maintenance Activity.
BASE HISTORY: 1801, first Navy shipyard built at foot of Federal St, downtown Philadelphia. Late 1860s, moved to present site at what was then known as League Island; mostly underwater and requiring extensive excavation and dredging. During Spanish-American War, 2 dry docks built. WWI, Naval aircraft factory built on E side of base. Following WWI, changed to center for developing and manufacturing experimental aircraft.

PHILADELPHIA NAVAL BASE *(continued)*

Shipyard, in over 188 years, built 127 ships, last one, USS *Blue Ridge*, 1971. Now specializes in revitalization and repair of ships under Service Life Extension Program (SLEP).

Key Contacts

COMMANDER: (215) 897-8706.
PUBLIC AFFAIRS: (215) 897-8775.
PROCUREMENT: (215) 897-8739, Autovon 443-8739.

Personnel and Expenditures

ACTIVE DUTY PERSONNEL: 3500
DEPENDENTS: 6000
Services *Housing:* Family units; BOQ cottages; BEQ units; Townhouse units 450; Trailer spaces 36; Apartment units 176. *Temporary Housing:* Transient living quarters 5; Units w/shared bath 140. *Commissary:* Base commissary; Retail store; Barber shop; Dry cleaners; Food shop; Florist; Banking; Service station; Military clothing sales; Convenience store/Shopette; Credit union; Package beverages; 3 exchanges and branch; Garden center; Toys; Beauty shop; Laundry; Tailor; Video rental; Photo finishing; Jewelry/watch sales and repair; Optical shop; Ice cream; Fast food. *Child Care/Capacities:* Day care center; Preschool/learning center; Summer day camp. *Schools:* Navy campus. *Base Library:* Yes. *Medical Facilities:* Hospital; Medical clinic; Dental clinic. *Recreational Facilities:* Bowling; Movie theater; Pool; Gym; Recreation center; Golf; Tennis; Racquetball; Fitness center; Softball field; Football field; Auto shop; Crafts; Officers club; NCO club; SATO; ITT; Youth activities; Equipment rental; Soccer field.

PHILADELPHIA NAVAL HOSPITAL

1701 Pattison Ave, Philadelphia, PA 19145-5199
(215) 897-8000; Autovon 443-8000
OFFICER-OF-THE-DAY: (215) 897-8000, Autovon 443-8000
Profile
BRANCH: Navy.
SIZE AND LOCATION: 49 acres. SE Philadelphia, approx 10 min from Philadelphia IAP. Use I-95 or I-76 Broad St Exit, N to Pattison Ave, left on Pattison, hospital on right; N of Naval Base, Philadelphia and is separate from base.
MAJOR UNITS: Naval Hospital.
BASE HISTORY: 1935, established. Current hospital provides general clinical and hospitalization services primarily for active duty military, subject to availability of space, facilities, and capabilities.
VISITOR ATTRACTIONS: Art and science museums; historical attractions within walking distance.
Key Contacts
COMMANDER: Capt William M Jackman.
PUBLIC AFFAIRS: (215) 897-8134, Autovon 443-8134.
PROCUREMENT: Lt Wellen; (215) 897-8340, Autovon 443-8340.
TRANSPORTATION: Lt Kelly; (215) 897-8314, Autovon 443-8314.
PERSONNEL/COMMUNITY ACTIVITIES: Ens Nixon; (215) 897-8103, Autovon 443-8103.
Personnel and Expenditures
ACTIVE DUTY PERSONNEL: 441
CIVILIAN PERSONNEL: 225
MILITARY PAYROLL EXPENDITURE: $18 mil
Services *Housing:* Family units 13; BEQ units 3; Additional housing on Naval Base. *Commissary and Exchange:* Barber shop. *Schools:* Space taken by one Philadelphia kindergarten. *Base Library:* Yes. *Medical Facilities:* Hospital 78. *Recreational Facilities:* Bowling; Tennis; Fitness center; Softball field.

PHILADELPHIA NAVAL SHIPYARD

Philadelphia, PA 19112-5287
OFFICER-OF-THE-DAY: (215) 897-3350, Autovon 443-3350
Profile
BRANCH: Navy.
SIZE AND LOCATION: 944 acres. On Philadelphia Naval Base at the confluence of the Delaware and Schuylkill Rivers within the city limits at the S border.
BASE HISTORY: Opened 1801, 1st Naval Shipyard. 1876, Navy Yard relocated to League Island S of city. PNSY has built 125 ships and repaired/overhauled thousands. Portion of "back channel" serves as anchorage for mothball ships in reserve. five dry docks, two of Navy's largest, can accommodate any ship currently in Navy. Navy's only propeller manufacturing facility, Navy's East Coast Amalgamated Foundry, East Coast Naval Tactical Data System Land Based Test and Restoration Facility, and East Coast Oil Free Engineering Calibration and Cleaning Facility housed here.
Key Contacts
COMMANDER: Capt Arthur D Clark; Code 100, (215) 897-5681, Autovon 443-5681.
PUBLIC AFFAIRS: Albert W Peterson; Code 103, (215) 897-3156, Autovon 443-3156.
PROCUREMENT: Capt Robert L Collette, Supply Officer; Code 500, (215) 897-3153, Autovon 443-3153.
TRANSPORTATION: Capt Duncan Hughes, Public Works Officer; Code 400, (215) 897-3170, Autovon 443-3170.
PERSONNEL/COMMUNITY ACTIVITIES: Mort Adelberg, Industrial Relations Officer; Code 150, (215) 897-2625, Autovon 443-2625.
Personnel and Expenditures
ACTIVE DUTY PERSONNEL: 100
CIVILIAN PERSONNEL: 8400
Services *Housing:* Family units 906; BOQ cottages 140; BEQ units 1803; Townhouse units (off-base). *Commissary:* Base commissary; Retail store; Barber shop; Dry cleaners; Food shop; Florist; Banking; Service station; Furniture store; Bakery; Book store; Item. *Child Care/Capacities:* Day care center; Home day care program. *Schools:* Kindergarten/Preschool; Elementary; Intermediate/Junior high; High school. *Base Library:* Yes. *Medical Facilities:* Hospital; Medical clinic; Dental clinic. *Recreational Facilities:* Bowling; Movie theater; Pool; Gym; Recreation center; Golf; Stables; Tennis; Racquetball; Skating rink; Fitness center; Softball field; Football field; Auto shop; Crafts; Officers club; NCO club; Camping; Fishing/Hunting.

438TH AERIAL PORT SQUADRON, DETACHMENT 1 (MAC)

Terminal D, Philadelphia IAP, Philadelphia, PA 19153
(215) 897-5645
Profile
BRANCH: Air Force.
SIZE AND LOCATION: 3 acres. At Philadelphia IAP.
MAJOR UNITS: 438th Aerial Port Squadron, Detachment 1.
BASE HISTORY: Provides services required to process, move, and receive DOD air transportation eligible passengers using DOD owned, controlled, or procured air transportation. Detachment located at commercial airport assigned to APS which is attached to MAW. This detachment reports to 438th APS, McGurie AFB, NJ. Prior to civilian contracting, staffed entirely by AF personnel. Departing on MAC flight, check-in counters in Concourse D and available at least 8 hours prior to departure time.

Personnel and Expenditures
ACTIVE DUTY PERSONNEL: 10
Services *Medical Facilities:* Red Cross office. *Recreational Facilities:* Interline baggage from connecting domestic flights; Transportation to and from Bayonne, NJ; USO facilities; VIP passenger facility; Contracts with local hotels to provide lodging for distressed passengers; SATO; Transportation to separation point at Ft Dix.

PITTSBURGH

PENNSYLVANIA AIR NATIONAL GUARD

Greater Pittsburgh International Airport, Pittsburgh, PA 15231-0459
(412) 269-8359; Autovon 277-8359
OFFICER-OF-THE-DAY: (412) 269-8378, Autovon 277-8378
Profile
BRANCH: Air National Guard.
LOCATION: At the Greater Pittsburgh IAP in Moon Township, 10 mi from downtown.
MAJOR UNITS: 171st Air Refueling Wing (SAC); 112th Tactical Fighter Group (TAC).
Key Contacts
COMMANDER: Brig Gen Robert G Chrisjohn; (412) 269-8359, Autovon 277-8359.
PUBLIC AFFAIRS: 1st Lt Sandra L Slaven; (412) 269-8350, 269-8378, Autovon 277-8350, 277-8378.
PROCUREMENT: Lt Col Brian Carroll; (412) 269-8354, Autovon 277-8354.
TRANSPORTATION: CMS John Campbell; (412) 269-8357, Autovon 277-8357.
PERSONNEL/COMMUNITY ACTIVITIES: Capt Robert Bundy; (412) 269-8314, Autovon 277-8314.
Personnel and Expenditures
ACTIVE DUTY PERSONNEL: 105
CIVILIAN PERSONNEL: 472
Services *Commissary and Exchange:* Retail store; Dry cleaners. *Schools:* College courses held on base. *Recreational Facilities:* Gym; Fitness center.

US ARMY CORPS OF ENGINEERS, PITTSBURGH DISTRICT

1000 Liberty Ave, William S Moorhead Federal Bldg, Pittsburgh, PA 15222
(412) 644-6924
Profile
BRANCH: Army.
SIZE: Offices only.

SCRANTON

SCRANTON ARMY AMMUNITION PLANT

156 Cedar Ave, Scranton, PA 18505-1138
(717) 342-7801; Autovon 247-1350
Profile
BRANCH: Army.
SIZE AND LOCATION: 15.3 acres. Downtown Scranton, PA; From the airport, take I-81 N to Exit 53 (Central Scranton Expy); then, 1st exit onto Cedar Ave; at the stop sign turn right; Scranton AAP is on left.
MAJOR UNITS: Government-owned, contractor operated, military industrial installation under jurisdiction of Army Armament, Munitions and Chemical Command (AMCCOM).
BASE HISTORY: 1951, established; converted 50 year old, privately owned, railroad maintenance facility to production plant for metal parts used in large caliber artillery projectiles. 1953, began manufacturing projectiles pursuant to GOCO agreement between Army and US Hoffman Machinery Co. 1962, contract awarded to

SCRANTON ARMY AMMUNITION PLANT (continued)

current operator, Chamberlain Manufacturing Co.

Key Contacts
COMMANDER: Lt Col Samuel E Mims.
PUBLIC AFFAIRS: Capt John D McDermott.
PROCUREMENT: Anthony Pisano.

Personnel and Expenditures
ACTIVE DUTY PERSONNEL: 2
CIVILIAN PERSONNEL: 17 DOD 600 contractors
CONTRACT EXPENDITURE: $33.6 mil

Services *Medical Facilities:* Industrial medical clinic with 1 nurse on duty.

TOBYHANNA

TOBYHANNA ARMY DEPOT
Tobyhanna, PA 18466
(717) 894-7000
OFFICER-OF-THE-DAY: (717) 894-7200

Profile
BRANCH: Army.
SIZE AND LOCATION: 1293 acres. Heart of Pocono Mountains, NE PA, just off I-380 approx 20 mi S of Scranton, PA; Airports, Scranton/Wilkes-Barre and Allentown/Bethlehem/Easton 22 and 50 mi, respectively, from depot.
MAJOR UNITS: New Weapon System Support; Supply Programs; Fabrication and Manufacturing; Directorate of Information Management; Quality Assurance; AMC Packaging, Storage, and Containerization Center; AMC Central Systems Design Activity-East, Resources Data Analysis Branch; Defense Reutilization and Marketing Office; Monroe County Memorial, US Army Reserve Center; US Army Health Clinic; Medical Equipment Maintenance Division; Department of the Army Joint Visual Information Activity; US Army Medical Materiel Agency; US Army Area TMDE Support Center; US Army Corps of Engineers, Baltimore District-Northeast Resident Office.
BASE HISTORY: 1913, Tobyhanna Military Reservation used Army and NG as artillery site. WWI, Ambulance and Tank Regiment Training Center. Following WWI, idle until 1938-41, when West Point cadets used it for field artillery training. 1942, reactivated as Army Air Force Unit Training Center; storage and supply depot for Air Service Command; POW camp for German prisoners. 1948, acquired by state from War Assets Administration. 1951, Corps of Engineers established Signal Depot; 1953, opened. Today, Army's prime supply and maintenance center for communications and electronics systems; designated Center of Technical Excellence (CTX) for 10 critical systems and space communications program.
VISITOR ATTRACTIONS: The Pocono Mts, resorts and recreation facilities.

Key Contacts
COMMANDER: Col Rex M Isley; (717) 894-7201.
PUBLIC AFFAIRS: Joan E Mier; Tobyhanna, PA 18466-5076, (717) 894-7308.
PROCUREMENT: Director of Contracting; (717) 894-7232.
PERSONNEL/COMMUNITY ACTIVITIES: Director of Military Personnel and Community Activities; (717) 894-6637.

Personnel and Expenditures
ACTIVE DUTY PERSONNEL: 36
CIVILIAN PERSONNEL: 4082
CONTRACT EXPENDITURE: $40 mil

Services *Housing:* Family units 1; BOQ cottages; BEQ units; Townhouse units 40; Barracks spaces 280; 1 bedroom efficiency apartments 9. *Temporary Housing:* VOQ cot-

tages 1; Guesthouse units 2. *Commissary:* Base commissary; Barber shop; Banking; Service station; Package beverages; Credit union. *Child Care/Capacities:* Day care center. *Base Library:* Yes. *Medical Facilities:* Medical clinic. *Recreational Facilities:* Movie theater; Gym; Racquetball; Fitness center (weight room); Softball field; Auto shop; Crafts; Fishing/Hunting; Youth center (activities); Community club; Snow sports; Barney's Lake; Picnicking; Equipment rental; Basketball; Volleyball; ITT.

WILLOW GROVE

WILLOW GROVE NAVAL AIR STATION
Naval Air Station, Willow Grove, PA 19090-5010
(215) 443-1776, 443-1777, 443-1779; Autovon 991-1776

Profile
BRANCH: Air Force; Army; Marines; Navy; Army National Guard.
SIZE AND LOCATION: 1000 acres. In town of Hatboro, 3.5 mi N of PA Tpke Exit 27; 20 mi N of Philadelphia at Horsham off I-276..
MAJOR UNITS: Patrol Squadron 64 & 66; Helicopter Antisubmarine Squadron Light 94; Fleet Logistics Support Squadron 52; Marine Aircraft Group 49; 79th Army Reserve Command; 913 Tactical Airlift Group-Air Force Reserve; 111th Pennsylvania Air National Guard.
VISITOR ATTRACTIONS: Antique aircraft display of WWII, Korean Conflict, and Vietnam era; base tour program.

Key Contacts
COMMANDER: Capt James R Shapard III; (215) 443-6051, Autovon 991-6051.
PUBLIC AFFAIRS: Ens Barbara MacStravic; (215) 443-1776, 443-1777, 443-1779, Autovon 991-1776.
TRANSPORTATION: LCDR M Zook; (215) 443-6221, Autovon 991-6221.
PERSONNEL/COMMUNITY ACTIVITIES: See Public Affairs Officer.

Personnel and Expenditures
ACTIVE DUTY PERSONNEL: 474
DEPENDENTS: 10
CIVILIAN PERSONNEL: 212
MILITARY PAYROLL EXPENDITURE: FY 89, $15.5 mil
CONTRACT EXPENDITURE: FY 89, $13 mil

Services *Housing:* Family units 6; Barracks spaces 5; RV/Camper sites Base housing 8 mi from base at Naval Air Development Center, Warminister, PA. *Temporary Housing:* BOQ units Barracks 1. *Commissary and Exchange:* Retail store; Barber shop; Dry cleaners; Food shop; Florist; Banking. *Child Care/Capacities:* Day care center 45-50. *Base Library:* Yes. *Medical Facilities:* Medical clinic; Dental clinic. *Recreational Facilities:* Bowling; Movie theater; Pool; Gym; Tennis; Racquetball; Fitness center; Softball field; Football field; Auto shop; Officers club.

WYOMING

92ND AERIAL PORT SQUADRON
1160 Wyoming Ave, Wyoming, PA 18644-0003
(717) 288-5427; Autovon 81-991-1290

Profile
BRANCH: Air Force Reserve.
SIZE AND LOCATION: 2 acres. In the town of Wyoming, on US Rte 11, 10 mi from I-81 and 10 mi from PA Tpke.
MAJOR UNITS: 92nd Aerial Port Squadron.
BASE HISTORY: Air Force Reserve Center with a building and C-130 training aid; mother unit is 512th MAW, Dover AFB, DE.

Key Contacts
COMMANDER: Lt Col Charles L Attardo, USAFR.

Personnel and Expenditures
CIVILIAN PERSONNEL: 2

RHODE ISLAND

NEWPORT

NAVAL EDUCATION AND TRAINING CENTER

Newport, RI 02841-5000
(401) 841-2311; Autovon 948-2311
OFFICER-OF-THE-DAY: (401) 841-3456,
    Autovon 948-3456

Profile

BRANCH: Navy.

SIZE AND LOCATION: 256 acres. Approx 30 mi from Providence Airport. Base located off Rte 138 and Rte 114.

MAJOR UNITS: Naval Education and Training Center; Naval War College; Naval Underwater Systems Center; Naval Surface Group Four, Newport; Surface Warfare Officers School Command; Senior Officer Ship Materiel Readiness Course; Naval Justice School; Navy Regional Data Automation Center; Trident Command and Control Systems Maintenance Activity; Naval Regional Contracting Center; Naval Telecommunications Center; Naval Hospital, Newport; Naval Legal Service Office; Naval Reserve Readiness Command, Region One; Naval Construction Battalion Unit 408. NETC operates nine schools: Officer Candidate School, International Officer Candidate School, Officer Candidate Preparatory School, Naval Academy Preparatory School, Officer Indoctrination School, Chaplains School, Communications School, Senior Enlisted Academy, and Instructors Training School.

BASE HISTORY: During Civil War, Naval Academy moved to Newport. 1869-1951 experimental torpedo station at Goat Island, replaced by Naval Underwater Ordnance Station. 1883, Coasters Harbor Island first recruit training station. 1884, Naval War College established. 1913, Navy acquired Government Landing downtown Newport. 1940, Coddington Cove as Supply Station; Melville as PT-Boat Training Center and Net Depot. 1941, Air Station operational and Advanced Base Depot at Davisville (later Construction Battalion Center). 1946, Naval complex in Bay area consolidated as US Naval Base. 1952, Naval Training Station, Newport transferred to Bainbridge, MD. 1973, Quonset Point Naval Air Station closed; drawdown of facilities at Davisville; active fleet moved from Newport.

VISITOR ATTRACTIONS: Naval War College Museum.

Key Contacts

COMMANDER: Capt F James Barnes III; (401) 841-3715, Autovon 948-3715.

PUBLIC AFFAIRS: Mary K Silvia; Public Affairs Office NETC, Newport, RI 02841-5000, (401) 841-3538, Autovon 948-3538.

PROCUREMENT: CDR James Parham, SC, USN; Comptroller/Director for Supply, (401) 841-3037, Autovon 948-3037.

TRANSPORTATION: Donald Guilfoyle.

PERSONNEL/COMMUNITY ACTIVITIES: Dennis Pucello; Director of Personnel.

Personnel and Expenditures

ACTIVE DUTY PERSONNEL: 5600

CIVILIAN PERSONNEL: 4100

MILITARY PAYROLL EXPENDITURE: $366 mil

CONTRACT EXPENDITURE: $24 mil

Services *Housing:* Family units 1479; BOQ cottages 580; BEQ units 400; Trailer spaces 40; Including student officer qtrs 380. *Commissary:* Base commissary; Retail store; Barber shop; Dry cleaners; Food shop; Florist; Banking; Service station; Bakery; Snacks; Beauty shop; Optical shop; Laundry; Tailor; Jewelry/watch sales and repair; Credit union; Package beverages; Thrift shop. *Child Care/Capacities:* Day care center; Home day care program. *Schools:* Kindergarten/Preschool. *Base Library:* Yes. *Medical Facilities:* Hospital 59; Naval dental clinic. *Recreational Facilities:* Bowling; Pool; Gym; Tennis; Racquetball; Softball field; Auto shop; Officers club; NCO club; Fishing/Hunting; Wives clubs; Newport Armed Services YMCA; Fleet Reserve Association-Branch 19.

PROVIDENCE

143RD TACTICAL AIRLIFT GROUP (ANG)

Quonset Point State Airport, Providence, RI 02852
(401) 885-3960; Autovon 476-3210

Profile

BRANCH: Air National Guard.

SIZE AND LOCATION: 79 acres. 20 mi S of Providence, off US Rte 1.

MAJOR UNITS: 143rd Tactical Airlift Group (ANG).

Personnel and Expenditures

ACTIVE DUTY PERSONNEL: 868

CIVILIAN PERSONNEL: 184

MILITARY PAYROLL EXPENDITURE: $10.6 mil

SOUTH CAROLINA

BEAUFORT

BEAUFORT MARINE CORPS AIR STATION

Beaufort, SC 29904-5001
(803) 522-7298; Autovon 832-7298
OFFICER-OF-THE-DAY: (803) 522-7121,
Autovon 832-7121
Profile
BRANCH: Marines.
SIZE AND LOCATION: 6600 acres. Approx 1.5
mi N of Beaufort, SC, on Hwy 21.
MAJOR UNITS: Headquarters and Headquarters Squadron; Marine Aircraft Group-31.
BASE HISTORY: Formerly location of Tidewater Hospital, Scott Crop Dusting Service, Busbee Pike Flying Service, and Blue Channel Freezer Plant prior to becoming airfield. 1943, Naval Auxiliary Air Station commissioned. During WWII, operated antisubmarine patrols on US southeastern seaboard. 1960, redesignated Marine Corps Air Station, named Merritt Field for Maj Gen Lewie Merritt, SC native. MCAS base of operations for Fleet Marine Force (FMF) units; also operates family housing area 3 mi W of base, Laurel Bay.
Key Contacts
COMMANDER: Col John J Sullivan; (803) 522-7158, Autovon 832-7158.
PUBLIC AFFAIRS: Capt Mark Hough; (803) 522-7201, Autovon 832-7201.
PROCUREMENT: Maj R M Welter; (803) 522-7845, Autovon 832-7845.
TRANSPORTATION: Mr Phillips; (803) 522-7507, Autovon 832-7507.
Personnel and Expenditures
ACTIVE DUTY PERSONNEL: 3373
DEPENDENTS: 5456
CIVILIAN PERSONNEL: 9554
MILITARY PAYROLL EXPENDITURE: $15 mil
CONTRACT EXPENDITURE: $12.5 mil
Services *Housing:* Family units 1276; Dormitory spaces 1643; Trailer spaces 120. *Temporary Housing:* BOQ units 119; Transient living quarters 156. *Commissary and Exchange:* Retail store; Barber shop; Dry cleaners; Food shop; Banking; Service station. *Child Care/Capacities:* Day care center 151. *Schools:* Kindergarten/Preschool; Elementary. *Base Library:* Yes. *Medical Facilities:* Medical clinic; Dental clinic. *Recreational Facilities:* Bowling; Movie theater; Pool; Gym; Recreation center; Tennis; Racquetball; Fitness center; Softball field; Football field; Auto shop; Officers club; NCO club; Fishing/Hunting.

BEAUFORT NAVAL HOSPITAL

Beaufort, SC 29902
(803) 525-5340
OFFICER-OF-THE-DAY: (803) 525-5400, 525-5401, emergency room

Profile
BRANCH: Navy.
SIZE AND LOCATION: 24 acres. On Ribaut Rd on Beaufort River approx halfway between MCAS Beaufort and Marine Corps Recruit Depot Parris Island.
MAJOR UNITS: Naval Hospital.
BASE HISTORY: One of most modern, small to medium sized Navy hospitals in southeastern US; provides medical care for all active duty and retired military personnel and their dependents in southeastern SC and northeastern GA.
Services *Housing:* Family units 53 (11 at Laurel Bay); BEQ units 3. *Commissary and Exchange:* Retail store; Barber shop; Service station; Convenience store/Shopette; Optical shop; Snacks. *Base Library:* Yes. *Medical Facilities:* Hospital 207; Dental clinic. *Recreational Facilities:* Pool; Recreation center; Tennis; Softball field; Auto shop; Recreational services; Volleyball; Equipment rental; Picnicking; Playgrounds.

CHARLESTON

CHARLESTON COAST GUARD BASE

196 Tradd St, Charleston, SC 29401-1899
(803) 724-7600; FTS 670-8600
Profile
BRANCH: Coast Guard.
SIZE AND LOCATION: 8.5 acres. In southernmost part of city of Charleston.
MAJOR UNITS: USCG Base/Group Charleston; USCGC *Madrona*; USCGC *Metompkin*; USCGC *Rambler*; Marine Safety Office; Reserve Group Charleston; Coast Guard Auxiliary Flotilla 12-8.
BASE HISTORY: 1914, US Lighthouse Service purchased "Dunkins Sawmill" for buoy depot. 1915, Navy established remote, wireless unit here and US Weather Service contracted to use radio tower for storm warning signals. 1930, Lighthouse Service merged with and became part of USCG. WWII, base under operational control of Sixth Naval District. Mission: buoy repair and logistical supply for visiting and assigned vessels. WWII to today, industrial buoy depot and host to various vessels. 1974, added search and rescue responsibilities and general law enforcement duties to existing functions.
Key Contacts
COMMANDER: CDR R F Duncan.
Services *Housing:* Barracks spaces. *Commissary and Exchange:* Small exchange. *Recreational Facilities:* Boating.

CHARLESTON NAVAL BASE

Charleston, SC 29408
(803) 743-4111; Autovon 563-4111
Profile
BRANCH: Navy.
SIZE AND LOCATION: 20,500 acres. Along Cooper River, 6 mi N of Charleston off I-26.
MAJOR UNITS: Naval Base Headquarters; Naval Weapons Station; Charleston Naval Shipyard; Naval Supply Center; Polaris Missile Facility, Atlantic; Cruiser-Destroyer Group 2; Submarine Group 6; Mine Warfare Command; Naval Hospital.
BASE HISTORY: 1901, present site established.
Personnel and Expenditures
ACTIVE DUTY PERSONNEL: 27,000
DEPENDENTS: 30,000
CIVILIAN PERSONNEL: 15,000
Services *Housing:* Family units 2680; Barracks spaces; Trailer spaces 6. *Temporary Housing:* BOQ units 227; Lodge units 45; Mobile home units 23. *Commissary:* Base commissary; Retail store; Barber shop; Convenience store/Shopette; Garden center. *Child Care/Capacities:* Day care center 170. *Medical Facilities:* Hospital 500. *Recreational Facilities:* Bowling; Movie theater; Pool; Gym; Golf; Tennis; Racquetball; Fitness center; Auto shop; Crafts; Camping; Youth center (activities); Picnicking; Boating; Skeet shooting; Lake Moultrie recreation area, 40 mi N.

CHARLESTON NAVAL WEAPONS STATION

Charleston, SC 29408-7000
(803) 764-7703; Autovon 794-7703
OFFICER-OF-THE-DAY: (803) 764-7901,
Autovon 794-7901
Profile
BRANCH: Navy.
SIZE AND LOCATION: 16,331 acres. Approx 25 mi from Charleston, SC; Exit 203 off of I-26, take US-78 to US-52, to SC-37 (Red Bank Rd) to main gate. Approx 17 mi from Charleston IAP.
MAJOR UNITS: Naval Weapons Station.
BASE HISTORY: 1941, established. Provides materiel and technical support for ammunition and assigned weapons and weapons systems; operates an explosive ordnance outloading facility; manages Navy family housing for Charleston area.
Key Contacts
COMMANDER: Capt S G Kmetz; (803) 764-7886, Autovon 794-7886.
PUBLIC AFFAIRS: J H Brooks; (803) 764-7703, Autovon 794-7703.
PROCUREMENT: Lt Coley; (803) 764-7721, Autovon 794-7721.
TRANSPORTATION: CDR Johnson; (803) 764-7991, Autovon 794-7991.
PERSONNEL/COMMUNITY ACTIVITIES: Mary Kirkman; (803) 764-7601, Autovon 794-7601.

CHARLESTON NAVAL WEAPONS STATION
(continued)
Personnel and Expenditures
ACTIVE DUTY PERSONNEL: 153
DEPENDENTS: 11,750
CIVILIAN PERSONNEL: 1004
MILITARY PAYROLL EXPENDITURE: FY 88, $2.9 mil
Services *Housing:* Family units 2275; Mobile home pads 60. *Commissary:* Base commissary; Retail store; Barber shop; Service station. *Child Care/Capacities:* Day care center. *Schools:* Elementary; Intermediate/Junior high. *Base Library:* Yes. *Medical Facilities:* Medical clinic; Dental clinic. *Recreational Facilities:* Bowling; Movie theater; Pool; Gym; Recreation center; Golf; Stables; Tennis; Racquetball; Fitness center; Softball field; Auto shop; Officers club; NCO club; Fishing/Hunting.

US ARMY CORPS OF ENGINEERS, CHARLESTON DISTRICT
PO Box 919, Charleston, SC 29402-0919
(803) 724-4201
Profile
BRANCH: Army.
SIZE: Offices only.

CHARLESTON AFB

CHARLESTON AIR FORCE BASE
Charleston AFB, SC 29404
(803) 554-0230; Autovon 583-0230
Profile
BRANCH: Air Force.
SIZE AND LOCATION: 3500 acres. 10 mi NW of Charleston, SC in city of North Charleston; shares runway with Charleston IAP; terminal on opposite side of runway.
MAJOR UNITS: 437th Military Airlift Wing (MAC); 315th Military Airlift Wing (Associate) (AFRES); 1968th Communications Squadron (AFCC); 437th Air Base Group; 437th Field Maintenance Squadron; 43rd Organization Maintenance Squadron; 437th Avionics Maintenance Squadron; 437th Aerial Port Squadron; 437th Civil Engineering Squadron; Detachment 7, 1361st Audiovisual Squadron; Detachment 1, 87th Fighter Interceptor Group; Detachment 6, 1600th Management Engineering Squadron; Detachment 21103, Office of Special Investigation; Field Training Detachment 317; Area Defense Counsel; Air Force Audit Agency Area Audit Office; Armed Forces Courier Station; Military Air Traffic Coordination Unit; Army Assistance Office; Air Force Commissary Services, Southeast Complex.
BASE HISTORY: 1919, airfield established. 1941, AFB established on airfield. WWII, Army Air Corps took full control of field; civilian use of runways still allowed; base used as training site for combat and ground crews for B-17 Flying Fortress and B-24 Liberator aircraft, under First Air Force. 1943, reassigned to Air Transport Command and trained transport crews. After WWII, closed and returned to city. 1952, Charleston and USAF agreed to establish troop carrier base and joint use of runways. 1985, new civilian terminal completed. 1990s, first operational wing of C-17 aircraft scheduled.
Key Contacts
COMMANDER: Col David B Marcrander; Wing Commander, Bldg 1600SE, 437 MAW/CC, (803) 554-3201, Autovon 583-3201.

PUBLIC AFFAIRS: Capt Rhonda K Lustig; Bldg 1600SE, 437 MAW/PA, Charleston AFB, SC 29404-5154, (803) 554-2454, Autovon 583-2454.
PROCUREMENT: LTC Thomas W Christensen; Chief of Supply, Bldg 611, (803) 554-2323, Autovon 583-2323.
TRANSPORTATION: LTC Robert W Francis; Bldg 234, (803) 554-3322, Autovon 583-3322.
PERSONNEL/COMMUNITY ACTIVITIES: Col Arthur G Ericson; Bldg 503, (803) 554-3456, Autovon 583-3456.
Personnel and Expenditures
ACTIVE DUTY PERSONNEL: 5217
DEPENDENTS: 5289
CIVILIAN PERSONNEL: 1378
MILITARY PAYROLL EXPENDITURE: $93.6 mil
CONTRACT EXPENDITURE: $201 mil
Services *Housing:* Family units 977; Senior NCO units 90; Junior NCO units 760; Trailer spaces 75; RV/Camper sites 10; Barracks/Dormitory spaces 1798. *Temporary Housing:* VIP cottages 7; VOQ cottages 128; VEQ units 400. *Commissary:* Base commissary; Retail store; Barber shop; Dry cleaners; Food shop; Florist; Service station; Optical shop; Jewelry/watch sales and repair; Car rental. *Child Care/Capacities:* Day care center 193; Home day care program. *Schools:* Kindergarten/Preschool. *Base Library:* Yes. *Medical Facilities:* Medical clinic; Dental clinic. *Recreational Facilities:* Bowling; Movie theater; Pool; Gym; Recreation center; Golf; Stables; Tennis; Racquetball; Fitness center; Softball field; Auto shop; Crafts; Officers club; NCO club; Camping; Soccer field.

COLUMBIA

FORT JACKSON
US Army Training Center, Columbia, SC 29207
(803) 751-7621; Autovon 88-734-7621
OFFICER-OF-THE-DAY: (803) 751-7611, Autovon 88-734-7611
Profile
BRANCH: Army.
SIZE AND LOCATION: 52,303 acres. In central SC, adj to city of Columbia on E. From Atlanta, take I-20 through Augusta to Columbia; From Knoxville, take Hwy 25 to I-40, then Hwy 26 to Columbia; From Fayetteville, NC, take I-95 until it joins I-20 to Columbia.
MAJOR UNITS: 1st BT Brigade; 2d BT Brigade; 4th CST Brigade; Troop Command; Training Command; 120th AG Battalion.
BASE HISTORY: 1917, Company E, 1st Regiment, SC Infantry first unit at Camp Jackson, named for Maj Gen Andrew Jackson, native of SC and president of US. Troops trained here part of American Expeditionary Forces in WWI. 1917, first all-black regiment of WWI, 1st Provisional Infantry Regiment (Colored) organized. Birthplace of Army unit patch, beginning with 81st "Wildcat" Division. 1925-39, reverted to Cantonment Lands Commission and used by SCNG for training exercises. 1940, designated Fort Jackson and organized under federal control as Infantry Training Center. WWII, "Old Hickory" Division trained. 1974, first all female brigade, 5th Basic Training Brigade, established. Today, designated training center.
VISITOR ATTRACTIONS: Ft Jackson Museum.
Key Contacts
COMMANDER: Maj Gen Krausz.
PUBLIC AFFAIRS: LTC Dan C Riney; Ernie Pyle Media Center, Bldg 3499, (803) 751-6719, Autovon 88-734-7650.
PROCUREMENT: Mr Paul Tuccio; (803) 751-5231, Autovon 88-734-5231.

TRANSPORTATION: Joel Winchip; (803) 751-7696, Autovon 88-734-7696.
PERSONNEL/COMMUNITY ACTIVITIES: LTC Paul Searle; (803) 751-7538, Autovon 88-734-7538.
Personnel and Expenditures
ACTIVE DUTY PERSONNEL: 67,000
DEPENDENTS: 3050
CIVILIAN PERSONNEL: 7334
MILITARY PAYROLL EXPENDITURE: $243.3 mil
CONTRACT EXPENDITURE: $152 mil
Services *Housing:* Family units 1149; BOQ cottages 62; BEQ units 76; Barracks spaces 15,192; Senior NCO units 44; Junior NCO units 32. *Temporary Housing:* VIP cottages 7; VOQ cottages 104; VEQ units 12; BOQ units 62; Guesthouse units 210. *Commissary:* Base commissary; Retail store; Barber shop; Dry cleaners; Food shop; Florist; Banking; Service station; Bakery; Book store; Toys; Garden center; Pharmacy. *Child Care/Capacities:* Day care center 392; Home day care program; Latchkey program; FCC. *Schools:* Kindergarten/Preschool; Elementary; Education center with 5 college branches. *Base Library:* Yes. *Medical Facilities:* Hospital 215; Medical clinic; Dental clinic; Veterinary clinic; Alcohol & drug abuse center; Wellness center; Red Cross. *Recreational Facilities:* Bowling; Movie theater; Pool; Gym; Recreation center; Golf; Tennis; Racquetball; Skating rink; Fitness center; Softball field; Auto shop; Crafts; Officers club; NCO club; Camping; Fishing/Hunting; Youth center; Picnicking; Alpine lodge; Video rental; Boy Scouts; Girl Scouts; SATO; Do-it-yourself center.

MCENTIRE ANGB

MCENTIRE AIR NATIONAL GUARD BASE
McEntire ANGB, SC 29044
(803) 776-5121; Autovon 583-8201
Profile
BRANCH: Air National Guard.
SIZE AND LOCATION: 2394 acres. 12 mi E of Columbia.
MAJOR UNITS: 169th Tactical Fighter Group (ANG); Army Guard Aviation Unit.
BASE HISTORY: 1961, named for Brig Gen B B McEntire Jr (ANG), killed in an F-104.
Personnel and Expenditures
ACTIVE DUTY PERSONNEL: 1114
CIVILIAN PERSONNEL: 244
MILITARY PAYROLL EXPENDITURE: $10.2 mil
Services *Medical Facilities:* Dispensary.

MYRTLE BEACH

MYRTLE BEACH AIR FORCE BASE
Myrtle Beach, SC 29579-5000
(803) 238-7211; Autovon 748-1110
Profile
BRANCH: Air Force.
SIZE AND LOCATION: 3944 acres. On S edge of Myrtle Beach, off Hwy 17 S.
MAJOR UNITS: 354th Tactical Fighter Wing (TAC); 2066th Communications Squadron; Detachment 3, 3rd Weather Squadron; Detachment 2105, Air Force Office of Special Investigations; Field Training Detachment 301; 73rd Tactical Control Squadron; Detachment 354, 4400th Management Engineering Squadron; USAF Judiciary Area Defense Counsel; Detachment 2, Operating Location I-1816 Advisory Squadron; Fort Fisher Recreation Area (TAC).
BASE HISTORY: 1940, Myrtle Beach Municipal Airport first used by Army Air Corps. 1942, troops arrived from Savannah Army Air Base. 1943, designated Myrtle Beach Army Air Field. 1954, Myrtle Beach officials offered Municipal Airport

MYRTLE BEACH AIR FORCE BASE
(continued)

to USAF and 727th Aircraft Control and Warning Squadron arrived. For most of its history, 354th TFW served as host. 1975, joint military and civilian use of runway commenced. Today, 4 terminals, American Airlines, ASA Delta Airlines, USAIR, and Eastern Metro.

Key Contacts
COMMANDER: Col Robert G Jenkins.

Personnel and Expenditures
ACTIVE DUTY PERSONNEL: 3264
DEPENDENTS: 7612
CIVILIAN PERSONNEL: 943
MILITARY PAYROLL EXPENDITURE: $73.3 mil
CONTRACT EXPENDITURE: $7.4 mil
Services *Housing:* Family units 800; BOQ cottages 6; Duplex units 448; Dormitory spaces 1260; Trailer spaces 65; BOQ/BAQ 8. *Temporary Housing:* VIP cottages 3; VOQ cottages 40; VAQ units 76; Apartment units 14; Transient living quarters 3; Advanced reservations advised during tourist season. *Commissary:* Base commissary; Retail store; Convenience store/Shopette; Credit union; Laundry; Construction materials; Thrift shop. *Child Care/Capacities:* Day care center 154. *Schools:* Elementary. *Base Library:* Yes. *Medical Facilities:* Hospital 31; Medical clinic; Dental clinic; Veterinary services. *Recreational Facilities:* Bowling; Movie theater; Pool; Gym; Recreation center; Golf; Tennis; Racquetball; Fitness center; Softball field; Football field; Auto shop; Crafts; Officers club; NCO club; Camping; Fishing/Hunting; Youth center; Skeet shooting; Aero Club; Picnic pavilion; Nearby public beach resorts; SATO.

NORTH

NORTH AUXILIARY AIR FIELD
437th ABG/OC-A, Rte 2, Box 141, North, SC 29112
(803) 247-2241
OFFICER-OF-THE-DAY: (803) 247-2241
Profile
BRANCH: Air Force.
SIZE AND LOCATION: 2270 acres. Approx 25 mi S of Columbia, SC between North and Orangeburg, SC.
MAJOR UNITS: 437th Military Airlift Wing; 437th Air Base Group/Operating Location Alpha.
BASE HISTORY: 1950s, B-29 bomber and test base. Currently used for Special Operations Low-Level (SOLL II) nighttime missions and air drops.
Key Contacts
COMMANDER: TSgt Harry E Smith III.
PUBLIC AFFAIRS: See Commanding Officer.
PROCUREMENT: See Charleston AFB.
TRANSPORTATION: See Charleston AFB.
PERSONNEL/COMMUNITY ACTIVITIES: See Commanding Officer.
Personnel and Expenditures
ACTIVE DUTY PERSONNEL: 1
CIVILIAN PERSONNEL: 9
MILITARY PAYROLL EXPENDITURE: $21,600
CONTRACT EXPENDITURE: $20,000
Services *Housing:* Mobile home units 1; RV/Camper sites 2. *Temporary Housing:* Mobile home units 1.

NORTH CHARLESTON

MILITARY TRAFFIC MANAGEMENT COMMAND, SOUTH ATLANTIC OUTPORT
1050 Remount Rd, North Charleston, SC 29406-3500
(803) 566-5219

Profile
BRANCH: Army.
SIZE: Offices only.

PARRIS ISLAND

PARRIS ISLAND MARINE CORPS RECRUIT DEPOT/EASTERN RECRUITING REGION
Parris Island, SC 29905-5001
(803) 525-2111; Autovon 832-1110
OFFICER-OF-THE-DAY: (803) 525-3712, Autovon 832-3712
Profile
BRANCH: Marines.
SIZE AND LOCATION: 7132 acres. On SC 802 just outside Port Royal, 5 mi from Beaufort, SC and 45 mi N of Savannah, GA; 40 mi N of Hilton Head Island, SC.
MAJOR UNITS: Recruit Training Regiment; Headquarters and Service Battalion; Support Battalion; Weapons Training Battalion.
BASE HISTORY: 1891, first Marine Corps presence at Parris Island; small security detachment attached to Naval Station, Port Royal, forerunner of Parris Island. 1891-WWI, military buildings and homes constructed form Parris Island Historic District, on National Register of Historic Places. Island named after Englishman, Alexander Parris, purchased island, 1715. 1915, male recruit training started here and continuous since. Prior to 1929 causeway, transportation by boat from Port Royal. 1949, separate battalion (now 4th Recruit Training Battalion), activated for sole purpose of training women Marine recruits. Parris Island also has Drill Instructor School.
VISITOR ATTRACTIONS: Parris Island Museum; Historic tours; Recruit graduation parades; Douglas Visitor's Center (provides maps, brochures, place to relax, receptionist on duty).
Key Contacts
COMMANDER: Maj Gen Jarvis D Lynch Jr; (803) 525-2535, Autovon 832-2535.
PUBLIC AFFAIRS: Maj Robert W Mclean; (803) 525-2943, Autovon 832-2943.
PROCUREMENT: Maj T E Fultz; Contracts & Purchasing, (803) 525-3427, Autovon 832-3427.
TRANSPORTATION: Lt William A Jones; (803) 525-2233, Autovon 832-2233.
PERSONNEL/COMMUNITY ACTIVITIES: Capt Sherri Hicks; Family Services Center, (803) 525-3788, Autovon 832-3788.
Personnel and Expenditures
ACTIVE DUTY PERSONNEL: 3000
DEPENDENTS: 5500
CIVILIAN PERSONNEL: 486
MILITARY PAYROLL EXPENDITURE: FY 88, $50 mil
CONTRACT EXPENDITURE: FY 88, $12.3 mil
Services *Housing:* Family units 464; Mobile home units 100. *Temporary Housing:* Transient living quarters. *Commissary:* Base commissary; Retail store; Barber shop; Dry cleaners; Food shop; Banking; Service station; Ice cream; Donuts; Fast food; Gifts; Shoe repair; Post office; Tailor; Credit union; Western Union. *Child Care/Capacities:* Day care center. *Schools:* Kindergarten/Preschool; Kindergarten & elementary schooling provided by MCAS Beaufort, 12 mi away. *Base Library:* Yes. *Medical Facilities:* Medical clinic; Dental clinic; Beaufort Naval Hospital, 5 mi away. *Recreational Facilities:* Bowling; Movie theater; Pool; Gym; Golf; Tennis; Racquetball; Fitness center; Softball field; Football field; Auto shop; Crafts; Officers club; Fishing/Hunting; SNCO club; Enlisted club; Marina; Rod & gun club.

SHAW AFB

SHAW AIR FORCE BASE
Shaw AFB, SC 29152
(803) 668-3621; 668-3816; Autovon 965-3621; 965-3816
OFFICER-OF-THE-DAY: (803) 668-3410, Autovon 965-3410
Profile
BRANCH: Air Force.
SIZE AND LOCATION: 11,746 acres. Off US Hwy 76/378, 10 mi W of Sumter, SC; approx 40 mi E of Columbia, SC.
MAJOR UNITS: 363rd Tactical Fighter Wing; 363rd Combat Support Group; 363rd Aircraft Generation Squadron; 363rd Component Repair Squadron; 363rd Equipment Maintenance Squadron; 363rd Transportation Squadron; 363rd Civil Engineering Squadron; 363rd Security Police Squadron; 363rd Services Squadron; 16th Tactical Reconnaissance Squadron; 17th Tactical Fighter Squadron; 19th Tactical Fighter Squadron; 33rd Tactical Fighter Squadron; 363rd Tactical Fighter Wing Hospital; 363rd Comptroller Squadron; Headquarters 9th Air Force; 507th Tactical Air Control Wing; 21st Tactical Air Support Squadron; 682nd Air Support Operations Center Squadron; 507th Tactical Air Control Center Squadron; 4507th Tactical Intelligence Squadron; Detachment 363, 4400th Management Engineering Squadron; 3rd Weather Squadron; Detachment 1, 2020th Communications Squadron; 3537th Recruiting Squadron; Detachment 307, 3751st Field Training Squadron; Detachment 1, 17th Military Intelligence Squadron; Detachment 7, Aircraft Delivery Squadron; Detachment 9, Tactical Communication Division; Detachment 2101, Air Force Office of Special Investigations; Detachment QD 20, Area Defense Counsel; Defense Investigation Service, District 22; Operating Location, Shaw, HQ Electronic Security Tactical; HQ SAC Operating Location Shaw; Detachment OAX3, Air Force Commissary Service; Detachment 261, Air Force Audit Agency.
BASE HISTORY: 1941, activated as Shaw Field; named for 1st Lt Ervin D Shaw, Sumter county native shot down in WWI; small basic flying school. After WWII, transferred to TAC. 1948, redesignated Shaw AFB. 1951, 363rd TFW (then 363rd TRW) became host unit and continues today. Cuban Missile Crisis, helped identify Russian missiles in Cuba. 1985, transition to F-16CS completed.
VISITOR ATTRACTIONS: Static aircraft: RB-66, RF-101, RF-4C, and O-2.
Key Contacts
COMMANDER: Col Linwood Snell; 363 CSG/CC, (803) 668-3112, Autovon 965-3211.
PUBLIC AFFAIRS: 1st Lt Thomas A Beath; 363 TFW/PA, (803) 668-3621, Autovon 965-3621.
PROCUREMENT: Capt Bruce Hall; (803) 668-2434, Autovon 965-2434.
TRANSPORTATION: LTC Larry D Yarbrough; 363 TRANSP/CC, (803) 668-3680, Autovon 965-3680.
PERSONNEL/COMMUNITY ACTIVITIES: Maj Simeon B Davis III; 363 MSSQ/CC, (803) 668-2324, Autovon 965-2324.
Personnel and Expenditures
ACTIVE DUTY PERSONNEL: 6500
DEPENDENTS: 10,023
CIVILIAN PERSONNEL: 840
MILITARY PAYROLL EXPENDITURE: $130.5 mil
CONTRACT EXPENDITURE: $27.6 mil
Services *Housing:* Family units 1704; BOQ cottages 1; Duplex units 563; Townhouse units 251; Senior NCO units 4. *Temporary Housing:* VIP cottages 4; VOQ cottages 84;

SHAW AIR FORCE BASE (*continued*)
VEQ units 134; VAQ units 69; BOQ units 8;
Guesthouse units 40; Dormitory units 3500;
Transient living quarters 40. *Commissary:*
Base commissary; Barber shop; Dry cleaners;
Food shop; Florist; Banking; Service station.
Child Care/Capacities: Day care center 150.
Base Library: Yes. *Medical Facilities:* Hospital 40; Medical clinic; Dental clinic; Veterinary clinic. *Recreational Facilities:* Bowling; Movie theater; Pool; Gym; Recreation
center; Golf; Tennis; Racquetball; Fitness
center; Softball field; Football field; Auto
shop; Crafts; Officers club; NCO club;
Camping; Fishing/Hunting; Aero club; Picnic
area; Recreation supply; Rod and gun club;
Wateree Recreation Area, off Hwy 97, 10 mi
past Camden, SC.

SOUTH DAKOTA

ELLSWORTH AFB

ELLSWORTH AIR FORCE BASE
Ellsworth AFB, SD 57706-5000
(605) 385-5056; Autovon 675-5056
OFFICER-OF-THE-DAY: (605) 385-2450,
Autovon 675-2450
Profile
BRANCH: Air Force.
SIZE AND LOCATION: 4933 acres. 12 mi E of
Rapid City, SD, Exit 66 off I-90.
MAJOR UNITS: 12th Air Division; 28th Bombardment Wing; 44th Strategic Missile
Wing; 2148th Communications Squadron;
812th Combat Support Group; 812th Security Police Group; 812th Strategic Hospital; Air Force Office of Special Investigation, Detachment 1302; Detachment
17, 9th Weather Squadron; Air Force Audit Agency Detachment; Field Training
Detachment 409; Detachment 2, 37th
Aerospace Rescue and Recovery Squadron (ARRS); Detachment A, 64th Flying
Training Wing; 15th Air Force Leadership
School and NCO Preparatory School; Detachment 15, 3904th Management Engineering Squadron, Strategic Air Command.
BASE HISTORY: 1942, activated as Rapid City
Army Air Force Base, training B-17
bomber crews. 1946-47, temporary inactive status. 1947, reactivated as part of
15th Air Force. 1948, renamed Weaver
AFB, for Brig Gen Walter R Weaver, pioneer in the Air Force, and renamed again
Rapid City AFB, in response to public
opinion and declared permanent installation. 1953, President Eisenhower dedicated base in honor of Brig Gen Richard
E Ellsworth, commander of 28th SRW,
killed in RB-36 crash. 1960, 850th Strategic Missile Squadron with Titan I missile
activated. 1962, 44th Strategic Missile
Wing formed with Minuteman I. 1958-71,
821st Aerospace Division HQ. 1988, HQs
12th Air Division. Primary aircraft, B-1B
bomber.
VISITOR ATTRACTIONS: Black Hills area.
Key Contacts
COMMANDER: Col Robert E Roberts; 812
CSG/CC, (605) 385-2450, Autovon 675-
2450.
PUBLIC AFFAIRS: Maj Joseph B Saxon; 12
AD/PA, (605) 385-5056, Autovon 675-
5056.
PROCUREMENT: Dick Rasmussen; 12 AD/
LGC, (605) 385-1718, Autovon 675-1718.
TRANSPORTATION: LTC David R Postell; 812
TRANS/CC, (605) 385-2952, Autovon
675-2952.
PERSONNEL/COMMUNITY ACTIVITIES: LTC
John Ford; Director of Personnel, 812
CSG/DP, (605) 385-2343, Autovon 675-
2343; Community Activities, See Base
Commander.

Personnel and Expenditures
ACTIVE DUTY PERSONNEL: 7000
DEPENDENTS: 5000
CIVILIAN PERSONNEL: 743
MILITARY PAYROLL EXPENDITURE: $133.1 mil
CONTRACT EXPENDITURE: $34 mil
Services *Housing:* Family units 1884; BOQ
cottages 4; BEQ units 76; Duplex units 830;
Barracks spaces 1362; Dormitory spaces;
Senior NCO units 238; Junior NCO units
1124; RV/Camper sites; Airman housing
194. *Temporary Housing:* VIP cottages 7;
VOQ cottages 43; VAQ units 144; Dormitory units 1277; Family units 21. *Commissary:* Base commissary; Retail store; Barber
shop; Dry cleaners; Food shop; Florist; Service station; Convenience store/Shopette;
Beauty shop; Credit union; Jewelry/watch
sales and repair; Optical shop; Video rental;
Fast food; Clothing sales; Snacks. *Child
Care/Capacities:* Day care center 120; Home
day care program. *Schools:* Kindergarten/
Preschool. *Base Library:* Yes. *Medical Facilities:* Hospital 40; Dental clinic. *Recreational
Facilities:* Bowling; Movie theater; Pool;
Gym; Recreation center; Stables; Tennis;
Racquetball; Fitness center; Softball field;
Auto shop; Crafts; Officers club; NCO club;
Camping; Fishing/Hunting.

FORT MEADE

FORT MEADE MILITARY RESERVATION
Ft Meade VA Medical Center, Fort Meade,
SD 57741
(605) 347-2511
Profile
BRANCH: Army.
SIZE AND LOCATION: 250 acres. In SW SD, 2
mi E of Sturgis, SD, off of I-90, on Hwy
34.
MAJOR UNITS: VA Medical Center.
BASE HISTORY: 1878, founded as military
post; number of different units assigned
including glider detachment. 1944, turned
over to Veterans Administration. All old
buildings on register of historic places. In
recent years SDNG using buildings for
training site; buildings restored and used
for classrooms, barracks, administration.
VISITOR ATTRACTIONS: Museum.

MITCHELL

MITCHELL NATIONAL GUARD COMPLEX
PO Box 610, Municipal Airport, Mitchell,
SD 57301-0610
(605) 996-6070

Profile
BRANCH: Army National Guard.
SIZE AND LOCATION: 25 acres. 4 mi N of
Mitchell, SD, on SD-37 at Mitchell Municipal Airport.
MAJOR UNITS: 665th Maintenance Company;
Battery A, 1st Battalion, 147th Field Artillery; 147th Army Band; Combined Support Maintenance Shop 1#1; Organizational Maintenance Shop 1#5.
BASE HISTORY: Since 1950, facility was Combined Support Maintenance Shop 1#1
(CSMS 1#1). Since 1957, Armory and Organizational Maintenance Shop 1#1. Presently, facility has outdoor baffled rifle
range serving units in 70 mi radius,
equipment cold storage, and vehicle storage buildings; responsible for majority of
maintenance of SD Army NG equipment.
Key Contacts
COMMANDER: LTC Rodger R Jacquet.
PUBLIC AFFAIRS: See Base Commander.
Personnel and Expenditures
ACTIVE DUTY PERSONNEL: 10
CIVILIAN PERSONNEL: 40
MILITARY PAYROLL EXPENDITURE: $2.2 mil
CONTRACT EXPENDITURE: $0.9 mil

RAPID CITY

CAMP RAPID
2823 W Main St, Rapid City, SD 57702-
8186
(605) 394-6702; Autovon 747-8702
OFFICER-OF-THE-DAY: (605) 394-6611
Profile
BRANCH: Army National Guard.
SIZE AND LOCATION: 600 acres. In the western portion of Rapid City approx 15 mi
W of Ellsworth AFB.
MAJOR UNITS: HQ State Area Command.
BASE HISTORY: 1933, established on 84 acres
of Rapid City Indian School land. 1950,
Secretary of Interior transferred 673 acres
of Sioux Sanatorium property for SDNG
(West Camp Rapid). 1962, 90 acres West
Camp David deeded to Rapid City
School District No 1 for a high school.
1963, NG designated 22 acres for Rapid
City NG Armory. Currently, Camp Rapid
a state-owned, federally-supported training site, consisting of cantonment area for
troop housing logistics and training facilities. West Camp Rapid provides training
in field. Used by units of SD Army NG,
reserve forces of the Army, Ellsworth
AFB, units of active Army and Office of
Adjutant General and support facilities of
SD Army NG.
Key Contacts
COMMANDER: Brig Gen Harold J Sykora.
PUBLIC AFFAIRS: LTC Duane D Long; (605)
394-6721, Autovon 747-8721.
PROCUREMENT: LTC Gary Vollmer; (605)
394-6743, Autovon 747-8743.

CAMP RAPID *(continued)*

TRANSPORTATION: Maj Susan Rodriguez; (605) 394-6747, Autovon 747-8747.

PERSONNEL/COMMUNITY ACTIVITIES: Col Paul A Hybertson; (605) 394-6710, Autovon 747-8710.

Personnel and Expenditures

ACTIVE DUTY PERSONNEL: 41

CIVILIAN PERSONNEL: 180

MILITARY PAYROLL EXPENDITURE: $23.4 mil

CONTRACT EXPENDITURE: $4.1 mil

Services *Housing:* BOQ cottages 20; Barracks spaces 400. *Commissary and Exchange:* Limited retail only during two-week annual training. *Medical Facilities:* Only during two-week annual training period. *Recreational Facilities:* Softball field; Officers club; NCO club.

SIOUX FALLS

114TH TACTICAL FIGHTER GROUP (ANG)

Joe Foss Field, Sioux Falls, SD 57104

(605) 336-0670; Autovon 939-7210

Profile

BRANCH: Air National Guard.

SIZE AND LOCATION: 145 acres. N side of Sioux Falls, between I-29 and I-229, and just S of I-90.

MAJOR UNITS: 114th Tactical Fighter Group (ANG).

BASE HISTORY: Named for Brig Gen Joseph J Foss, WWII ace, former governor of SD, and founder of SD ANG.

Personnel and Expenditures

ACTIVE DUTY PERSONNEL: 827

CIVILIAN PERSONNEL: 213

MILITARY PAYROLL EXPENDITURE: $8.5 mil

TENNESSEE

ARNOLD AFB

ARNOLD AIR FORCE BASE
Arnold Engineering Development Center, Arnold AFB, TN 37389
(615) 454-3000; Autovon 340-5011
OFFICER-OF-THE-DAY: (615) 454-7752, Autovon 340-7752
Profile
BRANCH: Air Force.
SIZE AND LOCATION: 40,000 acres. Off I-24, 65 mi S of Nashville; 12 mi from Manchester, Tullahoma, and Winchester.
MAJOR UNITS: Arnold Engineering Development Center.
BASE HISTORY: Part of Air Force Systems Command, named for Gen Henry H "Hap" Arnold, Commanding General of Army Air Forces during WWII and responsible for concept of engineering development center. 1950, construction begun at old Camp Forrest. Major divisions: Engine Test Facility, von Karman Gas Dynamics Facility, and Propulsion Wind Tunnel. 1951, AEDC Mission established to support development of aerospace systems by testing hardware in aerodynamic, propulsion, and space test facilities that simulate flight conditions.
VISITOR ATTRACTIONS: Woods Reservoir, boating, fishing, picnic areas.
Key Contacts
COMMANDER: Col Stephen P Condon; (615) 454-5201, Autovon 340-5201.
PUBLIC AFFAIRS: Capt Patricia Rogers; (615) 454-5586, Autovon 340-5586.
PROCUREMENT: Col William Sebren; (615) 454-7806, Autovon 340-7806.
TRANSPORTATION: Capt Steven Wells; (615) 454-4410, Autovon 340-4410.
PERSONNEL/COMMUNITY ACTIVITIES: 1st Lt Peg Zaniewski; (615) 454-4309, Autovon 340-4309.
Personnel and Expenditures
ACTIVE DUTY PERSONNEL: 150
DEPENDENTS: 75
CIVILIAN PERSONNEL: 3800
MILITARY PAYROLL EXPENDITURE: $44 mil
CONTRACT EXPENDITURE: $100 mil
Services *Housing:* Family units 40. *Temporary Housing:* VOQ cottages 40. *Commissary:* Base commissary; Retail store; Banking. *Medical Facilities:* Medical clinic (part-time facilities only); Dental clinic. *Recreational Facilities:* Recreation center; Golf; Softball field; Auto shop; Crafts; Officers club; NCO club; Camping; Fishing/Hunting; Marina.

BRISTOL

NAVAL WEAPONS INDUSTRIAL RESERVE PLANT
100 Vance Tank Rd, Bristol, TN 37620-5698
(615) 652-5000
Profile
BRANCH: Navy.
SIZE AND LOCATION: 99.9 acres. 10 mi S of I-81.
MAJOR UNITS: Defense Contract Administrative Services (DCAS) Residency, Raytheon; NAVSEA Technical Representative.
BASE HISTORY: 1952-53, constructed. 1954, manufacturing operations begun by Sperry Farragut Corp. 1957, Raytheon Co took over. A GOCO industrial production facility with capabilities in research and development, design engineering and testing associated with manufacture of advanced weapons systems, and fabrication and assembly of missiles.
Key Contacts
COMMANDER: LCDR J A Sanders; Officer-in-Charge, (615) 652-5866.
Personnel and Expenditures
ACTIVE DUTY PERSONNEL: 1
CIVILIAN PERSONNEL: 28
Services *Medical Facilities:* Contractor operated clinic.

CHATTANOOGA

NAVAL & MARINE CORPS RESERVE CENTER
12 Meadow St, Chattanooga, TN 37421
(615) 267-2111
Profile
BRANCH: Naval Reserve.
SIZE AND LOCATION: 9.11 acres. Downtown Chattanooga next to the Market St Bridge.
MAJOR UNITS: Reserve Units.
BASE HISTORY: Reserve Center only. 9 reserve units drill 2 weekends a month.
Key Contacts
COMMANDER: Lt Roxane M Young.
Personnel and Expenditures
ACTIVE DUTY PERSONNEL: 26

VOLUNTEER ARMY AMMUNITION PLANT
PO Box 22607, Chattanooga, TN 37422-2607
(615) 855-7100; Autovon 588-9100
Profile
BRANCH: Army.
SIZE AND LOCATION: 6000 acres. VAAP is about 12 mi NE of Chattanooga, TN, take I-75 N, Exit 7B W, facility on State Hwy 317, approx 2 mi from Exit.

BASE HISTORY: 1941-43, constructed; originally Volunteer Ordnance Works. Following WWII, shut down and placed on standby status. Rehabilitated for Korean War and produced TNT until placed on standby status, 1957. 1965, activated to produce TNT for Vietnam War. 1970, gradual phase down started. 1977, put on current inactive status.
Key Contacts
COMMANDER: James E Fry; Commander's Representative, (615) 855-7109, Autovon 588-9109.
Personnel and Expenditures
CIVILIAN PERSONNEL: 5

KINGSPORT

HOLSTON ARMY AMMUNITION PLANT
Kingsport, TN 37660-9982
(615) 247-9111; Autovon 748-9111
OFFICER-OF-THE-DAY: Security Officer, (615) 247-3767, Autovon 748-3767
Profile
BRANCH: Army.
SIZE AND LOCATION: 6000 acres. In Kingsport, TN, on Hwy 11-W.
MAJOR UNITS: Holston Defense Corp.
BASE HISTORY: 1942, constructed; originally Holston Ordnance Works, a GOCO facility. Mission is manufacture of military explosives. Current operating contractor, Holston Defense Corp.
Key Contacts
COMMANDER: (615) 247-3751, Autovon 748-3751.
PROCUREMENT: (615) 247-3757, Autovon 748-3757.
TRANSPORTATION: (615) 247-3766, Autovon 748-3766.
PERSONNEL/COMMUNITY ACTIVITIES: (615) 247-3753, Autovon 748-3753.
Personnel and Expenditures
ACTIVE DUTY PERSONNEL: 2
CIVILIAN PERSONNEL: 28

KNOXVILLE

134TH AIR REFUELING GROUP (ANG)
McGhee Tyson Airport, Knoxville, TN 37901
(615) 970-3077; Autovon 588-8210
Profile
BRANCH: Air National Guard.
SIZE AND LOCATION: 287 acres. 10 mi SW of Knoxville, off US-129.
MAJOR UNITS: 134th Air Refueling Group (ANG); 228th Combat Communications Squadron; I G Brown Professional Military Education Center (ANG).

134TH AIR REFUELING GROUP (ANG)
(continued)
Personnel and Expenditures
ACTIVE DUTY PERSONNEL: 1162
CIVILIAN PERSONNEL: 253
MILITARY PAYROLL EXPENDITURE: $11.9 mil
Services *Medical Facilities:* Dispensary.

MEMPHIS

MEMPHIS DEFENSE DEPOT
2163 Airways Blvd, Memphis, TN 38114-5000
(901) 775-6011; Autovon 683-6011
OFFICER-OF-THE-DAY: (901) 775-6677,
Autovon 683-6677
Profile
BRANCH: Joint Service Installation.
SIZE AND LOCATION: 642 acres. Near the center of Metro Memphis, two blocks from I-240 and Airways Blvd and 2.5 mi from Memphis IAP.
MAJOR UNITS: Defense Depot Memphis; HQ Defense Industrial Plant Equipment Center; Defense Reutilization and Marketing Region; Defense Logistics Agency Systems Automation Center.
BASE HISTORY: 1941, constructed. 1942, activated, originally operated by Corps of Engineers, later transferred to Quartermaster Corps. Depot names: Memphis General Depot, Memphis Quartermaster Depot, Army Service Forces Depot, Memphis General Depot (again), and Memphis Army Depot. 1964, under jurisdiction Defense Supply Agency (later, Defense Logistics Agency), name changed to Defense Depot Memphis. DLA has mission of supply, contract administration, and technical and logistical services. Also, stores materiels for National Defense Stockpile program. Primarily serves southeastern US, PR, and Panama Canal Zone.
Key Contacts
COMMANDER: Col James M Johnston, USAF; (901) 775-6411, Autovon 683-6411.
PUBLIC AFFAIRS: George L Dunn; (901) 775-6753, Autovon 683-6753.
PROCUREMENT: Bobbie Williams; (901) 775-6671, Autovon 683-6671.
TRANSPORTATION: Maj Perry R Metheny, USA; (901) 775-6396, Autovon 683-6396.
PERSONNEL/COMMUNITY ACTIVITIES: Ernest Lloyd; (901) 775-4940, Autovon 683-4940.
Personnel and Expenditures
ACTIVE DUTY PERSONNEL: 16
CIVILIAN PERSONNEL: 2600
MILITARY PAYROLL EXPENDITURE: $49.9 mil
CONTRACT EXPENDITURE: $33 mil
Services *Commissary and Exchange:* Retail store; Food shop. *Medical Facilities:* Medical clinic. *Recreational Facilities:* Pool; Golf; Softball field.

US ARMY CORPS OF ENGINEERS, MEMPHIS DISTRICT
B-202 Clifford Davis Federal Bldg,
Memphis, TN 38103-1894
(901) 521-3222; 521-3348
Profile
BRANCH: Army.
SIZE AND LOCATION: 157 acres, Shipyard. HQs in downtown Memphis, 10 mi to the airport, off I-40; Shipyard is 5 mi S of Memphis on McKellar Lake; Field Offices in Wynee, AR and Caruthersville, MO.
BASE HISTORY: Since 1882, has performed flood control and navigation works in Lower Mississippi Valley. Detailed account can be found in Clay, Floyd M, *A Century on the Mississippi: A History of the Memphis District US Army Corps of Engineers 1876-1981*, 1986.

Key Contacts
COMMANDER: Col O'Brene Richardson, CE; District Engineer, (901) 521-3221.
PUBLIC AFFAIRS: William C Schult; (901) 521-3348.
PROCUREMENT: Clinton E Hopkins; (901) 521-3116.
TRANSPORTATION: Robert E Brewer; (901) 521-3384.
PERSONNEL/COMMUNITY ACTIVITIES: Robert W Mays; Director of Personnel, (901) 521-3105.
Personnel and Expenditures
ACTIVE DUTY PERSONNEL: 3
CIVILIAN PERSONNEL: 650
Services *Base Library:* Yes.

164TH TACTICAL AIRLIFT GROUP (ANG)
Memphis IAP, Memphis, TN 38118
(901) 369-4111; Autovon 966-8210
Profile
BRANCH: Air National Guard.
SIZE AND LOCATION: 82 acres. 10 mi S of Memphis, use exit 24 off I-240.
MAJOR UNITS: 164th Tactical Airlift Group (ANG).
Personnel and Expenditures
ACTIVE DUTY PERSONNEL: 815
CIVILIAN PERSONNEL: 171
MILITARY PAYROLL EXPENDITURE: $7.5 mil
Services *Medical Facilities:* Medical clinic.

MILAN

MILAN ARMY AMMUNITION PLANT
Milan, TN 38358-5000
(901) 686-6087; Autovon 966-6087
OFFICER-OF-THE-DAY: (901) 686-6087,
Autovon 966-6087
Profile
BRANCH: Army.
SIZE AND LOCATION: 22,500 acres. Adj to E boundary of Milan, TN, approx 100 mi E/NE of Memphis via I-40 and US Hwy 45.
MAJOR UNITS: Martin Marietta Ordnance Systems, Inc (Operating Contractor).
BASE HISTORY: 1941-42, Milan Ordnance Depot constructed; operated by government personnel. 1943, merged with Wolf Creek Ordnance Plant operated by Procter & Gamble Defense Corp. 1945, redesignated Milan Arsenal. 1945-1953, deactivated. 1954, designated permanent installation. 1957, Harvey Aluminum Sales Inc became operating contractor and Arsenal placed in inactive status. 1960, activated. 1963, given present name. 1969, Martin Marietta Inc acquired Harvey Aluminum Sales and operates plant.
Key Contacts
COMMANDER: LTC Michael P Tucker; Commander, Milan Army Ammunition Plant, ATTN: SMCMI-CO, (901) 686-6087, Autovon 966-6087.
PUBLIC AFFAIRS: Frank R Claytor; Commander, Milan Army Ammunition Plant, ATTN: SMCMI-XC, (901) 686-6870, Autovon 966-6870.
TRANSPORTATION: Bruce S Laird; Milan Army Ammunition Plant, ATTN: SMCMI-TM, (901) 686-6895, Autovon 966-6895.
Personnel and Expenditures
ACTIVE DUTY PERSONNEL: 2
DEPENDENTS: 60
CIVILIAN PERSONNEL: 1900
CONTRACT EXPENDITURE: $100 mil
Services *Housing:* Family units 32. *Medical Facilities:* Medical clinic. *Recreational Facilities:* Pool; Recreation center; Tennis; Racquetball; Fishing/Hunting.

MILLINGTON

MEMPHIS NAVAL AIR STATION
Millington, TN 38054-5000
(901) 873-5500; Autovon 966-5500
OFFICER-OF-THE-DAY: (901) 873-5500,
Autovon 966-5500
Profile
BRANCH: Navy.
SIZE AND LOCATION: 3400 acres. In Millington, approx 11 mi N of Memphis.
MAJOR UNITS: Chief of Naval Technical Training (CNTECHTRA); Naval Air Technical Training Center; NAS Memphis; Marine Aircraft Group-42, Detachment B; Marine Aviation Training Support Group-90; Naval Air Reserve Memphis; Patrol Squadron-67; Fleet Logistics Support Squadron 60; Naval Hospital Millington; Naval Construction Battalion Unit-404; Naval Reserve Readiness Command Region Nine; Naval Oceanography Command Detachment; Personnel Support Activity; Naval Air Maintenance Training Group; Financial Information Processing Center, Memphis; Naval Legal Service Office; Naval Education and Training Program Management & Support Activity Detachment.
BASE HISTORY: 1942, first commissioned as Naval Reserve Air Base (NRAB). WWII, trained aviation cadets to pilot proficiency for action. 1943, designated NAS; northside area: administrative buildings, barracks, and runways. 1949, all support logistics requirements of commands aboard, except Naval Hospital, assigned to NAS. Major facelift recently.
Key Contacts
COMMANDER: Capt Jerry Baker II; (901) 873-5101, Autovon 966-5101.
PUBLIC AFFAIRS: Sue N Hosmer; (901) 873-5761, Autovon 966-5761.
Personnel and Expenditures
ACTIVE DUTY PERSONNEL: 14,000
DEPENDENTS: 2800
CIVILIAN PERSONNEL: 2500
Services *Housing:* Family units; BEQ units; BAQ units; Duplex units; Townhouse units; Barracks spaces; Trailer spaces; RV/Camper sites. *Temporary Housing:* BOQ units; Lodge units; Transient living quarters. *Commissary:* Base commissary; Retail store; Barber shop; Dry cleaners; Food shop; Florist; Banking; Service station; Furniture store; Bakery. *Child Care/Capacities:* Day care center. *Base Library:* Yes. *Medical Facilities:* Hospital; Medical clinic; Dental clinic. *Recreational Facilities:* Bowling; Movie theater; Pool; Gym; Recreation center; Golf; Stables; Tennis; Racquetball; Fitness center; Softball field; Football field; Auto shop; Crafts; Officers club; NCO club; Camping; Fishing/Hunting.

NASHVILLE

US ARMY CORPS OF ENGINEERS, NASHVILLE DISTRICT
PO Box 1070, Nashville, TN 37202-1070
(615) 736-7161
Profile
BRANCH: Army.
LOCATION: In the John Weld Peck Federal Office Bldg, downtown Nashville.
MAJOR UNITS: Army Corps of Engineers, Nashville.
Key Contacts
COMMANDER: Col Edward A Starbird; Nashville District Commander.
PUBLIC AFFAIRS: Dr M S Merriman; PAO.
Personnel and Expenditures
ACTIVE DUTY PERSONNEL: 4
CIVILIAN PERSONNEL: 400
Services *Base Library:* Yes.

118TH TACTICAL AIRLIFT WING (ANG)

Nashville Metropolitan Airport, Nashville, TN 37217

(615) 361-4600; Autovon 446-6210

Profile

BRANCH: Air National Guard.

SIZE AND LOCATION: 66 acres. 6 mi SE of Nashville, off I-40.

MAJOR UNITS: 118th Tactical Airlift Wing (ANG).

Personnel and Expenditures

ACTIVE DUTY PERSONNEL: 1156

CIVILIAN PERSONNEL: 286

MILITARY PAYROLL EXPENDITURE: $12.9 mil

TEXAS

ABILENE

DYESS AIR FORCE BASE
96th BMW, Abilene, TX 79607-5000
(915) 696-2863; 696-5609; 696-2864;
Autovon 461-2863; 461-5609; 461-2864;
461-2862
Profile
BRANCH: Air Force.
SIZE AND LOCATION: 6405 acres. On W side
of city of Abilene; bordered by city of
Tye; Hwy 80 runs through Abilene and
joins DUB Wright Blvd on W side of
town, Dyess is on right hand side of DUB
Wright Blvd; 9 mi from Abilene Municipal Airport.
MAJOR UNITS: 96th Bombardment Wing
(SAC); 463rd Tactical Airlift Wing
(MAC).
BASE HISTORY: 1852, first military base, only
used a few years, Fort Phantom. WWII,
Camp Barkley, became Army training
camp for recruits; Army Air Corps cadets
learned to fly light aircraft at Tye Army
Field. Following WWII, both installations
closed; Tye Army Field sold to city of
Abilene; site used by Texas NG as training facility. 1953, ground broken for SAC
base, originally Abilene AFB. 1956, dedicated and renamed for LTC William Edwin Dyess.
VISITOR ATTRACTIONS: Static display of aircraft on base.
Key Contacts
COMMANDER: Col Robert C Richards;
96CSG/CC, (915) 696-2141, Autovon
461-2141.
PUBLIC AFFAIRS: Maj Mary E Kilgore;
96CSG/PA, (915) 696-2862, Autovon
461-2862.
PROCUREMENT: Capt Peter V Stiglich; Con-
tracting, 96th BMW/LGC, (915) 696-
2352, Autovon 461-2352.
TRANSPORTATION: Maj Ford; 96TRANS/CC,
(915) 696-5018, Autovon 461-5018.
PERSONNEL/COMMUNITY ACTIVITIES: Maj
Vincent; 96CSG/DP, (915) 696-2960,
Autovon 461-2960.
Personnel and Expenditures
ACTIVE DUTY PERSONNEL: 5523
DEPENDENTS: 7606
CIVILIAN PERSONNEL: 690
MILITARY PAYROLL EXPENDITURE: $159.4 mil
CONTRACT EXPENDITURE: $24.3 mil
Services *Housing:* Family units 993; Bar-
racks spaces 1396. *Temporary Housing:* VIP
cottages 12; VOQ cottages 135; VEQ units
132; BAQ units 40; Guest cottages 22; Tran-
sient living quarters 40. *Commissary:* Base
commissary; Barber shop; Dry cleaners;
Food shop; Florist; Banking; Service station;
Bakery; Car rental. *Child Care/Capacities:*
Day care center 112. *Base Library:* Yes.
Medical Facilities: Hospital 35 (can be expanded when needed); Dental clinic. *Recreational Facilities:* Bowling; Movie theater;
Pool; Gym; Recreation center; Golf; Stables;
Tennis; Racquetball; Fitness center; Softball
field; Football field; Auto shop; Crafts; Officers club; All ranks club.

AUSTIN

BERGSTROM AIR FORCE BASE
Austin, TX 78743
(512) 479-4100; Autovon 685-4100
OFFICER-OF-THE-DAY: (512) 369-3375,
Autovon 685-3375
Profile
BRANCH: Air Force.
SIZE AND LOCATION: 3971 acres. On TX-71;
6 mi W of Garfield; 2 mi E of intersec-
tion US-183 and TX-71.
MAJOR UNITS: 67th Tactical Reconnaissance
Wing (TAC); 602nd Tactical Air Control
Group (TAC); Headquarters 12th Air
Force (TAC); Headquarters 10th Air
Force (AFRES); 924th Tactical Fighter
Group (AFRES); 712th Air Support Oper-
ations Center Squadron (TAC); 12th Tac-
tical Intelligence Squadron (TAC);
1882nd Communications Squadron
(AFCC); OL-J, 1816th Reserve Advisor
Squadron (AFRES); 25th Weather Squadron (MAC); Detachment 1, 1702nd Mobility Support Squadron (MAC); Detach-
ment 67, 4400th Management Engineer-
ing Squadron; Detachment 2, 4500th
School Squadron (TAC); Detachment 2,
17th Military Intelligence Company
(Army); Detachment 10, 25th Weather
Squadron (MAC); Detachment 12, Tactical Communications Division (TAC); Detachment 423, 3751st Field Training
Squadron (ATC); Detachment 502, Air
Force Audit Agency (HQ Command); Detachment 1001, AF Office of Special Investigations (AFOSI) at Pentagon; Operating Location TB, Electronic Security
Command (Tactical); AFHRL OL-AK/
IDDB (Human Resources Lab); Air Force
ROTC (ATC); Operating Location AB,
2500th Management Engineering Flight
(AFRES); Air Defense Counsel (HQ
USAF).
BASE HISTORY: 1942, activated as Del Valle
Army Air Base. 1943, at suggestion of
then Congressman Lyndon B Johnson, re-
named Bergstrom Army Air Field, for
Capt John Augus Earl Bergstrom, be-
lieved to be first man from Austin killed
in WWII. 1948, renamed Bergstrom AFB;
home of troop carrier units, some in Ber-
lin Airlift, 1948-49. 1949, transferred to
SAC. 1957, transferred to TAC. 1958,
12th Air Force; returned to SAC. 1966,
returned to TAC. 1968, HQ 12th Air
Force. 1971, 67th Tactical Reconnais-
sance Wing; regarded as home of tactical
reconnaissance.
VISITOR ATTRACTIONS: Reconnaissance Air
Park.
Key Contacts
COMMANDER: Col Robert Smith; 67 Combat
Support Group/CC, (512) 369-3321,
Autovon 685-3321.
PUBLIC AFFAIRS: Capt Guy C Thompson; 67
TRW/PA, (512) 369-2577, Autovon 685-
2577.
PROCUREMENT: Maj Jamie Adams; 67 TRW/
LGC, (512) 369-3441, Autovon 685-3441.
TRANSPORTATION: LTC David Ellison; 67
Transportation Squadron/CC, (512) 369-
4018, Autovon 685-4018.
PERSONNEL/COMMUNITY ACTIVITIES: Maj Al-
bert Johnson; 67 Mission Support
Squadron/CC, (512) 369-2998, Autovon
685-2998.
Personnel and Expenditures
ACTIVE DUTY PERSONNEL: 4951
DEPENDENTS: 8000
CIVILIAN PERSONNEL: 1057
MILITARY PAYROLL EXPENDITURE: FY 88,
$112.6 mil
CONTRACT EXPENDITURE: $47.2 mil
Services *Housing:* Family units 719. *Tem-
porary Housing:* VOQ cottages 81; VEQ
units 60; Transient living quarters 40. *Commissary:* Base commissary; Retail store; Barber shop; Dry cleaners; Food shop; Florist;
Service station. *Child Care/Capacities:* Day
care center. *Base Library:* Yes. *Medical Facilities:* Hospital 30; Medical clinic; Dental
clinic. *Recreational Facilities:* Bowling; Movie theater; Pool; Gym; Recreation center;
Golf; Stables; Tennis; Racquetball; Fitness
center; Softball field; Auto shop; Crafts; Officers club; NCO club.

CAMP MABRY
PO Box 5218, 2200 W 35th St, Austin, TX
78763
(512) 465-5001; Autovon 954-5001
OFFICER-OF-THE-DAY: (512) 465-5001,
Autovon 954-5001
Profile
BRANCH: Army National Guard.
SIZE AND LOCATION: 375 acres. In W Austin
at intersection of Loop 1 and 35th St.
MAJOR UNITS: Headquarters, Texas Army
National Guard; Headquarters, Texas Air
National Guard; Texas State Guard; 49th
Armored Division; Troop Command of
Texas Army National Guard; USPFO for
Texas; Texas National Guard Academy.
BASE HISTORY: 1982, original tract donated
to state of TX for establishing permanent
encampment for TX Volunteer Guard.
1898, named for Brig Gen Woodford H
Mabry, Adjutant Gen of TX at the time.
1916, arsenal constructed; on parade
field, Teddy Roosevelt once broke wild
mustangs, Jenny biplanes landed, citizen-
soldiers trained, and TX State Exposition
held. WWI and WWII, portions used as
active military installation by federal gov-

CAMP MABRY (continued)
ernment. Also occupied at various times by Department of Public Safety, Texas Rangers, and State Board of Control.
VISITOR ATTRACTIONS: Texas Guard all-faiths chapel with stained glass windows depicting 10 Battle Flags of TX; static displays of all military equipment; Statue of Audie Murphy, Medal of Honor winner.
Key Contacts
COMMANDER: Maj Gen James T Dennis; Adjutant Gen of TX, (512) 465-5006, Autovon 954-5006.
PUBLIC AFFAIRS: LTC Ed S Komandosky; (512) 465-5059, Autovon 954-5059.
PROCUREMENT: Col Fred R Jones.
TRANSPORTATION: Col Don Swayze.
PERSONNEL/COMMUNITY ACTIVITIES: Col William Byrd.
Personnel and Expenditures
ACTIVE DUTY PERSONNEL: 300
DEPENDENTS: 10
CIVILIAN PERSONNEL: 400
MILITARY PAYROLL EXPENDITURE: $10 mil
Services *Housing:* BEQ units 300; Barracks spaces 300; Senior NCO units 10; Mobile home units 4. *Temporary Housing:* VOQ cottages 6; BOQ units 10. *Commissary and Exchange:* Retail store; Dry cleaners; Banking. *Recreational Facilities:* Running.

BASYTOP

CAMP SWIFT (UNIT TRAINING AND EQUIPMENT SITE #3)
Rt 2, Box 151-X, Basytop, TX 78602-9737
(512) 321-2497
OFFICER-OF-THE-DAY: (512) 465-5001, Autovon 954-5001
Profile
BRANCH: Army National Guard.
SIZE AND LOCATION: 11,777 acres. On E side of TX Hwy 95 about half-way between towns of Elgin and Bastrop.
MAJOR UNITS: Company A, 386th Engineer Battalion.
BASE HISTORY: During WWII, used as training base for Army. After WWII, turned over to TX National Guard. Also used for federal prison and Boy Scout camp.
Key Contacts
COMMANDER: Lt James A Junot.
PUBLIC AFFAIRS: LTC Ed S Komandosky; PO Box 5218, Austin, TX 78763, (512) 465-5059.
Personnel and Expenditures
ACTIVE DUTY PERSONNEL: 10
CIVILIAN PERSONNEL: 5
MILITARY PAYROLL EXPENDITURE: $0.4 mil

BEEVILLE

CHASE FIELD NAVAL AIR STATION
Beeville, TX 78103
(512) 354-5119; Autovon 861-5119
OFFICER-OF-THE-DAY: (512) 354-5119, Autovon 861-5119
Profile
BRANCH: Navy.
SIZE AND LOCATION: 1772 acres. In S TX on Hwy 202, 4 mi E of Beeville, TX.
MAJOR UNITS: NAS Chase Field; Naval Oceanography Command Detachment Chase Field (NAVOCEANCOMDET); Training Airwing Three; Training Squadron Twenty-four (VT-24); Training Squadron Twenty-five (VT-25); Training Squadron Twenty-six (VT-26); Naval Air Maintenance Training Group 1004; Seabees Construction Battalion.
BASE HISTORY: Originally planned as Beeville Municipal Airport; opened 1943, as auxiliary of NAS Corpus Christi, TX, and named for LCDR Nathan Brown Chase, naval aviator killed in Pacific in 1925

training mission. Following WWII, reduced to caretaker status. 1952, purchased from city of Beeville. 1968, elevated to NAS; also operates two remote sites: NALF Goliad and McMullen Target Site.
Key Contacts
COMMANDER: Capt W P Dobbins; (512) 354-5516, Autovon 861-5516.
PUBLIC AFFAIRS: Lt Carter; (512) 354-5465, Autovon 861-5465.
PROCUREMENT: CDR Robertson; (512) 354-5403, Autovon 861-5403.
TRANSPORTATION: Walter Wallace; (512) 354-5535, Autovon 861-5535.
PERSONNEL/COMMUNITY ACTIVITIES: LTjg S Wright; (512) 354-5125, Autovon 861-5125.
Personnel and Expenditures
ACTIVE DUTY PERSONNEL: 1063
CIVILIAN PERSONNEL: 1440
Services *Housing:* Family units 415; BOQ cottages 128; BEQ units 480; Townhouse units 88; Mobile home units 19; Trailer spaces 20. *Temporary Housing:* BOQ units 34; Lodge units 5; Transient living quarters (on available basis). *Commissary:* Base commissary; Retail store; Barber shop; Dry cleaners; Food shop; Banking; Service station; Beauty shop; Package beverages. *Child Care/Capacities:* Day care center 67. *Base Library:* Yes. *Medical Facilities:* Medical clinic; Dental clinic. *Recreational Facilities:* Bowling; Movie theater; Pool; Gym; Recreation center; Golf; Stables; Tennis; Racquetball; Fitness center; Softball field; Football field; Auto shop; Officers club; NCO club; Camping; Fishing/Hunting.

GOLIAD NAVAL AUXILIARY LANDING FIELD
Beeville, TX 78103
(512) 354-5482; Autovon 861-5482
Profile
BRANCH: Navy.
SIZE AND LOCATION: 1180 acres. 25 mi NE of Beeville.
MAJOR UNITS: See NAS Chase Field.
BASE HISTORY: 1969, commissioned as Field Carrier Landing Practice (FCLP) field for NAS Chase Field, Beeville, TX. Primary mission to maintain and operate airport facilities in support of advanced pilot training under Commander, Training Air Wing Three; NALF self-supporting with jet fuel tanks, and all necessary GSE equipment for launching and serving on T-2C and TA-4J aircraft; fire and crash protection available.
Key Contacts
PUBLIC AFFAIRS: Lt Carter; NAS Chase Field, (512) 354-5465, Autovon 861-5465.
Personnel and Expenditures
ACTIVE DUTY PERSONNEL: 18
CIVILIAN PERSONNEL: 12
Services *Commissary and Exchange:* See NAS Chase Field. *Recreational Facilities:* Recreation center; Lake Langley, 10 acre lake with 19 hunting blinds.

BROOKS AFB

BROOKS AIR FORCE BASE
Brooks AFB, TX 78235-5000
(512) 536-1110; Autovon 240-1110
Profile
BRANCH: Air Force.
SIZE AND LOCATION: 873 acres. In SE part of San Antonio at corner of I-37 and Military Dr; approx 20 mi from San Antonio IAP.
MAJOR UNITS: Human Systems Division; USAF School of Aerospace Medicine; USAF Human Resources Laboratory; USAF Drug Testing Laboratory; USAF

Occupational and Environmental Health Laboratory; 6570th Air Base Group; 6570th Services Squadron; 6570th Civil Engineering Squadron; 6570th Security Police Squadron; USAF Clinic Brooks; San Antonio Real Property Maintenance Agency (SARPMA); Detachment 26, Management Engineering Team (MET); 2199th Communications Squadron (CS); 6575th School Squadron; Detachment 1018, AF Office of Special Investigation (AFOSI); 6906th Electronic Security Squadron (ESS); AF Office of Medical Support (AFOMS).
BASE HISTORY: Originally called Gosport Field, name derived from flight instruction system used. 1917, Army named site Kelly Field No 5. 1918, renamed Brooks Field for Cadet Sidney J Brooks Jr, native of San Antonio killed in training flight. 1919, pilot instructor school closed and Balloon and Airship School opened for pilots and ground crew members. 1922, series of mishaps closed school. 1922-31, became Primary Flying School of Army Air Corps; School of Aviation Medicine moved from Mitchell Field, NY. 1929, world's first successful mass parachute drop. 1930s, center of aerial observation activity. 1931, both schools transferred to newly constructed Randolph Field. 1940, special school for combat observers. 1943, home for training pilots in B-25 bomber. 1950s, transformed from flying training to center for modern medical research and development and education center. 1959, School of Aviation Medicine returned and HQs, Aerospace Medical Center. 1960, last plane took off Brook's runway. 1961, school's title changed to School of Aerospace Medicine. 1963, President Kennedy dedicated four buildings, his last official act before his assassination in Dallas. Today, researchers continue to study man's interaction with aerospace environment.
VISITOR ATTRACTIONS: USAF Museum of Flight Medicine; Hangar 9 (oldest Air Force hangar); Edward H White II Museum; Sidney J Brooks Jr Memorial Park; Schriever Heritage Park.
Key Contacts
COMMANDER: Maj Gen Fredric F Doppelt; HSD Commander; Col Herbert Klein; Base Commander.
PUBLIC AFFAIRS: HSD/PA.
Services *Housing:* Duplex units 150; Dormitory spaces 71; Single officers live off base; Capehart single units 20. *Temporary Housing:* VIP cottages 6; VOQ cottages 160; VAQ units 136; Transient living quarters 8. *Commissary:* Base commissary; Retail store; Barber shop; Dry cleaners; Banking; Service station; Convenience store/Shopette; Snacks; Optical shop; Video rental; Laundry; Beauty shop; Fabric care; Credit union; Thrift shop. *Child Care/Capacities:* Day care center. *Base Library:* Yes. *Medical Facilities:* Medical clinic; Dental clinic. *Recreational Facilities:* Bowling; Pool; Gym; Recreation center; Golf; Tennis; Racquetball; Softball field; Football field; Auto shop; Crafts; Officers club; NCO club; Camping; Youth center; Recreational supply; Picnicking; Ticket sales.

CORPUS CHRISTI

CORPUS CHRISTI ARMY DEPOT
Corpus Christi, TX 78419
(512) 939-3314
Profile
BRANCH: Army.
MAJOR UNITS: Army Depot (DARCOM).
Services *Housing:* Housing units 739. *Commissary:* Base commissary; Retail store; Package beverages. *Base Library:* Yes. *Medical Facilities:* Health center. *Recreational Fa-

CORPUS CHRISTI ARMY DEPOT *(continued)*
cilities: Bowling; Movie theater; Pool; Recreation center; Golf; Stables; Tennis; Racquetball; Fitness center; Auto shop; Crafts; Officers club; NCO club; Camping; Fishing/Hunting; Youth center; Boats; Skeet shooting; Lake; Fitness trail; Community Club.

CORPUS CHRISTI NAVAL AIR STATION
Corpus Christi, TX 78419-5000
(512) 939-2674; Autovon 861-2674
OFFICER-OF-THE-DAY: (512) 939-2383, Autovon 861-2383
Profile
BRANCH: Navy.
SIZE AND LOCATION: 4400 acres. 18 mi from downtown Corpus Christi.
MAJOR UNITS: Chief, Naval Air Training; Commander, Training Air Wing Four; VT-27; VT-28; VT-31; Corpus Christi Army Depot (CCAD).
BASE HISTORY: Naval Auxiliary Landing Field Waldron is part of NAS Corpus Christi.
Key Contacts
COMMANDER: Capt C L Reynolds; (512) 939-2332, Autovon 861-2332.
PUBLIC AFFAIRS: LTjg E A Vogel.
Personnel and Expenditures
ACTIVE DUTY PERSONNEL: 1700
DEPENDENTS: 4800
CIVILIAN PERSONNEL: 5000
MILITARY PAYROLL EXPENDITURE: $236 mil
CONTRACT EXPENDITURE: $43.5 mil
Services *Housing:* Family units 439; BEQ units 4; Senior NCO units 8; Trailer spaces 28. *Temporary Housing:* BOQ units 1; Lodge units 21. *Commissary:* Base commissary; Retail store; Barber shop; Dry cleaners; Florist; Banking; Service station; Book store. *Child Care/Capacities:* Day care center 110. *Schools:* Kindergarten/Preschool. *Base Library:* Yes. *Medical Facilities:* Hospital 195. *Recreational Facilities:* Bowling; Movie theater; Pool; Gym; Recreation center; Golf; Tennis; Racquetball; Fitness center; Softball field; Auto shop; Crafts; Officers club; NCO club; Camping; Fishing/Hunting.

CORPUS CHRISTI NAVAL HOSPITAL
Corpus Christi, TX 78419-5200
(512) 939-2688; Autovon 861-2688
OFFICER-OF-THE-DAY: Varies
Profile
BRANCH: Navy.
LOCATION: 10 mi from Corpus Christi IAP; 5 mi from I-37.
MAJOR UNITS: Naval Hospital Corpus Christi.
Key Contacts
COMMANDER: Capt Richard Gutshall; (512) 939-2684, Autovon 861-2684.
PUBLIC AFFAIRS: LCDR J Thomas Benson.
PROCUREMENT: Ens Kevin Kelley; (512) 939-2215, Autovon 861-2215.
TRANSPORTATION: Lt Tom Davis; (512) 939-3211, Autovon 861-3211.
PERSONNEL/COMMUNITY ACTIVITIES: Ltjg Brent Hayie; (512) 939-2257, Autovon 861-2257.
Services *Commissary:* Base commissary; Retail store; Barber shop; Dry cleaners; Food shop; Florist; Banking; Service station; SATO Travel Office. *Child Care/Capacities:* Day care center; Home day care program. *Schools:* Kindergarten/Preschool. *Base Library:* Yes. *Medical Facilities:* Hospital 195; Medical clinic; Dental clinic; Veterinary services. *Recreational Facilities:* Bowling; Movie theater; Pool; Gym; Recreation center; Golf; Tennis; Fitness center; Softball field; Auto shop; Crafts; Officers club; NCO club; Camping; Fishing/Hunting.

DALLAS

DALLAS NAVAL AIR STATION
Dallas, TX 75211-9501
(214) 266-6111; Autovon 874-6111
OFFICER-OF-THE-DAY: (214) 266-6120, 266-6215, Autovon 874-6120, 874-6215
Profile
BRANCH: Navy.
SIZE AND LOCATION: 840 acres. 13 mi W of Dallas, in Grand Prairie, on Jefferson Ave/Blvd. Take I-30 W and Loop 12 exit; take Loop 12 S and Jefferson Ave/Blvd W exit off Loop 12 S; NAS on left side of road clearly marked.
MAJOR UNITS: DINRIP; Reserve Readiness Command, Region 11 (REDCOM-11); Navy Reserve and Readiness Center (NAVRESREDCEN); Commander Fleet Logistics Support Wing (COMFLELOGSUPWING); Naval Logistics Squadron (VR-59); Naval Fighter Squadron (VF-202); Marine Air Group 41 (MAG-41); 14th Marines; CRUITCOR III; 136th Tactical Wing (Texas ANG); Reserve Naval Mobile Construction Battalion 22; US Coast Guard Reserve unit.
BASE HISTORY: 1941, commissioned to provide training of aircrews and aviation ground support personnel; test site for aircraft manufactured at adjacent North American aviation plant and training facility for Army Air Corps during WWII. Following WWII, assigned to Naval Air Reserve. USAF converted Hemsley Field, to Texas ANG. NAS under operational and administrative command of Commander Naval Air Reserve Force, New Orleans, LA; one of 15 major aviation reserve activities located throughout US.
Key Contacts
COMMANDER: Capt J D Olson II; Commanding Officer, NAS, (214) 266-6100, Autovon 874-6100.
PUBLIC AFFAIRS: PHCS H D Johnson; JO2 Chris Moilanen; PAO, NAS, (214) 266-6140, 266-6141, Autovon 874-6140, 874-6141.
PROCUREMENT: CDR John Hensley; Supply Department, NAS, (214) 266-6510, 266-6511, Autovon 874-6510, 874-6511.
TRANSPORTATION: LCDR Benjamin Spaulding; Public Works Office, NAS, (214) 266-6450, 266-6452, Autovon 874-6450, 874-6452.
Personnel and Expenditures
ACTIVE DUTY PERSONNEL: 1500
CIVILIAN PERSONNEL: 500
MILITARY PAYROLL EXPENDITURE: $24 mil
CONTRACT EXPENDITURE: $26 mil
Services *Housing:* BEQ units 240; Barracks spaces 240; Senior NCO units 39; Junior NCO units 201. *Temporary Housing:* VOQ cottages 2; VEQ units 300; BOQ units 180. *Commissary and Exchange:* Retail store; Barber shop; Dry cleaners; Florist; Banking; Service station; Military clothing sales; Convenience store/Shopette; Personal services shop; Optical shop; Beauty shop; Fast food. *Child Care/Capacities:* Day care center 50. *Base Library:* Yes. *Medical Facilities:* Medical clinic; Dental clinic. *Recreational Facilities:* Bowling; Pool; Gym; Tennis; Racquetball; Fitness center; Softball field; Football field; Auto shop; Officers club; NCO club; Fishing/Hunting; SATO office; Marina & picnic area; ITT office.

US ARMY CORPS OF ENGINEERS, SOUTHWESTERN DISTRICT
1114 Commerce St, Dallas, TX 75242-0216
(214) 767-2510

Profile
BRANCH: Army.
LOCATION: In downtown Dallas.
BASE HISTORY: 1937, established to oversee projects on Arkansas, White, Black, and North and South Canadian Rivers in Southwest; initially included Conchas (later Caddoa) District and Little Rock District; began functioning in Little Rock, AR. 1941, Galveston District transferred to Southwestern, adding most of TX, and parts of LA, CO, and NM. WWII, turned to military construction. 1941, moved to Dallas. 1950-1955, special study of Arkansas, White, and Red River basins, known as AWRBIAC. 1958, full-scale survey of water in TX. 1980s, reviewing and approving designs, plans, and specifications for hydroelectric plants at its water projects. Work on traditional dam and reservoir projects drawing to close, no new ones anticipated.
Key Contacts
COMMANDER: Brig Gen Robert C Lee; (214) 767-2500.
PUBLIC AFFAIRS: Lu DuCharme.
PROCUREMENT: Charles Free; (214) 767-2334.
PERSONNEL/COMMUNITY ACTIVITIES: Parker Greenwell; (214) 767-2491.

US ARMY CORPS OF ENGINEERS, SOUTHWESTERN DIVISION
1200 Main St, Main Tower Bldg, Dallas, TX 75202
(214) 767-2500
Profile
BRANCH: Army.
SIZE: Offices only.
Key Contacts
COMMANDER: Brig Gen Robert C Lee; Division Engineer.

136TH TACTICAL AIRLIFT WING (ANG)
Dallas Naval Air Station, Dallas, TX 75211
(214) 266-6111; Autovon 874-6111
Profile
BRANCH: Air National Guard.
SIZE AND LOCATION: 49 acres. On the Dallas Naval Air Station.
MAJOR UNITS: 136th Tactical Airlift Wing (ANG).
Personnel and Expenditures
ACTIVE DUTY PERSONNEL: 872
CIVILIAN PERSONNEL: 186
MILITARY PAYROLL EXPENDITURE: $9.2 mil

FORT BLISS

FORT BLISS
Headquarters, USADACEN and Ft Bliss, Bldg 2, Fort Bliss, TX 79916-5000
(915) 568-4505; Autovon 978-4505
Profile
BRANCH: Army.
SIZE AND LOCATION: 1.11 mil. Borders on El Paso City, along US Hwy 54.
MAJOR UNITS: US Army Sergeants Major Academy; 1st Spt. Battalion; 11th ADA Brigade; 70th Ordnance Battalion; 3rd Armored Cavalry Regiment; 6th ADA Brigade; Air Defense Artillery School; US Army Training Center; William Beaumont Army Medical Center.
BASE HISTORY: Roots go back to early infantry units dispatched more than 136 years ago to protect local ranchers from Indians and bandits.
VISITOR ATTRACTIONS: Memorial Circle; Japanese Gardens; Building 2 Headquarters; Pershing House; Officers Row; Old Barracks; Bliss Monument; Bradley Tree; Pace Hall; Air Defense Artillery Museum;

FORT BLISS (continued)
Replica Museum; 3rd Armored Cavalry Regiment Museum; Biggs Army Airfield.
Key Contacts
COMMANDER: Maj Gen Donald R Infante; Post Commander, ATTN: ATZC-CG, (915) 568-3898, 568-3401, Autovon 978-3898, 978-3401.
PUBLIC AFFAIRS: LTC James E Lawson Jr; Post Public Affairs, ATTN: ATZC-CGP-CI Bldg 15, (915) 568-4505, 568-4601, Autovon 978-4505, 978-4601.
PROCUREMENT: P Gill; ATTN: ATZC-DOC Bldg 2021, (915) 568-5150, Autovon 978-5150.
TRANSPORTATION: Maj Larry W Shields; ATTN: ATZC-DIT, (915) 568-1262, 568-1088, Autovon 978-1262, 978-1088.
PERSONNEL/COMMUNITY ACTIVITIES: Col Richard Miks; ATTN: ATZC-PA Bldg 1, (915) 568-3724, 568-4516, Autovon 978-3724, 978-4516.
Personnel and Expenditures
ACTIVE DUTY PERSONNEL: 19,535
DEPENDENTS: 9143
CIVILIAN PERSONNEL: 8737
MILITARY PAYROLL EXPENDITURE: $342.7 mil
CONTRACT EXPENDITURE: $63 mil
Services *Housing:* Family units 3575; BEQ units 239. *Temporary Housing:* VIP cottages 6; VOQ cottages 460; VEQ units 384; BOQ units 116; Guesthouse units 75; Guest cottages 9. *Commissary:* Base commissary; Retail store; Barber shop; Dry cleaners; Food shop; Florist; Banking; Service station; Book store. *Child Care/Capacities:* Day care center; Home day care program. *Schools:* Kindergarten/Preschool; Elementary; Intermediate/Junior high. *Base Library:* Yes. *Medical Facilities:* Hospital 340; Medical clinic; Dental clinic. *Recreational Facilities:* Bowling; Movie theater; Pool; Gym; Recreation center; Golf; Stables; Tennis; Racquetball; Fitness center; Softball field; Football field; Auto shop; Crafts; Officers club; NCO club; Camping; Fishing/Hunting; Rod and Gun Club.

FORT HOOD

FORT HOOD
Fort Hood, TX 76544
(817) 287-1110; Autovon 737-2131
Profile
BRANCH: Army.
SIZE AND LOCATION: 217,337 acres. In hill and lake country of central TX, approx 60 mi N of Austin and 50 mi S of Waco; adj to Killeen, TX on Rte 190.
MAJOR UNITS: III Corps; 1st Cavalry Division; 2d Armored Division; 6th Cavalry Brigade (Air Combat); 13th Support Command (Corps); 3rd Signal Brigade; 89th Military Police Brigade; Apache Training Brigade; Medical Department Activity (MEDDAC); Dental Activity (DENTAC); US Army Training and Doctrine Command Test and Experimentation Command (TEXCOM); AMC Liaison Office; Criminal Investigation Command; III Corps and Ft Hood Opposing Forces (OPFOR); Red Thrust; US Army Information Systems Command-Ft Hood; Detachment 1, 602nd Tactical Air Control Wing (USAF Air Liaison Detachment); 5th Weather Squadron; Apache Materiel Fielding Team; Texas Army National Guard; 47th Ordnance Detachment (EOD); RGAAF: 504th Military Intelligence Brigade; ½ 00th Aviation Platoon; 3rd Signal Brigade; ½ 00th 16th Air Traffic Control Battalion; 3rd Platoon, 507th Medical Company; 1st Cavalry Division, Combat Aviation Brigade; HAAF: 2d Armored Division; 6th Cavalry Brigade (Air Combat); Apache Training Brigade.

BASE HISTORY: 1942, construction of South Camp Hood began; North Camp Hood, 17 miles N, established shortly after founding of cantonment area; named for Confederate Gen John Bell Hood, Civil War commander of Hood's Texas Brigade. 1951, South Camp Hood designated Ft Hood, a permanent installation. North Camp Hood became North Ft Hood; training facilities used for summer training of Army Reserve and NG units. 1947, West Fort Hood, originally Killeen Base, constructed. 1952, USAF facility. 1952-1969 variously named Killeen Base and Robert Gray AFB, named after Capt Robert M Gray, WWII Army Air Corps pilot from Killeen, TX, under Defense Atomic Support Agency, manned by Army, Navy, and Air Force personnel. 1969, Robert Gray Army Air Field became part of Ft Hood with Hood Army Airfield (HAAF), a fully instrumented airfield (3,000 acres) capable of handling largest aircraft and FAA-approved helicopter instrument airfield (773 acres) exclusively rotary wing aircraft. Both restricted areas for security reasons. 2 paved, non-instrumented airstrips used for training at North Fort Hood: Longhorn and Shorthorn Strips used as summer training sites for NG and Reserve aviation units.
VISITOR ATTRACTIONS: 2nd Armored Division Museum; 1st Cavalry Museum (both open 9-3:30 M-F, Noon-3:30 Sat, Sun, holidays, closed Christmas, New Year's, Thanksgiving, and Easter).
Key Contacts
PUBLIC AFFAIRS: III Corps Public Affairs Office.
Personnel and Expenditures
ACTIVE DUTY PERSONNEL: 38,203
DEPENDENTS: 14,642
CIVILIAN PERSONNEL: 10,142
MILITARY PAYROLL EXPENDITURE: $177.8 mil
CONTRACT EXPENDITURE: $6.8 mil
Services *Housing:* Family units 5558; BEQ units 24,000; Junior NCO units 500; RV/Camper sites 40. *Temporary Housing:* VIP cottages 9; VOQ cottages; VEQ units 32; BAQ units; Guesthouse units 75; General officer guesthouse 1; Junior enlisted guest quarters rooms 48. *Commissary:* Base commissary; Retail store; Barber shop; Dry cleaners; Food shop; Service station; Military clothing sales; Convenience store/Shopette; Computer store; Garden center; Four Seasons shop; Laundry; Video rental; Ice cream; Snacks; Car rental; Shoe repair; Fast food; Package beverages. *Child Care/Capacities:* Day care center 499; Home day care program. *Schools:* Kindergarten/Preschool; Elementary; Intermediate/Junior high. *Base Library:* Yes. *Medical Facilities:* Hospital 264; Medical clinic; Dental clinic; Darnall Hospital; Veterinary services. *Recreational Facilities:* Bowling; Movie theater; Pool; Gym; Recreation center; Golf (and driving range); Tennis; Racquetball; Skating rink; Fitness center; Softball field; Football field; Auto shop; Crafts; Officers club; NCO club; Camping; Fishing/Hunting; Youth center; Rod and Gun Club; Picnicking; Equipment checkout center; Marina; Field house; Belton Lake Outdoor Recreation Area (BLORA), 64 camper spaces.

FORT SAM HOUSTON

CAMP BULLIS
HQ, Fort Sam Houston, Fort Sam Houston, TX 78234-5000
(512) 221-7611; 221-7622; Autovon 471-7611; 471-7622
OFFICER-OF-THE-DAY: (512) 221-7622, Autovon 471-7622

Profile
BRANCH: Army.
SIZE AND LOCATION: 28,000 acres. Adj to downtown San Antonio. City bus lines cross post in all directions. No gates or checkpoints on major thoroughfares. Airport approx 10 min away. Immediate access from IH-37 at N Braufels Ave.
MAJOR UNITS: Academy of Health Sciences; Joint Military Medical Readiness Group; 1st SOCOM 18D Course.
BASE HISTORY: Training facility for all services and many federal agencies; subpost of Ft Sam Houston.
VISITOR ATTRACTIONS: Post Museum; Medical Museum; Quadrangle; Quadrangle Gift Shoppe; Post on Grayline tour.
Key Contacts
COMMANDER: See Ft Sam Houston.
PUBLIC AFFAIRS: Public Affairs Officer, HQ, Ft Sam Houston (AFZG-PO), Ft Sam Houston, TX 78234-5000, (512) 221-5151, 221-2030, Autovon 471-5151, 471-2030.
PROCUREMENT: Contracting Officer; HQ, Ft Sam Houston, Ft Sam Houston, TX 78234-5000, (512) 221-2930, 221-2240, Autovon 471-2930, 471-2240.
TRANSPORTATION: Director of Logistics (ATTN: Trans Off); HQ, Ft Sam Houston, Ft Sam Houston, TX 78234-5000, (512) 221-2649, 221-2661, Autovon 471-2649, 471-2661.
PERSONNEL/COMMUNITY ACTIVITIES: Director of Personnel and Community Activities; HQ, Ft Sam Houston, Ft Sam Houston, TX 78234-5000, (512) 221-2412, 221-6933, Autovon 471-2412, 471-6933.
Personnel and Expenditures
ACTIVE DUTY PERSONNEL: Varies daily
DEPENDENTS: 23
CIVILIAN PERSONNEL: 37
MILITARY PAYROLL EXPENDITURE: See Ft Sam Houston
Services *Housing:* Family units 4. *Commissary and Exchange:* Class C retail store. *Medical Facilities:* Medical clinic.

FORT SAM HOUSTON
Fort Sam Houston, TX 78234-5000
(512) 221-1211; Autovon 475-1211
OFFICER-OF-THE-DAY: (512) 221-3810, 221-3105, Autovon 475-3810, 475-3105
Profile
BRANCH: Army.
SIZE AND LOCATION: 3000 acres. Adj to downtown San Antonio. City bus lines cross the post in all directions. There are no gates or checkpoints on major thoroughfares. Airport is approx 10 min away. Immediate access from IH-37 at N Braufels Ave.
MAJOR UNITS: HQ Fifth US Army; Health Services Command; Academy of Health Sciences; Fifth Recruiting Brigade; Defense Mapping Agency; Brooke Army Medical Center.
BASE HISTORY: The US Army Garrison at Ft Sam Houston can loosely trace its origins back to the very first troops to arrive in San Antonio in 1870; troops of the Department of TX were housed in rented buildings around the Alamo and the Arsenal areas of downtown; headquarters were located where the Gunter Hotel now stands at Houston and St Marys streets; most of the troops in TX were cavalry, sent here to protect the settlers and wagon trains from the Indians. Mission of Ft Sam Houston has passed from a Quartermaster Depot supplying frontier outposts to one of providing medical training to meet the Army's needs worldwide.
VISITOR ATTRACTIONS: Post Museum; Medical Museum; Quadrangle; Quadrangle Gift Shoppe; Post is on the Grayline tour.

FORT SAM HOUSTON *(continued)*
Key Contacts
COMMANDER: Lt Gen William H Schneider; Cdr, Fifth US Army and Ft Sam Houston, ATTN: AFKB-CG, Ft Sam Houston, TX 78234-7000, (512) 221-6865, Autovon 475-6865.
PUBLIC AFFAIRS: LTC Troy D Griffin Jr; Public Affairs Office, ATTN: AFZG-PO.
PROCUREMENT: Larry Roberts; (512) 221-2930, 221-2240, Autovon 475-2930, 475-2240.
TRANSPORTATION: Maj S R Todd; (512) 221-2649, 221-2661, Autovon 475-2649, 475-2661.
PERSONNEL/COMMUNITY ACTIVITIES: LTC Wayne Armour; (512) 221-6933, 221-6133, 221-2240, Autovon 475-6933, 475-6133.
Personnel and Expenditures
ACTIVE DUTY PERSONNEL: 15,000
DEPENDENTS: 3207
CIVILIAN PERSONNEL: 6359
MILITARY PAYROLL EXPENDITURE: $34.9 mil
Services *Housing:* Family units 1169; Barracks spaces 7546. *Temporary Housing:* BOQ units 506; Guesthouse units 28. *Commissary:* Base commissary; Retail store; Barber shop; Dry cleaners; Food shop; Florist; Banking; Service station; Furniture store. *Child Care/Capacities:* Day care center 250; Home day care program. *Schools:* Kindergarten/Preschool; Elementary; Intermediate/Junior high; High school. *Base Library:* Yes. *Medical Facilities:* Hospital 470; Medical clinic; Dental clinic; USAF Medical Ctr is also available 20 min away at Lackland AFB. *Recreational Facilities:* Bowling; Movie theater; Pool; Gym; Recreation center; Golf; Stables; Tennis; Racquetball; Softball field; Football field; Auto shop; Crafts; Officers club; NCO club; Canyon Lake Travel Camp/Recreation Area with camping and fishing 50 mi NW.

FORT WORTH

AIR FORCE PLANT REPRESENTATIVE OFFICE, AIR FORCE PLANT NO 4
PO Box 371, General Dynamics Fort Worth Division, Fort Worth, TX 76101-0371
Profile
BRANCH: Air Force.
SIZE AND LOCATION: 300 acres. Adj to Carswell AFB, 10 mi from downtown Fort Worth.
MAJOR UNITS: Air Force Plant Representative; Air Force Institute of Technology-Education with Industry; Air Force Systems Command/Central Technical Order Control Unit; Air Force Systems Command/Joint Test Force; Defense Contract Audit Agency; Military Airlift Command/Civilian Personnel Representative; Tactical Air Command Logistics Liaison Office; Air Force Operational Test and Evaluation Command/Air Force Electronic Warfare Evaluation Simulator; Resident Integrated Logistics Support Activity.
BASE HISTORY: 1941, construction began on Air Force Plant No 4, one of largest aircraft plants in world. WWII, 3034 B-24s assembled here. Subsequent production resulted in more than 5300 aircraft deliveries. AFPRO one of 28 plant representative offices under AFCMD, immediately subordinate to AF Systems Command (AFSC).
Key Contacts
COMMANDER: (817) 763-4422.

CARSWELL AIR FORCE BASE
Fort Worth, TX 76127
(817) 782-5000; Autovon 739-1110
Profile
BRANCH: Air Force.
SIZE AND LOCATION: 3274 acres. 7 mi W of downtown Ft Worth, TX; At the junction of I-30 and Hwy 183; 50 min from Dallas and 40 min from Dallas/Ft Worth IAP.
MAJOR UNITS: 7th Bombardment Wing (SAC); 301st Tactical Fighter Wing (Reserve)(TAC); 2048th Communication Squadron (AFCC); 1365th Audiovisual Squadron (MAC).
BASE HISTORY: 1941, Consolidated Vultee Aircraft Corp constructed Vultee plant and landing field, designated Tarrant Field Airdrome. 1942, field placed under Army Air Field Training Command; Vultee built B-24 bombers and military trained crews and maintained B-24s. 1942, became Tarrant County Army Air Field. 1946, renamed Ft Worth Army Air Field. 1946-1955, HQ, 8th Air Force. 1948, became Fort Worth AFB on Jan 2; Griffis AFB on Jan 13; finally, Jan 30, Carswell AFB, for Maj Horace S Carswell Jr, WWII hero and Ft Worth native (Only AFB to have namesake interred on base). 1951, HQ, 19th Air Division activated. 1965-1973, bombers deployed to Pacific for strikes against North Vietnam.
Key Contacts
COMMANDER: Col John B Sams Jr; Wing Commander.
PUBLIC AFFAIRS: Capt Barbara Carr; (817) 782-7154, Autovon 739-7154.
Personnel and Expenditures
ACTIVE DUTY PERSONNEL: 5258
DEPENDENTS: 1131
CIVILIAN PERSONNEL: 1280
MILITARY PAYROLL EXPENDITURE: $124 mil
CONTRACT EXPENDITURE: $46 mil
Services *Housing:* Family units 807; BAQ units 1144. *Temporary Housing:* VOQ cottages 106; VAQ units 80; Transient living quarters 18. *Commissary:* Base commissary; Retail store; Barber shop; Dry cleaners; Food shop; Florist; Banking; Service station; Computer store; Optical shop. *Child Care/Capacities:* Day care center 250. *Base Library:* Yes. *Medical Facilities:* Hospital (Robert L Thompson Strategic Hospital). *Recreational Facilities:* Bowling; Movie theater; Pool; Gym; Recreation center; Golf; Tennis; Racquetball; Fitness center; Softball field; Football field; Auto shop; Crafts; Officers club; NCO club; Camping; Fishing/Hunting.

GALVESTON

GALVESTON COAST GUARD BASE
PO Box 1912, Galveston, TX 77553-1912
(409) 766-5615
Profile
BRANCH: Coast Guard.
SIZE AND LOCATION: 100 acres. Eastern end of Galveston Island next to Galveston-Boliver Ferry Terminal; 50 mi from Houston via I-45S.
MAJOR UNITS: USCG Group Galveston; USCGC *Valiant*; USCGC *Buttonwood*; USCGC *Point Spencer*; USCGC *Clamp*; USCGC *Hatchet*; USCG ANT Galveston.
BASE HISTORY: 1938, established at current location, Fort Point. Controls units operating from Marsh Island, LA, to Matagorda, TX; primary missions include search and rescue, aids to navigation, and maritime law enforcement; group provides operational guidance, administrative support, materiel, and technical support for 10 sub-units, including USCG cutters, Aids to Navigation Team at Sabine, and USCG Station at Freeport.

Key Contacts
COMMANDER: Capt Michael F Cowan.
PUBLIC AFFAIRS: Lt Scott P LaRochelle.
PROCUREMENT: CWO2 Marc Schmidt.
TRANSPORTATION: See Procurement Officer.
Personnel and Expenditures
ACTIVE DUTY PERSONNEL: 130
CIVILIAN PERSONNEL: 20
Services *Temporary Housing:* Transient living quarters 10. *Commissary and Exchange:* Small store. *Medical Facilities:* Dental clinic; Small clinic. *Recreational Facilities:* Tennis; NCO club.

US ARMY ENGINEER DISTRICT, GALVESTON
PO Box 1229, Galveston, TX 77553-1229
Profile
BRANCH: Army.
SIZE: Offices only.

GARLAND

GARLAND AIR NATIONAL GUARD STATION
PO Box 461635, Garland, TX 75046
(214) 276-0521; Autovon 883-3420
Profile
BRANCH: Air National Guard.
SIZE AND LOCATION: 2 acres. Center of Garland, TX, in NE Dallas County.
MAJOR UNITS: Headquarters, 254th Combat Communications Group; 221st Combat Communications Squadron.
BASE HISTORY: 254th Combat Communications Group evolved from small squadron organized 1952, as 221st Radio Relay Squadron. 1968, redesignated 221st Mobile Communications Squadron. Following a few reassignments, designated 254th Combat Communications Group. First Guard unit to lead combat communications unit in Joint Chiefs of Staff directed joint exercise.
VISITOR ATTRACTIONS: Hall of Flags; Hall of Honor.
Key Contacts
COMMANDER: Col Fred E Ellis.
PUBLIC AFFAIRS: Maj Henry D Kaplan.
PROCUREMENT: Maj Joe Saucedo.
TRANSPORTATION: Maj Robert Starks.
PERSONNEL/COMMUNITY ACTIVITIES: Capt Mel Bohler.
Personnel and Expenditures
ACTIVE DUTY PERSONNEL: 5
CIVILIAN PERSONNEL: 2
MILITARY PAYROLL EXPENDITURE: $0.2 mil
Services *Recreational Facilities:* Weight room.

GOODFELLOW AFB

GOODFELLOW AIR FORCE BASE
Goodfellow AFB, TX 76908
(915) 657-3231; Autovon 477-3217
Profile
BRANCH: Air Force.
SIZE AND LOCATION: 1119 acres. Just E of San Angelo, TX on US-87.
MAJOR UNITS: Goodfellow Technical Training Center; 3480th Technical Training Wing; 3480th Air Base Group; 3480th Technical Training Group; 2081st Communication Squadron; 3490th Technical Training Group; 3495th Technical Training Group; 8th Missile Warning Squadron.
BASE HISTORY: 1941, established and named after Lt John J Goodfellow, Jr, native of San Angelo killed in plane crash in WWI. For most of its history served as pilot training site except 1958-1978, Security Service (later Electronic Security Command).

GOODFELLOW AIR FORCE BASE
(continued)
Personnel and Expenditures
ACTIVE DUTY PERSONNEL: 1924; students,
1500
DEPENDENTS: 2794
CIVILIAN PERSONNEL: 443
MILITARY PAYROLL EXPENDITURE: $38.5 mil
Services *Housing:* Family units 99; BAQ
units 520; BOQ/VOQ units 36. *Temporary
Housing:* VIP cottages 4; VOQ cottages 36;
VAQ units 618; Transient living quarters 12;
TDY reservations only. *Commissary:* Base
commissary; Barber shop; Food shop; Ser-
vice station; Convenience store/Shopette;
Optical shop; Beauty shop; Toys. *Child
Care/Capacities:* Day care center 126. *Medi-
cal Facilities:* Medical clinic; Veterinary ser-
vices. *Recreational Facilities:* Bowling; Movie theater; Pool; Gym; Recreation center;
Golf; Stables; Tennis; Racquetball; Fitness
center; Auto shop; Crafts; Fishing/Hunting;
Youth center (activities); Aero Club; Skeet
shooting; Consolidated Club; Lake Nasworth
recreation camp, 10 mi SW.

HOUSTON

ELLINGTON AIR NATIONAL GUARD BASE
147th Fighter Interceptor Group, Houston,
TX 77034-5546
(713) 929-2110; Autovon 954-2110
Profile
BRANCH: Air National Guard.
SIZE AND LOCATION: 2283 acres. 17 mi SE of
Houston; Take I-45 from Houston to El-
lington Field exit, proceed E for 2.5 mi to
field.
MAJOR UNITS: 147th Fighter Interceptor
Group; Houston Coast Guard Air Station;
NASA Operations; Army National Guard;
FAA; Military Sealift Command; ANG
Transition Caretaker Force.
BASE HISTORY: Named for Lt Eric L Elling-
ton, pilot killed in 1913.
VISITOR ATTRACTIONS: Johnson Space Flight
Center; Astro World theme park; Astro-
dome.
Key Contacts
PUBLIC AFFAIRS: 147 FIG/PA, 105 Ellington
Field, Houston, TX 77034-5586.
Personnel and Expenditures
ACTIVE DUTY PERSONNEL: 898
CIVILIAN PERSONNEL: 411
MILITARY PAYROLL EXPENDITURE: $13.6 mil
Services *Commissary and Exchange:* Retail
store. *Medical Facilities:* Pharmacy. *Recrea-
tional Facilities:* NCO club; SATO; Adjacent
to public golf course and driving range.

HOUSTON COAST GUARD AIR STATION
Houston, TX 77034
(713) 929-2110; Autovon 954-2110
Profile
BRANCH: Coast Guard.
LOCATION: 17 mi SE of Houston; Take I-45
from Houston to Ellington Field exit, pro-
ceed E for 2.5 mi to field.
MAJOR UNITS: Houston Coast Guard Air Sta-
tion.
VISITOR ATTRACTIONS: Johnson Space Flight
Center; Astro World theme park; Astro-
dome.
Key Contacts
PUBLIC AFFAIRS: 147 FIG/PA, 105 Ellington
Field, Houston, TX 77034-5586.
Services *Commissary and Exchange:* Retail
store. *Medical Facilities:* Pharmacy. *Recrea-
tional Facilities:* NCO club; SATO; Adjacent
to public golf course and driving range.

KELLY AFB

KELLY AIR FORCE BASE
Kelly AFB, TX 78241
(512) 925-1110; Autovon 945-1110
Profile
BRANCH: Air Force.
SIZE AND LOCATION: 4660 acres. 5 mi SW of
downtown San Antonio, TX; S of Hwy 90
and off Loop 13.
MAJOR UNITS: 2851st Air Base Group; San
Antonio Air Logistics Center (SA ALC);
2954th Combat Logistics Support Squad-
ron; Electronic Security Command; 433rd
Military Airlift Wing; 404th Combat Lo-
gistics Support Squadron; 149th Tactical
Fighter Group (Texas Air National
Guard); Air Force Service Information
and News Center; Air Force Commissary
Service; Defense Courier Service; 1827th
Electronics Installations Squadron; 1923rd
Communications Group; Air Force Audit
Agency Defense Reutilization and Mar-
keting Office; Detachment 4, 3025th
Management Engineering Squadron; De-
tachment 5, 375th Aeromedical Airlift
Wing; Detachment 7, 17th Weather
Squadron; DOD Dog Center.
BASE HISTORY: 1917, first aircraft from 3rd
Aero Squadron landed at then South San
Antonio Aviation Camp; became Camp
Kelly, and then Kelly Field, named for Lt
George E M Kelly, first American mili-
tary aviator killed in military plane crash.
WWI, reception and testing center for
new recruits and training center for mechanics, chauffeurs, engineering and supply officers, and cooks and bakers. 1917,
Aviation General Supply Depot moved
from San Antonio. Kelly unofficially divided into two adjoining fields: Kelly
Number 1, original site, became home of
warehouses, supply functions, and recruit
training; Kelly Number 2, to north, site of
flying training. 1921, Aviation Repair Depot moved from Dallas to Kelly Number
1, to form San Antonio Air Intermediate
Depot. 1922, Air Service Advanced Flying School opened at Kelly Number 2.
1925, field officially divided: Kelly Number 1 became Duncan Field; and, Number
2 retained Kelly name. Kelly hosted 1924
National Elimination Balloon Race, 1926
Pan American Goodwill Flight, and film-
ing of silent movie "Wings." 1943, bases
reunited as Kelly Field and transferred to
Air Service Command. WWII, developed
into industrial complex; acquired Nor-
moyle Ordnance Depot, known today as
East Kelly. 1946, logistics depot defined
as separate facility called San Antonio Air
Materiel Area (SA-ALC, 1974). 1948, be-
came Kelly AFB. Today, logistics center
operates independently within Kelly AFB.
Kelly also provides refueling facilities for
space shuttle's "piggy-back" mother ship.
Key Contacts
COMMANDER: Maj Gen Richard D Smith;
SA-ALC/CC; Col James T Jones, 2851st
ABG/CC.
PUBLIC AFFAIRS: LTC Edwin B Cooke; SA-
ALC/PA.
PROCUREMENT: Col J V Orsini Jr; Director
of Contracting & Manufacturing (PM).
TRANSPORTATION: M R Medley.
Personnel and Expenditures
ACTIVE DUTY PERSONNEL: 5800
DEPENDENTS: 2700
CIVILIAN PERSONNEL: 18,000
MILITARY PAYROLL EXPENDITURE: $43.5 mil
CONTRACT EXPENDITURE: $3.4 bil
Services *Housing:* Family units 46; Barracks
spaces 1337; Senior NCO units 18; Junior
NCO units 350. *Temporary Housing:* VIP
cottages 6; VOQ cottages 50; VAQ units 48.
Commissary: Base commissary; Retail store;

Service station; Convenience store/Shopette.
Child Care/Capacities: Day care center 200.
Base Library: Yes. *Medical Facilities:* Medical clinic; Dental clinic. *Recreational Facilities:* Bowling; Movie theater; Pool; Gym; Recreation center; Golf; Tennis; Racquetball;
Fitness center; Softball field; Football field;
Auto shop; Crafts; Officers club; NCO club;
Camping; Jogging; ITT; Aero Club; Youth
club; Sports equipment rental; Lindbergh
Park, 32 acres; Laguna Shores recreational
area at Corpus Christi NAS; Flying K Recreational Ranch, 5 mi W of Marble Falls, TX.

KINGSVILLE

KINGSVILLE NAVAL AIR STATION
Kingsville, TX 78363-5000
(512) 595-6136; Autovon 861-6136
Profile
BRANCH: Navy.
SIZE AND LOCATION: 3986 acres. 40 mi SW
of Corpus Christi, TX, in Kingsville off
Rte 77.
MAJOR UNITS: Chief of Naval Training
(CNATRA); Commander, Training Air
Wing Two; Training Squadron Twenty-
One (VT-21); Training Squadron Twenty-
Two (VT-22); Training Squadron Twenty-
Three (VT-23); Naval Auxiliary Landing
Field, Orange Grove; Naval Oceanog-
raphic Command Detachment (NOCD);
Naval Air Maintenance Training Group
Detachment 1017; Seabee Division.
BASE HISTORY: 1942, established to house
four "P-4" squadrons and as training base
for fighter and bomber tactics, gunnery
school for combat aircrews, and later tem-
porary basic training center for overflow
from Naval Training Center, Great Lakes,
IL. Following WWII, caretaker status;
leased to Texas A & I University, Kingsville, for agricultural station. 1951, reopened as Naval Auxiliary Station. 1968,
redesignated NAS. 1986, airfield named
for Vice Adm Alva D Bernhard, founder
of station.
Key Contacts
PUBLIC AFFAIRS: John L Caffey.
Personnel and Expenditures
ACTIVE DUTY PERSONNEL: 1200
DEPENDENTS: 750
CIVILIAN PERSONNEL: 1000
Services *Housing:* Family units 242; BOQ
cottages 159; BEQ units 402. *Temporary
Housing:* VIP cottages 3; VOQ cottages 10;
VEQ units 14; Guesthouse units 8; Transient
living quarters 19. *Commissary:* Base com-
missary; Retail store; Barber shop; Dry
cleaners; Florist; Service station; Military
clothing sales; Convenience store/Shopette;
Beauty shop; Laundry; Package beverages;
Credit union. *Child Care/Capacities:* Day
care center 50. *Base Library:* Yes. *Medical
Facilities:* Medical clinic; Dental clinic; Veterinary clinic. *Recreational Facilities:* Bowl-
ing; Movie theater; Pool; Gym; Recreation
center; Golf; Stables; Tennis; Racquetball;
Softball field; Football field; Auto shop;
Crafts; Officers club; NCO club; Camping;
Fishing/Hunting; Skeet range; Picnic area;
Equipment rental; Rod and Gun Club; ITT.

LACKLAND AFB

LACKLAND AIR FORCE BASE
AFMTC/PAM, Lackland AFB, TX 78236-
5000
(512) 671-2907; Autovon 473-2907
Profile
BRANCH: Air Force.
SIZE AND LOCATION: 6783 acres. 6 mi SW of
San Antonio, adj to Kelly AFB; at inter-
sections of US 90 and Military Dr, near
Loop 410 W; Served by San Antonio IAP.

LACKLAND AIR FORCE BASE (continued)

MAJOR UNITS: Basic Military Training School; Defense Language Institute English Language Center; 3250th Technical Training Wing; Officer Training School; Wilford Hall USAF Medical Center.

BASE HISTORY: 1941, constructed; designated Air Corps Replacement Training Center with mission to produce potential Army Air Corps pilots; named for Brig Gen Frank D Lackland, pioneer of military flying.

VISITOR ATTRACTIONS: History and Traditions Museum; Security Police Museum; Military Training Instructor Monument.

Key Contacts

COMMANDER: Maj Gen Larry N Tibbetts; Center Commander, Col Bruce W Sharer; Base Commander, 3700 Air Base Group.

PUBLIC AFFAIRS: Maj Johnny Whitaker.

TRANSPORTATION: Maj Suzanne L Cowan; 3700 Transportation Squadron, (512) 671-2855, Autovon 473-2855.

PERSONNEL/COMMUNITY ACTIVITIES: LTC Andrew M Stanley Jr; Director of Personnel, 3700 Personnel Resources Group, (512) 671-3907, Autovon 473-3907.

Personnel and Expenditures

ACTIVE DUTY PERSONNEL: 2900
DEPENDENTS: 1960
CIVILIAN PERSONNEL: 900
MILITARY PAYROLL EXPENDITURE: $242 mil
CONTRACT EXPENDITURE: $73 mil

Services Housing: Family units 724; Dormitory spaces 780. Temporary Housing: VIP cottages 60; VOQ cottages 225; VEQ units 60; VAQ units 800; Guesthouse units 230. Commissary: Base commissary; Retail store; Barber shop; Dry cleaners; Food shop; Florist; Banking; Service station; Furniture store; Computer store; Beauty shop; Garden center; Toys. Child Care/Capacities: Day care center 210; Home day care program. Schools: Kindergarten/Preschool; Elementary; High school. Base Library: Yes. Medical Facilities: Hospital 1000; Medical clinic; Dental clinic. Recreational Facilities: Bowling; Movie theater; Pool; Gym; Recreation center; Golf; Stables; Tennis; Racquetball; Skating rink; Fitness center; Softball field; Football field; Auto shop; Crafts; Officers club; NCO club; Camping and fishing at Medina Lake facility.

LAUGHLIN AFB

LAUGHLIN AIR FORCE BASE

47th Flying Training Wing, Laughlin AFB, TX 78843-5000
(512) 298-5044; Autovon 732-5044

Profile

BRANCH: Air Force.

SIZE AND LOCATION: 4194 acres. On perimeter of Del Rio, TX; 150 mi due W of San Antonio on Hwy 90.

MAJOR UNITS: 47th Fighter Training Wing; 85th Flying Training Squadron (FTS); 86th Flying Training Squadron (FTS); 47th Air Base Group (ABG); 47th Civil Engineering Squadron; 47th Mission Support Squadron; 47th Supply Squadron; 47th Security Police Squadron; 47th Field Maintenance Squadron; 47th Organizational Maintenance Squadron; 47th Student Squadron; USAF Hospital; 2108th Communications Squadron (AFCC); Area Defense Council, Detachment QD 30 (ADC); 3314th Management Engineering Squadron, Detachment 9 (ATC); 24th Weather Squadron, Detachment 20 (MAC); Defense Investigative Service (D42DL); AF Office of Special Investigations, Detachment 1014 (AFOSI); Defense Reutilization Marketing Office, Operating Location 32 (DRMO).

BASE HISTORY: 1942, activated as Laughlin Army Air Field, named for 1st Lt Jack T Laughlin, Del Rio native killed in WWII; primarily a pilot training base. Following WWII, closed until reactivated 1952 as jet fighter training base and transition to basic gunnery training. 1957, part of SAC. 1962, U-2s discovered Soviet missile sites in Cuba. 1962, Air Training Command took control; returned to pilot training mission.

Key Contacts

COMMANDER: Col Donald F Craigie.
PUBLIC AFFAIRS: Capt Michael G Young.
PERSONNEL/COMMUNITY ACTIVITIES: Elton W Graham; 47 FTW/PAC, 732-5201.

Personnel and Expenditures

ACTIVE DUTY PERSONNEL: 1657
DEPENDENTS: 3139
CIVILIAN PERSONNEL: 772
MILITARY PAYROLL EXPENDITURE: $53.9 mil
CONTRACT EXPENDITURE: $38.9 mil

Services Housing: Family units 603; BOQ cottages 221; BEQ units 604; Mobile home units 54; RV/Camper sites 24. Temporary Housing: Transient living quarters 22. Commissary: Base commissary; Retail store; Barber shop; Dry cleaners; Food shop; Florist; Service station. Child Care/Capacities: Day care center 100. Schools: Kindergarten/Preschool. Base Library: Yes. Medical Facilities: Hospital 60; Medical clinic; Dental clinic. Recreational Facilities: Bowling; Movie theater; Pool; Gym; Recreation center; Golf; Stables; Tennis; Racquetball; Fitness center; Softball field; Football field; Auto shop; Crafts; Officers club; NCO club; Camping; Water sports and recreational facilities (at Lake Amistad Reservoir).

MARSHALL

LONGHORN ARMY AMMUNITION PLANT

Commander, Longhorn Army Ammunition Plant, Marshall, TX 75671-1059
(214) 679-3181; Autovon 956-2010

Profile

BRANCH: Army.

SIZE AND LOCATION: 8493 acres. Approx 1 mi off State Hwy 43, 13 mi from Marshall, TX, 3.5 mi W of LA-TX border; served by Greater Shreveport Regional Airport.

BASE HISTORY: 1941, designated as Longhorn Ordnance Works until 1963; established to support mobilization requirements for WWII. 1941-46, operated by Monsanto Chemical Co; Plant 1 produced over 400 mil pounds of TNT flake and Plant 2, under construction 1945, designed to produce solid rocket fuel. 1945-52, standby and GOGO status. 1952, active status; operated by Universal Match Corp. 1955, Plant 3, designated to produce solid propellant rocket motors, operated by Thiokol Corp (later Morton Thiokol, Inc). GOCO plant, managed by operating contractor but under command of US Army Armament, Munitions and Chemical Command (AMCCOM). Current workload includes loading, assembly, and packout of illuminating munitions, infrared flares, signals and simulators.

Key Contacts

COMMANDER: LTC Allen L Germain; (214) 679-2100, Autovon 956-2100.
PUBLIC AFFAIRS: Dorothy P Grant; (214) 679-2228, Autovon 956-2228.

Personnel and Expenditures

ACTIVE DUTY PERSONNEL: 2
CIVILIAN PERSONNEL: 887

Services Base Library: Yes. Medical Facilities: Contractor operated dispensary. Recreational Facilities: Picnic area for employees.

ORANGE GROVE

ORANGE GROVE NAVAL AUXILIARY LANDING FIELD

Orange Grove, TX 78372

Profile

BRANCH: Navy.

LOCATION: 45 mi NW of Kingsville, TX; near Orange Grove at intersection of State Rte 359 and 624.

BASE HISTORY: Operates under an officer-in-charge to provide mirror landing facilities for three training squadrons out of NAS Kingsville; small installation, consisting of two 8,000 foot runways, air traffic control center, fuel farm, and crash crew.

Personnel and Expenditures

ACTIVE DUTY PERSONNEL: 40

RANDOLPH AFB

RANDOLPH AIR FORCE BASE

12th Flying Training Wing, Randolph AFB, TX 78150-5000
(512) 652-1110; Autovon 487-1110

Profile

BRANCH: Air Force.

SIZE AND LOCATION: 2956 acres. 17 mi NE of San Antonio. Co-located with small community of Universal City, TX. Main gate at intersection of Farm Rd 78 and Pat Booker Rd.

MAJOR UNITS: 12th Flying Training Wing; HQ, Air Training Command; HQ, Air Force Military Personnel Center; HQ, USAF Recruiting Service; Joint Military Medical Command.

BASE HISTORY: 1930, dedicated, partially completed, nicknamed "West Point of the Air," and named for Capt William Millican Randolph, native Texan and former adjutant of Advanced Flying School, Kelly Field. 1931, Air Corps Primary Flying School trained cadets and regular Army officers. 1943, trained instructor pilots and, briefly, B-29 crews. Following WWII, a series of different training programs: primary and basic pilot training; B-29, C-119, and B-57 crews, and helicopters. 1958-71, pilot training returned. 1971-present, home of USAF Pilot Instructor Training program.

VISITOR ATTRACTIONS: Called "Showplace of the Air Force." Buildings are Spanish Colonial design, accented by arches and red tile roofs. Hundreds of tall oak trees dot landscape. Bldg 100, The Taj Mahal, listed in National Registry of Historic Places; Randolph Air Park, with 7 historic aircraft used in pilot training; Hangar 12, Atterberry Hall, dedicated to Col Ed Atterberry, former POW who died in captivity; Freedom Hall; Missing Man Monument.

Key Contacts

COMMANDER: Col Michael J Wright; 12th Air Base Group, Commander, (512) 652-2939, Autovon 487-2939.
PUBLIC AFFAIRS: Capt Ingrid K Bradley; 12th Flying Training Wing, Public Affairs, (512) 652-4410, Autovon 487-4410.
TRANSPORTATION: LTC Ronald H Owen; 12th Transportation Squadron, Commander, (512) 652-4314, Autovon 487-4314.
PERSONNEL/COMMUNITY ACTIVITIES: LTC Melvin A Dumke; Chief of Personnel, 12th Air Base Group/DP, (512) 652-4423, Autovon 487-4423.

Personnel and Expenditures

ACTIVE DUTY PERSONNEL: 5800
DEPENDENTS: 16,000
CIVILIAN PERSONNEL: 4000
MILITARY PAYROLL EXPENDITURE: $165.3 mil
CONTRACT EXPENDITURE: $14.9 mil

RANDOLPH AIR FORCE BASE *(continued)*
Services *Housing:* Family units 430; BOQ cottages; BEQ units; BAQ units 150; Dormitory spaces 1500. *Temporary Housing:* VOQ cottages 50; VAQ units 100. *Commissary:* Base commissary; Retail store; Barber shop; Dry cleaners; Food shop; Florist; Banking; Service station. *Child Care/Capacities:* Day care center; Home day care program. *Schools:* Kindergarten/Preschool; Elementary; Intermediate/Junior high; High school. *Base Library:* Yes. *Medical Facilities:* Medical clinic; Dental clinic. *Recreational Facilities:* Bowling; Movie theater; Pool; Gym; Recreation center; Golf; Stables; Tennis; Racquetball; Fitness center; Softball field; Football field; Auto shop; Crafts; Officers club; NCO club; Camping; Fishing/Hunting.

REESE AFB

REESE AIR FORCE BASE
Reese AFB, TX 79489
(806) 885-4511; Autovon 838-1110
Profile
BRANCH: Air Force.
SIZE AND LOCATION: 3546 acres. Approx 10 mi W of Lubbock, TX, off Rte 114.
MAJOR UNITS: 64th Flying Training Wing; 64th Air Base Group; 1958th Communication Squadron.
BASE HISTORY: 1941, established as Lubbock Army Air Field as pilot training center. 1949, renamed for Lt Augustus F Reese, killed in action in WWII.
Personnel and Expenditures
ACTIVE DUTY PERSONNEL: 2067
DEPENDENTS: 2026
CIVILIAN PERSONNEL: 763
MILITARY PAYROLL EXPENDITURE: $61 mil
Services *Housing:* Family units 407; BOQ cottages 148; Barracks spaces. *Temporary Housing:* VIP cottages 4; VOQ cottages 18; VAQ units 20; Apartment units; Transient living quarters 25. *Commissary:* Base commissary; Garden center; Toys. *Child Care/Capacities:* Day care center 114; Home day care program. *Schools:* Elementary. *Medical Facilities:* Hospital 20; Dental clinic; Veterinary services. *Recreational Facilities:* Bowling; Pool; Gym; Golf; Tennis; Racquetball; Fitness center; Auto shop; Crafts; Officers club; NCO club; Picnic area; Skeet/trap range; Youth center.

SHEPPARD AFB

SHEPPARD AIR FORCE BASE
Sheppard Technical Training Center, Sheppard AFB, TX 76311-5000
(817) 676-2511; Autovon 736-1001
OFFICER-OF-THE-DAY: (817) 676-2621
Profile
BRANCH: Air Force.
SIZE AND LOCATION: 5406 acres. In N-central TX, 4 mi N of Wichita Falls off Rte 281; 12 mi S of OK border.
MAJOR UNITS: Sheppard Technical Training Center; 3700th Technical Training Wing; 3750th Technical Training Group; 3760th Technical Training Group; 3770th Technical Training Group; 3780th Student Group; 3785th Field Training Wing; School of Health Care Science; Sheppard Regional Hospital; Resource Management Deputate; 3750th Air Base Group; 80th Flying Training Wing; 2054th Communications Squadron; Detachment 12, 24th Weather Squadron; Detachment 5, 3314th Management Engineering Squadron; Area Defense Counsel; Air Force Audit Agency; Detachment 1024, Air Force Office of Special Investigations.

BASE HISTORY: 1941, opened, named for Senator Morris Sheppard, chairman of Senate Military Affairs Committee. WWII, conducted training for pilots and mechanics. 1946-48, deactivated. Today, conducts technical, health care, and flying training in one of five technical training centers.
Key Contacts
COMMANDER: Col Aulay MacRae; Commander, 375th Air Base Group, (817) 676-2336.
PUBLIC AFFAIRS: LTC Sally L Davidson; (817) 676-2732.
Personnel and Expenditures
ACTIVE DUTY PERSONNEL: 7575; 4448 students
DEPENDENTS: 5632
CIVILIAN PERSONNEL: 3502
Services *Housing:* Family units 200; Senior NCO units 1087. *Temporary Housing:* VIP cottages 18; VOQ cottages 112; VAQ units 1269; Apartment units 50. *Commissary:* Base commissary; Retail store; Barber shop; Dry cleaners; Food shop; Banking; Service station; Military clothing sales; Convenience store/Shopette; Beauty shop; Package beverages; Laundry; Credit union; Snacks; Jewelry/watch sales and repair; Four Seasons store. *Child Care/Capacities:* Day care center 200. *Schools:* Elementary. *Base Library:* Yes. *Medical Facilities:* Hospital 160. *Recreational Facilities:* Bowling; Movie theater; Pool; Gym; Recreation center; Golf; Stables; Tennis; Racquetball; Fitness center; Softball field; Football field; Auto shop; Crafts; Officers club; NCO club; Camping; Fishing/Hunting; Amusement center; Running track; Picnicking; Aero club; MWR supply; Skeetshooting; Gun club; Lake Texoma Recreation Annex, 356 acre site 120 mi E of base on TX side of lake, (817) 676-2876.

TEXARKANA

RED RIVER ARMY DEPOT
Texarkana, TX 75507-5000
(214) 334-2316; Autovon 829-2316
Profile
BRANCH: Army.
SIZE AND LOCATION: 19,081 acres. In NE TX, approx 17 mi W of Texarkana, TX; on I-30, exit 206 will lead into main entrance.
MAJOR UNITS: School of Engineering & Logistics.
BASE HISTORY: 1941, activated as ammunition storage site. Currently, Army's largest depot in terms of workload and personnel; part of Army Depot System Command and responsible for maintenance, supply, and ammunition; also serves as training site for Reserve and NG troops.
Personnel and Expenditures
ACTIVE DUTY PERSONNEL: 50
CIVILIAN PERSONNEL: 5300
MILITARY PAYROLL EXPENDITURE: $154 mil
CONTRACT EXPENDITURE: $10 mil
Services *Housing:* BOQ cottages; BEQ units. *Commissary and Exchange:* Retail store; Credit union. *Medical Facilities:* Medical clinic; Dispensary. *Recreational Facilities:* Gym; Golf; Officers club; Camping; Fishing/Hunting; Man-made lake.

UTAH

DUGWAY

DUGWAY PROVING GROUND

Dugway, UT 84022
(801) 831-2151; Autovon 789-2151
OFFICER-OF-THE-DAY: (801) 831-2020,
Autovon 789-2020
Profile
BRANCH: Army.
SIZE AND LOCATION: 840,941 acres. 1.5 hrs
SW of Salt Lake City and Salt Lake City
Airport by I 80; Tooele, UT, nearest city,
37 mi NE via Johnson's Pass. 100 mi
NW of Dugway is NV State Line and
Wendover, UT/NV, home of Bonneville
Speedway.
MAJOR UNITS: US Army Infantry School,
Ranger Detachment; Technical Escort and
Disposal Detachment; 6501st Range
Squadron; 65th Military Police Platoon.
BASE HISTORY: 1942, officially activated with
incendiary bombs, chemical weapons, and
modified agents as spray, disseminated
from aircraft, and pioneer work on mor-
tars, important projects. 1943, biological
warfare and testing facilities established.
1945, part of Wendover Bombing Range
transferred to proving ground. After
WWII, combined with Deseret Chemical
Depot to form Dugway Deseret Command, later renamed Western Chemical
Center and placed on stand-by basis.
1950, resumed active status with additional 279,000 acres. 1954, confirmed as
permanent installation. 1968, Ft Douglas
based Deseret Test Center and Dugway
Proving Ground combined as Deseret
Test Center. 1973, received present name.
Now aligned under Army's Test and Eval-
uation Command (TECOM), HQs Aber-
deen Proving Ground, MD, subordinate
command of Army Materiel Command,
HQs Alexandria, VA.
VISITOR ATTRACTIONS: Lincoln Memorial
Bridge, part of first transcontinental high-
way.
Key Contacts
COMMANDER: J A Van Prooyen; Command-
er, US Army Dugway Proving Ground,
ATTN: STEDP-CO, (801) 831-3314,
Autovon 789-3314.
PUBLIC AFFAIRS: Kathleen B Whitaker; Com-
mander, US Army Dugway Proving
Ground, ATTN: STEDP-PA, (801) 831-
2116, Autovon 789-2116.
PROCUREMENT: Robert Andrus; Director of
Contracting, US Army Dugway Proving
Ground, PO Box 538, Dugway, UT
84022-0538, (801) 831-2102, Autovon
789-2102.
TRANSPORTATION: Ned B Davis; Transporta-
tion Officer, US Army Dugway Proving
Ground, ATTN: STEDP-EN-M-T, (801)
831-2131, Autovon 789-2131.

PERSONNEL/COMMUNITY ACTIVITIES: LTC
Paul W Herrick; ATTN: STEDP-PT,
(801) 831-3414, Autovon 789-3414.
Personnel and Expenditures
ACTIVE DUTY PERSONNEL: 195
DEPENDENTS: 953
CIVILIAN PERSONNEL: 1569
MILITARY PAYROLL EXPENDITURE: $4.6 mil
CONTRACT EXPENDITURE: $24.9 mil
Services *Housing:* Family units 645; BOQ
cottages 57; Barracks spaces 153; Dormitory
spaces 100; Senior NCO units 1; RV/Camp-
er sites 1. *Temporary Housing:* BOQ units
38. *Commissary:* Base commissary; Retail
store; Barber shop; Dry cleaners; Food shop;
Banking; Service station; Video rental; Package beverages; Thrift shop; Laundry. *Child
Care/Capacities:* Day care center 91; Home
day care program; Latchkey program.
Schools: Elementary; High school. *Base Library:* Yes. *Medical Facilities:* Medical clinic;
Dental clinic; Eye clinic. *Recreational Facilities:* Bowling; Movie theater; Pool; Gym; Recreation center; Golf; Stables; Tennis; Racquetball; Fitness center; Softball field; Football field; Auto shop; Crafts; Community
Club.

HILL AFB

HILL AIR FORCE BASE

HQ Ogden Air Logistics Center, Hill AFB,
UT 84056
(801) 777-1411; Autovon 458-1110
Profile
BRANCH: Air Force.
SIZE AND LOCATION: 6666 acres; 962,100
acres including Test Range. Approx 5 mi
S of Ogden and 25 mi N of Salt Lake
City, off I-15.
MAJOR UNITS: Ogden Air Logistics Center;
2849th Air Base Group; Naval Explosive
Ordnance Technology Center; Air Force
Logistics Command Professional Military
Education Center; 2849th Security Police
Squadron; 2849th Civil Engineering
Squadron; 2701st Explosive Ordnance
Disposal Squadron; 2849th Support
Squadron (Range); 2952nd Combat Logis-
tics Support Squadron; 388th Tactical
Fighter Wing (TAC); 419th Tactical
Fighter Wing (AFRES); 6545th Test
Group (AFSC); 6514th Test Squadron;
6501st Range Squadron; 729th Tactical
Control Squadron (TAC); 4400th Main-
tenance Training Flight (TAC); Detach-
ment 6, 17th Weather Squadron (MAC);
Detachment 8, 1365th Audiovisual
Squadron (MAC); Detachment 3, 3025th
Management Engineering Squadron
(AFLC); Field Training Detachment 533
(ATC); Detachment 435, Audit Agency
Office (AFAA); Strategic Air Command
System Office (SAC); Office of Special
Investigations, Detachment 1404

(AFOSI); 84th Radar Evaluation Squad-
ron (TAC); 1881st Communications
Squadron (AFCC); Corps of Engineers
(USA); Defense Reutilization and Market-
ing Office (DLA); Operating Location
MA, Air Force Cryptologic Support Cen-
ter (ESC); Area Defense Counsel (HQ
USAF); Nontactical Generator and Rail
Shops (USA); Utah Test and Training
Range; Minuteman Hardness Testing Site;
Little Mountain Complex.
BASE HISTORY: Begun as Ogden Air Depot.
1939, Hill Field named for Maj Ployer P
Hill, who died piloting original model of
B-17. During WWII, aircraft rehabilitation major activity; crews of 509th Com-
posite Group practiced bombing runs
over Wendover Range from Hill in prep-
aration of Hiroshima and Nagasaki mis-
sions. 1948, became Hill AFB. Following
WWII, storage and deposition site for air-
planes and support equipment. 1955, Og-
den Arsenal property, now West Area of
Hill AFB, added. 1959, single assembly
and recycling point for Minuteman mis-
siles. 1974, Ogden Air Materiel Area be-
came Ogden Air Logistics Center.
VISITOR ATTRACTIONS: Hill AFB Heritage
Museum & Aerospace Park.
Key Contacts
COMMANDER: Maj Gen James W Hopp.
PUBLIC AFFAIRS: (801) 777-5201, Autovon
458-5201.
Personnel and Expenditures
ACTIVE DUTY PERSONNEL: 4896
DEPENDENTS: 15,000
CIVILIAN PERSONNEL: 14,537
MILITARY PAYROLL EXPENDITURE: FY 89,
$112.4 mil
CONTRACT EXPENDITURE: FY 89, $183.6 mil
Services *Housing:* Family units 1145; Du-
plex units 500; Dormitory spaces 1605.
Temporary Housing: VIP cottages 14; VOQ
cottages 107; VAQ units 120; Transient liv-
ing quarters 45; TDY reservations only.
Commissary: Base commissary; Retail store;
Barber shop; Dry cleaners; Food shop; Florist; Banking; Service station; Furniture
store; Military clothing sales; Convenience
store/Shopette; Tailor; Beauty shop; Credit
union; Optical shop; Package beverages;
Thrift shop. *Child Care/Capacities:* Day care
center 132. *Schools:* Kindergarten/Preschool;
Elementary. *Base Library:* Yes. *Medical Facilities:* Hospital 30; Medical clinic; Dental
clinic; Veterinary clinic. *Recreational Facilities:* Bowling; Movie theater; Pool; Gym; Recreation center; Golf; Stables; Tennis; Racquetball; Fitness center; Auto shop; Crafts;
Officers club; NCO club; Camping; Fishing/
Hunting; Youth center; Amusement center;
Aero Club; Skeet shooting; Skiing; MWR
supply/sports loan; Centennial Park; SATO.

UTAH TEST AND TRAINING RANGE

6501st Range Squadron, Hill AFB, UT 84056
(801) 777-1411; Autovon 458-1110

Profile

BRANCH: Air Force.

SIZE AND LOCATION: 1.8 mil acres. 48 mi (105 mi by road) W of Hill AFB; 18 mi N of Utah exit 62 off I-80.

MAJOR UNITS: 6501st Range Squadron (AFSC); 2849th Civil Engineering Squadron; 2849th Support Squadron (Range).

BASE HISTORY: Range equipped with radar, communications and mission control centers and threat systems to provide full-scale air combat maneuvering environment. AF Logistics Command, TAC, and SAC routinely conduct operational test and evaluation programs and operational exercises. UTTR capable of receiving real-time data and providing mission control function for missions being conducted from Western Space and Missile Center at Vandenberg AFB or Edwards AFB. In addition, test site for manned and unmanned aircraft programs and storage and testing of conventional munitions. Also provides facilities for combat units of TAC, SAC, Navy, Marines, and Army Aviation.

VISITOR ATTRACTIONS: No public access.

Key Contacts

COMMANDER: See Hill AFB.

PUBLIC AFFAIRS: See Hill AFB or Edwards AFB, CA.

Personnel and Expenditures

ACTIVE DUTY PERSONNEL: 70

MAGNA

NAVAL PLANT BRANCH REPRESENTATIVE OFFICE

c/o Hercules Inc, Bacchus Works, PO Box 157, Magna, UT 84044-0157
(801) 251-1140

Profile

BRANCH: Navy.

SIZE AND LOCATION: 534 acres. 20 mi from Salt Lake IAP; 25 mi from Salt Lake City on UT Rte 111 in Magna.

MAJOR UNITS: Naval Plant Branch Representative Office.

BASE HISTORY: NAVPBRO an office within Hercules Inc Complex; mission to monitor DOD contracts and rocket motor production, quality assurance, and shipping at Hercules Missile, Ordnance and Space Rocket Motor Plant, Magna; OIC is cognizant over operation of Naval Industrial Reserve Ordnance Plant (NIROP), government land maintained and operated by Hercules.

Key Contacts

COMMANDER: LCDR Gary L Brown; Officer in Charge.

TRANSPORTATION: Glen Wanczyk; (801) 251-1303.

Personnel and Expenditures

ACTIVE DUTY PERSONNEL: 5

CIVILIAN PERSONNEL: 83

OGDEN

GENERAL RAIL SHOPS

Hill AFB, Ogden, UT 84056
(801) 777-5913; Autovon 458-5913

Profile

BRANCH: Army.

LOCATION: At Hill AFB in Ogden, UT; 32 mi N of Salt Lake City Airport.

BASE HISTORY: Only rail overhaul shop in the Department of Defense and is part of the Tooele Army Depot.

Key Contacts

COMMANDER: Col Richard J Maksimowski; SDSTE-CO, Tooele Army Depot, Tooele, UT 84074, (801) 833-2211, Autovon 790-2211.

PUBLIC AFFAIRS: Susan Broadbent; SDSTE-PAO, Tooele Army Depot, Tooele, UT 84074, (801) 833-3216, Autovon 790-3216.

PROCUREMENT: Robert S Corrigan; Director of Contracting, SDSTE-CD, Tooele Army Depot, Tooele, UT 84074, (801) 833-2616, Autovon 790-2616.

TRANSPORTATION: Deroy Burt; Tooele Army Depot, Tooele, UT 84074, (801) 833-2914, Autovon 790-2914.

PERSONNEL/COMMUNITY ACTIVITIES: Blaine Kelley; SDSTE-PC, Tooele Army Depot, Tooele, UT 84074, (801) 833-2412, Autovon 790-2412.

OGDEN DEFENSE DEPOT

500 W 12th St, Ogden, UT 84407-5000
(801) 399-7011; Autovon 790-7011

OFFICER-OF-THE-DAY: (801) 399-7743, Autovon 790-7743

Profile

BRANCH: Defense Logistics Agency.

SIZE AND LOCATION: 1139 acres. Set at foot of Wasatch Mountain Range in city of Ogden. Approx 45 mi from Salt Lake City Airport via I-15 to 12th St Exit, approx 3 mi E on 12th St.

MAJOR UNITS: 1120th Army Signal Battalion; DLA Systems Automation Center; Defense Reutilization and Marketing Region.

BASE HISTORY: 1940, present site selected. 1941, UT General Depot activated as exempt station under control of War Department. 1942, name changed to UT Quartermaster Depot (Subsequent name changes: 1943, UT Army Services Depot; 1946, UT General Depot; 1947, UT General Distribution Depot; 1949, UT General Depot; 1962, UT Army Depot; and, 1964, Defense Depot Ogden). 1943, POW camp opened. Following WWII, employment scaled down until Korean Conflict. 1964, transferred to Defense Supply Agency (DSA), now Defense Logistics Agency.

Key Contacts

COMMANDER: Capt A P Tully, SC, USN; (801) 399-7743, Autovon 790-7743.

PUBLIC AFFAIRS: Joyce Fencl; (801) 399-7828, Autovon 790-7828.

PROCUREMENT: Barry Brunson; (801) 399-7541, Autovon 790-7541.

TRANSPORTATION: LTC Glenn Wimer, USAF; (801) 399-7398, Autovon 790-7398.

PERSONNEL/COMMUNITY ACTIVITIES: Fred Case; (801) 399-7356, Autovon 790-7356.

Personnel and Expenditures

ACTIVE DUTY PERSONNEL: 200

DEPENDENTS: 63

CIVILIAN PERSONNEL: 1946

CONTRACT EXPENDITURE: $14 mil

Services *Housing:* Family units 17; Duplex units 2. *Temporary Housing:* BAQ units 2. *Commissary and Exchange:* Retail store; Barber shop; Banking. *Child Care/Capacities:* Day care center 48. *Base Library:* Yes. *Medical Facilities:* Medical clinic. *Recreational Facilities:* Pool; Gym; Tennis; Racquetball; Fitness center; Softball field; Auto shop; Crafts; Officers club.

RIVERTON

CAMP W G WILLIAMS

RFD #1, Riverton, UT 84065-4999
(801) 524-3839; Autovon 924-3839

OFFICER-OF-THE-DAY: (801) 524-3669, Autovon 924-3669

Profile

BRANCH: Army National Guard.

SIZE AND LOCATION: 28,000 acres. Off UT Hwy 68, approx 20 mi S of Salt Lake City.

MAJOR UNITS: 1st Battalion, 19th SF Gp; 115th Heavy Equipment Maintenance Co; 115th Engineer Detachment (Util); 489th Engineer Detachment (Util); Utah Military Academy; Region V NCO Academy.

BASE HISTORY: Only rail overhaul shop in DOD and part of Tooele Army Depot.

Key Contacts

COMMANDER: Col Gerald L Cook; (801) 524-3727, Autovon 924-3727.

PUBLIC AFFAIRS: LTC Robert S Voyles; (801) 524-3727, Autovon 924-3727.

Personnel and Expenditures

ACTIVE DUTY PERSONNEL: 120

CIVILIAN PERSONNEL: 45

MILITARY PAYROLL EXPENDITURE: $6.2 mil

CONTRACT EXPENDITURE: $2.5 mil

Services *Housing:* Barracks spaces 2500. *Temporary Housing:* VIP cottages 1; VOQ cottages 50; VEQ units 200. *Commissary and Exchange:* Retail store; Branch annex of Hill AFB. *Base Library:* Yes. *Medical Facilities:* Medical clinic. *Recreational Facilities:* Pool; Recreation center; Fitness center; Officers club; NCO club.

SALT LAKE CITY

151ST AIR REFUELING GROUP (ANG)

Salt Lake City IAP, Salt Lake City, UT 84116
(801) 521-7070; Autovon 790-9210

Profile

BRANCH: Air National Guard.

SIZE AND LOCATION: 75 acres. 3 mi W of Salt Lake City, off I-215.

MAJOR UNITS: 151st Air Refueling Group (ANG); 130th Engineering Installation Squadron (ANG); 106th Tactical Control Flight (ANG); 109th Tactical Control Flight (ANG).

Personnel and Expenditures

ACTIVE DUTY PERSONNEL: 1265

CIVILIAN PERSONNEL: 276

MILITARY PAYROLL EXPENDITURE: $12 mil

Services *Medical Facilities:* Dispensary.

TOOELE

TOOELE ARMY DEPOT

Tooele, UT 84074-5000
(801) 833-3216; Autovon 790-3216

OFFICER-OF-THE-DAY: (801) 833-2304, Autovon 790-2304

Profile

BRANCH: Army.

SIZE AND LOCATION: North Area 24,732 acres; South Area 19,364 acres. North Area adj to Tooele, UT; South Area in desert valley 15 mi S of main HQs.

BASE HISTORY: 1942, construction of Tooele Ordnance Depot began; administrative area included hospital, POW camp, troop barracks, housing facilities, and storage depot for Chemical Corps toxics 15 mi S in Rush Valley (Deseret Chemical Warfare Depot); mission to store vehicles, small arms, and fire control equipment; later, maintenance shop and shops to rebuild, modify and reclaim 75mm howitzer motor carriages and artillery pieces established. 1956, Ammunition Equipment Directorate began. 1961, assimilation of Deseret Depot Activity. 1962, name changed to Tooele Army Depot. 1977, CAMDS mission added. Command expanded to include four additional depot activities: Umatilla, 1973; Fort Wingate, Navajo, and Pueblo in 1975.

TOOELE ARMY DEPOT (*continued*)
Key Contacts
COMMANDER: Col Richard J Maksimowski; SDSTE-CO, (801) 833-2211, Autovon 790-2211.
PUBLIC AFFAIRS: Susan Broadbent; SDSTE-PAO, (801) 833-3216, Autovon 790-3216.
PROCUREMENT: Director of Contracting, SDSTE-CD, (801) 833-2616, Autovon 790-2616.
PERSONNEL/COMMUNITY ACTIVITIES: Director of Personnel/Community Affairs, SDSTE-PC, (801) 833-2412, Autovon 790-2412.
Personnel and Expenditures
ACTIVE DUTY PERSONNEL: 62
CIVILIAN PERSONNEL: 3500
MILITARY PAYROLL EXPENDITURE: $110 mil
CONTRACT EXPENDITURE: $40 mil
Services *Housing:* Family units 5; BOQ cottages 8; Barracks spaces 14; Wherry housing 25. *Temporary Housing:* VIP cottages 2; VOQ cottages 2. *Commissary and Exchange:* Retail store. *Medical Facilities:* Medical clinic. *Recreational Facilities:* Bowling; Pool; Gym; Golf (driving range); Stables; Racquetball; Fitness center; Softball field; Auto shop; Crafts; NCO club; Camping.

VERMONT

BURLINGTON IAP

158TH FIGHTER INTERCEPTOR GROUP

Burlington IAP, VT 05401-5895
(802) 658-0770; Autovon 689-4390

Profile

BRANCH: Air National Guard.

SIZE AND LOCATION: 240 acres. At the Burlington IAP.

MAJOR UNITS: 158th FIG; 134th FIS; 158th CAM; 158th CES; 158th MSS; 158th RMS; 158th TAC Clinic.

BASE HISTORY: 1946, organized Burlington Municipal Airport as 134th Fighter Squadron; first air unit in VT. 1951, activated Korean War unit, assigned to Eastern Air Defense Commander until Oct 1952. Part of Air Defense Runway Alert program 1960; reorganized as 158th Fighter Group under USAF Air Defense Command. 1973, became Defense Systems Evaluation Group. 1982, became 158th TFG. 1988, became operational at Bangor IAP, Maine Air Guard Base.

Key Contacts

COMMANDER: Col John D Leonard.

PUBLIC AFFAIRS: Maj Christine Desmond.

PROCUREMENT: MSgt Gordon Lesperance.

Personnel and Expenditures

ACTIVE DUTY PERSONNEL: 100 AGR, 225 technicians, 600 guardsmen

MILITARY PAYROLL EXPENDITURE: $12.5 mil

CONTRACT EXPENDITURE: $3 mil

Services *Medical Facilities:* Medical clinic. *Recreational Facilities:* NCO club.

JERICHO

ETHAN ALLEN FIRING RANGE

RR 1 Box 57, Jericho, VT 05465-9706
(802) 899-2811

OFFICER-OF-THE-DAY: (802) 899-2811

Profile

BRANCH: Army National Guard.

SIZE AND LOCATION: 11,218 acres. Approx 15 mi E of Burlington, VT, off Rte 15; served by Burlington IAP.

MAJOR UNITS: HQ 3-172d IN; ARNG MWS; Det 2, HQ STARC-VT; Vermont Military Academy.

BASE HISTORY: 1926, 6000 acres acquired for artillery range. 1941, expanded. 1952, ownership transferred to Air Force. 1965, ownership transferred to Army. AMCCOM is current agent for Army. Currently, test facility for General Electric (GOCO) and training site for ARNG.

Key Contacts

COMMANDER: Col Gerald N Katgle.

PERSONNEL/COMMUNITY ACTIVITIES: Maj Shawn W Bryan.

Personnel and Expenditures

ACTIVE DUTY PERSONNEL: 50

CIVILIAN PERSONNEL: 6

Services *Temporary Housing:* BOQ units 45; Barracks 750. *Commissary and Exchange:* Small Imprest Fund BX from Plattsburgh AFB, open limited hours. *Medical Facilities:* Troop medical clinic operational when troops are in training.

VIRGINIA

ALEXANDRIA

ARMY MATERIEL COMMAND HEADQUARTERS

5001 Eisenhower Ave, Alexandria, VA 22333
(703) 545-6700
Profile
BRANCH: Army.
SIZE: Offices only.
MAJOR UNITS: Army Materiel Command.
Key Contacts
COMMANDER: Gen Louis C Wagner Jr; Commanding General, (703) 274-9625.

CAMERON STATION, MILITARY DISTRICT OF WASHINGTON

5010 Duke St, Alexandria, VA 20304-5050
(202) 274-6059; Autovon 284-6059
OFFICER-OF-THE-DAY: Police Desk, (202) 274-6516, Autovon 284-6516
Profile
BRANCH: Army.
SIZE AND LOCATION: 163 acres. Approx 3 mi from Alexandria's central business district on VA Rte 236 within 1.5 mi of the Capital Beltway.
MAJOR UNITS: HQ Cameron Station, DCSLOG; Defense Logistics Agency; Defense Fuel Supply Center; Defense Tech Information Center; Defense Contract Audit Agency; US Army Recruiting Support Command; The Institute of Heraldry; USAF Detachment 29 (Aero Space Fuel); *Soldiers Magazine* (Official Army Publication); US Army Aeronautical Service; WRAMC Food Inspection; Navy Petroleum Office; Civilian Personnel, Ft Myer; Army/Air Force Exchange Service (AAFES) Capital Exchange Regional HQ.
BASE HISTORY: 1869, known as Washington General Depot. 1941, Quartermaster Depot under command of Army Quartermaster General. 1950, transferred to Military District of Washington, redesignated Cameron Station. Site of one of world's largest commissaries, and one of its missions is to provide commissary and exchange facilities to over 60,000 service families in WA area.
VISITOR ATTRACTIONS: Institute of Heraldry in Bldg 15, upstairs.
Key Contacts
COMMANDER: Col Roger J Tancreti Jr; Post Commander, (202) 274-6505, Autovon 284-6505.
PUBLIC AFFAIRS: See Military District of Washington; (202) 475-0849, Autovon 335-0849.
PROCUREMENT: L Piasecki; Directorate of Contracting, (202) 274-6592, Autovon 284-6592.
TRANSPORTATION: Samuel Heermans; ANLOG-T, Bldg 17, (202) 274-6503, Autovon 284-6503.

PERSONNEL/COMMUNITY ACTIVITIES: See Ft Myer for Personnel Office; Community Affairs, Deputy Post Commander, LTC L H Gilbertson; (202) 274-6059, Autovon 284-6059.
Personnel and Expenditures
ACTIVE DUTY PERSONNEL: 338
CIVILIAN PERSONNEL: 4000
Services *Temporary Housing:* Overnight sites for self-contained campers at small fee. No hook-up for electricity/water. *Commissary:* Base commissary; Retail store; Barber shop; Dry cleaners; Food shop; Florist; Banking; Service station; Bakery; Beauty shop; Personal items; Four Seasons store; Joint Personal Property Shipping Office; Optical shop; Outdoor recreation shop; Jewelry/watch sales and repair. *Medical Facilities:* Medical clinic. *Recreational Facilities:* Tennis; Fitness center; Softball field; Officers club; NCO club; Wildlife sanctuary; Manmade lakes; Picnicking; All-purpose court; Volleyball; Jogging.

DEFENSE MAPPING AGENCY

6801 Telegraph Rd, Alexandria, VA 22310
(703) 325-7060
Profile
BRANCH: Department of Defense.
SIZE AND LOCATION: Offices only. In Brookmont, MD.
MAJOR UNITS: Aerospace Center, St Louis, MO (Production Center); Hydrographic/Topographic Center, Washington, DC (Production Center); Reston Center, Reston, VA (Production Center); Defense Mapping School, Ft Belvoir, VA (Distribution Organization); Systems Center, Fairfax, VA (Special Mission Support Organization); Telecommunications Services Center, Fairfax, VA (Special Mission Support Organization).
BASE HISTORY: 1972, established, when mapping activities of all services combined for greater efficiency; organized into HQs, Fairfax, VA, and seven primary components.
VISITOR ATTRACTIONS: Generally closed to the public.
Key Contacts
PUBLIC AFFAIRS: Carl W Goodman; DMA, Hydrographic/Topographic Center, Washington, DC 20315-0030, (202) 227-2032.
PERSONNEL/COMMUNITY ACTIVITIES: DMA, ATTN: POR-25, Hydrographic/Topographic Center, Washington, DC 20315 (East of Mississippi); DMA, ATTN: POR-25, Hydrographic/Topographic Center, 3200 S 2nd St, St Louis, MO 63118 (West of Mississippi).
Personnel and Expenditures
ACTIVE DUTY PERSONNEL: 500
CIVILIAN PERSONNEL: 8500
Services *Base Library:* Yes.

NAVAL FACILITIES ENGINEERING COMMAND HEADQUARTERS

200 Stovall St, Alexandria, VA 22332-2300
(202) 325-0310; Autovon 221-0310
OFFICER-OF-THE-DAY: (202) 325-0400, Autovon 221-0400
Profile
BRANCH: Navy.
LOCATION: Near the intersection of Telegraph Rd and Duke St in Alexandria, VA, in the Hoffman complex, 10th through 12th floors, directly across from the Eisenhower Metro (subway) station.
BASE HISTORY: 1942, Board of Navy Commissioners replaced by Bureau Systems and Bureau of Yards and Docks; charged with responsibility for building and maintaining Navy's shore establishment. 1966, reorganized as Naval Facilities Engineering Command. Currently manages planning, design and construction of Navy's shore facilities; physical work done through subordinate commands, Engineering Field Divisions in Norfolk, VA, Pearl Harbor, HI, Charleston, SC, San Bruno, CA, Washington, DC, and Philadelphia, PA.
Key Contacts
COMMANDER: Rear Adm Benjamin F Montoya, CEC, USN; (202) 325-0400, Autovon 221-0400.
PUBLIC AFFAIRS: Elaine McNeil.
PROCUREMENT: Capt Louis A Fermo; (202) 325-8577, Autovon 221-8577.
TRANSPORTATION: Gary Lind; (202) 325-8185, Autovon 221-8185.
PERSONNEL/COMMUNITY ACTIVITIES: Capt David J Nash; (202) 325-8542, Autovon 221-8542.
Personnel and Expenditures
ACTIVE DUTY PERSONNEL: 47
CIVILIAN PERSONNEL: 460
Services *Base Library:* Yes. *Recreational Facilities:* Gym.

ARLINGTON

FORT MYER

Post Headquarters, Bldg 59, Arlington, VA 22211
(703) 696-3250; Autovon 226-3250
OFFICER-OF-THE-DAY: (703) 696-3250, Autovon 226-3250
Profile
BRANCH: Army.
SIZE AND LOCATION: 256 acres. Off of US Rte 50 and Rte 27 in Arlington, VA. The post is adj to Arlington National Cemetery and is min from I-395 and 10-15 min from National Airport.
MAJOR UNITS: US Army Band (Pershing's Own); 3d US Infantry Regiment (The Old Guard); Headquarters, US Army Garrison; Headquarters Company Special Activities; MDW Military Police Company;

FORT MYER *(continued)*

US Army Information Systems Command, Operations Command; Walter Reed Army Medical Center, Company D; US Army Criminal Investigation Command, Washington District; US Army Engineering Activity, Capital Area; Army Chorus.

BASE HISTORY: Owned by Martha Custis Washington's son, John Parke Custis. 1861, confiscated by federal government. Some became what is now Arlington National Cemetery and remainder became Ft Whipple. Signal Corps took over by late 1860s. Brig Gen Albert J Myer, after whom fort was renamed, was Army's first Chief Signal Officer and Commander at Ft Whipple. First military test flight of an aircraft made from parade grounds Sept 1908 by Orville Wright. Cavalry Regiments stationed beginning in 1881. Since early 1900s, known as "Home of the Generals." Quarters Number One, official residence of Chief of Staff of Army since 1899. WWII, served as inprocessing and outprocessing station. 1942, Army School of Music. 1948, 3rd Infantry Regiment, oldest regular infantry regiment, reactivated and assigned to Ft Myer and Ft McNair.

VISITOR ATTRACTIONS: The 3d US Infantry Museum; 3d US Infantry Caisson Platoon Stables; Summerall Field (burial site of Black Jack); Arlington National Cemetery and Tomb of the Unknowns; Whipple Field.

Key Contacts

COMMANDER: Col Daniel Shamanski.
PUBLIC AFFAIRS: Col David H Burpee; Public Affairs Officer, US Army Military District of Washington, Bldg 42, Ft Lesley J McNair, Washington DC 20319, (202) 475-0856, Autovon 335-0856.
Services *Housing:* Family units; Barracks spaces. *Temporary Housing:* VOQ cottages; VEQ units; Guesthouse units. *Commissary:* Base commissary; Retail store; Barber shop; Dry cleaners; Food shop; Florist; Banking; Service station; Beauty shop; Clothing store; Optical shop; Shoe repair. *Child Care/Capacities:* Day care center. *Base Library:* Yes. *Medical Facilities:* Medical clinic; Dental clinic; Veterinary services. *Recreational Facilities:* Bowling; Movie theater; Pool; Gym; Recreation center; Tennis; Racquetball; Fitness center; Softball field; Football field; Auto shop; Crafts; Officers club; NCO club; Equipment check-out.

HENDERSON HALL
Arlington, VA 22214
(202) 694-2200; Autovon 224-2908
Profile
BRANCH: Marines.
SIZE AND LOCATION: 21 acres. 2 mi S of the Pentagon off Columbia Pike, adj to Ft Myer and Arlington National Cemetery.
MAJOR UNITS: Headquarters, US Marine Corps.
Personnel and Expenditures
ACTIVE DUTY PERSONNEL: 3700
Services *Housing:* BEQ units 500. *Commissary and Exchange:* Retail store; Barber shop; Dry cleaners; Food shop; Florist; Bakery; 7 day store; Garden center. *Recreational Facilities:* Movie theater; Pool; Gym; Tennis; Racquetball; Fitness center; NCO club.

NAVAL SEA SYSTEMS COMMAND
Washington, DC 20362-5101, Arlington, VA 22202
(703) 602-6920

Profile
BRANCH: Navy.
SIZE AND LOCATION: Offices only. On Rte 1 in Arlington, VA on the Crystal City metrorail stop.
MAJOR UNITS: Headquarters, Naval Sea Command.
BASE HISTORY: Navy Department's central activity for designing, engineering, integrating, building, and procuring naval ships and shipboard weapons and combat systems. NAVSEA employs over 107,000 military and civilian personnel at 63 field activities and 32 detachments, nationwide.
Key Contacts
PUBLIC AFFAIRS: Barbara Jyachosky; 2531 Jefferson Davis Hwy, Zachary Taylor Office Bldg, National Center Bldg Three, Arlington, VA 22202.

NAVAL SUPPLY SYSTEMS COMMAND
Washington, DC 20376-5000, Arlington, VA 22202
Profile
BRANCH: Navy.
SIZE AND LOCATION: Offices only. In Crystal Mall, Bldg #3, 1931 Jeff Davis Hwy, Arlington, VA 22202.
MAJOR UNITS: Naval Supply Systems Command; Spares Competition and Logistics Technology Program; Navy Field Contracting System; Navy Resale System; Navy Publications and Printing Service; Navy Petroleum Office; Transportation Directorate; Financial Subsystem; Navy Food Service Program; Navy Security Assistance Program; Fleet Hospital Program Office.
BASE HISTORY: Navy's professional staff corps responsible for supply phases of naval logistics. Since 1795, supplied Navy with items essential to operation of ships, facilities, and later, aircraft, and missiles.
Key Contacts
COMMANDER: (202) 695-4009.
PUBLIC AFFAIRS: (703) 697-3795.
Personnel and Expenditures
ACTIVE DUTY PERSONNEL: 100
CIVILIAN PERSONNEL: 500

THE PENTAGON
Washington, DC 20301, Arlington, VA 22211
(202) 545-6700
Profile
BRANCH: Joint Service Installation.
SIZE AND LOCATION: 583 acres, Bldg 29. Adj to Arlington National Cemetery and Ft Myer; Exits off I-395 and I-66.
MAJOR UNITS: Department of Defense.
BASE HISTORY: Original site a swampy area into which over 40,000 concrete piles and tons of sand and gravel were added. Building constructed in 16 months, completed 1943. One of world's largest office buildings; twice size of Merchandise Mart, Chicago and 3 times floor space of Empire State Building, NY. Virtually a city in itself; 17.5 miles of corridors; takes 7 minutes to walk between any two points in building; consolidated 17 buildings of War Department. DOD managed by civilian Secretary of Defense, appointed by President. Highest ranking military position, Chairman, Joint Chiefs of Staff. While not a member of DOD, USCG one of five Armed Forces.
VISITOR ATTRACTIONS: Daily tours.
Key Contacts
COMMANDER: Secretary of Defense.
PUBLIC AFFAIRS: Tour Director, Rm 1E776-The Pentagon, (202) 695-1776; Col James D Weiskopf, Fort McNair, Headquarters, US Military District of Washington,

Washington, DC 20319-5050, (202) 475-0856, 475-0855, Autovon 335-0856, 335-0855.
Personnel and Expenditures
ACTIVE DUTY PERSONNEL: 11,500
CIVILIAN PERSONNEL: 11,500
Services *Base Library:* Yes. *Medical Facilities:* Medical clinic; Dental clinic. *Recreational Facilities:* Gym; Racquetball; Fitness center; Restaurant; 2 cafeterias; 6 snack bars; 1 outdoor snack bar.

WASHINGTON, DC, COAST GUARD AIR STATION
Washington National Airport, Hangar 6, Washington, DC, Arlington, VA 20001-4964
(202) 576-2520
Profile
BRANCH: Coast Guard.
LOCATION: At Washington National Airport.
BASE HISTORY: Facility consists only of aircraft used mainly for VIP travel.
Key Contacts
PUBLIC AFFAIRS: HQ, USCG, (202) 267-0930.

BOWLING GREEN

FORT A P HILL
Bowling Green, VA 22427
(804) 633-5041; Autovon 934-8110
Profile
BRANCH: Army.
SIZE AND LOCATION: 76,096 acres. Approx 10 mi SE of Fredericksburg, VA; 2 mi E of Bowling Green, VA on Rte 301.
BASE HISTORY: Formerly a subpost of Ft Lee, VA. Training installation for Ft George G Meade, MD.
Key Contacts
PUBLIC AFFAIRS: See Ft George G. Meade, MD 20755.
Personnel and Expenditures
ACTIVE DUTY PERSONNEL: 33
CIVILIAN PERSONNEL: 130
Services *Housing:* Trailer spaces 10; RV/Camper sites 48; Housing units 28. *Temporary Housing:* VOQ cottages 3; BOQ/BEQ units 46. *Commissary and Exchange:* Small exchange. *Medical Facilities:* Medical clinic. *Recreational Facilities:* Bowling; Movie theater; Pool; Gym; Tennis; Fitness center; Auto shop; Crafts; Camping; Skeet shooting; Skiing; Lakeside cabins.

CHESAPEAKE

FENTRESS NAVAL AUXILIARY LANDING FIELD
Chesapeake, VA 23322
(804) 433-2000
Profile
BRANCH: Navy.
LOCATION: 6 mi SW of NAS Oceana in Chesapeake, VA.
MAJOR UNITS: See Naval Air Station Oceana.
BASE HISTORY: Under operational control of NAS Oceana and used as primary training field for fleet carrier landing practice by operational units based in area; average number of total operations range from 80,000 to 100,000 annually.
Key Contacts
PUBLIC AFFAIRS: Naval Air Station Oceana, (804) 433-3131.

NORTHWEST NAVAL SECURITY GROUP ACTIVITY
Chesapeake, VA 23322-5002
(804) 421-8000
Profile
BRANCH: Navy.
SIZE AND LOCATION: 4500 acres. In city of Chesapeake, near Rte 125 and 337.

NORTHWEST NAVAL SECURITY GROUP ACTIVITY (*continued*)

MAJOR UNITS: Naval Security Group Activity Northwest; NAVCAMSLANTSATCOMM Facility; NATO SATCOMM Facility; Coast Guard Communications Station.

BASE HISTORY: Situated on wooded farm and swamp lands; all NAVSECGRU operational elements located at Northwest except for COMSEC Materiel Issuing Office (CMIO) and a division of Signal Security Department, both located on Naval Base, Norfolk.

Key Contacts

PUBLIC AFFAIRS: (804) 421-8352.

Personnel and Expenditures

ACTIVE DUTY PERSONNEL: 500

Services *Housing:* Family units; BOQ cottages; BEQ units; Mobile home units. *Commissary and Exchange:* Retail store; Credit union. *Medical Facilities:* Medical clinic; Dental clinic. *Recreational Facilities:* Bowling; Pool; Gym; Tennis; Racquetball; Fitness center (weight room); Softball field; NCO club; Camping; Fishing/Hunting; Youth center (teen club); Water sports; Archery range.

DAHLGREN

NAVAL SURFACE WARFARE CENTER

Code C12, Dahlgren, VA 22448-5000
(703) 663-8291; Autovon 249-8291
OFFICER-OF-THE-DAY: (703) 663-8291, Autovon 249-8291

Profile

BRANCH: Navy.

SIZE AND LOCATION: 4300 acres. From Fredericksburg, VA, 28 mi, take Rte 3 E, left on Rte 206 at King George, follow to Dahlgren. From Richmond, VA, take I-95 to Rte 208, Carmel Church Exit, to Rte 301 N, right on Rte 206 to Dahlgren. From Washington, DC, take I-95 S to Rte 5, Waldorf, MD, Exit, S to Rte 301 S, across Harry W Nice Bridge, left on Rte 206 to Dahlgren.

MAJOR UNITS: Naval Space Command; Naval Space Surveillance Center; AEGIS Training Center.

BASE HISTORY: 1974, established with merger of Naval Ordnance Laboratory, Silver Spring, MD. Country's largest research and development center. Formed 1918, as Naval Proving Ground, Dahlgren's Potomac River range tests naval guns and ammunition, WWII. Today, gun line and 20-mile down river range still used for projectile testing. Primarily civilian organization with military commander and civilian technical director. two main sites: Dahlgren and White Oak, MD, and field test facilities Ft Monroe, VA, Ft Lauderdale, FL, and, Wallops Island, VA.

VISITOR ATTRACTIONS: During special events, such as, Armed Forces Day and 4th of July, public invited to tour, witness gun firings (up to 16" guns), and view exhibits. Area located near sports and recreational activities with Potomac River, Blue Ridge Mountains, Chesapeake Bay and Atlantic Ocean within easy driving distance. Many historical sites associated with Colonial America and Revolutionary and Civil Wars, nearby.

Key Contacts

COMMANDER: Capt Robert P Fuscaldo, USN; (703) 663-8101, Autovon 249-8101.

PUBLIC AFFAIRS: R Diane Palermo; (703) 663-8154, Autovon 249-8154.

PROCUREMENT: CDR Terrence A Conner, SC, USN; (703) 663-8391, Autovon 249-8391.

TRANSPORTATION: CDR Michael T Hadbavny; (703) 663-8251, Autovon 249-8251.

PERSONNEL/COMMUNITY ACTIVITIES: LTjg Gretchen Merryman; (703) 663-8216, Autovon 249-8216.

Personnel and Expenditures

ACTIVE DUTY PERSONNEL: 89

DEPENDENTS: 384

CIVILIAN PERSONNEL: 3000

Services *Housing:* Family units 154; BOQ cottages 14; BEQ units 171. *Temporary Housing:* VIP cottages 2; VOQ cottages 41; VEQ units 46; Transient living quarters 14. *Commissary:* Base commissary; Barber shop; Dry cleaners; Food shop; Banking. *Child Care/Capacities:* Day care center 35. *Schools:* Kindergarten/Preschool; Elementary; (K-8). *Base Library:* Yes. *Recreational Facilities:* Bowling; Movie theater; Pool; Gym; Recreation center; Golf; Tennis; Racquetball; Fitness center; Softball field; Crafts; Officers club; NCO club; Camping; Fishing/Hunting.

FALLS CHURCH

ARMY CRIMINAL INVESTIGATION COMMAND

5611 Columbia Pike, Nassif Bldg, Falls Church, VA 22041
(703) 756-2263

Profile

BRANCH: Army.

SIZE: Offices only.

Key Contacts

COMMANDER: Maj Gen Eugene R Cromartie.

FORT BELVOIR

FORT BELVOIR

Fort Belvoir, VA 22060
(703) 664-5001; Autovon 354-5001
OFFICER-OF-THE-DAY: Duty Officer, (703) 664-1308, Autovon 354-1308

Profile

BRANCH: Army.

SIZE AND LOCATION: 8656 acres. In N VA on the peninsula just below Mount Vernon, approx 50 minutes SE of Washington, DC. Enter main gate from Richmond Hwy, Rte 1. 30 minutes from National Airport. Borders city of Alexandria.

MAJOR UNITS: Intelligence and Security Command; HQ, Army Corps of Engineers; Army Criminal Investigation Command; Defense Mapping School; Defense Systems Management College; 310th Theater Army Area Command; HQ, 29th Infantry Division (light), VA Army National Guard; US Army Engineer School (until 1990); 610th Ordnance Battalion; US Army Information Systems Software Center; US Army Belvoir Research Development and Engineering Center; Center for Night Vision and Electro-Optics; US Army Davison Aviation Command.

BASE HISTORY: Original tract acquired for use of District of Columbia. 1912, transferred to War Department to establish rifle range and summer camp for engineering troops stationed at Washington Barracks, DC. 1917, first camp held at Camp Belvoir, named after mansion built on property by Col Fairfax in 1741. 1918, designated training center for engineers. 1922, made permanent post, Camp Humphreys, later Fort Humphreys. 1935, became Ft Belvoir. Currently in transition from Army Engineers School to Military District of Washington post.

VISITOR ATTRACTIONS: Accotink Bay Wildlife Refuge (1100 acres); Jackson Miles Abbott Wetland Refuge (150 acres).

Key Contacts

COMMANDER: Brig Gen Arvid E West Jr; Bldg 269, (703) 664-1241, Autovon 354-1241.

PUBLIC AFFAIRS: Martha Rudd; Bldg 269, (703) 664-5001, Autovon 354-5001.

TRANSPORTATION: L Anderson; Bldg 1170, ANFB/DOL/MB, (703) 664-3557, Autovon 354-3557.

PERSONNEL/COMMUNITY ACTIVITIES: Lt Col P J Tuohig; Bldg 498, (703) 664-6447.

Personnel and Expenditures

ACTIVE DUTY PERSONNEL: 7338

DEPENDENTS: 5943

CIVILIAN PERSONNEL: 8765

MILITARY PAYROLL EXPENDITURE: $115 mil

Services *Housing:* Family units 1655; BEQ units 12; Duplex units 770; Townhouse units 325; Barracks spaces 4063; Senior NCO units 144; Junior NCO units 719. *Temporary Housing:* VOQ cottages 552; VEQ units 26; BOQ units 1; VOQ units 9. *Commissary:* Base commissary; Retail store; Barber shop; Dry cleaners; Food shop; Florist; Banking; Service station; Furniture store; Bakery. *Child Care/Capacities:* Day care center. *Schools:* Kindergarten/Preschool; Elementary; Intermediate/Junior high; High school. *Base Library:* Yes. *Medical Facilities:* Hospital; Medical clinic; Dental clinic. *Recreational Facilities:* Bowling; Movie theater; Pool; Gym; Recreation center; Golf; Tennis; Racquetball; Fitness center; Softball field; Football field; Auto shop; Crafts; Officers club; NCO club; Camping.

HUMPHREYS ENGINEER CENTER

Leaf and Telegraph Rd, Fort Belvoir, VA 22060-5580
(202) 355-2214; Autovon 345-2214

Profile

BRANCH: Army.

SIZE AND LOCATION: 500 acres. On Ft Belvoir; 6 mi from US-1; 6 mi from I-95; 8 mi S of Capital Beltway, I-495.

MAJOR UNITS: Corps of Engineers FOA's.

BASE HISTORY: 1973, developed by Army Corps of Engineers.

Key Contacts

COMMANDER: Maj Gen R S Kem; 20 Massachusetts Ave NW, Washington, DC 20001, (202) 272-0002, Autovon 285-0002.

PUBLIC AFFAIRS: Col William Garber; 20 Massachusetts Ave NW, Washington, DC 20001, (202) 272-0010, Autovon 285-0010.

PROCUREMENT: John Carpenter; (202) 355-2153, Autovon 345-2153.

TRANSPORTATION: Sharon Patrick; (202) 355-2548, Autovon 345-2548.

Personnel and Expenditures

ACTIVE DUTY PERSONNEL: 200

CIVILIAN PERSONNEL: 1145

Services *Commissary and Exchange:* Credit union; See Ft Belvoir for other services. *Base Library:* Yes. *Recreational Facilities:* Fitness center; Softball field; SATO.

FORT MONROE

FORT MONROE

Fort Monroe, VA 23651-6000
(804) 727-3241; Autovon 680-3241
OFFICER-OF-THE-DAY: (804) 727-3241, Autovon 680-3241

Profile

BRANCH: Army.

SIZE AND LOCATION: 1068 acres. Adj to the city of Hampton, 1 mi E of I-64; 17 mi SE of Patrick Henry Airport and 17 mi NW of the Norfolk Airport.

MAJOR UNITS: Training and Doctrine Command Headquarters.

FORT MONROE (continued)

BASE HISTORY: 1819, formed as irregular polygon with 7 fronts and 7 bastions, largest stone fort in US. Nicknamed "Gibraltar of the Chesapeake," one of few federal military installations in South not to fall to Confederate forces at outbreak of Civil War. WWII, Headquarters for Harbor Defenses of Chesapeake Bay. Later, headquarters for US Ground Forces. Third oldest continuously operating fort in US and registered National Landmark 1960.

VISITOR ATTRACTIONS: Casemate Museum; Chamberlin Hotel.

Key Contacts

COMMANDER: Col Eugene Scott; ATZG-CO.
PUBLIC AFFAIRS: Wayne Kanoy; ATZG-PAO, 23651-6035, (804) 727-3207, Autovon 680- 3207.
PROCUREMENT: T R Ryan; ATZG-C, 23651-6070, (804) 727-2630, Autovon 680-2630.
TRANSPORTATION: Henry Richardson; ATZG-LT, 23651-6600, (804) 727-2141, Autovon 680-2141.
PERSONNEL/COMMUNITY ACTIVITIES: Capt Roberta Antry; ATZG-PA, 23651-6100, (804) 727-3737, Autovon 680-3737.

Personnel and Expenditures

ACTIVE DUTY PERSONNEL: 1181
DEPENDENTS: 982
CIVILIAN PERSONNEL: 2350
MILITARY PAYROLL EXPENDITURE: $40 mil
CONTRACT EXPENDITURE: $78 mil

Services *Housing:* Family units 188; BOQ cottages 18; BEQ units 106; Senior NCO units 18; RV/Camper sites 10. *Temporary Housing:* VIP cottages 4; VOQ cottages 2; VEQ units 4; BOQ units 18. *Commissary:* Base commissary; Retail store; Barber shop; Dry cleaners; Food shop; Banking; Service station; Furniture store; Book store. *Child Care/Capacities:* Day care center 60; Home day care program. *Base Library:* Yes. *Medical Facilities:* Medical clinic; Dental clinic. *Recreational Facilities:* Bowling; Movie theater; Pool; Recreation center; Tennis; Racquetball; Fitness center; Softball field; Football field; Auto shop; Crafts; Officers club; NCO club; Camping.

FORT STORY

FORT STORY

Fort Story, VA 23459
(804) 422-7210; Autovon 927-9201

Profile

BRANCH: Army.
SIZE AND LOCATION: 1451 acres. On Cape Henry off Atlantic Ave, I-60.
MAJOR UNITS: 11th Transportation Battalion; US Army Information Systems Command; 4th Brigade (IN-OSUT), 80th Division (Training) USAR; 680th Transportation Detachment (LARC LX) USAR; Area Maintenance Support Activity No 90 Sub-shop USAR; Directorate of Training and Doctrine (DTD); US Army Element, School of Music; Directorate of Evaluation/Standardization (DOES); Combined Service Support Program; Atlantic Ordnance Disposal Group Two; Mobile Technical Unit Two; Electronic Countermeasures Test Site; US Navy Helicopter Mine Countermeasures Squadron Twelve; Naval Sea Combat Systems Engineering Station; Naval Surface Weapons Center, Ft Monroe Facility; Navy Public Works, Ft Story; Landing Force Training Command Atlantic (Amphibious Reconnaissance School); Naval Station Norfolk (Shipboard Marines); Cape Henry Lighthouse (USCG Group Hampton Roads).
BASE HISTORY: 1914, commonwealth of VA gave land to federal government to build fortifications; named after Gen John Patton Story, noted coast artilleryman. WWI, integrated into Coast Defense of Chesapeake Bay including Ft Monroe (HQ) and Ft Wool. 1925, designated a Harbor Defense Command. Following period of inactivity, extensive development, 1941. 1944, transition from heavily fortified coast artillery garrison to convalescent hospital for returning veterans. 1946, hospital closed and first amphibious training began. 1961, declared permanent installation. 1962, redesignated Class I sub-installation of Ft Eustis.

VISITOR ATTRACTIONS: Old Cape Henry Lighthouse; Jamestown Landing Site; Get visitor's pass to see historic sites at gate.

Key Contacts

PUBLIC AFFAIRS: Olivia C Alfriend; (804) 422-7755.

Services *Housing:* BOQ cottages; Barracks spaces; Housing units 164. *Temporary Housing:* Transient living quarters 12. *Commissary:* Base commissary; Retail store; Barber shop; Dry cleaners; Banking; Service station; Convenience store/Shopette; Credit union; Snacks; Tailor; Package beverages; Thrift shop. *Child Care/Capacities:* Day care center; Latch key program. *Base Library:* Yes. *Medical Facilities:* Medical clinic; Dental clinic; Veterinary clinic. *Recreational Facilities:* Bowling; Movie theater; Gym; Recreation center; Tennis; Fitness center; Softball field; Football field; Auto shop; Crafts; Officers club; NCO club; Youth center; Soccer; Go-cart track; Beach.

LANGLEY AFB

LANGLEY AIR FORCE BASE

Langley AFB, VA 23665
(804) 764-9990; Autovon 574-1110

Profile

BRANCH: Air Force.
SIZE AND LOCATION: 5511 acres. 3 mi N of city of Hampton on VA Peninsula; separated from Norfolk by Hampton Roads; SE from Richmond on I-64, take Armistead Ave exit; NE from Norfolk on I-64 take LaSalle Ave exit.
MAJOR UNITS: 1st Tactical Fighter Wing; Tactical Air Command Headquarters; Headquarters First Air Force; 1st Combat Support Group; Headquarters Tactical Communications Division; 5th Weather Wing; 2d Aircraft Delivery Group; 6th Airborne Command and Control Squadron; 48th Fighter Interceptor Squadron; 480th Reconnaissance Technical Group; 1913th Communications Group; Detachment 1, 1402nd Military Airlift Squadron; TAC Management Engineering Team; Detachment 6, 2000th Management Engineering Squadron; 4400th Management Engineering Squadron; 564th Air Force Band; Air Force Audit Agency, HQ Eastern District; Field Training Detachment 201; Operating Location B, HQ Air Weather Service; District 21, Air Force Office of Special Investigations; 1912th Computer Systems Group; 4700th Operations Support Squadron; 425th Munitions Support Squadron; Tactical Air Combat Operations Staff (TACOPS); Detachment 4, HQ AFCC; HQ AFCC, OL-D; US Army Corps of Engineers; 71st Aerial Port Squadron (AFRES); 1816th Reserve Advisor Squadron; AF Commissary Service; Detachment 7, 3rd Weather Squadron; HQ EST; 4400th Tactical Control Squadron; 4525th Combat Applications Squadron; 4444th Operations Squadron; 72nd Tactical Control Flight; 74th Tactical Control Flight; 5th Combat Communications Squadron; Training and Doctrine Command Flight Detachment; 4400th Contracting Squadron; 4410th Transportation Flight; 4500th Field Printing Squadron; 4500th School Squadron; 4545th Security Assistance Manager Squadron (TACSAO); AF Legal Services Center; Commander-in-Chief, Atlantic Airborne Command Post.
BASE HISTORY: Langley AFB makes a claim to being oldest continuously active air base in US. 1916, Army, Navy, and National Advisory Committee for Aeronautics agreed to construct a facility for government sponsored aviation research and development center and purchased land for Aviation Experimental Station and Proving Ground. 1917, officially named Langley Field for Samuel Pierpont Langley, former Secretary of Smithsonian Institute and pioneer in American aviation. 1920s, used by Brig Gen William "Billy" Mitchell to demonstrate use of airplanes as offensive weapons against ships anchored in Chesapeake Bay; conducted experiments with lighter-than-air machines, part of Langley still called LTA area. 1935, General Headquarters Air Force located here. WWII, antisubmarine operations. Following WWII, HQs TAC established. 1965-75, home for number of MAC units. 1976, 1st TFW arrived.

Key Contacts

COMMANDER: Col Richard B Myers; (804) 764-3252, Autovon 574-3252.

Personnel and Expenditures

ACTIVE DUTY PERSONNEL: 9955
DEPENDENTS: 4423
CIVILIAN PERSONNEL: 1544
MILITARY PAYROLL EXPENDITURE: $252.4 mil
CONTRACT EXPENDITURE: $56.4 mil

Services *Housing:* Family units 938; BAQ units 14; Dormitory spaces 1604; Senior NCO units; Family housing also available at Bethel Manor 5 mi from base. *Temporary Housing:* VIP cottages 29; VOQ cottages 78; VAQ units 110; Family units 100. *Commissary:* Base commissary; Retail store; Barber shop; Dry cleaners; Food shop; Florist; Banking; Service station; Military clothing sales; Convenience store/Shopette; Credit union; Tailor; Ice cream; Snacks; Thrift shop; Beauty shop; Laundry; Optical shop; Video rental; Construction materials. *Child Care/Capacities:* Day care center 224. *Schools:* Kindergarten/Preschool. *Base Library:* Yes. *Medical Facilities:* Hospital 75; Dental clinic; Veterinary clinic. *Recreational Facilities:* Bowling; Movie theater; Pool; Gym; Recreation center; Golf (driving range); Stables; Tennis; Racquetball; Fitness center; Softball field; Auto shop; Crafts; Officers club; NCO club; Fishing/Hunting; Youth center; Marina; Big Bethel Recreation Area; Tickets & Tour; Jr Rifle Club; MWR supply; Yacht Club; Skeet Club; Aero Club.

NEWPORT NEWS

FORT EUSTIS

Newport News, VA 23604
(804) 878-5251; Autovon 927-1110

Profile

BRANCH: Army.
SIZE AND LOCATION: 73,118 acres. On W side of Newport News on Mulberry Island.
MAJOR UNITS: US Army Transportation School; US Army Aviation Logistics School; NCO Academy; Joint Strategic Deployment Training Center; 8th Transportation Brigade; Felker Army Airfield; 7th Transportation Group (Terminal); 6th Transportation Battalion (Truck); 10th Transportation Battalion (Terminal); 11th Transportation Battalion (Terminal); 24th Transportation Battalion (Terminal); US Army Training Support Center (ATSC); Aviation Applied Technology Directorate (AATD); Military Traffic Management

FORT EUSTIS (continued)

Command Transportation Engineering Agency (MTMCTEA); National Oceanic and Atmospheric Administration Officer Training Center; US Army Information Systems Command (USAISC); TRADOC Management Engineering Activity (TRAMEA); McDonald Army Community Hospital.

BASE HISTORY: 1918, began as artillery training area camp; named for Brevet Brig Gen Abraham Eustis, artillery officer. 1946, became principal training post, Army Transportation Corps. Felker Army Airfield, Army's first military heliport; remains only Army heliport with at least one of every Army helicopter in active Army. McDonald Army Community Hospital opened 1964, with major outpatient clinic added, 1976.

VISITOR ATTRACTIONS: Army Transportation Museum.

Personnel and Expenditures

ACTIVE DUTY PERSONNEL: 10,400

DEPENDENTS: 6000

Services *Housing:* Trailer spaces 32; Housing units 1338. *Temporary Housing:* VIP cottages 9; VOQ cottages 272; VEQ units 229; Guesthouse units; Transient living quarters 32. *Commissary:* Base commissary; Retail store; Barber shop; Dry cleaners; Food shop; Florist; Banking; Service station; Convenience store/Shopette; Credit union; Tailor; Clothing sales; Laundry; Optical; Shoe repair; Ice cream; Snacks; Fast food; Package beverages; Video rental. *Child Care/Capacities:* Day care center 61; Home day care program; Latch key program. *Schools:* Kindergarten/Preschool. *Base Library:* Yes. *Medical Facilities:* Hospital 57; Medical clinic; Dental clinic; Veterinary services. *Recreational Facilities:* Bowling; Movie theater; Pool; Gym; Recreation center; Golf; Stables; Tennis; Racquetball; Skating rink; Fitness center; Softball field; Football field; Auto shop; Crafts; Officers club; NCO club; Fishing/Hunting; Youth center; Soccer; ITT; Water sports; Skeet shooting; Picnicking.

NEWPORT NEWS SUPERVISOR OF SHIPBUILDING, CONVERSION AND REPAIR

Newport News, VA 23607-2787
(804) 380-4122

Profile

BRANCH: Navy.

SIZE AND LOCATION: Offices only. Within the shipyard, Newport News.

BASE HISTORY: SUPSHIPNN is a command which oversees the contractors building of aircraft carriers and submarines.

Key Contacts

COMMANDER: Capt Charles D Wasson.

PUBLIC AFFAIRS: LTjg Mary C Jenson; ATTN: Code 184, (804) 380-3687.

PERSONNEL/COMMUNITY ACTIVITIES: See Public Affairs.

Personnel and Expenditures

ACTIVE DUTY PERSONNEL: 60

Services *Commissary and Exchange:* Retail store; Barber shop.

NORFOLK

ARMED FORCES STAFF COLLEGE

Norfolk, VA 23511-6097
(804) 444-5252

Profile

BRANCH: Joint Service Installation.

LOCATION: On Naval Station, Norfolk.

BASE HISTORY: 1946, established as part of National Defense University, a joint intermediate-level college under Joint Chiefs of Staff to prepare selected mid-career officers for joint and combined

staff duty. Course 5 ½ months long and presented twice each academic year; approx 280 resident students from Great Britain, Canada, Australia, France, New Zealand, West Germany, Japan, Korea, Luxembourg, Spain, and Turkey attend each session. Navy has responsibility for fiscal and logistic support of college through Commanding Officer, Naval Administrative Command, who serves concurrently as Dean.

Key Contacts

PUBLIC AFFAIRS: Naval Station, Norfolk, Public Affairs Ctr X-18, Norfolk, VA 23511-6199.

Services *Housing:* See Norfolk Naval Station. *Temporary Housing:* See Norfolk Naval Station. *Base Library:* Yes. *Recreational Facilities:* Bowling; Movie theater; Recreation center; Officers club.

ATLANTIC DIVISION, NAVAL FACILITIES ENGINEERING COMMAND

Norfolk, VA 23511
(804) 444-9870

Profile

BRANCH: Navy.

LOCATION: On Naval Station, Norfolk.

MAJOR UNITS: Atlantic Division, Naval Facilities Engineering Command.

BASE HISTORY: One of six engineering field divisions of Naval Facilities Engineering Command (NAVFAC), established 1942, as agent of Bureau of Yards and Docks to decentralize and expedite Bureau actions in Atlantic area. WWII, support of actions in Africa and chain of advance bases from Iceland to Brazil. Majority of employees located on Naval Base, Norfolk; field offices in VA, WV, NC, Iceland, Bermuda, Caribbean, Africa, and Mediterranean countries; design, construct, manage, and maintain shore-based facilities for Navy, DOD, and other government agencies.

Key Contacts

PUBLIC AFFAIRS: Naval Station, Norfolk, Public Affairs Ctr X-18, Norfolk, VA 23511-6199.

Personnel and Expenditures

ACTIVE DUTY PERSONNEL: 1000 (military and civilian)

CONTRACT EXPENDITURE: $600 mil

Services *Housing:* See Norfolk Naval Station. *Temporary Housing:* See Norfolk Naval Station.

CAMP ELMORE

Norfolk, VA 23515
(804) 444-6005; Autovon 564-6005

Profile

BRANCH: Marines.

SIZE AND LOCATION: 4 acres. Adj to Norfolk Naval Base; off Terminal Blvd.

MAJOR UNITS: Headquarters and Service Battalion; Headquarters Fleet Marine Force, Atlantic (FMFLANT).

BASE HISTORY: 1950s, established; named after recipient of Navy Cross. One of smallest Marine Corps facilities.

Personnel and Expenditures

ACTIVE DUTY PERSONNEL: 600

CIVILIAN PERSONNEL: 5

Services *Commissary and Exchange:* Retail store; Barber shop; Dry cleaners; Food shop; Service station. *Recreational Facilities:* Gym.

FLEET ANTISUBMARINE WARFARE TRAINING CENTER, ATLANTIC

Norfolk, VA 23511-6495
(804) 444-0000

Profile

BRANCH: Navy.

LOCATION: On Naval Station, Norfolk.

MAJOR UNITS: Fleet Antisubmarine Warfare Training Center, Atlantic.

BASE HISTORY: A major shore activity within Training Command, US Atlantic Fleet; mission to provide Atlantic Fleet with antisubmarine warfare training, conduct training for individuals, shipboard teams, and trainers; provides basic to advanced training in five buildings on Naval Station, Norfolk.

Key Contacts

PUBLIC AFFAIRS: Naval Station, Norfolk, Public Affairs Ctr X-18, Norfolk, VA 23511-6199.

Services *Housing:* See Norfolk Naval Station. *Temporary Housing:* See Norfolk Naval Station.

LITTLE CREEK NAVAL AMPHIBIOUS BASE

Norfolk, VA 23521-5000
(804) 464-7000; Autovon 680-7000
OFFICER-OF-THE-DAY: (804) 464-7385, Autovon 680-7385

Profile

BRANCH: Navy.

SIZE AND LOCATION: 12,000 acres. At extreme NW corner of Virginia Beach along Shore Dr, Rte 60; 2 mi W of Chesapeake Bay Bridge-Tunnel off I-60.

MAJOR UNITS: Naval Amphibious Base; Naval Beach Group Two; Assault Craft Two; Amphibious Construction Battalion; Beachmaster Unit Two; Naval Special Warfare Group Two; Landing Force Training Command, Atlantic; Homeport for 30 ships.

BASE HISTORY: Grew out of four bases constructed during WWII—Amphibious Training Base, Naval Frontier Base, and Camps Bradford and Shelton. Consisted of three annexes, named for former owners, Shelton on E, Bradford in center, and Whitehurst on W. 1945, established as base. 1946, designated permanent base.

VISITOR ATTRACTIONS: Amphibious Training Demonstrator; Ship tours.

Key Contacts

COMMANDER: Capt Paul A Canady; Bldg 3129, (804) 464-7231, Autovon 680-7231.

PUBLIC AFFAIRS: Karen Parkinson; Bldg 3006, (804) 464-7923, 464-7161, Autovon 680-7923, 680-7761.

PROCUREMENT: LCDR Robert Leake; Bldg 3015, (804) 464-7442, 464-7443, Autovon 680-7442, 680-7443.

TRANSPORTATION: Donald French; Bldg 3662, (804) 464-7911, Autovon 680-7911.

Personnel and Expenditures

ACTIVE DUTY PERSONNEL: 4100

DEPENDENTS: 7000

CIVILIAN PERSONNEL: 415

MILITARY PAYROLL EXPENDITURE: $9.6 mil

CONTRACT EXPENDITURE: $6.6 mil

Services *Housing:* Family units 1962; BOQ cottages 1; BEQ units 5. *Temporary Housing:* VIP cottages 4; VOQ cottages 198; BOQ units 79; Naval Lodge Units (15 day max occupancy) 90. *Commissary:* Base commissary; Retail store; Barber shop; Dry cleaners; Food shop; Florist; Banking; Service station; Furniture store; Book store; Convenience store/Shopette; Ice cream; Beauty shop; Photo studio; Package beverages; Frame shop; Jewelry/watch sales and repair; Optical shop; Shoe repair; Wood shop; Camera shop; Home entertainment center; Personalized engraving services; Sound shop; Photo finishing; Credit union; Country store. *Child Care/Capacities:* Day care center 238; Before & after school care. *Schools:* Kindergarten/Preschool. *Base Library:* Yes. *Medical Facilities:* Medical clinic; Dental clinic; Ports-

LITTLE CREEK NAVAL AMPHIBIOUS BASE (continued)

mouth Naval Hospital. *Recreational Facilities:* Bowling; Movie theater; Pool; Gym; Recreation center; Golf (and Pro shop); Tennis (and Pro shop); Racquetball; Fitness center; Softball field; Football field; Auto shop; Crafts; Officers club; NCO club; Fishing/Hunting; Youth center (and teen center); ITT office; Miniature golf; Sailing center; Beaches, boat piers; Storage lot for recreational vehicles; Picnicking; Boat/Camper shop; Rugby field; Amusement center.

NORFOLK FLEET TRAINING CENTER

Norfolk, VA 23511-6285
(804) 444-0000
Profile
BRANCH: Navy.
LOCATION: On Naval Station, Norfolk.
MAJOR UNITS: Fleet Training Command.
BASE HISTORY: A fleet, shore-based activity providing practical, operational and maintenance training in shipboard operations; training officers and enlisted in advanced and/or specialized courses; and, providing reactivation or precommissioning training. 65,000 students taught annually in 198 courses.
Key Contacts
PUBLIC AFFAIRS: Naval Station, Norfolk, Public Affairs Ctr X-18, Norfolk, VA 23511-6199.
Personnel and Expenditures
ACTIVE DUTY PERSONNEL: 608
CIVILIAN PERSONNEL: 25
Services *Housing:* See Norfolk Naval Station. *Temporary Housing:* See Norfolk Naval Station.

NORFOLK NAVAL AIR STATION

Norfolk, VA 23511
(804) 444-0000
Profile
BRANCH: Navy.
SIZE AND LOCATION: 1950 acres. Bounded on N & W by James and Elizabeth Rivers and on E by Chesapeake Bay; off I-64 in Norfolk.
MAJOR UNITS: Commander, Naval Air Force, US Atlantic Fleet; Commander, Naval Safety Center; Naval Aviation Depot (Repair Facility).
BASE HISTORY: 1918, commissioned on historic site of 1907 Jamestown Exhibition. Initially, NAS provided support for operational and experimental flights; grew into major sea plane base, training pilots and crews. During WWI and WWII, provided antisubmarine patrols in mid-Atlantic. Presently, home to five aircraft carriers and 26 aircraft squadrons.
Key Contacts
PUBLIC AFFAIRS: See Norfolk Naval Base.
Personnel and Expenditures
ACTIVE DUTY PERSONNEL: 21,500 (military and civilian)
Services *Housing:* BOQ cottages; BEQ units; Barracks spaces; See Norfolk Naval Station. *Temporary Housing:* See Norfolk Naval Station. *Commissary and Exchange:* Retail store; Barber shop; Dry cleaners; Food shop; Service station; Convenience store/Shopette; Beauty shop; Laundry; Tailor; Jewelry/watch sales and repair; Credit union. *Schools:* Kindergarten/Preschool. *Base Library:* Yes. *Medical Facilities:* Naval Hospital Portsmouth. *Recreational Facilities:* Bowling; Pool; Gym; Recreation center; Auto shop; Officers club; NCO club; Breezy Park Recreation Area.

NORFOLK NAVAL AVIATION DEPOT

Norfolk, VA 23511
(804) 444-0000
Profile
BRANCH: Navy.
SIZE AND LOCATION: 172 acres. On Naval Station, Norfolk.
MAJOR UNITS: Naval Aviation Depot.
BASE HISTORY: Since 1917, mission to perform depot level maintenance, engineering, logistic management in support of tactical naval aviation. Largest tenant command at NAS Norfolk and largest employer in Norfolk. Aircraft inducted at NADEP for Standard Depot Level Maintenance, damage repair, and major modifications. One of two depots for repair and maintenance on air-launched missiles for Navy, Air Force, and NATO countries.
Key Contacts
PUBLIC AFFAIRS: Naval Station, Norfolk, Public Affairs Ctr X-18, Norfolk, VA 23511-6199.
Personnel and Expenditures
ACTIVE DUTY PERSONNEL: 4000 (military and civilian)
Services *Housing:* See Norfolk Naval Station. *Temporary Housing:* See Norfolk Naval Station.

NORFOLK NAVAL BASE

Norfolk, VA 23511
(804) 444-0000; Autovon 564-1521
Profile
BRANCH: Navy.
SIZE AND LOCATION: 3327 acres. Sewell's Point area of Norfolk off I-64, Terminal Blvd.
MAJOR UNITS: Commander-in-Chief, Atlantic Fleet; Supreme Allied Commander, Atlantic; Fleet Marine Force, Atlantic; Naval Surfaces Forces, Atlantic; Submarine Forces, Atlantic; Naval Air Forces, Atlantic; Commander, Naval Base, Norfolk; Armed Forces Staff College; Norfolk Naval Air Station; Norfolk Naval Station; Commander-in-Chief, Atlantic Fleet; Naval Amphibious Base, Little Creek; Naval Air Station Oceana. Other major US commands also headquartered here: Commander Naval Surface Force, Atlantic; Commander Naval Air Force, Atlantic; Commander Submarine Force, Atlantic; Commanding General, Fleet Marine Force Atlantic; and, Commander Second Fleet, one of four numbered fleets and major antisubmarine warfare strike force..
BASE HISTORY: Situated near site of battle of Monitor and Merrimac; World's largest naval complex; HQs Commander, Naval Base, Norfolk; Navy's largest supply center; Naval Aviation Depot (second largest employer in VA), Naval Station, and NAS, Norfolk. Also part of Naval Base complex HQs for Commander-in-Chief, Atlantic/Supreme Allied Commander, Atlantic, North Atlantic Treaty Organization (NATO) command (under command of four-star admirals who oversee defense of entire Atlantic area). Homeported about 156 ships, 50 aircraft squadrons and 252 shore activities.
VISITOR ATTRACTIONS: Tours; Hampton Roads Naval Museum.
Key Contacts
PUBLIC AFFAIRS: (804) 444-2163; Autovon 564-2163.
Personnel and Expenditures
ACTIVE DUTY PERSONNEL: 108,000
CONTRACT EXPENDITURE: $510.5 mil
Services *Housing:* Family units 750; BEQ units 225; Townhouse units 1730; Also see Naval Public Works Center. *Temporary Housing:* VIP cottages; Lodge units. *Commissary:* Base commissary; Retail store; Barber shop; Dry cleaners; Food shop; Service station; Credit union; Sporting goods; Hardware store; Toys; Beauty shop; Laundry; Tailor; Jewelry/watch sales and repair. *Child Care/Capacities:* Day care center 750. *Base Library:* Yes. *Medical Facilities:* Medical clinic; Dental clinic; Portsmouth Naval Hospital. *Recreational Facilities:* Bowling; Movie theater; Pool; Gym; Recreation center; Golf; Tennis; Auto shop; Crafts; Officers club; NCO club; Fishing/Hunting; Picnic areas.

NORFOLK NAVAL STATION

Norfolk, VA 23511
(804) 444-0000
Profile
BRANCH: Navy.
SIZE AND LOCATION: 1950 acres. Bounded on N & W by James and Elizabeth Rivers and on E by Chesapeake Bay; off I-64 in Norfolk.
MAJOR UNITS: Naval Training Station.
BASE HISTORY: 1917, construction began on Naval Operating Base on historic site of 1907 Jamestown Exhibition. Late 1930s-early 1940s, additional construction. 1942, recruit training ended. 1945, name changed to present name. 1946, Naval Station made separate command under military command of Commandant (later Commander), Naval Base.
VISITOR ATTRACTIONS: Ship tours; Hampton Roads Naval Museum.
Key Contacts
PUBLIC AFFAIRS: Public Affairs Ctr X-18, Norfolk, VA 23511-6199.
Services *Housing:* Family units 5989; Mobile home units 195 (homesites); Waiting list 2-30 months. *Temporary Housing:* Navy Lodge units (each, 15 day max occupancy), 90; Naval Base, 7811 Hampton Blvd, Norfolk, VA 23505, (804) 489-2656; Naval Amphibious Base, Little Creek, Norfolk, VA 23521 (804) 464-6215. *Commissary:* Base commissary; See Naval Base, Norfolk. *Child Care/Capacities:* Day care center. *Base Library:* Yes. *Medical Facilities:* Portsmouth Naval Hospital. *Recreational Facilities:* Bowling; Movie theater; Pool; Recreation center; Golf; Auto shop; Officers club; NCO club; Fishing/Hunting; Sailing.

NORFOLK NAVAL SUPPLY CENTER

Norfolk, VA 23512-5000
(804) 445-2525
Profile
BRANCH: Navy.
SIZE AND LOCATION: 2900 acres. On Naval Station, Norfolk.
MAJOR UNITS: Navy Supply Center.
BASE HISTORY: Headquartered on Naval Station, Norfolk, NSC Navy's largest supply operation. Includes Craney Island and Yorktown fuel terminals; main complex on Naval Base, Norfolk, also, South Annex, and Cheatham Annex. Provides services to Atlantic Fleet ships homeported in Norfolk, Second Fleet Atlantic, and Sixth Fleet in Mediterranean. Support also provided to Middle East Force ships in Persian Gulf and Atlantic Fleet ships in Indian Ocean. Shore activities worldwide also receive support.
Key Contacts
PUBLIC AFFAIRS: Naval Station, Norfolk, Public Affairs Ctr X-18, Norfolk, VA 23511-6199.
Personnel and Expenditures
ACTIVE DUTY PERSONNEL: 82
CIVILIAN PERSONNEL: 3400
Services *Housing:* See Norfolk Naval Station. *Temporary Housing:* See Norfolk Naval Station. *Commissary and Exchange:* Credit union.

NORFOLK NAVY PUBLIC WORKS CENTER
Hampton Blvd & Ingram St, Norfolk, VA 23511-6098
(804) 444-4694
Profile
BRANCH: Navy.
LOCATION: On Naval Station, Norfolk.
MAJOR UNITS: Navy Public Works Center.
BASE HISTORY: Provides maintenance services throughout entire Atlantic and European area.
Key Contacts
PUBLIC AFFAIRS: Naval Station, Norfolk, Public Affairs Ctr X-18, Norfolk, VA 23511-6199.
Services *Housing:* See Norfolk Naval Station. *Temporary Housing:* See Norfolk Naval Station. *Commissary and Exchange:* Credit union.

TRAINING COMMAND, US ATLANTIC FLEET
Naval Station Norfolk, Norfolk, VA 23511-6597
(804) 444-0000
Profile
BRANCH: Navy.
LOCATION: On Naval Station, Norfolk.
MAJOR UNITS: Training Command, US Atlantic Fleet.
BASE HISTORY: Conducts more than 550 courses, ranging from fire fighting to celestial navigation.
Key Contacts
PUBLIC AFFAIRS: Naval Station, Norfolk, Public Affairs Ctr X-18, Norfolk, VA 23511-6199.
Services *Housing:* See Norfolk Naval Station. *Temporary Housing:* See Norfolk Naval Station.

PETERSBERG

FORT LEE AIR FORCE STATION
Petersberg, VA 23801
(804) 734-1011; Autovon 687-4008
Profile
BRANCH: Air Force.
MAJOR UNITS: Fort Lee AFS (TAC).

PETERSBURG

FORT LEE
US Army Quartermaster Center, Bldg T-2600, C Ave, Fort Lee, Petersburg, VA 23801
(804) 734-3110; Autovon 687-3110
OFFICER-OF-THE-DAY: (804) 734-2326, Autovon 687-2326
Profile
BRANCH: Army.
SIZE AND LOCATION: 5575 acres. 22 mi S of Richmond and 35 mi from Richmond IAP. Surrounding cities include, Petersburg, Colonial Heights, and Hopewell. I-95 runs to the W of the post and I-85 begins in nearby Petersburg.
BASE HISTORY: 1917, first Camp Lee selected as state mobilization camp and later division training camp; named for Gen Robert E Lee, Confederate Civil War commander. After WWI, Camp Lee taken over by state and designated game preserve. Later, portions incorporated into National Military Park of Petersburg. 1940, construction of another Camp Lee on site of earlier installation. 1941, Quartermaster Replacement Training Center (QMRTC) started operation; also home of Medical Replacement Training Center (MRTC), later relocated to Camp Pickett; QMRTC redesignated as Army Service Forces Training Center; when Quarter-

master School transferred to Camp Lee, full program of courses conducted, including Officer Candidate School. 1950, redesignated as Fort Lee. 1962, became Class 1 military installation under Second US Army; school, part of Continental Army Command service school system, served as home of Quartermaster Corps and Corps Historian. 1963, Camp Pickett and Camp A P Hill established as subinstallations of Fort Lee. 1973, came under US Army Training and Doctrine Command.
VISITOR ATTRACTIONS: Quartermaster Museum located on A Ave just inside main gate.
Key Contacts
COMMANDER: Maj Gen William T McLean.
PUBLIC AFFAIRS: Joy C Whitmore; Acting.
PROCUREMENT: A A Swanson; Director of Contracting, Bldg 7124, Ft Lee, (804) 734-1068, Autovon 687-1068.
TRANSPORTATION: R H Silva; Bldg T-1105, Ft Lee, (804) 734-4743, Autovon 687-4743.
PERSONNEL/COMMUNITY ACTIVITIES: LTC J P DeBiase; Bldg 4320, Ft Lee, (804) 734-3012, Autovon 687-3012.
Personnel and Expenditures
ACTIVE DUTY PERSONNEL: 3769
DEPENDENTS: 2874
CIVILIAN PERSONNEL: 3730
MILITARY PAYROLL EXPENDITURE: $153 mil
Services *Housing:* Family units 1461; Barracks spaces 3974; RV/Camper sites 19. *Temporary Housing:* VIP cottages 16; VOQ cottages 482; BOQ units 45; Guesthouse units 37; Transient living quarters 582. *Commissary:* Base commissary; Retail store; Barber shop; Dry cleaners; Food shop; Florist; Banking; Service station; Book store. *Child Care/Capacities:* Day care center 110; Home day care program. *Schools:* Kindergarten/Preschool. *Base Library:* Yes. *Medical Facilities:* Hospital 120; Medical clinic; Dental clinic. *Recreational Facilities:* Bowling; Movie theater; Pool; Gym; Recreation center; Golf; Stables; Tennis; Racquetball; Fitness center; Softball field; Football field; Auto shop; Crafts; Officers club; NCO club; Camping; Skeet range; Track; Skateboarding pit; Playhouse.

PORTSMOUTH

FIFTH COAST GUARD DISTRICT
431 Crawford St, Portsmouth, VA 23704-5004
(804) 398-6000
OFFICER-OF-THE-DAY: Operations Duty Officer (804) 398-6231
Profile
BRANCH: Coast Guard.
SIZE AND LOCATION: Offices only. In the historic waterfront area of downtown Portsmouth, the Fifth District Office overlooks the Elizabeth River near Portsmouth's Portside area and across from the Norfolk Shipyards and Norfolk Waterside area.
MAJOR UNITS: Fifth District Command; Ship Introductory Unit (HQ Command); Maintenance & Logistics Command; Atlantic Civilian Personnel Branch.
Key Contacts
COMMANDER: Rear Adm Alan D Breed; (804) 398-6287.
PUBLIC AFFAIRS: LTjg D J Rose; Commander (dpa), (804) 398-6275.
PROCUREMENT: Capt P E Prindle; Administrative Division Chief, (804) 398-6332.
PERSONNEL/COMMUNITY ACTIVITIES: See Public Affairs Officer.
Personnel and Expenditures
ACTIVE DUTY PERSONNEL: 125
CIVILIAN PERSONNEL: 38

NORFOLK NAVAL SHIPYARD
Portsmouth, VA 23709
(804) 396-3000; 396-8615; Autovon 961-8615
Profile
BRANCH: Navy.
SIZE AND LOCATION: 1294 acres. On Elizabeth River in Portsmouth; 1 mi from I-264; main gate at Effington St and Portsmouth Blvd.
MAJOR UNITS: Norfolk Naval Shipyard; Naval Electronic Systems Engineering Center; Supervisor of Shipbuilding, Conversion, and Repair; Planning and Engineering for Repairs and Alterations.
BASE HISTORY: 1767, established by British; During American Revolution taken over by VA. 1794, leased by Navy. 1801, purchased. 1833, Dry Dock One, first in Western Hemisphere, opened. 1889-1942, six graving docks added; responsible for a number of firsts, among them: converted USS *Merrimack* into first ironclad, CSS *Virginia*, 1862; built first battleship commissioned by Navy (USS *Texas*); built first platform for first plane flight from ship; and, converted a collier into first aircraft carrier (USS *Langley*), 1922. 1939-45, built 101 new ships from landing craft to aircraft carriers. 1983-88, repaired and returned 96 ships to fleet operations, more than any other shipyard. Part of Naval Sea Systems Command.
VISITOR ATTRACTIONS: Portsmouth Naval Shipyard Museum.
Key Contacts
COMMANDER: Capt Edward S McGinley II.
PUBLIC AFFAIRS: Joe Law; Code 103.
Personnel and Expenditures
ACTIVE DUTY PERSONNEL: 678
CIVILIAN PERSONNEL: 14,486
MILITARY PAYROLL EXPENDITURE: $319 mil
CONTRACT EXPENDITURE: $135 mil
Services *Housing:* Family units 35; Dormitory spaces; Senior NCO units 125; Junior NCO units 247. *Temporary Housing:* Temporary units for personnel from ships being overhauled 75. *Commissary:* Base commissary; Service station; Credit union. *Child Care/Capacities:* Day care center 75. *Medical Facilities:* Medical clinic; Portsmouth Naval Hospital, 3 mi away. *Recreational Facilities:* Bowling; Pool; Gym; Recreation center; Tennis; Racquetball; Softball field; Auto shop.

PORTSMOUTH NAVAL HOSPITAL
Portsmouth, VA 23708
(804) 398-5000; Autovon 564-0111
Profile
BRANCH: Navy.
SIZE AND LOCATION: 110 acres. In city of Portsmouth off I-264.
MAJOR UNITS: Naval Medical Command, Mid-Atlantic Region.
BASE HISTORY: 1827, cornerstone laid. 1830, first patients admitted. 1960, modern 15-story addition built.
Personnel and Expenditures
ACTIVE DUTY PERSONNEL: 2234
Services *Housing:* Family units 2234; BOQ cottages 19. *Temporary Housing:* Guesthouse units. *Commissary and Exchange:* Credit union. *Base Library:* Yes. *Medical Facilities:* Hospital 445; Dental clinic. *Recreational Facilities:* Bowling; Movie theater; Pool; Gym; Recreation center (pool tables); Softball field; NCO club; Picnicking.

PORTSMOUTH SUPERVISOR OF SHIPBUILDING, CONVERSION AND REPAIR
PO Box 215, Portsmouth, VA 23705
(804) 396-3579; Autovon 961-3579
OFFICER-OF-THE-DAY: (804) 396-3736, Autovon 961-3736

PORTSMOUTH SUPERVISOR OF SHIPBUILDING, CONVERSION AND REPAIR
(continued)
Profile
BRANCH: Navy.
SIZE AND LOCATION: 10 acres. On the banks of S branch of the Elizabeth River opposite Norfolk, VA. Immediate access to I-64, I-264, US 13, US 17. Serviced by Norfolk Airport approx 10 mi away.
MAJOR UNITS: Norfolk Naval Shipyard (co-located); Naval Electronics Systems Engineering Center, Portsmouth.
BASE HISTORY: 1947, Commander, Norfolk Naval Shipyard designated as Industrial Manager, USN, Fifth Naval District. 1951, Office of Industrial Manager established independently of Shipyard. 1967, Industrial Manager redesignated Supervisor of Shipbuilding, Conversion and Repair, USN Fifth Naval District. 1975, Command title changed to current title. 1985, NAVSEA established detachment, Chester, PA, and Bethlehem Steel Corp, Baltimore, MD, to administer new construction contracts.
Key Contacts
COMMANDER: Capt Richard E Westerbrook.
PUBLIC AFFAIRS: Betty A Liverman.
PROCUREMENT: LCDR C B McGaughey, USN; (804) 396-5153, Autovon 961-5153.
TRANSPORTATION: See Public Affairs Officer.
PERSONNEL/COMMUNITY ACTIVITIES: See Public Affairs Officer.
Personnel and Expenditures
ACTIVE DUTY PERSONNEL: 23
CIVILIAN PERSONNEL: 575
MILITARY PAYROLL EXPENDITURE: $20.7 mil
CONTRACT EXPENDITURE: $331 mil
Services *Commissary:* Base commissary; Retail store; Barber shop; Dry cleaners; Food shop; Florist; Service station. *Child Care/ Capacities:* Day care center 40. *Medical Facilities:* Medical clinic; Dental clinic. *Recreational Facilities:* Bowling; Movie theater; Pool; Gym; Recreation center; Tennis; Racquetball; Fitness center; Softball field; Football field; Auto shop; NCO club.

SHORE INTERMEDIATE MAINTENANCE ACTIVITY
St Julien's Creek Annex, Portsmouth, VA 23702-5001
(804) 396-0117; Autovon 961-0117
OFFICER-OF-THE-DAY: (804) 396-0117, Autovon 961-0117
Profile
BRANCH: Navy.
SIZE AND LOCATION: 50 acres. On Victory Blvd between George Washington Hwy and NNSY.
Key Contacts
COMMANDER: LCDR J R Hosking; (804) 396-0120, Autovon 961-0120.
PUBLIC AFFAIRS: MMCM W K Dowell Jr; (804) 396-0145, Autovon 961-0145.
PROCUREMENT: Lt Hanna; (804) 396-0119, Autovon 961-0119.
TRANSPORTATION: SKCM Trinidad; (804) 396-0217, Autovon 961-0217.
Personnel and Expenditures
ACTIVE DUTY PERSONNEL: 320
CIVILIAN PERSONNEL: 7
Services *Commissary:* Base commissary; Retail store; Barber shop; Dry cleaners; Food shop; Florist; Service station. *Child Care/ Capacities:* Day care center. *Medical Facilities:* Medical clinic; Dental clinic. *Recreational Facilities:* Bowling; Pool; Gym; Recreation center; Tennis; Racquetball; Fitness center; Softball field; Auto shop; Camping; Fishing/Hunting.

QUANTICO

QUANTICO MARINE CORPS COMBAT DEVELOPMENT COMMAND
Quantico, VA 22134
(703) 640-2415; Autovon 278-2415
OFFICER-OF-THE-DAY: (703) 640-2707, Autovon 278-2707
Profile
BRANCH: Marines.
SIZE AND LOCATION: 60,000 acres. Approx 30 mi S of Washington, DC, on I-95 or Rte 1; surrounds town of Quantico, VA on three sides with Potomac River running adj to base.
MAJOR UNITS: Marine Corps Base Quantico; Marine Air-Ground Task Force Warfighting Center; Marine Corps Wargaming and Assessment Center; The Intelligence Center; Marine Air-Ground Training and Education Center; Staff Noncommissioned Officers Academy; Officers Candidates School; The Basic School, Camp Barrett; Marine Corps University; Amphibious Warfare School; Communication Officers School; Command and Staff College; Computer Sciences School; Instructional Management School; Weapons Training Battalion; Information Technology Center; Headquarters and Service Battalion; Security Battalion; Marine Corps Air Station Quantico; Marine Corps Band; Range Control; Natural Resources and Training Area Management; Marine Corps Research, Development and Acquisition Command; Marine Helicopter Squadron One (HMX-1); Marine Security Guard Battalion; Marine Corps Operational Test and Evaluation Activity; Marine Corps Central Design and Programming Activity; Morale, Welfare and Recreation Support Activity; Naval Investigative Service; Marine Corps Association; Federal Bureau of Investigation Academy.
BASE HISTORY: "By the large stream," Indian meaning of Quantico aptly describes this Marine installation on Potomac River. 1917, first Marines arrived; thousands trained during WWI, including 4th Marine Brigade. 1920, Marine Corps Schools founded. 1935-41, tactical units became Fleet Marine Force, developed amphibious warfare techniques used during WWII. Air facility and HMX-1 continue to aid in development, training and education, and support of president. 1968, redesignated as Marine Corps Development and Education Command (MCDEC), forerunner of today's MCCDC, created Nov 10, 1987.
VISITOR ATTRACTIONS: Marine Corps Air Ground Museum.
Key Contacts
COMMANDER: Lt Gen William Etnyre; MCCDC CG; Brig Gen Gail Reals; MCB CG.
PUBLIC AFFAIRS: LTC R W McLean; Public Affairs Office, MCCDC, Quantico, VA 22134-5001, (703) 640-2741, 640-2742, 640-3341, Autovon 278-2741, 278-2742, 278-3341.
PERSONNEL/COMMUNITY ACTIVITIES: Sgt William Roberts Jr; Community Relations NCO, Public Affairs Office, (703) 640-3250, 640-3341, Autovon 278-3250, 278-3341.
Personnel and Expenditures
ACTIVE DUTY PERSONNEL: 10,000
DEPENDENTS: 4200
CIVILIAN PERSONNEL: 2100
Services *Housing:* Family units 2030; BOQ cottages 860; BEQ units 4782; Trailer spaces 31. *Temporary Housing:* VIP cottages 3; Hostess house units 73. *Commissary:* Base commissary; Retail store; Barber shop; Dry cleaners; Food shop; Florist; Banking; Service station; Bakery; Credit union; 7 day stores. *Child Care/Capacities:* Day care center; Home day care program. *Schools:* Kindergarten/Preschool; Elementary; Intermediate/Junior high; High school; Northern VA Community College; Univ of Denver, Park College; Univ of VA. *Base Library:* Yes. *Medical Facilities:* Medical clinic; Dental clinic; Branch clinics: TBS, OCS, and Camp Usher; Seasonal-open during officer candidate training. *Recreational Facilities:* Bowling; Movie theater; Pool; Gym; Golf; Stables; Tennis; Racquetball; Fitness center; Softball field; Football field; Auto shop; Officers club; NCO club; Camping; Fishing/Hunting.

RADFORD

RADFORD ARMY AMMUNITION PLANT
Caller Service 2, Radford, VA 24141-0298
(703) 639-6376
Profile
BRANCH: Army.
SIZE AND LOCATION: 4080 acres Radford; 2821 acres New River Unit. Radford Unit: near city of Radford and town of Blacksburg, N of I-81, 47 mi from Roanoke and 108 mi NE from Bristol, TN; New River Unit: just outside city of Dublin, VA, off US Rte 11.
MAJOR UNITS: US Army Armament, Munitions and Chemical Command (AMCCOM).
BASE HISTORY: 1940, construction began on site where Byron McDonald made gun powder for Revolutionary War. After WWII, standby status. Korean Conflict, reactivated. Remained in operation since. Divided between two sites: Radford Unit, all manufacturing operations, producing explosives and propellants; New River Unit, propellant storage site.
Key Contacts
COMMANDER: LTC R E D'Andrea.
Personnel and Expenditures
CIVILIAN PERSONNEL: 4000
Services *Commissary:* Base commissary.

RESTON

DEFENSE MAPPING AGENCY
12310 Sunrise Valley Dr, Reston, VA 22091-3414
(703) 264-2100
Profile
BRANCH: Department of Defense.
SIZE: Offices only.
MAJOR UNITS: See Defense Mapping Agency, Alexandria, VA 22310.
Key Contacts
COMMANDER: Capt Channing M Zucker; Director.

RICHMOND

DEFENSE GENERAL SUPPLY CENTER
8000 Jefferson Davis Hwy, Richmond, VA 23297-5000
(804) 275-3861
Profile
BRANCH: Defense Logistics Agency.
LOCATION: 8 mi S of Richmond, VA; 14 mi N of Petersburg on US Hwy-1 and 301; easily accessible from Richmond-Petersburg Tpke (I-95) via Exits 6 or 7.
MAJOR UNITS: Defense General Supply Center.

DEFENSE GENERAL SUPPLY CENTER
(continued)
BASE HISTORY: Occupies one of oldest inhabited parcels of land in US. Early 1600s settled by colonists who ventured upriver from Jamestown. 1942, established as Richmond Quartermaster Depot. 1960, became Military General Supply Agency. 1962, changed to present name upon activation of Defense Supply Agency as parent command. 1977, that headquarters became Defense Logistics Agency, extension of supply systems of individual services. Mission: supply management of military general supplies for Armed Services worldwide; also major procurement and supply responsibility for school and library materials for overseas military dependents and service libraries.
Key Contacts
COMMANDER: Rear Adm Peter A Bondi, SC, USN.
PUBLIC AFFAIRS: Scott Church; (804) 275-3139.
TRANSPORTATION: ATTN: DDRV-TT.
Personnel and Expenditures
ACTIVE DUTY PERSONNEL: 40
CIVILIAN PERSONNEL: 3400
CONTRACT EXPENDITURE: $713.8 mil

VIRGINIA OFFICE OF THE ADJUTANT GENERAL
501 E Franklin St, Richmond, VA 23219-2317
Profile
BRANCH: Air National Guard; Army National Guard.
MAJOR UNITS: See: State Military Reservation, Camp Pendleton; 192nd Tactical Fighter Group.
BASE HISTORY: HQs for VA National Guard.
Key Contacts
COMMANDER: Maj Gen John G Castles; Adjutant Gen.
PUBLIC AFFAIRS: Capt Stewart D MacInnis; (804) 344-4107.

SANDSTON

192ND TACTICAL FIGHTER GROUP
Richmond IAP, Byrd Field, Sandston, VA 23150
(804) 222-8884
Profile
BRANCH: Air National Guard.
SIZE AND LOCATION: 143 acres. 4 mi SE of Richmond directly adj to Richmond IAP; Access from I-64 and I-295 and VA Hwy 60 and 33.
MAJOR UNITS: 192nd Tactical Fighter Group.
BASE HISTORY: Units can trace lineage directly back to 328th Fighter Squadron, one of top Army Air Force fighter units of WWII. Following WWII, 328th redesignated 149th Fighter Squadron and assigned to VAANG, 1946; and 1947, located at Byrd Field. 1947, federal recognition. 1951, called to active duty and served 21 months in Korea and other overseas areas. 1953, reorganized into 149th Bombardment Squadron. 1958, redesignated Tactical Fighter Squadron. 1961-62, active duty for Berlin Crisis. 1962, received present designation.
Key Contacts
PUBLIC AFFAIRS: Capt Stewart D MacInnis; Office of the Adjutant General of Virginia, 501 E Franklin St, Richmond, VA 23219-2317, (804) 344 4107.
Personnel and Expenditures
ACTIVE DUTY PERSONNEL: 1048 Guardsmen
CIVILIAN PERSONNEL: 304
MILITARY PAYROLL EXPENDITURE: $14.8 mil
CONTRACT EXPENDITURE: $0.9 mil

VIRGINIA BEACH

DAM NECK, FLEET COMBAT TRAINING CENTER, ATLANTIC
Virginia Beach, VA 23461-5200
(804) 433-2000; Autovon 433-2000
Profile
BRANCH: Navy.
SIZE AND LOCATION: 1200 acres. On Atlantic coast, about 5 mi S of downtown resort area of Virginia Beach; 2 mi E of Rte 615.
MAJOR UNITS: Fleet Combat Training Center, Atlantic; Naval Guided Missiles School; Tactical Training Group, Atlantic; Fleet Combat Direction System Support Activity; Naval Ocean Processing Facility; Readiness Training Facility; Navy & Marine Corps Intelligence Training Center; Marine Air Control Squadron; Fleet Composite Squadron Six; Naval Education and Training Support Center, Atlantic.
BASE HISTORY: 1941, established as Anti-Aircraft Training and Test Center (Anti-Aircraft Range) to provide live firing range to train fleet gunnery crews. Only half of facility used due to wetlands. One of few Navy commands with all-military police force. Smallest Naval base in Tidewater area. Has only open ocean gunline in US.
VISITOR ATTRACTIONS: federal game preserve; Trained Sailor Statue; Gallery Plaza with two original twin 40 guns from battleship USS *Missouri*.
Key Contacts
COMMANDER: Capt R E Zunich.
PUBLIC AFFAIRS: ENS D S Watson; FCTCL PAO, (804) 433-6595; 433-6027.
Personnel and Expenditures
ACTIVE DUTY PERSONNEL: 6825
CIVILIAN PERSONNEL: 775
MILITARY PAYROLL EXPENDITURE: $105 mil (military and civilian)
Services *Housing:* Family units 31; BOQ cottages 206; BEQ units 3558; Barracks spaces. *Commissary and Exchange:* Retail store; Service station; Convenience store/Shopette; Credit union; Fast food. *Base Library:* Yes. *Medical Facilities:* Medical clinic; Dental clinic. *Recreational Facilities:* Bowling; Movie theater; Pool; Gym; Recreation center; Tennis; Softball field; Auto shop; Officers club; NCO club; Fishing/Hunting; Equipment gear rental; Weight room; Jogging trail; Beach with cabanas.

OCEANA NAVAL AIR STATION
Virginia Beach, VA 23460
(804) 433-2000; Autovon 433-1110
OFFICER-OF-THE-DAY: (804) 433-2366, Autovon 433-2366
Profile
BRANCH: Navy.
SIZE AND LOCATION: 5916 acres. Within city limits of Virginia Beach; approx 3 mi S of resort area off I-264.
MAJOR UNITS: NAS Oceana; Commander Tactical Wings, Atlantic (TACWINGSLANT); Fighter Wing One; Fighter Squadron-101 (VF-101); Fighter Squadron-43 (VF-43); Medium Attack Wing One; Attack Squadron-42 (VA-42); Fighter Squadron Composite-12 (VFC-12); Carrier Air Wing One (CVW-1); Fighter Squadron-33 (VF-33); Fighter Squadron-102 (VF-102); Attack Squadron-85 (VA-85); Carrier Air Wing Three (CVW-3); Fighter Squadron-14 (VF-14); Fighter Squadron-32 (VF-32); Attack Squadron-75 (VA-75); Carrier Air Wing Six (CVW-6); Fighter Squadron-11 (VF-11); Fighter Squadron-31 (VF-31); Attack Squadron-176 (VA-176); Carrier Wing Seven (CVW-7); Fighter Squadron-142 (VF-142); Fighter Squadron 143 (VF-143); Attack Squadron-34 (VA-34); Car-

rier Air Wing Eight (CVW-8); Fighter Squadron-41 (VF-41); Fighter Squadron-84 (VF-84); Attack Squadron-35 (VF-35); Attack Squadron-36 (VF-36); Carrier Air Wing Thirteen (CVW-13); Attack Squadron-55 (VA-55); Attack Squadron-65 (VA-65); Carrier Air Wing Seventeen (CVW-17); Fighter Squadron-74 (VF-74); Fighter Squadron-103 (VF-103); Fleet Area Control and Surveillance Facility, Virginia Capes; Naval Air Maintenance Training Group Detachments; Fleet Aviation Specialized Operational Training Group, Atlantic Fleet; Naval Construction Battalion Unit 45; Detachment 2, Southeast Air Defense Sector TAC, USAF; Naval Oceanography Command Detachment Oceana; Fleet Imaging Center Atlantic Oceana; Naval Auxiliary Landing Field Fentress.
BASE HISTORY: 1940, commissioned as auxiliary airfield; wartime growth pushed status to Naval Auxiliary Air Station. 1952, designated NAS. 1953, designated all-weather air station. 1957, designated master jet base with longest runways in Tidewater region.
Key Contacts
PUBLIC AFFAIRS: (804) 433-3131, Autovon 433-3131.
PERSONNEL/COMMUNITY ACTIVITIES: Director of Civilian Personnel; Bldg 280/282, (804) 433-3221, Autovon 433-3221.
Personnel and Expenditures
ACTIVE DUTY PERSONNEL: 10,727
DEPENDENTS: 11,500
CIVILIAN PERSONNEL: 1834
MILITARY PAYROLL EXPENDITURE: $228.6 mil
CONTRACT EXPENDITURE: $179.2 mil
Services *Housing:* Family units 528; BOQ cottages; BEQ units 13. *Commissary:* Base commissary; Retail store; Barber shop; Dry cleaners; Food shop; Florist; Banking; Service station; Convenience store/Shopette; Credit union; Laundry; Personal services center; Optical shop; Video rental; Jewelry/watch sales and repair; Package beverages; Fast food. *Child Care/Capacities:* Nursery. *Base Library:* Yes. *Medical Facilities:* Medical clinic; Dental clinic. *Recreational Facilities:* Bowling; Movie theater; Pool; Gym; Recreation center; Golf; Stables; Tennis; Racquetball; Fitness center; Softball field; Football field; Auto shop; Officers club; NCO club; Fishing/Hunting; Skeet shooting; Picnicking; Squash; Gear issue checkout.

STATE MILITARY RESERVATION, CAMP PENDLETON
PO Box 9, Virginia Beach, VA 23458
(804) 491-5140
Profile
BRANCH: Army National Guard.
SIZE AND LOCATION: 390 acres. Just S of Rudee Inlet in Virginia Beach; adj to US Fleet Anti-Air Warfare Training Center; off Atlantic Ave, extension of I-60 S.
MAJOR UNITS: 29th Light Infantry Division.
BASE HISTORY: 1887, roots at National Encampment held at Camp Fitz Lee, Montgomery County and NC; training moved to State Fair Grounds, Richmond. 1904, 71st Infantry held first paid camp at Ocean View. 1908-12, appropriated funds, land purchased, and opened as State Rifle Range. WWI, known as US Navy Rifle Range. 1920, reverted to state control. 1928, renamed State Military Reservation and Camp named for each current governor. 1930s, units from reserves, Regular Army, Navy, Marine Corps, Coast Guard, VA State Police and aviators (used parade ground as emergency landing field). 1940, Army redesignated SMR as Camp Pendleton, for Civil War general, VA native (continued in

WASHINGTON

BREMERTON

BREMERTON NAVAL HOSPITAL
Bremerton, WA 98312
(206) 479-6600; Autovon 439-6600
Profile
BRANCH: Navy.
SIZE AND LOCATION: 49 acres. 4 mi N of
    Bremerton on Rte 3.
MAJOR UNITS: Naval Hospital.
Personnel and Expenditures
ACTIVE DUTY PERSONNEL: 506
DEPENDENTS: 732
Services *Housing:* Housing administered by
Bangor NSB. *Commissary and Exchange:*
Small exchange, also use Bangor NSB and
Puget Sound Naval Shipyard. *Medical Facilities:* Hospital 155. *Recreational Facilities:*
Tennis; Softball field; Fishing/Hunting; Picnicking.

PUGET SOUND NAVAL SHIPYARD
Bremerton, WA 98314
(206) 476-3466; Autovon 439-3466
Profile
BRANCH: Navy.
SIZE AND LOCATION: 1393 acres. 60 mi W of
    Seattle on Rte 3 and 16 in Bremerton.
MAJOR UNITS: Naval Shipyard.
Personnel and Expenditures
ACTIVE DUTY PERSONNEL: 4542
DEPENDENTS: 6260
Services *Housing:* Family units 1090; BOQ
cottages 215; Barracks spaces 2500. *Commissary:* Base commissary; Retail store; Convenience store/Shopette. *Child Care/Capacities:* Day care center 85. *Medical Facilities:*
Bremerton Naval Hospital nearby. *Recreational Facilities:* Bowling; Pool; Gym; Tennis; Crafts; Park on lake.

CHENEY

FOUR LAKES COMMUNICATIONS STATION
Rte 2, Box 153A, Cheney, WA 99004-9659
(509) 459-6496; Autovon 820-7496
OFFICER-OF-THE-DAY: (509) 459-6481,
    Autovon 820-7481
Profile
BRANCH: Air National Guard.
SIZE AND LOCATION: 10 acres. 13 mi SW of
    Spokane, WA; 3.5 mi N of Cheney, WA;
    7 mi W of Fairchild AFB, WA.
MAJOR UNITS: 105th Tactical Control Squadron.
BASE HISTORY: 1955, originally built as home
    for Army Nike Missile Battery, to protect
    Fairchild AFB. 1961, closed and property
    transferred to USAF, then, leased to
    ANG, known as Four Lakes Communications Station; first ANG occupants of
    "The Hill" HQ 252nd Mobile Communications Groups and Squadron. 1971,

105th Tactical Control Squadron, "Big
    Willy" established with working agreements with USAF, ANG, Navy, and
    Army flying activities.
Key Contacts
COMMANDER: Michael D Burkhalter; (509)
    459-6492.
PUBLIC AFFAIRS: Frank E Thompson; (509)
    459-6482.
PROCUREMENT: John T Wittman; (509) 459-
    6481, Autovon 820-7481.
TRANSPORTATION: John E Rosen; (509) 459-
    6478, Autovon 820-7480.
PERSONNEL/COMMUNITY ACTIVITIES: See Public Affairs Officer.
Personnel and Expenditures
ACTIVE DUTY PERSONNEL: 5
CIVILIAN PERSONNEL: 35
Services *Medical Facilities:* Medical clinic.
Recreational Facilities: Recreation center
(base club).

FAIRCHILD AFB

FAIRCHILD AIR FORCE BASE
Fairchild AFB, WA 99011-5000
(509) 247-1212; Autovon 352-1110
OFFICER-OF-THE-DAY: (509) 247-2566,
    Autovon 352-2566
Profile
BRANCH: Air Force.
SIZE AND LOCATION: 5300 acres. Approx 12
    mi from Spokane, WA, on US Hwy 2, in
    the community of Airway Heights.
MAJOR UNITS: 92nd Bombardment Wing;
    92nd Combat Support Group; 141st Air
    Refueling Wing (ANG).
BASE HISTORY: 1942, opened on donated
    land as Spokane Army Air Depot; site
    chosen partly because of strategic defense
    location 300 miles inland behind mountain range. 1950, renamed for Gen Muir
    S Fairchild, native of Bellingham, WA.
VISITOR ATTRACTIONS: Air Force History
    Museum.
Key Contacts
COMMANDER: Col Steve Smith; 92CSG/CC,
    (509) 247-2113, Autovon 352-2113.
PUBLIC AFFAIRS: Capt Brad Peck; 92BMW/
    PA, (509) 247-5704, Autovon 352-5704.
PROCUREMENT: Maj Robert Myers; 92BMW/
    LGC, (509) 247-2161, Autovon 352-2161.
TRANSPORTATION: Maj Thomas W Ollie;
    92BMW/LGT, (509) 247-5375, Autovon
    352-5375.
PERSONNEL/COMMUNITY ACTIVITIES: Maj
    Turner Willford Jr; 92CSG/DP, (509)
    247-5063, Autovon 352-5063.
Personnel and Expenditures
ACTIVE DUTY PERSONNEL: 4368
DEPENDENTS: 4644
CIVILIAN PERSONNEL: 1252
MILITARY PAYROLL EXPENDITURE: $80.7 mil
CONTRACT EXPENDITURE: $10.3 mil

Services *Housing:* Family units 1056; BOQ
cottages 2. *Temporary Housing:* VIP cottages
2; VOQ cottages 27; VEQ units 18; VAQ
units 58; BOQ units 2; Dormitory units
1326; Transient living quarters 8. *Commissary:* Base commissary; Retail store; Barber
shop; Dry cleaners; Food shop; Florist;
Banking; Service station; Bakery; Video rental. *Child Care/Capacities:* Day care center
50; Home day care program. *Schools:* Elementary. *Base Library:* Yes. *Medical Facilities:* Hospital 45; Medical clinic; Dental clinic. *Recreational Facilities:* Bowling; Movie
theater; Pool; Gym; Recreation center; Tennis; Racquetball; Skating rink; Fitness center;
Softball field; Football field; Auto shop;
Crafts; Officers club; NCO club.

FORT LEWIS

FORT LEWIS
HQ I Corps and Ft Lewis, Fort Lewis, WA
98433-5000
(206) 967-2662; Autovon 357-2662
OFFICER-OF-THE-DAY: (206) 967-5128,
    Autovon 357-5128
Profile
BRANCH: Army.
SIZE AND LOCATION: 86,176 acres. 10 mi S of
    Tacoma, WA on I-5 Exit 120.
MAJOR UNITS: Headquarters I Corps; Headquarters 9th Infantry Division; First Brigade, 9th Infantry; Second Brigade, 9th
    Infantry; Third Brigade, 9th Infantry;
    Ninth Cavalry Brigade (Air Attack); 9th
    Infantry, Division Air Defense Artillery;
    9th Infantry Division Support Command;
    15th Engineer Battalion; 109th Military
    Intelligence Battalion; 9th Signal Battalion; Headquarters 4th ROTC Region;
    Madigan Army Medical Center; 593rd
    Area Support Group; 864th Engineer Battalion; 80th Ordnance Battalion; 29th Signal Battalion; 62nd Medical Group; 35th
    Air Defense Artillery; 502nd Military Intelligence Battalion; Law Enforcement
    Command; 2d Battalion (Ranger), 75th
    Infantry; First Special Group Readiness
    Group Ft Lewis; Army Development and
    Employment Agency; School Command.
BASE HISTORY: 1917, began service as Camp
    Lewis on land donated to federal government; named after Meriwether Lewis of
    Lewis and Clark expedition. 1926, permanent barracks constructed. 1927, became
    Ft Lewis, full-fledged Army post. During
    WWII, IX Corps and 3rd and 41st Divisions trained at Ft Lewis/Camp Murray.
    1943, POW camp established. 1944, redesignated as Army Service Forces training center, training medics and engineers.
    Following WWII, became separation center and basic training center for overseas
    occupation troops. During Korean Conflict, trained US and Canadian troops.

STATE MILITARY RESERVATION, CAMP PENDLETON *(continued)*

popular use to present although ceased to be official with state control, 1946), trained and billet coastal artillery units and later boot camp. Following WWII, annual amphibious exercises including Naval Academy and West Point. 1948, VANG resumed summer training. 1950s, received little use except classroom instruction and meetings. 1960s, rehabilitation and annual training by 107th Artillery Brigade. 1970-80s, period of rebirth. Today, a Major Training Area (MTA), Category D site, capable of supporting 900 personnel.

Key Contacts

COMMANDER: LTC T E Mendenhall; Training Site Commander.

PUBLIC AFFAIRS: Capt Stewart D MacInnis; Office of the Adjutant General of Virginia, 501 E Franklin St, Richmond, VA 23219-2317, (804) 344-4107.

Personnel and Expenditures

ACTIVE DUTY PERSONNEL: 3

CIVILIAN PERSONNEL: 20

CONTRACT EXPENDITURE: $1 mil

Services *Housing:* BOQ cottages; BEQ units; Barracks spaces 1780. *Temporary Housing:* VIP cottages; BOQ units; Guest cottages; Trailers. *Commissary and Exchange:* Barber shop; PX shoppette at Ft Story. *Medical Facilities:* Dispensary. *Recreational Facilities:* Exercise room; Sauna; Beach; Lake Christine.

WARRENTON

VINT HILL COMMUNICATIONS AND ELECTRONICS SUPPORT ACTIVITY

USACEA-VH, Warrenton, VA 22186

(703) 347-6730; Autovon 249-6730

OFFICER-OF-THE-DAY: (703) 347-6730, Autovon 249-6730

Profile

BRANCH: Army.

SIZE AND LOCATION: 721 acres. In north central VA, about 40 mi from Washington, DC, and about 15 mi W of Manassas, VA.

MAJOR UNITS: USAG-VH, HQ Co; 201st Military Intelligence Battalion; Information Systems Command.

BASE HISTORY: June 1942, government purchased all or part of 11 separate farms. Name "Vint Hill Farms" given by previous owner. 1942, troops arrived from Forts Monmouth and Hancock, NJ, to garrison post. WWII, served as Signal School, Signal Training Center and Refitting Station for selected signal units returning from combat prior to further overseas deployment.

VISITOR ATTRACTIONS: About 15 mi from Manassas Battlefield.

Key Contacts

COMMANDER: Col LeRoy A Adam; (703) 347-6212, Autovon 249-6212.

PUBLIC AFFAIRS: 1st Lt Erin C Hutson; Adjutant's Office, (703) 347-6730, Autovon 249-6730.

PROCUREMENT: Kenneth Roberts; SELCE-PC, Bldg 160, (703) 347-6245, Autovon 249-6245.

TRANSPORTATION: Anthony Fromm; SELVH-LO, Transportation Division, Bldg 228, (703) 347-6330, Autovon 249-6330.

PERSONNEL/COMMUNITY ACTIVITIES: Albert L Hutchens Jr, Acting Director; SELVH-CA, Bldg 230, (703) 347-6750, Autovon 249-6750.

Personnel and Expenditures

ACTIVE DUTY PERSONNEL: 655

DEPENDENTS: 575

CIVILIAN PERSONNEL: 990

Services *Housing:* Family units 253; BEQ units 20; Barracks spaces 445. *Temporary Housing:* VIP cottages 1; VOQ cottages ~ VEQ units 8; BOQ units 2; Guesth~ 13. *Commissary:* Base commissary; ~ store; Barber shop; Food shop; Bankin~ vice station. *Child Care/Capacities:* Day center; Home day care program. *Schools:* Kindergarten/Preschool. *Base Library:* Yes. *Medical Facilities:* Medical clinic; Dental clinic. *Recreational Facilities:* Bowling; Movie theater; Pool; Gym; Tennis; Racquetball; Softball field; Auto shop; Crafts; Officers club; NCO club.

WILLIAMSBURG

CAMP PEARY

Williamsburg, VA 23185

Profile

BRANCH: Department of Defense.

LOCATION: Off I-64 Camp Peary Exit, Rte 143; just E of Williamsburg, along York River.

MAJOR UNITS: Armed Forces Experimental Training Activity.

Key Contacts

PUBLIC AFFAIRS: Geri Taylor; Army Public Affairs Office, The Pentagon, (202) 694-0739.

NAVAL SUPPLY CENTER, CHEATHAM ANNEX

Williamsburg, VA 23187-8792

(804) 887-7108; 887-7109; Autovon 953-7108; 953-7109

OFFICER-OF-THE-DAY: (804) 887-7222, Autovon 953-7222

Profile

BRANCH: Navy.

SIZE AND LOCATION: 1579 acres. On the York River approx 5 mi outside of Williamsburg on Rte 199, approx 2 mi off of Rte 64.

MAJOR UNITS: Navy Cargo Handling & Port Group (NAVCHAPGRU); Defense Reutilization & Marketing Office (DRMO); Defense Logistics Agency (DLA); Navy Cargo Handling Training Battalion (NCHTB); Emergency Ship Salvage Materiel (ESSM); Naval Inshore Undersea Warfare Group II (IUWG2).

BASE HISTORY: Built on site of munitions plant named for Russell S Penniman, inventor of ammonia dynamite. Following WWI, plant all but disappeared, returning to farm land. A number of old buildings still stand, in use, as Ranger's Field Office and Paint Storage. Old timers still refer to area as Penniman. 1943, Naval Supply Depot named for Rear Adm Joseph Johnston Cheatham, former Chief of Bureau of Supplies and Accounts.

Key Contacts

COMMANDER: Capt K A Kowalski, SC, USN; Officer in Charge.

PUBLIC AFFAIRS: LCDR D J Hughes, SC, USN; Assistant Officer in Charge.

PROCUREMENT: Lincoln O'Brian; Code BX.43, (804) 887-7371, 887-7372, Autovon 953-7371, 953-7372.

TRANSPORTATION: Jim Haynie; Code BX.53, (804) 887-7369, Autovon 953-7369.

Personnel and Expenditures

ACTIVE DUTY PERSONNEL: 350

DEPENDENTS: 30

CIVILIAN PERSONNEL: 150

Services *Housing:* Family units 13; BEQ units 112; RV/Camper sites 19; Chiefs Qts 6. *Temporary Housing:* VIP cottages 2; Guesthouse units 8. *Commissary and Exchange:* Retail store; Barber shop; Service station. *Recreational Facilities:* Bowling; Pool; Gym; Golf; Tennis; Softball field; Camping; Fishing/Hunting.

A~
DE~
Ser~
rary ~
Excha~
ties: Dis~
Bowling; ~
Racquetba~

YORKTOW~ STATION

Yorktown, VA 2~
(804) 887-4000; A~

Profile

BRANCH: Navy.

SIZE AND LOCATION: 12~ 64, approx 5 mi S of ~ on border of Newport ~

MAJOR UNITS: Naval Mine~ ing Activity; Naval Ophth~ and Training Activity; Mar~ curity Force Company.

BASE HISTORY: 1918, established ~ Mine Depot to support laying ~ mine North Sea barrage in WW1, that time, world's largest naval res~ tion, covering about 20 sq mi. Dur~ WWII, developed mines, depth charg~ and new ordnance devices. 1953, Skif~ Creek Annex commissioned with Guide~ Missile Service Unit No 211. 1956, Nava~ Mine Engineering Facility (later Naval Mine Warfare Engineering Activity) established for mines and depth charges. 1958, name changed to US Naval Weapons Station.

VISITOR ATTRACTIONS: Lee House, circa 1650.

Personnel and Expenditures

ACTIVE DUTY PERSONNEL: 900

DEPENDENTS: 750

Services *Housing:* Family units 470; Trailer spaces 40. *Commissary:* Base commissary; Small exchange; Credit union. *Child Care/ Capacities:* Day care center 65. *Base Library:* Yes. *Recreational Facilities:* Bowling; Movie theater; Pool; Gym; Recreation center (pool tables); Golf; Stables; Tennis; Auto shop; Officers club; NCO club; Fishing/Hunting; Picnicking; Skeet shooting.

BR~
BR~
Bre~
(20~
P~
S~

FORT LEWIS (continued)

Since 1954, home to various divisions, 2nd, 3rd, 4th, 33rd, 40th, 41st, 44th, 71st, and 96th. Since 1981, home of newly reorganized I Corps.
VISITOR ATTRACTIONS: Ft Lewis Museum.

Key Contacts

COMMANDER: Lt Gen William H Harrison.
PUBLIC AFFAIRS: LTC Jay A Craig; ATTN: AFZH-PO.
PROCUREMENT: James Edwards; Director of Contracting, HQ Ft Lewis, WA 98466-5000, (206) 967-2151, Autovon 357-2151.
TRANSPORTATION: LTC James Tutton; Joint Personal Property Shipping Office, HQ Ft Lewis, WA 98466-5000, (206) 967-5099, Autovon 357-5099.
PERSONNEL/COMMUNITY ACTIVITIES: LTC James McKay; HQ Ft Lewis, WA 98466-5000, (206) 967-5335, Autovon 357-5335.

Personnel and Expenditures

ACTIVE DUTY PERSONNEL: 23,857
DEPENDENTS: 9800
CIVILIAN PERSONNEL: 6029
MILITARY PAYROLL EXPENDITURE: $502 mil
CONTRACT EXPENDITURE: $200.1 mil
Services *Housing:* Family units 3508; BOQ cottages 30; Senior NCO units 87. *Temporary Housing:* VIP cottages 5; VOQ cottages 16; Guesthouse units 75; All ranks facility 30. *Commissary:* Base commissary; Retail store; Barber shop; Dry cleaners; Food shop; Florist; Banking; Service station; Furniture store; Book store. *Child Care/Capacities:* Day care center; Home day care program. *Schools:* Kindergarten/Preschool; Elementary. *Base Library:* Yes. *Medical Facilities:* Hospital 378; Dental clinic. *Recreational Facilities:* Bowling; Movie theater; Pool; Gym; Recreation center; Golf; Tennis; Racquetball; Skating rink; Fitness center; Softball field; Football field; Auto shop; Crafts; Officers club; NCO club; Camping; Fishing/Hunting; Boating; Flying and parachuting clubs.

HADLOCK

NAVAL UNDERSEA WARFARE ENGINEERING STATION, INDIAN ISLAND DETACHMENT

Hadlock, WA 98339-5000
(206) 385-5307; Autovon 744-5307
OFFICER-OF-THE-DAY: (206) 396-5261, Autovon 744-5261

Profile

BRANCH: Navy.
SIZE AND LOCATION: 2800 acres. On Puget Sound in NE portion of Olympic Peninsula. Traveling W on Rte 104, approx 18 mi from Hood Canal Bridge. Detachment bounded on E by Marrowstone Island and on W by Hadlock. 11 mi to NW by land, and 2 mi by water, lies Port Townsend.
MAJOR UNITS: Explosive Ordnance Disposal Mobile Unit Nine, Detachment Keyport.
BASE HISTORY: 1939, bought for stowing ammunition and arming area for aircraft at NAS, Seattle. 1939-early 40s, constructed. 1959, reduced activity status and used basically for stowage purpose. 1979, reactivated as Detachment of Naval Undersea Warfare Engineering Station, Keyport. Today, active as Ordnance Depot for stowage of ammunition and on- and off-loading of Naval vessels.

Key Contacts

COMMANDER: LCDR Carroll D Bernier.
PUBLIC AFFAIRS: John Curtis; Naval Underseas Warfare Engineering Station, Keyport, WA 98345-0580, (206) 396-2699, Autovon 744-2699.
PROCUREMENT: LCDR Ben Holland; Naval Underseas Warfare Engineering Station, Keyport, WA 98345-0580, (206) 396-5236, Autovon 744-5236.

TRANSPORTATION: Bill Blazer; Naval Undersea Warfare Engineering Station, Keyport, WA 98345-0580, (206) 396-2447, Autovon 744-2447.
PERSONNEL/COMMUNITY ACTIVITIES: Lyn Coleman; Naval Undersea Warfare Engineering Station, Keyport, WA 98345-0580, (206) 396-2431, Autovon 744-2431.

Personnel and Expenditures

ACTIVE DUTY PERSONNEL: 32
DEPENDENTS: 29
CIVILIAN PERSONNEL: 170
CONTRACT EXPENDITURE: $1.2 mil
Services *Housing:* Family units 14; Townhouse units 17. *Commissary and Exchange:* Convenience store/Shopette. *Medical Facilities:* Branch medical clinic with duty corpsman. *Recreational Facilities:* Bowling; Gym; Tennis; Racquetball; Softball field.

KEYPORT

NAVAL UNDERSEA WARFARE ENGINEERING STATION

Keyport, WA 98345-0580
(206) 396-2699; Autovon 744-2699
OFFICER-OF-THE-DAY: (206) 396-2551, Autovon 744-2551

Profile

BRANCH: Navy.
SIZE AND LOCATION: 250 acres. 12 mi N of Bremerton & Puget Sound Naval Shipyard; 5 mi E of Submarine Base, Bangor, on State Hwy 308.
MAJOR UNITS: Naval Undersea Warfare Engineering Station.
BASE HISTORY: 1914, Pacific Coast Torpedo Station commissioned. 1930, name changed to US Naval Torpedo Station. 1950, NTS and Naval Ammunition Depot, Bangor merged to become US Naval Ordnance Depot, Puget Sound. 1970, NAD Bangor disestablished and residual functions transferred to NTS. 1974, HI detachment established. 1976, Social, Hawthorne, and Indian Island Detachment established. 1978, name changed to current name.
VISITOR ATTRACTIONS: The Naval Museum of Undersea Warfare.

Key Contacts

COMMANDER: Capt Robert W Hoag II.
PUBLIC AFFAIRS: John L Curtis; Code 06PAO.
PROCUREMENT: LCDR Benjamin Holland; (206) 396-2211, Autovon 744-2211.
TRANSPORTATION: See Procurement Officer.
PERSONNEL/COMMUNITY ACTIVITIES: L R Coleman; (206) 396-2431, Autovon 744-2431.

Personnel and Expenditures

ACTIVE DUTY PERSONNEL: 300
DEPENDENTS: 150
CIVILIAN PERSONNEL: 3200
MILITARY PAYROLL EXPENDITURE: $300 mil
CONTRACT EXPENDITURE: $6 mil
Services *Housing:* Family units 25; BEQ units 1; Senior NCO units 1; Junior NCO units 13. *Commissary and Exchange:* Retail store; Barber shop; Food shop; Service station; Credit union. *Base Library:* Yes. *Medical Facilities:* Medical clinic. *Recreational Facilities:* Gym; Tennis; Softball field; Auto shop; Crafts; All hands club.

MCCHORD AFB

MCCHORD AIR FORCE BASE

62nd Military Airlift Wing, McChord AFB, WA 98438-5000
(206) 984-1910; Autovon 976-1110

Profile

BRANCH: Air Force.
SIZE AND LOCATION: 4535 acres. 3 mi S of Tacoma, WA; I-5 passes approx 0.5 mi away.
MAJOR UNITS: 62nd Military Airlift Wing (Host); 25th Air Division; 446th Military Airlift Wing (Reserve).
BASE HISTORY: 1920s-1930s, Tacoma Pierce County Airport occupied site of McChord Field. 1938, airfield deeded to federal government. 1940, dedicated as McChord Field, named for Col William C McChord killed in bomber crash in VA, 1937. 1941, British crews trained on British Fortress I versions of Flying Fortress bombers. During WWII, McChord trained fliers; participated in 1942 Doolittle bombing raid on Tokyo. 1944, massive overhaul center established to refurbish fighters. Postwar, became major airlift center. 1947, 62nd Troop Carrier Group and Wing came to McChord. 1950, became part of Air Defense Command's 25th Air Division. 1960s-early 1970s, major port for equipment and troops during Vietnam War. 1968, transferred to MAC.
VISITOR ATTRACTIONS: McChord Air Museum.

Key Contacts

COMMANDER: Col Edwin E Tenoso; 62nd MAW/CC, (206) 984-2621, Autovon 976 2601.
PUBLIC AFFAIRS: Capt John Litten; 62nd MAW/PA, (206) 984-5637, Autovon 976 5630.

Personnel and Expenditures

ACTIVE DUTY PERSONNEL: 5662
DEPENDENTS: 2431
CIVILIAN PERSONNEL: 1982
MILITARY PAYROLL EXPENDITURE: $134.2 mil (military and civilian)
CONTRACT EXPENDITURE: $66.6 mil
Services *Housing:* Family units 981. *Temporary Housing:* BOQ units; BAQ units; Dormitory units. *Commissary:* Base commissary; Retail store; Barber shop; Dry cleaners; Food shop; Florist; Banking; Service station; Bakery; Book store; Convenience store/Shopette; Garden center; Computer store; Deli; Jewelry/watch sales and repair; Video rental; Snacks. *Child Care/Capacities:* Day care center 200. *Schools:* Kindergarten/Preschool; Elementary. *Base Library:* Yes. *Medical Facilities:* Medical clinic; Dental clinic; Madigan Army Medical Center 4 mi away. *Recreational Facilities:* Bowling; Movie theater; Pool; Gym; Recreation center; Golf; Tennis; Racquetball; Fitness center; Softball field; Football field; Auto shop; Crafts; Officers club; NCO club; Camping; Fishing/Hunting; Rod and Gun Club; Picnicking; Horseshoe pit.

NEAH BAY

MAKAH AIR FORCE STATION

Neah Bay, WA 98357
(206) 645-2231

Profile

BRANCH: Air Force.
MAJOR UNITS: Makah AFS (TAC).

OAK HARBOR

WHIDBEY ISLAND NAVAL AIR STATION

Oak Harbor, WA 98278-5000
(206) 257-2211; Autovon 820-2211
OFFICER-OF-THE-DAY: (206) 257-2631, Autovon 820-2631

WHIDBEY ISLAND NAVAL AIR STATION
(continued)
Profile
BRANCH: Navy.
SIZE AND LOCATION: Ault Field 4362 acres; Seaplane Base 2793 acres. In middle of Puget Sound, 80 mi NW of Seattle. Oak Harbor 2 mi from NAS. Driving: take I-5 N, exit on Anacortes/Whidbey exit 230, continue W on Hwy 20 following signs to Oak Harbor/Whidbey Island. Ferry N of Seattle at Mukilteo, watch for Mukilteo exit on I-5 in Everett area; ferry crosses on hourly basis to S Whidbey, from there 45 min drive to NAS.
MAJOR UNITS: Commander, Medium Attack Tactical Electronic Warfare Wing, US Pacific Fleet; Marine Aviation Training Support Group; Marine Aircraft Group 42, Detachment C; Naval Oceanography Command Detachment; Naval Communications Detachment, Whidbey Island; Fleet Aviation Specialized Operational Training Group Pacific, Detachment Whidbey Island; Explosive Ordnance Disposal Group 1 Detachment Whidbey Island; Naval Air Reserve; Navy Calibration Laboratory; Naval Hospital.
BASE HISTORY: 1942, commissioned on largest island in continental US. 1943, field designated Ault Field for CDR William B Ault, missing, Battle of Coral Sea. Originally built for seaplane patrol operations, rocket firing training, torpedo overhaul, and recruit and petty officer training. End of WWII-1949, reduced operating status. Today, home of all Navy electronic warfare squadrons flying EA-6B "Prowler," carrier-based tactical jamming aircraft; W coast training and operations center for A-6 "Intruder" attack bomber squadrons; and, Naval and Marine Air Reserve training activities center, Northwest. Composed of two bases 5 mi apart: Seaplane Base and NAS, known as Ault Field. NAS contains most of station's military activities. Seaplane Base on eastern shore at edge of Oak Harbor. Also under jurisdiction of NAS is Outlying Field, Coupeville; Boardman Bombing Range, Boardman OR; and, Radar Bomb Scoring Unit, Spokane, WA.
Key Contacts
COMMANDER: Capt Donald B Sehlin; (206) 257-2345, Autovon 820-2345.
PUBLIC AFFAIRS: Howard Thomas; (206) 257-2287, Autovon 820-2287.
PROCUREMENT: CDR Don Pendarvis; (206) 257-2441, Autovon 820-2441.
TRANSPORTATION: CDR Terry Dillon.
PERSONNEL/COMMUNITY ACTIVITIES: LCDR Richard Littke; (206) 257-2641, Autovon 820-2641.
Personnel and Expenditures
ACTIVE DUTY PERSONNEL: 8100
DEPENDENTS: 13,600
CIVILIAN PERSONNEL: 1750
MILITARY PAYROLL EXPENDITURE: $205.8 mil
CONTRACT EXPENDITURE: $15.3 mil
Services *Housing:* Family units 1446; BOQ cottages 174; BEQ units 1131; RV/Camper sites 20. *Commissary:* Base commissary; Retail store; Barber shop; Dry cleaners; Food shop; Florist; Banking; Service station; Furniture store; Bakery; Book store. *Child Care/Capacities:* Day care center. *Base Library:* Yes. *Medical Facilities:* Hospital 35; Dental clinic; (addition to be completed by March 1991). *Recreational Facilities:* Bowling; Movie theater; Gym; Recreation center; Golf; Tennis; Racquetball; Fitness center; Softball field; Football field; Auto shop; Crafts; Officers club; NCO club; Camping; Fishing/Hunting; Archery; Motorcross.

PACIFIC BEACH

PACIFIC NORTHWEST FLEET RECREATION AND EDUCATION SUPPORT CENTER
Pacific Beach, WA 98571
(206) 526-3600; Autovon 941-3600
Profile
BRANCH: Navy.
SIZE AND LOCATION: 53 acres. On W coast of WA, 150 mi SW of Seattle and reached by highways connecting to I-5 from Seattle and Portland; from US-101 Coastal Hwy and US-12 from Yakima.
BASE HISTORY: Operated expressly for active duty military community; retired military personnel and DOD civilians welcome on space available basis; reservations must be made in advance.
Key Contacts
PUBLIC AFFAIRS: Reservations; Ocean Getaway, Recreation Services, Bldg 47/Code 60, Naval Station Puget Sound, Seattle, WA 98115-5014.
Services *Housing:* RV/Camper sites 43. *Temporary Housing:* Cabins 28; Suites 4. *Recreational Facilities:* Fishing/Hunting; Beach; Hiking.

SEATTLE

FORT LAWTON
4575 36th Ave W, Seattle, WA 98199-5000
(206) 281-3026; Autovon 744-3026
Profile
BRANCH: Army.
SIZE AND LOCATION: 75 acres. Approx 5 mi NW of downtown Seattle in Magnolia Community area; approx 17 mi N of Seattle-Tacoma IAP; adj to Discovery Park, operated by city of Seattle. From airport, take I-5 N to Mercer St Exit, turn right on Fairview Ave N, turn left on Valley St, turn right on Westlake Ave N, continue onto Nickerson, turn left on W Emerson, turn right on Gilman, turn right on 36th W.
MAJOR UNITS: Headquarters 124th US Army Reserve Command; 104th Training Division (USAR).
Key Contacts
COMMANDER: Maj Gen Clyde R Cherberg; Commander, 124th USARCOM, (206) 281-3019, Autovon 744-3019.
PUBLIC AFFAIRS: Maj Wanda Arceneaux; HQ 124th USARCOM, ATTN: AFKC-ACD-PAO, (206) 281-3026, Autovon 744-3026.
PROCUREMENT: DCSLOG; HQ 124th USARCOM, ATTN: AFKC-ACD-LG, (206) 281-3022, Autovon 744-3022.
PERSONNEL/COMMUNITY ACTIVITIES: DCSPER; HQ 124th USARCOM, ATTN: AFKC-ACD-PR, (206) 281-3031, Autovon 744-3031.
Personnel and Expenditures
ACTIVE DUTY PERSONNEL: 50
CIVILIAN PERSONNEL: 110
CONTRACT EXPENDITURE: $0.5 mil
Services *Housing:* Family units; Operated by Commander, Naval Base, Seattle. *Commissary and Exchange:* Retail store.

PUGET SOUND NAVAL STATION
7500 Sandpoint Way, Seattle, WA 98115-5001
(206) 526-3487; Autovon 941-3487
OFFICER-OF-THE-DAY: (206) 526-3212, Autovon 941-3212
Profile
BRANCH: Navy.
LOCATION: 15 min from Seattle on Lake Washington; 1 hr from Seattle Airport; 5 min E of Univ of Washington.
MAJOR UNITS: COMNAVBASE Seattle; SUPSHIPS Seattle; DCASMA; Reserve Readiness Command Region 22; COMINEGRU 1.
BASE HISTORY: 1925, NAS Seattle at Sand Point established on land donated by King County. Army's first around-the-world flight began and ended. WWII, operated cargo flights to AK and Aleutian Islands; escort carriers and seaplane tenders built in Tacoma and Vancouver outfitted at station prior to fleet duty. Following WWII, designated Naval Reserve Air Station. 1970, aviation operations ceased when NAS Seattle decommissioned and Naval operations such as supply, billeting, and administration transferred to Commandant, 13th Naval District, DOD activities and federal agencies, as well as ships in Seattle area. 1982, Naval Station Seattle established as echelon 4 activity under Commander, Naval Logistics Command, Pacific Fleet. 1986, name changed to Naval Station Puget Sound to reflect expanded fleet support mission at both Seattle and Everett locations.
Key Contacts
COMMANDER: Capt Eugene S Dvornick; (206) 526-3325, Autovon 941-3325.
PROCUREMENT: Lt E Eichenmiller; (206) 526-3437, Autovon 941-3437.
TRANSPORTATION: LCDR Cowan; (206) 526-3844, Autovon 941-3844.
Personnel and Expenditures
ACTIVE DUTY PERSONNEL: 3600
Services *Housing:* Family units; BEQ units; BAQ units; Barracks spaces; Total units 195. *Temporary Housing:* BOQ units; BAQ units; Transient living quarters. *Commissary:* Base commissary; Retail store; Barber shop; Dry cleaners; Food shop; Florist; Banking; Service station; Furniture store; Bakery. *Base Library:* Yes. *Medical Facilities:* Medical clinic; Dental clinic. *Recreational Facilities:* Bowling; Movie theater; Pool; Gym; Recreation center; Tennis; Racquetball; Fitness center; Softball field; Football field; Auto shop; Crafts; Officers club; NCO club.

SEATTLE COAST GUARD SUPPORT CENTER
1519 Alaskan Way S, Seattle, WA 98134
(206) 286-9650; FTS 396-9650
OFFICER-OF-THE-DAY: (206) 286-9696, FTS 396-9696
Profile
BRANCH: Coast Guard.
SIZE AND LOCATION: 2 acres. In downtown Seattle at waterfront Pier 36; approx 10 mi from Seattle-Tacoma Airport, and North Annex on Lake Washington Ship Canal.
MAJOR UNITS: USGC Group Seattle; Marine Safety Office Seattle; Vessel Traffic Service Seattle; CGC *Polar Sea*; CGC *Polar Star*; CGC *Boutwell*; Ship Repair Detachment.
BASE HISTORY: 1926, Pier 36 built by Pacific Steamship Terminal Co. 1940, Pier 36 acquired for Port of Embarkation. 1941, Pier 37 constructed to expand port facilities. 1960, occupied by Army Corps of Engineers and used as district HQs. 1966, USCG acquired site. 1975, commissioned to provide services and support to Thirteenth Coast Guard District commands in Seattle area. Since commissioning, Center home to numerous vessels and various commands. Today, host to six ships and five shore based units. Planned acquisition of Pier 35 would bring all personnel together. Responsibilities include moorage and port services for floating units, office and work space for shore based commands, personnel and pay support ser-

SEATTLE COAST GUARD SUPPORT CENTER *(continued)*

vices, logistics support and transient personnel administration.

VISITOR ATTRACTIONS: Polar class ice breakers; 378 ft cutter; Coast Guard Museum; Tours of MSO and UTS facilities.

Key Contacts

COMMANDER: Capt Michael B Dunn.

PUBLIC AFFAIRS: LTjg Bryan Beard; (206) 286-9695, FTS 396-9695.

PROCUREMENT: Lt Melsesto Gonzalez; (206) 286-9721, FTS 396-9721.

TRANSPORTATION: LCDR Brian White; (206) 286-9672, FTS 396-9672.

PERSONNEL/COMMUNITY ACTIVITIES: CWO2 Mark Carter; (206) 286-9650, FTS 396-9650.

Personnel and Expenditures

ACTIVE DUTY PERSONNEL: 300

CIVILIAN PERSONNEL: 25

Services *Housing:* BEQ units 20. *Commissary:* Base commissary; Retail store; Barber shop; Dry cleaners; Food shop; Florist. *Medical Facilities:* Medical clinic; Dental clinic. *Recreational Facilities:* Gym; Tennis; Racquetball; Fitness center.

13TH COAST GUARD DISTRICT OFFICE

915 Second Ave, Seattle, WA 98174-1067

(206) 442-5078

OFFICER-OF-THE-DAY: (206) 442-5886

Profile

BRANCH: Coast Guard.

SIZE AND LOCATION: Offices only. In the Federal Bldg, downtown Seattle.

MAJOR UNITS: 13th District Office.

Key Contacts

COMMANDER: Rear Adm Robert E Kramek; Commander.

PUBLIC AFFAIRS: Lt E K Delong Jr; (206) 442-5896.

Personnel and Expenditures

ACTIVE DUTY PERSONNEL: 153

CIVILIAN PERSONNEL: 50

Services *Commissary and Exchange:* At Pier 36 Coast Guard Complex, 0.5 mi away. *Recreational Facilities:* At Pier 36 Coast Guard Complex, 0.5 mi away.

SILVERDALE

BANGOR NAVAL SUBMARINE BASE

Silverdale, WA 98315-5000

(206) 396-4843; Autovon 744-4843

OFFICER-OF-THE-DAY: (206) 396-4800, Autovon 744-4800

Profile

BRANCH: Navy.

SIZE AND LOCATION: 7000 acres. On the Hood Canal, approx 1 hr drive from Seattle/Tacoma area; nearby communities of Bremerton and Silverdale.

MAJOR UNITS: Trident Training Facility, Bangor; Trident Refit Facility, Bangor; Strategic Weapons Facility, Pacific; Commander, Submarine Group 9; Commander, Submarine Squadron 17; Naval Communications Station, Puget Sound; Personnel Support Activity, Puget Sound; Marine Corps Security Force Company, Bangor.

BASE HISTORY: 1945, commissioned as Naval Ammunition Depot, Bangor Annex; Pacific Coast transshipment point for ammunition and explosives. 1963, Polaris Missile Facility, Pacific established. 1974, redesignated Strategic Weapons Facility, Pacific; work began at Bangor support site. 1973, homeport for new OHIO-class submarine. 1977, commissioning of Naval Submarine Base, Bangor. 1981, base fully operational with arrival of first Trident submarine, USS *Ohio*.

VISITOR ATTRACTIONS: Not open to the public.

Key Contacts

COMMANDER: Capt William D Hahn; (206) 396-4949, Autovon 744-4949.

PUBLIC AFFAIRS: LCDR Keith Arterburn; Code 005, Public Affairs Office, (206) 396-4843, Autovon 744-4843.

PROCUREMENT: CDR Mike Moran; Supply Officer, Code N5, (206) 396-4216, Autovon 744-4216.

TRANSPORTATION: K Dean Robison; Code 822, (206) 396-4216, Autovon 744-4216.

PERSONNEL/COMMUNITY ACTIVITIES: Project Manager, Morale, Welfare & Recreation, (206) 779-9907.

Personnel and Expenditures

ACTIVE DUTY PERSONNEL: 5441

DEPENDENTS: 2157

CIVILIAN PERSONNEL: 2682

MILITARY PAYROLL EXPENDITURE: $141 mil

CONTRACT EXPENDITURE: $40 mil

Services *Housing:* Family units 799; BEQ units 600; BAQ units 66. *Temporary Housing:* VIP cottages 1; BOQ units 46; BEQ 308. *Commissary:* Base commissary; Retail store; Barber shop; Dry cleaners; Food shop; Florist; Banking; Service station. *Child Care/ Capacities:* Day care center 112. *Base Library:* Yes. *Medical Facilities:* Medical clinic; Dental clinic; Naval Hospital Bremerton, 10 mi away. *Recreational Facilities:* Bowling; Movie theater; Pool; Gym; Recreation center; Tennis; Racquetball; Fitness center; Softball field; Football field; Auto shop; Crafts; Officers club; NCO club; Fishing/Hunting.

SPOKANE

MICA PEAK AIR FORCE STATION

Spokane, WA 99023

(509) 247-2669

Profile

BRANCH: Air Force.

MAJOR UNITS: Mica Peak AFS (TAC).

TACOMA

MADIGAN ARMY MEDICAL CENTER

PO Box 323, Tacoma, WA 98431

(206) 967-6230; 967-6594; Autovon 357-6230; 357-6594

Profile

BRANCH: Army.

SIZE AND LOCATION: 120 acres. Fort Lewis, WA.

MAJOR UNITS: Company A; Company B.

BASE HISTORY: Originally established as Ft Lewis Station Hospital during WWI. 1944, became Madigan General Hospital named for Col Patrick Sarsfield Madigan, assistant to Surgeon General, US Army from 1940-43, known as Father of Army Neuropsychiatry. 1973, redesignated Madigan Army Medical Center and assigned to US Army Health Services Command, Ft Sam Houston, TX. Responsibilities include Army, Navy, and Air Force installations in WA, OR, MT, ID, and AK; 8 troop clinics and 21 aid stations at Ft Lewis; and, health clinics at Yakima Firing Center and Umatilla, OR; also provides training, research, and logistical support; largest and busiest military hospital on West Coast.

Key Contacts

COMMANDER: Brig Gen John Hutton.

PUBLIC AFFAIRS: Chris Hober.

Personnel and Expenditures

ACTIVE DUTY PERSONNEL: 1190

CIVILIAN PERSONNEL: 930

Services *Temporary Housing:* BOQ units; BAQ units; Guesthouse units 10. *Commissary and Exchange:* Retail store; Barber shop; Dry cleaners; Florist; Banking. *Base*

Library: Yes. *Medical Facilities:* Hospital 378; Medical clinic; Dental clinic. *Recreational Facilities:* Pool; Gym; Recreation center; Tennis; Racquetball; Fitness center; Softball field; Football field; Crafts; Officers club; NCO club.

WALLA WALLA

US ARMY CORPS OF ENGINEERS, WALLA WALLA DISTRICT

Bldg 602, City-County Airport, Walla Walla, WA 99362-9265

(509) 522-6660

Profile

BRANCH: Army.

SIZE AND LOCATION: Offices only. At the City-County Airport in Walla Walla.

MAJOR UNITS: Corps of Engineers.

BASE HISTORY: History of District linked directly to development of water resource projects on Columbia and Snake rivers. 1948, establishment coincided with work on McNary Dam on Columbia River near Tri-Cities, WA. District generally follows Snake River drainage and includes more than 114,000 sq mi in 6 states: WA, OR, ID, WY, and small portions of NV and UT.

Personnel and Expenditures

CIVILIAN PERSONNEL: 585

CONTRACT EXPENDITURE: $70.8 mil

YAKIMA

WASHINGTON ARMY NATIONAL GUARD MOBILIZATION AND TRAINING EQUIPMENT SITE

Bldg 951, Yakima Firing Center, Yakima, WA 98901-5000

(509) 575-2602; Autovon 355-8261

Profile

BRANCH: Army National Guard.

SIZE AND LOCATION: 20 acres. 10 mi N of Yakima off of I-82; take Firing Center exit, E approx 1.5 mi.

MAJOR UNITS: Washington Army National Guard.

BASE HISTORY: MATES, tenant facility located on Yakima Firing Center; NG equipment pool and maintenance facility.

Key Contacts

COMMANDER: LTC Garold W Luthy.

PUBLIC AFFAIRS: Maj Joe Jimenez; Camp Murray, Tacoma, WA 98430-5000, (206) 581-1481, Autovon 355-7481.

PROCUREMENT: USPFO for WA, Camp Murray, Tacoma, WA 98430-5000, (206) 581-1290, Autovon 355-7290.

TRANSPORTATION: CWO Bud Newman; USPFO for WA, Camp Murray, Tacoma, WA 98430-5000, (206) 581-1301, Autovon 355-7301.

Personnel and Expenditures

CIVILIAN PERSONNEL: 76

Services *Commissary and Exchange:* Through the Yakima Firing Center.

YAKIMA FIRING CENTER

Yakima, WA 98901-5000

(509) 454-8206; Autovon 355-8206

OFFICER-OF-THE-DAY: (509) 454-8300, Autovon 355-8300

Profile

BRANCH: Army.

SIZE AND LOCATION: 263,131 acres. Approx 10 mi from Yakima City; take Firing Center Exit from I-82.

MAJOR UNITS: Company A, USAG; Company B, USAG (MPIS); 53rd EOD; 1119th Signal Battalion; Washington Army National Guard; 81st Infantry Brigade; 95th Heavy Equipment Maintenance Company.

YAKIMA FIRING CENTER *(continued)*

BASE HISTORY: Just before WWII, Army leased land for what was to become Yakima Anti-Aircraft Artillery Range. 1941, used for both range firing and small unit tests. 1942, first camp constructed on Umtanum Ridge, 13 mi NE of present cantonment area. 1942-43, Yakima Firing Center constructed on present site. 1946-47, use greatly curtailed and approx 60,000 acres returned to original owners. 1949-50, used for summer training of WA NG Units. 1951, Army expanded facility for training requirements. 1955, 10 ranges named for Yakima Valley war heroes: William H Perkins, Merl H Todd, Frank R Goulet, James Russell, Dolph Barnett Jr, Winfield M Black, Joseph H Carvo, Herbert E Lane, Jack J Pendleton, and James B Kinyon. 1965-72, used by Reservists and Guardsmen on weekend and summer camp training; with activation of 9th Infantry Division, Center became training center for Ft Lewis. 1977-78, test site for Improved TOW Vehicle (ITV); terrain ideal for artillery, tank, mortar, recoilless weapons, and small arms training exercises.

Key Contacts

COMMANDER: ATTN: AFZH-Y-IC.

PUBLIC AFFAIRS: Kenneth Cooper; ATTN: AFZH-Y-DPCA, (509) 454-8201, Autovon 355-8201.

PROCUREMENT: Barbara Champlin; ATTN: AFZH-Y-DOC, (509) 454-8420, Autovon 355-8420.

TRANSPORTATION: Robert Hester; ATTN: AFZH-Y-TMP, (509) 454-8409, Autovon 355-8409.

PERSONNEL/COMMUNITY ACTIVITIES: See Public Affairs Officer.

Personnel and Expenditures

ACTIVE DUTY PERSONNEL: 107

CIVILIAN PERSONNEL: 61

CONTRACT EXPENDITURE: $0.5 mil

Services *Housing:* Senior NCO units 9; Junior NCO units 60. *Temporary Housing:* VIP cottages 1; VOQ cottages 7; VEQ units 4; Transient living quarters 12. *Commissary and Exchange:* Retail store; Barber shop; Food shop; Cafeteria. *Base Library:* Yes. *Medical Facilities:* Medical clinic; Dental clinic. *Recreational Facilities:* Gym; Recreation center; Racquetball; Softball field; Auto shop; Crafts; Camping (trailer rental); Combined club.

WEST VIRGINIA

CHARLESTON

130TH TACTICAL AIRLIFT GROUP (ANG)

Kanawha Airport, Charleston, WV 25311
(304) 342-6194; Autovon 366-9210
Profile
BRANCH: Air National Guard.
SIZE AND LOCATION: 218 acres. 4 mi NE of Charleston, off US-119.
MAJOR UNITS: 130th Tactical Airlift Group (ANG).
Personnel and Expenditures
ACTIVE DUTY PERSONNEL: 900
CIVILIAN PERSONNEL: 179
MILITARY PAYROLL EXPENDITURE: $7.9 mil
Services *Medical Facilities:* Dispensary; Clinic.

KINGWOOD

CAMP DAWSON, ARMY TRAINING SITE

Rte 2, Box 1, Kingwood, WV 26537
(304) 329-3350; Autovon 366-9376
OFFICER-OF-THE-DAY: (304) 329-3350, Autovon 366-9376
Profile
BRANCH: Army National Guard.
SIZE AND LOCATION: 1 mil acres. Served by nearby airports, Morgantown, WV, approx 30 mi NW; Clarksburg, WV, approx 45 mi SW; and Elkins, WV, approx 60 mi S. Major highways serving the area are US 48, 50, and 219. Routes into Camp Dawson are WV State Rte 7, 26, and 72.
MAJOR UNITS: Det 3, HD WV-STARC; WV Military Academy; Co C, 2/19th Special Forces Group; Service Btry ½ 01st Field Artillery; 229th Engineer Detachment.
BASE HISTORY: Regional "major training area" for many types of units from all branches of Armed Forces. Nestled in WV Hills, offers unique terrain and serenity. Ideal site for conferences and most types of management training; also offers rugged mountainous regions for readiness training.
VISITOR ATTRACTIONS: Within driving distance of many historic sites and resort areas.
Key Contacts
COMMANDER: Col Bruce Moss.
PUBLIC AFFAIRS: SSG F E Onestinghel.
PROCUREMENT: CW3 Wilber Bolyard.
PERSONNEL/COMMUNITY ACTIVITIES: CW4 Terry Butcher.
Personnel and Expenditures
ACTIVE DUTY PERSONNEL: AGR14; NG236
CIVILIAN PERSONNEL: 14
Services *Housing:* BOQ cottages 4; BEQ units 4; Duplex units 30; Barracks spaces 1000; Senior NCO units 3; RV/Camper sites 1. *Temporary Housing:* VIP cottages 2; VOQ cottages 2; VEQ units 2; Guest cottages 1. *Commissary and Exchange:* PX. *Medical Facilities:* Troop clinic. *Recreational Facilities:* Golf; Softball field; Football field; Camping; Fishing/Hunting.

MARTINSBURG

167TH TACTICAL AIRLIFT GROUP (ANG)

Eastern West Virginia Regional Airport, Martinsburg, WV 25401
(304) 263-0801; Autovon 242-9210
Profile
BRANCH: Air National Guard.
SIZE AND LOCATION: 279 acres. 4 mi S of Martinsburg.
MAJOR UNITS: 167th Tactical Airlift Group (ANG).
Personnel and Expenditures
ACTIVE DUTY PERSONNEL: 880
CIVILIAN PERSONNEL: 175
MILITARY PAYROLL EXPENDITURE: $7.7 mil
Services *Medical Facilities:* Dispensary.

SUGAR GROVE

SUGAR GROVE NAVAL RADIO STATION

Sugar Grove, WV 26815
(304) 246-6300; Autovon 564-7276
OFFICER-OF-THE-DAY: (304) 246-6300, Autovon 564-7276
Profile
BRANCH: Navy.
SIZE AND LOCATION: 500 acres. 5 mi S of Brandywine, WV on State Rte 21.
MAJOR UNITS: Naval Security Group Detachment.
BASE HISTORY: Established 1965; operates as a radio receiving station since then.
Key Contacts
COMMANDER: LCDR Jerry Dearbeck.
PUBLIC AFFAIRS: See Base Commander.
PROCUREMENT: SKC Buckholtz; (304) 246-6370, Autovon 564-6370.
TRANSPORTATION: Marge Cowser; (304) 246-6305, Autovon 564-6305.
PERSONNEL/COMMUNITY ACTIVITIES: Bob Hoops; (304) 249-6360, Autovon 564-6360.
Personnel and Expenditures
ACTIVE DUTY PERSONNEL: 160
DEPENDENTS: 150
CIVILIAN PERSONNEL: 42
MILITARY PAYROLL EXPENDITURE: $1.5 mil
CONTRACT EXPENDITURE: $1.2 mil
Services *Housing:* Family units 50; BEQ units 30. *Commissary:* Base commissary; Retail store; Barber shop; Food shop. *Base Library:* Yes. *Medical Facilities:* Medical clinic. *Recreational Facilities:* Bowling; Pool; Gym; Recreation center; Tennis; Racquetball; Fitness center; Softball field; Football field; Auto shop; Crafts; NCO club.

WISCONSIN

BARABOO

BADGER ARMY AMMUNITION PLANT

Baraboo, WI 53913-5000
(608) 356-5525; Autovon 280-9600
Profile
BRANCH: Army.
SIZE AND LOCATION: 7400 acres. On US Hwy 12, 8 mi S of Baraboo, WI, 6 mi N of Prairie du Sac/Sauk City, 38 mi NW of Madison, WI.
Personnel and Expenditures
CIVILIAN PERSONNEL: 350
CONTRACT EXPENDITURE: $12 mil
Services *Base Library:* Yes.

CAMP DOUGLAS

HARDWOOD AIR-TO-GROUND WEAPONS RANGE

Camp Douglas, WI 54618
(608) 427-1210; Autovon 798-3210
Profile
BRANCH: Air National Guard.
SIZE AND LOCATION: 7680 acres. N of Necedah, WI, near the town of Finley.
BASE HISTORY: 1954, when federal government leased Volk Field from WI State as permanent air training site, work also began on this air-to-ground range. 1955, initial construction completed; range used to meet variety of missions, from tactical fighter units to specialized weapons systems testing, such as "Strike Eagle" F 15 field testing. Today, used by units from all over mid-west, including all flying units assigned to Volk Field. Class A range: manned, scoring capability from ground, and Range Control Officer on ground who controls aircraft using range. Munitions employed are all inert or practice ordnance; also capable of night bombing and providing simulated threats to aircrews.
VISITOR ATTRACTIONS: Visits to range in operation can be arranged, call (608) 565-2884; annual open house also held.
Key Contacts
COMMANDER: Capt James E Pitchford.
PUBLIC AFFAIRS: See Volk Field Air National Guard Base.

VOLK FIELD AIR NATIONAL GUARD BASE

Camp Douglas, WI 54618-5001
(608) 427-1210; Autovon 798-3210
OFFICER-OF-THE-DAY: (608) 427-1212, Autovon 798-3212

Profile
BRANCH: Air National Guard.
SIZE AND LOCATION: 2336 acres. One-half mi N of Village of Camp Douglas; on I-90/94 N off Exit 55; approx 90 mi NW of Madison; 50 mi E of LaCrosse.
MAJOR UNITS: ANG Field Training Site (FTS).
BASE HISTORY: Military post can be traced back to 1889. 1927, named Camp Williams, for LTC Charles R Williams, Chief Quartermaster of post, 1917-1926. 1935-36, first hard-surfaced runways constructed. Following WWII, WI NG grew into Army and ANG. 1947, Army NG began training at Camp McCoy and ANG squadron Camp Williams. 1954, federal government leased field as permanent air training site. 1957, name changed to present name for 1st Lt Jerome A Volk, first WI ANG pilot killed in Korean War. Today, used year-round for training of ANG and deploying military units representing all branches.
VISITOR ATTRACTIONS: Wisconsin National Guard Museum; Static display of ANG aircraft.
Key Contacts
COMMANDER: LTC Robert D Green; (608) 427-1200, Autovon 798-3200.
PUBLIC AFFAIRS: TSgt Leo V Clark; (608) 427-1271, Autovon 798-3271.
PROCUREMENT: SMSgt Richard A Sommerfeldt; (608) 427-1234, Autovon 798-3234.
TRANSPORTATION: MSgt John A Greenwell; (608) 427-1233, Autovon 798-3233.
PERSONNEL/COMMUNITY ACTIVITIES: See Public Affairs Officer.
Personnel and Expenditures
ACTIVE DUTY PERSONNEL: 60 ANG Active Guard-Reserve
CIVILIAN PERSONNEL: 45
MILITARY PAYROLL EXPENDITURE: FY 88 $2.8 mil
CONTRACT EXPENDITURE: FY 88 $2.5 mil
Services *Housing:* Barracks spaces; RV/Camper sites 16; NCO dorms. *Temporary Housing:* VIP cottages 8; VOQ cottages 57; VAQ units 1129; Transient living quarters 13. *Commissary and Exchange:* Retail store; Branch Exchange of Ft McCoy. *Medical Facilities:* Hospital 6; Medical clinic; Dental clinic. *Recreational Facilities:* Movie theater; Recreation center; Tennis; Softball field; Camping; All Ranks Club; Snow sports.

FORT MCCOY

FORT MCCOY

Commander, Headquarters Fort McCoy, Fort McCoy, WI 54656-5000
(608) 388-2222; Autovon 280-1110
OFFICER-OF-THE-DAY: (608) 388-2216, Autovon 280-2216

Profile
BRANCH: Army.
SIZE AND LOCATION: 60,000 acres. In W-central WI, between Sparta and Tomah. Hwy 16 and 21 and I-90 and I-94 provide easy access to reservation. Nearest commercial airport 35 mi W, LaCrosse, WI.
MAJOR UNITS: Army Reserve Readiness Training Center; Fourth US Army Consolidated Training Activity; Readiness Group-McCoy; 88th Explosive Ordnance Detachment; 86th Army Reserve Command Equipment Concentration Site; WI National Guard Mobilization and Training Equipment Site; Regional Office of Test, Measurement & Diagnostic Equipment.
BASE HISTORY: 1909, founded, on what is known today as "south post"; northern half, maneuver camp named Camp Emory Upton set up; artillery camp, known as Camp Robinson, set up in south. 1910, named Ft McCoy for Bruce Elisha McCoy, Civil War captain. 1923-25, training stopped; redesignated Sparta Ordnance Depot, mission changed to handling, shipping, and storage of explosives. 1925, transferred to Dept of Agriculture. 1926, reestablished and named for Robert Bruce McCoy, son of Bruce McCoy and prominent local resident. 1933-1935, supply base for Civilian Conservation Corps (CCC). 1935, put on standby status. 1940, chosen as site for Second Army maneuvers. 1942, "new camp" today's cantonment area, begun. WWII, POW and relocation camp for European, Japanese prisoners, and Japanese-Americans relocated from W coast. Nation's first ordnance regiment, 301st, organized here. 1943, hospital built and induction and basic training center for Army nurses; Limited Service School established to train physically handicapped soldiers. 1945, discharge center; induction center; then on inactive status except summer training camps. 1950, reactivated with Fifth Army units. 1953, deactivated again. 1955, Wisconsin State Patrol Academy. 1966-1968, Jobs Corps Training center. 1971, Mobilization and Training Equipment Site (MATES) established. 1973, designated Forces Command installation with formation of FORSCOM. 1974, renamed Ft McCoy. 1980, 15,000 Cubans, relocated here. Only installation to have its own insignia. 1987, operational control to Army NG. 1988, Sparta-Ft McCoy Airport, civilian/military facility dedicated.
Key Contacts
COMMANDER: Col Raymond G Boland; Commander, Headquarters Fort McCoy, ATTN: AFZR-CO, (608) 388-3001, Autovon 280-3001.

FORT MCCOY (continued)
PUBLIC AFFAIRS: Mary A Binder; Commander, Headquarters Fort McCoy, ATTN: AFZR-XO-PA, (608) 388-4209, Autovon 280-4209.
PROCUREMENT: Gary Friedl; Commander, Headquarters Fort McCoy, ATTN: AFZR DC, (608) 388-3818, Autovon 280-3818.
TRANSPORTATION: William Kasten; Commander, Headquarters Fort McCoy, ATTN: AFZR-DLT, (608) 388-3714, Autovon 280-3714.
PERSONNEL/COMMUNITY ACTIVITIES: Maj Ronald Kettleson; Commander, Headquarters Fort McCoy, ATTN: AFZR-PA, (608) 388-2201, Autovon 280-2201.
Personnel and Expenditures
ACTIVE DUTY PERSONNEL: 400
DEPENDENTS: 38
CIVILIAN PERSONNEL: 1600
MILITARY PAYROLL EXPENDITURE: $190.5 mil
CONTRACT EXPENDITURE: $17.6 mil
Services *Housing:* Family units 96; BEQ units 66; RV/Camper sites 117. *Temporary Housing:* VOQ cottages 519; VEQ units 276; Guesthouse units 4; Guest cottages 5; Mobile home units 16; Transient living quarters 4. *Commissary and Exchange:* Retail store; Barber shop; Dry cleaners; Food shop; Service station; Credit union; Snacks. *Child Care/Capacities:* Day care center 51. *Base Library:* Yes. *Medical Facilities:* Medical clinic; Dental clinic. *Recreational Facilities:* Movie theater; Pool; Gym; Recreation center; Stables; Tennis; Racquetball; Fitness center; Softball field; Auto shop; Crafts; Officers club; NCO club; Camping; Fishing/Hunting; Ski hill operation with tow bar and tubing run.

MADISON

TRUAX AIR NATIONAL GUARD BASE
Truax Field, 3110 Mitchell St, Madison, WI 53704-2591
(608) 241-6200; Autovon 273-8210
Profile
BRANCH: Air National Guard.
SIZE AND LOCATION: 156 acres. In Madison, adj to Dane County Regional Airport, off E Washington Ave (Hwy 151) or Hwy 51 N or intersection with Hwy 151.
MAJOR UNITS: 128th Tactical Fighter Wing (ANG); 176th Tactical Fighter Squadron; 115th Maintenance Support Squadron; 115th Mission Support Flight; 115th Tactical Clinic; 115th Civil Engineering Squadron; 115th Resource Management Squadron; 115th Consolidated Aircraft Maintenance Squadron; 115th Weapons Systems Security Flight.
BASE HISTORY: 1949, 128th TFW established. During Korean Conflict, active duty. 1974, transferred from Aerospace Command to TAC. Today, combat ready with A-10 fighters.
Key Contacts
COMMANDER: Col Fred R Sloan; (608) 241-6202, Autovon 273-8202.
PUBLIC AFFAIRS: Maj Jay Poster; (608) 241-8395, Autovon 273-8395.
PROCUREMENT: CMSgt Bob Copas; (608) 241-6248, Autovon 273-8248.
PERSONNEL/COMMUNITY ACTIVITIES: Maj Cheryl Miller; (608) 241-6282, Autovon 273-8282.
Personnel and Expenditures
ACTIVE DUTY PERSONNEL: 949
CIVILIAN PERSONNEL: 35
MILITARY PAYROLL EXPENDITURE: FY 88, $3.8 mil
CONTRACT EXPENDITURE: FY 88, $2.5 mil

Services *Commissary and Exchange:* Retail store. *Medical Facilities:* Medical clinic; Dental clinic. *Recreational Facilities:* Softball field; All Ranks Club.

WISCONSIN NATIONAL GUARD
PO Box 8111, Office of the Adjutant General, Madison, WI 53708-8111
Profile
BRANCH: Air National Guard; Army National Guard.
SIZE: Offices only.

MILWAUKEE

MILWAUKEE COAST GUARD BASE
2420 S Lincoln Memorial Dr, Milwaukee, WI 53207-1997
(414) 291-1882
OFFICER-OF-THE-DAY: (414) 291-1919
Profile
BRANCH: Coast Guard.
SIZE AND LOCATION: 4 acres. 3 mi S of downtown Milwaukee on Lakefront, at S end of Hoan Bridge via I-794E.
MAJOR UNITS: USCG Group Milwaukee; Marine Safety Office Milwaukee; Western Region Director of Auxiliary; USCG Station Milwaukee.
BASE HISTORY: 1877-1970, USCG station operated at McKinley Park. 1968, present base constructed. Responsible for conducting and coordinating: rescue operations, boating safety, law enforcement, marine safety, commercial vessel inspections, icebreaking, and aids to navigation on Lake Michigan. Open 0700-1600 daily, duty officer present all other times.
Key Contacts
COMMANDER: CDR R J Losea.
PUBLIC AFFAIRS: LTjg B A Minnick; (414) 291-3425.
Personnel and Expenditures
ACTIVE DUTY PERSONNEL: 95
CIVILIAN PERSONNEL: 7
Services *Housing:* BEQ units. *Commissary and Exchange:* Small exchange. *Medical Facilities:* Corpsman for active duty personnel only. *Recreational Facilities:* Tennis; Basketball.

128TH AIR REFUELING GROUP
1919 E Grange Ave, Gen Mitchell Field, WI ANGB, Milwaukee, WI 53207-6199
(414) 747-4405
Profile
BRANCH: Air National Guard.
SIZE AND LOCATION: 123 acres. In city of Milwaukee.
MAJOR UNITS: 128th Air Refueling Group; 128th Air Refueling Squadron; 128th Mission Support Squadron; 128th Consolidated Aircraft Maintenance Squadron; 128th Resource Management Squadron; 128th Civil Engineering Squadron; 128th Mission Support Flight; 128th USAF Clinic; 128th Security Police Flight; Operating Location C, 1819th Reserve Advisor Squadron; 128th Tactical Control Flight; 128th Weather Flight.
BASE HISTORY: June 25, 1947 formed. Korean Conflict, served 21 months of active duty. Aug 1961, redesignated from Fighter Group to Refueling Group (TAC). Oct 1976, reassigned to SAC.
Key Contacts
COMMANDER: Col Eugene Schmitz.
Personnel and Expenditures
ACTIVE DUTY PERSONNEL: 946
CIVILIAN PERSONNEL: 30
MILITARY PAYROLL EXPENDITURE: FY 88, $5.7 mil
CONTRACT EXPENDITURE: FY 88, $1.2 mil

Services *Commissary:* Base commissary; Credit union. *Medical Facilities:* Medical clinic; Dental clinic. *Recreational Facilities:* All ranks club.

84TH DIVISION (TRAINING), HEADQUARTERS
4828 W Silver Spring Dr, Milwaukee, WI 53218-3498
(414) 438-6100
OFFICER-OF-THE-DAY: (414) 438-6100
Profile
BRANCH: Army Reserve.
SIZE AND LOCATION: 70 acres. In N-central Milwaukee.
MAJOR UNITS: HQ 84th Division (TNG); 961st Engineer Battalion; 5091st AG Battalion; 452nd General Hospital; 521st Maintenance Battalion; 84th Division 3rd Brigade; 84th Division 4th Brigade; 84th Division Training Group; 84th Division Logistics Group.
BASE HISTORY: Formerly a NIKE air defense site. Facilities consist of helipad, tank simulation center and outdoor training areas.
VISITOR ATTRACTIONS: Half of complex turned over to establishment of an environmental awareness center called "Havenwoods".
Key Contacts
COMMANDER: Maj Gen Vance Coleman.
PUBLIC AFFAIRS: Capt Zan Martin; (414) 438-6151.
PROCUREMENT: See Ft McCoy, WI.
Services *Commissary and Exchange:* Retail store; Branch BX of Ft Sheridan.

WYOMING

CHEYENNE

153RD TACTICAL AIRLIFT GROUP (ANG)
Cheyenne Municipal Airport, Cheyenne, WY 82001
(307) 772-6201; Autovon 943-6201
Profile
BRANCH: Air National Guard.
SIZE AND LOCATION: 46 acres. Within the corporate limits of Cheyenne.
MAJOR UNITS: 153rd Tactical Airlift Group (ANG).
Personnel and Expenditures
ACTIVE DUTY PERSONNEL: 724
CIVILIAN PERSONNEL: 179
MILITARY PAYROLL EXPENDITURE: $7.6 mil

F E WARREN AFB

FRANCIS E WARREN AIR FORCE BASE
90 SMW, F E Warren AFB, WY 82005
(307) 775-1110; Autovon 481-1110
Profile
BRANCH: Air Force.
SIZE AND LOCATION: 5866 acres. Immediately adj and W of Cheyenne, WY; 2 mi N of I-80 and adj to I-25.
MAJOR UNITS: Headquarters, 90th Strategic Missile Wing (Strategic Air Command).
BASE HISTORY: Oldest continuously active USAF base. On active duty since 1867, when Fort D A Russell, largest old cavalry post, established. 1885, Ft Russell made permanent post and fort rebuilt. 1930, presidential decree changed name to Fort Francis E Warren, for Senator Warren, Congressional Medal of Honor winner in Civil War. WWII, Quartermaster Training Center, Women's Auxiliary Army Corps, Transportation Corps, and POW camp. 1947, Army relinquished jurisdiction to USAF with 463rd AFB unit, Aviation Engineer School. 1948, School redesignated USAF Technical School under Air Training Command. 1949, designated Francis E Warren AFB (no runway) with aircraft stationed at Cheyenne Municipal Airport. 1957, first operational ICBM base. 1959, SAC base. 1984, Peacekeeper support facilities added. 1986, part of US Strategic Triad.
VISITOR ATTRACTIONS: Warren Historical Association museum, covering base history from 1800s to 1947; Reunion Center, with Warren's AF history, 1947-present; National Historic Site.
Key Contacts
COMMANDER: Col John A Gordon; Installation Commander.
PUBLIC AFFAIRS: Capt Liz Lane-Johnson; 90 SMW/PA, (307) 775-3381, Autovon 481-3381.

Personnel and Expenditures
ACTIVE DUTY PERSONNEL: 3800
DEPENDENTS: 1900
CIVILIAN PERSONNEL: 815
MILITARY PAYROLL EXPENDITURE: $76 mil
CONTRACT EXPENDITURE: $29.7 mil
Services *Housing:* Family units 831; BOQ cottages 2; BAQ units 13. *Temporary Housing:* VIP cottages 4; VOQ cottages 16; Guesthouse units 13. *Commissary:* Base commissary; Retail store; Barber shop; Dry cleaners; Food shop; Florist; Banking; Service station; Bakery; Convenience store/Shopette; Fast food. *Child Care/Capacities:* Day care center; Home day care program. *Base Library:* Yes. *Medical Facilities:* Hospital 40; Medical clinic; Dental clinic. *Recreational Facilities:* Bowling; Movie theater; Pool; Gym; Recreation center; Golf; Stables; Tennis; Racquetball; Skating rink; Fitness center; Softball field; Football field; Auto shop; Crafts; Officers club; NCO club; Camping; Fishing/Hunting.

GUERNSEY

CAMP GUERNSEY, WYOMING ARMY NATIONAL GUARD TRAINING SITE
PO Box 399, Guernsey, WY 82214-0399
(307) 836-2619; Autovon 943-6295; 943-6396
OFFICER-OF-THE-DAY: (307) 772-6296, 772-6396, Autovon 943-6396
Profile
BRANCH: Army National Guard.
SIZE AND LOCATION: 32,752 acres. In SE WY on North Platte River between Wheatland and Torrington, at elevation of 4338 ft. Adj to town of Guernsey on Hwy 26 not far from I-25, approx 30 mi from NE border and approx 100 mi N of CO border.
MAJOR UNITS: Detachment 2, STARC (Training Site); 475th Medical Detachment; 197th Engineer Detachment; 1041st Engineer Detachment.
BASE HISTORY: Originally, WYANG used Pole Mountain, on Ft Warren Military Reservation, for annual training maneuvers. 1938, summer camp site moved and Camp Guernsey became training center. WWII, Ft Warren sent troops to train here. Following WWII, deactivated and used as state maintenance site. 1950s, NG reactivated camp and used yearly ever since for NG training. 1980s, night land navigation course, air operations building, USPFO, and maintenance shop built; includes 25,000 acre artillery firing range. Airstrip at E edge of main camp.
VISITOR ATTRACTIONS: In heart of Wyoming's Oregon Trail area with Ft Laramie National Historic Site about 13 mi E.

Key Contacts
COMMANDER: Col Castillion; FA, WY ARNG, Commanding, (307) 836-2399, Autovon 943-6396.
PUBLIC AFFAIRS: LTC John Cornelison; PO Box 1709, Cheyenne, WY 82003-1709, (307) 772-6229, Autovon 943-6229.
PROCUREMENT: CW4 George Branscom; (307) 836-2823, Autovon 943-6396.
TRANSPORTATION: Capt Jerry Stround; (307) 836-2315, Autovon 943-6396.
Services *Housing:* BEQ units 1204; BAQ units 96; Barracks spaces 1300; Trailer spaces 8; RV/Camper sites 40. *Commissary and Exchange:* Retail store. *Medical Facilities:* Medical clinic. *Recreational Facilities:* Softball field; Officers club; NCO club; Camping; Fishing/Hunting.

ALPHABETICAL LISTING OF BASES

Aberdeen Proving Ground, Aberdeen Proving Ground, MD

Adak Naval Air Station, Adak, AK

Adak Naval Security Group Activity, Adak, AK

Adelphi Laboratory Center, Adelphi, MD

Air Force Plant Representative Office, Air Force Plant No 4, Fort Worth, TX

Air Reserve Personnel Center, Denver, CO

Alabama State Military Department, Montgomery, AL

Alameda Coast Guard Island, Alameda, CA

Alameda Naval Air Station, Alameda, CA

Albany Marine Corps Logistics Base, Albany, GA

Alternate Joint Communications Center/Site R, Fort Ritchie, MD

Altus Air Force Base, Altus AFB, OK

Anacostia Naval Station, Washington, DC

Andrews Air Force Base, Andrews AFB, MD

Annapolis Naval Station, Annapolis, MD

Anniston Army Depot, Anniston, AL

Armed Forces Institute of Pathology, Washington, DC

Armed Forces Staff College, Norfolk, VA

Army Aviation Support Facility, Winder, GA

Army Aviation Support Facility #1, Greensburg, OH

Army Cold Regions Research and Engineering Laboratory, Hanover, NH

Army Criminal Investigation Command, Falls Church, VA

Army Materiel Command Headquarters, Alexandria, VA

Army Materiels Technology Laboratory, Watertown, MA

Army Natick Research, Development & Engineering Center, Natick, MA

Army Publications Distribution Center, Baltimore, MD

Army Research Office, Research Triangle Park, NC

Army Reserve Personnel Center, Saint Louis, MO

Army Tank-Automotive Command, Warren, MI

Army Troop Support Command, Saint Louis, MO

Arnold Air Force Base, Arnold AFB, TN

Atlanta Naval Air Station, Marietta, GA

Atlantic Division, Naval Facilities Engineering Command, Norfolk, VA

Aviation Supply Office Compound, Philadelphia, PA

Badger Army Ammunition Plant, Baraboo, WI

Ballston Spa Nuclear Power Training Unit, Ballston Spa, NY

Bangor Air National Guard Base, Bangor, ME

Bangor Naval Submarine Base, Silverdale, WA

Barbers Point Naval Air Station, Barbers Point, HI

Barksdale Air Force Base, Barksdale AFB, LA

Barstow Marine Corps Logistics Base, Barstow, CA

Bath Supervisor of Shipbuilding, Conversion and Repair, Bath, ME

Battle Creek Air National Guard Base, Battle Creek, MI

Bayonne Military Ocean Terminal, Bayonne, NJ

Beale Air Force Base, Beale AFB, CA

Beaufort Marine Corps Air Station, Beaufort, SC

Beaufort Naval Hospital, Beaufort, SC

Bellows Air Force Station, Waimanalo, HI

Bergstrom Air Force Base, Austin, TX

Bolling Air Force Base, Bolling AFB, DC

Bremerton Naval Hospital, Bremerton, WA

Brooklyn Coast Guard Air Station, Brooklyn, NY

Brooklyn Coast Guard Supply Center, Brooklyn, NY

Brooks Air Force Base, Brooks AFB, TX

Brunswick Naval Air Station, Brunswick, ME

Buckley Air National Guard Base, Aurora, CO

Buffalo Coast Guard Group, Buffalo, NY

Calumet Air Force Station, Calumet, MI

Cameron Station, Military District of Washington, Alexandria, VA

Camp Beauregard, Pineville, LA

Camp Blanding Training Site, Starke, FL

Camp Bullis, Fort Sam Houston, TX

Camp Dawson, Army Training Site, Kingwood, WV

Camp Dodge Iowa, Johnston, IA

Camp Edwards, ARNG Training Site, Camp Edwards, MA

Camp Elmore, Norfolk, VA

Camp Grayling Army and Air National Guard Training Center, Grayling, MI

Camp Gruber Training Site, Braggs, OK

Camp Guernsey, Wyoming Army National Guard Training Site, Guernsey, WY

Camp Lejeune Marine Corps Base, Camp Lejeune, NC

Camp Lincoln, Springfield, IL

Camp Mabry, Austin, TX

Camp Peary, Williamsburg, VA

Camp Pendleton Marine Corps Base, Camp Pendleton, CA

Camp Rapid, Rapid City, SD

Camp Rilea, Oregon National Guard Training Site, Warrenton, OR

Camp Joseph T Robinson, North Little Rock, AR

Camp San Luis Obispo, San Luis Obispo, CA

Camp Shelby Training Site, Camp Shelby, MS

Camp H M Smith, Camp H M Smith, HI

Camp Smith Training Site, Peekskill, NY

Camp Swift (Unit Training and Equipment Site #3), Basytop, TX

Camp W G Williams, Riverton, UT

Campion Air Force Station, Campion Air Force Station, AK

Cannon Air Force Base, Cannon AFB, NM

Cape Canaveral Air Force Station, Cocoa Beach, FL

Cape Lisburne Air Force Station, Cape Lisburne Air Force Station, AK

Cape May Coast Guard Training Center, Cape May, NJ

Cape Newenham Air Force Station, Cape Newenham Air Force Station, AK

Cape Romanzof Air Force Station, Cape Romanzof Air Force Station, AK

Carlisle Barracks, Carlisle Barracks, PA

Carswell Air Force Base, Fort Worth, TX

Castle Air Force Base, Castle AFB, CA

Catoosa Area Training Center, Tunnel Hill, GA

Cavalier Air Force Station, Cavalier, ND

Cecil Field Naval Air Station, Jacksonville, FL

Cecil Field Naval Air Station, Detachment, Astor, FL

Centerville Beach Naval Facility, Ferndale, CA

Chanute Air Force Base, Chanute AFB, IL

Charleston Air Force Base, Charleston AFB, SC

Charleston Coast Guard Base, Charleston, SC

Charleston Naval Base, Charleston, SC

Charleston Naval Weapons Station, Charleston, SC

Chase Field Naval Air Station, Beeville, TX

Cherry Point Marine Corps Air Station, Cherry Point, NC

Cheyenne Mountain Air Force Base, Colorado Springs, CO

China Lake Naval Weapons Center, China Lake, CA

Clearwater Coast Guard Air Station, Clearwater, FL

Clover Field Civil Air Patrol Station, Santa Monica, CA

Coast Guard Communication Area Master Station Pacific, San Francisco, Point Reyes Station, CA

Coast Guard Communication Area Master Station Pacific Transmitter Site, Bolinas, CA

Coast Guard Pacific Strike Team, Novato, CA

Cold Bay Air Force Station, Cold Bay, AK

Columbus Air Force Base, Columbus, MS

Concord Naval Weapons Station, Concord, CA

Concrete MEWS, Concrete, ND

Cornhusker Army Ammunition Plant, Grand Island, NE

Corona Naval Weapons Station, Corona, CA

Coronado Naval Amphibious Base, San Diego, CA

Corpus Christi Army Depot, Corpus Christi, TX

Corpus Christi Naval Air Station, Corpus Christi, TX

Corpus Christi Naval Hospital, Corpus Christi, TX

Corry Station Naval Technical Training Center, Pensacola, FL

Cortez Coast Guard Station, Cortez, FL

Crescent City Air Force Station, Klamath, CA

Crows Landing Naval Auxiliary Landing Field, Crows Landing, CA

Cudjoe Key Air Force Station, Sugarloaf Shores, FL

Cumberland Naval Reserve Center, Cumberland, MD

Cutler Naval Communications Unit, East Machias, ME

Dallas Air Force Station, Dallas AFS, OR

Dallas Naval Air Station, Dallas, TX

Dam Neck, Fleet Combat Training Center, Atlantic, Virginia Beach, VA

Davis-Monthan Air Force Base, Tucson, AZ

Defense Construction Supply Center, Columbus, OH

Defense Depot Tracy, Tracy, CA

Defense General Supply Center, Richmond, VA

Defense Industrial Plant Equipment Facility, Atchison, KS

Defense Mapping Agency, Alexandria, VA

Defense Mapping Agency, Reston, VA

Defense Mapping Agency Aerospace Center, Saint Louis, MO

Defense Personnel Support Center, Philadelphia, PA

Defense Reutilization and Marketing Service, Battle Creek, MI

Detroit Arsenal, Warren, MI

Detroit Coast Guard Group/Base, Detroit, MI

Detroit Naval Air Facility, Selfridge ANG Base, MI

Dobbins Air Force Base, Dobbins AFB, GA

Dover Air Force Base, Dover AFB, DE

Dugway Proving Ground, Dugway, UT

Dyess Air Force Base, Abilene, TX

Eaker Air Force Base, Blytheville, AR

Edwards Air Force Base, Edwards AFB, CA

Eglin Air Force Base, Fort Walton Beach, FL

Egmont Key Coast Guard Light Station, Saint Petersburg, FL

Eielson Air Force Base, Eielson AFB, AK

Eighth Coast Guard District, New Orleans, LA

El Centro Naval Air Facility, El Centro, CA

El Toro Marine Corps Air Station, Santa Ana, CA

Elizabeth City Coast Guard Air Station, Elizabeth City, NC

Elizabeth City Coast Guard Aircraft Repair & Supply Center, Elizabeth City, NC

Ellington Air National Guard Base, Houston, TX

Ellsworth Air Force Base, Ellsworth AFB, SD

Elmendorf Air Force Base, Anchorage, AK

Empire Air Force Station, Empire AFS, MI

England Air Force Base, Alexandria, LA

Ethan Allen Firing Range, Jericho, VT

Fairchild Air Force Base, Fairchild AFB, WA

Falcon Air Force Base, Falcon AFB, CO

Fallbrook Naval Weapons Station, Fallbrook, CA

Fallon Naval Air Station, Fallon, NV

Fentress Naval Auxiliary Landing Field, Chesapeake, VA

Fifth Coast Guard District, Portsmouth, VA

Finley Air Force Station, Finley, ND

1st Combat Evaluation Group, Detachment 18 (SAC), Forsyth, MT

1st Combat Evaluation Group, Detachment 10 (SAC), Hastings, NE

1st Marine Corps District Headquarters, Long Island, NY

Fitzsimons Army Medical Center, Aurora, CO

Fleet Antisubmarine Warfare Training Center, Atlantic, Norfolk, VA

Fleet Antisubmarine Warfare Training Center, Pacific, San Diego, CA

Fleet Combat Training Center, Pacific, San Diego, CA

Fort Belvoir, Fort Belvoir, VA

Fort Benning, Fort Benning, GA

Fort Bliss, Fort Bliss, TX

Fort Bragg, Fort Bragg, NC

Fort Campbell, Fort Campbell, KY

Fort Carson and 4th Infantry Division (Mechanized), Fort Carson, CO

Fort Chaffee, Fort Chaffee, AR

Fort DeRussy, Honolulu, HI

Fort Detrick, Frederick, MD

Fort Devens, Fort Devens, MA

Fort Dix, Fort Dix, NJ

Fort Drum, Fort Drum, NY

Fort Eustis, Newport News, VA

Fort Fisher Air Force Station, Kure Beach, NC

Fort Fisher Recreation Area, Kure Beach, NC

Fort Gillem, Forest Park, GA

Fort Gordon, Fort Gordon, GA

Fort Greely, Fort Greely, AK

Fort Hamilton, Brooklyn, NY

Fort Benjamin Harrison, Fort Benjamin Harrison, IN

Fort William Henry Harrison, Helena, MT

Fort A P Hill, Bowling Green, VA

Fort Hood, Fort Hood, TX

Fort Huachuca, Fort Huachuca, AZ

Fort Hunter Liggett, Fort Hunter Liggett, CA

Fort Indiantown Gap, Annville, PA

Fort Irwin, National Training Center, Fort Irwin, CA

Fort Jackson, Columbia, SC

Fort Kamehameha, Honolulu, HI

Fort Knox, Fort Knox, KY

Fort Lawton, Seattle, WA

Fort Leavenworth, Fort Leavenworth, KS

Fort Lee, Petersburg, VA

Fort Lee Air Force Station, Petersberg, VA

Fort Leonard Wood, Fort Leonard Wood, MO

Fort Lewis, Fort Lewis, WA

Fort Mason, San Francisco, CA

Fort McClellan, Anniston, AL

Fort McCoy, Fort McCoy, WI

Fort Lesley J McNair, Washington, DC

Fort McPherson, Fort McPherson, GA

Fort George G Meade, Fort Meade, MD

Fort Meade Military Reservation, Fort Meade, SD

Fort Monmouth, Fort Monmouth, NJ

Fort Monroe, Fort Monroe, VA

Fort Myer, Arlington, VA

Fort Myers Beach Coast Guard Station, Fort Myers Beach, FL

Fort Ord, Fort Ord, CA

Fort Polk, Fort Polk, LA

Fort Richardson, Fort Richardson, AK

Fort Riley, Fort Riley, KS

Fort Ritchie, Fort Ritchie, MD

Fort Rodman, US Army Reserve Center, New Bedford, MA

Fort Rucker, Fort Rucker, AL

Fort Ruger, Honolulu, HI

Fort Sam Houston, Fort Sam Houston, TX

Fort Shafter, Fort Shafter, HI

Fort Sheridan, Fort Sheridan, IL

Fort Sill, Fort Sill, OK

Fort Stewart, Hinesville, GA

Fort Story, Fort Story, VA

Fort Tilden, Fort Tilden, NY

Fort Totten, Queens, NY

Fort Wainwright, Fort Wainwright, AK

Fort Wingate Depot Activity, Gallup, NM

Fort Yukon Air Force Station, Fort Yukon, AK

Fortuna Air Force Station, Fortuna AFS, ND

Four Lakes Communications Station, Cheney, WA

Fresno Air National Guard Base, Fresno Air Terminal, CA

Galena Airport, Galena, AK

Galveston Coast Guard Base, Galveston, TX

Garland Air National Guard Station, Garland, TX

General Rail Shops, Ogden, UT

Gentile Air Force Station, Dayton, OH

George Air Force Base, George AFB, CA

Georgia Air National Guard Field Training Site, Headquarters, Savannah, GA

Georgia Department of Defense, Military Division, Atlanta, GA

Gibbsboro Air Force Station, Gibbsboro, NJ

Gila Bend Air Force Auxiliary Field, Gila Bend AF Auxiliary Field, AZ

Glenview Naval Air Station, Glenview, IL

Goliad Naval Auxiliary Landing Field, Beeville, TX

Goodfellow Air Force Base, Goodfellow AFB, TX

Governors Island Coast Guard Support Center, Governors Island, NY

Gowen Field, Boise, ID

Grand Forks Air Force Base, Grand Forks AFB, ND

Great Lakes Naval Training Center, Great Lakes, IL

Griffiss Air Force Base, Griffiss AFB, NY

Grissom Air Force Base, Grissom AFB, IN

Gulfport Naval Construction Battalion Center, Gulfport, MS

Gunter Air Force Base, Gunter AFB, AL

Hamilton Army Airfield, Novato, CA

Hammond Air National Guard Station, Hammond, LA

Hanscom Air Force Base, Bedford, MA

Hardwood Air-to-Ground Weapons Range, Camp Douglas, WI

Hawthorne Army Ammunition Plant, Hawthorne, NV

Henderson Hall, Arlington, VA

Hickam Air Force Base, Hickam AFB, HI

Hill Air Force Base, Hill AFB, UT

Holloman Air Force Base, Holloman AFB, NM

Holston Army Ammunition Plant, Kingsport, TN

Homestead Air Force Base, Homestead, FL

Houston Coast Guard Air Station, Houston, TX

Humphreys Engineer Center, Fort Belvoir, VA

Hunter Army Air Field, Savannah, GA

Hurlburt Field, Hurlburt Field, FL

Idaho Falls Naval Administrative Unit, Idaho Falls, ID

Idaho Falls Naval Nuclear Power Training Unit, Idaho Falls, ID

Indian Head Naval Ordnance Station, Indian Head, MD

Indian Mountain Air Force Station, Indian Mountain Air Force Station, AK

Iowa Air National Guard, Des Moines, IA

Iowa Army Ammunition Plant, Middletown, IA

Jackson Barracks, New Orleans, LA

Jacksonville Naval Air Station, Jacksonville, FL

Jacksonville Naval Hospital, Jacksonville, FL

Jacksonville Naval Supply Center, Jacksonville, FL

Jefferson Proving Ground, Madison, IN

Joliet Army Ammunition Plant, Joliet, IL

Kallspell Air Force Station, Lakeside, MT

Kaneohe Bay Marine Corps Air Station, Kaneohe Bay, HI

Kansas Army Ammunition Plant, Parsons, KS

Keesler Air Force Base, Biloxi, MS

Kelly Air Force Base, Kelly AFB, TX

Charles E Kelly Support Facility, Oakdale, PA

Key West Naval Air Station, Key West, FL

Kilauea Military Camp, Armed Forces Recreation Center, Hawaii National Park, HI

Kings Bay Naval Submarine Base, Kings Bay, GA

Kingsville Naval Air Station, Kingsville, TX

Kirtland Air Force Base, Albuquerque, NM

Kotzebue Air Force Station, Kotzebue, AK

Kulis Air National Guard Base, Anchorage, AK

La Junta Strategic Training Range, La Junta, CO

Lackland Air Force Base, Lackland AFB, TX

Lake Seneca Naval Underwater Systems Center Detachment, Lake Seneca, NY

Langley Air Force Base, Langley AFB, VA

Laughlin Air Force Base, Laughlin AFB, TX

Lemoore Naval Air Station, Lemoore, CA

Letterkenny Army Depot, Chambersburg, PA

Letterman Army Medical Center, San Francisco, CA

Lexington-Blue Grass Army Depot, Lexington, KY

Lima Army Tank Plant, Lima, OH

Lincoln Air National Guard Base, Lincoln, NE

Little Creek Naval Amphibious Base, Norfolk, VA

Little Rock Air Force Base, Little Rock AFB, AR

Long Beach Combined Support Maintenance Shop, Long Beach, CA

Long Beach Naval Station, Long Beach, CA

Long Beach Navy Regional Medical Center, Long Beach, CA

Long Beach Supervisor of Shipbuilding, Conversion and Repair, Long Beach, CA

Longhorn Army Ammunition Plant, Marshall, TX

Loring Air Force Base, Loring AFB, ME

Los Angeles Air Force Base, El Segundo, CA

Louisiana Army Ammunition Plant, Shreveport, LA

Louisville Naval Ordnance Station, Louisville, KY

Lowry Air Force Base, Lowry AFB, CO

Luke Air Force Base, Luke AFB, AZ

MacDill Air Force Base, MacDill AFB, FL

Madigan Army Medical Center, Tacoma, WA

Makah Air Force Station, Neah Bay, WA

Malmstrom Air Force Base, Great Falls, MT

March Air Force Base, March AFB, CA

Mare Island Naval Complex, Vallejo, CA

Marine Barracks, Hawaii, Pearl Harbor, HI

Marine Barracks, Washington, Washington, DC

Massachusetts Military Reservation/Otis Air National Guard Base, Cape Cod, MA

Mather Air Force Base, Mather AFB, CA

Maxwell Air Force Base, Maxwell AFB, AL

May Air National Guard Base, Reno, NV

Mayport Naval Station, Mayport, FL

McAlester Army Ammunition Plant, McAlester, OK

McChord Air Force Base, McChord AFB, WA

McClellan Air Force Base, McClellan AFB, CA

McConnell Air Force Base, McConnell AFB, KS

McEntire Air National Guard Base, McEntire ANGB, SC

McGuire Air Force Base, McGuire AFB, NJ

Mechanicsburg Defense Depot, Mechanicsburg, PA

Memphis Defense Depot, Memphis, TN

Memphis Naval Air Station, Millington, TN

Meridian Naval Air Station, Meridian, MS

Miami Beach Coast Guard Base, Miami Beach, FL

Miami Coast Guard Air Station, Opa-Locka, FL

Mica Peak Air Force Station, Spokane, WA

Michigan National Guard Mobilization and Training Equipment Site, Grayling, MI

Milan Army Ammunition Plant, Milan, TN

Military District of Washington, Washington, DC

Military Traffic Management Command, South Atlantic Outport, North Charleston, SC

Military Traffic Management Command, Western Area, Oakland, CA

Milwaukee Coast Guard Base, Milwaukee, WI

Minot Air Force Base, Minot AFB, ND

Miramar Naval Air Station, San Diego, CA

Mississippi Air National Guard Field Training Site, Headquarters, Gulfport, MS

Mississippi Army Ammunition Plant, Stennis Space Center, MS

Mitchell National Guard Complex, Mitchell, SD

Mobile Coast Guard Aviation Training Center, Mobile, AL

Mobile Coast Guard Base, Mobile, AL

Moffett Field Naval Air Station, Moffett Field, CA

Moody Air Force Base, Moody AFB, GA

Mount Hebo Air Force Station, Hebo, OR

Mountain Home Air Force Base, Mountain Home AFB, ID

Murphy Dome Air Force Station, Murphy Dome Air Force Station, AK

Myrtle Beach Air Force Base, Myrtle Beach, SC

National Naval Medical Center, Bethesda, MD

Navajo Depot Activity, Bellemont, AZ

Naval Air Engineering Center, Lakehurst, NJ

Naval Air Propulsion Center, Trenton, NJ

Naval & Marine Corps Reserve Center, Raleigh, NC

Naval & Marine Corps Reserve Center, Chattanooga, TN

Naval & Marine Corps Reserve Center, Tallahassee, Tallahassee, FL

Naval Avionics Center, Indianapolis, Indianapolis, IN

Naval Civil Engineering Laboratory, Port Hueneme, CA

Naval Clothing and Textile Research Facility, Natick, MA

Naval Coastal Systems Center, Panama City, FL

Naval Communication Unit, Washington, Cheltenham, MD

Naval Education and Training Center, Newport, RI

Naval Education and Training Program Management Support Activity, Pensacola, FL

Naval Facilities Engineering Command Headquarters, Alexandria, VA

Naval Oceanography Command, Stennis Space Center, MS

Naval Plant Branch Representative Office, Magna, UT

Naval Postgraduate School, Monterey, CA

Naval Research Laboratory, Washington, DC

Naval Research Laboratory, Underwater Sound Reference Laboratory, Orlando, FL

Naval Reserve Readiness Center Portland, Portland, ME

Naval Sea Systems Command, Arlington, VA

Naval Security Station, Washington, DC

Naval Ship Weapons Systems Engineering Station, Port Hueneme, CA

Naval Station New York (Brooklyn), Brooklyn, NY

Naval Station New York (Staten Island), Staten Island, NY

Naval Supply Center, Cheatham Annex, Williamsburg, VA

Naval Supply Systems Command, Arlington, VA

Naval Surface Warfare Center, Dahlgren, VA

Naval Training Systems Center, Orlando, FL

Naval Undersea Warfare Engineering Station, Keyport, WA

Naval Undersea Warfare Engineering Station, Indian Island Detachment, Hadlock, WA

Naval Underwater Systems Center, New London, CT

Naval Weapons Industrial Reserve Plant, Bristol, TN

Naval Weapons Support Center Crane, Crane, IN

NAVMAG Lualualei, Waianae, HI

Navy and Marine Corp Reserve Readiness Center, Bridgeton, MO

Navy Finance Center, Cleveland, OH

Navy Recreation Center, Solomons, MD

Navy Recruiting District Boston, Boston, MA

Navy Ships Parts Control Center, Mechanicsburg, PA

Navy Supply Corps School, Athens, GA

Nellis Air Force Base, Las Vegas, NV

Nevada National Guard Headquarters, Carson City, NV

New Cumberland Army Depot, New Cumberland, PA

New London Naval Submarine Base, Groton, CT

New Mexico National Guard State Headquarters, Santa Fe, NM

New Orleans Naval Air Station, Belle Chasse, LA

New Orleans Naval Support Activity, New Orleans, LA

New River Marine Corps Air Station, Jacksonville, NC

Newark Air Force Base, Newark AFB, OH

Newport News Supervisor of Shipbuilding, Conversion and Repair, Newport News, VA

Norfolk Fleet Training Center, Norfolk, VA

Norfolk Naval Air Station, Norfolk, VA

Norfolk Naval Aviation Depot, Norfolk, VA

Norfolk Naval Base, Norfolk, VA

Norfolk Naval Shipyard, Portsmouth, VA

Norfolk Naval Station, Norfolk, VA

Norfolk Naval Supply Center, Norfolk, VA

Norfolk Navy Public Works Center, Norfolk, VA

North Auxiliary Air Field, North, SC

North Bend Air Force Station, North Bend AFS, OR

North Island Naval Air Station, San Diego, CA

North Truro Air Force Station, North Truro, MA

Northwest Naval Security Group Activity, Chesapeake, VA

Norton Air Force Base, Norton AFB, CA

Oakland Army Base, California, Oakland, CA

Oakland Naval Hospital/Naval Medical Command Northwest Region, Oakland, CA

Oakland Naval Supply Center, Oakland, CA

Oceana Naval Air Station, Virginia Beach, VA

Offutt Air Force, Offutt AFB, NE

Ogden Defense Depot, Ogden, UT

O'Hare Air Reserve Forces Facility, O'Hare ARFF, IL

Ohio National Guard, Unit Training Equipment Site #1, Newton Falls, OH

Oklahoma City Air Force Station, Oklahoma City AFS, OK

Onizuka Air Force Base, Sunnyvale, CA

Operating Location Alpha Bravo South East Air Defense Sector, Old Town, FL

Orange Grove Naval Auxiliary Landing Field, Orange Grove, TX

Orlando Recruit Training Command, Orlando, FL

Pacific Missile Range Facility, Hawaiian Area, Kekaha, Kauai, HI

Pacific Northwest Fleet Recreation and Education Support Center, Pacific Beach, WA

Papago Military Installation, Phoenix, AZ

Parks Reserve Forces Training Area, Dublin, CA

Parris Island Marine Corps Recruit Depot/ Eastern Recruiting Region, Parris Island, SC

Pascagoula Supervisor of Shipbuilding, Conversion and Repair, Pascagoula, MS

Patrick Air Force Base, Patrick AFB, FL

Patuxent River Naval Air Station, Patuxent River, MD

Pearl Harbor Fleet Training Group, Pearl Harbor, HI

Pearl Harbor Naval Station, Pearl Harbor, HI

Pearl Harbor Naval Submarine Base, Pearl Harbor, HI

Pearl Harbor Navy Public Works Center, Pearl Harbor, HI

Pease Air Force Base, Pease AFB, NH

Pennsylvania Air National Guard, Pittsburgh, PA

Pensacola Coast Guard Station, Pensacola, FL

Pensacola Naval Air Station, Pensacola, FL

Pensacola Naval Aviation Depot, Pensacola, FL

Pensacola Naval Hospital, Pensacola, FL

The Pentagon, Arlington, VA

Petaluma Coast Guard Training Center, Petaluma, CA

Peterson Air Force Base, Peterson AFB, CO

Phelps Collins Air National Guard Base, Alpena, MI

Philadelphia Coast Guard Marine Safety Office and Group, Philadelphia, PA

Philadelphia Naval Base, Philadelphia, PA

Philadelphia Naval Hospital, Philadelphia, PA

Philadelphia Naval Shipyard, Philadelphia, PA

Pillar Point Air Force Station, El Granada, CA

Plattsburgh Air Force Base, Plattsburgh, NY

Pohakuloa Training Area, Hilo, HI

Point Arena Air Force Station, Point Arena AFS, CA

Point Mugu Naval Air Station, Point Mugu, CA

Pomona Naval Weapons Station, Pomona, CA

Pope Air Force Base, Pope AFB, NC

Port Austin Air Force Station, Operating Location Alpha Nancy, Northeast Air Division Sector, Port Austin, MI

Port Hueneme, Naval Construction Battalion Center, Port Hueneme, CA

Portsmouth Naval Hospital, Portsmouth, VA

Portsmouth Naval Shipyard, Portsmouth, NH

Portsmouth Supervisor of Shipbuilding, Conversion and Repair, Portsmouth, VA

Presidio of Monterey, Monterey, CA

Presidio of San Francisco, San Francisco, CA

Charles Melvin Price Support Center, US Army, Granite City, IL

Production Flight Test Installation, Air Force Plant 42, Palmdale, CA

Pueblo Army Depot Activity, Pueblo, CO

Puget Sound Naval Shipyard, Bremerton, WA

Puget Sound Naval Station, Seattle, WA

Quantico Marine Corps Combat Development Command, Quantico, VA

Radford Army Ammunition Plant, Radford, VA

Randolph Air Force Base, Randolph AFB, TX

Recruit Training Command, Great Lakes, Great Lakes, IL

Red River Army Depot, Texarkana, TX

Redstone Arsenal, Redstone Arsenal, AL

Reese Air Force Base, Reese AFB, TX

Richards-Gebaur Air Force Base, Richards-Gebaur AFB, MO

Richmond Heights Air Force Station, Homestead, FL

Rickenbacker Air National Guard Base, Columbus, OH

Robins Air Force Base, Robins AFB, GA

Rock Island Arsenal, Rock Island, IL

Roslyn Air National Guard Station, Roslyn, NY

Sacramento Army Depot, Sacramento, CA

St Louis Coast Guard Base, Saint Louis, MO

St Petersburg Coast Guard Station, Saint Petersburg, FL

San Diego Coast Guard Group, San Diego, CA

San Diego Marine Corps Recruit Depot, San Diego, CA

San Diego Naval Station, San Diego, CA

San Diego Naval Submarine Base, San Diego, CA

San Diego Naval Supply Center, San Diego, CA

San Diego Naval Training Center, San Diego, CA

San Diego Recruit Training Command, Naval Training Center, San Diego, CA

San Francisco Coast Guard Air Station, San Francisco, CA

San Francisco Coast Guard Base, San Francisco, CA

San Nicholas Island Naval Facility, Point Mugu, CA

Sand Island Coast Guard Station, Honolulu, HI

Sault Ste Marie Coast Guard Base, Sault Ste Marie, MI

Savanna Army Depot Activity, Savanna, IL

Savannah Air Force Station, Savannah, GA

K I Sawyer Air Force Base, K I Sawyer, MI

Schofield Barracks, Schofield Barracks, HI

Scott Air Force Base, Scott AFB, IL

Scranton Army Ammunition Plant, Scranton, PA

Seal Beach Naval Weapons Station, Seal Beach, CA

Seattle Coast Guard Support Center, Seattle, WA

Selfridge Air National Guard Base, Selfridge ANG Base, MI

Seneca Army Depot, Romulus, NY

Seymour Johnson Air Force Base, Goldsboro, NC

Sharpe Army Depot, Lathrop, CA

Shaw Air Force Base, Shaw AFB, SC

Shemya Air Force Base, Shemya AFB, AK

Sheppard Air Force Base, Sheppard AFB, TX

Shore Intermediate Maintenance Activity, Portsmouth, VA

Sierra Army Depot, Herlong, CA

Skaggs Island Naval Security Group Activity, Sonoma, CA

Smith Air National Guard Base, Birmingham, AL

Soctia Naval Administrative Unit, Soctia, NY

South Weymouth Naval Air Station, South Weymouth, MA

Space & Naval Warfare Systems Command, Washington, DC

Sparrevohn Air Force Station, Sparrevohn Air Force Station, AK

State Military Reservation, Camp Pendleton, Virginia Beach, VA

Stewart Air National Guard Base, Newburgh, NY

Stockton Naval Communications Station, Stockton, CA

Sugar Grove Naval Radio Station, Sugar Grove, WV

Sunny Point Military Ocean Terminal, Southport, NC

Tampa Coast Guard Marine Safety Office, Tampa, FL

Tatalina Air Force Station, McGrath, AK

David Taylor Research Center, Bethesda, MD

David Taylor Research Center, Annapolis Laboratory, Annapolis, MD

Tin City Air Force Station, Tin City Air Force Station, AK

Tinker Air Force Base, Tinker AFB, OK

Tobyhanna Army Depot, Tobyhanna, PA

Tooele Army Depot, Tooele, UT

Training Command, US Atlantic Fleet, Norfolk, VA

Travis Air Force Base, Travis AFB, CA

Travis Field, Garden City, GA

Treasure Island Naval Station, San Francisco, CA

Tripler Army Medical Center, Tripler AMC, HI

Truax Air National Guard Base, Madison, WI

Tustin Marine Corps Air Station, Tustin, CA

Twentynine Palms Marine Corps Air Ground Combat Center, Twentynine Palms, CA

Tyndall Air Force Base, Tyndall AFB, FL

Umatilla Army Depot Activity, Hermiston, OR

US Air Force Academy, United States Air Force Academy, CO

US Army Corps of Engineers, Baltimore District, Baltimore, MD

US Army Corps of Engineers, Buffalo District, Buffalo, NY

US Army Corps of Engineers, Charleston District, Charleston, SC

US Army Corps of Engineers, Chicago District, Chicago, IL

US Army Corps of Engineers, Detroit District, Detroit, MI

US Army Corps of Engineers, Headquarters, Washington, DC

US Army Corps of Engineers, Huntsville Division, Huntsville, AL

US Army Corps of Engineers, Jacksonville District, Jacksonville, FL

US Army Corps of Engineers, Kansas City District, Kansas City, MO

US Army Corps of Engineers, Little Rock District, Little Rock, AR

US Army Corps of Engineers, Lower Mississippi Valley Division, Vicksburg, MS

US Army Corps of Engineers, Memphis District, Memphis, TN

US Army Corps of Engineers, Missouri River Division, Omaha, NE

US Army Corps of Engineers, Mobile District, Mobile, AL

US Army Corps of Engineers, Nashville District, Nashville, TN

US Army Corps of Engineers, New England Division, Waltham, MA

US Army Corps of Engineers, North Atlantic Division, New York, NY

US Army Corps of Engineers, North Central Division, Chicago, IL

US Army Corps of Engineers, North Pacific Division, Portland, OR

US Army Corps of Engineers, Ohio River Division, Cincinnati, OH

US Army Corps of Engineers, Omaha District, Omaha, NE

US Army Corps of Engineers, Pacific Ocean Division, Honolulu, HI

US Army Corps of Engineers, Pittsburgh District, Pittsburgh, PA

US Army Corps of Engineers, Portland District, Portland, OR

US Army Corps of Engineers, Rock Island District, Rock Island, IL

US Army Corps of Engineers, Sacramento District, Sacramento, CA

US Army Corps of Engineers, St Louis District, Saint Louis, MO

US Army Corps of Engineers, St Paul District, Saint Paul, MN

US Army Corps of Engineers, South Atlantic Division, Atlanta, GA

US Army Corps of Engineers, South Pacific Division, San Francisco, CA

US Army Corps of Engineers, Southwestern District, Dallas, TX

US Army Corps of Engineers, Southwestern Division, Dallas, TX

US Army Corps of Engineers, Tulsa District, Tulsa, OK

US Army Corps of Engineers, Walla Walla District, Walla Walla, WA

US Army Corps of Engineers Waterways Experiment Station, Vicksburg, MS

US Army Engineer District, Galveston, Galveston, TX

US Coast Guard Academy, New London, CT

Traverse City Coast Guard Air Station, Traverse City, MI

US Coast Guard Headquarters, Washington, DC

Kodiak Coast Guard Support Center, Kodiak, AK

US Coast Guard Yard, Curtis Bay, MD

US Marine Corps Mountain Warfare Training Center, Bridgeport, CA

US Marine Corps Reserve Support Center, Overland Park, KS

United States Military Academy, West Point, NY

US Naval Academy, Annapolis, MD

US Naval Observatory, Washington, DC

US Property & Fiscal Office for Mississippi, Jackson, MS

US Property and Fiscal Office-NY, Rochester Warehouse, Rochester, NY

Utah Test and Training Range, Hill AFB, UT

Van Nuys Air National Guard Base, Van Nuys, CA

Vance Air Force Base, Vance AFB, OK

Vandenberg Air Force Base, Vandenberg AFB, CA

Vint Hill Communications and Electronics Support Activity, Warrenton, VA

Virginia Office of the Adjutant General, Richmond, VA

Volk Field Air National Guard Base, Camp Douglas, WI

Volunteer Army Ammunition Plant, Chattanooga, TN

Wahiawa Naval Communications Area Master Station, Eastern Pacific, Wahiawa, HI

Waianae Army Recreation Center, Waianae, HI

Walter Reed Army Medical Center, Washington, DC

Francis E Warren Air Force Base, F E Warren AFB, WY

Washington Army National Guard Mobilization and Training Equipment Site, Yakima, WA

Washington, DC, Coast Guard Air Station, Arlington, VA

Washington, DC, Naval Air Facility, Andrews AFB, MD

Washington Navy Yard, Naval District of Washington, Washington, DC

Watervliet Arsenal, Watervliet, NY

Westover Air Force Base, Westover AFB, MA

Wheeler Air Force Base, Wheeler AFB, HI

Whidbey Island Naval Air Station, Oak Harbor, WA

Whidbey Island Naval Facility, Detachment Coos Head, Charleston, OR

White Sands Missile Range, White Sands Missile Range, NM

Whiteman Air Force Base, Whiteman AFB, MO

Whiting Field Naval Air Station, Milton, FL

Wilder Air Force Station, Wilder, ID

Williams Air Force Base, Williams AFB, AZ

Willow Grove Naval Air Station, Willow Grove, PA

Winter Harbor Naval Security Group Activity, Winter Harbor, ME

Wisconsin National Guard, Madison, WI

Woods Hole Coast Guard Group, Woods Hole, MA

Wright-Patterson Air Force Base, Wright-Patterson AFB, OH

Wurtsmith Air Force Base, Wurtsmith AFB, MI

Yakima Firing Center, Yakima, WA

Yankeetown Coast Guard Station, Yankeetown, FL

Yorktown Coast Guard Reserve Training Center, Yorktown, VA

Yorktown Naval Weapons Station, Yorktown, VA

Yuma Marine Corps Air Station, Yuma, AZ

Yuma Proving Ground, Yuma, AZ

103rd Tactical Fighter Group (ANG), Windsor Locks, CT

104th Tactical Fighter Group (ANG), Westfield, MA

105th Tactical Air Support Group (ANG), White Plains, NY

106th Aerospace Rescue and Recovery Group (ANG), Westhampton Beach, NY

109th Tactical Airlift Group (ANG), Schenectady, NY

114th Tactical Fighter Group (ANG), Sioux Falls, SD

114th Tactical Fighter Training Squadron, Klamath Falls, OR

118th Tactical Airlift Wing (ANG), Nashville, TN

119th Fighter Interceptor Group, Fargo, ND

120th Fighter Interceptor Group Air National Guard Base, Great Falls, MT

122nd Tactical Fighter Wing (ANG), Fort Wayne, IN

123rd Tactical Airlift Wing/Kentucky Air National Guard, Louisville, KY

125th Fighter Interceptor Group, Florida Air National Guard, Jacksonville, FL

128th Air Refueling Group, Milwaukee, WI

129th Tactical Control Squadron, Kennesaw, GA

130th Tactical Airlift Group (ANG), Charleston, WV

131st Tactical Fighter Wing (ANG), Saint Louis, MO

133rd Tactical Airlift Wing, Minneapolis-Saint Paul IAP, MN

134th Air Refueling Group (ANG), Knoxville, TN

136th Tactical Airlift Wing (ANG), Dallas, TX

137th Tactical Airlift Wing (ANG), Oklahoma City, OK

138th Tactical Fighter Group (ANG), Tulsa, OK

139th Tactical Airlift Group (ANG), Saint Joseph, MO

13th Coast Guard District Office, Seattle, WA

142nd Fighter Interceptor Group (ANG), Portland, OR

143rd Tactical Airlift Group (ANG), Providence, RI

145th Tactical Airlift Group, Charlotte, NC

145th Tactical Airlift Group (ANG), Charlotte, NC

148th Combat Communications Group (ANG), Ontario, CA

148th Tactical Reconnaissance Group (ANG), Duluth, MN

151st Air Refueling Group (ANG), Salt Lake City, UT

153rd Tactical Airlift Group (ANG), Cheyenne, WY

158th Fighter Interceptor Group, Burlington IAP, VT

161st Air Refueling Group (ANG), Phoenix, AZ

162nd Tactical Fighter Group, Tucson, AZ

164th Tactical Airlift Group (ANG), Memphis, TN

166th Tactical Airlift Group (ANG), Wilmington, DE

167th Tactical Airlift Group (ANG), Martinsburg, WV

172nd Tactical Airlift Group (ANG), Jackson, MS

174th Tactical Fighter Wing (ANG), Syracuse, NY

175th Tactical Airlift Group (ANG), Baltimore, MD

177th Fighter Interceptor Group, NJANG, Pleasantville, NJ

178th Tactical Fighter Group (ANG), Springfield, OH

179th Tactical Airlift Group (ANG), Mansfield, OH

180th Tactical Fighter Group, Swanton, OH

181st Tactical Fighter Group (ANG), Terre Haute, IN

182nd Tactical Air Support Group, Peoria, IL

183rd Tactical Fighter Group (ANG), Springfield, IL

185th Tactical Fighter Group (ANG), Sergeant Bluff, IA

186th Tactical Reconnaissance Group (ANG), Meridian, MS

187th Tactical Reconnaissance Group (ANG), Montgomery, AL

188th Tactical Fighter Group, Fort Smith, AR

190th Air Refueling Group, Forbes Field, Topeka, KS

192nd Tactical Fighter Group, Sandston, VA

193rd Electronic Combat Group (ANG), Middletown, PA

3545th US Air Force Recruiting Squadron, Saint Louis, MO

438th Aerial Port Squadron, Detachment 1 (MAC), Philadelphia, PA

84th Division (Training), Headquarters, Milwaukee, WI

910th Tactical Airlift Group (AFRES), Vienna, OH

914th Tactical Airlift Group, Niagara Falls, NY

926th Tactical Fighter Group, Headquarters, Belle Chasse, LA

92nd Aerial Port Squadron, Wyoming, PA

BRANCH OF SERVICE INDEX

AIR FORCE

Alabama
Gunter Air Force Base, Gunter AFB
Maxwell Air Force Base, Maxwell AFB

Alaska
Campion Air Force Station, Campion Air Force Station
Cape Lisburne Air Force Station, Cape Lisburne Air Force Station
Cape Newenham Air Force Station, Cape Newenham Air Force Station
Cape Romanzof Air Force Station, Cape Romanzof Air Force Station
Cold Bay Air Force Station, Cold Bay
Eielson Air Force Base, Eielson AFB
Elmendorf Air Force Base, Anchorage
Fort Yukon Air Force Station, Fort Yukon
Galena Airport, Galena
Indian Mountain Air Force Station, Indian Mountain Air Force Station
Kotzebue Air Force Station, Kotzebue
Murphy Dome Air Force Station, Murphy Dome Air Force Station
Shemya Air Force Base, Shemya AFB
Sparrevohn Air Force Station, Sparrevohn Air Force Station
Tatalina Air Force Station, McGrath
Tin City Air Force Station, Tin City Air Force Station

Arizona
Davis-Monthan Air Force Base, Tucson
Gila Bend Air Force Auxiliary Field, Gila Bend AF Auxiliary Field
Luke Air Force Base, Luke AFB
Williams Air Force Base, Williams AFB

Arkansas
Eaker Air Force Base, Blytheville
Little Rock Air Force Base, Little Rock AFB

California
Beale Air Force Base, Beale AFB
Castle Air Force Base, Castle AFB
Crescent City Air Force Station, Klamath
Edwards Air Force Base, Edwards AFB
George Air Force Base, George AFB
Los Angeles Air Force Base, El Segundo
March Air Force Base, March AFB
Mather Air Force Base, Mather AFB
McClellan Air Force Base, McClellan AFB
Norton Air Force Base, Norton AFB
Onizuka Air Force Base, Sunnyvale
Pillar Point Air Force Station, El Granada
Point Arena Air Force Station, Point Arena AFS
Presidio of Monterey, Monterey
Production Flight Test Installation, Air Force Plant 42, Palmdale
Travis Air Force Base, Travis AFB
Vandenberg Air Force Base, Vandenberg AFB

Colorado
Air Reserve Personnel Center, Denver
Falcon Air Force Base, Falcon AFB
La Junta Strategic Training Range, La Junta
Lowry Air Force Base, Lowry AFB
Peterson Air Force Base, Peterson AFB
US Air Force Academy, United States Air Force Academy

Delaware
Dover Air Force Base, Dover AFB

District Of Columbia
Bolling Air Force Base, Bolling AFB

Florida
Cape Canaveral Air Force Station, Cocoa Beach
Cudjoe Key Air Force Station, Sugarloaf Shores
Eglin Air Force Base, Fort Walton Beach
Homestead Air Force Base, Homestead
Hurlburt Field, Hurlburt Field
MacDill Air Force Base, MacDill AFB
Operating Location Alpha Bravo South East Air Defense Sector, Old Town
Patrick Air Force Base, Patrick AFB
Richmond Heights Air Force Station, Homestead
Tyndall Air Force Base, Tyndall AFB

Georgia
Dobbins Air Force Base, Dobbins AFB
Moody Air Force Base, Moody AFB
Robins Air Force Base, Robins AFB
Savannah Air Force Station, Savannah

Hawaii
Bellows Air Force Station, Waimanalo
Hickam Air Force Base, Hickam AFB
Wheeler Air Force Base, Wheeler AFB

Idaho
Mountain Home Air Force Base, Mountain Home AFB
Wilder Air Force Station, Wilder

Illinois
Chanute Air Force Base, Chanute AFB
Scott Air Force Base, Scott AFB

Indiana
Grissom Air Force Base, Grissom AFB

Kansas
McConnell Air Force Base, McConnell AFB

Louisiana
Barksdale Air Force Base, Barksdale AFB
England Air Force Base, Alexandria

Maine
Loring Air Force Base, Loring AFB

Maryland
Andrews Air Force Base, Andrews AFB
Fort George G Meade, Fort Meade

Massachusetts
Hanscom Air Force Base, Bedford
Massachusetts Military Reservation/Otis Air National Guard Base, Cape Cod
North Truro Air Force Station, North Truro

Michigan
Calumet Air Force Station, Calumet
Empire Air Force Station, Empire AFS
Port Austin Air Force Station, Operating Location Alpha Nancy, Northeast Air Division Sector, Port Austin
K I Sawyer Air Force Base, K I Sawyer
Wurtsmith Air Force Base, Wurtsmith AFB

Mississippi
Columbus Air Force Base, Columbus
Keesler Air Force Base, Biloxi

Missouri
Richards-Gebaur Air Force Base, Richards-Gebaur AFB
Whiteman Air Force Base, Whiteman AFB
3545th US Air Force Recruiting Squadron, Saint Louis

Montana
1st Combat Evaluation Group, Detachment 18 (SAC), Forsyth
Kallspell Air Force Station, Lakeside
Malmstrom Air Force Base, Great Falls

Nebraska
1st Combat Evaluation Group, Detachment 10 (SAC), Hastings
Offutt Air Force, Offutt AFB

Nevada
Nellis Air Force Base, Las Vegas

New Hampshire
Pease Air Force Base, Pease AFB

New Jersey
Gibbsboro Air Force Station, Gibbsboro
McGuire Air Force Base, McGuire AFB

New Mexico
Cannon Air Force Base, Cannon AFB
Holloman Air Force Base, Holloman AFB
Kirtland Air Force Base, Albuquerque

New York
Griffiss Air Force Base, Griffiss AFB
Plattsburgh Air Force Base, Plattsburgh
Stewart Air National Guard Base, Newburgh

North Carolina
Fort Fisher Air Force Station, Kure Beach
Fort Fisher Recreation Area, Kure Beach
Pope Air Force Base, Pope AFB
Seymour Johnson Air Force Base, Goldsboro

North Dakota
Cavalier Air Force Station, Cavalier
Concrete MEWS, Concrete
Finley Air Force Station, Finley
Fortuna Air Force Station, Fortuna AFS
Grand Forks Air Force Base, Grand Forks AFB
Minot Air Force Base, Minot AFB

Ohio
Newark Air Force Base, Newark AFB
Wright-Patterson Air Force Base, Wright-Patterson AFB

AIR FORCE *(continued)*
Oklahoma
Altus Air Force Base, Altus AFB
Oklahoma City Air Force Station, Oklahoma City AFS
Tinker Air Force Base, Tinker AFB
Vance Air Force Base, Vance AFB
Oregon
Dallas Air Force Station, Dallas AFS
Mount Hebo Air Force Station, Hebo
North Bend Air Force Station, North Bend AFS
Pennsylvania
Willow Grove Naval Air Station, Willow Grove
438th Aerial Port Squadron, Detachment 1 (MAC), Philadelphia
South Carolina
Charleston Air Force Base, Charleston AFB
Myrtle Beach Air Force Base, Myrtle Beach
North Auxiliary Air Field, North
Shaw Air Force Base, Shaw AFB
South Dakota
Ellsworth Air Force Base, Ellsworth AFB
Tennessee
Arnold Air Force Base, Arnold AFB
Texas
Air Force Plant Representative Office, Air Force Plant No 4, Fort Worth
Bergstrom Air Force Base, Austin
Brooks Air Force Base, Brooks AFB
Carswell Air Force Base, Fort Worth
Dyess Air Force Base, Abilene
Goodfellow Air Force Base, Goodfellow AFB
Kelly Air Force Base, Kelly AFB
Lackland Air Force Base, Lackland AFB
Laughlin Air Force Base, Laughlin AFB
Randolph Air Force Base, Randolph AFB
Reese Air Force Base, Reese AFB
Sheppard Air Force Base, Sheppard AFB
Utah
Hill Air Force Base, Hill AFB
Utah Test and Training Range, Hill AFB
Virginia
Fort Lee Air Force Station, Petersberg
Langley Air Force Base, Langley AFB
Washington
Fairchild Air Force Base, Fairchild AFB
Makah Air Force Station, Neah Bay
McChord Air Force Base, McChord AFB
Mica Peak Air Force Station, Spokane
Wyoming
Francis E Warren Air Force Base, F E Warren AFB

AIR FORCE RESERVE
Illinois
O'Hare Air Reserve Forces Facility, O'Hare ARFF
Massachusetts
Westover Air Force Base, Westover AFB
New York
Fort Totten, Queens
914th Tactical Airlift Group, Niagara Falls
Pennsylvania
92nd Aerial Port Squadron, Wyoming

AIR NATIONAL GUARD
Alabama
Smith Air National Guard Base, Birmingham
187th Tactical Reconnaissance Group (ANG), Montgomery
Alaska
Kulis Air National Guard Base, Anchorage
Arizona
Papago Military Installation, Phoenix
161st Air Refueling Group (ANG), Phoenix
162nd Tactical Fighter Group, Tucson
Arkansas
188th Tactical Fighter Group, Fort Smith

California
Fresno Air National Guard Base, Fresno Air Terminal
Van Nuys Air National Guard Base, Van Nuys
148th Combat Communications Group (ANG), Ontario
Colorado
Buckley Air National Guard Base, Aurora
Connecticut
103rd Tactical Fighter Group (ANG), Windsor Locks
Delaware
166th Tactical Airlift Group (ANG), Wilmington
Florida
125th Fighter Interceptor Group, Florida Air National Guard, Jacksonville
Georgia
Dobbins Air Force Base, Dobbins AFB
Georgia Air National Guard Field Training Site, Headquarters, Savannah
Georgia Department of Defense, Military Division, Atlanta
Travis Field, Garden City
129th Tactical Control Squadron, Kennesaw
Idaho
Gowen Field, Boise
Illinois
182nd Tactical Air Support Group, Peoria
183rd Tactical Fighter Group (ANG), Springfield
Indiana
122nd Tactical Fighter Wing (ANG), Fort Wayne
181st Tactical Fighter Group (ANG), Terre Haute
Iowa
Iowa Air National Guard, Des Moines
185th Tactical Fighter Group (ANG), Sergeant Bluff
Kansas
190th Air Refueling Group, Forbes Field, Topeka
Kentucky
123rd Tactical Airlift Wing/Kentucky Air National Guard, Louisville
Louisiana
Camp Beauregard, Pineville
Hammond Air National Guard Station, Hammond
Jackson Barracks, New Orleans
Maine
Bangor Air National Guard Base, Bangor
Maryland
175th Tactical Airlift Group (ANG), Baltimore
Massachusetts
Massachusetts Military Reservation/Otis Air National Guard Base, Cape Cod
104th Tactical Fighter Group (ANG), Westfield
Michigan
Battle Creek Air National Guard Base, Battle Creek
Camp Grayling Army and Air National Guard Training Center, Grayling
Phelps Collins Air National Guard Base, Alpena
Selfridge Air National Guard Base, Selfridge ANG Base
Minnesota
133rd Tactical Airlift Wing, Minneapolis-Saint Paul IAP
148th Tactical Reconnaissance Group (ANG), Duluth
Mississippi
Mississippi Air National Guard Field Training Site, Headquarters, Gulfport
172nd Tactical Airlift Group (ANG), Jackson
186th Tactical Reconnaissance Group (ANG), Meridian

Missouri
131st Tactical Fighter Wing (ANG), Saint Louis
139th Tactical Airlift Group (ANG), Saint Joseph
Montana
120th Fighter Interceptor Group Air National Guard Base, Great Falls
Nebraska
Lincoln Air National Guard Base, Lincoln
Nevada
May Air National Guard Base, Reno
Nevada National Guard Headquarters, Carson City
New Jersey
177th Fighter Interceptor Group, NJANG, Pleasantville
New Mexico
New Mexico National Guard State Headquarters, Santa Fe
New York
Roslyn Air National Guard Station, Roslyn
Stewart Air National Guard Base, Newburgh
105th Tactical Air Support Group (ANG), White Plains
106th Aerospace Rescue and Recovery Group (ANG), Westhampton Beach
109th Tactical Airlift Group (ANG), Schenectady
174th Tactical Fighter Wing (ANG), Syracuse
North Carolina
145th Tactical Airlift Group, Charlotte
145th Tactical Airlift Group (ANG), Charlotte
North Dakota
119th Fighter Interceptor Group, Fargo
Ohio
Rickenbacker Air National Guard Base, Columbus
178th Tactical Fighter Group (ANG), Springfield
179th Tactical Airlift Group (ANG), Mansfield
180th Tactical Fighter Group, Swanton
910th Tactical Airlift Group (AFRES), Vienna
Oklahoma
137th Tactical Airlift Wing (ANG), Oklahoma City
138th Tactical Fighter Group (ANG), Tulsa
Oregon
114th Tactical Fighter Training Squadron, Klamath Falls
142nd Fighter Interceptor Group (ANG), Portland
Pennsylvania
Pennsylvania Air National Guard, Pittsburgh
193rd Electronic Combat Group (ANG), Middletown
Rhode Island
143rd Tactical Airlift Group (ANG), Providence
South Carolina
McEntire Air National Guard Base, McEntire ANGB
South Dakota
114th Tactical Fighter Group (ANG), Sioux Falls
Tennessee
118th Tactical Airlift Wing (ANG), Nashville
134th Air Refueling Group (ANG), Knoxville
164th Tactical Airlift Group (ANG), Memphis
Texas
Ellington Air National Guard Base, Houston
Garland Air National Guard Station, Garland
136th Tactical Airlift Wing (ANG), Dallas
Utah
151st Air Refueling Group (ANG), Salt Lake City

AIR NATIONAL GUARD (continued)

Vermont
158th Fighter Interceptor Group, Burlington IAP

Virginia
Virginia Office of the Adjutant General, Richmond
192nd Tactical Fighter Group, Sandston

Washington
Four Lakes Communications Station, Cheney

West Virginia
130th Tactical Airlift Group (ANG), Charleston
167th Tactical Airlift Group (ANG), Martinsburg

Wisconsin
Hardwood Air-to-Ground Weapons Range, Camp Douglas
Truax Air National Guard Base, Madison
Volk Field Air National Guard Base, Camp Douglas
Wisconsin National Guard, Madison
128th Air Refueling Group, Milwaukee

Wyoming
153rd Tactical Airlift Group (ANG), Cheyenne

ARMY

Alabama
Anniston Army Depot, Anniston
Fort McClellan, Anniston
Fort Rucker, Fort Rucker
Redstone Arsenal, Redstone Arsenal
US Army Corps of Engineers, Huntsville Division, Huntsville
US Army Corps of Engineers, Mobile District, Mobile

Alaska
Fort Greely, Fort Greely
Fort Richardson, Fort Richardson
Fort Wainwright, Fort Wainwright

Arizona
Fort Huachuca, Fort Huachuca
Yuma Proving Ground, Yuma

Arkansas
Fort Chaffee, Fort Chaffee
US Army Corps of Engineers, Little Rock District, Little Rock

California
Fort Hunter Liggett, Fort Hunter Liggett
Fort Irwin, National Training Center, Fort Irwin
Fort Mason, San Francisco
Fort Ord, Fort Ord
Hamilton Army Airfield, Novato
Letterman Army Medical Center, San Francisco
Military Traffic Management Command, Western Area, Oakland
Oakland Army Base, California, Oakland
Parks Reserve Forces Training Area, Dublin
Presidio of Monterey, Monterey
Presidio of San Francisco, San Francisco
Sacramento Army Depot, Sacramento
Sharpe Army Depot, Lathrop
Sierra Army Depot, Herlong
US Army Corps of Engineers, Sacramento District, Sacramento
US Army Corps of Engineers, South Pacific Division, San Francisco

Colorado
Fitzsimons Army Medical Center, Aurora
Fort Carson and 4th Infantry Division (Mechanized), Fort Carson
Pueblo Army Depot Activity, Pueblo

District Of Columbia
Fort Lesley J McNair, Washington
Military District of Washington, Washington
US Army Corps of Engineers, Headquarters, Washington
Walter Reed Army Medical Center, Washington

Florida
US Army Corps of Engineers, Jacksonville District, Jacksonville

Georgia
Fort Benning, Fort Benning
Fort Gillem, Forest Park
Fort Gordon, Fort Gordon
Fort McPherson, Fort McPherson
Fort Stewart, Hinesville
Hunter Army Air Field, Savannah
US Army Corps of Engineers, South Atlantic Division, Atlanta

Hawaii
Fort DeRussy, Honolulu
Fort Kamehameha, Honolulu
Fort Ruger, Honolulu
Fort Shafter, Fort Shafter
Pohakuloa Training Area, Hilo
Schofield Barracks, Schofield Barracks
Tripler Army Medical Center, Tripler AMC
US Army Corps of Engineers, Pacific Ocean Division, Honolulu
Waianae Army Recreation Center, Waianae

Illinois
Fort Sheridan, Fort Sheridan
Joliet Army Ammunition Plant, Joliet
Charles Melvin Price Support Center, US Army, Granite City
Rock Island Arsenal, Rock Island
Savanna Army Depot Activity, Savanna
US Army Corps of Engineers, Chicago District, Chicago
US Army Corps of Engineers, North Central Division, Chicago
US Army Corps of Engineers, Rock Island District, Rock Island

Indiana
Fort Benjamin Harrison, Fort Benjamin Harrison
Jefferson Proving Ground, Madison

Iowa
Iowa Army Ammunition Plant, Middletown

Kansas
Defense Industrial Plant Equipment Facility, Atchison
Fort Leavenworth, Fort Leavenworth
Fort Riley, Fort Riley
Kansas Army Ammunition Plant, Parsons

Kentucky
Fort Campbell, Fort Campbell
Fort Knox, Fort Knox
Lexington-Blue Grass Army Depot, Lexington

Louisiana
Fort Polk, Fort Polk
Louisiana Army Ammunition Plant, Shreveport
New Orleans Naval Support Activity, New Orleans

Maryland
Aberdeen Proving Ground, Aberdeen Proving Ground
Adelphi Laboratory Center, Adelphi
Army Publications Distribution Center, Baltimore
Fort Detrick, Frederick
Fort George G Meade, Fort Meade
Fort Ritchie, Fort Ritchie
US Army Corps of Engineers, Baltimore District, Baltimore

Massachusetts
Army Materiels Technology Laboratory, Watertown
Army Natick Research, Development & Engineering Center, Natick
Fort Devens, Fort Devens
US Army Corps of Engineers, New England Division, Waltham

Michigan
Army Tank-Automotive Command, Warren
US Army Corps of Engineers, Detroit District, Detroit

Minnesota
US Army Corps of Engineers, St Paul District, Saint Paul

Mississippi
Mississippi Army Ammunition Plant, Stennis Space Center
US Army Corps of Engineers, Lower Mississippi Valley Division, Vicksburg
US Army Corps of Engineers Waterways Experiment Station, Vicksburg
US Property & Fiscal Office for Mississippi, Jackson

Missouri
Army Reserve Personnel Center, Saint Louis
Army Troop Support Command, Saint Louis
Fort Leonard Wood, Fort Leonard Wood
US Army Corps of Engineers, Kansas City District, Kansas City
US Army Corps of Engineers, St Louis District, Saint Louis

Nebraska
Cornhusker Army Ammunition Plant, Grand Island
US Army Corps of Engineers, Missouri River Division, Omaha
US Army Corps of Engineers, Omaha District, Omaha

Nevada
Hawthorne Army Ammunition Plant, Hawthorne

New Hampshire
Army Cold Regions Research and Engineering Laboratory, Hanover

New Jersey
Bayonne Military Ocean Terminal, Bayonne
Fort Dix, Fort Dix
Fort Monmouth, Fort Monmouth

New Mexico
Fort Wingate Depot Activity, Gallup
Kirtland Air Force Base, Albuquerque
White Sands Missile Range, White Sands Missile Range

New York
Fort Drum, Fort Drum
Fort Hamilton, Brooklyn
Fort Tilden, Fort Tilden
Seneca Army Depot, Romulus
US Army Corps of Engineers, Buffalo District, Buffalo
US Army Corps of Engineers, North Atlantic Division, New York
United States Military Academy, West Point
Watervliet Arsenal, Watervliet

North Carolina
Army Research Office, Research Triangle Park
Fort Bragg, Fort Bragg
Sunny Point Military Ocean Terminal, Southport

Ohio
Army Aviation Support Facility #1, Greensburg
Lima Army Tank Plant, Lima
US Army Corps of Engineers, Ohio River Division, Cincinnati

Oklahoma
Fort Sill, Fort Sill
McAlester Army Ammunition Plant, McAlester
US Army Corps of Engineers, Tulsa District, Tulsa

Oregon
Umatilla Army Depot Activity, Hermiston
US Army Corps of Engineers, North Pacific Division, Portland
US Army Corps of Engineers, Portland District, Portland

Pennsylvania
Carlisle Barracks, Carlisle Barracks
Fort Indiantown Gap, Annville
Charles E Kelly Support Facility, Oakdale
Letterkenny Army Depot, Chambersburg
New Cumberland Army Depot, New Cumberland
Scranton Army Ammunition Plant, Scranton
Tobyhanna Army Depot, Tobyhanna

ARMY (continued)

US Army Corps of Engineers, Pittsburgh District, Pittsburgh
Willow Grove Naval Air Station, Willow Grove

South Carolina
Fort Jackson, Columbia
Military Traffic Management Command, South Atlantic Outport, North Charleston
US Army Corps of Engineers, Charleston District, Charleston

South Dakota
Fort Meade Military Reservation, Fort Meade

Tennessee
Holston Army Ammunition Plant, Kingsport
Milan Army Ammunition Plant, Milan
US Army Corps of Engineers, Memphis District, Memphis
US Army Corps of Engineers, Nashville District, Nashville
Volunteer Army Ammunition Plant, Chattanooga

Texas
Camp Bullis, Fort Sam Houston
Corpus Christi Army Depot, Corpus Christi
Fort Bliss, Fort Bliss
Fort Hood, Fort Hood
Fort Sam Houston, Fort Sam Houston
Longhorn Army Ammunition Plant, Marshall
Red River Army Depot, Texarkana
US Army Corps of Engineers, Southwestern District, Dallas
US Army Corps of Engineers, Southwestern Division, Dallas
US Army Engineer District, Galveston, Galveston

Utah
Dugway Proving Ground, Dugway
General Rail Shops, Ogden
Tooele Army Depot, Tooele

Virginia
Army Criminal Investigation Command, Falls Church
Army Materiel Command Headquarters, Alexandria
Cameron Station, Military District of Washington, Alexandria
Fort Belvoir, Fort Belvoir
Fort Eustis, Newport News
Fort A P Hill, Bowling Green
Fort Lee, Petersburg
Fort Monroe, Fort Monroe
Fort Myer, Arlington
Fort Story, Fort Story
Humphreys Engineer Center, Fort Belvoir
Radford Army Ammunition Plant, Radford
Vint Hill Communications and Electronics Support Activity, Warrenton

Washington
Fort Lawton, Seattle
Fort Lewis, Fort Lewis
Madigan Army Medical Center, Tacoma
US Army Corps of Engineers, Walla Walla District, Walla Walla
Yakima Firing Center, Yakima

Wisconsin
Badger Army Ammunition Plant, Baraboo
Fort McCoy, Fort McCoy

ARMY NATIONAL GUARD

Alabama
Alabama State Military Department, Montgomery

Arizona
Navajo Depot Activity, Bellemont
Papago Military Installation, Phoenix

Arkansas
Camp Joseph T Robinson, North Little Rock

California
Camp San Luis Obispo, San Luis Obispo
Long Beach Combined Support Maintenance Shop, Long Beach

Florida
Camp Blanding Training Site, Starke

Georgia
Army Aviation Support Facility, Winder
Catoosa Area Training Center, Tunnel Hill
Georgia Department of Defense, Military Division, Atlanta

Idaho
Gowen Field, Boise

Illinois
Camp Lincoln, Springfield

Iowa
Camp Dodge Iowa, Johnston

Louisiana
Camp Beauregard, Pineville
Jackson Barracks, New Orleans

Massachusetts
Camp Edwards, ARNG Training Site, Camp Edwards
Massachusetts Military Reservation/Otis Air National Guard Base, Cape Cod

Michigan
Camp Grayling Army and Air National Guard Training Center, Grayling
Michigan National Guard Mobilization and Training Equipment Site, Grayling

Mississippi
Camp Shelby Training Site, Camp Shelby

Montana
Fort William Henry Harrison, Helena

Nevada
Nevada National Guard Headquarters, Carson City

New Mexico
New Mexico National Guard State Headquarters, Santa Fe

New York
Camp Smith Training Site, Peekskill
US Property and Fiscal Office-NY, Rochester Warehouse, Rochester

Ohio
Ohio National Guard, Unit Training Equipment Site #1, Newton Falls

Oklahoma
Camp Gruber Training Site, Braggs

Oregon
Camp Rilea, Oregon National Guard Training Site, Warrenton

Pennsylvania
Willow Grove Naval Air Station, Willow Grove

South Dakota
Camp Rapid, Rapid City
Mitchell National Guard Complex, Mitchell

Texas
Camp Mabry, Austin
Camp Swift (Unit Training and Equipment Site #3), Basytop

Utah
Camp W G Williams, Riverton

Vermont
Ethan Allen Firing Range, Jericho

Virginia
State Military Reservation, Camp Pendleton, Virginia Beach
Virginia Office of the Adjutant General, Richmond

Washington
Washington Army National Guard Mobilization and Training Equipment Site, Yakima

West Virginia
Camp Dawson, Army Training Site, Kingwood

Wisconsin
Wisconsin National Guard, Madison

Wyoming
Camp Guernsey, Wyoming Army National Guard Training Site, Guernsey

ARMY RESERVE

Massachusetts
Fort Rodman, US Army Reserve Center, New Bedford

Wisconsin
84th Division (Training), Headquarters, Milwaukee

COAST GUARD

Alabama
Mobile Coast Guard Aviation Training Center, Mobile
Mobile Coast Guard Base, Mobile

Alaska
Kodiak Coast Guard Support Center, Kodiak

California
Alameda Coast Guard Island, Alameda
Coast Guard Communication Area Master Station Pacific, San Francisco, Point Reyes Station
Coast Guard Communication Area Master Station Pacific Transmitter Site, Bolinas
Coast Guard Pacific Strike Team, Novato
Petaluma Coast Guard Training Center, Petaluma
Presidio of Monterey, Monterey
San Diego Coast Guard Group, San Diego
San Francisco Coast Guard Air Station, San Francisco
San Francisco Coast Guard Base, San Francisco

Connecticut
US Coast Guard Academy, New London

District Of Columbia
US Coast Guard Headquarters, Washington

Florida
Clearwater Coast Guard Air Station, Clearwater
Cortez Coast Guard Station, Cortez
Egmont Key Coast Guard Light Station, Saint Petersburg
Fort Myers Beach Coast Guard Station, Fort Myers Beach
Miami Beach Coast Guard Base, Miami Beach
Miami Coast Guard Air Station, Opa-Locka
Pensacola Coast Guard Station, Pensacola
St Petersburg Coast Guard Station, Saint Petersburg
Tampa Coast Guard Marine Safety Office, Tampa
Yankeetown Coast Guard Station, Yankeetown

Hawaii
Sand Island Coast Guard Station, Honolulu

Louisiana
Eighth Coast Guard District, New Orleans

Maryland
US Coast Guard Yard, Curtis Bay

Massachusetts
Massachusetts Military Reservation/Otis Air National Guard Base, Cape Cod
Woods Hole Coast Guard Group, Woods Hole

Michigan
Detroit Coast Guard Group/Base, Detroit
Sault Ste Maric Coast Guard Base, Sault Ste Marie
Traverse City Coast Guard Air Station, Traverse City

Missouri
St Louis Coast Guard Base, Saint Louis

New Jersey
Cape May Coast Guard Training Center, Cape May

New York
Brooklyn Coast Guard Air Station, Brooklyn
Brooklyn Coast Guard Supply Center, Brooklyn
Buffalo Coast Guard Group, Buffalo
Governors Island Coast Guard Support Center, Governors Island

COAST GUARD (continued)

North Carolina
Elizabeth City Coast Guard Air Station, Elizabeth City
Elizabeth City Coast Guard Aircraft Repair & Supply Center, Elizabeth City

Pennsylvania
Philadelphia Coast Guard Marine Safety Office and Group, Philadelphia

South Carolina
Charleston Coast Guard Base, Charleston

Texas
Galveston Coast Guard Base, Galveston
Houston Coast Guard Air Station, Houston

Virginia
Fifth Coast Guard District, Portsmouth
Washington, DC, Coast Guard Air Station, Arlington
Yorktown Coast Guard Reserve Training Center, Yorktown

Washington
Seattle Coast Guard Support Center, Seattle
13th Coast Guard District Office, Seattle

Wisconsin
Milwaukee Coast Guard Base, Milwaukee

DEFENSE LOGISTICS AGENCY

California
Defense Depot Tracy, Tracy

Michigan
Defense Reutilization and Marketing Service, Battle Creek

Ohio
Defense Construction Supply Center, Columbus

Pennsylvania
Defense Personnel Support Center, Philadelphia
Mechanicsburg Defense Depot, Mechanicsburg

Utah
Ogden Defense Depot, Ogden

Virginia
Defense General Supply Center, Richmond

DEPARTMENT OF DEFENSE

District Of Columbia
Armed Forces Institute of Pathology, Washington

Missouri
Defense Mapping Agency Aerospace Center, Saint Louis

Pennsylvania
Defense Personnel Support Center, Philadelphia
Mechanicsburg Defense Depot, Mechanicsburg

Virginia
Camp Peary, Williamsburg
Defense Mapping Agency, Alexandria
Defense Mapping Agency, Reston

JOINT SERVICE INSTALLATION

Colorado
Cheyenne Mountain Air Force Base, Colorado Springs

District Of Columbia
Armed Forces Institute of Pathology, Washington

Hawaii
Kilauea Military Camp, Armed Forces Recreation Center, Hawaii National Park

Maryland
Alternate Joint Communications Center/Site R, Fort Ritchie

Ohio
Defense Construction Supply Center, Columbus
Gentile Air Force Station, Dayton

Tennessee
Memphis Defense Depot, Memphis

Virginia
Armed Forces Staff College, Norfolk
The Pentagon, Arlington

MARINES

Arizona
Yuma Marine Corps Air Station, Yuma

California
Barstow Marine Corps Logistics Base, Barstow
Camp Pendleton Marine Corps Base, Camp Pendleton
El Toro Marine Corps Air Station, Santa Ana
Presidio of Monterey, Monterey
San Diego Marine Corps Recruit Depot, San Diego
Tustin Marine Corps Air Station, Tustin
Twentynine Palms Marine Corps Air Ground Combat Center, Twentynine Palms
US Marine Corps Mountain Warfare Training Center, Bridgeport

District Of Columbia
Marine Barracks, Washington, Washington

Florida
Naval & Marine Corps Reserve Center, Tallahassee, Tallahassee

Georgia
Albany Marine Corps Logistics Base, Albany

Hawaii
Camp H M Smith, Camp H M Smith
Kaneohe Bay Marine Corps Air Station, Kaneohe Bay
Marine Barracks, Hawaii, Pearl Harbor

Kansas
US Marine Corps Reserve Support Center, Overland Park

Maryland
Fort George G Meade, Fort Meade

Massachusetts
Massachusetts Military Reservation/Otis Air National Guard Base, Cape Cod

New York
1st Marine Corps District Headquarters, Long Island
Stewart Air National Guard Base, Newburgh

North Carolina
Camp Lejeune Marine Corps Base, Camp Lejeune
Cherry Point Marine Corps Air Station, Cherry Point
New River Marine Corps Air Station, Jacksonville

Pennsylvania
Willow Grove Naval Air Station, Willow Grove

South Carolina
Beaufort Marine Corps Air Station, Beaufort
Parris Island Marine Corps Recruit Depot/ Eastern Recruiting Region, Parris Island

Virginia
Camp Elmore, Norfolk
Henderson Hall, Arlington
Quantico Marine Corps Combat Development Command, Quantico

NAVAL RESERVE

Florida
Naval & Marine Corps Reserve Center, Tallahassee, Tallahassee

Georgia
Atlanta Naval Air Station, Marietta

Maryland
Cumberland Naval Reserve Center, Cumberland
Washington, DC, Naval Air Facility, Andrews AFB

Massachusetts
South Weymouth Naval Air Station, South Weymouth

Missouri
Navy and Marine Corp Reserve Readiness Center, Bridgeton

Tennessee
Naval & Marine Corps Reserve Center, Chattanooga

NAVY

Alaska
Adak Naval Air Station, Adak
Adak Naval Security Group Activity, Adak

California
Alameda Naval Air Station, Alameda
Centerville Beach Naval Facility, Ferndale
China Lake Naval Weapons Center, China Lake
Concord Naval Weapons Station, Concord
Corona Naval Weapons Station, Corona
Coronado Naval Amphibious Base, San Diego
Crows Landing Naval Auxiliary Landing Field, Crows Landing
El Centro Naval Air Facility, El Centro
Fallbrook Naval Weapons Station, Fallbrook
Fleet Antisubmarine Warfare Training Center, Pacific, San Diego
Fleet Combat Training Center, Pacific, San Diego
Lemoore Naval Air Station, Lemoore
Long Beach Naval Station, Long Beach
Long Beach Navy Regional Medical Center, Long Beach
Long Beach Supervisor of Shipbuilding, Conversion and Repair, Long Beach
Mare Island Naval Complex, Vallejo
Miramar Naval Air Station, San Diego
Moffett Field Naval Air Station, Moffett Field
Naval Civil Engineering Laboratory, Port Hueneme
Naval Postgraduate School, Monterey
Naval Ship Weapons Systems Engineering Station, Port Hueneme
North Island Naval Air Station, San Diego
Oakland Naval Hospital/Naval Medical Command Northwest Region, Oakland
Oakland Naval Supply Center, Oakland
Point Mugu Naval Air Station, Point Mugu
Pomona Naval Weapons Station, Pomona
Port Hueneme, Naval Construction Battalion Center, Port Hueneme
Presidio of Monterey, Monterey
San Diego Naval Station, San Diego
San Diego Naval Submarine Base, San Diego
San Diego Naval Supply Center, San Diego
San Diego Naval Training Center, San Diego
San Diego Recruit Training Command, Naval Training Center, San Diego
San Nicholas Island Naval Facility, Point Mugu
Seal Beach Naval Weapons Station, Seal Beach
Skaggs Island Naval Security Group Activity, Sonoma
Stockton Naval Communications Station, Stockton
Treasure Island Naval Station, San Francisco

Connecticut
Naval Underwater Systems Center, New London
New London Naval Submarine Base, Groton

District Of Columbia
Anacostia Naval Station, Washington
Naval Research Laboratory, Washington
Naval Security Station, Washington
Space & Naval Warfare Systems Command, Washington
US Naval Observatory, Washington
Washington Navy Yard, Naval District of Washington, Washington

Florida
Cecil Field Naval Air Station, Jacksonville
Cecil Field Naval Air Station, Detachment, Astor
Corry Station Naval Technical Training Center, Pensacola
Jacksonville Naval Air Station, Jacksonville

NAVY *(continued)*

Jacksonville Naval Hospital, Jacksonville
Jacksonville Naval Supply Center, Jacksonville
Key West Naval Air Station, Key West
Mayport Naval Station, Mayport
Naval Coastal Systems Center, Panama City
Naval Education and Training Program Management Support Activity, Pensacola
Naval Research Laboratory, Underwater Sound Reference Laboratory, Orlando
Naval Training Systems Center, Orlando
Orlando Recruit Training Command, Orlando
Pensacola Naval Air Station, Pensacola
Pensacola Naval Aviation Depot, Pensacola
Pensacola Naval Hospital, Pensacola
Whiting Field Naval Air Station, Milton

Georgia
Kings Bay Naval Submarine Base, Kings Bay
Navy Supply Corps School, Athens

Hawaii
Barbers Point Naval Air Station, Barbers Point
NAVMAG Lualualei, Waianae
Pacific Missile Range Facility, Hawaiian Area, Kekaha, Kauai
Pearl Harbor Fleet Training Group, Pearl Harbor
Pearl Harbor Naval Station, Pearl Harbor
Pearl Harbor Naval Submarine Base, Pearl Harbor
Pearl Harbor Navy Public Works Center, Pearl Harbor
Wahiawa Naval Communications Area Master Station, Eastern Pacific, Wahiawa

Idaho
Idaho Falls Naval Administrative Unit, Idaho Falls
Idaho Falls Naval Nuclear Power Training Unit, Idaho Falls

Illinois
Glenview Naval Air Station, Glenview
Great Lakes Naval Training Center, Great Lakes
Recruit Training Command, Great Lakes, Great Lakes

Indiana
Naval Avionics Center, Indianapolis, Indianapolis
Naval Weapons Support Center Crane, Crane

Kentucky
Louisville Naval Ordnance Station, Louisville

Louisiana
New Orleans Naval Air Station, Belle Chasse
926th Tactical Fighter Group, Headquarters, Belle Chasse

Maine
Bath Supervisor of Shipbuilding, Conversion and Repair, Bath
Brunswick Naval Air Station, Brunswick
Cutler Naval Communications Unit, East Machias
Naval Reserve Readiness Center Portland, Portland
Winter Harbor Naval Security Group Activity, Winter Harbor

Maryland
Annapolis Naval Station, Annapolis
Fort George G Meade, Fort Meade
Indian Head Naval Ordnance Station, Indian Head
National Naval Medical Center, Bethesda
Naval Communication Unit, Washington, Cheltenham
Navy Recreation Center, Solomons
Patuxent River Naval Air Station, Patuxent River
David Taylor Research Center, Bethesda
David Taylor Research Center, Annapolis Laboratory, Annapolis
US Naval Academy, Annapolis

Massachusetts
Naval Clothing and Textile Research Facility, Natick
Navy Recruiting District Boston, Boston

Michigan
Detroit Naval Air Facility, Selfridge ANG Base

Mississippi
Gulfport Naval Construction Battalion Center, Gulfport
Meridian Naval Air Station, Meridian
Naval Oceanography Command, Stennis Space Center
Pascagoula Supervisor of Shipbuilding, Conversion and Repair, Pascagoula

Nevada
Fallon Naval Air Station, Fallon

New Hampshire
Portsmouth Naval Shipyard, Portsmouth

New Jersey
Naval Air Engineering Center, Lakehurst
Naval Air Propulsion Center, Trenton

New Mexico
Kirtland Air Force Base, Albuquerque

New York
Ballston Spa Nuclear Power Training Unit, Ballston Spa
Lake Seneca Naval Underwater Systems Center Detachment, Lake Seneca
Naval Station New York (Brooklyn), Brooklyn
Naval Station New York (Staten Island), Staten Island
Soctia Naval Administrative Unit, Soctia

North Carolina
Naval & Marine Corps Reserve Center, Raleigh

Ohio
Navy Finance Center, Cleveland

Oregon
Whidbey Island Naval Facility, Detachment Coos Head, Charleston

Pennsylvania
Aviation Supply Office Compound, Philadelphia
Navy Ships Parts Control Center, Mechanicsburg
Philadelphia Naval Base, Philadelphia
Philadelphia Naval Hospital, Philadelphia
Philadelphia Naval Shipyard, Philadelphia
Willow Grove Naval Air Station, Willow Grove

Rhode Island
Naval Education and Training Center, Newport

South Carolina
Beaufort Naval Hospital, Beaufort
Charleston Naval Base, Charleston
Charleston Naval Weapons Station, Charleston

Tennessee
Memphis Naval Air Station, Millington
Naval Weapons Industrial Reserve Plant, Bristol

Texas
Chase Field Naval Air Station, Beeville
Corpus Christi Naval Air Station, Corpus Christi
Corpus Christi Naval Hospital, Corpus Christi
Dallas Naval Air Station, Dallas
Goliad Naval Auxiliary Landing Field, Beeville
Kingsville Naval Air Station, Kingsville
Orange Grove Naval Auxiliary Landing Field, Orange Grove

Utah
Naval Plant Branch Representative Office, Magna

Virginia
Atlantic Division, Naval Facilities Engineering Command, Norfolk
Dam Neck, Fleet Combat Training Center, Atlantic, Virginia Beach
Fentress Naval Auxiliary Landing Field, Chesapeake
Fleet Antisubmarine Warfare Training Center, Atlantic, Norfolk
Little Creek Naval Amphibious Base, Norfolk
Naval Facilities Engineering Command Headquarters, Alexandria
Naval Sea Systems Command, Arlington
Naval Supply Center, Cheatham Annex, Williamsburg
Naval Supply Systems Command, Arlington
Naval Surface Warfare Center, Dahlgren
Newport News Supervisor of Shipbuilding, Conversion and Repair, Newport News
Norfolk Fleet Training Center, Norfolk
Norfolk Naval Air Station, Norfolk
Norfolk Naval Aviation Depot, Norfolk
Norfolk Naval Base, Norfolk
Norfolk Naval Shipyard, Portsmouth
Norfolk Naval Station, Norfolk
Norfolk Naval Supply Center, Norfolk
Norfolk Navy Public Works Center, Norfolk
Northwest Naval Security Group Activity, Chesapeake
Oceana Naval Air Station, Virginia Beach
Portsmouth Naval Hospital, Portsmouth
Portsmouth Supervisor of Shipbuilding, Conversion and Repair, Portsmouth
Shore Intermediate Maintenance Activity, Portsmouth
Training Command, US Atlantic Fleet, Norfolk
Yorktown Naval Weapons Station, Yorktown

Washington
Bangor Naval Submarine Base, Silverdale
Bremerton Naval Hospital, Bremerton
Naval Undersea Warfare Engineering Station, Keyport
Naval Undersea Warfare Engineering Station, Indian Island Detachment, Hadlock
Pacific Northwest Fleet Recreation and Education Support Center, Pacific Beach
Puget Sound Naval Shipyard, Bremerton
Puget Sound Naval Station, Seattle
Whidbey Island Naval Air Station, Oak Harbor

West Virginia
Sugar Grove Naval Radio Station, Sugar Grove

STATE AND BRANCH OF SERVICE INDEX

ALABAMA
Air Force
Gunter Air Force Base, Gunter AFB
Maxwell Air Force Base, Maxwell AFB
Air National Guard
Smith Air National Guard Base, Birmingham
187th Tactical Reconnaissance Group (ANG), Montgomery
Army
Anniston Army Depot, Anniston
Fort McClellan, Anniston
Fort Rucker, Fort Rucker
Redstone Arsenal, Redstone Arsenal
US Army Corps of Engineers, Huntsville Division, Huntsville
US Army Corps of Engineers, Mobile District, Mobile
Army National Guard
Alabama State Military Department, Montgomery
Coast Guard
Mobile Coast Guard Aviation Training Center, Mobile
Mobile Coast Guard Base, Mobile

ALASKA
Air Force
Campion Air Force Station, Campion Air Force Station
Cape Lisburne Air Force Station, Cape Lisburne Air Force Station
Cape Newenham Air Force Station, Cape Newenham Air Force Station
Cape Romanzof Air Force Station, Cape Romanzof Air Force Station
Cold Bay Air Force Station, Cold Bay
Eielson Air Force Base, Eielson AFB
Elmendorf Air Force Base, Anchorage
Fort Yukon Air Force Station, Fort Yukon
Galena Airport, Galena
Indian Mountain Air Force Station, Indian Mountain Air Force Station
Kotzebue Air Force Station, Kotzebue
Murphy Dome Air Force Station, Murphy Dome Air Force Station
Shemya Air Force Base, Shemya AFB
Sparrevohn Air Force Station, Sparrevohn Air Force Station
Tatalina Air Force Station, McGrath
Tin City Air Force Station, Tin City Air Force Station
Air National Guard
Kulis Air National Guard Base, Anchorage
Army
Fort Greely, Fort Greely
Fort Richardson, Fort Richardson
Fort Wainwright, Fort Wainwright

Coast Guard
Kodiak Coast Guard Support Center, Kodiak
Navy
Adak Naval Air Station, Adak
Adak Naval Security Group Activity, Adak

ARIZONA
Air Force
Davis-Monthan Air Force Base, Tucson
Gila Bend Air Force Auxiliary Field, Gila Bend AF Auxiliary Field
Luke Air Force Base, Luke AFB
Williams Air Force Base, Williams AFB
Air National Guard
Papago Military Installation, Phoenix
161st Air Refueling Group (ANG), Phoenix
162nd Tactical Fighter Group, Tucson
Army
Fort Huachuca, Fort Huachuca
Yuma Proving Ground, Yuma
Army National Guard
Navajo Depot Activity, Bellemont
Marines
Yuma Marine Corps Air Station, Yuma

ARKANSAS
Air Force
Eaker Air Force Base, Blytheville
Little Rock Air Force Base, Little Rock AFB
Air National Guard
188th Tactical Fighter Group, Fort Smith
Army
Fort Chaffee, Fort Chaffee
US Army Corps of Engineers, Little Rock District, Little Rock
Army National Guard
Camp Joseph T Robinson, North Little Rock

CALIFORNIA
Air Force
Beale Air Force Base, Beale AFB
Castle Air Force Base, Castle AFB
Crescent City Air Force Station, Klamath
Edwards Air Force Base, Edwards AFB
George Air Force Base, George AFB
Los Angeles Air Force Base, El Segundo
March Air Force Base, March AFB
Mather Air Force Base, Mather AFB
McClellan Air Force Base, McClellan AFB
Norton Air Force Base, Norton AFB
Onizuka Air Force Base, Sunnyvale
Pillar Point Air Force Station, El Granada
Point Arena Air Force Station, Point Arena AFS
Presidio of Monterey, Monterey

Production Flight Test Installation, Air Force Plant 42, Palmdale
Travis Air Force Base, Travis AFB
Vandenberg Air Force Base, Vandenberg AFB
Air National Guard
Fresno Air National Guard Base, Fresno Air Terminal
Van Nuys Air National Guard Base, Van Nuys
148th Combat Communications Group (ANG), Ontario
Army
Fort Hunter Liggett, Fort Hunter Liggett
Fort Irwin, National Training Center, Fort Irwin
Fort Mason, San Francisco
Fort Ord, Fort Ord
Hamilton Army Airfield, Novato
Letterman Army Medical Center, San Francisco
Military Traffic Management Command, Western Area, Oakland
Oakland Army Base, California, Oakland
Parks Reserve Forces Training Area, Dublin
Presidio of San Francisco, San Francisco
Sacramento Army Depot, Sacramento
Sharpe Army Depot, Lathrop
Sierra Army Depot, Herlong
US Army Corps of Engineers, Sacramento District, Sacramento
US Army Corps of Engineers, South Pacific Division, San Francisco
Army National Guard
Camp San Luis Obispo, San Luis Obispo
Long Beach Combined Support Maintenance Shop, Long Beach
Coast Guard
Alameda Coast Guard Island, Alameda
Coast Guard Communication Area Master Station Pacific, San Francisco, Point Reyes Station
Coast Guard Communication Area Master Station Pacific Transmitter Site, Bolinas
Coast Guard Pacific Strike Team, Novato
Petaluma Coast Guard Training Center, Petaluma
Presidio of Monterey, Monterey
San Diego Coast Guard Group, San Diego
San Francisco Coast Guard Air Station, San Francisco
San Francisco Coast Guard Base, San Francisco
Defense Logistics Agency
Defense Depot Tracy, Tracy
Marines
Barstow Marine Corps Logistics Base, Barstow
Camp Pendleton Marine Corps Base, Camp Pendleton

CALIFORNIA (continued)
El Toro Marine Corps Air Station, Santa Ana
Presidio of Monterey, Monterey
San Diego Marine Corps Recruit Depot, San Diego
Tustin Marine Corps Air Station, Tustin
Twentynine Palms Marine Corps Air Ground Combat Center, Twentynine Palms
US Marine Corps Mountain Warfare Training Center, Bridgeport

Navy
Alameda Naval Air Station, Alameda
Centerville Beach Naval Facility, Ferndale
China Lake Naval Weapons Center, China Lake
Concord Naval Weapons Station, Concord
Corona Naval Weapons Station, Corona
Coronado Naval Amphibious Base, San Diego
Crows Landing Naval Auxiliary Landing Field, Crows Landing
El Centro Naval Air Facility, El Centro
Fallbrook Naval Weapons Station, Fallbrook
Fleet Antisubmarine Warfare Training Center, Pacific, San Diego
Fleet Combat Training Center, Pacific, San Diego
Lemoore Naval Air Station, Lemoore
Long Beach Naval Station, Long Beach
Long Beach Navy Regional Medical Center, Long Beach
Long Beach Supervisor of Shipbuilding, Conversion and Repair, Long Beach
Mare Island Naval Complex, Vallejo
Miramar Naval Air Station, San Diego
Moffett Field Naval Air Station, Moffett Field
Naval Civil Engineering Laboratory, Port Hueneme
Naval Postgraduate School, Monterey
Naval Ship Weapons Systems Engineering Station, Port Hueneme
North Island Naval Air Station, San Diego
Oakland Naval Hospital/Naval Medical Command Northwest Region, Oakland
Oakland Naval Supply Center, Oakland
Point Mugu Naval Air Station, Point Mugu
Pomona Naval Weapons Station, Pomona
Port Hueneme, Naval Construction Battalion Center, Port Hueneme
San Diego Naval Station, San Diego
San Diego Naval Submarine Base, San Diego
San Diego Naval Supply Center, San Diego
San Diego Naval Training Center, San Diego
San Diego Recruit Training Command, Naval Training Center, San Diego
San Nicholas Island Naval Facility, Point Mugu
Seal Beach Naval Weapons Station, Seal Beach
Skaggs Island Naval Security Group Activity, Sonoma
Stockton Naval Communications Station, Stockton
Treasure Island Naval Station, San Francisco

COLORADO
Air Force
Air Reserve Personnel Center, Denver
Falcon Air Force Base, Falcon AFB
La Junta Strategic Training Range, La Junta
Lowry Air Force Base, Lowry AFB
Peterson Air Force Base, Peterson AFB
US Air Force Academy, United States Air Force Academy

Air National Guard
Buckley Air National Guard Base, Aurora

Army
Fitzsimons Army Medical Center, Aurora
Fort Carson and 4th Infantry Division (Mechanized), Fort Carson
Pueblo Army Depot Activity, Pueblo

Joint Service Installation
Cheyenne Mountain Air Force Base, Colorado Springs

CONNECTICUT
Air National Guard
103rd Tactical Fighter Group (ANG), Windsor Locks

Coast Guard
US Coast Guard Academy, New London

Navy
Naval Underwater Systems Center, New London
New London Naval Submarine Base, Groton

DELAWARE
Air Force
Dover Air Force Base, Dover AFB

Air National Guard
166th Tactical Airlift Group (ANG), Wilmington

DISTRICT OF COLUMBIA
Air Force
Bolling Air Force Base, Bolling AFB

Army
Fort Lesley J McNair, Washington
Military District of Washington, Washington
US Army Corps of Engineers, Headquarters, Washington
Walter Reed Army Medical Center, Washington

Coast Guard
US Coast Guard Headquarters, Washington

Joint Service Installation
Armed Forces Institute of Pathology, Washington

Marines
Marine Barracks, Washington, Washington

Navy
Anacostia Naval Station, Washington
Naval Research Laboratory, Washington
Naval Security Station, Washington
Space & Naval Warfare Systems Command, Washington
US Naval Observatory, Washington
Washington Navy Yard, Naval District of Washington, Washington

FLORIDA
Air Force
Cape Canaveral Air Force Station, Cocoa Beach
Cudjoe Key Air Force Station, Sugarloaf Shores
Eglin Air Force Base, Fort Walton Beach
Homestead Air Force Base, Homestead
Hurlburt Field, Hurlburt Field
MacDill Air Force Base, MacDill AFB
Operating Location Alpha Bravo South East Air Defense Sector, Old Town
Patrick Air Force Base, Patrick AFB
Richmond Heights Air Force Station, Homestead
Tyndall Air Force Base, Tyndall AFB

Air National Guard
125th Fighter Interceptor Group, Florida Air National Guard, Jacksonville

Army
US Army Corps of Engineers, Jacksonville District, Jacksonville

Army National Guard
Camp Blanding Training Site, Starke

Coast Guard
Clearwater Coast Guard Air Station, Clearwater
Cortez Coast Guard Station, Cortez
Egmont Key Coast Guard Light Station, Saint Petersburg
Fort Myers Beach Coast Guard Station, Fort Myers Beach
Miami Beach Coast Guard Base, Miami Beach
Miami Coast Guard Air Station, Opa-Locka
Pensacola Coast Guard Station, Pensacola
St Petersburg Coast Guard Station, Saint Petersburg
Tampa Coast Guard Marine Safety Office, Tampa
Yankeetown Coast Guard Station, Yankeetown

Marines
Naval & Marine Corps Reserve Center, Tallahassee, Tallahassee

Navy
Cecil Field Naval Air Station, Jacksonville
Cecil Field Naval Air Station, Detachment, Astor
Corry Station Naval Technical Training Center, Pensacola
Jacksonville Naval Air Station, Jacksonville
Jacksonville Naval Hospital, Jacksonville
Jacksonville Naval Supply Center, Jacksonville
Key West Naval Air Station, Key West
Mayport Naval Station, Mayport
Naval Coastal Systems Center, Panama City
Naval Education and Training Program Management Support Activity, Pensacola
Naval Research Laboratory, Underwater Sound Reference Laboratory, Orlando
Naval Training Systems Center, Orlando
Orlando Recruit Training Command, Orlando
Pensacola Naval Air Station, Pensacola
Pensacola Naval Aviation Depot, Pensacola
Pensacola Naval Hospital, Pensacola
Whiting Field Naval Air Station, Milton

GEORGIA
Air Force
Dobbins Air Force Base, Dobbins AFB
Moody Air Force Base, Moody AFB
Robins Air Force Base, Robins AFB
Savannah Air Force Station, Savannah

Air National Guard
Georgia Air National Guard Field Training Site, Headquarters, Savannah
Georgia Department of Defense, Military Division, Atlanta
Travis Field, Garden City
129th Tactical Control Squadron, Kennesaw

Army
Fort Benning, Fort Benning
Fort Gillem, Forest Park
Fort Gordon, Fort Gordon
Fort McPherson, Fort McPherson
Fort Stewart, Hinesville
Hunter Army Air Field, Savannah
US Army Corps of Engineers, South Atlantic Division, Atlanta

Army National Guard
Army Aviation Support Facility, Winder
Catoosa Area Training Center, Tunnel Hill

Marines
Albany Marine Corps Logistics Base, Albany

Naval Reserve
Atlanta Naval Air Station, Marietta

Navy
Kings Bay Naval Submarine Base, Kings Bay
Navy Supply Corps School, Athens

HAWAII
Air Force
Bellows Air Force Station, Waimanalo
Hickam Air Force Base, Hickam AFB
Wheeler Air Force Base, Wheeler AFB

Army
Fort DeRussy, Honolulu
Fort Kamehameha, Honolulu
Fort Ruger, Honolulu
Fort Shafter, Fort Shafter
Pohakuloa Training Area, Hilo
Schofield Barracks, Schofield Barracks
Tripler Army Medical Center, Tripler AMC
US Army Corps of Engineers, Pacific Ocean Division, Honolulu
Waianae Army Recreation Center, Waianae

HAWAII (continued)
Coast Guard
Sand Island Coast Guard Station, Honolulu
Joint Service Installation
Kilauea Military Camp, Armed Forces Recreation Center, Hawaii National Park
Marines
Camp H M Smith, Camp H M Smith
Kaneohe Bay Marine Corps Air Station, Kaneohe Bay
Marine Barracks, Hawaii, Pearl Harbor
Navy
Barbers Point Naval Air Station, Barbers Point
NAVMAG Lualualei, Waianae
Pacific Missile Range Facility, Hawaiian Area, Kekaha, Kauai
Pearl Harbor Fleet Training Group, Pearl Harbor
Pearl Harbor Naval Station, Pearl Harbor
Pearl Harbor Naval Submarine Base, Pearl Harbor
Pearl Harbor Navy Public Works Center, Pearl Harbor
Wahiawa Naval Communications Area Master Station, Eastern Pacific, Wahiawa

IDAHO
Air Force
Mountain Home Air Force Base, Mountain Home AFB
Wilder Air Force Station, Wilder
Air National Guard
Gowen Field, Boise
Navy
Idaho Falls Naval Administrative Unit, Idaho Falls
Idaho Falls Naval Nuclear Power Training Unit, Idaho Falls

ILLINOIS
Air Force
Chanute Air Force Base, Chanute AFB
Scott Air Force Base, Scott AFB
Air Force Reserve
O'Hare Air Reserve Forces Facility, O'Hare ARFF
Air National Guard
182nd Tactical Air Support Group, Peoria
183rd Tactical Fighter Group (ANG), Springfield
Army
Fort Sheridan, Fort Sheridan
Joliet Army Ammunition Plant, Joliet
Charles Melvin Price Support Center, US Army, Granite City
Rock Island Arsenal, Rock Island
Savanna Army Depot Activity, Savanna
US Army Corps of Engineers, Chicago District, Chicago
US Army Corps of Engineers, North Central Division, Chicago
US Army Corps of Engineers, Rock Island District, Rock Island
Army National Guard
Camp Lincoln, Springfield
Navy
Glenview Naval Air Station, Glenview
Great Lakes Naval Training Center, Great Lakes
Recruit Training Command, Great Lakes, Great Lakes

INDIANA
Air Force
Grissom Air Force Base, Grissom AFB
Air National Guard
122nd Tactical Fighter Wing (ANG), Fort Wayne
181st Tactical Fighter Group (ANG), Terre Haute

Army
Fort Benjamin Harrison, Fort Benjamin Harrison
Jefferson Proving Ground, Madison
Navy
Naval Avionics Center, Indianapolis, Indianapolis
Naval Weapons Support Center Crane, Crane

IOWA
Air National Guard
Iowa Air National Guard, Des Moines
185th Tactical Fighter Group (ANG), Sergeant Bluff
Army
Iowa Army Ammunition Plant, Middletown
Army National Guard
Camp Dodge Iowa, Johnston

KANSAS
Air Force
McConnell Air Force Base, McConnell AFB
Air National Guard
190th Air Refueling Group, Forbes Field, Topeka
Army
Defense Industrial Plant Equipment Facility, Atchison
Fort Leavenworth, Fort Leavenworth
Fort Riley, Fort Riley
Kansas Army Ammunition Plant, Parsons
Marines
US Marine Corps Reserve Support Center, Overland Park

KENTUCKY
Air National Guard
123rd Tactical Airlift Wing/Kentucky Air National Guard, Louisville
Army
Fort Campbell, Fort Campbell
Fort Knox, Fort Knox
Lexington-Blue Grass Army Depot, Lexington
Navy
Louisville Naval Ordnance Station, Louisville

LOUISIANA
Air Force
Barksdale Air Force Base, Barksdale AFB
England Air Force Base, Alexandria
Air National Guard
Camp Beauregard, Pineville
Hammond Air National Guard Station, Hammond
Jackson Barracks, New Orleans
Army
Fort Polk, Fort Polk
Louisiana Army Ammunition Plant, Shreveport
New Orleans Naval Support Activity, New Orleans
Coast Guard
Eighth Coast Guard District, New Orleans
Navy
New Orleans Naval Air Station, Belle Chasse
926th Tactical Fighter Group, Headquarters, Belle Chasse

MAINE
Air Force
Loring Air Force Base, Loring AFB
Air National Guard
Bangor Air National Guard Base, Bangor
Navy
Bath Supervisor of Shipbuilding, Conversion and Repair, Bath
Brunswick Naval Air Station, Brunswick
Cutler Naval Communications Unit, East Machias

Naval Reserve Readiness Center Portland, Portland
Winter Harbor Naval Security Group Activity, Winter Harbor

MARYLAND
Air Force
Andrews Air Force Base, Andrews AFB
Fort George G Meade, Fort Meade
Air National Guard
175th Tactical Airlift Group (ANG), Baltimore
Army
Aberdeen Proving Ground, Aberdeen Proving Ground
Adelphi Laboratory Center, Adelphi
Army Publications Distribution Center, Baltimore
Fort Detrick, Frederick
Fort Ritchie, Fort Ritchie
US Army Corps of Engineers, Baltimore District, Baltimore
Coast Guard
US Coast Guard Yard, Curtis Bay
Joint Service Installation
Alternate Joint Communications Center/Site R, Fort Ritchie
Marines
Fort George G Meade, Fort Meade
Naval Reserve
Cumberland Naval Reserve Center, Cumberland
Washington, DC, Naval Air Facility, Andrews AFB
Navy
Annapolis Naval Station, Annapolis
Indian Head Naval Ordnance Station, Indian Head
National Naval Medical Center, Bethesda
Naval Communication Unit, Washington, Cheltenham
Navy Recreation Center, Solomons
Patuxent River Naval Air Station, Patuxent River
David Taylor Research Center, Bethesda
David Taylor Research Center, Annapolis Laboratory, Annapolis
US Naval Academy, Annapolis

MASSACHUSETTS
Air Force
Hanscom Air Force Base, Bedford
Massachusetts Military Reservation/Otis Air National Guard Base, Cape Cod
North Truro Air Force Station, North Truro
Air Force Reserve
Westover Air Force Base, Westover AFB
Air National Guard
104th Tactical Fighter Group (ANG), Westfield
Army
Army Materiels Technology Laboratory, Watertown
Army Natick Research, Development & Engineering Center, Natick
Fort Devens, Fort Devens
US Army Corps of Engineers, New England Division, Waltham
Army National Guard
Camp Edwards, ARNG Training Site, Camp Edwards
Massachusetts Military Reservation/Otis Air National Guard Base, Cape Cod
Army Reserve
Fort Rodman, US Army Reserve Center, New Bedford
Coast Guard
Massachusetts Military Reservation/Otis Air National Guard Base, Cape Cod
Woods Hole Coast Guard Group, Woods Hole

MASSACHUSETTS (*continued*)
Naval Reserve
South Weymouth Naval Air Station, South Weymouth
Navy
Naval Clothing and Textile Research Facility, Natick
Navy Recruiting District Boston, Boston

MICHIGAN
Air Force
Calumet Air Force Station, Calumet
Empire Air Force Station, Empire AFS
Port Austin Air Force Station, Operating Location Alpha Nancy, Northeast Air Division Sector, Port Austin
K I Sawyer Air Force Base, K I Sawyer
Wurtsmith Air Force Base, Wurtsmith AFB
Air National Guard
Battle Creek Air National Guard Base, Battle Creek
Camp Grayling Army and Air National Guard Training Center, Grayling
Phelps Collins Air National Guard Base, Alpena
Selfridge Air National Guard Base, Selfridge ANG Base
Army
Army Tank-Automotive Command, Warren
US Army Corps of Engineers, Detroit District, Detroit
Army National Guard
Michigan National Guard Mobilization and Training Equipment Site, Grayling
Coast Guard
Detroit Coast Guard Group/Base, Detroit
Sault Ste Marie Coast Guard Base, Sault Ste Marie
Traverse City Coast Guard Air Station, Traverse City
Defense Logistics Agency
Defense Reutilization and Marketing Service, Battle Creek
Navy
Detroit Naval Air Facility, Selfridge ANG Base

MINNESOTA
Air National Guard
133rd Tactical Airlift Wing, Minneapolis-Saint Paul IAP
148th Tactical Reconnaissance Group (ANG), Duluth
Army
US Army Corps of Engineers, St Paul District, Saint Paul

MISSISSIPPI
Air Force
Columbus Air Force Base, Columbus
Keesler Air Force Base, Biloxi
Air National Guard
Mississippi Air National Guard Field Training Site, Headquarters, Gulfport
172nd Tactical Airlift Group (ANG), Jackson
186th Tactical Reconnaissance Group (ANG), Meridian
Army
Mississippi Army Ammunition Plant, Stennis Space Center
US Army Corps of Engineers, Lower Mississippi Valley Division, Vicksburg
US Army Corps of Engineers Waterways Experiment Station, Vicksburg
US Property & Fiscal Office for Mississippi, Jackson
Army National Guard
Camp Shelby Training Site, Camp Shelby
Navy
Gulfport Naval Construction Battalion Center, Gulfport
Meridian Naval Air Station, Meridian

Naval Oceanography Command, Stennis Space Center
Pascagoula Supervisor of Shipbuilding, Conversion and Repair, Pascagoula

MISSOURI
Air Force
Richards-Gebaur Air Force Base, Richards-Gebaur AFB
Whiteman Air Force Base, Whiteman AFB
3545th US Air Force Recruiting Squadron, Saint Louis
Air National Guard
131st Tactical Fighter Wing (ANG), Saint Louis
139th Tactical Airlift Group (ANG), Saint Joseph
Army
Army Reserve Personnel Center, Saint Louis
Army Troop Support Command, Saint Louis
Fort Leonard Wood, Fort Leonard Wood
US Army Corps of Engineers, Kansas City District, Kansas City
US Army Corps of Engineers, St Louis District, Saint Louis
Coast Guard
St Louis Coast Guard Base, Saint Louis
Department Of Defense
Defense Mapping Agency Aerospace Center, Saint Louis
Naval Reserve
Navy and Marine Corp Reserve Readiness Center, Bridgeton

MONTANA
Air Force
1st Combat Evaluation Group, Detachment 18 (SAC), Forsyth
Kallspell Air Force Station, Lakeside
Malmstrom Air Force Base, Great Falls
Air National Guard
120th Fighter Interceptor Group Air National Guard Base, Great Falls
Army National Guard
Fort William Henry Harrison, Helena

NEBRASKA
Air Force
1st Combat Evaluation Group, Detachment 10 (SAC), Hastings
Offutt Air Force, Offutt AFB
Air National Guard
Lincoln Air National Guard Base, Lincoln
Army
Cornhusker Army Ammunition Plant, Grand Island
US Army Corps of Engineers, Missouri River Division, Omaha
US Army Corps of Engineers, Omaha District, Omaha

NEVADA
Air Force
Nellis Air Force Base, Las Vegas
Air National Guard
May Air National Guard Base, Reno
Nevada National Guard Headquarters, Carson City
Army
Hawthorne Army Ammunition Plant, Hawthorne
Navy
Fallon Naval Air Station, Fallon

NEW HAMPSHIRE
Air Force
Pease Air Force Base, Pease AFB
Army
Army Cold Regions Research and Engineering Laboratory, Hanover

Navy
Portsmouth Naval Shipyard, Portsmouth

NEW JERSEY
Air Force
Gibbsboro Air Force Station, Gibbsboro
McGuire Air Force Base, McGuire AFB
Air National Guard
177th Fighter Interceptor Group, NJANG, Pleasantville
Army
Bayonne Military Ocean Terminal, Bayonne
Fort Dix, Fort Dix
Fort Monmouth, Fort Monmouth
Coast Guard
Cape May Coast Guard Training Center, Cape May
Navy
Naval Air Engineering Center, Lakehurst
Naval Air Propulsion Center, Trenton

NEW MEXICO
Air Force
Cannon Air Force Base, Cannon AFB
Holloman Air Force Base, Holloman AFB
Kirtland Air Force Base, Albuquerque
Air National Guard
New Mexico National Guard State Headquarters, Santa Fe
Army
Fort Wingate Depot Activity, Gallup
White Sands Missile Range, White Sands Missile Range
Navy
Kirtland Air Force Base, Albuquerque

NEW YORK
Air Force
Griffiss Air Force Base, Griffiss AFB
Plattsburgh Air Force Base, Plattsburgh
Stewart Air National Guard Base, Newburgh
Air Force Reserve
Fort Totten, Queens
914th Tactical Airlift Group, Niagara Falls
Air National Guard
Roslyn Air National Guard Station, Roslyn
Stewart Air National Guard Base, Newburgh
105th Tactical Air Support Group (ANG), White Plains
106th Aerospace Rescue and Recovery Group (ANG), Westhampton Beach
109th Tactical Airlift Group (ANG), Schenectady
174th Tactical Fighter Wing (ANG), Syracuse
Army
Fort Drum, Fort Drum
Fort Hamilton, Brooklyn
Fort Tilden, Fort Tilden
Seneca Army Depot, Romulus
US Army Corps of Engineers, Buffalo District, Buffalo
US Army Corps of Engineers, North Atlantic Division, New York
United States Military Academy, West Point
Watervliet Arsenal, Watervliet
Army National Guard
Camp Smith Training Site, Peekskill
US Property and Fiscal Office-NY, Rochester Warehouse, Rochester
Coast Guard
Brooklyn Coast Guard Air Station, Brooklyn
Brooklyn Coast Guard Supply Center, Brooklyn
Buffalo Coast Guard Group, Buffalo
Governors Island Coast Guard Support Center, Governors Island
Marines
1st Marine Corps District Headquarters, Long Island

NEW YORK (continued)
Navy
Ballston Spa Nuclear Power Training Unit, Ballston Spa
Lake Seneca Naval Underwater Systems Center Detachment, Lake Seneca
Naval Station New York (Brooklyn), Brooklyn
Naval Station New York (Staten Island), Staten Island
Soctia Naval Administrative Unit, Soctia

NORTH CAROLINA
Air Force
Fort Fisher Air Force Station, Kure Beach
Fort Fisher Recreation Area, Kure Beach
Pope Air Force Base, Pope AFB
Seymour Johnson Air Force Base, Goldsboro
Air National Guard
145th Tactical Airlift Group, Charlotte
145th Tactical Airlift Group (ANG), Charlotte
Army
Army Research Office, Research Triangle Park
Fort Bragg, Fort Bragg
Sunny Point Military Ocean Terminal, Southport
Coast Guard
Elizabeth City Coast Guard Air Station, Elizabeth City
Elizabeth City Coast Guard Aircraft Repair & Supply Center, Elizabeth City
Marines
Camp Lejeune Marine Corps Base, Camp Lejeune
Cherry Point Marine Corps Air Station, Cherry Point
New River Marine Corps Air Station, Jacksonville
Navy
Naval & Marine Corps Reserve Center, Raleigh

NORTH DAKOTA
Air Force
Cavalier Air Force Station, Cavalier
Concrete MEWS, Concrete
Finley Air Force Station, Finley
Fortuna Air Force Station, Fortuna AFS
Grand Forks Air Force Base, Grand Forks AFB
Minot Air Force Base, Minot AFB
Air National Guard
119th Fighter Interceptor Group, Fargo

OHIO
Air Force
Newark Air Force Base, Newark AFB
Wright-Patterson Air Force Base, Wright-Patterson AFB
Air National Guard
Rickenbacker Air National Guard Base, Columbus
178th Tactical Fighter Group (ANG), Springfield
179th Tactical Airlift Group (ANG), Mansfield
180th Tactical Fighter Group, Swanton
910th Tactical Airlift Group (AFRES), Vienna
Army
Army Aviation Support Facility #1, Greensburg
Lima Army Tank Plant, Lima
US Army Corps of Engineers, Ohio River Division, Cincinnati
Army National Guard
Ohio National Guard, Unit Training Equipment Site #1, Newton Falls

Joint Service Installation
Defense Construction Supply Center, Columbus
Gentile Air Force Station, Dayton
Navy
Navy Finance Center, Cleveland

OKLAHOMA
Air Force
Altus Air Force Base, Altus AFB
Oklahoma City Air Force Station, Oklahoma City AFS
Tinker Air Force Base, Tinker AFB
Vance Air Force Base, Vance AFB
Air National Guard
137th Tactical Airlift Wing (ANG), Oklahoma City
138th Tactical Fighter Group (ANG), Tulsa
Army
Fort Sill, Fort Sill
McAlester Army Ammunition Plant, McAlester
US Army Corps of Engineers, Tulsa District, Tulsa
Army National Guard
Camp Gruber Training Site, Braggs

OREGON
Air Force
Dallas Air Force Station, Dallas AFS
Mount Hebo Air Force Station, Hebo
North Bend Air Force Station, North Bend AFS
Air National Guard
114th Tactical Fighter Training Squadron, Klamath Falls
142nd Fighter Interceptor Group (ANG), Portland
Army
Umatilla Army Depot Activity, Hermiston
US Army Corps of Engineers, North Pacific Division, Portland
US Army Corps of Engineers, Portland District, Portland
Army National Guard
Camp Rilea, Oregon National Guard Training Site, Warrenton
Navy
Whidbey Island Naval Facility, Detachment Coos Head, Charleston

PENNSYLVANIA
Air Force
Willow Grove Naval Air Station, Willow Grove
438th Aerial Port Squadron, Detachment 1 (MAC), Philadelphia
Air Force Reserve
92nd Aerial Port Squadron, Wyoming
Air National Guard
Pennsylvania Air National Guard, Pittsburgh
193rd Electronic Combat Group (ANG), Middletown
Army
Carlisle Barracks, Carlisle Barracks
Fort Indiantown Gap, Annville
Charles E Kelly Support Facility, Oakdale
Letterkenny Army Depot, Chambersburg
New Cumberland Army Depot, New Cumberland
Scranton Army Ammunition Plant, Scranton
Tobyhanna Army Depot, Tobyhanna
US Army Corps of Engineers, Pittsburgh District, Pittsburgh
Army National Guard
Willow Grove Naval Air Station, Willow Grove
Coast Guard
Philadelphia Coast Guard Marine Safety Office and Group, Philadelphia

Department Of Defense
Defense Personnel Support Center, Philadelphia
Mechanicsburg Defense Depot, Mechanicsburg
Marines
Willow Grove Naval Air Station, Willow Grove
Navy
Aviation Supply Office Compound, Philadelphia
Navy Ships Parts Control Center, Mechanicsburg
Philadelphia Naval Base, Philadelphia
Philadelphia Naval Hospital, Philadelphia
Philadelphia Naval Shipyard, Philadelphia

RHODE ISLAND
Air National Guard
143rd Tactical Airlift Group (ANG), Providence
Navy
Naval Education and Training Center, Newport

SOUTH CAROLINA
Air Force
Charleston Air Force Base, Charleston AFB
Myrtle Beach Air Force Base, Myrtle Beach
North Auxiliary Air Field, North
Shaw Air Force Base, Shaw AFB
Air National Guard
McEntire Air National Guard Base, McEntire ANGB
Army
Fort Jackson, Columbia
Military Traffic Management Command, South Atlantic Outport, North Charleston
US Army Corps of Engineers, Charleston District, Charleston
Coast Guard
Charleston Coast Guard Base, Charleston
Marines
Beaufort Marine Corps Air Station, Beaufort
Parris Island Marine Corps Recruit Depot/Eastern Recruiting Region, Parris Island
Navy
Beaufort Naval Hospital, Beaufort
Charleston Naval Base, Charleston
Charleston Naval Weapons Station, Charleston

SOUTH DAKOTA
Air Force
Ellsworth Air Force Base, Ellsworth AFB
Air National Guard
114th Tactical Fighter Group (ANG), Sioux Falls
Army
Fort Meade Military Reservation, Fort Meade
Army National Guard
Camp Rapid, Rapid City
Mitchell National Guard Complex, Mitchell

TENNESSEE
Air Force
Arnold Air Force Base, Arnold AFB
Air National Guard
118th Tactical Airlift Wing (ANG), Nashville
134th Air Refueling Group (ANG), Knoxville
164th Tactical Airlift Group (ANG), Memphis
Army
Holston Army Ammunition Plant, Kingsport
Milan Army Ammunition Plant, Milan
US Army Corps of Engineers, Memphis District, Memphis
US Army Corps of Engineers, Nashville District, Nashville
Volunteer Army Ammunition Plant, Chattanooga

TENNESSEE (continued)
Joint Service Installation
Memphis Defense Depot, Memphis

Naval Reserve
Naval & Marine Corps Reserve Center, Chattanooga

Navy
Memphis Naval Air Station, Millington
Naval Weapons Industrial Reserve Plant, Bristol

TEXAS
Air Force
Air Force Plant Representative Office, Air Force Plant No 4, Fort Worth
Bergstrom Air Force Base, Austin
Brooks Air Force Base, Brooks AFB
Carswell Air Force Base, Fort Worth
Dyess Air Force Base, Abilene
Goodfellow Air Force Base, Goodfellow AFB
Kelly Air Force Base, Kelly AFB
Lackland Air Force Base, Lackland AFB
Laughlin Air Force Base, Laughlin AFB
Randolph Air Force Base, Randolph AFB
Reese Air Force Base, Reese AFB
Sheppard Air Force Base, Sheppard AFB

Air National Guard
Ellington Air National Guard Base, Houston
Garland Air National Guard Station, Garland
136th Tactical Airlift Wing (ANG), Dallas

Army
Camp Bullis, Fort Sam Houston
Corpus Christi Army Depot, Corpus Christi
Fort Bliss, Fort Bliss
Fort Hood, Fort Hood
Fort Sam Houston, Fort Sam Houston
Longhorn Army Ammunition Plant, Marshall
Red River Army Depot, Texarkana
US Army Corps of Engineers, Southwestern District, Dallas
US Army Corps of Engineers, Southwestern Division, Dallas
US Army Engineer District, Galveston, Galveston

Army National Guard
Camp Mabry, Austin
Camp Swift (Unit Training and Equipment Site #3), Basytop

Coast Guard
Galveston Coast Guard Base, Galveston
Houston Coast Guard Air Station, Houston

Navy
Chase Field Naval Air Station, Beeville
Corpus Christi Naval Air Station, Corpus Christi
Corpus Christi Naval Hospital, Corpus Christi
Dallas Naval Air Station, Dallas
Goliad Naval Auxiliary Landing Field, Beeville
Kingsville Naval Air Station, Kingsville
Orange Grove Naval Auxiliary Landing Field, Orange Grove

UTAH
Air Force
Hill Air Force Base, Hill AFB
Utah Test and Training Range, Hill AFB

Air National Guard
151st Air Refueling Group (ANG), Salt Lake City

Army
Dugway Proving Ground, Dugway
General Rail Shops, Ogden
Tooele Army Depot, Tooele

Army National Guard
Camp W G Williams, Riverton

Defense Logistics Agency
Ogden Defense Depot, Ogden

Navy
Naval Plant Branch Representative Office, Magna

VERMONT
Air National Guard
158th Fighter Interceptor Group, Burlington IAP

Army National Guard
Ethan Allen Firing Range, Jericho

VIRGINIA
Air Force
Fort Lee Air Force Station, Petersberg
Langley Air Force Base, Langley AFB

Air National Guard
Virginia Office of the Adjutant General, Richmond
192nd Tactical Fighter Group, Sandston

Army
Army Criminal Investigation Command, Falls Church
Army Materiel Command Headquarters, Alexandria
Cameron Station, Military District of Washington, Alexandria
Fort Belvoir, Fort Belvoir
Fort Eustis, Newport News
Fort A P Hill, Bowling Green
Fort Lee, Petersburg
Fort Monroe, Fort Monroe
Fort Myer, Arlington
Fort Story, Fort Story
Humphreys Engineer Center, Fort Belvoir
Radford Army Ammunition Plant, Radford
Vint Hill Communications and Electronics Support Activity, Warrenton

Army National Guard
State Military Reservation, Camp Pendleton, Virginia Beach

Coast Guard
Fifth Coast Guard District, Portsmouth
Washington, DC, Coast Guard Air Station, Arlington
Yorktown Coast Guard Reserve Training Center, Yorktown

Defense Logistics Agency
Defense General Supply Center, Richmond

Department Of Defense
Camp Peary, Williamsburg
Defense Mapping Agency, Alexandria
Defense Mapping Agency, Reston

Joint Service Installation
Armed Forces Staff College, Norfolk
The Pentagon, Arlington

Marines
Camp Elmore, Norfolk
Henderson Hall, Arlington
Quantico Marine Corps Combat Development Command, Quantico

Navy
Atlantic Division, Naval Facilities Engineering Command, Norfolk
Dam Neck, Fleet Combat Training Center, Atlantic, Virginia Beach
Fentress Naval Auxiliary Landing Field, Chesapeake
Fleet Antisubmarine Warfare Training Center, Atlantic, Norfolk
Little Creek Naval Amphibious Base, Norfolk
Naval Facilities Engineering Command Headquarters, Alexandria
Naval Sea Systems Command, Arlington
Naval Supply Center, Cheatham Annex, Williamsburg
Naval Supply Systems Command, Arlington
Naval Surface Warfare Center, Dahlgren
Newport News Supervisor of Shipbuilding, Conversion and Repair, Newport News
Norfolk Fleet Training Center, Norfolk
Norfolk Naval Air Station, Norfolk
Norfolk Naval Aviation Depot, Norfolk
Norfolk Naval Base, Norfolk
Norfolk Naval Shipyard, Portsmouth
Norfolk Naval Station, Norfolk
Norfolk Naval Supply Center, Norfolk
Norfolk Navy Public Works Center, Norfolk

Northwest Naval Security Group Activity, Chesapeake
Oceana Naval Air Station, Virginia Beach
Portsmouth Naval Hospital, Portsmouth
Portsmouth Supervisor of Shipbuilding, Conversion and Repair, Portsmouth
Shore Intermediate Maintenance Activity, Portsmouth
Training Command, US Atlantic Fleet, Norfolk
Yorktown Naval Weapons Station, Yorktown

WASHINGTON
Air Force
Fairchild Air Force Base, Fairchild AFB
Makah Air Force Station, Neah Bay
McChord Air Force Base, McChord AFB
Mica Peak Air Force Station, Spokane

Air National Guard
Four Lakes Communications Station, Cheney

Army
Fort Lawton, Seattle
Fort Lewis, Fort Lewis
Madigan Army Medical Center, Tacoma
US Army Corps of Engineers, Walla Walla District, Walla Walla
Yakima Firing Center, Yakima

Army National Guard
Washington Army National Guard Mobilization and Training Equipment Site, Yakima

Coast Guard
Seattle Coast Guard Support Center, Seattle
13th Coast Guard District Office, Seattle

Navy
Bangor Naval Submarine Base, Silverdale
Bremerton Naval Hospital, Bremerton
Naval Undersea Warfare Engineering Station, Keyport
Naval Undersea Warfare Engineering Station, Indian Island Detachment, Hadlock
Pacific Northwest Fleet Recreation and Education Support Center, Pacific Beach
Puget Sound Naval Shipyard, Bremerton
Puget Sound Naval Station, Seattle
Whidbey Island Naval Air Station, Oak Harbor

WEST VIRGINIA
Air National Guard
130th Tactical Airlift Group (ANG), Charleston
167th Tactical Airlift Group (ANG), Martinsburg

Army National Guard
Camp Dawson, Army Training Site, Kingwood

Navy
Sugar Grove Naval Radio Station, Sugar Grove

WISCONSIN
Air National Guard
Hardwood Air-to-Ground Weapons Range, Camp Douglas
Truax Air National Guard Base, Madison
Volk Field Air National Guard Base, Camp Douglas
Wisconsin National Guard, Madison
128th Air Refueling Group, Milwaukee

Army
Badger Army Ammunition Plant, Baraboo
Fort McCoy, Fort McCoy

Army Reserve
84th Division (Training), Headquarters, Milwaukee

Coast Guard
Milwaukee Coast Guard Base, Milwaukee

WYOMING
Air Force
Francis E Warren Air Force Base, F E Warren AFB

WYOMING *(continued)*
Air National Guard
153rd Tactical Airlift Group (ANG), Cheyenne

Army National Guard
Camp Guernsey, Wyoming Army National Guard Training Site, Guernsey

BASE REALIGNMENT AND CLOSURES

*DEFENSE SECRETARY
PROPOSED BASE
CLOSINGS January 29, 1990*

*DOMESTIC CANDIDATES FOR
POSSIBLE CLOSING BY
SERVICE*

US ARMY

Charlestown Army Ammunition Plant, IN 47111*
Desoto Army Ammunition Plant, KS 66018*
Detroit Army Tank Plant, MI 48397-5000
Fort McClellan, AL 36205
Fort Ord, CA 93941
Karnack Army Ammunition Plant, TX 75661*
Lima Army Tank Plant, OH 45804-1898
Minden Army Ammunition Plant, LA 71055*
Parsons Army Ammunition Plant, KS 67357-9107
Mississippi (Picayune) Army Ammunition Plant, MS 39466
Sacramento Army Depot, CA 95813
Scranton Army Ammunition Plant, PA 18505-1138
Troop Support Command, St. Louis, MO 63120-1798

US NAVY

Alameda Naval Air Station, CA 94501
Alameda Naval Aviation Depot, CA 94501
Chase Field Naval Air Station, TX 78103
Detroit Naval Air Facility, MI 48043
El Centro Naval Air Facility, CA 92243
Long Beach Naval Shipyard, CA 90822
Louisville Naval Ordnance Station, KY 40214-5001
Moffett Field Naval Air Station, CA 94035
Oakland Naval Hospital, CA 94627
Oakland Naval Supply Center, CA 94625
Philadelphia Naval Shipyard, PA 19112-5287
Philadelphia Naval Station, PA 19112-5084
South Weymouth Naval Air Station, MA 02190
Treasure Island Naval Station, CA 94130

US AIR FORCE

Bergstrom Air Force Base, TX 78743
Eaker Air Force Base, AR 72317
Los Angeles Air Force Base, CA 90009-2960
Myrtle Beach Air Force Base, SC 29577

DEFENSE LOGISTICS AGENCY

Defense Contract Administration Regional Offices:
Cleveland, OH
Dallas, TX
New York, NY
St. Louis, MO

*DOMESTIC FACILITIES
CANDIDATES FOR FORCE
REALIGNMENT OR
REDUCTION*

US ARMY

Army Materiel Command Headquarters, Alexandria, VA 22333
Depot Systems Command, Letterkenny Depot, PA 17201-4150 (and 11 management engineering activities)
Fort Gillem, GA 30050
Fort Hood, TX 76544
Fort Knox, KY 40121
Fort Lewis, WA 98433
Fort Meade, MD 20755
Fort Sam Houston, TX 78234
Fort Sheridan, IL 60037
Information Systems Command (parts)
Management Engineering Activities (11 activities)
Red River Army Depot, TX 75507
Reserve Component (elements of)

US AIR FORCE

Andrews Air Force Base, MD 20331
Bangor Air Guard Station, ME 04401-3099
Davis-Monthan Air Force Base, AZ 85707
Edwards Air Force Base, CA 93523
Eglin Air Force Base, FL 32542
Hanscom Air Force Base, MA 01731
Hill Air Force Base, UT 84406
Kelly Air Force Base, TX 78241
Kirtland Air Force Base, NM 87117
Luke Air Force Base, AZ 85309
MacDill Air Force Base, FL 33608
McClellan Air Force Base, CA 95652
Nellis Air Force Base, NV 89191
Robins Air Force Base, GA 31098
Tinker Air Force Base, OK 73145
Tonopah Research Site, NV 89049*
Wright-Patterson Air Force Base, OH 45433

*DEFENSE SECRETARY'S
COMMISSION ON BASE
REALIGNMENTS AND
CLOSURE Public Law 100-526
December 29, 1988*

*DOMESTIC CANDIDATES FOR
POSSIBLE CLOSING BY
SERVICE*

US ARMY

Aberdeen Proving Ground (Former Nike Site), MD 21005 (Closure)
Alabama Ammunition Plant, AL 35044 (Closure)
Army Materiel Technology Laboratory (AMTL), MA 02172-0001 (Closure)
Cameron Station, VA 20304 (Closure)
Cape St. George, FL (Closure)*
Coosa River Annex, AL 36201 (Closure)*
Fort Devens, MA 01433 (Closure)
Fort Dix, NJ 08640 (Realignment to semi-active status)
Fort Douglas, UT 84113 (Closure)*
Fort Holabird, MD 21219 (Closure)*
Fort Meade, MD 20755 (Closure)
Fort Sheridan, IL 60037 (Closure)
Fort Wingate Ammunition Storage Depot, NM 87301 (Closure)
Hamilton Army Airfield, CA 94949 (Closure)
Jefferson Proving Ground, IN 47250 (Closure)
Kapalama Military Reservation Phase III, HI (Closure)*
Lexington-Bluegrass Army Depot, KY 40511 (Lexington portion) (Closure)
Navajo Depot Activity, AZ 86015 (Closure)
New Orleans Military Ocean Terminal, LA 70115 (Closure)*
Pontiac Storage Facility, MI 48053 (Closure)*
Presidio of San Francisco, CA 94129-6520 (including Letterman Army Medical Center) (Closure)

---

* inactive (not listed in this *Directory*)

Pueblo Army Depot, CO 81001
    (Realignment)
Tacony Warehouse, Philadelphia, PA
    19135 (Closure)*
Umatilla Army Depot, OR 97838-9544
    (Realignment)

US NAVY

Naval Hospital Philadelphia, PA
    19145-5199 (Closure)
Naval Station Galveston, TX 77553-5615
    (Closure)
Naval Station Lake Charles, LA 70601
    (Closure)
Naval Station New York (Brooklyn), NY
    11251-5000 (Closure)
Naval Station Puget Sound (Sand Point),
    WA 98115 (Closure)
Naval Station San Francisco (Hunters
    Point), CA 94102 (Realignment)

US AIR FORCE

Chanute Air Force Base, IL 61868
    (Closure)
George Air Force Base, CA 92394
    (Closure)
Mather Air Force Base, CA 95655
    (Closure)
Norton Air Force Base, CA 92409-5154
    (Closure)
Pease Air Force Base, NH 03803-5270
    (Closure)

MISCELLANEOUS PROPERTIES

Army Reserve Center, Gaithersburg, MD
    (Closure)*
Bennett Army National Guard Facility,
    Arapahoe County, CO (Closure)*
Defense Mapping Agency, Herndon, VA
    22091-3414 (Closure)

Fort Des Moines, IA 50320 (Partial
    Closure)*
Indiana Army Ammunition Plant, IN
    47111 (Partial Closure)*
Naval Reserve Center (Coconut Grove),
    Miami, FL (Closure)*
Nike Philadelphia 41/43, New Jersey
    (Closure)*
Nike Kansas City 30, Missouri (Closure)*
Salton Sea Test Base, Imperial County,
    CA (Closure)*
Various Stand-Alone Housing Installations
    (Closure)*

---

* inactive (not listed in this *Directory*)

WILLIAM R. EVINGER

William Evinger is the president of CompuRite, Ltd., an information consulting firm located in Arlington, VA. He is the compiler of *Federal Statistical Data Bases: A Comprehensive Catalog of Current Machine-Readable and Online Files; Federal Statistical Directory, 28th Edition; Directory of Federal Libraries;* and the *Guide to Federal Government Acronyms,* all published by The Oryx Press.